Pedophilia & Empire: Satan Sodomy and the Deep State Book 2

The United Kingdom – The World's Pedophilia Epicenter

By Joachim Hagopian

Copyright Page

Individual chapters are available free online with foreign language translation and a tag cloud at

https://pedoempire.org.

Published by Joachim Hagopian via Amazon CreateSpace.   October 2020

Cover Graphic by Nora Maccoby. The Fever Dreams of a Shadow.Visit her at www.noramaccoby.com.

LIBRARY OF CONGRESS CATALOGING-IN-PUBLICATION DATA

Hagopian, Joachim

Pedophilia & Empire: Satan Sodomy and the Deep State Book 1: A Quarter Million Millenia of Human Enslavement, Child Rape and Blood Sacrifice from Antiquity to the Modern Catholic Church

p, cm.

Includes bibliographic references as footnotes and an index.

1. Adrenochrome. 2. Anunnaki. 3. Baal. 4. Blood Drinking. 5. Cannibalism. 6. Catholic Church. 7. Child Abuse. 8. Deep State. 9. Enki. 10. Freemasons. 11 Human Trafficking. 12. Illuminati. 13. Jesuits. 14. Jews. 15. Knights of Malta. 16. Lucifer. 17. Niburu. 18. Opus Dei. 19. Paedophilia. 20. Pedophilia. 21. Rothschilds. 22. Sabbatean. 23. Satan. 24. Satanic Ritual Abuse. 25. Skull and Bones Society. 26. Torture. 27. Vatican. 28. Zionism.

MDS 364.153

Table of Contents

Preface

As a licensed Marriage Family Therapist in Los Angeles, California for many years, I worked with many victims of pedophilia. I saw the horrific damage done.

The self-blame, the guilt, anger, self-loathing, distrust toward adults, and low self-esteem that caused clients to struggle with Post Traumatic Stress Disorder and Depression, drug abuse, suicidal impulses, self-cutting to relieve the psychic pain.

The effects and trauma of child sexual abuse often last a lifetime. The decades working in mental health provided me the sensitivity and experience necessary to take on this monster of a topic, chronicling the extent of organized pedophilia around the world.

Pedophilia has become humanity's scourge, with global child sex trafficking the world's fastest growing organized crime, largely unchecked by the political, legal and child welfare systems that to a great extent are an enormous part of the problem.

As a journalist beginning in 2014, I began focusing on this egregious epidemic that was avoided or denied by mainstream press. When WikiLeaks released the Hillary Clinton and John Podesta emails in October 2016, and citizen journalists picked up on the Pizzagate scandal, drawing wide internet attention to the coded language that the FBI has documented as terms commonly used by pedophiles, I was among the few independent journalists that wrote about the Washington DC pedophile ring centered around the Comet Ping Pong pizza parlor.

Immediately dismissed as fake news, even alternative news sites where I regularly contributed articles would not even touch the topic.

I began researching, investigating and writing extensively on this topic. Within several months I was independently approached by two individuals I respect. After reading the more than half dozen articles I'd written about Pizza-turned Pedogate, James Fetzer asked me to write the book on this much needed, overlooked and under-reported issue.

With my professional background as a West Point graduate, former Army officer, mental health clinician and journalist, I came to realize I was in a unique position to expose the elite's pedophilia network. Since I possess the passion, compassion and sensibility suited to taking on this horrendous enterprise, once James suggested it, I knew it had to be done. In April 2017 I began work on what I initially believed would be a yearlong writing project.

Two months later, Robert David Steele also contacted me, encouraging me to write the book. Robert has been extremely supportive throughout this marathon endeavor, and I'm very grateful for his providing venues allowing me to get the word out beyond my own blog site. I appreciate both James Fetzer for getting me started and Robert's continued encouragement throughout. Robert also devised the book title, secured its cover art, created the website https://pedoempire.org with tags, and was instrumental in facilitating this five-volume print edition.

As I've progressed completing dozens of chapters, several friends have also been instrumental in providing links related to my work. I'm additionally grateful that this disturbing topic, just since I've been writing, has gradually become embraced by more and more people, recognizing that this scourge must be stopped. Public awareness and commitment to eradicate the global pedophilia network has never been greater, and together we can make a difference.

It is not possible to understand the Deep State – and how the Deep State maintains control over key figures across all domains from government at all levels to the world of banking, across law enforcement, the media, and the military – without understanding pedophilia and all that surrounds it, including the torture and murder of innocent children in the millions.

Joachim Hagopian

Foreword by Robert David Steele

Although I have been a spy for my country – a clandestine operations officer or case officer for the Central Intelligence Agency (CIA) – and am very familiar with blackmail, bribery, and the assorted perversions common at all levels of society from the wealthiest elite to the basest rogues in the gutters and slums – it was not until recently that I have realized that every aspect of our government, economy, and society is controlled by a Satanic elite using a Deep State construct to manage all people, all corporations, all property, all land, and even all social conventions including the legalization of homosexuality and (had Hillary been elected) the legalization of bestiality and pedophilia.

The Deep State begins with the Rothschild family and their centuries-old genius in bribing monarchs and later parliaments and other forms of legislature into allowing them to literally own and control the central banks of all countries. The Federal Reserve in the USA is neither federal nor a reserve. It is a "front" for the Rothschild family and their assigns. In combination with the City of London and Wall Street, the central banks are the means by which every political-legal, socio-economic, ideo-cultural, techno-demographic, and natural-geographic condition is controlled Of, By, and For a tiny elite – 1% of 1%.

The Rothschild family is joined by the Black Pope, the Superior General of the Society of Jesus (the Jesuit Order), and other elements of the Vatican (the Catholic Church) often far beyond the control of the White Pope, the nominal head of the Catholic Church. In the case of the Jesuits, their power has come from being the confessors and counselors to monarchs and mandarins for centuries, in one of the most complex sustained clandestine operations of global scope ever achieved, and from their control of trade in drugs and gold alongside the East India Company and its now infamous Hong Kong and Shanghai Bank controlled by the Rothschilds.

The Freemasons and the Knights of Malta are among the two most important secret societies that serve as transnational – which is to say, without national allegiance of any kind – consiglieri and "fixers" able to achieve any desired outcome at any level of any organization.

Using a mix of bribery and blackmail, the elite control every government, generally by sustaining a "two-party tyranny" that blocks seventy percent of the eligible voters – and candidates from small parties or candidates who wish to be independent – from ballot access. The politicians, together with senior bureaucrats hand-picked to be Freemason or Knights of Malta or merely hired hands, and most particularly, senior executives of the secret intelligence services able to spy on and then blackmail politicians, judges, and celebrities, comprise "the

1

best of the servant class" in this construct. Mind control, begun and used in the 1950's and far advanced today, is the special purview of the secret intelligence services.

Pedophilia is generally understood to be about the rape of children by adults – children as young as two to four years old. Many children abused by pedophiles have been kidnapped and sold into slavery, and many have also been bred – from birth to sale – for pedophilia.

In the USA, although the Catholic Church and its pedophile priests – roughly ten percent of the total priestly population – have been known as major enablers in the cover-up of pedophilia – pedophilia is in fact very widespread across all demographic and religious groups, but generally trending at the elite level where it is considered a "privilege" of elite status, one that can be enjoyed with impunity as long as the Federal Bureau of Investigation (FBI) and 18,000 individual law enforcement jurisdictions continue to dishonor all of us by ignoring this scourge. One law enforcement organization, the Los Angeles County Sheriff's Department – with arguably the highest percentage of elite pedophiles in the county within its jurisdiction – actually has a pedophilia symbol on its badge.

Pizzagate and Pedogate, rooted in the discovery by a Romanian taxi driver of many emails to and from John Podesta that contain clear references to pedophilia in all its forms – from art to swimming parties with children by name as "special guests" – helped expose pedophilia to a much broader audience of Internet-savvy citizens. Its impact on public consciousness has been far greater than the Boy's Town scandal in Nebraska documented in Nick Bryant's book *The Franklin Scandal: A Story of Powerbrokers, Child Abuse & Betrayal* (Trine Day, 2012), or the Boston Catholic Church scandal covered by the movie "Spotlight." While somewhat reminiscent of the White House and Congressional pedophilia scandals centered on Speaker of the House Dennis Hastert (R-IL-14), for the first time the public began to realize that pedophilia is pervasive across both the Republican and the Democratic political leadership.

The arrest and conviction of Jeffrey Epstein, a Mossad agent and fake billionaire whose assignment has been to lure as many US politicians, judges, and celebrities as possible to his "Lolita Island" in the Caribbean (or "no name" hotels in Washington, DC and New York City) so as to get them on videotape doing terrible things to children of both sexes, was a major but largely covered up window into how pedophilia pervades every aspect of Wall Street as well as Washington and Hollywood.

Now here is what is not yet being properly covered:

First, that close to one million children a year go missing across the USA.

Second, that beyond pedophilia lie Satanic murder rituals in which children who have been kidnapped or bought into slavery or exported from Haiti by the Clinton Foundation and its surrogates and others, are tortured and murdered with impunity.

Third, that the drinking of adrenalized child's blood – blood is adrenalized when the victim is tortured and terrified before death – think of the Chinese boiling dogs alive to adrenalize the blood and "improve" the flavor of the meat – is the ultimate pedophile "high." Silicon Valley's Peter Thiel is on record as receiving transfusions of children's blood. This is legal – and a stark confirmation of what the elite have known for centuries.

A final form of child exploitation appears to be rooted in the secret US Government programs substituting children for chimpanzees and black people as subjects for medical experimentation and long-range space missions – disposable children!

How we treat children, in my view, defines us as a society. I am gravely concerned by the decades long endeavor of the elite to dumb-down and fatten-up the population, weaponizing food and medicine to produce millions of people who are less able to think critically, less able to move with agility, and less able to be effective citizens in what should be, but is not, a democracy.

Around the world pedophilia is a scourge. The United Kingdom stands out as the worst of the Western countries, where members of the Royal Family and Parliamentary leaders including a former Prime Minister are clearly deeply immersed in both sodomizing children as well as murdering them and drinking their blood. Many other countries, such as Saudi Arabia, treat children as commodities that can be abused and traded and murdered with impunity.

I find it particularly troubling that the annual report on human trafficking by the US Department of State is so mediocre, lacking in substantive data and being more of a comic book narrative than a serious report. Indeed, it can be said that not only is the USA among the worst in terms of practice, it is also – along with the UK – the top funder of human trafficking and trade in body parts and bone marrow transplants and other forms of mutilating and exploiting the soon to be dead bodies of children. Separately, the enslavement of children, women, and men – generally of color – is thriving.

There are a number of published books on pedophilia and the author is to be commended for not only having extraordinary linked endnotes [in the Kindle and free online chapters] – the mark of both a responsible academic and a serious investigative journalist – but he has also compiled a bibliography of major works spanning the range from child abuse to slavery to sexual torture to Satanic ritual murder to the use of children's blood, body parts, and bone marrow as anti-aging tonics for the elite who can kill others with impunity that they might be refreshed.

3

This is the real world. It is time we all understood that this is the real world. Public understanding of the scourge of pedophilia in all its forms is a useful starting point for restoring dignity, integrity, and justice to our various governments and institutions. The Deep State – from central banks to pedophilia networks – must be put to death.

Robert David Steele

Robert David Steele is a former Marine Corps infantry officer and former spy for the Central Intelligence Agency who went on to create the Marine Corps Intelligence Activity, the for-profit company Open Source Solutions, Inc., and the non-profit Earth Intelligence Network.

He is the founder of the modern Open Source Intelligence (OSINT) movement and the lead pioneer in the broader field of Open Source Everything Engineering (OSEE).

In January 2017 he was recommended for the Nobel Peace Prize. In May 2017 he founded #UNRIG, and was soon joined by Dr. Cynthia McKinney as a co-founder. #UNRIG seeks to destroy the Deep State, restore integrity to the US Government, and thereby eliminate pedophilia, among other ills.

He is a Commissioner for the International Tribunal of International Justice and Chief Counsel for the Judicial Commission of Inquiry into Human Trafficking and Child Sex Abuse.

His analysis of global to local matters is aided by his being a top reviewer, with over 2,000 reviews of non-fiction books spanning 98 categories of inquiry.

He strongly supports a Truth & Reconciliation approach toward the elite, seeking only to restore integrity to the matter in politics, economics, and culture.

His primary website is https://robertdavidsteele.com; he curates https://phibetaiota.net and maintains the online counterpart to this book, https://pedoempire.org.

Chapter 1: The British Royal Family, Pedophilia and the End of a 1200 Year Parasitic Monarchy

This first chapter of Book 2 exposes the fraudulent British royal family as a key component of why the British nation is the planet's pedophilia epicenter, unmasking the puppet masters themselves that control the obscene worldwide Luciferian operation. From the Anunnaki colonization to the hybrid Black Nobility unhuman bloodlines left on earth as humanity's slavemasters, this Merovingian lineage is historically steeped in the international slave and drug trade, literally bleeding our children dry through their cannibalistic satanic practice of ritual blood sacrifice, torture and systematic child sexual abuse of the planet's most defenseless, vulnerable population. This chapter will graphically demonstrate how Britain's so called royal family imposters, with their Illuminati-Zionist roots, have been earth's underlying powerbrokers among others behind all war, genocide, an economic system of human enslavement, and globally organized pedophilia trafficking network predatorily feeding off of, sacrificing and destroying our children, and how this growing cancerous scourge on humanity must be excised off the face of this earth sooner than later.

This book like the first will not mince words tracing the demon seed planted on earth near a half million millennia ago as over-the-top, hardwired evidence of how this same diabolical, nonhuman, genetically engineered, off-planet hybrid lineage still tragically controls us to keep our battered and bruised, always divided human family dying on our toxically scorched, ecocided earth to the present day. Profound changes are already in process, resisting and opposing the New World Order's Luciferian control agenda. But our most potent weapon in this epic good vs. evil war of the ages is what the dark forces fear the most - exposure and spread of the truth to slay the dragon of enslavement and death.

This chapter in particular and Books 2 and 3 unveiling the United Kingdom as the world's pedo-epicenter will illustrate the most flagrant cases of the planet's pedophilia web, invariably linking the royal family's active hand, including unindicted criminal violations exposing both direct and indirect involvement in every one of UK's major child abuse scandals. This presentation is an encapsulated summary of the Windsors' royal involvement in the worldwide pedophilia network, serving as the connecting bookend to Book 1's exposure of the Catholic Church. Together through control over both church and state throughout history, they have completely hijacked humanity for eons of time and incredibly through stealth and deception they're still pulling the puppet strings that continue plundering the earth today. The global establishment can't handle this truth because it knows that a tipping point of public mass awareness is fast approaching, unveiling the mountain of crimes committed against humanity through the ages by the same genocidal perpetrators subversively entrenched as our planetary overlords and slavemasters, personified and held together by the British Crown's unjustified, archaic, feudalistic monarchy.

Europe is a pedophilia haven and the home of the ancient aristocratic bloodlines that control the planet. Pedophilia is what bloodlines do, feeding parasitically off youth's energy and blood. As the world's largest landowner at 6.6 billion acres,[1] one-sixth of the earth's entire landmass surface, Queen Elizabeth II of the Merovingian Illuminati bloodline that originally emerged out of the Near and Middle East,[2] is among the supreme movers and shakers today, controlling the power structure behind the globalized mass child sex raping-sacrificing-trafficking network. The Queen of 32 nations and head of the 54 nation Commonwealth where a quarter of the world population resides, is the furthest thing from a benign symbolic figurehead. As earth's top landowner, the Black Nobility Queen of England is aided by the Black Nobility Jesuit pope as the third largest landowner behind the planet's second biggest single landowner, the Wahhabist (compliments of British Empire) House of Saud[3] (at only a little more than a half billion acres or only one eleventh of total British royal turf), together with their legions of secret societies - the Illuminati, Sabbatean-Frankist Zionists, Freemasons, Knights of Malta, Jesuits, Templars, Opus Dei and the Queen's own Order of the Garter among numerous others, working closely with the global intelligence community, acting as the planetary controllers' child sex slavery pimps and blackmailers to ensure ownership of all major world leaders as obedient puppet slaves doing the dirty bidding of the Illuminati-Zionist led international crime cabal's New World Order agenda.

For near a half millennium, Freemasonry rules the British Isles, having roots traced back to the escaping Knights of Templar from mainland Europe during the 14th century (as covered in Book 1).[4] Many of the royal family males have been Freemasons over numerous centuries. Both Queen Elizabeth's husband and father are/were senior members along with her first cousin, the 84-year old Duke of Kent who, until recently, presided as United Kingdom's Grand Master for over a half century.[5] The Duke's brother, Prince Michael of Kent is still Grand Master of the Grand Lodge of Mark Master Masons, and Provincial Grand Master of the Provincial Grand Lodge of Middlesex.

The younger brother of the queen's father – her uncle Prince George, was father of the current Kent duke and prince, but mysteriously died when his sons were both very young. Prince George was a suave, drug addicted party animal and Nazi sympathizer who, along with his abdicated king brother Edward VIII,[6] planned a coup against Prime Minister Winston Churchill

---

[1] Thornton McEnery, "The World's 15 Biggest Landowners," *Business Insider*, March 18, 2011.
[2] David Icke, "The Windsor-Bush Bloodline," *bibliotecapleyades.net*.
[3] Abdullah Mohammad Sindi, "Britain and the Rise of Wahhabism and the House of Saud," *Kana'an Bulletin*, January 16, 2004.
[4] "From Templars to Freemasonry," *bibliotecapleyades.net*.
[5] Charlie Proctor, "The Royal Family's Links to Freemasonry," *royalcentral.co.uk*, February 8, 2018.
[6] "What is the Evidence that King Edward VIII was a Nazi Sympathizer?" *open.edu*, August 30, 2019.

and a truce with Germany.[7] The 39-year old Prince George was likely murdered in a suspicious air accident over Scotland in 1942 on his way to Sweden. After all, both George and Edward were still loyal to their Saxe-Coburg and Gotha German cousins (having just changed their name to Windsor little more than a couple decades earlier[8]) and maintained not-so-secret ties to Nazi dictator Adolf Hitler and his Nazi deputy Rudolf Hess. But more on that embarrassing Gotha-Nazi rabbit hole later.

The British royal family is estimated to be worth more than a staggering $33 trillion.[9] Yet each year the queen justifies stealing £100 million ($128 million USD)[10] more from over-taxed commoners who she only holds in contempt. Plus, she has legally fixed it so she's making a killing through tax-free breaks and insider trading.

The English royals are also up their eyeballs for centuries in racial discrimination and deportation of darker skinned people.[11] Like the Rothschilds, the royal family were profiteers in the African slave trade, starting in 1564 with the first Queen Elizabeth I as the Anglican Church's first Supreme Governor.[12] Both Queen Elizabeth I and II and their regal lineage have benefited from both the abhorrent slave trade and the East India Company's illegal drug trade and opium wars against China, and to this very day are still turning a profit from illicit drugs, still killing and harming millions.[13] Though in 1807 the British slave trade was legally abolished on paper, the covert illegal slave trade only continued operating around the globe,[14] and today is larger than any previous time in recorded history.[15] 27% of human slaves today are children[16] in the fastest growing, most lucrative illegal enterprise on earth.[17] The Crown uses its secret societies to do its bidding and killing, and war and human suffering is the profitable driving force behind Luciferianism. These coldhearted, psychopathy-diseased, non-human creatures actually get off on afflicting mass casualties and human suffering, including blood sacrifice and sodomy of children.

---

[7] Steve Myall, "Was Royal behind a Secret Plot to Use Nazi Rudolf Hess to Topple Winston Churchill?" *Mirror*, May 10, 2016.

[8] Richard Nelsson, "British Royal Family Change their Name to Windsor – Archive 1917," *The Guardian*, July 17, 2017.

[9] Dick Eastman, "Queen Elizabeth Worth $33 Trillion," *rense.com*, December 6, 2009.

[10] Katherine Hignett, "Royal Finances Explained: Where does Queen Elizabeth II Actually Get her Money?" *Newsweek*, June 25, 2019.

[11] Emily C. Bartels, "Too Many Blackamoors: Deportation, Discrimination, and Elizabeth I," *English.rutgers.edu*, Spring 2006..

[12] Kwame Dallas, "Removing of Queen Elizabeth I," *changingthetimes.net*, May 15, 2011.

[13] Michel Chossudovsky, "Colonial Drug Trafficking and the British Empire," *Global Research*, June 25, 2020.

[14] Kenan Malik, "Let's Put an End to the Delusion that Britain Abolished Slavery," *The Guardian*, February 10, 2018.

[15] Helena Horton, "There are More Slaves Today than Ever before in the History of the world," *Mirror*, October 14, 2014.

[16] "The Fight against Child Trafficking," *savethechildren.org*.

[17] "Human Trafficking Fact Sheet," *Homeland Security Digital Library*.

As alluded to earlier, it's important to note that when the First World War broke out in 1914, the Windsors were the German family Saxe-Coburg-Gotha, not changing their name until 1917 to conveniently avoid bad press resulting from British soldiers dying in stalemated bloody trench warfare against the German enemy. Short-lived King Edward VIII was a hardcore Nazi sympathizer, a diehard Hitler ally and British traitor colluding with Berlin in the bombing of England. The queen herself at 6, prompted by her Queen Mother and Nazi Uncle Edward, in 2015 were all caught on film zealously practicing their Nazi arm salute in loyal alliance to the German fascist Nazis.[18] As if that's not enough, Elizabeth's husband, Prince Philip lived with an older sister in Germany, schooled as a boy indoctrinated in Nazi Youth groups, with all four sisters marrying German husband princes from Black Nobility bloodlines, three of whom were prominent Nazi Party officials and SS officers.[19] At barely 15, Philip's underage youngest sister Sophie was engaged to Prince Christoff of Hesse, nearly twice her age, a German SS colonel and second cousin once removed.[20] Like Prince Philip and Queen Elizabeth, Christoff was also a great grandchild of Queen Victoria. Sophie and her SS husband were such fans of their Nazi leader, they even named their kid Karl Adolf.

Fuhrer Hitler actively courted German aristocracy ties with their German Crypto-British relatives embedded as imposters in the "English" royal family. Though the House of Saxe-Coburg-Gotha deceptively changed its stripes during the First World War, the royals could never quite shake their Nazi loyalties.[21] Even in 2005 Prince Harry's Nazi armband prank, worn at a party as his mischievous way of brazenly paying loyal homage to his Nazi-roots, created a mini-scandal digging up the family's buried shameful past.[22]

With both sides of the British royal family, through Queen Elizabeth's Windsor clan and husband Prince Philip's Mountbatten lineage, hiding their German Nazi roots behind willfully deceiving surnames and royal title first names, Prince Philip's family's name is actually Schleswig-Holstein-Sonderburg-Glücksburg.[23] The royal couple, Queen Elizabeth II and her consort hubby, the Duke of Edinburgh, are second cousins once removed, and both are great grandchildren of Queen Victoria who married her first cousin German Saxe-Coburg-Gotha Prince Albert. The royal bloodline obsession for inbreeding to greedily keep their power, their Anunnaki-Merovingian DNA lineage and their unlimited wealth within the family leads to both pervasive genetic and mental disorders.[24]

---

[18] Tom Morgan and Jonathan Reilly, "Their Royal Heilnesses," *The Sun*, July 17, 2015.

[19] Scott Thompson, "The Nazi Roots of the House of Windsor," *bibliotecapleyades.net*, August 25, 1997.

[20] "Princess George of Hanover," *The Telegraph*, November 30, 2001.

[21] Steven MacMillan, "The Nazi-Connected British Royal Family Still Wields Incredible Power," *New Eastern Outlook*, December 23, 2015.

[22] Neil Tweedy and Michael Kallenbach, "Prince Harry Faces Outcry at Nazi Outfit," *The Telegraph*, January 14.

[23] Paul Callan, "Prince Philip and the Nazis," *Express*, February 20, 2008 .

[24] Mandi Kerr, "Deadly Diseases the Royal Family has been Plagued with throughout History, *cheatsheet.com*, June 17, 2018.

On top of all this, the House of Windsor itself is also an illegitimate claimant to the British throne. Looks like one of the many skeletons in Queen Elizabeth II's family closet may have slipped out when King Richard III's skeleton was unearthed in a Leicester car park in 2012.[25] Leicester University scientists subsequently discovered through genetic analysis that on two accounts, Queen Elizabeth's reign is illegitimate because a break in the DNA hereditary bloodline was found.[26] In 1441 while Edward IV's "father" the Duke of York was busily fighting in France, his mother Cecily Neville is believed to have been busily fucking around on him, having sex with a local archer named Blaybourne. Though there were whispered rumors in Tudor court at the time, a recent uncovered Shakespeare document confirms that the Duke of York was in France during July and August, confirming Edward IV to be illegit. Even his mother admitted to legal sources that Edward IV was born a bastard. This fact renders every royal reign since illegitimate as well.

A second even more gaping anomaly arose over the genetic disorder hemophilia.[27] Since Queen Victoria had hemophilia and her afflicted son died from the deadly blood disease over a century ago, not one descendent since has inherited hemophilia, leaving only a one in 50,000 chance that Queen Elizabeth's monarchy is legitimate.

Scientists have shown that the madness of King George III (and countless other European royals) almost certainly suffered from the genetically inherited disorder called porphyria. Queen Victoria's granddaughter Charlotte, her mother Vicky and Queen Elizabeth's 30-year old cousin William of Gloucester killed in a plane crash,[28] all suffered from porphyria.[29] One in two royals is believed to carry the faulty gene that causes the disease and out of that half, about one in ten family members is estimated to show varying levels of porphyria symptoms, that's one in twenty total and five among any 100 royals.[30] Symptoms include red or purple urine, physical lameness (disabled bodily limb), abdominal pain, skin blisters, nervous system ailments and mental illness. The cause of porphyria most often results from the body's inability to produce required hemoglobin enzymes in red blood cells.[31] The disorder is not exclusive to only European aristocracy bloodlines, but as the numbers convey, a sizeable percentage experience it.

Though there is no cure, medical treatment can help manage symptoms.[32] With access to the best healthcare in the world, the royal family can no doubt effectively mask symptoms in afflicted family members. Depending on the type of porphyria, blood transfusions and dialysis

---

[25] Sarah Knapton, "Richard III DNA Shows British Royal Family may not have Royal Bloodline," *The Telegraph*, December 2, 2014.
[26] Maev Kennedy, "Questions Raised over Queen's Ancestry after DNA Test on Richard III's Cousins," *The Guardian*, December 2, 2014.
[27] Ekaterina Blinova, "Does the House of Windsor have Right to the British Throne?" *Sputnik*, February 28, 2015..
[28] Jon Rogers, "Who was Prince William of Gloucester? The Queen's 'Lost Cousin' who Died in a Plane Crash Aged just 30," *The Sun*, May 26, 2018.
[29] "Porphyria in the Royal Family," *englishmonarchs.co.uk*.
[30] "The Royal Family's Toxic Time Bomb," *archive.sussex.ac.uk*, June 25, 1999.
[31] "Porphyria in the Royal Family," http://www.englishmonarchs.co.uk/hanover_15.html.
[32] "Porphyria," *webmd.com*.

are often standard forms of treatment for hemophilic porphyria. This may also explain the royal bloodline's addiction to fresh children's blood, be it in satanic ritual blood sacrifice or through medical blood transfusion. A fresh supply of children is required. At least in part it also explains why so many royals are mentally and emotionally disturbed, erratic, and exercise gross lack of judgment. The mental disorder of psychopathy is of course also rampant not just among royal bloodlines but in occupants within the highest echelons of power wherein the system itself propagates, breeds and protects psychopaths as a mandatory inner club membership requirement. Plus, their Anunnaki DNA is rooted in psychopathy.

In a related matter, cases of royals debilitated by mental illness and/or porphyria and how they've historically been treated by the ruling family speaks volumes. The queen's first cousins – Nerissa and Katharine Bowes-Lyon – children belonging to the Queen Mother's older brother, were diagnosed with learning disabilities and with three second cousins were all conveniently hidden away in the same mental institution on the very same day in 1941. This royal purge resulted in "out of sight, out of mind" convenience for the royal family, with discarded cousins eventually dying, Nerissa in 1987 and Katherine hanging on till 2014 at age 87.[33] Queen Elizabeth even went so far as to make sure that the 1963 edition of *Burke's Peerage*, an aristocracy lineage sourcebook,[34] was fed lies reporting that the two royal sisters had already died off in 1940 and 1961. This deception was exposed when a private investigator actually found cousin Katherine still alive, wasting away neglected shortly before her 2014 death. Katherine's caregiving staff refute the lie that the royals faithfully looked after their interests and regularly visited, setting the record straight that none of them either visited nor showed up for their funerals as they'd essentially been falsely disowned in 1940 and 1961. Another Windsor "mutated" defective was Queen Elizabeth's mildly retarded, partially deaf great-uncle Victor who also happened to be a Jack the Ripper suspect.[35]

These sad cases bear striking resemblance to the disgraceful bloodline patriarch Joe Kennedy ordering the lobotomy on his secret oldest daughter Rosemary, leaving her at 23 with the intellectual capacity of a toddler, subsequently locked away in institutions the rest of her life in family shame.[36] Whenever genetic embarrassments to elite bloodline families come along, throughout history they're virtually always cast aside, inhumanely forgotten and imprisoned behind insane asylum walls. It's simply the coldhearted, aristocratic bloodline way of dealing with their genetic "blemishes" as inconvenient byproducts of habitual in-fucking.

Similarly, Prince Philip's own mother was also institutionalized in Switzerland in 1930 for many years as a paranoid schizophrenic while Philip's father ran off with a mistress to Monaco, leaving Philip as a young boy to be taken in by relatives, aside from his German sisters, his recently turned "English" Mountbatten uncles George and "Dickie", the family nickname for Louis Mountbatten. Dickie's 8-year older brother George was addicted to sado-masochistic

---

[33] Richard Palmer, "The Queen's 'Hidden away' Cousin Katharine Bowes-Lyon Dies at 87," *Express*, March 6, 2014.
[34] Burke's Peerage website, *burkespeerage.com*.
[35] "The House of Dan," *spencorp.info*.
[36] Liz McNeil, "The Untold Story of JFK's Sister, Rosemary Kennedy, and her Disastrous Lobotomy," *People*, September 6, 2018.

pornography, proudly maintaining an enormous collection of family crest engraved photo albums depicting the most memorable highlights of their family orgies that include bestiality, pedophilia and incest.[37] The Mountbatten photo albums are locked away inside a British Museum vault due to their vile, pornographic content. When not brainwashed by Nazism in Germany, young Philip was exposed to the degenerate surrogate parenting of his uncles in Britain. Once his Uncle George died in 1938 at age 45 of bone marrow cancer, pedophile Uncle Dickie assumed full command in Philip's royal mentorship of the future British Crown consort.

At 16-years of age in 1937 Germany, Philip and Louis Mountbatten attended one of Philip's older sisters' funeral after her fatal plane crash. An infamous, inconvenient photograph portrays Philip flanked by his German relatives all decked out in their Nazi regalia. One row behind Philip in the cortege is his mentor Uncle Louis wearing his royal navy uniform. Two years later at 18, Philip was hot to trot after the 13-year old future Queen Elizabeth, but had to wait 8 more years before tying the knot in 1947.[38] Outside of Dickie, Philip's only family member from his German side allowed to attend the royal wedding was his delusional mother who, believing she was a nun, came dressed for the part.

A year after the Prince Harry armband caper, a book published in 2006 unveiled the "secret" royal family ties to the Nazis, including the infamous photo of a teenage Philip and Uncle Louie marching in lockstep with the Nazi funeral procession. The unveiling of the Mountbatten-Windsor treasonous German loyalties and hidden heritage had been resisted, long swept under the rug. But after 60 years of silence, Prince Philip was compelled to comment on his family's German past. Via the *Daily Mail* Prince Philip stated:

They [the British royals] *found Hitler's attempts to restore Germany's power and prestige 'attractive' and admitted they had 'inhibitions about the Jews.'*[39]

Notice his third person frame of reference. Calling the Nazis "attractive" with anti-Semitic overtones went over like a lead balloon, not unlike last November's train wreck of an interview that Philip's un-princely second son Andrew botched, feebly dodging the truth with the BBC, nervously denying he ever had sex with underage trafficked sex slave Virginia (nee Giuffre) Roberts.[40] But more on the fallen, shameful Duke of York's criminal shenanigans later in this chapter.

In fact, males from the Queen's royal family, beginning with her husband to her two older sons, Prince Charles and Prince Andrew, all share an incredulous history of claiming ignorance when it comes to maintaining super intimate ties to men who serially rape children. But then this sickness really runs deep in the incest-infested family history. As already mentioned, the queen's firstborn Prince Charles and his father Prince Philip share a favorite mentoring uncle in

---

[37] Chris Spivey, "Who Murdered Mountbatten?" *chrisspivey.org*, January 5, 2015.
[38] Chris Spivey, http://chrisspivey.org/who-murdered-mountbatten/.
[39] Andrew Levy, "Prince Philip Pictured at Nazi Funeral," *Daily Mail*, March 6, 2006.
[40] "Prince Andrew & Epstein Scandal: The Newsnight Interview – BBC News," YouTube video, November 17, 2019, 49:26.

common, the Lord Louis Mountbatten, a confirmed pedophile who helped raise and indoctrinate both father and son into the pedophilic royal tradition. In England it was in fact Dickie Mountbatten who was most instrumental lobbying for the intermarriage merger of the two German transplant blood-related families shortly after the war in 1947. A *Daily Beast* article emphasized the close bond between Dickie and Chucky:

Mountbatten was a strong influence in the upbringing of Charles. They fondly called each other, 'Honorary Grandfather' and 'Honorary Grandson,' according to the Jonathan Dimbleby biography of the Prince.[41]

Mountbatten's German father, Prince Louis of Battenberg, became a naturalized British citizen, also changing his family name in 1917, just like the Saxe-Coburg-Gothas. Born a German prince in 1900, the royal matchmaker Lord Dickie and the son of Dickie's sister Alice, Prince Philip, born in 1921, both serving as British naval officers fighting during the war against the German enemy that included all their family members in Germany. While serving in the Royal Navy, throughout the war Philip and Dickie along with Dickie's sister Louise, the crown princess soon-to-be queen of pro-Nazi Sweden, Queen Elizabeth's uncles - the abdicated King Edward VIII and his fellow pro-Nazi brother Prince George (till that 1942 suspicious plane "accident") and all their Black Nobility cousins back in Germany high up in the Nazi government and military, all of them maintained a covert line of communication, fraternizing, aiding and abetting Britain's enemy, allegedly giving away vital secrets costing Allied troops' lives.[42]

Hitler even sent a Windsor cousin, the German Duke of Coburg who was actually born and bred British, as his go-between for frequent visitation to Sandringham and Buckingham Palaces. Despite being born in Surry and raised in the Claremont House, the Duke of Coburg, or Prince Charles Edward (1884-1954) was disgracefully hung out to dry by his own family in Britain. He was Queen Victoria's favorite grandson, Etonian educated and a knight in the Order of the Garter.[43] But when his German cousin, Emperor Wilhelm II, needed to fill a vacancy in the German Empire, Victoria went along with making Charles Edward the Duke of Coburg, named after her husband Prince Albert's German family, which proved Charles Edward's kiss of death. At age 16 his cruel fate intervened, uprooting his world to send him off to Germany not even speaking the language. Kaiser Wilhelm II enrolled him at the Sandhurst equivalent, a military academy in Bavaria and by 1914 as a married military officer in his late 20s, the British Duke of Coburg was forced to fight on the German side against his country of birth. During the war UK King George V abandoned their Saxe-Coburg-Gotha name and through no fault of his own, the exiled Prince Charles Edward's destiny was sealed on the wrong side of history. After WWI, cousin King George V stripped him of his British titles, including his Order of Garter, unjustly branding him a traitor.

Meanwhile, Hitler was emerging as the power in Europe and sent the Duke of Coburg off as president of the Anglo-German Fellowship to recruit his British royal relatives sympathetic to

---

[41] Tom Sykes, "Prince Charles Makes Peace with the Past," *Daily Beast*, April 14, 2017.

[42] Scott Thompson, https://www.bibliotecapleyades.net/sociopolitica/esp_sociopol_blacknobil09.htm.

[43] Michael Thornton, "The Nazi Relative that the Royals Disowned," *Daily Mail*, December 1, 2007.

the Nazi cause.[44] Of course he found receptive cousins in the short-lived British King Edward VIII and brother Duke of Kent. Heading the German Red Cross during WWII, atrocities were committed. Eventually Charles was captured as a prisoner of war and though exonerated for war crimes, based on his nobility he was judged "an important Nazi." Stripped of all royal German assets, he lived out the rest of his days a penniless convicted criminal, cruelly disowned by both his own British family and birth nation, only to be airbrushed out of history. He cherished his one possession he'd brought over from Claremont House, his bed from his Surry home back in England. And it was on that bed he died a pauper at age 69 in 1954. His daughter gave birth to Gustav the King of Sweden, but another daughter accused him of sexually abusing her, backed up by her brother. Despite getting screwed over by his British "Windsor" family, the duke apparently kept up the royal family tradition - incestuous pedo-perversion.[45]

In stark contrast, the Duke of Coburg's year older sister, Princess Alice, Countess of Athlone (1883-1981), lived a charmed life for almost a century as Britain's revered, longest lived princess and last surviving grandchild of Queen Victoria. She became one of Britain's best loved royals, the only one to travel by public transport. 90 years apart, she stood proudly on the Buckingham Palace balcony for both Queen Victoria's and Queen Elizabeth's silver jubilee celebrations, waving to adoring British subjects while her disowned and dishonored year older brother remained forgotten as persona non grata... royal family hypocrisy and injustice on full display.[46]

As part of the plan to avoid war with Britain, the Fuhrer's right hand man Rudolf Hess parachuted into the UK on a secret mission to collaborate with the pro-Nazi British royalty to incite a coup against Churchill to forge an Anglo-German peace alliance.[47] Meanwhile, Edward VIII was prepared on standby in Portugal or Spain awaiting his return to the throne. The former king actually called for Hitler to bomb Britain into submission and capitulation.

Deemed the black sheep of the royal family, Edward VIII has been outed a traitor by MSM per a German microfilm dossier found by US troops in Germany at the end of the war.[48] But other Mountbatten-Windsor members were also in bed with their Nazi cousins, though the mainstream media refuses to slam them because Lord Louis Mountbatten is portrayed as a national war hero and British history's longest serving military leader and his nephew Prince Philip Mountbatten is the current queen's husband. Yet during wartime they and other family members secretly communicated with their German cousins atop Hitler's Third Reich. Somehow content from that dossier will never be discovered, much less released to the public, in order to spare the royal family justifiable accusations of treason. The royals have made certain that all content of correspondence from pedophile-treasonous spy Anthony Blunt's

---

[44] Michael Thornton, https://www.dailymail.co.uk/news/article-498894/The-Nazi-relative-Royals-disowned.html.

[45] Karina Urbach, *Go-Betweens for Hitler* (Oxford: Oxford University Press, 2015), p. 178.

[46] Michael Thornton, https://www.dailymail.co.uk/news/article-498894/The-Nazi-relative-Royals-disowned.html.

[47] Jim Mitchell, "A Brief History of the British Royals and their Alleged Nazi Connections," *sbs.com.au*, August 28, 2017.

[48] Andrew Morton, "Unmasked, Edward the Nazi King of England: Princess Diana's Biographer Reveals the Duke of Windsor's Collusion with Hitler... and a Plot to Regain his Throne," *Daily Mail*, February 28, 2015.

retrieved suitcase snuck out of Germany just prior to war's end is permanently suppressed, erased from history, just like Prince Charles Edward.

On behalf of Elizabeth's father King George VI, just weeks after the German surrender in August 1945, distant relative to the Queen Mother as her favorite palace employee, the art curator Anthony Blunt, friend of planetary overlord and fellow treasonous spy Victor Rothschild (fully covered in Book 3) was assigned a top secret mission, dispatched to Germany to retrieve the slew of criminally incriminating correspondence exchanged during the war between English royals and their many German relatives that would give away the Windsors' ultra-cozy Nazi ties and true treasonous loyalties.[49] Elizabeth's father King George VI scrambled with Churchill to make a deal with General-turned-President Dwight Eisenhower, whose American troops had taken possession of the critical documents gathered up from Kronberg Castle in Germany by Blunt, and of course ever since, the royals have ensured that the family secrets remain classified off limits under national security and buried from the public.[50]

Due to the royal family's willful suppression of its own traitorous history for well over a half century, the German-British royals' loyalty, or more apt their disloyalty, has never been fully called into question. And considering the abdicated British king, his prince of a brother as well as a British Supreme Allied Commander and a royal naval officer the future British royal consort, all maintained open back-channel communications throughout the war with their supposed German enemy, but the fact remains regardless of whether they were family members, it's still treason. How do you adequately fight an enemy when the enemy's leaders are family relatives with whom you continue talking to and sharing information? Yet a number of Mountbatten-Windsors did just that throughout the entire war. But what they talked about and shared will never be publicly revealed because less-than-human planetary controllers tightly control history.

In 1979 when pedophile Blunt was exposed a traitor in Rothschild's Cambridge spy ring having given away British top secrets to the Soviets, Queen Elizabeth made it explicitly clear that Blunt was never to be questioned about his secret mission to recover the royals' damaging pro-Nazi evidence. What are they so afraid of? That if the British people ever found out that their crypto-Nazi royal family are disloyal traitors, the German imposters masquerading as the House of Windsor would become history. That's why it's so important that the full truth about this Satanic bloodline ultimately be revealed, even if it takes till now in eye-opening hindsight.

Back to royal perversions... Edward VIII, his younger brother Prince George Duke of Kent, Lord Mountbatten and Prince Philip are not only traitors but one time or another, all have been accused of indulging their homosexual pedophilic impulses. As teenagers into young adulthood, Mountbatten and Edward VIII were reportedly kissing cousins, involved in a torrid 10-year romantic affair,[51] while pedo-Anthony Blunt, alleged to be illegitimately conceived by the

---

[49] Paul Callan, https://www.express.co.uk/expressyourself/35562/Prince-Philip-and-the-Nazis.
[50] Scott Thompson, https://www.bibliotecapleyades.net/sociopolitica/esp_sociopol_blacknobil09.htm.
[51] "Lord Louis Mountbatten," *whale.to*.

14

queen's father King George VI, was also reputedly a onetime lover of his own half-brother Prince George.

Rather than reveal the real reason - Nazi treason - the former King Edward VIII stepped down from the throne using the fake excuse that his professed love of his life - the twice divorced American Wallis Simpson, prohibited his continued reign. Wallis Simpson was a reputed nympho, afflicted with Androgen Insensitivity Syndrome, conceived a male but cut short of transitioning to female prior to her birth. One of their sexual roleplays was for Edward to dress up as an infant in diapers and be pushed around in a baby stroller by mommy Wallis... sick shit, compliments of the Windsor family tradition.[52] In between promiscuous homosexual romps and acting on pedophilic urges, cousin Lord Louis Mountbatten also chose to marry a notorious nymphomaniac as well.[53] Wild boy drug addict Prince George the Duke of Kent, his illegit half-brother boyfriend Anthony Blunt and future MI6 head Maurice Oldfield (the latter pedo-pair both linked to Northern Ireland's Kincora child abuse to be taken up in Book 3) during early WWII were allegedly arrested drunk, picking up underage boys off the London streets.[54]

Throughout history, the royals' addiction to incestuous perversion, engaging in countless extramarital affairs,[55] bearing countless illegitimate children,[56] maintaining seedy, blatant pedophilic affiliations and sexually abusing children is despicably rampant as known facts.[57] A September 2004 *Telegraph* article examines the queen and her consort's union in "Portrait of a Marriage," mentioning and quoting Nicholas Davies' 1994 unauthorized biography - *Queen Elizabeth II: A Woman who is not Amused*:

'A shocking world of royal adultery, passion and betrayal' and stated - as fact, not surmise - that the Duke of Edinburgh's liaisons with his cousin, Princess Alexandra, with the film star Merle Oberon, and with the Duchess of York's mother, Susan Barrantes (among others!) were the reason 'why the Queen banned her husband from her bed.'[58]

Considering the royal family is the head of the Church of England, and British subjects' taxes pay for all their exorbitant weddings, they insult the people of Britain by trashing the sanctity of marriage and fidelity. The queen's own favorite son Andrew is likely the product of an affair with Lord Porchester.[59] Additionally, Prince Charles is likely not Prince Harry's real father as that's reputedly James Hewitt. There's good chance that Princess Anne's daughter Zara Philips' real father is police officer Peter Cross and on and on their sleazy family history goes.

---

[52] Robert Gottlieb, "Duke, Duchess and Jimmy D.: Question Time for the Windsors," *Observer*, March 5, 2001.

[53] Tony Rennell, "My Mummy the Maneater: How the Wild Promiscuity of Edwina Mountbatten – Wife of Prince Charles' Mentor – Took a Heartbreaking Toll on her Children," *Daily Mail*, November 30, 2012.

[54] John Costello, *Mask of Treachery: Spies, Lies, Buggery and Betrayal*, p.465.

[55] Jessie Quinn, "Is Cheating Accepted in the Royal Family?" *cheatsheet.com*, April 26, 2019.

[56] Simon Edge, "The Illegitimate Royals," *Express*, July 2, 2009.

[57] "Royal Sex," *aangirfan.blogspot.com*, December 27, 2013.

[58] "Portrait of a Marriage," The Telegraph, September 5, 2004.

[59] Chris Spivey, "Monsters Inc: The Satanic British Royal Family," chrisspivey.org, August 7, 2012.

Apparently, Camilla Parker-Bowles wasn't the only adulterer Prince Charles used to cheat on his wife Diana. From another secret affair comes a now 71-year old Welsh born Toronto woman and her Prince Charles' love child - a 35-year old illegitimate Canadian son named Jason.[60] His mother Janet alleges she carried on a 16-year affair with Charles from 1976 to 1992, spanning his estranged marriage to Diana. Janet claims that during trysts at Sandringham and Balmoral Castle, Queen Elizabeth found out about their relationship and reports have surfaced that she threatened to deny Charles the inherited Crown. As of 2017 when this story broke, Janet was seeking a paternity test to confirm their love child Jason.

Yet another inconvenient "love child" claimant desiring a paternity test, insists that he's the illegitimate offspring of Charles and Camilla.[61] A 53-year old British born engineer adopted by an Australian family is taking his claim to high court. The alleged parents were seen together as teenagers in 1965 and Camilla is further alleged to have "disappeared" for 9 months afterwards. Another little bastard belonging to Charles and Camilla awaited a far more diabolical fate, but more on that scandalous part of their demonic saga later.

The Northern Ireland scandal has established proven links between Lord Mountbatten and Kincora boys trafficked south across the border to the royal's summer estate in the Republic of Ireland for sexual abuse.[62] One of the raped boys committed suicide months later. As last Viceroy of India and after its 1947 independence, its first governor-general, the Earl Mountbatten of Burma was notorious for also raping little Indian boys from the peasant class while his Jewish heiress nympho wife Edwina (whose great grandfather was banking financier Sir Ernest Cassel) had sex with India's first Prime Minister Nehru.[63]

Lord Mountbatten was also implicated in the Playland amusement arcade scandal in Piccadilly Square where homeless, so called rent boys were preyed upon during the early to mid-1970s.[64] In September 1975 five men were convicted, each receiving 5- or 6-year sentences. Among them was one highbrow Etonian named Charles Hornby, who occasionally had Prince Charles over as his dinner guest.[65] Suddenly a little more than a year later, the convicted were all mysteriously released from prison in a blatant cover-up to protect the rich and powerful. It's been nearly wiped clean from history because numerous members of the elite were involved, including Lord Mountbatten, which was revealed in his biography published a half dozen years after his death.

---

[60] "The Queen's Fury over Love Child Scandal," *Woman's Day/pressreader.com*, September 18, 2017.

[61] Zoe Zaczek and Martin Robinson, "Megxit was a Cover-up to Hide Truth about Me, Claims Builder as he Launches Legal Bid to Prove he's Charles and Camilla's Secret Love Child... Despite being Laughed out of Court Three Times," *Daily Mail*, January 27, 2020.

[62] Joseph de Burca, "Second Update: Kincora Boy Abused by Mountbatten Committed Suicide Months Later," *Village Magazine*, August 26, 2019.

[63] Tom Parry, "Lord Mountbatten's 'Lust for Young Boys' Exposed in FBI Files," *Mirror*, August 18, 2019.

[64] "The Playland Cover-Up," *spotlightonabuse.wordpress.com*, May 10, 2014.

[65] Richard Wright, "The Squire's Secret Life in the Playland of Vice," *Daily Express/spotlightonabuse.wordpress.com*, September 20, 1975.

Dickie and Edwina Mountbatten were the sleaziest, most promiscuous couple known amongst all modern degenerate royals.[66] Yet outside procreating two daughters, even Dickie admitted they hardly slept in the same bed together. New Zealand researcher-author of *Hitler was a British Agent*,[67] Greg Hallett has called both Lord Mountbatten and Prince Philip pedophiles.[68] Both Prince Philip and Prince Charles were "looked after" by their surrogate father, pedophile uncle who "royally mentored" them, i.e., more than likely broke them in as genetic royal perverts. And it's a scientific fact that child victims often identify with their adult familial abusers, growing up to also become child abusers themselves.

A long history exists of allegations against royal family members sexually abusing underage children. A former Metro Police officer in March 2015 came forward to state that an investigation of a pedophile ring in the late 1980s revealed that a member of the royal family was implicated.[69] But as always when VIPs are guiltily caught red-handed, the police probe is suddenly aborted for "national security" reasons. So many high crimes have been committed by those in high places, conveniently covered up under the phony pretense of that same overused, totally unjustifiable excuse of "national security" than any other.

Another case reinforcing contention that royal family members are pedophiles comes from the likely murdered 65-year old former MI6 spy, journalist and author James Rusbridger. Found hanging in his home in February 1994 just a week after MP Stephen Milligan's similarly strange autoerotic asphyxiation (covered fully in Chapter 6 of this book), an account of Rusbridger's bizarre death scene states:

He was dressed in a green protective suit for use in nuclear, biological or chemical warfare, green overalls, a black plastic mackintosh and thick rubber gloves. His face was covered by a gas mask and he was also wearing a sou'wester [hat]. His body was suspended from two ropes, attached with shackles fastened to a piece of wood across the open loft hatch, and was surrounded by pictures of men and mainly black women in bondage. Consultant pathologist Dr Yasai Sivathondan said he died from asphyxia due to hanging 'in keeping with a form of sexual strangulation.' Rusbridger was allegedly starting work on a book about the Royal Family.[70]

Rusbridger was extremely critical of both the UK government and the monarchy, especially the royal family's fleecing of British taxpayers.[71] Moreover, according to *Scallywag Magazine*, the investigative journalist had been about to disclose "material from within the royal family."[72]

---

[66] Tony Rennell, "My Mummy the Maneater: How the Wild Promiscuity of Edwina Mountbatten – Wife of Prince Charles' Mentor – Took a Heartbreaking Toll on her Children," *Daily Mail*, November 30, 2012.

[67] Greg Hallett, "Hitler was a British Agent," whale.to.

[68] Brandon Turbeville, "The Prince and the Pedophile: Charles' Connections to Pedophilia Networks," *Activist Post*, November 16, 2012.

[69] Jon Stone, "Royal Family Member was Investigated as Part of a Paedophile Ring before Cover-up, Ex-Cop Says," *Independent*, March 23, 2015.

[70] Sally Ramage, "Cold Case: The 1994 Death of MP Stephen David Wyatt Milligan," *Criminal Law News*, January 2016.

[71] Andrew Lownie, "Obituary: James Rusbridger," Independent, February 18, 1994.

[72] "Paedophiles from within the Royal Family," *Scallywag/forums.richieallen.co.uk*, Issue 21 1994.

Insiders are certain both Milligan and Rusbridger's so called suicides were coldblooded murders for knowing too much. It's remarkable how easily and frequent it's been for the murdering pedophilia protectors to keep getting away with neutralizing all the truth tellers who pose a threat. They can be MPs, ex-security services, authors (John Costello), journalists (Danny Casolero) princesses (Diana), news presenters (Jill Dando), investigators (Gary Coradori), even former CIA Directors (William Colby), Defense Secretaries (James Forester) and US Presidents (JFK), every one of them insiders who vowed to speak up and tell the truth. This is the tragic, all too common fate and reality that evildoers remain in power and control by simply eliminating their opposition in mobster-style assassination ad nauseam. Let these truth tellers who gave their lives not die in vain, nor all the victims, the millions of innocent ones who deserved a better life than the tragic hand dealt them. We owe all of them our collective efforts to eradicate pedophilia.

Then there was 17-year old Alisa Dmitrijeva, a murdered Latvian immigrant teenager whose body was found on the royal grounds of the Sandringham Estate New Year's Day 2011.[73] Though the case quickly went cold after suspects were released, police treated it as foul play from the very start. The royal family was at their holiday home at the time her decaying body was discovered several hundred yards away, believed to have been murdered and discarded in the wooded area three months earlier. Alisa was last seen in the nearby town of King's Lynn and a year after her body was found, a Vietnamese boy went missing. This area of Britain has been taken over by the Russian mafia, notorious for child sex trafficking. With the steady supply of abducted children blood sacrificed in royal elite's satanic ritual torture, there may well be a link between the two.

An unnamed royal family member was again alleged to have raped a young courtier in Buckingham Palace. In November 2002 a half dozen years after Diana's ritual blood sacrifice and on the heels of her butler Paul Burrell's acquittal over charges that he had pilfered 310 of her personal belongings from her Kensington Palace apartments, he was rescued by the queen herself, claiming Paul had previously mentioned in 1997 to her that he was "safekeeping" some of her items.[74] But right afterwards two thirds of the British people polled saw through it, believing that Queen Elizabeth lied in order to cover-up more of her family's dark secrets from public exposure, timed just prior to the butler taking the witness stand. However, the transparent royal ploy didn't work as immediate fallout from the acquittal followed.

Former palace valet George Smith alleged that he'd been raped by a "trusted" aide to Prince Charles and witnessed another sexual "incident" between a royal family member and another palace employee.[75] Once Burrell dodged a bullet in court, he secured $468,000 payoff from the *Mirror* in a "tell-all" deal. Other sour grapes tabloids began slinging arrows against Burrell as a spurned homosexual. Quite an intriguing soap opera those royals weave of bread and circuses fodder for the easily tantalized consuming masses, no doubt mere diversionary machinations to

---

[73] "Body on Queen's Estate – Suspects Released," *aangirfan.blogspot.com*, September 25, 2012.
[74] Alex Tresniowski, "Palace Intrigue," *People*, November 25, 2002.
[75] Alex Tresniowski, https://people.com/archive/palace-intrigue-vol-58-no-22/.

prevent deeper sinister disclosures about those lovable royals from oozing out, exposing the unsightly emperors in birthday suits left at crime scenes all over the palaces.

Speaking of which, the plot thickened with the unveiling of a "red tape" recording apparently made by Diana of George Smith's admission that he'd been raped.[76] Shortly after Lady Di's demise, her Spencer sister Sarah McCorquodale found a box containing the controversial tape along with letters and a ring from one of Diana's lovers, alleged biological father to Prince Harry, James Hewitt. But the box and contents soon turned up missing. In January 2001 police searched the butler's home resulting in "the butler did it" charges, though the butler wasn't in possession of the still missing red tape. Having been employed as a palace footman and valet for 11 years till 1997, in response to newspaper articles George Smith went public in November 2002 with his rape confession. His allegations triggered an anonymous denier's countercharges that Smith was a story changing alcoholic. Amidst all this swirling royal subterfuge in late 2002, Butler Burrell told the press about a December 1997 meeting he had with the queen when, according the Burrell, she stated:

Be careful, Paul. No one has been as close to a member of the Royal Family as you have. There are powers at work in this country of which we have no knowledge. Do you understand?[77]

The queen was warning him of "dark forces at work" that could threaten him, for knowing too much about "the family Firm" and how it operates just like the mafia. As the stomach turns… again, more bread and circuses misdirection from perennial titillating teaser *People Magazine* diverting public attention away from the royals' real crimes of blood sacrifice and murder.

Dueling banjos, competing in the soap opera froth, produced more headlines. Not to be outdone, the king of gossip, the *National Enquirer* published an update of the above squalid cloak and dagger story in July 2019.[78] Alleged rape victim-ex-valet George Smith who accused longtime Prince Charles senior aide Michael Fawcett of raping him, died mysteriously at the early age of 44 in August 2005. Privately George had consistently maintained that Fawcett had invited him to his home and they drank beer and champagne prior to Smith falling asleep, reporting that when he awoke, he was bare-bottom naked feeling the dreaded evidence he'd been sodomized by his creepy predator host Fawcett. A November 2002 *New Statesman* article weighed in:

… evidence certainly suggests that it wasn't investigated properly at the time. And as each new revelation emerges, a picture builds up of a royal household in which some gay men expect to be immune from the processes of the law, their crimes covered up, their victims silenced, or paid off.[79]

---

[76] Alex Tresniowski, https://people.com/archive/palace-intrigue-vol-58-no-22/.

[77] "What the Butler Paul Burrell Said about the Queen, Prince Philip, Charles… and Himself," Daily Mail, January 15, 2008.

[78] Karleigh Smith, "Prince Charles Gay Cover-Up Exposed," National Enquirer, July 19, 2019.

[79] Malcolm Clark, "Carry on the Windsors," *New Statesman*, November 18, 2002.

As of July 2019, George Smith's family was calling for the case to be reopened, asserting that the rape victim never recovered from the assault and subsequent 2003 whitewashed inquiry that allowed Michael Fawcett to walk free for "insufficient evidence," no doubt due to the accused being Prince Charles' favorite all-time, indispensable aide. Prince Charles has said of his trusted longtime employee Fawcett:

I can manage without just about anyone, except for Michael.[80]

"Insufficient evidence" and the "national security" mantras are standby wheel-turning cover-up devices deployed ad nauseam by the pedo-Establishment in order to let guilty perps live above the law. Once again, another victim ends up in an early grave without any justice while the perpetrator lives high off the hog. To this day Fawcett's business services to Prince Charles alone - running the prince's charity foundation and organizing his parties, bring in a hefty near half million dollars annually after a $630,000 severance package as Charles longtime, most trusted aide. Twice Fawcett was forced to resign, yet Charles then turned around and rehired him with promotions.

Rumors of a gay future king in the 71-year old Prince of Wales have been circulating for a half century now. According to George Smith, his accused rapist Michael Fawcett was spotted having sex with Prince Charles when George entered the prince's bedroom one morning to serve breakfast.[81] Tabloids of course feed off this kind of prurient bullshit all the time, but based on historical fact, a long line of Windsor males has been consistently outed as homosexual pedo-predators, gravitating in their close orbit other hardcore child rapists as both mentors and intimate friends.

On June 3, 2013, the sensational tabloid *Globe* ran the "risqué" headline "Prince Charles Is Gay!" followed less than three years later with revealing photos of Charles kissing a very young man with the racy headline "Gay Prince Charles Caught with Boy Toy" in another *Globe* dated May 19, 2016.[82] For what it's worth, the gossip rag *Enquirer* announced in December 2019 that Queen Elizabeth decided that the only royals who can save the sagging, scandalous-prone monarchy is Prince William and Duchess Kate.[83] Both articles proclaim that a disgusted Queen Elizabeth is determined to make her successor not her own irreversibly tainted first and second born sons, but her favorite grandson Prince William,[84] who's the odds on favorite to not only be the next British king but some say the antichrist as well.[85]

Joye Jeffries Pugh, Ph.D., a researcher-author with a doctorate in education, has even made a case for Prince William actually being a clone of Jesus from a DNA blood sample taken from the

[80] Karleigh Smith, https://www.nationalenquirer.com/royal-gossip/prince-charles-gay-cover-up-exposed/.

[81] Karleigh Smith, https://www.nationalenquirer.com/royal-gossip/prince-charles-gay-cover-up-exposed/.

[82] Vivek, Surendran, "US Tabloid Explains Prince Charles is Gay, Splashes Photos of Scandalous Kiss," *India Today*, June 1, 2016.

[83] "William Named King," *National Enquirer*, December 13, 2019.

[84] "Gay Prince Charles Caught with Boy Toy," *Globe*, May 19, 2016.

[85] House of Windsor and the New World Order," YouTube video, 2:51:32.

Shroud of Turin, and that he will be the international crime cabal's antichrist.[86] Short of advocating her hypothesis as gospel truth, it's worth examining further to draw one's own conclusions.[87]

For many years those "dark [occult] forces" that Queen Lizzie Bizzie referred to and is a big part of,[88] have been methodically setting the stage for the ascendancy of King William. The possibility of William turning out to be the antichrist amongst many convinced observers defies popular belief.[89] But again, hidden forces have been at work for a very long time preparing us to accept William as a viable world leader. His carefully cultivated, crafted image as the one reasonable, responsible, down-to-earth royal Windsor to ascend to the throne has been meticulously engineered. With his heavily promoted, positive media image and benign reputation of both William and his always supportive, gracious, stand-by-her-man "commoner" wife, Kate Middleton, is designed to restore the fairytale luster that every little girl can grow up dreaming of one day becoming a queen, as long as she finds her perfect prince first. From an Aril 2011 *Express* article:

As Kate Middleton prepares to marry a prince, her family biographer explains why their remarkable rise from the most humble background is a triumph of social mobility.[90]

... One scripted for the lowly masses to keep buying into the "rags to riches" dream myth, though Kate's great-great-great grandfather may have been a 19th century coalminer, according to another *Express* genealogist:

[The Duchess of Cambridge] *can claim direct blood ties with every crowned head of Europe and the majority of the British peerage.[91]*

We knew there had to be a catch. Her "distant" nobility descendant can be traced back to Henry Percy, the 3rd Earl of Northumberland (1421-1461). Also turns out that Will and Kate are 14th cousins once removed, and that they, along with both his parents Charles and Diana, are related to Yorkshire knight named Sir William Gascoigne who died in 1487.[92] The 2011 William-Kate royal marriage breaks family tradition to mark the first time in British history that an heir to the throne is not marrying a foreign princess or titled British aristocracy; since Kate's teeny weeny trace of blue blood was confined to her big toe after stubbing it while waiting for her

---

[86] Joye Jeffries Pugh, "Is Prince William the Cloned Image from the Shroud? Has the History Channel Proven that Prince William has the same Face as that on the Shroud of Turin?" *drjoye.com*.

[87] "Prince William – The Cloned Antichrist," *Truth Frequency Radio*, September 16, 2014.

[88] Steve Bird and Sam Lister, "The Queen Warned Butler to be Aware of 'Dark Forces at Work," *The Times*, November 6, 2002..

[89] Alfred Lambremont Weber, "Prince William Is the Antichrist Future King of One World Government," *bibliotecapleyades.net*, June 15, 2011.

[90] Claudia Joseph, "Kate Middleton: Princess from the Pit Family," *Express*, April 23, 2011.

[91] "Kate has her own Royal Family," *Express*, November 6, 2007.

[92] "Royal Wedding: Will and Kate are (very) Distant Cousins," *Channel 4*, April 28, 2011.

prince to finally ask her to marry him (i.e., their on again-off again courtship lasting almost a decade[93]).

Despite all the hype, the coalminer's granddaughter isn't so common after all, but the royal fairytale romance propaganda plays so well to the world audience. MSM's 24/7 portrayal of Kate's respectability, humility and selfless service to the greater Commonwealth endears her to throngs of admirers wherever her royal duties take her. In contrast to that controversial royal American "troublemaker" Meghan Markle, this one fits like a glove, another Diana minus all her drama of course. It's nothing more than an occult magician's sleight of hand deception, using the magical mythical fairytale dust to cover up the dark evil forces propelling us off the cliff towards worldwide collapse as the necessary precursor for one world government and a single, unifying savior-type leader to rescue humanity from doom and gloom. Enter our hero, antichrist King William.

That said, even the appearance of William and Kate's perfect marriage may be illusive. As of April 2019, the rumor mill of royal infidelity hit fever pitch, prompting their lawyers to warn tabloids to back off.[94] During the preceding year numerous publications were featuring insider scoops that Prince William was cheating on his pregnant wife with the also married former model Rose Hanbury. Both 33-year old Rose and her 58-year old husband David Rocksavage, the 7th Marquess of Cholmondeley, shared mutual play dates with their children living just three miles away, and both couples were extremely close friends… until under the heavy cloud of gossip hovering over Kate allegedly forced William to sever all ties to an otherwise intimate, close friendship.

It's impossible to say one way or the other whether Willy boy got caught, afflicted by the catchy Windsor adultery bug, embedded in virtually every single royal marriage throughout history. Especially during this last year, with so much scandal already rocking the royal family to its very foundation, seriously jeopardizing the future monarchy's survivability, Kate and William had no choice but to be good actors playing out their assigned scripted roles on the world stage, at least appearing to be in love as a happy royal family couple in order to quell more bad publicity, gnawingly undermining the Crown's very existence. Too much is at stake riding on the Duke and Duchess of Cambridge's fairytale marriage to fall apart now.

Induced birth by C-section, occult powers ensured that Prince William was born on the summer solstice,[95] June 21st, 1982,[96] on the longest day of the year immediately following a solar eclipse, a day occultists like the royals faithfully worship their ancient Sun God as a critical pagan holiday (i.e., among the peak times for blood sacrificing children).[97] Princess Diana herself, used solely for her breeding purposes, carried the House of Stuart bloodline allegedly

[93] "Timeline: Prince William's 9-Year Courtship of Kate Middleton," *macleans.ca*, November 16, 2010.
[94] Caitlin Yilek, "Royal Lawyers Issue Warning over Rumors of Prince William Affair with Marchioness of Cholmondeley," *Washington Examiner*, April 9, 2019.
[95] "Summer Solstice," *BBC*.
[96] "Prince William Taking Two Huge Steps to Become the 'Masonic Christ,'" *cuttingedge.org*, 2008..
[97] "Occult Holidays and Sabbats," *bibliotecapleyades.net*.

linked to Merovingian-King David-Jesus lineage,[98] which will be used to justify establishment of a Judaic royal throne, not just over Europe but entire world per the secret society Priory of Sion.[99] At four months pregnant with Prince William, a depressed and love-starved Diana desperately threw herself down a flight of stairs,[100] knowing she was carrying the one destined to be King, Messiah and leader of the New World Order.[101] A decade later in 1991 Diana recorded audio tapes explaining her melodramatics as a cry for her husband's attention, but his reaction accused her of crying wolf, that her histrionics were aimed purely at manipulation, and he refused to allow it to get in the way of his scheduled horse ride. But a genuinely alarmed Queen Elizabeth instinctively knew what was at stake, and that Diana was struggling with misgivings over being the deliverer of the NWO's future antichrist.

In her 2009 Christmas message, Queen Elizabeth announced:

The Commonwealth in a lot of ways is the face of the future.[102]

An October 2015 article declaring the truth that the younger generation of the royal family "are all Jews" astutely stated that prior to Harry even meeting his future mixed race African American wife Meghan Markle:

Royal rumour has it that Prince Harry is under great pressure, especially from the Queen, to marry a black woman to help promote the racial genocide of the indigenous British people through mass immigration, cultural Marxism and Zioncorp promoted miscegenation.[103]

William is the only living royal who can claim the Merovingian lineage of every English king.[104] He married a "commoner" also possessing traces of the Merovingian bloodline. And as the son of a Jewish mother (whose own mother's maiden name was Roche), Prince William was born a Jew who married another Jew. Diana's Jewish mother was unhappily married to a heavy drinking Earl Spencer and cheated on him with banker-publisher-Rothschild cousin Sir James Goldsmith, and out came Lady Di nine months later.[105] What are the odds that Kate Middleton's mother's maiden name is also Goldsmith?[106] And Sir James had two daughters marry Rothschilds[107]... an unholy trinity of House of Rothschild, House of Goldsmith and House of Windsor, all coming not that long ago from Germany, making one big fat Jewish wedding of a

[98] "The Royals and the Antichrist," *prophecy.go-cephas.com*.

[99] Barbara Aho, "The Merovingian Dynasty Satanic Bloodline of the Antichrist and False Prophet: Identity of the False Christ" *bibliotecapleyades.net*, 1997.

[100] Loulla-Mae Eleftheriou-Smith, "Princess Diana 'Threw Herself Down the Stairs while Pregnant," *Independent*, June 13, 2017.

[101] Grace Powers, *Prince William: Even before his Birth, Princess Diana Knew that her Firstborn was Destined to be King, Messiah and Leader of the New World Order* (Amazon.com, 2014.

[102] Liam Halligan, "Why the Commonwealth is the Key to a Trade Boom," *The Telegraph*, April 21, 2018.

[103] "The Truth about the so called British 'Royal Family': They are all Jews!" *inspiretochangeworld.com*, October 8, 2015..

[104] "The Royals and the Antichrist."

[105] "The Truth about the so called British 'Royal Family': They are all Jews!"

[106] Warren Boroson, "Will the Future King of England be Jewish?" *Jewish Standard*, June 2, 2011.

[107] Zoe Brennan, "Goldsmith and Rothschild Dynasties Head for divorce," *The Telegraph*, June 8, 2012.

happy Jewish royal family to deceitfully rule the world. A royal insider had this to say about the British monarchy turning Jewish:

An insecure immigrant Royal family who have never felt at ease with the British people, and always more secure with immigrants and outsiders, and an alliance with the richest Jewish family in the world, heads of what is increasingly being re-Christened 'The Jew World Order,' who also seek to raise their status, is perceived by the Queen and the Duke of Edinburgh as the best guarantor of their family's future and safety. In short, we will one day see a Rothschild Royal family.[108]

So the Priory of Sion and the Protocols of Zion merge to both get what they came for, in this messianic Jewish royal family claiming the Jesus-King David bloodline to take over the world with one of their own fast tracked bluebloods anointed the antichrist savior in a dangerous, forlorn world. Add the creepy, apocalyptic, end-of-world murals displayed in the lobby of the Bank of America building in North Carolina, the Denver Airport and the United Nations,[109] featuring a blondish young Prince William, with "William" even boldly written on his sleeve, it all becomes all the more compellingly incriminating, damning evidence of what the sinister New World Order hell-on-earth has in store for humanity.[110]

In May 1995 the *Washington Post* reported that 12-year old Prince William had a microchip surgically implanted in his right hand for location anywhere on the planet if abducted.[111] Some Christians would say it's the mark of the beast.[112] In April 2008 Prince William was welcomed into the Most Noble Order of the Garter, the world's oldest surviving order of chivalry,[113] that also happens to be the queen's secret Illuminati society and parent organization to Freemasonry. William and Kate married on April 29, 2011, exactly 66 years to the day after Hitler married Eva Braun. With three children and his marriage appearing stronger than ever in 2020, William and his happy, smiling, perfect little family seem well on their way to bigger and better things to come, according to the Unholy Destiny's Plan. But who's running this show? Lucifer or God? At surface appearance, the answer's too obvious. But ultimately God rules.

In the face of constant scandal and loss of Crown favor amidst a growing ever-wary public, Queen Elizabeth has come to the realization that her future British monarchy can only survive if such a popular, benign figure as William becomes her successor. As the 1000th knight in the Order of the Garter since its 1348 inception, it's believed that over this last decade Prince William stands as the ideal candidate for the heady, "wolf in sheep's clothing" role he's been

[108] "The Truth about the so called British 'Royal Family': They are all Jews!" .

[109] "United Nations Mural Shows NWO Coming. Illuminati Freemason Symbolism," YouTube video, 08:32, posted on February 10, 2015.

[110] "Analysis of the Occult Symbols Found on the Bank of America Murals," *bibliotecapleyades.net*, November 23, 2010.

[111] Rauni Kilde, "Microchip Mind Control, Implants and Cybernetics," *rense.com*, December 6, 2001.

[112] Holly Meyer, "'Mark of the Beast?' Microchipping Employees Raises Apocalyptic Questions," *The Tennessean*, April 4, 2017.

[113] "Revealed: William's Touching Tribute to Princess Diana in his Knight of the Garter Quest," *Daily Mail*, July 23, 2008.

groomd for all his life.[114] The New World Order has deemed the prince, for his due diligence and careful on the job training, fit to be king, and in due time, many conclude the NOW's favored choice to be antichrist.[115]

As mentioned, Kate Middleton's mother's maiden name is Goldsmith. In October 2017 her 52-year old younger brother Gary coldcocked his wife unconscious in front of a shocked taxi driver after driving them home from a celebrity auction in London with the couple both intoxicated.[116] His fourth wife Julie-Ann had to be rushed to the hospital and Gary Goldsmith faced an assault by beating charge and was fined £5,000 and given a 12-month community order in November.[117] Apparently the argument in the taxi preceding the violence was over his wife accusing Goldsmith of leaving her for most of the night to use cocaine. After hitting the ground hard and remaining unconscious for about 15 seconds, after his wife came to, she told the taxi driver to call the police. A millionaire with an estimated worth of £30million, Gary Goldsmith has a history with cocaine, fast cars, fast women and a snazzy residence in Ibiza, Spain. In 2006 William and Kate spent a holiday at his Spanish villa worth $8.25 million. A scathing piece in the *Evening Standard* titled Gary Goldsmith, the family's "black sheep" and worse:

Not to put too fine a point on it: a pimp and drug dealer who lives in a house called Maison de Bang Bang.[118]

Since so many royal family members are pedophiles, it's no wonder nor surprise that through the years the royal household has been a longtime magnet attracting scores, if not hundreds of fellow child sexual abusers. Buckingham Palace is in fact at the center of a vast pedophilia network extending to every corner of the 54 Commonwealth nations and beyond.[119] Through its government representatives all taking oaths of loyalty not toward their nation but the queen, the Crown has stacked the deck in the UK and throughout the Commonwealth with agents working on behalf of the queen-linked pedophilia network.

Queen Elizabeth has an uncanny habit of granting knighthood to the worst pedo-offenders. The examples that follow will either be prominent pedophiles who've enjoyed intimate, highly influential relationships with senior royal family members or are outed, known pedophiles who've been busted as royal staff employees or as her important appointees representing the queen.

---

[114] Sabine Vlaming, "Will I Am: Forthtelling Portraits of a Wounded Prince," *forthtell.wordpress.com*, October 10, 2015.

[115] "Is Prince William the AntiChrist? It Seems Possible," *abovetopsecret.com*, May 2, 2011.

[116] Richard Spillett, "Kate Middleton's Uncle is Banned from Family Home as he Admits Drunkenly Punching his Wife Unconscious with Left Hook after she Slapped him in Taxi on their Way from Charity Event," *Daily Mail*, November 14, 2017.

[117] Nina Massey, "Duchess of Cambridge's Uncle Fined £5,000 for Assaulting Wife after Drunken Row over Drugs," Independent, November 29, 2017.

[118] Rachel Johnson, "Look Kate Middleton, All the Best Families have a Black Sheep," *Evening Standard*, July 20, 2009.

[119] "VIP Pedophile Ring Operating out of Buckingham Palace and Balmoral Castle," *hangthebankers.com*, December 8, 2014.

Anthony Blunt, the illegitimate cousin to the queen and monarchy's longtime royal art curator and pedophile-traitor showing up at the Elm Guest House and Northern Ireland scandals, like BBC DJ Jimmy Savile, is mentioned in virtually every UK chapter. The royal family was complicit in protecting all of Blunt's "bad habits." Speaking of Elm Guest House guests, aside from Blunt, two other Buckingham Palace employees allegedly partied at the infamous boy brothel - senior palace aide Richard Langley and Commander Michael Trestrail, the Queen's lead bodyguard.[120] The July 1982 headlines explained that the Met officer in charge of Buckingham Palace security in the face of a serious recent breach when a man wandered into the queen's bedroom was hardly the basis of Trestrail's resignation, admitting to carrying on a homosexual affair with a male prostitute.[121] The vast majority of workers in all the royal palaces have a long history of being predominantly gay. With it the established historical norm to hire homosexual servants to the queen, that's definitely not why Trestrail quit. Add one more puzzling piece via the *Scotsman*:

It later emerged that Trestrail, 51, had protected the Queen and supervised her security for years, but had only been security vetted some three or four months before his resignation.[122]

Hmm, an unvetted Elm Guest House partaker, compliments of the queen, leads to a ventured guess that pedophilia blackmail might be a closer to the truth reason for resigning, although pedophilia is a palace norm too.

According to insiders' disclosures in recent years, the royal service staff is ruthlessly run by a gay mafia,[123] many of whom are pedophiles as will be demonstrated. For over 50 years William Tallon was Queen Mother's confidant and master of ceremonies at Clarence House. Tallon and the Mother Queen had a symbiotic love affair of mutual trust and respect, and both shared a fondness for alcohol.[124] At night she allowed her head servant be the rooster ruling the castle roost, hosting gay orgies, having sex on her favorite sofa, picking up underage rent boys in Soho and bringing them back for midnight palace tours and virtually raping younger staff of his choosing at will. "Backstairs Billy" as he was called was a ruthless, petty, campy bully and sexual predator. Prince Charles' right hand man Michael Fawcett was less campy but the same kind of ruthless gay mafia boss. As peas in a pod, Fawcett, Tallon and Tallon's boyfriend Wilcock all got along swimmingly well but as alleged predation mobsters, they cruelly mistreated junior staff in the most abusive, rigidly dictatorial pecking order way. From a poignant *New Statesman* article:

[120] "Buckingham Palace at the Centre of a Vast Paedophile Network," *robinwestenra.blogspot.com*, December 4, 2019.

[121] Barry James, "Royal Bodyguard Confesses to Homosexual Relationship," *UPI*, July 19, 1982.

[122] "Your Humbled Servant," *The Scotsman/indymedia.org.uk*, November 1982.

[123] Nick Craven, "Backstairs Bully: The Real Story of the Servant to the Queen Mother," *Daily Mail*, November 30, 2007.

[124] Tom Quinn, "Outrageous Secrets of Backstairs Billy: Gay Sex on the Queen's Favorite Sofa. Predatory Advances on Junior Butlers. Casual Pickups Left to Roam Clarence House: The Explosive True Story of a Favoured Retainer," *Daily Mail*, March 14, 2015.

It was from the royals they learnt that social 'inferiors' would not dare to answer back; and absorbed the conviction that they were above the law. There is a mafia at work at the Palace. But it's the Queen's, not the queens'.[125]

This insight is hugely significant. The predatory gay-pedo-culture permeating the royal House of Windsor comes straight from the Head of State Crown. That's why Prime Minister Thatcher's Parliamentary Private Secretary MP Peter Morrison, like the other pedo MI6 Deputy Peter Hayman, would wind up so brazenly in all the British scandals. What are the odds that one of UK's biggest government pedophile's sister happens to be Queen Elizabeth's closest confidant and for over a half century her lady-in-waiting.[126] In 2013 the Queen made Mary Anne Morrison a Dame Grand Cross of the Royal Victorian Order.[127] Another close advisor to the queen is senior judge Lord Justice Fulford, who during the 1970s actively campaigned for pedophile rights.[128] Oft accused pedophile, the late Rev. Ronald Selby Wright, was such a close mentor to former Prime Minister Tony Blair during his crossdressing days at Fettes. Turns out from 1963 to 1978, the Rev Selby was also the queen's chaplain in Scotland and one of her favorite preachers.[129] But how spiritually and morally upright can a church leader be if he's abusing children?

Queen Elizabeth personally selects the top law officers on the tax dodging Commonwealth haven – the Island of Jersey in the Channel Islands. One of the suppressors that has spent years directly interfering and sabotaging child victim-witnesses from testifying about their abuse at Haut de la Garenne children's home, finally closed after a century in 1986, is a queen honored judge and politician. An island infested by Freemasons, the police investigation into child abuse over a decade ago was constantly hampered and undermined, flagrantly protecting VIPs of both prominent island residents as well as infamous visitors from Britain. For many decades from the 1960s to the present, severe child sexual and physical abuse has occurred, including murder, linked to visiting VIP perpetrators like Jimmy Savile and former Prime Minister Edward Heath as well as Jersey VIPs like Zionist Senator Wilfred Krishevsky.[130] It's been documented that Jersey children were also trafficked to Britain as part of the larger pedo-network.

From an in-depth March 2009 article from *The Guardian* entitled "Home to Something Evil":

The assembly - made up of the connétables, their deputies and 12 elected senators, many of them multimillionaires - is supervised by the bailiff, Jersey's highest officer, who is appointed by the Queen, while the task of upholding the law and keeping the hobby bobbies in check falls to

---

[125] Malcolm Clark, https://www.newstatesman.com/node/194566.

[126] Simon Johnson, "Queen Leads Royal Family on Island Cruise," *The Telegraph*, July 23, 2010.

[127] Katie Harris, "The Queen "Shocked as Lady-in-Waiting Falls Down Stairs Missing Monarch 'by Inches,'" *Express*, September 22, 2018.

[128] Martin Beckford, "High Court Judge and the Child Sex Ring: Advisor to Queen was Founder of Paedophile Support Group to Keep Offenders out of Jail," *Daily Mail*, January 22, 2015.

[129] Tam Dalyell, "Obituary: The Very Rev Ronald Selby Wright," *Independent*, October 26, 1995.

[130] "British High Level Pedophile and Murder Ring on the Island of Jersey," *tapnewswire.com*, October 9, 2017.

the attorney general. These two key posts are currently held by brothers, Sir Philip and William Bailhache, members of one of the oldest and most powerful families on Jersey.[131]

These two Queen Elizabeth appointed brothers have been key Jersey Island gatekeepers, seemingly forever willfully obstructing justice. Sir Philip Bailhache was Jersey Attorney General (1986-1993) and Bailiff (Chief Justice), knighted in 1996 and further rewarded with Queen Council honors in 1989, later serving in the Jersey Senate from 2013-2018. But in the 1970s and 1980s when so much of the abuse was raging out of control, Bailhache was Governor of Haut de la Garenne.[132] His brother William was queen appointed Jersey Attorney General from 2000 to 2009 while the police investigation of the children's home was sabotaged and eventually aborted. These two brothers stand out among the conspiracy of high-powered queen supported government officials on the island that effectively cover up the notorious scandal.[133]

Even after an Independent Jersey Care Inquiry, only 5% of the pedophiles have been named with a meager handful convicted while scores of child rapists have gotten away with their rampant crimes. The Jersey scandal implicates the queen's deep complicity in one of the most corrupt and subverted courses of pedo-justice ever on record with crimes linked to the House of Rothschild. Other royal ties to Jersey and the "fat man" Senator Wilfred Krishevsky are the queen's cousin Princess Alexandra of Kent and her husband Sir Angus Ogilvy. So, we have pedophiles in child procuring Savile, Heath and Fat Man linked to the princess on Jersey and Savile and the same princess again linked in child sex abuse at Duncroft Approved School in Surrey. There's a well-worn pattern here that only grows more incriminating.

Longtime Welsh Labor MP from Cardiff (1945-1983) and Speaker of the House, George Thomas, upon retirement was granted the title Viscount Tonypandy. Though he died in 1997 at age 88, allegations were covered up that he had raped a nine-year old boy in the late 1960s and early 1970s after befriending the child's foster parents who were avid supporters of the Labor Party.[134] Around the time of the abuse, as Wales Secretary of State, Thomas was all in with the investiture of Charles in 1969 as Prince of Wales, helping the royal learn the language for the ceremony, which many Welsh nationalists and republicans criticized Thomas for hypocritically kissing royal ass to the extreme. He especially adored Queen Mother.[135] Bottom line, Tonypandy's mutual love affair with the royals likely shielded him from any police investigation. Upon the pedo's death, the queen fondly reminisced:

---

[131] Cathy Scott-Clark, "Home to Something Evil," *The Guardian*, March 13, 2009.

[132] "State Protected Paedophile Ring in Jersey?" *indymedia.org.uk*, February 25, 2008.

[133] Joel van der Reijden, "The Haut de la Garenne Child Abuse Scandal: Senators Implicated; Ties to Rothschild, the Epstein Affair, Iran Contra, BCCI, IraqGate," *isgp-studies.com*, January 11, 2020.

[134] Nick Sommerlad, "Police Investigating Child Rape Allegation against Ex-Labour Peer and Commons Speaker Viscount Tonypandy," *Mirror*, July 18, 2014.

[135] "Reluctant Queen's Links to Wales," *BBC*, March 30, 2002.

Like so many people who knew him, or heard his voice, I will remember his warm personality, his dignity as Speaker of the House of Commons, his wonderful Welsh accent and his long and courageous battle against throat cancer.[136]

The viscount's victim remembered him for his brutal rapes, repeatedly reporting the crimes to the South Wales police to no avail. In 2014 a police apology and belated investigation was impotently initiated as to why no action had been taken earlier. The answer to that question is the same answer to this question. Why are VIP child fuckers always allowed to go peacefully to their graves?

Peter Bick, a 57-year old friend of Prince Philip that shared a mutual interest in carriage racing, was suddenly bludgeoned to death in January 2011 by a sex abuse victim, 27-year old Christopher Hunnisett.[137] Peter Bick had boasted to neighbors that he had raced in Prince Philip's carriage. Bick's killer Christopher was first raped by his vicar as an altar boy, which resulted in the clergy's murder by 18-year old Hunnisett, sent to prison for life in 2002. But an appeals court acquitted the abuse victim in September 2010 upon learning the murdered vicar had sexually abused Hunnisett for years as a boy. The former choirboy was a ticking time bomb, making a target list of who he believed were pedophiles that when a free man he planned to exterminate one by one as a self-appointed one-man vigilante force. Irreversible damage to Hunnisett had already been inflicted, festering eight long years in prison. Upon his release he was bent on a mission of revenge against pedophiles and the royal friend Bick happened to be at the top of his list, though other than rumor no apparent evidence at his trial allegedly supported Hunnisett's claim.[138] But the question remains, did Bick and the Duke of Edinburgh share more than just carriage racing in common?

Paul Kidd while in his 20s and 30s working as the queen and queen mother's butler for a decade in the mid-1970s to mid-1980s, all the while sexually assaulted young boys for 30 years at least up to 2006 prior to his arrest, trial and sentencing in 2008.[139] Exploiting his royal status to gain access to grooming boys as young as 13, the derelict audaciously even brought one victim to Christmas tea at the Queen Mother's Clarence House. Police found over 19,000 images of child pornography on his home computer, some of which he both created and distributed. He was convicted of abusing at least three boys (though no doubt he had many more victims) and sentenced to no less than six years in prison in December 2008. It was clear that Kidd ran an open pedophile ring during his decade tenure with the royal family that of course, as always, claimed total ignorance of his sordid illegal activities.[140]

---

[136] "Lord Tonypandy, Popular Speaker of the House of Commons, Dies at 88," *Associated Press*, September 23, 1997.

[137] "Former Alter Boy Arrested after "Duke of Edinburgh's Friend' Found Bludgeoned to Death," *Daily Mail*, January 14, 2011.

[138] "Christopher Hunnisett Guilty of Peter Bick Murder," BBC, May 11, 2012.

[139] "Paedophile Royal Butler 'Took Victims to Tea with Queen Mother,'" *The Telegraph*, October 2, 2008.

[140] "Buckingham Palace 'Ran Paedophile Sex Ring while Working for the Royal Family," *Daily Mail*, October 1, 2008.

Just prior to butler Paul Kidd violating kids while running his royal pedo-operation, allegations surfaced by a 16-year old working in the kitchens at Buckingham Palace, indicating that an ongoing pedo-ring was already in place, flourishing within the royal household by the early 1970s. The boy's parents were initially approached by a close family friend who was also a royal staff member that:

... got wind of this after an incident at Balmoral when he [the boy] screamed in the night.[141]

The parents had noticed a change in their son's behavior soon after beginning his palace employment but, as is typical with abused adolescent boys, he refused to disclose. Ultimately the parents found a note written by their son that read:

What Buckingham Palace did for me was exploitation of the highest order.[142]

According to UK Home Office files, the boy's parents contacted whistleblowing MP Geoffrey Dickens for help. A letter written by the mother detailing the complaints wound up on the desk of pedophile Home Office Secretary Leon Brittan, who dismissed the claims outright as unsubstantiated, not warranting further investigation... the typical brick wall of deceitful denial that gatekeeper Sir Leon is infamous for.[143] Another deeply disturbing element to this story is that another high profile pedophile, Sir Peter Hayman, onetime Deputy MI6 Director and Queen Elizabeth's choice as UK High Commissioner to Canada, had learned through the royal pedo-ring grapevine that the 16-year old was fair game and began aggressively pursuing him to join his staff in Canada. That's how brazenly open these untouchable predatory sick fucks are.

In 2015 a video went viral of a naked young man desperately climbing out a top floor window at Buckingham Palace to lower himself on what appear as ropes of knotted sheets but halfway down he falls.[144] Per royally controlled press, all the mainstream media outlets claimed it was an internet hoax. Yet no hoax explanation adequately disproved what was clearly observed on film. Within the cultural climate of out of control gay sex orgies, rape and pedophilia running rampant within the royal milieu, someone attempting to avoid being further abused was desperate enough to risk his life trying to escape was inadvertently caught on film for the world to see.

The child sex abuse in the royal household has been shielded and allowed to go on for many years. Lt. Col. Benjamin Herman, a personal assistant or equerry to the queen's husband Prince Philip from 1971 to 1974, was arrested and charged in July 2014 for sexually assaulting a 12-year old girl while in his late 30s.[145] Then there was BBC entertainer and convicted pedophile

[141] "VIP Pedophile Ring Operating out of Buckingham Palace and Balmoral Castle," *hangthebankers.com*, December 8, 2014.
[142] "VIP Pedophile Ring Operating out of Buckingham Palace and Balmoral Castle."
[143] "VIP Pedophile Ring Operating out of Buckingham Palace and Balmoral Castle."
[144] Sam Rkaina, "Buckingham Palace Naked Man: Watch Shocking Clip of Nude Man Appearing to Climb out of Royal Residence Window," *Mirror*, February 27, 2015.
[145] "Prince Philip Ex-Aide Up on Charges," *The Guardian*, July 30, 2014.

Rolf Harris who back in 2005 could do no wrong, unveiling his royal commissioned portrait of Queen Elizabeth at her Buckingham Palace art gallery.[146] Once Harris was sentenced to five years in prison in 2015, after bestowing him with a CBE honor, the embarrassed queen quietly stripped the disgraced Australian born derelict of his knighthood, having been exposed for serially abusing girls as young as 7 including his own daughter.[147] He's a free man now.

In November 2015, 77-year old Roger Benson who did "high profile work" for many years with Prince Charles' Youth Business Trust charity was convicted and sentenced to five years in prison for repeated sexual assaults against a 14-year old girl nearly three decades earlier.[148] No sooner had Benson been headhunted for the lofty position of the trust director of operations in Northern Ireland where he worked for the next 14 years,[149] less than four months into his new job interfacing with disadvantaged youth, he began sexually abusing a local girl. Because of his prestigious post working for Prince Charles at his royal children's charity trust, when the girl reported the crimes to the police, it was simply his word against hers. In all likelihood, Benson went on to perpetrate abuse toward other child victims as well, prior to his 2014 arrest when he called his victim "a malicious nutcase and a liar." Despite not being listened to in 1986, during the post-Savile era when victims of historic child sexual abuse reported their past trauma to authorities by the thousands, 29 years later with the perp's guilty plea, conviction, half decade prison sentence and registered for life as sex offender, in 2015 the court finally listened to the 43-year old woman, still struggling with the ill effects, telling Benson in court29 years later, "I feel dirty, damaged, ashamed and rubbish." That's what abuse does to victims, often posing a lifetime sentence.

The man in charge of Prince Charles' public trust for youth from 1977 to 1988 who likely hired Roger Benson was Sir Harold Haywood, the prince's trusted charity aide, implicated as a pedophile himself. While heading the Albany Trust in 1975, he sponsored a Q&A pamphlet with Paedophile Information Exchange members, claiming that pedophiles "represent no special threat to society," advocating in favor of them working with children.[150] Working more for child predators' interests than children's, the queen awarded him an OBE in 1973 and then in 1988 bestowed knighthood for his many years with charity trusts. While Director of Youth Work for over 20 years prior to the prince's public trust, Haywood worked with the queen's cousin Princess Alexandra, selecting her husband Sir Angus Ogilvy as president and Jimmy Savile vice president... again the same pedo-connection between the royal princess and Savile. Again, the royals knew full well who they were so busy trusting and honoring all those years.

[146] Jonathan Jones, "I Saw Rolf Harris's Dark Side when I Questioned his Portrait of the Queen," *The Guardian*, July 2, 2014.

[147] "Disgraced Entertainer Rolf Harris Stripped of CBE," *BBC*, March 3, 2015.

[148] Jenifer Loweth, "Retired Lecturer Jailed for Historic Child Sexual Abuse of Child," *The Telegraph & Argus*, November 14, 2015.

[149] "Roger Howard Benson," *cbetta.com*.

[150] "1975-1977: Who was 'John', Albany Trust's Representative, on Paedophile Drafting Committee," *bitsofbooksblog.wordpress.com*, February 10, 2015.

Hubert Chesshyre has lived a charmed life turning 81 in June this year. Educated at Cambridge and Oxford hailing from aristocratic stock, serving the queen for over 40 years as the second most senior heraldic officer in Britain, Australia, New Zealand and several other Commonwealth nations. He's been secretary to the queen's very powerful secret society, her Order of the Garter, the Honorary Genealogist to the Royal Victorian Order and Registrar of the College of Arms.[151] He is the author of seven books including the official history of the Order of the Garter. In other words, this dude remains protected. That's why when it was learned at Britain's Independent Inquiry for Child Sexual Abuse in March 2018 that Chesshyre in 2015 was found to have sexually abused a teenage chorister back in the 1990s, nothing happened.[152] He wasn't convicted of any crime, no criminal status was placed on his record, and absolutely no consequence came his way, despite the fact that "he was found to have committed the acts in question" in a trial of the facts jury. Adding headaches to police detectives investigating this royal "Cheshire cat" was his repeatedly misspelled name that further permitted him to evade justice.

Virtually it's a déjà vu case of Lord Greville Janner, a Zionist serial pedophile that was never indicted nor brought to justice because the system found him too far gone with dementia to put him on trial, allowing him to escape justice going to his grave in 2015 without prosecution. Virtually the same situation again is occurring with Hubert Chesshyre because he allegedly had a stroke and now dementia, so despite a trial admitting he committed sexual assault on a minor, which the Janner case never got to, there will be no conviction and therefore no consequence. His victim wrote to all his abuser's societies and honorary memberships including the Royal Garter, and none of them are willing to remove this criminal's honorable standing or membership. So once again, another royal pedophile is allowed to slither to his grave, unconsequenced and unblemished since everything stays intact right to the end, and then even after death his awards and honors remain, nothing revoked despite a jury unanimously deciding he is guilty of a very serious crime... sick. And the only reason this still alive man escapes justice is his "royal" standing.

From the queen's officer of arms turning 81 this year to the queen's driver behind her chauffeur driven wheels who died at 81, it seems a common occurrence for perverts who rape children but are employed by Queen Elizabeth to escape justice. While Chesshyre cat worked for the queen for over four decades, her pedo-chauffeur for two decades from 1972 to 1992. The royal wheels of non-justice turn ever so slowly to allow this particular pedophile Alwyn Stockdale to sexually assault a 9- and a 10-year old back in 1972 and 1975 and not have to pay for his crimes.[153] This royal child abuser sexually assaulted one of the young boys at his Buckingham Palace living quarters and the other in the home of the boy's relative, also a palace employee. After a man in his 50s told police about his abuse that occurred in the 1970s, it took

[151] "College of Arms," college-of-arms.gov.uk.

[152] Jamie Doward, "Honours System under Scrutiny after Sex Abuser Kept Title for Years," The Guardian, March 30, 2018.

[153] "Royal Chauffeur Died before Child Abuse Charges could be Brought," BBC, December 10, 2018..

Met officers 19-months to catch up to the old codger.[154] When the police finally did interview Stockdale, he even admitted his crimes, prompting the lame Crown Prosecution Service (CPS) after finally receiving the case file in August, to set up a prosecution date for November 30th, 2018. But the former driver to the queen died within the week and thus successfully joined a long line of royal rapists living out their long, unencumbered lives escaping justice. This happens way too often to simply be by chance. If child sexual abusers are gainfully employed by the royal family, they rarely if ever have to pay for their crimes. That way the protected royal pedo-network continues unchanged.

In June 2018 Tony Aslett, a 52-year old visitor services warden for Buckingham Palace's Royal Collection Trust, was sentenced to nine months in prison for amassing 15,000 indecent photo images and video clips between 2009 and 2015 of child pornography on his home electronic devices, with victims as young as 18-months.[155]

Another former butler to the queen, 57-year old Andrew Lightwood, someone his attorney said was "a respectable, outstanding member of society," exposed himself to a young boy, masturbated in front of him and then began sexually assaulting him. He was sentenced to 28 months in prison in July 2019.[156] The boy's mother reported that boy suffers from insomnia, becomes easily frustrated and upset, despite receiving counseling, adding that what the ex-butler did to him "will stay with him the rest of his life."

Senior Foreign Office diplomat and linguist for 33 years, Robert Coughlin, who in February 1995 accompanied Princess Diana on her visit to Japan, was found guilty in September 1996 of smuggling 109 videotapes of obscene material, 70 of which were child pornography.[157] The 54-year old received a three-year prison sentence. Authorities believed Coughlin was likely part of a wider pedophilia network operating within the diplomatic service corps as convenient cover for production, distribution and sale of child pornographic material.

Retired Scottish railway stationmaster Trevor Francis, whose station was often voted the best floral arrangement on display during his 21 years of service, was recognized in 2012 by the Queen and Prince Charles with an MBE at Buckingham Palace for his decades of community service.[158] But in reality, similar to the royal family, outward appearances are deceiving. Francis lived a Jekyll and Hyde life as a serial sexual abuser. Back in the mid-1970s, he sadistically beat and sexually assaulted vulnerable children under his care at a group home. The predator was known to creep into girl's rooms at night to viciously sexually attack them. Due apparently to his "upstanding" status per the Crown, the twisted 71-year old pervert received a remarkably

---

[154] Mike Sullivan, "Palace Pervert Queen's Former Driver Attacked Boy, 10, at Buckingham Palace But Died before Charges could be Brought," *The Sun*, December 9, 2018.

[155] Andy Crick, "Perv Caged Buckingham Palace Paedophile Caught with 15,000 Indecent Snaps and Clips of Kids," *The Sun*, June 6, 2018.

[156] "Queen's Former Butler Jailed for Abusing a Boy," *BBC*, July 5, 2019.

[157] Stephen Farrell, "Diplomat Faces Prison over Paedophile Videos," *The Times/spotlightonabuse.wordpress.com*, September 6, 1996.

[158] Paul Harper and Robert Collins, "Perv at the Palace Paedophile Trevor Francis who Received MBE from Prince Charles at Buckingham Palace is Exposed as a Serial Child Abuser," *The Sun*, March 31, 2017.

light prison sentence of only 9-months in May 2017, forcing the royals in another embarrassing move several months later to strip him of his regal honors.[159]

Cristopher Exley, a 33-year old Met Police Officer assigned to the elite Special Operations Division protecting the royal family, was caught in an undercover sting possessing dozens of indecent images of children, including level four penetration.[160] Believing he was chatting online with a 10-year old boy, the cop let it be known he desired having "naked coffee" with him. But after making contact with another Met officer from the pedophile unit, a police raid on his home found child pornography on his computer in February 2012. Since the officer pled guilty to possession of indecent child images, the prosecutor opted to only charge him with the lesser child porn crime rather than intent to have sex with an underage victim. Likely due to the link to the royal family and the perp being one of their own, Exley was spared jail time.

Another on duty police officer from Royalty and Special Protection Police at a Queen's tea party parade hit on a 16-year old girl who maintains she repeatedly told him her age, asking for her phone number while he was on duty supposedly guarding the royal family.[161] The young girl in court said she gave it to him because he was a police officer with a gun. Married Officer Andrew Daly then began sending lewd messages asking if she was a virgin. At a hearing, Daly admitted to misconduct. Yet somehow, he's been allowed to keep his job. Apparently the royals have no issue with their police protectors also being married pedophiles.

Another derelict was also charged with four counts of making indecent images of children while employed as a Home Office chief responsible for security at Buckingham Palace, other royal palaces and 10 Downing Street. 48-year old David Tracey was arrested, suspended and then fired from his job in November 2012, admitting he had downloaded an incredible 90,000 photos and videos off the internet.[162] He too was also not sent to prison but received a similar light sentence – an order to attend internet sex offender class, a three-year community order, a sex offenses prevention order and a fine. 90,000 files of child pornography yet not one day in jail? Seems crime almost pays for these sickos as long as they're even remotely connected to the royal family.

Yet another Buckingham palace butler collecting and distributing yet more child pornography sent 33-year old Nicholas Greaves to prison for two years back in July 2006.[163] After employed as a royal footman from 2002 to 2004, he moved on as servant at the private Belgravia residence of Jordanian King Abdullah. He possessed over 450 indecent photos and 15 indecent films on his laptop, some with victims only a few months old and some involving torture. He made several gestures to try and commit suicide. One has to ask how come so many seriously

[159] Ross Hart, "Jailed Former Aberdour Stationmaster Trevor Francis Stripped of MBE," *Dunfermline Press*, December 12, 2017.
[160] "Christopher Exley – Clapton," *theukdatabase,net*, December 10, 2012.
[161] "Buckingham Palace Police Officer 'Should be Sacked Immediately after Sending Girl Sexualized Messages,'" *The Gazette*, December 4, 2018.
[162] "Royal Security Chief Found Guilty of Downloading Porn," *echo-news.co.uk*, April 5, 2013.
[163] "Former Royal Butler Jailed over Obscene Child Pictures," *Daily Mail*, July 27, 2006.

disturbed child perverts end up working for the royal family. Of course the answer is obvious, because the British monarchy is full of sexually deviant predatory child abusers. It's simply the universal law of "like attracts like" operating.

What's a pedo-scandal without the holier than thou clergy mucking it up with their raping of innocent children? The predator, Dr. Stephen Palmer, enticed an underage girl into his church under the false pretense to help her with her religious studies in 1975 and 1976, only to pounce on her and cause her nightmares, struggling with suicidal thoughts and attempts for years afterwards.[164] And then the creep goes on to be hired by the queen as one of her chaplains bringing the Anglican ministry that she presides over to serve her monarchy. And though court and karma finally caught up to this 68-year old prick 39 years later with a 39-month prison sentence in July 2015, you know that this girl wasn't his only victim as child rapists invariably repeat their crimes. And to receive but one-month incarceration for every year his crimes went unpunished is a slap on the hand. Could it be once again the queen's hand intervened on his behalf?

This next case looks even more suspect. Queen Elizabeth is a patron of her Church of England charity the Society for Promoting Christian Knowledge (SPCK). Patrick Gilbert, the Oxford educated secretary general of SPCK from 1971 to 1991 was a close friend of the queen, often attending her royal garden parties.[165] One of the SPCK governors that Gilbert worked with was Sir Angus Ogilvy, late husband of queen cousin Princess Alexandra. Children's charities, Prince Charles' buddy Jimmy Savile, pedo-linked charity head Sir Harold Haywood, Jersey pedo Senator Wilfred Krishevsky and this royal couple as the queen's royal charity patrons keep coming up over and over again and over again, indicating linkage between the royal family and the larger pedophilia network coordinated by the likes of "deep cover" Jimmy.

Serial sodomite Patrick Gilbert was already a convicted pedophile after sexually assaulting two 13-year old boys. Yet his prior didn't stop him from becoming a who's who in the Queen's Church of England, working for at risk children for decades in his queen sponsored church charity. Gilbert became obsessed with an 11-year old boy who began attending dance classes operated by the church trust. The derelict paid for the boy's ballet lessons, groomed him with new clothes and jewelry, and began a sexual relationship when the victim was 14. For the next four years he frequently traveled with the boy. Senior church officials knew of the abusive sexual relationship yet chose to do nothing, just like the royal family. Yet the crimes were allowed to continue year after year because of Patrick Gilbert's standing in both the church community and his close ties to royalty. After his November 1991 arrest, the judge gave him a 9-month suspended sentence allowing the VIP to escape justice with no prison time. It's almost like Jeffrey Epstein's sweetheart deal except even sweeter. Judge Michael McMullen said Gilbert's heart condition would likely kill the child rapist if he had to endure the discomfort of a jail cell. Obviously the judge exhibited more concern for the well-being of the perp than the victim. Here the sicko has a prior conviction and he was still allowed to carry on for years

---

[164] "Ex-Chaplain to Queen Jailed for Sex Assault on Teenage Churchgoer which Left her Suicidal and Suffering Nightmares," *Daily Mail*, July 24, 2015.
[165] Neil Syson, "This Church Pervert Abuses Lad and doesn't go to Prison," *The Sun/theadreaderapp.com*, 1992.

without consequence. This is yet another cover-up and disgrace of the entire British justice system.

Reason for calling this a cover-up is this asshole's crimes have been completely purged from the internet. Had an article in *The Sun* written by journalist Neil Syson in the early 1990s not been screen saved and placed on spotlightonabuse.wordpress.com or Twitter threadreaderapp.com,[166] this entire travesty would have simply been swept under the rug and effectively erased from history.[167] None of the past media coverage on any other royal palace pedophiles has been deleted from the net. That's why it's highly probable that Patrick Gilbert, the Church of England and its church head Queen Elizabeth have a lot more to hide, removing this man's perversions linked to her church and family from public access. Again, charity organizations are notorious for providing the convenient cover for clandestine pedophilia operations worldwide.

Sticking with the holy roller theme of degenerates, the queen's once renowned former organist and choirmaster Jonathan Rees-Williams in August 2004 was sentenced to five years and three months in prison for numerous sexual assaults against 5 boys and one girl back in the 1970s and 1980s.[168] He also had 127 indecent images of children on two computers, padding his jail time by just three months. He was forced to step down from his royal duties in 2002 when allegations first came to light. The now 71-year old is indefinitely registering as a sex offender. According to the August 26, 2004 *Daily Mail*, his crime scenes were:

...in a cathedral organ loft, a church crypt and on public transport as well as at home.[169]

If it's not a degenerate hiding behind the church, it's one in military uniform guarding the queen's castle or yacht. Retired Royal Navy Lt. Commander Douglas Slade cooked the queen's dinners on the Royal Yacht Britannica.[170] Also a notorious PIE founder and pedophile, Slade was arrested and extradited to the UK from the Philippines in 2016 to face a litany of serial sex crimes committed in Britain from 1965 to 1980.[171] Slade fled to the Philippines in 1985 and grew rich operating a meat supply company in Asia. He built a home overlooking a primary school in a poor section of Angeles City where the 308 pound (22 stone) monster regularly preyed on young local boys. But back in the UK, the child rapist was sentenced to 24 years in prison. The now morbidly obese 78-year old child rapist will no doubt die behind bars.

Yet another Royal Navy Commander, this time the Queen's harbormaster, honored with an OBE no less, was arrested for both making and storing indecent photos of underage girls as young as

---

[166] "Isabella," *thereaderapp.com*.

[167] Neil Syson, https://spotlightonabuse.files.wordpress.com/2013/12/sun150693.jpg.

[168] "Queen's Ex-Choirmaster Jailed for Child Sex Attacks," *Daily Mail*, August 25, 2004.

[169] David Wilkes, "Jailed, the Royal Choirmaster Who Abused Children," *Daily Mail/spotlightonabuse.wordpress.com*, August 26, 2004.

[170] "British Accused of Child Sexual Abuse," *News of the World/preda.org*, May 8, 2006.

[171] Simon Parry, "'I was Frightened… I bit his Arm and Ran': How Brave Boy Aged Ten was Paid 2 Pounds for Sex then Ran for his Life after 22-Stone Paedophile Douglas Slade Brandished Gun," *Daily Mail*, July 5, 2016.

11 on his computer.[172] But 48-year old Tom Herman, father of three, was allowed to keep his job after the Portsmouth Crown Court cleared him of all child pornography charges. You think his royal employer and OBE had any bearing on the outcome?

37-year old royal guardsman Simon Davies and his 44-year old primary schoolteacher wife Fiona Parsons Davies were arrested at their home within two miles from Windsor Castle for both raping a girl under 13 in late August 2011.[173] Apparently in late January 2011 the perps filmed their sexual attacks on the prepubescent girl and then shared it on the internet with fellow members of their pedophile ring. After completing a combat tour in Afghanistan serving with the Household Cavalry Blues and Royals, the same outfit of both Prince William and Prince Harry, they very likely know this child rapist. Three days after the married couple's arrest came another royal guardsman's arrest who lives several houses down. Police suspect a larger pedophile ring operating within the royal protection force.[174] Ya think?

Another soldier, chief warrant officer Stephen Salmon with the Royal Marines, was assigned as a bodyguard on the Royal Yacht Britannica during Prince Charles and Princess Diana's 1981 16-day honeymoon cruise in the Mediterranean.[175] But prior to his military duty, back in the 1970s after befriending the family living next door, the now 72-year old committed a string of sexual assaults on the family's daughter Natalie when she was aged 7 to 12. He was married and living in Spain when returning to Britain in 2012, he was arrested, tried and convicted for his brutal crimes. In 2014 he was sentenced to four years in prison. But less than a year later, two more of his victims came forward. At the time of their sexual attacks, they were 6- and 9-years old. But only six more months were tacked on in prison, that's an additional 3 months each for raping a 6- and a 9-year old.

Another pedophilia scandal also hit the tabloids in 2018, centered on 51-year old ex-paratrooper Wayne Domeney who'd gone on the lam after being convicted of 13 child sex crimes in Birmingham Crown Court. In 2018 his 18-year old stepdaughter waved anonymity to disclose that when she was 12 in 2012 the ex-soldier began raping her for the next two and a half years before she finally told her mother and police, culminating with a 17-year prison sentence in 2018 after two weeks on the run.[176] The media sensationalized the case, hyping it with a photograph of the perp shaking hands with Prince Charles, both clad in military uniform prior to reportedly downing Guinness beers together at the local pub. Domeney earned more media mileage claiming he'd had tea with Queen Elizabeth, escorted Princess Diana through a minefield on a visit to Bosnia, helped train Prince William and served with Prince Harry in Afghanistan over a 25-year career spanning tours in Iraq, Afghanistan and Northern Ireland. In

---

[172] Geoffrey Lakeman, "Sin the Navy; Royal Officer Keeps Job after Viewing Sick Photos of Kids," *Mirror/thefreelibrary.com*, May 12, 2005..

[173] Jamie Pyatt, Mike Sullivan and David Willetts, "Paedo Probe at Windsor Castle," *The Sun*, August 31, 2011.

[174] Damien Gayle, "Police Arrest another of the Queen's Guards in Windsor Castle Paedophile Ring Probe," *Daily Mail*, September 3, 2011.

[175] Jon Livesey, "Princess Diana's Ex-Royal Marine Bodyguard Jailed again for Child Abuse after more Victims Emerge," *Mirror*, May 20, 2015.

[176] Nicola Moors and Hayley Richardson, "Sexual Predator My Sick Stepdad who Said he Trained Prince William in the Army Raped me when I was 12 – then Went on the Run when I Reported him," *The Sun*, September 18, 2018.

2009 he left the army a diagnosed sergeant major with PTSD. This story was exploited by all the tabloid rags due to the perp claiming he had interaction with every senior royal family member. Bragging to the press about all his royal ties, clearly backfired, probably adding at least a decade onto his 17-year sentence.

One more pedophile person of interest indirectly related to the royal family - Reginald Forester-Smith, became wealthy as a photographer to the rich and famous back in the 1970s with royal clients Queen Elizabeth and Prince Philip along with race car driver Sir Jackie Stewart. But it was his incestuous pedophilia crimes inflicted on his two daughters and another schoolgirl that led to his last eight years on earth spent in prison and his will that became a contested source of controversy.[177] For near 20 years this star photographer in demand sexually abused daughters starting at 9- and 6-years old. Eventually as adults, they reported the abuse to police and Forester-Smith was arrested, tried and found guilty of his decades of abuse in 1999. After filing divorce, two years later their mother died. Then eight years into his prison sentence, the 77-year old wacko also died. For sending him to prison, his last act of hateful revenge against his victimized daughters was through his will, leaving them nothing with over a million pounds going to charity, two-thirds to two cancer organizations. But the 400,000 pounds left to the Girl Guides was ethically challenged by the two sisters, asking that the charity give the money back to the estate.

Incidentally, when the above story emerged, the Girl Guides was in the middle of celebrating its centennial in 2010. After the pedophile ex-military general Lord Baden-Powell had founded the Boy Scouts for males,[178] which is currently in bankruptcy due to too many rapes,[179] its founder Baden-Powell and his wife were asked to come up with an equivalent for girls, the Girl Guides or Girl Scouts.[180]

The abused daughters' mother had been a volunteer of the Girl Guides for years, where she chaperoned girls on camping trips on the family estate's land. It was during this time every year that Reginald would sexually assault his daughters and another girl. It was through Girl Guides that the pedophile was able to do his damage, so the victims made a public plea appealing to the charity to not accept the gift from their deceased father. The story was splashed across the media but, other than the dilemma facing the three charities that acknowledged the daughters' request, no further coverage of the final outcome is on the internet.

The three dozen cases presented here of professional pedophiles in official capacity hired by and serving Queen Elizabeth and her monarchy were all caught red-handed. Yet it's merely a drop in the bucket of the vast number of never caught child rapists historically surrounding the royal family whose job is to follow their every move, catering to their every whim wherever

---

[177] Lesley Roberts, "Paedophile's Will is Last Slap in the Face for Daughters he Abused," *Daily Record*, April 25, 2010.
[178] Michael Bronski, "Queering the Scouts," *Z Magazine*, May 1, 1998.
[179] Nathan Bomey, "Boy Scouts Bankruptcy: What we Know about Victims, Assets and the Future of Scouting," *USA Today*, February 18, 2020.
[180] "Lady Baden-Powell, 88, Girl Scouts' Chief Guide," *The New York Times*, June 27, 1977.

they go, regardless of palace, castle, yacht or travel. It's important to note that many of the royal staff whose crimes either went unpunished or were treated with excessive lenience were likely deemed of high enough status on the royal pecking order for the monarchy to quietly intervene and protect them from a fair and just consequence befitting their crimes. Only the lowest level of junior staff gets prosecuted, convicted and serves any length of time in prison. Just as child raping MPs never are brought to justice, neither are senior royal staff and of course never a royal family member regardless of how despicable their child sex crimes are. This is a clear discernable fact based on the aforementioned presentation. Moreover, it's also a fair and accurate assessment to conclude that based on its historical record of normative standard hiring practice policies, the British monarchy has knowingly chosen to permit severe, pathologically disturbed, dangerous criminal predators in its employment while knowingly posing extremely grave risk of harm to children. And the most obvious reason is that the royal family itself is comprised of an inordinate number of hardcore child sexual abusers. A royal infestation of sickos has been sponsored by sexually deviant predators within royalty because they're the born and bred bloodline of inherited planetary overlords secretly behind the massive child sex trafficking slavery trade on this earth that has and still is destroying and murdering millions and millions of innocent, defenseless children.

Next we turn to the long list of questionable, if not seedy, pedophilic company that Prince Charles has chosen to keep as a reflection of who this guy really is. From longtime MP Michael Colvin's obit in *The Guardian*:

He [Colvin] *was a friend of the Prince of Wales, but a sharp critic of Princess Diana.*[181]

MP Colvin was implicated in both corruption and the North Wales pedo-scandal. According to *indymedia.org*:

Five witnesses to child sexual abuse at Bryn Estyn reportedly 'died in a fire which was said to have been 'arranged' by Michael Colvin.'[182]

Apparently there was an "oversight" at Clarence House when Prince Charles sent out his guest list to join the royal family on the barge the Spirit of Chartwell celebrating the 2012 Diamond Jubilee Pageant on the Thames. As of 1986 a court of law ruled Harbinder Singh Rana a convicted pedophile for posing as a doctor to carry out his predatory sexual assaults on children, and was sentenced to four years in prison.[183] Despite his criminal past, because Rana is a recognized Sikh leader as honorary director of the Anglo Sikh Heritage Trail, promoting positive relations in the British Sikh community, raping a few kids in the past never got in the way of a good friendship with the future king. Of course, once again the usual claim of ignorance was evoked as the royal excuse for the sex offender's onboard presence. Prince

[181] Andrew Roth, "Michael Colvin," *The Guardian*, February 24, 2000.
[182] "The Royal Family - 32 Reasons why they must be Required to Answer Police Questions," *indymedia.org.uk*, December 30, 2014.
[183] Lauren Turner, "Sex Offender Invited on to Queen's Jubilee Barge by Prince Charles," *Belfast Telegraph*, June 7, 2012.

Charles's Clarence House spokesperson made no apology for his invitation but admitted had the office known of Rana's prior conviction, he would never have been invited…. famous last "would've, should've, could've" words come mighty cheap.

More from the prince's infamously enormous, "oops, I never knew" file comes his shady friendship with yet another high profile convicted child sexual predator - Bishop Peter Ball, involved in a friendship with Charles lasting at least 30 years. Despite being investigated by police for child sex abuse crimes back in the early 1990s, due to Ball's powerful friends, he was simply issued a caution, which in effect amounts to a "get out of jail card" for admitting guilt.[184] If the same evidence applied to you or me, we'd be locked up for years. But the bishop had the royal family standing proactively behind him, so he avoided prosecution in spite of the mounting clear-cut evidence. Peter Ball must have figured he was immune from the law for having cultivated such key strategic alliances with top Church of England officials including its Supreme Governor Queen Elizabeth and her heir-to-the-throne son Prince Charles. Though he received the police caution in 1993 for "committing an act of gross indecency against a teenager," apparently it had little to no impact to deter the brazenly ballsy Ball, who chose to continue committing acts of serial sodomy against targeted young boys, often even boasting to victims about his tight friendship with royalty, as if to say "I'm untouchable." And just like with Sir Jimmy Savile, Charles conveniently pretends he never knew.

Peter and his twin brother Michael Ball began their Community of the Glorious Ascension in 1960. For over a half century, the pedo-cabal system either looked the other way or rushed to his defense whenever victims came forward to report abuse. Despite the dozens of victims, Peter Ball rose through the clergy ranks to become Bishop of Lewes and then diocesan Bishop of Gloucester.[185] Finally, over the decades so much overwhelming evidence was gathered that victims and activists forced the hand of law enforcement and Crown Prosecution Service to finally act, and in 2015, Bishop Ball pleaded guilty to raping 18 underage victims yet was only given a light 32-month prison sentence for his mountain of abuse. Due to such a soft punishment and travesty of justice, the Church of England's senior ranking clergy, the Archbishop of Canterbury, was forced to launch a new investigation of church complicity. The current Archbishop Justin Welby finally apologized to all the victims and admitted the obvious:

The church colluded and concealed rather than seeking to help those who were brave enough to come forward.[186]

Right up to Ball's less than 3-year prison conviction, Prince Charles was the child rapist's biggest defender. Little more than a year after the police caution, Charles wrote in a letter of support:

I wish I could do more. I feel so desperately strongly about the monstrous wrongs that have been done to you and the way you have been treated.[187]

---

[184] "Bishop Ball Sex Charges Caution 'Wrong' Admits CPS," *BBC*, September 13, 2015..
[185] Amando Flavio, "Church of England Admits Protecting Pedophile Priests for Years," *anonymous-news.com*, June 25, 2017.
[186] Amando Flavio.

Look at the empathy showered upon his poor little martyred victim. Meanwhile, Charles' predatory friend is free to continue wrecking boys' lives for another 20 years. How disgustingly sickening that the future king always seems so caring and loyal toward the worst monsters in the world... unless he's one himself. Back in 1993, Charles was pissed at then Archbishop of Canterbury who had promised Charles that he'd restore Ball to "some form of ministry," but instead the disgraced bishop was forced to resign from the church. Vowing to find the bishop and his twin brother a nice place to live very close to Charles through his Duchy of Cornwall, Prince Charles ended up providing a home they rented from the prince near his royal Highgrove House from 1997 to 2011.

According to Charles, Ball had explained that his 1993 church resignation resulted from an accused "indiscretion" from someone with an apparent vendetta. Charles wrote that he had no idea about the abuse with which his bishop friend "regretfully misled" him. All this information only came to light because the Independent Inquiry on Child Sexual Abuse (IICSA) in July 2018 requested a written statement from the prince related to its probe into Church of England's institutional abuse. The same year 1993 the police caution was issued, the prince invited the bishop to give holy communion at his Highgrove House.

After Ball's caution, the following year even Queen Elizabeth publicly lent her support to the pedophile, seeking him out at an Anglican event to say in a loud clear voice in front of the gathered crowd, "My love and encouragement, Bishop."[188] So both the queen and future king went out of their way to show public support to a serial child sexual predator. And again, intelligence services would have kept the royal family abreast of their fond bishop's deviant proclivity. Even more incriminating is the fact that Jimmy Savile was also a close friend to both the prince and his fellow high-profile pedophile in the church.

In 2005 Peter Ball was a guest at Charles and Camilla's wedding at Windsor Castle, the following year the former bishop spoke at the prince's father-in-law's funeral. Clearly, for many decades the derelict ex-bishop and the derelict DJ both remained within Prince Charles' innermost circle of intimate friends. Not until the 2015 conviction, according to the heir to the throne, did he realize that the police caution was "an acceptance of guilt."[189] Despite being so close for over three decades, Prince Charles pretended all along he was absolutely clueless. The attorney representing many of Peter Ball's victims wasn't buying Charles' feigned ignorance that this princely man of the world didn't even know what a police caution was. Guess when you're so used to living your entire life so far above the law, ignorance is bliss:

Prince Charles had access to the best legal advice that money can buy and, as a man in his position, a particular responsibility to check the facts. It is difficult to see his failure to do so as anything other than willful blindness. His evidence, together with that of Lord Carey, the then

---

[187] Harriet Sherwood, "Prince Charles Rued 'Monstrous Wrongs' against Bishop Later Convicted of Abuse," *The Guardian*, July 27, 2018.
[188] Richard Kay.
[189] Harriet Sherwood, https://www.theguardian.com/uk-news/2018/jul/27/prince-charles-rued-monstrous-wrongs-against-bishop-later-convicted-of-abuse.

archbishop of Canterbury, and other establishment figures who have given evidence this week, will do little to dissuade survivors from the conclusion that the British establishment aided and protected Ball and even now have failed to give a transparent account of their actions.[190]

I second the motion. Under strict state protocol, as the future king of England, any personal friend of the prince who's a regular guest at his home must have been thoroughly vetted by security services. Thus, just like with intimate royal friend Jimmy Savile, Charles had to have been briefed over these high-profile child rapists who repeatedly found themselves under police investigation. Sorry Charlie, you are guilty as charged.

A sister of one of Ball's many abuse victims who took his own life claimed in a recent documentary that the pedophile's "friends in high places," like Prince Charles, "are categorically to blame" for her 38-year old brother's premature death.[191] And who could argue against her after he was violated at 13 and suffered the next quarter century before it became too much. As is a common fate, the lifelong tortured victim goes to his early grave still a young man while the parasitic perpetrator outlives his victim by a near half century. Disgraced bishop Ball was released from his overly-lenient prison stint in February 2017, and after sustaining injuries from falls in his home, in June 2019 at the ripe old age of 87, another one of Prince Charles' sexual predator intimates was dead.

Aside from Prince Charles and past Archbishops of Canterbury, yet another Peter Ball protector in high places is the Baroness Butler-Sloss. Judge Sloss was ex-Prime Minister Theresa May's first choice to lead (and protect) VIP pedophiles in the anything but "Independent," Home Office controlled Inquiry for Child Sexual Abuse (IICSA). No doubt Sloss was selected in 2015 on the basis that in 2011 when the head of the Anglican Church asked her to investigate Peter Ball, she went soft on the abuser in order to protect the church.[192] Pedo-enabling Lady Sloss was kicked off her IICSA perch because her late brother, Lord Michael Havers, the reputed pedophile Attorney General under Thatcher, was actually a big part of the problem, as a gatekeeping abuser himself instrumental in the national cover-up.[193]

Baroness Sloss was appointed to chair the nation's official child abuse investigation simply because Theresa May saw her as a safe pair of hands to continue the British government's longtime, unbroken policy of whitewashing all child abuse. But within a month, her plan backfired and Sloss was forced to resign due to mounting public pressure.[194] Based on both her brother's and her own abysmal track record, Sloss was the last person who'd be fair and objective. So what does May do? She selects never prosecuted pedophile Leon Brittan's next-

---

[190] Harriet Sherwood, https://www.theguardian.com/uk-news/2018/jul/27/prince-charles-rued-monstrous-wrongs-against-bishop-later-convicted-of-abuse.

[191] Monica Greep, "Sister of a Man who Took his own Life after being Abused by Bishop Ball Claims the Paedophile's 'Friends in High Places' like Prince Charles are 'to Blame' for her Brother's Death in a New Documentary," *Daily Mail*, January 14, 2020.

[192] David Barrett, "Baroness Butler-Sloss Criticized over Previous Flawed Paedophile Report, *The Telegraph*, July 9, 2014.

[193] "Sir Michael Havers, Brother of Baroness Butler-Sloss," *spotlightonabuse.wordpress.com*, July 8, 2014.

[194] Nicholas Watt, "'Conflict of Interest' Raised over Butler-Sloss Role in Child Abuse Inquiry," *The Guardian*, July 9.

door neighbor who also was a no-go. We're on our fourth IISCA chair in five years now, with social work professor Alexis Jay still at the helm moving nowhere fast, dying a slow ineffectual death on the vine, just as the elite intended all along. Jay's safe pair of hands found no organized pedophile network operating in Westminster involving MPs, PMs and ministers.[195] Nothing to see, just move along. During the Savile post-bombshell years, Britain's riled up public demanding justice for victims needed to be placated, and the IISCA has done its pedo-enabling, placating duty to keep VIP child rapists out of both newspaper headlines and federal prison. Meanwhile, in plain sight, Britain's vast child trafficking-rape network quietly lives on, by design out of sight and out of mind.

Next comes the story of the royal family's worst PR nightmare – its shameless love affair with Britain's worst all-time child rapist in history and how Sir Jimmy Savile's incredibly close ties to royalty are best explained by the covered-up truth. It all started back in 1966 when the then Royal Marine Commandant, "Dickie" Mountbatten, did the honor of awarding the green beret to BBC DJ Jimmy Savile as the first civilian recipient.[196] Allegedly Savile had completed the 30-mile Royal Marine Commando speed march in less than 8 hours with full 30-pound backpack to earn the symbolic accolade,[197] marking the beginning of a very long and special relationship Sir Jimmy enjoyed over the next 45 years with unprecedented access and inexplicable intimacy with the entire British royal family.

Apparently Lord Mountbatten saw something in the highly eccentric DJ that would prove useful to the royals, so he promptly introduced Savile to Prince Philip that same year. Considering that Savile and Mountbatten shared a mutual common interest as adult men who relished sodomizing young boys especially, the Savile-royal family common bond was quickly cemented. Savile has been proven to be a child procurer for the rich and famous, be they prime ministers (as in Edward Heath), politicians or entertainers. Savile's own nephew Guy Marsden implicated Britain's most infamous child predator as a supplier of children at sex orgies inside posh London mansions in the 1960s. During an *Esquire* interview, in the same breath Savile boasted:

The thing about me is I get things done and I work deep cover. I've known the Royal Family for a million years.[198]

Regarding how Savile was readily accepted into the royal circle right after his Marine beret ceremony:

Coming from Lord Louis, who was the favourite uncle of Prince Philip, that was quite something. So obviously I hooked up with the Prince – what was good enough for Lord Louis was good enough for him.[199]

---

[195] "Allegations of Child Sexual Abuse Linked to Westminster Investigation Report Part K1: Conclusions," *iicsa.org.uk*, February 2020.

[196] Simon Edge, "How Jim Really Did Fix It," *Express*, May 8, 2008.

[197] "Royal Marines Destroy Savile Memory," *The Sun*, October 18, 2012.

[198] Simon Edge, https://www.express.co.uk/expressyourself/43798/How-Jim-really-did-fix-it.

What asshole meant by "what" in the above quote has to be defiling children.

In the 1970s Savile got to know Prince Charles reportedly through mutual charity causes, gradually growing closer throughout the 1980s so that the pedophile became the prince's intimate confidant, reportedly on the short list to be Prince Harry's godfather.[200] During the seething "cold war" years of the 15-year royal marriage between Diana and Charles during the latter half, Jimmy Savile played a major role as informal marriage counselor. According to Princess Diana's biographer Andrew Morton:

Savile's opinions carry weight in both camps. He articulates opinions that courtiers can only think.[201]

In a taped conversation Diana had with one of her lovers James Gilbey in 1989, she described Savile "as a kind of mentor" to Charles. In her *Palace Diaries*, former Duke of Wales secretary Sarah Goodall noted a Savile office visit that went beyond working on a shared Stoke-Mandeville Hospital charity together:

Today is a strange day, a middle-aged man with a shock of white hair, dressed in a white boiler suit and covered in gold jewellery, has entered one of the offices… in another capacity altogether – as a marriage guidance counsellor.[202]

Savile was also called in to rescue the Duchess of York, Sarah Ferguson's sagging PR image during Prince Andrew and her adulterous years, ostensibly to manage lowering her scandalously high profile. The DJ also finagled Charles' siblings Andrew and Anne to each appear on separate episodes of Savile's 20-year run on BBC television show "Jim'll Fix It."[203] It appeared that the child sex parasite had the entire royal family wrapped around his little finger. As reputed child procurer for the royals according to multiple sources,[204] [205] [206] [207] the queen's "Firm" was highly invested in protecting Sir Jimmy as a means of protecting themselves, since the dirty lowdown that Savile had on them served as his own potentially unveiled blackmail threat of guaranteed self-protection.

---

[199] Simon Edge, https://www.express.co.uk/expressyourself/43798/How-Jim-really-did-fix-it.

[200] Richard Kay, "How Savile Seduced the Royals: As it's Claimed he nearly Became Godfather to Harry, how the Predatory DJ Wormed his way into the very Heart of Palace Life," *Daily Mail*, June 12, 2015.

[201] Richard Kay, https://www.dailymail.co.uk/news/article-3122130/How-Savile-seduced-royals-s-claimed-nearly-godfather-Harry-predatory-DJ-wormed-way-heart-Palace-life.html.

[202] Richard Kay, https://www.dailymail.co.uk/news/article-3122130/How-Savile-seduced-royals-s-claimed-nearly-godfather-Harry-predatory-DJ-wormed-way-heart-Palace-life.html.

[203] Richard Kay, https://www.dailymail.co.uk/news/article-3122130/How-Savile-seduced-royals-s-claimed-nearly-godfather-Harry-predatory-DJ-wormed-way-heart-Palace-life.html.

[204] J. Beverly Greene, *Illustrated Guide for the Politically Incorrect Looney Tunes Edition* (US: self-published, 2016), p. 217..

[205] Brandon Turbeville, https://www.activistpost.com/2012/11/the-prince-and-pedophile-charles.html.

[206] David Icke, "Jimmy Savile Doorway to the Cesspit," *davidicke.com*, November 2, 2012.

[207] "Prince Andrew, Part of the Evil Paedophile Family which has Abused and Murdered Poor Children for Centuries," *google-law.blogspot.com*, January 7, 2015.

Palace staff would note that Savile regularly solicited them for the latest gossip on royal family secrets, again as likely usable insurance in the foreseeable future if necessary.[208] Savile gloated about always remaining so tightlipped regarding his royal superiors, who of course fiercely protected him as well. Regarding his uncharacteristic discretion when it came to the royals, he asserted:

I'm the man who says nothing. Anything to do with matters royal is a no-go area.[209]

Obviously both Savile and the Windsors had/have much to hide and lose should their sins ever become fully exposed.

That said, Jimmy Savile had a knack for speaking in riddle tongue, frequently pushing his bodacious personality close to the limit of unacceptability, in hindsight dropping not-so-subtle truth bomb hints of his deeply pathological nature and sordid crimes in plain sight. An illustration of this Savile dynamic in action, as the procurer of children to the pedophilic royal family, cloaked in "benign" storytelling, he's seen yukking it up on a national talk show, boasting how he cleverly delivered an underage girl to Prince Philip at Buckingham Palace, receiving belly laughs from his unsuspecting captured audience throughout.[210] On full manic display, his satanic wizardry was at work, masterfully weaving his thinly disguised magic wand of child rape right before our eyes. Once he was exposed as British history's biggest, most vile child rapist ever, the criminal implications of his encrypted comedic gibberish suddenly became crystal clear.

As the initial shock of the 2012 Savile revelations began wearing off after his October 2011 death, British tabloids began running articles scratching just beneath the surface in efforts to explain the creepy showman's unprecedented access to the royal family, particularly inside Prince Charles' bizarro world. Describing how Savile used his wild court jester persona to liven up the deadpan stuffiness of an aging crusty old royal family, increasingly out of touch with the public, apparently brought Jimmy Savile into their intimate fold as a breath of albeit raunchy fresh air. His oddball, ingratiating "charm" is said to have seduced the royals, permitting him a status no outsider ever held, able to drop by the royal palaces at any given time, unannounced and unopposed, mingling freely as much with household staff as senior royals, unchallenged, Savile ruled the roost at Buckingham Palace, Kensington Palace, St. James' Palace or Highgate, his power over the Windsor family made it his kingdom, not unlike the BBC studios, Stoke-Mandeville hospital and Broadmoor prison asylum.[211]

---

[208] Richard Kay, https://www.dailymail.co.uk/news/article-3122130/How-Savile-seduced-royals-s-claimed-nearly-godfather-Harry-predatory-DJ-wormed-way-heart-Palace-life.html.

[209] Richard Kay, https://www.dailymail.co.uk/news/article-3122130/How-Savile-seduced-royals-s-claimed-nearly-godfather-Harry-predatory-DJ-wormed-way-heart-Palace-life.html.

[210] Jimmy Savile Took Young Girl to Prince Philip in Buckingham Palace," YouTube video, 03:49, posted November 21, 2019.

[211] Richard Kay, https://www.dailymail.co.uk/news/article-3122130/How-Savile-seduced-royals-s-claimed-nearly-godfather-Harry-predatory-DJ-wormed-way-heart-Palace-life.html.

Dickie Arbiter, the queen's longtime spokesperson in charge of media relations for Charles and Diana from 1988 to 2000, stated his observation of Savile's all too frequent visits:

He would walk into the office and do the rounds of the young ladies taking their hands and rubbing his lips all the way up their arms if they were wearing short sleeves. If it was summer [and their arms were bare] *his bottom lip would curl out and he would run it up their arms. This was at St James's Palace. The women were in their mid to late 20s doing typing and secretarial work.*[212]

Princess Diana's bodyguard Ken Wharfe commented:

He would turn up unannounced at Kensington Palace. He would bamboozle the police on the gate and just breeze in. He would tell Diana he was on a mission 'from the boss,' in other words her husband, but he just wanted to check up on her.[213]

To hear it from Savile:

Royalty are surrounded by people who don't know how to deal with it. I have a freshness of approach which they obviously find to their liking. I think I get invited because I have a natural, good fun way of going on and we have a laugh.[214]

What made this unpolished derelict DJ from a "lowly" working class background already past his career prime by the mid-1980s so enduringly popular to both the monarchy and public, allowing his bawdy, uncouth crudeness, "naughty" sleaziness and unpredictable, erratic behavior to be so pleasantly indulged, tolerated and even admired by the queen and her taken in family, especially her son Prince Charles? As the "deep cover" cabal operative known for "getting things done," evidence more than suggests that Jimmy Savile procured children for the royal pedophiles as part of his undercover utilitarian function, providing key linkage between sources of funneled child victims and their VIP perpetrators.

In all probability this bottom-line fact is the inherent value to the royals that pedo-Lord Mountbatten most likely first saw in Savile back in 1966 when the up and coming DJ was busily furnishing the kiddie entertainment at the mansion parties. One victim reported that a fleet of Savile taxis would drive up to the care home to pick up and traffic children to the sex parties for abuse. Again, Savile's own nephew Guy Marsden spoke of him supplying kids to the pedo-elite's orgies. Working "deep cover" with security services setting up sexual blackmail kiddie honey-traps,[215] "Jim fixed it" alright, so that the UK child care system pipelines were in place trafficking

---

[212] Robert Booth, https://www.theguardian.com/media/2012/oct/29/jimmy-savile-behaviour-prince-charles.

[213] Richard Kay, https://www.dailymail.co.uk/news/article-3122130/How-Savile-seduced-royals-s-claimed-nearly-godfather-Harry-predatory-DJ-wormed-way-heart-Palace-life.html.

[214] Robert Booth, "Jimmy Savile Cause Concern with Behaviour on Visits to Prince Charles," *The Guardian*, October 29, 2012.

[215] Roderick Russell, "Jimmy Savile – Pedophile, Friend of Royalty – and the Cover-up to Pervert Justice," *Daily Kos*, October 18, 2012.

victims to powerful VIP pedophile rings throughout the British Isles, Jersey Island and links across the channel to continental Europe.

After Savile proved himself a most frequent royal palace guest (similar to his 11 yearend holidays spent with the Thatchers), in 1999 it was finally the derelict's turn to invite Prince Charles over for dinner at his humble Scottish highland home in Glencoe, where the hired after dinner entertainment appeared as three dancing women dressed in pinafores. The British definition of a pinafore dress is a collarless, sleeveless dress worn over a blouse or sweater, a jumper, most often worn by young girls.[216] With nothing on underneath and decorated with only the letters HRH, it was a provocative gesture by the perverted host making a lasting impression on the prince who wrote in his Christmas card that year:

Jimmy, with affectionate greetings from Charles. Give my love to your ladies in Scotland.[217]

Considering Savile sexually abused at least 20 children in that same cottage that after his death was sold for twice the original asking price, but apparently has been left to rot, still begs the question, were the "ladies" Charles was referring to in his Christmas card, grown up ladies or more aptly Savile's underage victims?[218]

In one of Sir Jimmy's more than half dozen police interviews spanning his half century crime spree, during his final probe, under caution with Surrey police in 2009, two years before his death, Savile made countless references to the royal family, using his ever-tight bond as a guaranteed buffer against accountability for all his rapes.[219] A released transcript of the interview contained an astounding 96 redacted lines blacked out, making certain all references to the royals were completely censored. Breaching standard protocol, the Surrey police traveled to Savile's "home" office at Stoke-Mandeville Hospital where he raped the infirm, including dead corpses,[220] to question him regarding abuse allegations filed by three former students at Duncroft Approved School for girls. With Queen Elizabeth's cousin Princess Alexandra, a Duncroft patron and friend of Savile's, in his 1974 autobiography, Savile mentions attending a garden party with the princess at the state-run residential facility in Surrey that closed in the 1980s. In that same book, Savile even admitted to having sex with a 14-year old runaway.[221] Bottom line, MI5 knew, the police knew, Charles knew and the royal family knew Savile was a child sodomite but loved him and protected him anyway. And we know why. His autobiography states:

---

[216] "Pinafore," *Collins Dictionary*..

[217] Robert Booth, https://www.theguardian.com/media/2012/oct/29/jimmy-savile-behaviour-prince-charles.

[218] Holly Christdoulou, "Left to Rot Paedo Jimmy Savile's Scottish Highlands Cottage where Cops Fear 20 People were Abused Lays Empty Three Years after it Sold for Double the Asking Price," *The Sun*, November 22, 2017.

[219] "Police 'Censored' 2009 Interview with Jimmy Savile so it Removed all Reference to the Royal Family," *Daily Mail*, October 20, 2013.

[220] David Collins and Steve Robson, "Jimmy Savile 'Seen having Sex with Bodies and Wheeling Body of Four-Year Old in Pram into Hospital Mortuary," *Daily Record*, February 27, 2015.

[221] Hugo Rifkind, "Jimmy Savile's Affections Laid Bare," *The Times*, October 3, 2012.

With Angus Olgilvy and his super missus Princess Alexandra one feels a great friendship from the off. I am the vice-president to his Presidency of the National Association of Youth Clubs and he is often down with us at headquarters in Devonshire Street, wanting to know what's happening. Princess Alex is a patron of a hostel for girls in care. At this place I'm a cross between a termtime boyfriend and a fixer of special trips out. Girls in care don't take kindly to royal rules, protocol and the like, but Alex just steams in, captures them and anyone else that's around, and steams out.[222]

As a deceitful goodwill ambassador for children, UK's #1 sexual predator of all time enjoyed virtually unlimited VIP access and accommodations for many decades at Britain's National Health Services and care system facilities. In the police interview the royal name dropper of course denied any wrongdoing while police officers kissed the celebrity's ass during the near hour-long chitchat, heavily criticized for not challenging the guilty as sin criminal's cocky assertions. Despite 22 Duncroft abuse victims coming forth, no charges were ever brought against either Savile in 2009 or the enabling staff investigated a half decade later.[223] The reason Surrey police so strongly urged Crown Prosecution Service not to prosecute Savile was not from lack of evidence but simply the royal family's involvement.[224] With his monarchy connection automatically giving him a free pass, the scum of the earth was allowed to go to his grave dying "a legend" and "national treasure" two days shy of his 85th birthday, topped off by eulogized tributes led by a deeply "saddened" Prince Charles.[225] The function of security services, police, CPS and parliament render all criminal evidence leading to royalty off limits by media and redacted blackout, destroyed evidence or strict royal privacy laws ensuring the truth never sees the light of day for the sake of defense of the realm.[226] So an archaic abomination of a monarchy can still parasitically get away with murder and rape.

Repeated instances are on record of Charles seeking advice, guidance and assistance from Sir Jimmy, the lifetime bachelor, in response to his marital difficulties with Diana as well as consultation and feedback over selecting personal aides, leaning on Savile for the distasteful task of firing a particular staff that Diana said was a task Charles didn't have the stomach for.[227] Prior to becoming the royal couple's private secretary and treasurer in 1990, Charles asked Savile to sit in and essentially co-interview Sir Christopher Airy. In 1988 the heir to the throne asked Savile to become his royal party organizer for a Kensington Palace cocktail party with a group of television producers after a successful ITV telethon.[228] The Prince of Wales leaned on Savile's sway over the National Health Services, requesting his presence at a Highgate meeting with all of Britain's health chiefs. After the prince left, Savile threatened the health officials to

[222] Jimmy Savile, *As It Happens* (London: Barrie and Jenkins, 1974), p. 150.

[223] "Duncroft School: No Prosecutions over Jimmy Savile Inquiry," *BBC*, December 4, 2014.

[224] William Turvill, "Police 'Urged Prosecutors not to Pursue Child Sex Abuse Claims against Jimmy Savile after 2009 Interview," *Daily Mail*, December 15, 2013..

[225] Jimmy Savile Dead: Prince Charles Leads Tributes to TV Legend," *Mirror*, October 30, 2011.

[226] Eamonn McCann, "Savile Hides Beeb's other Crimes against Journalism," Belfast Telegraph, October 25, 2012..

[227] Richard Kay, https://www.dailymail.co.uk/news/article-3122130/How-Savile-seduced-royals-s-claimed-nearly-godfather-Harry-predatory-DJ-wormed-way-heart-Palace-life.html.

[228] Robert Booth, "Jimmy Savile Invited Royal Guests to a Party on Prince Charles' Behalf," *The Guardian*, November 7, 2012.

not piss Charles off or it could cost them their knighthood.[229] The more the future king relied on him, the more the over-the-hill megalomaniacal DJ relished throwing the full weight of his power around.

Doing so much for the Crown secured the legendary child predator boosted status, power and protection. Again and again situations arose where Prince Charles entrusted the Disc Jockey for his constant support, be it handling the prince's delicate personal affairs like the royals' disintegrating marriages or important day-to-day royal decisions involving the hiring and firing of key palace personnel to checking the prince's speeches, all illustrate the enormous significance of the intimate role Sir Jimmy played as Charles' trusted mentor and life supporter.[230] Though Diana saw through Savile's self-serving creepiness, especially after licking her hand, the princess's own observations confirm the fact that the pedophile was super close and extremely influential to Prince Charles.

The "Jim'll Fix It" persona made Jimmy the royal fixer in Charles' life for many years, because as Savile boasted, he earned the reputation for "getting things done" in "deep cover" service to the realm. Based on decades of mounting trust and proven reliance, Charles felt he could count on Savile to get him out of any fix, scrape or jam, regardless of how sticky or tricky. And Jimmy counted on Charles having his back as well. That's the kind of deep bonded survival trust the prince and pedophile shared, developed over several decades with the aging DJ as the MI5 vetted child procurer for the rich and powerful. The future king grew more confident that, no matter what, Savile would always have his back as well, no matter what, cementing their symbiotic "special" bond based upon decades of trust and mutually shared tastes and interests that extended far beyond their joint work together in various child charities.

After all, Jimmy Savile filled an emotional void for Charles, especially after violently losing his earliest family mentor and confidant - pedophile Uncle Dickie assassinated in August 1979.[231] With the prince's relationship with his own father Philip always cold, strained and contentious, Charles never quite passed Germanic muster as the stoic, manly kind of future king expected of his firstborn son, at least not by Prince Philip's Nazi standards.[232] The ingratiating Sir Jimmy was always soliciting, reassuring and never coldly rejecting like his sourpuss father. Charles' dependence on supportive, trustworthy older male role models from Lord Mountbatten transferred over to Jimmy Savile and Church of England Bishop Peter Ball. But they all shared one thing in common – they were all coldblooded predatory pedophiles to the nth degree. Now what does that tell you about Charles?

[229] Richard Kay, https://www.dailymail.co.uk/news/article-3122130/How-Savile-seduced-royals-s-claimed-nearly-godfather-Harry-predatory-DJ-wormed-way-heart-Palace-life.html.

[230] Gordon Raynor, "Charles Biography: 8 Most Intriguing Disclosures about Prince of Wales," *The Telegraph*, February 3, 2015.

[231] Alice Scarsi, "Prince Charles' Heartbreaking Speech after Tragic Loss – 'Ruthless and Irresistible,'" *Express*, August 27, 2019.

[232] Chelena Goldman, "Royal Family Secrets Reveal Why Prince Charles Has Always Hayed His Father," *cheatsheet.com*, August 27, 2018.

And what does it say when papal knight Sir Jimmy is best buds for over three decades with UK's top religious leaders from both churches. Britain's highest ranking Catholic Cardinal Keith O'Brien was forced to resign in disgrace in February 2013 after exposure for repeatedly making unwanted sexual advances on young priests, one as young as 18.[233] Then both the future king and Savile remained close loyal friends with Church of England's celebrity Bishop Peter Ball, the highest ranking convicted pedophile within the Queen's own church.[234] All these facts speak ever so loud and clear – "birds of a feather, flock together."

Gifting Savile a box of cigars and pair of gold cufflinks for his 80th birthday, Prince Charles wrote an encrypted thank you message on behalf of the entire British Establishment (pedo-network) that read:

Nobody will ever know what you have done for this country Jimmy. This is to go some way in thanking you for that.[235]

Counting on Savile's dark secrets staying safe with him, from the get-go Charles always had security services filling him in on the DJ's "deep cover" work in spite of a minority of royal advisors warning the prince to distance himself from the creepy pervert. But needing Savile's services and support emotionally, Charles chose not to listen.

Let's face it, no other single individual on the planet has left such indelibly distinctive fingerprints of "his services" rendered in every major pedophilia scandal in British history from the 1960s right into the 21st century as Sir Jimmy Savile. His name will uniquely come up invariably in virtually every scandalous chapter of this book, and, as a result, Savile is a huge reason why the United Kingdom is the world's pedophilia epicenter. With Savile's far-reaching tentacles uniquely dipped so deep in the darkest bowels of every public domain, from government, health, education, entertainment, charity, religion, military, law enforcement to royalty, Savile was the central spoke or common link to Britain's growing pedophilia network. And with all his tolerated grand scale abuse perpetrated in plain sight, indefinitely embedded for over a half century, Savile's criminal services as national child procurer was duly rewarded with a lifetime guarantee of shielded protection by police, security services, the BBC, prime ministers and especially the royal family.

Savile was an untouchable and arrogantly knew it, that's why everyone on the inside was very well aware of what he was really up to, but in deference to his unbridled evil power, all remained silent until it was safe after death. Savile was a self-described loner who had few true friends.[236] Colleagues who knew him for decades maintain they hardly knew him at all.[237] His

---

[233] Steve White, "Jimmy Savile and the Cardinal: Britain's Top Catholic Cleric was Friend of Disgraced IV Host," *Mirror*, February 26, 2013.

[234] Richard Kay, "Jimmy Savile and Prince Charles' Very Close Friendship with Sex Abuse Bishop Ball," *Daily Mail*, October 8, 2015.

[235] Richard Kay.

[236] Tracey McVeigh, "Jimmy Savile, Eccentric King of Children's TV, Dies at 84," *The Guardian*, October 29, 2011.

[237] Dan Davies, "'Little Slaves,' Sordid Beasts and the Dark Truth about my 'Friend' Jimmy Savile, by the Biographer who Tried to Unmask him," Daily Mail, October 6, 2012,.

sleaziness and self-serving, psychopathic, ruthlessly aggressive nature was secretly reviled and feared by those who got to know him up close and personal. Psychologist Oliver James concluded that Savile was Machiavellian, narcissistic and psychopathic, projecting and acting out his own deep pathology onto innocent victims.[238] Not exactly the fun-loving, altruistic, iconic entertainer generations of British kids fondly remember.

So there must be only one explanation as to why Satanist Savile was so much "revered" and honored while alive, he had the dirt on everybody in power as the kiddie procurer who "got things done" working "deep cover" with security services on expansion of UK's pedo-network. And for all his efforts, he was made a Malta Knight and Esteemed Friend of Israel.[239] Granted an early OBE from the Queen in 1972 on recommendation from then PM Edward Heath, a child rapist-murderer and fellow Satanist, and then knighted by the Queen in 1990 on PM Thatcher's 5th nominated go-round only a month after her safely leaving office. Then a month later as the "world's most Jewish Roman Catholic," Pope John Paul II, head of the biggest pedo-racket on earth, bestowed papal knighthood on "the saint" who could do no wrong in our upside-down Luciferian world. You might consider all these undeserved accolades as Jimmy Savile's hush rewards, his covert payoff thanking him as much for his many years of pedo-service as his bought, mum's-the-word, wink, wink silence.

In July 2014 even the cabal-controlled *Time Magazine* finally got one right with the feature story entitled "England: Land of Royals, Tea and Horrific Pedophilia Coverups."[240] But mainstream media can only go so far in raising questions about Prince Charles' incredibly poor judgment, explaining how the future king foolishly succumbed to the evil predator's charm, but never dare cross the line to actually suggest that Savile was ever pimping kids to the rich and powerful, among them the royals, despite the fact that a number of the Windsor men based on confirmed documented history unrelated to Savile indicate strong likelihood, if not certainty, that they are/were pedophiles. This kind of bottom line allegation, if ever accepted as truth, in a heartbeat would bring down the House of Windsor and end Britain's more than a millennium monarchal reign. So the controller-owned media will never bite the hand that feeds it.

Meanwhile, the truth's been staring us in the face for decades, from Lord Mountbatten to Prince Andrew's unlawfully despicable improprieties to Prince Charles' choice of "mentors and best friends." The controlled corporate media can never explicitly state the obvious. But in the case of the worst of the lot - Jimmy Savile, the "all too obvious" remained within our plain sight for over half a century. When it's all added up, too much credible evidence speaks louder than the British Establishment's feeble blackout of the truth. When all that is readily available and known within the public domain is taken fully into account, it makes for a formidably persuasive, if not open and shut case. Beyond his crude charm, mainstream media bothering to take on the topic of Savile's "special" relationship with the royals, always chalk it up to Prince Charles' naiveté and gullibility. That's attributing to a far from stupid man the much too feeble

---

[238] Oliver James, "Inside the Mind of Jimmy Savile," *The Guardian*, January 26, 2014.

[239] Tracey McVeigh, https://www.theguardian.com/tv-and-radio/2011/oct/30/jimmy-savile-top-of-pops-dead.

[240] Martin Hickman, "England: Land of Royals, Tea and Horrific Pedophilia Coverups," *Time Magazine*, July 10, 2014.

and lame an excuse and benefit of doubt that fails miserably to stand up as anything remotely plausible. Bottom line, the propensity for the Windsor men to surround themselves with sexual child predators has everything to do with them being child sexual predators themselves.

The confirmed pedophile Mountbatten helped raise both Philip and Charles during their impressionable, formative years while both were young lads, acting as a significant mentoring role model as well as surrogate father to both. Dickie's sexual urges to act on his impulses are almost for certain since pedophiles are compulsively driven to repeat their pedophilic behavior, particularly when ample opportunity affords itself. With Charles' father reportedly a pedophile,[241] and Charles' four great uncles Prince Edward VIII, his brother Prince George along with Lord Mountbatten and his older brother George Mountbatten all reputed pedophile perverts, and Charles' brother Andrew's evidential pedo-leanings, it's more than fair to assert that Charles possesses a strong genetic predisposition, additionally reinforced experientially by close contact with familial child abusers. Given this reality, it totally fits that Charles' two closest friends and mentors would be the all-time most infamous pedophile in British history and the most notorious Church of England bishop as UK's most senior cleric convicted of pedophilia. What are the odds of all that? It makes perfect sense when pedophilia runs so pervasively deep in royal family.

In Noel Botham's 2004 exposé *The Murder of Princess Diana*, he writes:

Lord Mountbatten, known affectionately around the palace as the biggest queen in the royal family, had surrounded Charles with homosexuals during the period when he had been entrusted by Queen Elizabeth with her eldest son's social upbringing. Diana did not like the clique that was similarly intended to be around her two sons and had systematically got rid of over 40 gay members of her husband's staff by forcing resignations or personally firing them.[242]

When from day one, Charles' primary conditioning years were inundated by the normalcy of homosexual pedophilia, the long-term effect was to predispose him toward the same behavior, replicating the same dynamic for his sons. But as much as she could, the princess's protective, maternal instinct sabotaged the overwhelming Windsor male legacy.

But it didn't stop Charles from gravitating to one pedophile after another, all taking on roles as close confidants and mentors heavily shaping and influencing him, making up for his lack of closeness and accessibility to his own preoccupied, emotionally distant parents. South African writer Laurens van der Post (1906-1996) is considered Charles' most influential guru and lifelong mentor. The prince even asked the aging van der Post to be Prince William's godfather. For decades Prince Charles sought out his personal sage for advice and guidance, Prime Minister Margaret Thatcher also often relied on van der Post's counsel for support. And just like Charles, she too grew incredibly close to Savile and as later chapters will show, was notoriously surrounded and protective of her pedo-saturated cabinet ministers as well. But it turns out

---

[241] Brandon Turbeville, https://www.activistpost.com/2012/11/the-prince-and-pedophile-charles.html.
[242] Noel Botham, *The Murder of Princess Diana* (New York: Kensington Publishing Corporation, 2004), p. 53.

Charles' guru was also a child abuser, while in his late 40s impregnating a 14-year old girl who bore him a secret love child.[243] Only after the womanizing "wise man" died did his shameful secret emerge. And then apparently even Charles' current wife Camilla Duchess of Cambridge doesn't care if her close friend with whom she travels on a 2005 holiday to Italy is a reputed sadistic homosexual pedophile and VIP child procurer – Derek Laud (also to be further documented).[244] These people have no shame.

Another pedophile was the science fiction writer Arthur C. Clarke. The expatriate author of *2001 Space Odyssey* living the second half of his life in Sri Lanka, in 1998 was granted knighthood by the Queen. But reporters from the *Mirror* went to the Sri Lankan capital Colombo and interviewed him, including men who claimed Clarke had sexually abused them as young boys.[245] In his *Mirror* interview Clarke as much as admitted he'd taken to enjoying boys for sex, incredibly even justifying his actions as harmless,[246] though insisting that in recent years his medical issues had prohibited him. But the head of current affairs at the Sri Lankan Broadcasting Company maintained that "just a few months ago" Clarke was sexually active with underage boys.[247] At the time of the controversy in 1998, Clarke insisted that defaming him with such allegations was aimed to embarrass Prince Charles who was the designated royal honoring him. Clarke contacted his lawyer and the *Mirror* was wrongly pressured into an apology.

In view of the fact that places like Sri Lanka, Thailand, the Philippines and Cambodia are notorious for sex tourism attracting hordes of Western pedophiles, there was an establishment urgency to deny that Arthur C. Clarke was ever a child abuser living abroad, for the sake of upholding his renowned literary reputation, tourism and the Queen's honors for knighthood. So in the end, it went forward. Bottom line, though a great writer, Clarke was a pedophile who in 2008 died a 90-year old in denial. The hypocritical irony is granting knighthood to known pedophiles has never, ever been an issue for the Queen or Prince. To the contrary, royalty has always cozied right up to child raping knights every chance they ever get.

Turning to Charles' brother born nearly a dozen years after Charles, Prince Andrew also has a thing for pedophiles. Due to his exposure in the still ongoing Epstein-Maxwell pedo-scandal (taken up in Book 4), as of December 2019, Prince Andrew the Duke of York has been relieved of all official royal duties due to the humiliation caused by his unbreakable ties to convicted pedophile and indicted trafficker Jeffrey Epstein. But the cat was let out of the bag more than a half decade earlier with an April 4, 2014 *Daily Mail* headline:

[243] Vanessa Thorpe, "Secret Life of Guru Revealed, The Guardian, February 3, 2001.
[244] Tim Spanton, "The Queen and Camilla," *The Sun/documen.tips*, May 30, 2005.
[245] Jane Kerr, Kevin McGuire and Gerard Couzens, "Arthur C. Clarke may Lose his Knighthood over Child Sex Claims," *Mirror/thefreelibrary.com*, February 2, 1998.
[246] "It doesn't do any Harm… Most of the Damage Comes from Fuss Made by Hysterical Parents," *Mirror/thefreelibrary.com*, February 1, 1998.
[247] Peter Popham, "The Mysterious Sri Lankan World of Arthur C. Clarke," *Independent*, February 3, 1998.

Bombshell Court Document that Claims Prince Andrew Knew about Billionaire Friend's Abuse of Under-age Girls[248]

The "party prince" was checkmated from the sleazy start, compliments of his pimping good buddies Jeffrey Epstein and Ghislaine Maxwell, daughter of media mogul and spy Robert Maxwell. Prince Andrew's innocence of any wrongdoing rings completely hollow in the face of alleged victim Virginia Roberts' persistent claims she was forced to have sex with the royal three times.[249] Meanwhile, according to an October 2019 tabloid headline from *The Sun*:

Prince Andrew admits 'best friend' Jeffrey Epstein was Jimmy Savile-style 'undercover paedo.'[250]

And then former assigned royal police officers insist that the prince's alibi, his bogus pizza story with his daughters, is false,[251] and an Epstein employee-witness on Epstein's sex slave island Little St. James went public insisting he observed Prince Andrew kissing, fondling and groping underage victim Virginia.[252] In December 2019 yet another damaging witness came forth to report that she was within feet of Prince Andrew and Virginia Roberts on the Tramp nightclub dancefloor in March 2001.[253]

The royal bleeding just doesn't stop. Prince Andrew attended an elite Canadian prep school in Ontario, Canada back in the 1970s as a youngster. In 2008 Andrew went back to his alma mater, Lakefield College School, to publicly honor the Anglican priest who worked there and attended the prince's 1986 wedding but had died in 2001.[254] Keith Gleed was employed as the Anglican priest at the school from 1974 to 1980, the same years the young prince attended. Subsequent to Andrew's 2008 tribute, former students have come forth to report that Andrew's favorite priest was yet another pedophile. At least five of Gleed's victims prompted an investigation that in 2015 determined that the cleric preyed on young boys throughout his Lakefield tenure. So by historical fact, every single male that Prince Andrew and Prince Charles get closest to and most admire, turns out to be yet another hardcore child sexual predator. Odds?

---

[248] Guy Adams and Daniel bates, "Bombshell Court Document that Claims Prince Andrew Knew about Billionaire Friend's Abuse of Under-age Girls," *Daily Mail*, April 4, 2014.

[249] Jenny Awford and Jon Lockett, "'He was an Abuser' Prince Andrew Virginia Roberts Claims She had Sex with Royal in Loo Aged 17 after he Plied her with Vodka at London Nightclub," *The Sun*, September 20, 2019.

[250] Christy Cooney, "Prince Andrew Admits 'Best Friend' Jeffrey Epstein was Jimmy Savile-Style 'Undercover Paedo.'" *The Sun*, October 7, 2019.

[251] Lee Brown, "Former Royal Cop Challenges Prince Andrew's Alibi in Virginia Roberts Giuffre Sex Scandal," *New York Post*, February 23, 2020.

[252] James Beal, Greg Woodfield and Dan Bates, "Royal Crisis Witness Claims He Saw Prince Andrew Kiss and Grope Virginia Roberts on Jeffrey Epstein's 'Paedo Island,'" *The Sun*, February 22, 2020.

[253] Richard Wheatstone, "New Evidence Witness who 'Saw Prince Andrew and Virginia Roberts in Tramp Nightclub in 2001' Comes Forward to Epstein Victims Lawyer," *The Sun*, December 3, 2019.

[254] Martha Ross, "Prince Andrew's Other Pedophile Friend: Prep School Priest who Came to his 1986 Wedding to Sarah Ferguson," *Mercury News*, September 18, 2019.

An additional link between Prince Andrew and Jeffrey Epstein, aside from the royals' gal pal spy Ghislaine Maxwell introducing the two back in the late 1990s,[255] is film and television producer Tim O'Brien.[256] An apparent mystery man, he's largely been scrubbed from the internet. Tim O'Brien was a close friend of Epstein, who in turn helped finance some of O'Brien's films.[257] His most notable Hollywood entry from 1996, "The Boy's Club," stars Sean Penn's deceased younger brother Michael Penn. Tim O'Brien is said to be the prince's friend since their schooldays at Lakefield together with pedo-priest Gleed back in the 1970s. Since the prince was close to O'Brien ever since the 1970s, who is also close to Epstein, it raises the possibility that Andrew may have met Epstein earlier through O'Brien. Though at the time the Duke of York's private secretary Alastair Watson wrote in a letter defending his boss, it ended up contradicting Andrew's insistence that he met Epstein in 1999:

The duke has known Mr Epstein since being introduced to him in the early 1990s.[258]

It's been noted that British articles written about Prince Andrew's liaisons with the pimping couple from the 1990s and early 2000s prior to Epstein's arrest are no longer available online. However, an incisive series of dot connecting pieces written by talented journalist Whitney Webb for *Mint Press News* has managed to access a number of disappearing British media coverage written many years prior to Epstein's 2006 arrest. Whitney mentions how manipulative the sexual blackmail entrapment of the unsuspecting prince was, based on observations made by friends of the blackmailing duo Jeffrey and Ghislaine in 2001.[259] The articles' reference Andrew's travels and his massages where he brought along his own massage mattress. Embedded in the word massage was Epstein's code word for sex with underage girls.

The senior royal traveled to not only all of Epstein's pleasure pads but Maxwell and Epstein both joined him on a holiday excursion to Phuket, Thailand. In January 2015 photos of Andrew in 2001 surfaced with him surrounded by topless young girls lounging on a yacht.[260] In fact, the London press reported Maxwell accompanied the prince on eight separate vacations, five of which also included Epstein. Andrew invited his secret blackmailers as his personal guests to his mother's 74th birthday bash in 2000. An *Evening Standard* article on January 22, 2001 commented:

Ghislaine is also now organising Andrew's social life in much the same way, introducing him to attractive women and encouraging his relationships with, among others, lingerie model Heidi Klum and PR girl Emma Gibbs. Indeed Ghis-laine, Epstein and Andrew now appear to

[255] Whitney Webb, "Scrubbed Reports Reveal New Secrets of the Prince Andrew-Jeffrey Epstein Relationship," *Mint Press News*, October 14, 2019.

[256] "Tim O'Brien," *IMDb*.

[257] @Kirby Sommers Twitter #princeandrew, *threadreaderapp.com*, February 23, 2020.

[258] Khaleda Rahman, "Prince Andrew Met Jeffrey Epstein Long before 1999, Buckingham Palace Letter Claims," *Newsweek*, November 20, 2019.

[259] Whitney Webb, https://www.mintpressnews.com/scrubbed-reports-reveal-new-secrets-of-the-prince-andrew-jeffrey-epstein-relationship/262330/.

[260] Flora Drury, "Pictured: Prince Andrew Surrounded by Topless Women on Thai Holiday with Paedophile Epstein as Friend says Duke 'has always been a T**s and Bums Man,'" Daily Mail, January 7, 2015.

have evolved a curious symbiotic relationship wherever Ghislaine is seen with Andrew, Epstein is never far behind.[261]

Less than a month away from 40, divorced for four years, Prince Andrew appeared to be undergoing a midlife crisis sowing his wild oats and Ghislaine was dubbed in the press as "his fixer." With the child traffickers taking over his life, the article reflected the very legitimate concerns of the prince's family and close friends:

His erratic behaviour has greatly upset Buckingham Palace and his ex-wife Fergie. No saint herself in the past, Fergie has been complaining he is so busy clubbing he doesn't even have time to babysit Princesses Beatrice, 12, and Eugenie, 10.[262]

The two quotations above were printed just 7 weeks before Andrew sexually assaulted Virginia Roberts.

Back in 2001 the man who is alleged to have set up the topless girl Asian getaway for the prince is another of old friends, sports equipment tycoon from Monaco Johan Eliasch.[263] In 2002 he and Andrew became business partners, launching Naples Gold Limited under the prince's fake name Andrew Inverness, registered in the British Virgin Islands by shady financier David "Spotty" Rowland. The prince has a habit of getting his hand caught in the crooked, crumbling cookie jar. Then while trade envoy there was that trip to Libya that Spotty and the prince took together to discuss some shady dealings with Muammar Gaddafi,[264] himself accused of having "kidnapped and raped hundreds of girls and boys."[265] Was there a mutual agenda exploring investment in the global pedophilia network?

A 2001 UK newspaper article even linked Epstein's business deals to Bill Gates, something the killer virus promiser-deliverer has repeatedly denied, that is until photographic proof shut him up. Since the 1990s, Epstein was always presented in the press as the flashy mystery man, garishly slinging billions around the world. Of course we now know the sexual blackmail-trafficking game raked in gobs of cold hard laundered cash while transparently the pedophile-Israeli intelligence operative was disguised as the maverick "property management" mogul, easily enticing corrupt banks like Deutsche, Citi and HSBC to launder his dirty "billions."[266]

---

[261] "Andrew's Fixer: She is the Daughter of Robert Maxwell and She's Manipulating his Jetset Lifestyle," *The Evening Standard/reddit.com*, January 22, 2001.
[262] "Andrew's Fixer: She is the Daughter of Robert Maxwell and She's Manipulating his Jetset Lifestyle."
[263] Guy Adams, "Revealed: How Prince Andrew Used Pseudonym to Set UP a Secret Firm with a Sports Tycoon who 'Organized 2001 Thailand Trip' during which Duke was Spotted on Yacht with Topless Women," *Daily News*, December 13, 2019.
[264] Lowrie Holmes and Simon Walters, "Why did Prince Andrew Visit Gaddafi in Libya with 'Shady' Tory?" *Daily Mail*, March 19, 2011.
[265] Tom Porter, "Colonel Gaddafi 'Kidnapped and Raped Hundreds of Girls and Boys,'" *IBT*, January 26, 2014..
[266] Whitney Webb, https://www.mintpressnews.com/scrubbed-reports-reveal-new-secrets-of-the-prince-andrew-jeffrey-epstein-relationship/262330/.

Once again it bears re-mentioning that MI5 vets anyone who even remotely enters the life of a senior royal family member, so Andrew's claims of ignorance about what his buddies were up to is pure bullshit as he had to have known exactly what he was getting himself into. Nor was he oblivious as to the life of his close chum Ghislaine and her mentoring relationship with her master spy daddy Robert Maxwell. The planetary controllers like the English royal family are cocksure of their untouchable status and that any involvement in seedy cesspit operations will automatically be shielded, granted total impunity, brazenly not fearing any public scrutiny or exposure whatsoever. And even though Andrew's blown it with a permanently disgraced reputation that from now on will only draw public scorn and contempt, due to the cabal's level of Deep State corruption, it's doubtful he'll ever be required to either give testimony to the FBI or ever have to answer for his own crimes against multiple underage victims… unless a miracle or revolution occurs first.

A 2003 *Evening Standard* article is eerily revealing:

*Ghislaine has risen, largely thanks to property developer Epstein bankrolling her, to become queen of the billionaires' social circuit, [adding] Jeffrey only likes billionaires or **very young women** and uses Ghislaine as his social **pimp**.[267]* [Boldface for bold]

With the above statement, even the mainstream British press appears to be giving away pre-knowledge of the true Epstein-Maxwell criminal honeytrap operation. Several pre-arrest articles as far back as 1992 state that Epstein was working for intelligence services, including both the CIA and Mossad. We've come to learn that Epstein and Maxwell knew each long before November 1991 when her father allegedly died, which is when she allegedly moved to New York. The couple are pictured together in a New York City tribute to her deceased father, with Ghislaine flanked by Epstein and actor Tony Randall. But the Mossad linked duo had met years earlier. Journalist Dylan Howard stated that longtime former Mossad insider Ari Ben-Menashe told him:

The business that Robert Maxwell had was turned over to Jeffrey Epstein almost in a switch before Maxwell died in mysterious circumstances in 1991.[268]

So the Maxwell-Epstein global honeytrap blackmail operation set up by Israeli military intelligence and financed by Mega Group Zionist syndicate tycoon Les Wexner that began in the mid-1980s was very much connected to CIA-connected Craig Spence, the Washington DC pedophile ringleader partnering with trafficker Lawrence King's Nebraska Franklin scandal during the Reagan and George Bush senior era.[269] Even military intelligence Lt. Colonels MK-Ultra Michael Aquino and "Iran-Contra" player Oliver North were involved in the global

---

[267] Whitney Webb, https://www.mintpressnews.com/scrubbed-reports-reveal-new-secrets-of-the-prince-andrew-jeffrey-epstein-relationship/262330/.

[268] Hattie Hamilton and Jenny Ky, "Jeffrey Epstein was a Mossad Spy, says Investigative Journalist Dylan Howard," *7news.com.au*, December 9, 2019.

[269] Whitney Webb, "Government by Blackmail: Jeffrey Epstein, Trump's Mentor and the Dark Secrets of the Reagan Era," *unz.com*, July 25, 2019.

entrapment operation in conjunction with Maxwell-Epstein Israeli intelligence. The pedo-torch was simply passed seamlessly from one administration and generation to the next criminal network pimping blackmailers. The early Epstein-Maxwell operation segued right into the Clinton-Bush junior crime family era.

In fact, a long unbroken history of the CIA-Mossad pedophilia blackmail web had been going on since the 1950s with the likes of Trump mentor Roy Cohn, Jewish mobster Meyer Lansky in cahoots with FBI director J. Edgar Hoover. And in the UK it was an unfolding parallel process with the Kray brothers in the late 1950s into the 1960s and then undercover operative Jimmy Savile taking over up through the 1980s, joined by the motley British crew of Colin Peters, Peter Righton, the Sidney Cooke gang, John Allen and Derek Laud in the 1980s right into the 1990s (all covered in full detail later in this book and next). And largely because the global Establishment's total cover-up of every scandal on both sides of the pond, today the sad pathetic tragedy is that the globalized child sex slave trade is currently booming larger than ever. Exposing this blight on humanity is but a first major step to bringing down this international criminal house of cards.

By 2000, an unnamed company with the same business address as Epstein's financial office on Madison Avenue bought British socialite Ghislaine Maxwell's NYC townhouse for $4.95 million from previous owner Lyn Forester, who that same year married Evelyn de Rothschild to become Lyn Forester de Rothschild.[270] The same planetary overlords are the recurring usual suspects. Some sources claim that Evelyn and Lyn de Rothschild first introduced Epstein to Bill Clinton while others claim since Clinton daughter Chelsea and Ghislaine were such chummy friends, it was Chelsea who introduced them to her parents. Though the Clinton camp have attempted to propagate the deception that it wasn't until Bill was out of office that he and sex offender Epstein hooked up, documented evidence clearly shows that Epstein had access to the Clinton White House many times beginning in the early 1990s throughout Bill's presidency.[271] By 1996, the future Mrs. Rothschild was also busy introducing Epstein to the later accused sex abuser Alan Dershowitz, Epstein's friend and lawyer that a decade later would lead the dream team alongside Kenneth Starr to his sweetheart deal.[272] The same criminal cabal players invariably keep reappearing, linking the House of Rothschild and House of Windsor to the global pedophilia operations.

Meanwhile, until early July 2020 the "free as a bird," co-trafficker-Israeli intel agent Ghislaine Maxwell remains Prince Andrew's loyal pedo-pal. Illustrating their small circle of elitist friends within the pedophilic cabal, a released photograph features a trio of sexual predator criminals, convicted rapist pig Harvey Weinstein[273] all smiles back in 2006 posing with soon-to-be arrested

[270] Katie Warren, "Ghislaine Maxwell, Jeffrey Epstein's Alleged Madam, Lived in a $5 Million NYC Mansion with Ties to Epstein and Ran a Mysterious Private Foundation. Here's What we Know about the British Socialite's Finances and Assets," Business Insider, August 14, 2019.

[271] Emily Shugerman and Suzi Parker, "Jeffrey Epstein Visited Clinton White House Multiple Times in Early '90s," The Daily Beast, August 19, 2019.

[272] Andrew Rice, "Alan Dershowitz Can't Stop Talking Accused of a Slew of Terrible Things, the Defense has no Intention of Resting," Intelligencer, July 19, 2019.

[273] Austa Somvichian-Clausen, "Harvey Weinstein was Convicted of 3rd Degree Rape. Here's What That Means," The Hill, February 24, 2020.

pedophile Jeffrey Epstein and now imprisoned honeytrap operative Ghislaine Maxwell, celebrating Prince Andrew's older daughter Beatrice's 18th birthday at Windsor Castle.[274] This year the now 32-year old Beatrice walked down the royal aisle, arm-in-arm with her forever disgraced pedo-daddy Andrew. With Harvey and Jeffrey predisposed, this was one wedding the soon to be detained Ghislaine also had to miss.

A former UK royal protection officer recently reported that the close bond between Prince Andrew and Ghislaine had her visiting Buckingham Palace up to four times a day with intimate picnics together on the grounds in view of the Queen's bedroom window.[275] Constantly staying in contact with one another, as recently as June 6, 2019, Maxwell was sighted together with Andrew at Buckingham Palace, just a month prior to the Epstein re-arrest.[276] The photo of Harvey, Jeffrey and Ghislaine at Windsor Palace is a glancing snapshot representing the unholy Luciferian marriage between British royalty, Jewish Hollywood royalty and Zionist pimping royalty.

In yet another episode of "noose around the neck gets tighter," the phony Andrew story about pizza time in Woking with daughter Beatrice, then straight to bed at his Sunninghill home like a good princely dad, got shot to pieces when a respected former protection officer maintains the prince arrived in the early hours of March 11, 2001 at Buckingham Palace.[277] He recalls Andrew yelling, "Open these gates you bloody buffoons!" This strongly corroborates Virginia Roberts-Giuffre's timeline contention that earlier that night in Ghislaine Maxwell's upstairs townhouse, the prince had sex with her before his belligerent return to the palace in the middle of the night. Virginia rebutted the prince's lies for BBC Panorama in early December 2019, convincingly blowing away all doubt of his innocence.[278] Met Police in 2015 briefly "investigated" the allegations against the prince, but by 2016 closed its inquiry, deferring to US law enforcement as lead investigators.[279] And to prove who the Scotland Yard works for, the Met's police records on the evening in question in March 2001 have been destroyed.[280] Despite being a crime, willfully destroying evidence is a favorite pastime utilized by the state to cover-up its stately crimes, in this case a British prince fucking an underage American girl and then forever lying about it.

---

[274] "Harvey Weinstein, Jeffrey Epstein and Ghislaine Maxwell at 18th Birthday Celebration for Andrew's Older Daughter Beatrice, at Windsor Castle in 2006," *imgur.com*, February 20, 2020.

[275] Patrick Hill, "Prince Andrew 'had Visits from Ghislaine Maxwell 4 Times a Day' Says Ex-Protection Officer," *Mirror*, January 25, 2020.

[276] Nick Pisa, "'Unswerving Loyalty' Prince Andrew has Kept in Constant Touch with Ghislaine Maxwell during Jeffrey Epstein Crisis," *The Sun*, December 1, 2019.

[277] Michael Gillard and Mark Hookham, "Former Royal Protection Officer Says 'Rude' Prince may have Stayed at Buckingham Palace and not his Sunninghill Home as he Claimed on Night he is Accused of Sex with Epstein Victim Virginia Roberts, February 22, 2020.

[278] Hana Carter, "'I'm Calling BS on him' Virginia Roberts Interview – What did she Say about Prince Andrew on Panorama?" *The Sun*, December 3, 2019.

[279] "Prince Andrew: Met Police Defend Decision to Drop Investigation," Sky News, November 29, 2019.

[280] Michael Gillard, "Met Police Destroyed Records for the Night Prince Andrew Allegedly had Sex with Teenager in London, Says Former Royal Protection Officer," *Daily Mail*, August 1, 2020.

For such a tireless children's advocate busily founding one child charity after another for young kids suffering across the world, in an interview with *Vogue Arabia*, Andrew's ex-wife Sarah Ferguson gives zero thought for the hundreds, if not thousands of Epstein-Maxwell victims.[281] In reaction to the anti-Andrew backlash after his disastrous November 2019 BBC interview, all she could yak about was how her ex-husband has been so brutally raked over the coals, calling it "appalling" and insisting the prince has suffered "enormous pain" over this entire unfair ordeal for her poor little picked on victim of an ex- husband.

The Sun unearthed another damning photo from 2003 showing a smiling Prince Andrew hanging out with former New Mexico Governor Bill Richardson, himself linked to the Epstein scandal with Virginia Giuffre claiming Epstein forced her to have sex with him too.[282] The photo places both the politician and prince at Epstein's New Mexico crime scene ranch... more proof of their longstanding intimate involvement with the infamous pedo-trafficker.[283] In fact, Epstein's housekeeper at his New Mexico ranch stated that in 2001 Prince Andrew stayed for three days with "a beautiful young neurosurgeon" supplied by Epstein who wasn't present, all for the prince's pleasure.[284]

Another shady revelation that's come to light is that once Andrew's affiliations with Epstein got him booted off his cushy government gig as Britain's trade envoy in 2011, the prince has been secretly setting up at least four linked investment fund companies under the assumed name "Andrew Inverness."[285] Since this information only surfaced in December 2019, critics view it as an obvious ploy to avoid potential scrutiny, especially since this royal has so much to hide. It was disclosed last October that despite losing his lofty post, Andrew has amassed a fortune of £57million pounds, only less than Charles at £100million and the Queen at £1.6billion.[286] With an estimate family fortune of 33 trillion pounds, these publicly issued "official" numbers are a paltry joke as each royal's individual worth is deeply buried from all prying eyes.

With last November's BBC interview only inviting more scrutiny, it appears Andrew's extravagant spending lifestyle far exceeds whatever legitimate sources of income he may actually still have, which raises yet more serious red flag legal and ethical issues. His annual naval pension amounts to just £20,000 and his mommy dearest's yearly allowance as a senior royal, amounts to £250,000, but that's supposedly been snatched since the prince is no longer

[281] Aurora Bosotti, "'Appalling' Sarah Ferguson Savaged over Reaction to Prince Andrew Epstein Scandal," *Express*, December 13, 2019.

[282] "Former NM Governor Bill Richardson Accused of Using Bribes to Fund 'Sexual Services and Favors,'" *thestreetjournal.org*, September 28, 2020.

[283] Emma Parry, "Prince's Pal Prince Andrew Pictured with Sex Scandal Governor – Amid Concern He Stayed at Infamous Epstein Ranch on Official Visit," *The Sun*, January 13, 2020.

[284] Jennifer Smith, "Former Epstein Housekeeper Says Prince Andrew was Entertained 'by a Beautiful Young Neurosurgeon' who she Believes was 'Given' to him by the Pedophile during three-day Visit his New Mexico Ranch in 2001," *Daily Mail*, November 21, 2019.

[285] Robert Mendick, Victoria Ward and James Cook, "Revealed: Duke of York Set up Secret Investment Fund under Assumed Name 'Andrew Inverness,'" *The Telegraph*, December 26, 2019.

[286] Dan Hall, "Prince of Cash Prince Andrew Faces Questions over £57 million Fortune and Lavish Lifestyle as It's Revealed He's Third Richest Royal," *The Sun*, October 20, 2019.

doing official royal business. Yet he spends so much more than whatever legitimate income he still has. He manages to live the lavish lifestyle above his legal means through people like David Spotty Rowland and his family owned Luxembourg based bank for the rich. In November 2019 it was learned that for at least the last decade the prince has been unlawfully cheating British taxpayers, misusing his publicly funded trade missions to create private income by secretly diverting funding streams into hidden Caribbean tax haven accounts while luring his trade contacts to invest in his own tax-free offshore fund.[287] This partially explains how he's been able to albeit illegally live such an opulent lifestyle after yanked from his official UK trade job way back in 2011.

Like his father, Prince Andrew has always been prone to sticking his big foot in his mouth. With such insensitive, highly revealing remarks as the ones displayed right after the false flag Lockerbie plane tragedy,[288] no doubt feeling put upon as the single royal representative forced to attend the Lockerbie, Scotland aftermath just before Christmas in 1988, longtime royalty journalist Richard Kay commented:

Not only did he upset the people of Lockerbie – where 11 residents were killed on the ground – by declaring that it was 'much worse for the Americans' (259 passengers and crew were on the U.S. airliner) but he added that it had been 'only a matter of time' before a plane fell out of the sky.[289]

The sullen Prince Andrew also has a long history of bullying his staff, frivolously chasing hedonistic pleasure at all cost and never really growing up, despite putting in 22 years with the Royal Navy, yet only reaching the rank of commander. Journalist Richard Kay wrote an article in 2001 openly critical in his assessment, asking whether the 41-year old prince in view of his shortcomings was actually up for the task as roving ambassador for British Trade International.[290] Had it not been for the strong lobbying efforts of the power-broking Rothschild agent and known pedophile Lord Mandelson, Prince Andrew would never have stood a chance securing such an important gig as official promoter of British trade in 2001. Former minister Lord Peter Mandelson first met the prince while Mandelson was heading the National Society for the Prevention of Cruelty to Children (NSPCC). Only in the world's pedo-epicenter would a pedophile prince and pedophile politician be the leading patrons in the nation's largest children's charity organization whose sole purpose is to prevent child abuse. As likeminded pervs, naturally Mandelson and Andrew swiftly hit it off and fast became friends. Chalk up yet another pedo friend for the prince. Soon enough, through pedo-pimping matchmaker Ghiz, so

---

[287] Isabel Oakshott and Mark Hookham, "Exposed: The Damning Details of Prince Andrew's Deals with Tax Haven Tycoons... So Does This Help Explain how he Funds his Billionaire Lifestyle?" *Daily Mail*, November 30, 2019.

[288] "Lockerbie Bombing 1988 – Another False-Flag Terror Act," schou.de, July 21, 2010..

[289] Anna Kretschmer, "Queen Heartbreak: Greatest Regrets of Her Majesty's Reign Revealed," Express, December 14, 2019.

[290] Richard Kay, "Boorish Jokes, Topless Beauties and the Question: Is this Man really the Right Person to Represent British Business?" *Daily Mail/forums.richieallen.co.uk*, February 24, 2001.

were Mandy and Epstein friends.[291] That's the key in how they keep getting away with it – stack all gatekeeping posts with pedophiles and enablers, from their point of view, the more pedophiles, always the better for the cabal.

A source claiming to know both Prince Andrew and Epstein well was quoted in a June 2011 *Vanity Fair* article:

I remember when Andrew and Jeffrey Epstein first became friends, Jeffrey had Andrew put on a pair of sweatpants for the first time in his life. He had him wear blue jeans for the first time. It was Jeffrey who taught Andrew how to relax.[292]

But the same friend called Andrew after Epstein was arrested in 2006 and said:

You cannot have a relationship with Jeffrey. You can't do these things. And he said, 'Stop giving me a hard time. You're such a puritan.' From there, our conversation descended into a screaming match, and finally Andrew said, 'Leave me alone. Jeffrey's my friend. Being loyal to your friends is a virtue. And I'm going to be loyal to him.'[293]

According to the same *Vanity Fair* article, Juan Alessi, a former Epstein employee at his Palm Beach estate, stated in a sworn deposition:

Andrew attended naked pool parties and was treated to massages by a harem of adolescent girls.[294]

Andrew's blind loyalty to continue friendship with Jeff and Ghiz, the king and queen of the turn-of-the-century pedo-trafficking empire, resulted in the loss of his employment and deep fall from grace. But during the entire decade as the Crown's poster boy for international trade, Andrew kept some bad company aside from just Jeff and Ghiz. The prince regularly hosted, wined and dined oppressive tyrants from Tunisia, Azerbaijan and Kazakhstan, accepting a £20,000 diamond necklace for his daughter Beatrice's 21st birthday from a convicted Libyan drug and arms dealer.[295] He even sold his Sunninghill mansion in 2007, given to him and Sarah by the queen as their wedding gift, to the Kazakhstan president's son-in-law for £3 million more than the £12m asking price, listed the previous 5 years without a buyer, after claiming Andrew wasn't the "fixer" in a £385m deal for a Kazakh oligarch.[296] Three years after losing his function as UK trade envoy, in 2014 Andrew shamelessly flew to oil-gas rich Azerbaijan, kowtowing to

---

[291] Guy Adams and Daniel Bates, "Peter Mandelson Pictured with Jeffrey Epstein: Labour Ex-Minister Who's Friends with Prince Andrew Shops with Paedophile Financier in 2005 after being Introduced by Ghislane Maxwell," *Daily Mail*, August 30, 2019.

[292] "Prince Andrew: Ties to Jeffrey Epstein and his Tenuous Position in 'the Firm,'" *Vanity Fair*, June 29, 2011.

[293] "Prince Andrew: Ties to Jeffrey Epstein and his Tenuous Position in 'the Firm.'"

[294] "Prince Andrew: Ties to Jeffrey Epstein and his Tenuous Position in 'the Firm.'"

[295] Stephen Bates, "Prince Andrew's Daughter was Given Necklace by Libyan Businessman," *The Guardian*, March 27, 2011.

[296] Adam Lusher, "Prince Andrew Facing Questions over the Sale of his Mansion to Kazakh Oligarch," *Independent*, May 23, 2016.

one of the most oppressive, corrupt billionaire dictators in the world, Ilham Aliyev.[297] Though this visit was one of his many private trips to Baku, officially as an envoy he went there another dozen times.

"Airmiles Andy" was repeatedly criticized for misallocating public funds while partaking of too many holidays on the ski slopes and golf courses during his envoy tenure. The prince constantly took gross advantage, misusing his public function designed to increase UK trade, but instead used it to hustle making private business deals for himself with the sleaziest despots possessing the world's worst human rights records. On top of his ongoing pedo-problem, the last straw for his piss-poor on the job performance came in December 2010 when WikiLeaks published a US diplomat's classified cable based on an October 2008 meeting with the US Ambassador in Kyrgyzstan prior to a meeting with the Kyrgyz prime minister. The report noted the prince's "rude" behavior and attitude over the Serious Fraud Office "idiocy" daring to probe a Saudi arms deal. But the royal prince's pure arrogance and imperialistic hubris shot off the page with the remark:

The United Kingdom, Western Europe (and by extension you Americans too) *were now back in the thick of playing the Great Game. And this time we aim to win!*[298]

After the pompous ass lost his trade job, and after a near decade of hiding behind feeble palace denials over the Epstein debacle, mounting pressure finally forced Andrew to face the music in last November's train wreck BBC broadcast, lying through his teeth, fumbling foolishly to obstinately defend his disastrous choice to stay friends with the infamous pedophile, even laughably claiming his loyalty showed him to be "too honorable" and that his military combat experience left him with an odd condition that he's incapable of sweating.[299] Everyone watching his public performance absolutely knew he was lying. At the queen's behest, it led directly to his being forced to give up his official royal duties. The queen then gave her favorite son his walking papers, ordering him to move his private business offices out of Buckingham Palace.[300] For the queen to publicly distance herself from her all-time favorite son is an indicator that it's sink or swim time for the overly-scandalized royal family, with each royal for him or herself.

Andrew's "what goes around, comes around" bad karma came home to roost in time for his 60th birthday in February 2020, leaving the unpopular prince without even enough invitees willing to join his pathetic birthday soiree on February 19th, embarrassingly having to send out

[297] Rebecca English, "Another Date for Airmiles Andy and his Despot Friend: Prince Secretly Flies to Azerbaijan for Meeting with Country's Billionaire President," *Daily Mail*, November 13, 2014..

[298] Prince Andrew, "US Embassy Cables: Prince Andrew Rails against France, the SFO and The Guardian," *The Guardian*, October 29, 2008.

[299] "The Psychology of Prince Andrew," YouTube video, 32:27, posted November 25, 2019.

[300] Julius Young, "Prince Andrew Forced to Move Office out of Buckingham Palace: Report," Fox News, November 22, 2019.

more invitations for his downsized Royal Lodge gathering.[301] With Andrew's spiraling downfall causing such humiliating disgrace, destroying the reputation of the royal family Firm, and with his shady finances exposed, all of this co-timed with the public fallout over the princely brother feud of William and Harry, the British royal family is looking to just stay alive, rescued just in time by the "wag the dog" Prince Philip's Corona-crowned "killer virus." Saved by the pandemic, now it's back to the benign gossip of what the rebellious "ex-royals" Meghan and Harry are wearing to their latest public appearance in Southern California.[302]

With Andrew's pedo-buddy Jeffrey laying low since August 2019, assumedly 6 feet under but perhaps cosmetically hidden away incognito in Israel, to fill the void left by his giant absence, the Andrew and Ghislaine story have hooked up where Epstein left off. That would at least account for both the prince's inexplicably inflated income and why he and his gal pal have maintained so much contact in recent years. With all of Andrew's closest associates busted as VIP pedophiles and pedo-pimp traffickers, as his next big gig and latest life choice, perhaps the prince has taken up child sex trafficking himself since it's so sinisterly lucrative, not to mention it being in such demand for Black Nobility occult rituals. Taking for granted living his entire pampered, spoiled, "princely" life as a royal untouchable, naturally the smug prince would arrogantly believe he's fully protected with guaranteed impunity from all possibility of arrest and prosecution, regardless of how sickeningly deplorable his crimes might be.

What's most obvious is all the high-end pedophiles compromised and blackmailed by their associations with Epstein are doing everything in their power to ensure that 58-year old Ghislaine Maxwell doesn't spill the rotten pedo-cabal beans to save her own bony ass. During her year as a fugitive after Epstein's staged death, a sensationalizing media hyped up her stealth as a licensed pilot able to travel by submarine or helicopter for quick, on-the-go getaways,[303] and, via her superspy dad, she's the "Bonnie and Clyde" darling of Israel intelligence, as well as holder of both US and British citizenship and a half dozen passports. Tabloids like the *Daily Mail* also propagated the myth that as a globetrotting international socialite, she must be well protected, reportedly hidden in a safe house inside Israel or Europe.[304] Meanwhile, Prince Andrew begged her to dutifully come forward to rescue him, and vouch for his boldface lie that he never had sex with any underage girls.[305] But looking out for #1, the Prima Dona Ghislaine chose to secretly buy her million dollar backwoods mansion in New Hampshire. There are those operating within Epstein's orbit that maintain that Maxwell

[301] Richard Kay, "Prince Andrew's Sorrowful 60th: There'll be no Palace Celebration or Fanfare for the Fallen Royal after Epstein Scandal Cost him his Job, his Official Role and even his Promotion to Admiral," *Daily Mail*, February 18, 2020.

[302] Bianca Betancourt, "Meghan Markle and Prince Harry Appear in a Stunning New Black-and-White Portrait," *Harpers Bazaar*, October 16, 2020.

[303] Aaron Tinney, "Prince Andrew's Pal Ghislaine Maxwell 'could be Hiding beneath Sea in Submarine,'" Daily Star, February 29, 2020.

[304] Keith Griffith, "Jeffrey Epstein's Socialite 'Madame' 'is being Hidden from the FBI in a Series of Safe Houses because of the Information she has on Powerful People,'" *Daily Mail*, January 1, 2020.

[305] Martin Robinson, "Prince Andrew 'Begged Ghislaine Maxwell to Clear his Name as the Only Witness on Night Virginia Roberts Claim they had Sex' – But she Refused because it 'wasn't in her Interests,'" *Daily Mail*, January 3, 2020.

was the behind-the-scenes boss and mastermind all along, running the Israeli blackmail operation with the same ruthless, cutthroat style her dad used. Nearing three decades since his mysterious disappearance, it was her turn. In October 2019, both Ghislaine and fellow pedophile-in-crime, French "modeling scout" Jean-Luc Brunel, were reportedly spotted hiding out together in Brazil, but vanished soon after.[306]

In the meantime, the damaging news keeps getting more damaging for Prince Andrew. During his infamous December 2011 visit to Epstein's NYC pad, the largest residence in all of Manhattan, when he and Jeffrey went for their infamous Central Park walk together, allegedly telling the recently released sex offender that the English royal just couldn't be his friend anymore, film footage surfaced in August 2019 showing young attractive, questionable-of-age females freely coming and going from Epstein's townhouse.[307] One of the visitors, Katherine Keating, was the young daughter of former Australian Prime Minister Paul Keating. As Katherine leaves the mansion, from behind the door the prince sheepishly smiles waving goodbye. Katherine Keating's father is one of three former Australian prime minister pedophiles accused by courageously outspoken MK-Ultra sex victim-survivor-activist Fiona Barnett,[308] and equally brave politician Franca Arena who confronted her peers in Parliament with Australia's large pedophile ring involving politicians, judges, doctors and media moguls, naming Katherine's father among the ring (to be taken up in Book 5).[309] So what's the daughter of an accused pedo-prime minister doing at the world's most infamous convicted pedophile's residence? To date, she and the prince avoided answering that question.

One thing we do know about Ms: Keating, she interviewed Ghislaine Maxwell for *Huffington Post* in July 2014, showcasing the child pimp's TerraMar project, a non-profit organization ostensibly devoted to saving the oceans.[310] If Maxwell only put that much effort into saving the children she abused. Instead of referring to her as a pimping pedophile-trafficker-child rapist, Keating's fluffy piece charitably calls her "a philanthropist." An embarrassed *Huffington Post* has since deleted the interview. Six days after Epstein's July 2019 arrest, Maxwell abruptly shut down her TerraMar "philanthropic" operation.

With all the same usual suspects uncannily showing up on the crime cabal radar screen in a high stakes, deceitful world of what you see is the opposite of what you get, let's look at how big money, royalty, charity, elite schools and the global pedo-network all work hand-in-hand together. Andrew's ex-wife Sarah Ferguson and their longtime close friend Ghislaine were very close to Epstein, having both been recipients of his ample cash reserves, the debt-ridden

[306] Victoria Elms and Laura Bundock, "Jeffrey Epstein's Inner Circle Ghislaine Maxwell and Jean-Luc Brunel Traced to Brazil," Sky News, October 15, 2019.

[307] Nick Miller, "'Randy' Prince Andy, the Paedophile and the Australian Ex-PM's Daughter," *The Sydney Morning Herald*, August 23, 2019..

[308] Fiona Barnett, "Jeffrey Epstein Linked to Aussie Pedo Prime Minister Paul Keating – Told You So!" *fionabarnett.org*, August 20, 2019.

[309] Makia Freeman, "Satanic Pedophilia Network Exposed in Australia (Just like the USA)," *thefreedomarticles.com*, August 30, 2019.

[310] Katherine Keating "One on One: Ghislaine Mazwell on Protecting the Blue Heart of the Planet," *Huffington Post*, May 20, 2014.

Duchess receiving a loan from Epstein.[311] But with Epstein on the low these days, they're seemingly tighter than ever with the disgraced, yet apparently substantially richer prince. Both Fergie and Ghiz knew full well what their "other halves" were up to all those years hanging out with so many underage minors.

Additionally, both Fergie and Ghiz are connected to same Street Child charity with Fergie the founder and Ghiz the supporter. They're also both linked to the same high-powered transatlantic investment firm Cantor Fitzgerald, though its New York offices were on the uppermost floors of One World Trade Center (CEO Howard "Lucky" Lutnick said he was taking his kid to school that morning).[312] Cantor Fitzgerald is a major fundraiser for Stowe School which both Fergie and Ghiz are again linked to. To this day the property management company of "Lucky" Larry Silverstein,[313] the 9/11 profiteer who leased the New York trade towers just in time to grow $5 billion richer,[314] and Cantor Fitzgerald are in land development partnership out in Sheldon Adelson's mafia stomping grounds of Las Vegas.[315] On top of that, Epstein lived at 9 East 71st Street and Lutnick his next-door neighbor at 11 East 71st Street. Epstein had a history at that address connected to the property next door.

Another anecdotal "coincidence" from the redhead – Fergie's charity Chances for Children also occupied an office on the WTC 101st floor, which happened to be on the exact same floor as Cantor Fitzgerald. Her charity mascot "Little Red," the Sarah lookalike ragdoll, was miraculously found in the rubble intact and nearly unblemished that same day of the 9/11 attack,[316] similar to how "lead terrorist" Mohammad Atta's passport was conveniently found a couple days later.[317] Sarah Ferguson said she too was in New York City on that 9/11 morning heading to her office, but due to heavy traffic, was running 20 minutes late when the twin towers blew, and just like her red-headed ragdoll, the redhead was saved by her own little miracle. God bless the royals.

The former head of the London Cantor Fitzgerald office, Lee Amaitis, is current owner of CG Technology, a Las Vegas based Cantor Fitzgerald gambling subsidiary that paid the bulk of $22.5 million in bribery to end an illegal gambling and money laundering investigation.[318] Amaitis' company also fundraises for another Fergie founded charity Children in Crisis. The Stowe School headmaster, Dr. Anthony Wallersteiner, is the trustee and chair of Children in Crisis, and son of

---

[311] Christopher Bucktin, "Fergie's 'Call Me' Message to Sex Abuser Epstein Found, *Express*, August 1, 2019,.

[312] "Epstein – The Bigger Picture," *aanirfan.blogpot.com*, August 20, 2019.

[313] Sean Adl-Tabatabai, "9/11: Larry Silverstein Designed New WTC-7 One Year before Attacks," *Mint Press News*, March 16, 2016.

[314] Kevin Barrett, "911 Suspect Silverstein Launches New $500 Million WTC Scam," *Veterans Today*, November 5, 2015.

[315] "Cantor Fitzgerald and Silverstein Properties Close Opportunity Zone Land Acquisition in Las Vegas, NV," *nevadabusiness.com*, January 13, 2020.

[316] Nicholas Frakes, "Sarah Ferguson Reveals How She Nearly Died on 9/11 – 'I Take Every Minute as a Blessing,'" *The Telegraph*, November 29, 2018.

[317] Anne Karpf, "Uncle Sam's Lucky Finds," *The Guardian*, March 18, 2002.

[318] Nate Raymond, "Cantor Fitzgerald Affiliate Pays $22.5 Million to End U.S. Gambling Probe," *Reuters*, October 4, 2016.

the late Kurt Wallersteiner, business associate of Daddy Maxwell, whom the FBI considered both to be Soviet espionage agents. Robert Maxwell at one time was the Stowe School's Buckinghamshire MP. In 2018 Anthony Wallerstein attended the wedding of Andrew and Fergie's younger daughter Princess Eugenie and her husband Jack Brooksbank who also attended Stowe.[319] Headmaster Wallerstein's sister Rebecca was a lover of boy loving artist Lucian Freud,[320] the brother of pedophile MP Clement and friend of pedo-procuring gangster twins, the Krays. Pedo-enabling former Canterbury Archbishop Lord Carey[321] disclosed at the IICSA that another former Stowe headmaster, Jeremy Nichols, "had a personal friendship with serial pedophile Bishop Peter Ball,"[322] best buddy to both Prince Charles and Sir Jimmy. The prestigious private coed boarding school for the elite generated some negative publicity of its own back in 2014 when a sex scandal erupted over "pupils having competition to have sex everywhere" in all the school buildings.[323]

Additionally, an alumni list of Stowe School reads like a who's who of pedo-movers and shakers.[324] Lord Alistair McAlpine exposed as a pedophile in the North Wales scandal (covered in Book 3), virtually every scandal pedophile Sir Peter Hayman's name comes up (throughout this book), Lord John Sainsbury and Lord Henniker, a Stowe governor, who after pedophile-child "expert" Peter Righton's child porn bust in 199, provided a safe haven for the procuring network Righton and his convicted pedo-lover PIE co-founder Richard Alston, brother to foreign diplomat Robert Alston, a colleague of Prince Andrew.[325] All these prominent UK pedophiles will be repeatedly mentioned throughout the remaining chapters of this book.

Another private Caribbean island owner and billionaire, Sir Richard Branson, and pedo-pimp Ghislaine herself were both students at the posh Stowe School. NXIVM financier Clare Bronfman of the infamous Canadian crime family just received a near 7-year prison sentence for her role.[326] In 2007 and again in 2010 Bronfman sponsored the sex cult co-founder Nancy Salzman and sex trafficking actress Allison Mack to conduct "seminars and wild sex parties" at Branson's Necker Island retreat in an overt attempt to entice Branson to join the pedo-trafficking cult.[327] Though Bronfman and Branson remained on friendly terms, word has it Branson was more interested in the sex parties than the seminars. Yet his phone number made

[319] Naomi Gordon, "Jack Brooksbank Said Something very Touching about Princess Eugenie in his Speech," *Harper's Bazaar*, October 13, 2018.

[320] Rebecca Wallersteiner, "The Woman Who Says 9Much) Older Men Make the Best Lovers: That's Why she's Taken so many – Artist Lucian Freud Included. Shameless, Maybe. But her Reasoning may Intrigue You," *Daily Mail*, November 12, 2015.

[321] "Ex-Archbishop Lord Carey Resigns after Child Abuse Review," *BBC*, June 26, 2017.

[322] "Witness Statement of Lord Carey," *The Independent Inquiry into Child Sexual Abuse*, May 2, 2018.

[323] Liv Stevens, "'Pupils had Competition to have Sex Everywhere': Former Stowe Sixth Former Lifts Lid on Steamy Relationships at Prestigious School in Wake of 'Morning after Pills' Scandal Exposed by MoS," *Daily Mail*, July 5, 2014.

[324] "Epstein – The Bigger Picture."

[325] "Epstein – The Bigger Picture."

[326] David K. Li, "NXIVM Sex Cult Benefactor Clare Bronfman Sentenced to More than 6 Years behind Bars," NBC News, September 30, 2020.

[327] Oliver Hardy, Emma Parry, James Beal and Nick Parker, "Horror Cult's Wild Parties NXIVM 'Held Wild Parties and Seminars' on Sir Richard Branson's Private Island Necker," *The Sun*, April 22, 2018.

the infamous Epstein black book, alongside Tony Blair, Mick Jagger, Peter Mandelson and in all, over 300 powerful Britons and numbers to Balmoral and Sandringham castles were also listed.[328] Goes without saying that Prince Andrew and Sarah had multiple listed numbers - 16 and 18 respectively.

Fergie and her two daughters Eugenie and Beatrice have all supported the Cantor Fitzgerald Relief Fund that provides money in crisis zones around the world. But in recent years it's been determined that humanitarian aid workers in various NGO charities such as Oxfam and the UN peacekeepers have been increasingly brutal in sexually exploiting vulnerable women and children in crisis nations such as Haiti.[329] Often NGO charities serve as deceptive cover or front companies for intelligence services' sexual blackmail operations like the CIA,[330] Mossad and MI6, actively involved in coordinating interfacing agencies in the global child sex trafficking trade[331]... dirty bidders in the Zionist-Sabbatean-Frankist-Illuminati-Masonic-Malta Knight-Jesuit-Luciferian NWO agenda.[332] An awful lot of links going on between Prince Andrew, Fergie, Epstein, Ghislaine, all their charities, Stowe School, Kantor Fitzgerald, 9/11 false flag terrorism and the worldwide pedophilia network, all driven and bound by the same dark forces behind the same worldwide Luciferian New World Order agenda.

Two weeks after pervert Oscar winner Kevin Spacey publicly apologized for making sexual advances on actor Anthony Rapp when he was only 14-years old,[333] it was revealed that Spacey visited Prince Andrew at Buckingham Palace. Having spent considerable time in the company of mutual friends Jeffrey Epstein and Ghislaine Maxwell, it later surfaced that Spacey was joined on his palace tour by Ghislaine Maxwell. A day after her arrest July on 2nd, 2020, *The Telegraph* released a photo of Maxwell and Spacey sitting on Queen Elizabeth's throne.[334] Their personal tour guide Prince Andrew had invited his fellow accused child abusers to explore the inner reaches of the royal palace, strictly off limits to lowly commoners.[335]

Having already collected an OBE in 2010, in 2016 the former "House of Cards" star was awarded honorary knighthood (only "honorary" for not being born in UK), personally and privately presented by Andrew's big brother Prince Charles.[336] Spacey's work in London theater and embracing the global pedo network with rides on Epstein's Lolita Express and raping young boys (15 accusers as of early November 2017[337]) no doubt made him the apple of the royals'

[328] Simon Osborne, "Tony Blair in US Paedophile Jeffrey Epstein's 'Little Black Book,'" *Express*, August 14, 2019..

[329] Lizzie Dearden, "Oxfam was Told of Aid Workers Raping and Sexually Exploiting Children in Haiti a Decade Ago," Independent, February 16, 2018..

[330] Greg Miller, "CIA's Secret Agents Hide under a Variety of Covers," July 5, 2005.

[331] Stephen Lendman, "CIA Involved in Child Sex Trafficking?" *thesleuthjournal.com*, February 8, 2018.

[332] "Sabbateans are the Illuminati," *henrymakow.com*, November 12, 2019.

[333] Madison Park, "Kevin Spacey Apologizes for Alleged Sex Assault with a Minor," *CNN*, October 31, 2017.

[334] Robert Mendick, "Exclusive: How Ghislaine Maxwell and Kevin Spacey Relaxed at Buckingham Palace 'as Guests of Prince Andrew,'" *The Telegraph*, July 3, 2020.

[335] Tom Wells and Emily Andrews, "Sleazy Kevin Spacey was Given a Private Tour of Buckingham Palace – and he even Sat on the Throne," *The Sun*, November 12, 2017.

[336] "Prince Charles Presents Honorary Knighthood to Kevin Spacey," *ca.hellomagazine.com*, June 16, 2016.

[337] Maria Puente, "Kevin Spacey Scandal: A Complete List of 15 Accusers," *USA Today*, November 7, 2017.

radar roving eye for attracting pedophile best friends into their pedo-web. Andy and Chucky's personal princely touch once again reflects either their chronically impaired judgment, their contempt for public perception or their pedophilia sponsorship, or more likely all three.

In yet another regrettable turn,[338] Prince Andrew played joker to convicted pedophile BBC host Stuart Hall in June 1987.[339] As if pedophiles Epstein, Savile, Spacey, Ball, Hall and Mandelson aren't quite incriminating enough associations, in February 2020 the latest in the never-ending stream of Prince Andrew's busted high powered pedo-friends is 78-year old fashion tycoon Peter Nygard, accused of luring girls as young as 14 to his yet another Caribbean mansion in the Bahamas, and just like Epstein, promising to make them models, plying them with alcohol and drugs prior to allegedly raping them.[340] The Duke of York and his family stayed at Nygard's estate near Nassau in 2000, the same year that Andrew and Fergie pulled their daughter Beatrice out of her exclusive Swiss school after its headmaster, a close friend of Andrew's, was yet another close associate arrested for molesting two children.[341]

Before Nygard's recent civil lawsuit filed in New York, like Epstein, the Canadian fashion exec appears to have been running yet another Caribbean child trafficking operation. It's alleged he paid off Nassau police, politicians and Bahamian government officials to look the other way. Why is it that the Windsor boys Andrew and Charles never quite learn? They just can't keep themselves away from vile child sexual predators. If it was once or maybe twice, it might be passed off as chance coincidence. But when it's over and over and over and over ad nauseam, it points to something far more sinister and darker, leading even a most casual, objective observer to the conclusion that top royal family members must be bigtime pedophiles and/or involved in pedophilia trafficking. Guilt by association combined in Andrew's case with plausible accusations from more than one victim, and a sordid, despicable picture emerges of the next supposed heir and the fourth in line to the British throne. Incredibly, Andrew's ex-wife Sarah Ferguson doesn't fare much better. Attending a luncheon in 2016 with the NXIVM sex cult Bronfman sister Sara (the other heiress from the notorious Zionist Rothschild-linked Canadian crime family), the NXIVM cult is currently being prosecuted for child sex trafficking.[342] And of course the Bronfmans[343] and the Rothschilds share the same family business interests, one might conclude in more ways than one.[344]

---

[338] "The Duke of Hazard: Embarrassing Stunts, Shocking Misjudgments, and very Shady Friends… The Photos that Show Prince Andrew has Never Been Far from a Crisis," *Daily Mail*, November 20, 2019.

[339] "Pictured: Paedophile and Former TV Star Stuart Hall is Living on a Modest South Manchester Estate," *Manchester Evening News*, November 11, 2016.

[340] Guy Adams and Vanessa Allen, "Pictured: Prince Andrew's on Bahamas Visit to Second Tycoon Facing Child Sex Claims – Duke and Family Stayed with Peter Nygard who is Accused of Raping Teenagers and Plying them with Wine and Drugs," *Daily Mail*, February 14, 2020.

[341] "Beatrice is Pulled out of Scandal School," *Daily Record/thefreelibrary.com*, June 24, 2000..

[342] Frank Parlato, "NXIVM Sex Cult Financier Sara Bronfman Once Attended Luncheon for Children in Crisis with Duchess of York – While Raniere's Son was in Hiding," *frankreport.com*, February 11, 2020,.

[343] "The Bronfmans – Empire on the Rocks," *centipedenation.com*, July 25, 2018.

[344] "Bronfman E.I. Rothschild," *fintel.io*.

More criminal linkage beyond mere happenchance: Epstein's only investment customer and sole benefactor, the Zionist Mega group member and Victoria's Secret retail mogul Les Wexner,[345] is married to Abigail Koppel,[346] daughter of Yehuda Koppel, who launched Israel's first commercial airline El Al in New York. The first El Al airline hostess was Livia (nee Eisen) Chertoff, mother of Michael Chertoff, Israeli national under Bush junior who rose to become America's second Homeland Security czar. Wexner's wife's father and Chertoff's mother while with El Al airline both worked together as Israeli Mossad operatives.[347] Co-author of the infamous Patriot Act, Michael Chertoff is a US traitor for his Israeli Firster role in the 9/11 false flag cover-up[348] and using his DHS insider status to make millions in a conflict of interest enterprise securing private contracts to sell and install his company's full body scanning machines at airports around the world.[349]

Today Michael Chertoff sits on the board of advisors for the Israeli security company Carbyne911 headed by former Mossad agents.[350] Carbyne collects instant data from 911 emergency callers, handy at state sponsored terrorism events like mass shootings. The company's biggest investors include Jeffrey Epstein, Carbyne's chairman, Epstein buddy, former Israeli prime minister Ehud Barak[351] (also a frequent flier on Epstein's Lolita Express as well as guest at both sex slave island and NYC love mansion[352]) and Silicon billionaire and Facebook investor Peter Thiel[353] (owner of a service company supplying children's blood to highflying customers for anti-aging benefits[354]). So there you have it, Wexner, Epstein, Chertoff, Barak, Thiel, the Zionist Adrenochrome world takeover in a nutshell using pedo-blackmail and wars for Israel to lead the way to our Brave New World turned Orwellian nightmare come true. It's not in the least bit surprising that the same sleazy Zionist criminals keep creeping, crawling and cropping up time and time again, thriving and prospering off their self-created NWO pedo-cabal at humanity's expense.

But this trail of criminal thuggery and treasonous deceit parasitically feeding off the not-so-silent or hidden tears of child victims is nothing new. In 1964 Canada, Queen Elizabeth and Prince Philip touched down for a brief Commonwealth visit to Canadian West Coast Province of British Columbia, and specifically to a Catholic operated residential primary school for the

[345] Whitney Webb, "Mega Group, Maxwells and Mossad: The Spy Story at the Heart of the Jeffrey Epstein Scandal," *Mint Press News*, August 7, 2019.

[346] "Weddings; Abigail Koppel, Leslie Wexner," *The New York Times*, January 24, 1993..

[347] Christopher Bollyn, "Michael Chertoff's Childhood in Israel," *bollyn.com*, October 26, 2007.

[348] "All the Necessary Proofs! Israel Did 9/11," *bibliotecapleyades.net*, May 6, 2009.

[349] Steve Benen, "Page 7 vs. Page 15," *Washington Monthly*, January 1, 2010.

[350] Carbyne911 website "About Us," *carbyne911.com*.

[351] Tomer Ganon, Amir Kurz and Ran Abramson, "The Ties that Bind: Ehud Barak's Business Network," *calcalistech.com*, July 18, 2019.

[352] Martin Gould, "Exclusive: Married Israeli Politician Ehud Barak is Seen Hiding his Face Entering Jeffrey Epstein's NYC Townhouse as Bevy of Young Beauties were also Spotted going into Mansion –Despite his Claim he never Socialized with Pedophile and his Girls," *Daily Mail*, July 16, 2019.

[353] Whitney Webb, "How the CIA, Mossad and the 'Epstein Network' are Exploiting Mass Shootings to Create an Orwellian Nightmare," *Mint Press News*, September 6, 2019.

[354] Maya Kosoff, "This Anti-Aging Start-up is Charging Thousands of Dollars for Teen Blood," *Vanity Fair*, June 1, 2017.

indigenous population. Though the royal couple was at the school for only a few minutes, a group of school pupils and staff accompanied the queen and prince on a picnic outing to a field near Dead Man's Creek near Kamloops. Witnesses have made sworn statements that "10 little Indians" were selected to leave the picnic area alone with the queen and prince - never to be seen again.[355] Despite this startling fact, apparently so accustomed to living above the law, the British monarchy has never been required to answer in a court of law for this tragic, unsolved criminal mystery.

Disappearing children and women among the aboriginal tribes of Canada (as well as the US, Central and South America) have become so alarming, painting a bigger, darker picture again that demands both authorities' explanation and justice (covered in Book 4). Even a Canadian government report in 2019 is calling the thousands of Native American women and girls murdered or missing since the 1970s "genocide."[356] A survivor of the queen's school outing, now an aboriginal elder, remarked:

The buck stops at Buckingham Palace. The Queen, and the Pope, are the ones responsible for the genocide their government and churches did to my people. She has to be held accountable. She has the power to help bring our children home, finally.[357]

As the last to see them alive, the British royal couple knows exactly what happened to those lost kids that fateful day but their disgraceful silence has never been sufficiently challenged or confronted legally with any teeth, despite heartfelt letters demanding an explanation. Moreover, a witness who sent a letter to the queen just prior to giving testimony was suddenly suspiciously dead. As the head of the Anglican Church, the queen along with the Catholic pope operated 80 Canadian residential schools across the nation that imprisoned up to 150,000 native schoolchildren with an appalling more than 50,000 winding up missing or murdered in what amounts to the imperial Commonwealth's systematic policy of indigenous ethnic purging.[358] The 1964 British Columbia incident with the queen and prince is connected directly to this genocidal policy against aboriginal peoples across the planet. And with so many children missing each year around the globe for so many years, satanic ritual sexual abuse, torture and murder account for millions of forgotten lost souls who were once innocent, vibrant children deserving our failed protection.

This was Canada's Commonwealth policy from the 1880s through the 1980s, with the last of the school closures not until the 1990s.[359] This inhumane pattern parallels the fate of 130,000 British children swept up in the migrant program banishing orphaned children to mostly Australia and Canada where they were forced into hard labor and horrid abuse from the 1920s

---

[355] "The Queen of England and the Children who Disappeared," *Daily Kos*, July 4, 2010.

[356] Jane Dalton, "Murdered and Missing Women and Girls in Canada Tragedy is Genocide Rooted in Colonialism, Official Inquiry Finds," *Independent*, June 1, 2019.

[357] "The Queen of England and the Children who Disappeared."

[358] Mark Cherrington, "Oh, Canada," *Cultural Survival Quarterly Magazine*, September 2007.

[359] Mark Cherrington.

to the 1970s.[360] Modeled after the Indian boarding school system in the United States, of the 150,000 aboriginal children rounded up in Canada, yanked from their families and sent to be "assimilated" in residential schools prior to the 1940s, the mortality rate was upwards of near 50% killed.[361] Near half these defenseless kids sent to state-monarchal-church run schools died in inhumane death camps, many willfully murdered under the direct satanic "care" of Canadian and British Commonwealth authorities.

One such shameful example among 31 mass grave sites discovered is the Mohawk Institute, shut down in 1970, where forensic evidence has unearthed hundreds of bones belonging to slaughtered Mohawk children.[362] Witnesses claim that red robed clergy from Queen Elizabeth's Anglican Church engaged in satanic torture rituals. Of course similar mass grave sites at residential schools also under the queen's Sovereign Crown in Jersey and Ireland are also well documented. Again, both royalty as well as popes have been granted the sanctified license for wholesale slaughter of children and to this day, there's been nothing we humans have done about it. In view of the gravity of House of Windsor crimes against both children and humanity on this earth for so many centuries, it's time we finally hold these demonically driven controllers accountable.

Three years before the royals abducted ten missing indigenous children in western Canada, in 1961 the queen and her princely consort went on another shopping spree to India so that the "warrior" hunter Philip could get his jollies off shooting Bengal tigers as trophy kills along with a rare rhinoceros, both the tiger and rhino endangered species along with killing mother elephants and terrorizing orphaned calves. Several months later ex Nazi-Bilderberg founder-Dutch Prince Bernhardt (father of Queen Beatrice) and "conservationist" Prince Philip co-founded the World Wildlife Fund (WWF),[363] resulting only in more endangered species. WWF raises funds to globally power grab land, push native populations off the soil used for farming. In other words, the WWF has a deceptive track record of doing exactly the opposite of what it advertises. Not only is it a scam causing animal species to disappear at a faster rate, in 2019 it's been accused of funding paramilitary groups allegedly torturing and murdering innocent people in large national parks and refuges across Africa and Asia,[364] similar to the rape and pillage of UN "peacekeeping" forces.[365] A consistent pattern has emerged - Illuminati royal aristocratic bloodlines behind many philanthropic global organizations ostensibly created to do good, in today's Lucifer controlled world are found to always do bad.

---

[360] Caroline Davies, "Britain's Child Migrant Programme: Why 130,000 were Shipped Abroad," *The Guardian*, February 27, 2017.

[361] Colin Perkel, "'Missing Children' at Residential Schools ID'd," *Huffington Post*, July 31, 2012..

[362] Alfred Lambremont Webre, "Mass Genocide of Mohawk Children by UK Queen and Vatican Uncovered in Canada," *bibliotecapleyades.net*, October 8, 2011.

[363] "Prince Bernhard of the Netherlands – Personal Background and his Part in Starting the Bilderberg Conferences," *bilderberg.org*.

[364] Karen McVeigh, "WWF Accused of Funding Guards who Tortured and Killed People," *The Guardian*, March 4, 2019.

[365] Lucy Johnston, "Now UN Peacekeepers Stand Accused after 612 Cases of Sex Abuse," *Express*, February 18, 2018.

A Windsor male rite of passage is hunting and killing as much wildlife species as possible, the royals' notorious lethal hunts for pure lustful blood sport typically kill scores or hundreds of birds, foxes, rabbits at a time along with many other hunted big game species, including the human species, just for the thrill of the kill, power and bloodthirst for slaying the beast.[366] The whiff of blood in the air is notoriously the royals' "Apocalypse Now" moment of "smells like victory." Despite having Diana their mother, who frowned on the needless bloodbath slaughter, without her, William and Harry have each reportedly become zealots upholding the royal Windsor male tradition of mass kills. And the public paying for all these abominable bloodbaths of pure gluttony and orgiastic overkill is supposed to admire this less-than-human alien hybrid?

In November 1962, Prince Philip made a trip to Bohemian Grove, infamous stomping grounds in the northern California redwoods where child blood sacrifice and ritual orgies are reported amongst mostly US elite, but British royalty of course are always welcomed.[367] Referring to his Bohemian rendezvous, a quote from *aangirfan.blogspot.com*, showcasing a summary of the royal philanderer's many conquests:

The rich and powerful sometimes made their way to the nearby town of Guerneville, where 10 bars were enhanced by call girls. According to Manu Kanaki, who operated one such establishment, Northwood Lodge, Philip was a visitor and was seen in the company of the girls.[368]

Prince Philip has another association that's proven to be dubiously embarrassing and suspect. An accredited partner of the Duke of Edinburgh awards program happens to be with Indian guru Sai Baba who claims he is the reincarnation of God in spite of decades of allegations that he sexually assaults youth. Yet the Duke of Edinburgh happily sends 200 kids from Sai Youth UK to India on a humanitarian medical mission in honor of the cult leader's 80th birthday.[369] Based on history of past affiliations, some might suspect the royal connection is a front for a child sex trafficking operation.

The queen's deceased younger sister Princess Margaret back in her wild and free, younger days also ran with some shady characters, like London gangster John Bindon.[370] She held court on her own Caribbean Island playground of Mustique. The infamous £500,00 London's Lloyds Bank heist on Baker Street in September 1971 allegedly ended up in possession of some rather compromising raunchy photos of Prince Margaret. On Mustique she was known to party hardy with sex, drugs and rock n' roll, entertaining pop star icon from the Mamas and Papas John Phillips,[371] who raped his daughter Mackenzie at 19 and proceeded with a consensual

[366] "Royal Babylon by Heathcote Williams," YouTube video, 1:11:53, posted May 11, 2012.
[367] Joel van der Reijden, "Bohemian Grove: Summer Hideout for America's Republican Establishment," *isgp-studies.com*, September 7, 2005.
[368] "The Crown – Philip – Sex," *aanirfan.blogspot.com*, March 18, 2017.
[369] Paul Lewis, "The Indian Living God, the Paedophilia Claims and the Duke of Edinburgh Awards," *The Guardian*, November 4, 2006.
[370] Elaine McCahill, "Princess Margaret's Scandalous Love Affair with Gangster had very X-Rated Party Trick," *Mirror*, December 15, 2018.
[371] Chris Champion, "King of the Wild Frontier," *The Guardian*, March 14, 2009.

incestuous affair for the next decade.[372] Another close loyal friend was writer Gore Vidal,[373] whose half-sister and nephew claim was a pedophile.[374] Again, the company one keeps is a telling reflection. A year after her centenarian mom the Mother Queen and drug-addicted incest pappy Papa Phillips died, Margaret also ran out of steam at 71 in 2002.

In keeping with this Luciferian theme, as the world's largest landowner, the House of Windsor largely controls the world food supply, owning a cartel of about 10-12 multinational corporations, assisted by another three dozen companies.[375] This cartel is primarily responsible for the global food production, distribution and sale of the earth's total food source output. While tens of millions are dying of hunger and starvation each year, Queen Elizabeth and her controllers could easily stop it in a heartbeat, but of course choose not to. Instead, the elite increasingly maintains an unconscionable policy of global austerity and impoverishment. Mass population control is far more manageable when people are hungry, living in fear, uncertainty and ongoing shortages brought on by endlessly induced crises like the current pandemic hoax. Plus, controlling the earth's human food supply can easily become a highly effective means of depopulation, which along with "killer viruses" tops Prince Philip's wish list.

In recent years the enigmatic Windsor clan have been at it again, changing their stripes, this time moving 180 degrees away from their proven German Nazi heritage to spawning the next generations as King of the Jews. Through Judaic law carried through maternal lineage, all the Windsor men – from Prince Charles to his son Prince William, both married and have offspring through Jewish wives and mothers. Once the now 94-year old queen dies, the next King will be the longest serving heir apparent – the near 72-year old Prince Charles, that is if he's not bypassed in line to the throne due to lack of popular support in Parliament and amongst British commoners.[376] A growing majority of the Crown's subjects desire Prince William as their next king rather than the aging, stodgy, "politically opinionated," largely unpopular senior citizen some call "Big Ears." Additionally, Britons have never forgotten how Prince Charles cheated on his globally adored first wife Princess Diana with fellow adulterer Duchess Camilla.[377] They'll never forget his sickening desire to be Camilla's tampon while still married to the "People's Princess."[378] In any event, beginning with William and then William's successor, his older son

[372] Christopher Luu, "One Day at a Time Star Says Coming Clean about Incest Caused a Rift in her Family," *refinery29.com*, February 9, 2017.

[373] Parul Sehgal, "Beauty, Bad Temper and Scandal in a Riveting Look at Princess Margaret," *The New York Times*.

[374] "Gore Vidal's Nephew and Half-Sister Claim the Celebrated Writer was a Pedophile who Carried out 'Jerry Sandusky Acts' on Underage Boys as they Challenge his $37 Million Will," Daily Mail, November 9, 2013.

[375] Richard Freeman, "The Windsors' Global Food Cartel: Instrument of Starvation," *EIR*, December 8, 1995.

[376] Giles Sheldrick, "Prince Charles Snubbed: "Prince William should Leapfrog Dad to be King' to Save Windsors," *Express*, January 25, 2020.

[377] Toby Jones, "Princess Diana was Delighted by Charles's 'Camillagate' Humiliation, New Book Reveals," *Independent*, August 10, 2017.

[378] Amalie Henden, "Royal Shock: How Prince Charles Told Camilla he Wanted to 'Live Inside her Trousers,'" *Express*, June 25, 2019.

Prince George, if the British monarchy lasts that long, the next royal reigns for generations to come will be by no accident ruled by Kings of the Jews.

Just like the other King of the Jews - the Jewish House of Rothschild they've been merging with, the British royal family emerged in recent centuries also from Germany as a prominent Royal Black Nobility bloodline, historically also purposely keeping their bloodline power within the family through practicing intergenerational incest. After all, if their DNA's spread too thin, the myth that "all men are created equal" might actually turn out true, and Lucifer only knows, that would never work in their satanically driven, war-ravaging, debtor enslaved, divided and ruled, demonically controlled regal world.

This chapter's dissection of the thoroughly dysfunctional equally controversial British royal family, from its traditionally inbred history full of sexual deviance and perversion, right up to its intimate close ties to the planet's two most infamous Zionist pedophiles of all time – Prince Charles' mentor and confidant (and chosen marriage counselor) Sir Jimmy Savile and now thoroughly disgraced younger brother Prince Andrew's "no regrets" pal, Israel's blackmailer Jeffrey Epstein[379] and their despicable key roles spanning the last half century in the global child sex trafficking trade, both exposed for procuring underage children for the world's most powerful, Zionist blackmail controlled, degenerate VIP scum of the earth. By both their undeniably intimate associations alone, and Andrew's all but prosecuted underage child sex abuse history, this chapter has laid out the extremely high probability that most of the senior royal family males are or have been pedophiles. It simply runs in this satanic family's blood. Further, this chapter also exposes how humanity has been hijacked and enslaved by these subhuman pedophilic black nobility imposters that have controlled the earth and human species going back to the Anunnaki roots for a mind boggling near half million millennia by willfully falsifying our own birthright history.

In typical Orwellian doublespeak deceit, laws that are ostensibly passed to make government more transparently open and accountable to public taxpayer scrutiny actually contain a special hidden clause buried in small print that when it comes to the royals, they're once again exclusively exempted and entitled even more secrecy than ever before.[380] Clearly this latest draconian move is designed to cover-up the royal family's known direct connections to the most infamous pedophiles on the planet - Sir Jimmy Savile and Jeffrey Epstein. All communication between the most senior royal family members, including their staff, and the government has been made completely off limits to the public.[381] Additionally, as it is, the

---

[379] Naomi Adedokun, "'Grotesque' – Prince Andrew an 'Embarrassment' to Royals Amid Meghan and Harry Outcry," *Express*, January 24, 2020.
[380] Eleanor Harding, "Royals to be Shrouded in Deeper Secrecy under Controversial Law Change," *Daily Mail*, January 7, 2011.
[381] Yasmin Alibhai-Brown, "The Royal Family Are Exempt from Freedom of Information Requests and can Veto BBC Programmes. Why do we put up with this?" *Independent*, January 4, 2015.

British monarchy holds the power of consultation on any potential legislation prior to parliamentary vote that could affect royal self-interests, by law it must first be run by the queen and Prince Charles for their veto power and input.[382]

After passage of the Freedom of Information Act of 2005, resulting in Queen Elizabeth, the world's largest landowner worth 33 trillion pounds, caught attempting to divert tax paid funds explicitly allocated for the poor and needy to heat her own plush Buckingham Palace in the winter, new secrecy laws went into further effect sparing her embarrassment for unconscionably fleecing her taxpaying subjects out of their hard earned cash for her own selfish purposes.[383] But even worse, recent secrecy laws effectively seal off protection of pedophilic royalty raping underage children. The queen has it in writing that under the guise of her Sovereign Crown, just like the sovereign pope's and sovereign Malta Knights, she enjoys immunity from any and all prosecution and is fully exempt from all accountability for violating any and all British laws.[384] She and her royals' unlimited sense of entitlement, like all VIPs, has always granted them permission to live above the law. Born into absolute godlike power and deference, not for their ability or accomplishment, but simply by their bloodline birthright ownership over the planet earth, is obscene and in itself criminal. That's how they keep their peace of mind, able to legally get away with murder and blood sacrifice, after torturing and sodomizing children in cannibalistic satanic rituals. But more on that favorite royal pastime shortly.

As the queen alluded to in her last annual Christmas broadcast, with photos of Prince Andrew, Prince Harry and Duchess Meghan all conspicuously absent from her royal desktop, she acknowledged 2019 was a "bumpy" year for the Windsors.[385] The Queen's personal favorite son Andrew's pedo-fall, or more apt leap from grace based upon his infamous BBC interview, combined with the queen's 99-year old Freemason husband (for the last two-thirds of a century),[386] and the longest living male royal in British history, Prince Philip's hospitalization just before Christmas last year for a medically serious precondition after his car accident and police probe, all made for an extremely rough and tumble year that had to be excruciatingly embarrassing and humiliating for the crusty, proper old queen.[387]

[382] Robert Booth, "Prince Charles has been Offered a Veto over 12 Government Bills since 2005," *The Guardian*, October 30, 2011.

[383] "Secrecy Laws Passed to Hide Pedophile Ring Connection to Royal Family," *hangthebankers.com*, July 14, 2014.

[384] Stephen Bates, "Is the Queen Above the Law?" *The Guardian*, May 16, 2007.

[385] Vanessa Allen and Rebecca English, "One's Bumpy Year: The Queen Uses her Christmas Message to Acknowledge a Turbulent 2019 for the Royals (But there's no Harry and Meghan on her Desk like Last Year... and Definitely no Andrew!" *Daily Mail*, December 23, 2019.

[386] Peter Lowndes, "Prince Philip, Duke of Edinburgh, Reaches 60 Years as a Member of the Craft," *Freemasonry Today*, September 5, 2013.

[387] Melissa Roberto, "Prince Philip Released from the Hospital just in Time to Celebrate Christmas with the Queen," *Fox News*, December 24, 2019.

Then there was and still is the publicly aired feuding between grandson princes William and Harry,[388] climaxed in January 2020 with Harry's decision to relocate to Canada with biracial American wife Meghan Markle who never quite fit in as a Windsor, and their rejection of the royal life in their so called Megxit circus.[389] With their official resignation as senior royal family members, and the couple's litigious lawsuits against the media,[390] including a recent court defeat,[391] the ongoing royal high drama casts an already divisively dark, foreboding shadow on the future of a most uncertain, perhaps dying monarchy. As a last vestige throwback to Middle Age feudalism, perhaps the enslaved human race has finally outgrown its blind servitude to the British Crown's 1200-year monarchy run.

In early 2020 the press reported that Andrew, fresh from nursing his own wounds spent a week in January consoling the aging queen who fell ill after their long "bumpy" year,[392] undoubtedly due to the nonstop royal stress and strain, witnessing both her family and Crown fall apart before the world's eyes. After 77 straight years of annually attending an affair at the Woman's Institute at Norfolk, the queen suddenly took ill, having to cancel a half hour prior to her scheduled engagement on January 23rd.[393]

Seems the unending royal scandals are beginning to take their toll on the aging, fragile, wary queen. Current gossip's going around among tongue wagging odds makers after increasing her 1 in 5 chance to 4 in 6 odds, Queen Elizabeth will be abdicating her throne prior to the end of 2020.[394] It appears she may beat the oddsmakers after all. In December 2019, Queen Elizabeth dispelled rumors of her stepping down upon her 95th birthday in June 2021.[395] It's been reaffirmed she plans to keep her vow as Britain's monarch till death do her part.

But in damage control mode for many months, the exhausted, run down queen who hadn't been seen for months with the Coronavirus hype, she held Harry and Meghan in contempt for tarnishing the increasingly fragile royal Firm. She went public in their banishment, feeling

[388] Monique Jessen and Simon Perry, "Prince Harry and Prince William 'Didn't Leave on Good Terms,' Says Family Friend," *People Magazine*, February 5, 2020.

[389] Suzanne Moore, "It's Not just Meghan and Harry. I'd Like us all to Escape this Dire Royal Circus," *The Guardian*, January 14, 2020.

[390] Audrey McNamara, "Meghan Markle Could Face Father in Legal Battle with British Tabloid," *CBS News*, January 15, 2020.

[391] "Prince Harry Loses Ipso Complaint over Mail on Sunday Story that Criticized his Wildlife Photographs that didn't Reveal the Fact that an Elephant was 'Drugged and Tethered,'" *Daily Mail*, January 30, 2020.

[392] Dan Wooton, "Handy Andy Disgraced Prince Andrew has Become the Queen's 'Rock' during Megxit, Royal Insiders have Revealed," *The Sun*, January 19, 2020.

[393] Rosa Sanchez, "Queen Elizabeth Falls Ill after Prince Harry and Meghan's Dramatic Royal Exit," *radaronline.com*, January 23, 2020.

[394] Clive Hammond, "Queen on the Brink: The Huge Clue that has Left Fans Convinced Her Majesty Will Abdicate," *Express*, February 10, 2020.

[395] Nicolas Bieber and Jamie Hawkins, "Officials Respond to Rumours that the Queen will Step down for Prince Charles at 95," *devonlive.com*, December 23, 2019.

they're bickering and squabbling has hurt the Crown long enough.[396] She as much as said the little ingrates are on their own.

As the Duke and Duchess of Sussex branched out on their own, the Queen put her foot down about them not cashing in on their "Sussex Royal" brand. As petulant children, they defiantly sniped back at ruling grandma's hardline approach with their website[397] statement on February 21, 2020:

While there is not any jurisdiction by The Monarchy or Cabinet Office over the use of the word 'Royal' overseas, The Duke and Duchess of Sussex do not intend to use 'Sussex Royal' or any iteration of the word 'Royal' in any territory.[398]

Harry and Meghan are also crying foul, never having felt welcomed into the Windsor tribe,[399] bitter over their perceived unfair, harsh treatment by the queen compared to other royal couples and members:

While there is precedent for other titled members of the royal family to seek employment outside of the institution, for the Duke and Duchess of Sussex, a 12-month review has been put in place.[400]

In tit for tat entertainment, the royal brand of petty little bread and circuses played on. Many grew wary of their gossipy feuding that the media to this day is still rehashing ad nauseam.[401] But humanity may be finally waking up to realize Europe's Black Nobility royal families are not humanity's friends but enemies.

Meanwhile, incredibly for over 67 years, Queen Elizabeth has been the British head of state, head of the British Crown's constitutional monarch, head of both the Anglican Church and the British Crown Commonwealth of 54 Nations. Far from the propagated myth that the longest running monarch in British history is but a "figurehead," that commonly held deception by design is analogous to America's Federal Reserve being part of the US government when the Rothschild private central bank controlling America's money supply is neither "federal" nor "a reserve." Another hidden historical falsehood is that the so called "sovereign" nation of America earned its independence upon winning its Revolutionary War when in fact it still

---

[396] Katie Nicholls, "She Wants It Done and Over With': Inside the Queen's Final Decision on Harry and Meghan," *Vanity Fair*, February 22, 2020.

[397] "The Duke and Duchess of Sussex Spring 2020 Transition," *sussexroyal.com*.

[398] Blake Montgomery, "Prince Harry and Meghan Snipe at the Queen for Banning 'Royal' from their Brand," *Daily Beast*, February 22, 2020.

[399] Tom Sykes and Tim Teeman, "Prince Harry and Meghan Markle Felt 'Totally Unwelcome' in the Royal Family – So They Split," *Daily Beast*, January 8, 2020.

[400] Tom Sykes, "Prince Harry and Meghan Markle Urged: 'Be More Gracious,'" *Daily Beast*, February 24, 2020.

[401] Zoe Forsey, "Lip Reader Confirms William's 'Weird' Whisper to Kate at Meghan and Harry's Final Event," *Mirror*, October 19, 2020.

secretly remains a British colony.[402] Seems if the queen owned Royal Crown's not covertly in control, by more calculated deceit, it's the Rothschild's Crown with the separate sovereign City of London Crown that is even more powerful. By following the money, the City of London Crown truly owns the world, including America.[403] As will be explained shortly, the off-planet, earth controlling, sneaky, lying bastards have managed to own and control the human race from its very first breath - literally.

So much shocking truth has been carefully and methodically concealed from us for a very, very long time, really from the very beginning. As addressed in Book 1, the ruling elite has willfully denied us – the Homo sapiens species - knowledge of our own human history as archeological finds that don't fit neatly into the Darwinian control matrix to this day have been suppressed, attacked or ignored.[404] Bad science rules this corrupt world of academia and the body politic because dishonest, evil gatekeepers have always been in charge. Just one prime example is the scientific "dictatorship" claiming that human-caused rising CO_2 levels are exclusively responsible for the so-called global climate change crisis when in fact it's been decades of toxic geoengineering poisoning the planet that's the real culprit along with EMF weather modification that's behind the current climate upheaval. The government cabal, its "scientific" establishment and corporate media are the elite purveyors of deception as only through trickery and deceit have ruling bloodlines kept the masses in check and completely in the dark as the necessary means to retain their tight megalomaniacal power and control over the earth's population for hundreds of millennia.

As much as any single institution today, the British royal monarchy epitomizes what's gone most wrong on planet earth. To hyper-glorify the public lives of the most visible of all elite Luciferians in such favorable, saccharine spin and façade, media propaganda spun 24/7 follows the family's every move, what they wear, how they comport themselves, and hang on their every word. As the darker truth about them continues to emerge, the powers of deception are having to work overtime to paint a positive, benevolent image that the global masses will still readily accept, without vomiting over the nauseatingly dripping duplicity. Two such Oscar winning Hollywood films, "The Queen" and "The King's Speech" were made to resuscitate the stale, cold image of Queen Elizabeth's monarchy. The mass media propaganda ministry is all about shaping and molding public opinion by portraying the royal family as caring and deserving of public worship and taxpayer support. So in desperation, the NWO propaganda machine continues endlessly churning out dozens more television soap opera series and films on the royals as an overtly transparent, feeble attempt to negate and erase history, hiding their ever-emerging darker reality.[405]

As more of their ugly shit gets exposed, you can see the cabal's publicity machine's frenzied, uptick tempo of glossed over bullshit is flimsily designed as necessary window dressing to

[402] "The United States is Still a British Colony - Part 1," *The Millennium Report*, October 26, 2017..

[403] Dick Eastman, "The City of London – Who the 'Crown' Really is," *rense.com*, August 13, 2011.

[404] Jonathan Gray, "The Suppressed History of Planet Earth," *bibliotecapleyades.net*.

[405] Nika Shakhnazarova, "Netflix Teases New Pictures from The Crown's Fourth Season Ahead of Release Date, *Mirror*, October 18, 2020.

hideously cover-up the royals' Luciferian agenda. As if further embellishing and glamourizing the commoditized, artificially manufactured brand of the Windsor "mystique" will stop the shockingly naked, appalling truth from seeping out. The latest episode of the emperor's new clothes cannot possibly shield them or their pedo-crime cabal any longer. Cultivating their benignly magnanimous, if not heroic, totally fake image and reputation as worldly do-gooders, pillars of humanity, ambassadors of goodwill and universal charity, honorably upholding tradition as a "stabilizing," benevolent global force for good, this completely false image projected 24/7 by the cabal propaganda machine cannot possibly save them as truth will prevail.

Just like the decaying criminal institutions of the Catholic Church and the Rothschild controlled global economic enslavement system, the Crown is the artificially manufactured institutionalized glue holding their house of cards power infrastructure together, in the face of its crumbling, corrosive, demonic core rapidly unraveling. In order to hold onto their power, they are stepping up their destructive permanent war agenda, planet-wide ecocide, spiraling global economy collapse, increasing spread of fear, infectious diseases, injustice, poverty, globalized pedophilia and human genocide. We are amidst their war on humanity. Rather than work towards reducing these mounting life-threatening killers, the Black Nobility bloodlines epitomized by the House of Windsor are our planetary destroyers, our true executioners in worship of Lucifer parasitically feeding off all human suffering but literally living off the flesh and blood of our innocents.

Throughout this series of books the royal family pedophiles are referred to as nonhuman. It was first reported in the *Inquisitr* in May 2014 that Russian President Vladimir Putin claimed he had witnessed Queen Elizabeth shapeshift from human to reptilian form upon meeting her during D-Day's 70th anniversary. Putin was hardly the first to accuse the queen of being a reptilian. Princess Diana confided in her confidant, healer Christine Fitzgerald that the Windsor family is not human, calling them "lizards," confirming their reptilian form.[406] Former MK-Ultra mind control sex slave and onetime Illuminati High Priestess Arizona Wilder described conducting ritual occult ceremonies for the elite. She maintains that she witnessed George HW Bush and Henry Kissinger as well as Queen Elizabeth and Prince Charles actually shapeshift during ceremonies.

At one secret ceremony a visibly drugged Diana was forced to attend a few weeks prior to her marriage to Prince Charles, she witnessed both the queen and Charles shapeshift. A few years later after Charles was caught cheating on his wife with Camilla Parker-Bowles, Diana wrote in a note to her butler Paul Burrell ten months before her death that she feared that Charles would have her vehicle's brakes tampered with,[407] a la Princess Grace Kelly's demise. And when the queen reportedly heard Diana died in a car accident, she too mentioned "the brakes." Sharing her concerns she would be murdered to close others, Diana actually predicted her own assassination at the bloody hands of the royal family.

---

[406] David Icke, *Tales from the Time Loop* (Rye: Bridge of Love Publications, 2003.

[407] Loulla-Mae Eleftheriou-Smith, "Princess Diana Letter Claims Prince Charles was 'Planning an Accident' in her Car just 10 Months before her Fatal Crash," *Independent,* August 30, 2017.

Former Illuminati insider Arizona Wilder stated that reptilians she observed in satanic rituals are generally of beige or brown color, stand 7 feet or taller, and possess a long hairy tongue, claws, a tail and scales that ethereally disappear into one another.[408] Wilder stated that when reptilians sleep, they will often shapeshift back into their natural nonhuman form. She asserted that Princess Diana no doubt knew that her husband was reptilian as when she underwent monthly menstrual cycles, the presence of blood would also automatically cause the royal lizard to shapeshift. As a result, female palace employees reportedly aren't permitted to work while menstruating.

In June 2016, during BBC2's primetime coverage of Queen Elizabeth's 90th birthday celebration parade, apparently thousands of observers adamantly claimed they saw Queen Elizabeth shapeshifting on live TV, immediately causing a Twitter uproar where the hashtag *#reptilianqueen* instantly skyrocketed as the #1 feed most commented topic on during the hours and day following, prior to Twitter abruptly scrubbing it from the net like it never happened.[409] At the same time, someone at the queen's own website actually addressed this remarkable phenomenon that so many viewers had witnessed on live television. On her official *royal.uk* website[410] appeared the following subheading: "Queen seen by her subjects in a different form." The word-for-word content of the amazing announcement is below:

*The Queen has ruled for longer than any other Monarch in British history, becoming a much loved and respected figure across the globe. Her extraordinary reign has seen her travel more widely than any other monarch, undertaking many historic overseas visits. Known for her sense of duty and her devotion to a life of service, she has been an important **figurehead** for the UK and the Commonwealth during times of enormous social change.[411]* [**Emboldened** Emphasis mine]

*Earlier this week the Queen was seen by thousands of people in a form they are not acquainted with. We seek to reassure the public that the Queen is still their Queen, and remains the respected and loved figure they have always known. While **she may not be human**, she is a devoted leader and Monarch, and she believes her subjects will grow to accept her and her family for what they are.[412]* [Again **boldface** because this is an incredibly revealing royal admission, followed by the Queen's own personal statement]:

I pay tribute to the commitment, selfless devotion and generosity of spirit shown by my millions of human subjects and I fully expect them to digest this news in a mature and humble fashion. Nothing has changed. Together we shall march on.[413]

---

[408] "David Icke – Revelations, Arizona Wilder," 1998, YouTube video, 1:30:42.
[409] "#ReptilianQueen | Queen Elizabeth 'Shapeshifting' On Live TV Goes Viral | The Queen of England Admits She Is 'Not Human' and We'll 'Learn to Accept Her for What She Is,'" *truth11.com*, June 12, 2016.
[410] British royal website, *royal.uk*.
[411] "Queen Elizabeth 'Is Not Human' – Confirmed by Buckingham Palace." *disclose.tv*, July 5, 2016.
[412] "Queen Elizabeth 'Is Not Human' – Confirmed by Buckingham Palace."
[413] "Queen Elizabeth 'Is Not Human' – Confirmed by Buckingham Palace."

Apparently realizing the stunned reaction of a fully informed world knowing Queen Elizabeth is a nonhuman reptile should that news spread around the world, again just like the fleeting Twitter frenzy, the above bombshell disclosure on her website quickly disappeared never to be seen nor heard nor commented on ever again. As if it never really even took place, it must've been some holographic dream, an apparition, figment of delusional conspiracy theorists' imagination, buried deep in the subconscious, under a heap of fast-fading "here today, gone tomorrow" memories. But fortunately, hundreds of quick-thinking observers did capture screenshots of the queen's "coming out" party, confirming what a growing number of us already suspected. Queen Elizabeth II is a coldblooded reptilian, a child eating, adrenochrome drinking, scaly, creepy alien from down under – not her Commonwealth colony Australia, Hell would be much closer in accuracy. But in this case, down under could easily refer to the subterranean environment where the bulk of her fulltime fellow reptilians are said to call their home in the underground caverns within the earth's interior. Other advanced races of ETs like the fair-haired Nordics, are also reportedly inner earth inhabitants. Greys are allegedly smaller ET's, malevolent but subservient to the reptilians. Michael Mott, author of *Caverns, Cauldrons and Concealed Creatures,*[414] encapsulates the alien dwellers of the subterranean world:

They are mostly reptilian or reptilian humanoids or 'fair' and Nordic; they are telepathic with superior mental powers; they can shape-shift and create illusions; they want to interbreed with humans and need human blood, flesh and reproductive materials; they have advanced technology; they have the secret of immortality; they can fly, either by themselves or with their technology; they mostly have a malevolent agenda for humans; they cannot survive for long in direct sunlight; they have been banished from the surface world or are in hiding from surface people and/or the Sun; they want to keep their treasures, knowledge and true identity a secret; they covertly manipulate events on the surface world; they have surface humans working for them through the priesthoods, cults and secret societies; they have a putrid smell like 'sulphur and brimstone.'[415]

All around the planet ancient passageways and tunnels to an inner hollow earth have been documented.[416] No accident that so much of the elite's occult satanic ritual abuse, MK torture and sacrifice of children on a massive scale occur in bulk volume in the thousands of black budgeted Deep Underground Military Bases (DUMBs) around the globe, the notorious Area 51 base in Nevada, New Mexico's Dulce base and in the California desert the China Lake facility all being prime examples.

After Illuminati whistleblowing former priestess Arizona Wilder performed satanic ritual sacrifices for the royal family, she stated:

There are changes going on in the Earth that seems they're [reptilians] *not able to hold their shape like they once were able to and people see them shapeshift more and more and they need the blood to try and maintain it. I believe there is a time coming, because of what I've been told,*

[414] Michael Mott, *Caverns, Cauldrons and Concealed Creatures* (Nashville: Grave Distractions Publications, 2011).
[415] David Icke, https://www.bibliotecapleyades.net/biggestsecret/taltimloop/tales_timeloop10.htm.
[416] Dennis Crenshaw, "An Introduction to the Hollow Earth," *bibliotecapleyades.net*, 2000.

when they are not going to bother having to hold that human shape as they had to before and they want that time to come.[417]

The above statement goes far in explaining the Queen's initial response of rosy optimism over her subjects accepting her nonhuman status. Aside from Arizona Wilder, another MK-Ultra survivor - Cathy O'Brien - in her *Trance Formation of America* autobiography accused other infamous public figures of being shapeshifting reptiles. Cathy maintains that her six-year old daughter was repeatedly raped by the late pedophile President George HW Bush who she said shapeshifted in Cathy's presence, explaining to her that he was a member of the Draco Anunnaki reptilian race that had taken over the earth but kept it secret due to the capacity to take on the human form.[418] Cathy also encountered reptilians among close presidential advisers from Reagan to George HW to Clinton. Cathy wrote how she caught the Jesuit educated brothers William and Robert S. Bennett shapeshifting when they unveiled their multidimensional superpowers. Bill Bennett as an MK-Ultra mind control programmer proclaimed:

Being alien, I simply make my thoughts your thoughts by projecting them into your mind. My thoughts are your thoughts.[419]

With literally millions of other mind control victims across the planet, Cathy O'Brien's been a courageous spokesperson disclosing the evil power and control of the CIA's MK-Ultra program, exposing pedophile presidents and their cabinet members, apparently feeling boldly at ease to reveal top secret revelations, confident that Cathy was destined to either be killed by her aging out planned obsolescence as a used up slave or smug in their belief that as a victim of Dissociative Disorder, her programmed amnesic state would hold, blocking all memories indefinitely. Fortunately for her and us, it didn't and instead their cocky misjudgment failed and has backfired on them. Sent as prototypical sex slave prototype and spy to service another president, this time Miguel de la Madrid, Mexico's leader from 1982 to 1988, in her book Cathy writes:

De la Madrid had relayed the 'legend of the Iguana' to me, explaining that lizard-like Aliens had descended upon the Mayans. The Mayan pyramids, their advanced astronomical technology, including the sacrifice of virgins, was supposedly inspired by the lizard aliens. He told me that when the aliens interbred with the Mayans to produce a form of life they could inhabit, they fluctuated between a human and Iguana appearance through chameleon-like abilities. 'A perfect vehicle for transforming into world leaders.' De la Madrid claimed to have Mayan/alien ancestry in his blood, whereby he transformed 'back into an Iguana at will.'[420]

Illuminati indoctrinated, sexually abused, tortured and mind-controlled slave trained to be an Illuminati goddess priestess, Arizona Wilder is actually Jennifer Ann (nee Nagel) Kealey. She met

[417] "David Icke – Revelations, Arizona Wilder."
[418] Cathy O'Brien, "Reptoid Rape: A Multi-Part Series," *reptilianagenda.com*, October 7, 1999.
[419] Cathy O'Brien, http://www.reptilianagenda.com/exp/e100799i.shtml.
[420] Cathy O'Brien, *Trace Formation of America* (US: Reality Marketing Inc., 1995).

David Icke while he was gathering information researching his seminal tome *The Biggest Secret* published in 1998. As Jennifer Ann Kealey writing from her blogsite *antinewworldorder.com* in June 2011, she refuted her earlier interviews with Icke, alluding to being programmed at the time to disclose what she revealed.[421] Naturally it's led to speculation over whether she was forced to recant her earlier testimony under death threats as those who share Illuminati secrets and attempt to leave their Illuminati past behind are often either murdered or harassed into oblivion. Sadly, it appears the latter fate may have befallen her as just last December 2019, Jennifer Kealey's whistleblowing husband Glen, who bravely exposed deep corruption at the top of Canada's Mulroney government during the early 1990s,[422] according to Jennifer, was poisoned to death.[423] The Canadian government had banned her from even entering Canada to be with her dying lawful husband.

The content of Arizona Wilder's interview disclosures with David Icke has been independently corroborated by multiple sources. She told David that while coordinating Illuminati satanic rituals as a priestess, she witnessed Presidents Lyndon Johnson, Gerald Ford, Ronald Reagan and George Bush senior along with Illuminati globalists Henry Kissinger, Jay Rockefeller (brother of David and Nelson), Clinton Secretary of State Madeleine Albright and former GOP House Speaker Newt Gingrich amongst numerous reptilian shapeshifters in attendance.[424] She also stated Bill and Hillary Clinton, George W. and Jeb Bush had also attended satanic rituals though she never observed them shapeshift. David Icke has encountered numerous others also claiming that they've seen Hillary Clinton, Henry Kissinger and George Bush senior as reptilians. It's believed to be common enough that sensitive, psychic individuals can attune to an energy frequency beyond the five physical senses of the human form to detect reptilians allegedly walking among us.[425]

The former Illuminati priestess also claimed experience conducting satanic ritual ceremonies in Europe at a number of occult locations such as Stonehenge, Westminster Abbey where the queen's coronation took place in 1953, the Queen Mother's old haunt Glamis Castle and Balmoral Castle, both in Scotland with the latter the seasonal royal family residence from July to October. Arizona maintained that she witnessed the following royal family members shapeshift into reptilian form during blood ritual child sacrifices – the Queen Mother, Queen Elizabeth, Prince Philip, Prince Charles, Prince Andrew and the queen's deceased sister Princess Margaret, in addition to Guy de Rothschild and Tony Blair.[426] Arizona Wilder stated that during child sacrifice rituals, animalistic beasts in the royal family lusting for blood would often fail to restrain themselves prior to the end of the rituals. Wilder witnessed the Queen Mother, Elizabeth II and Prince Charles all tearing open the jugular and devouring children's flesh, unable or unwilling to hold their human form prior to the ceremony's completion.

---

[421] Jennifer Ann Kealey, "Open Missive from Jennifer Ann Kealey," *antinewworldorder.com*, June 10, 2011.

[422] Mary Williams Walsh, "Politics: A Scandal Rocks Canada: One Man's Crusade against Corruption has the already Troubled Mulroney Government Squirming," *Los Angeles Times*, August 2, 1991.

[423] Jennifer Ann Kealey, "Silence Is Betrayal," *antinewworldorder.com*, December 10, 2019.

[424] "David Icke – Revelations, Arizona Wilder."

[425] David Icke, https://www.bibliotecapleyades.net/biggestsecret/taltimloop/tales_timeloop10.htm.

[426] "David Icke – Revelations, Arizona Wilder."

Arizona Wilder name-dropped a surprising Illuminati ritual attendee - the Anunnaki-Nibiru author himself Zecharia Sitchin, calling him a "dis-informer." David Icke added that Sitchin "tried warning me off from investigating the reptilians." So even though Zecharia singlehandedly put ancient Sumer's Anunnaki records on the public map so to speak, he did not want the ET race that he alleged had created humans to be associated with the reptillian Anunnaki brand of villainous earth controllers because according to Arizona Wilder, Sitchin himself was one of them.

In late 1970s prior to Charles' marriage to Princess Diana, Illuminati insider Arizona Wilder claimed that Charles impregnated Camilla Parker-Bowles, Duchess of Cornwall, but his firstborn child was sacrificed in a satanic blood ritual. The whistleblowing priestess said that the royals drink blood from their own jewel embedded goblets stirring the blood with daggers as a phallic symbol while wearing blood red or purple robes with Merovingian design. To hold their human form, these reptilian predators must have a steady diet of adrenalized blood from ritualized child rape, torture and sacrifice of infants and young children.[427] To meet the rising demand, it's why abduction of missing children, secret Illuminati cult infant breeding, and global child sex trafficking are all off the charts in recent times.

Arizona Wilder asserted that in late 1980s while Diana and Charles were still married, at both the Balmoral Castle and at the Mothers of Darkness Castle in Belgium,[428] the priestess overheard billionaire Mohamed Fayed and the Queen Mother (whom she described as "cold and cruel" while Diana called her downright "evil"[429]) speaking of an arranged future marriage between Fayed's son Dodi and Princess Diana. In other words, as a fellow Illuminati who fraternized with the royals at blood sacrifice rituals, Mohamed Fayed was prearranging a decade earlier Diana and Dodi ending up together while she was still married to the future lizard king. This statement illustrates how virtually all major future events are long planned out in advance, plotted behind the scenes years prior to them unfolding. That's how the cabal operates, there are no accidents, not with the biggest earth events involving humans.

Though a number of insiders have cited the head of the House of Rothschild (currently the 4th Baron Jacob) as the recognized Illuminati head honcho, Arizona Wilder insisted that this title known as Pindar in the Illuminati hierarchy (which means Phallus of the Dragon) belonged to Marquis de Libeaux, who may actually be a code for a Rothschild. Arizona stated in Icke's *The Biggest Secret* about the second in charge:

The Queen makes cruel remarks about lesser initiates, but is afraid of the man code-named 'Pindar' (the Marquis de Libeaux) *who is higher than her in Satanic rank. Pindar, apparently, bears a resemblance to Prince Charles.[430]*

---

[427] David Icke, "The Reptilian Connection," *bibliotecapleyades.net*.
[428] "Chateaux Des Amerois: Mothers of Darkness Castle," *The Millennium Report*, December 8, 2016.
[429] David Icke, https://www.bibliotecapleyades.net/biggestsecret/taltimloop/tales_timeloop10.htm.
[430] Dee Finney, "Pindar – The Lizard King?" *bibliotecapleyades.net*.

Arizona Wilder even went so far as to maintain that the Pindar de Libeaux is Charles' real father and that the Marquis' chateau in the Alsace-Lorraine region of eastern France contains an underground dungeon with an entrance to where menstrual blood is stored for handy ritual use among glowing green rocks that turn the blood black.[431] She also said that the entrance leads to the earth's warm interior where reptilian eggs are incubated. Arizona went on to say that full-blooded Anunnaki Reptilians live far longer than 100 years and that they will choose to inhabit a younger cloned body with shapeshifting capacity as a means of prolonging life. With all the blood drinking and cloning, the Queen Mother herself lived to be 101 and the shapeshifting queen's now 94 with her hubby 99. The inner royal circle has their ancient occult secrets for staying young and they all seem to involve adrenalized youngblood.

Princess Diana's close friend and healer for the final decade of her life in a recorded conversation with David Icke had lots to say about the royals, beginning with little old royal lady herself the Queen Mother:

The Queen Mother … now that's a serious piece of wizardry. The Queen Mother is a lot older than people think. To be honest, the royal family hasn't died for a long time, they have just metamorphosized. It's sort of cloning, but in a different way. They take pieces of flesh and rebuild the body from one little bit. Because it's lizard, because it's coldblooded, it's much easier to do this Frankenstein shit than it is for us. The different bodies are just different electrical vibrations and they have got that secret; they've got the secret of the micro-currents; it's so micro, so specific, these radio waves that actually create the bodies. These are the energies I work with when I'm healing. They know the vibration of life and because they're cold-blooded, they are reptiles, they have no wish to make the Earth the perfect harmony it could be, or to heal the Earth from the damage that's been done. The Earth's been attacked for zeons by different extraterrestrials. It's been like a football for so long. This place is a bus stop for many different aliens. All these aliens, they could cope with anything, including the noxious gases. They're landing all the time and coming up from the bowels of the Earth. They looked like reptiles originally, but they look like us when they get out now through the electrical vibration, that key to life I talked about. They can manifest how they want to. All the real knowledge has been taken out and shredded and put back in another way. The Queen Mother is 'Chief Toad' of this part of Europe and they have people like her in every continent. Most people, the hangers on, don't know, you know, about the reptiles. They are just in awe of these people because they are so powerful.[432]

Arizona Wilder also mentioned this about dear old grandma Windsor:

I have seen her sacrifice people. I remember her pushing a knife into someone's rectum the night that two boys were sacrificed. One was 13 and the other 18.[433]

---

[431] "David Icke – Revelations, Arizona Wilder."

[432] David Icke, https://www.bibliotecapleyades.net/biggestsecret/taltimloop/tales_timeloop10.htm.

[433] David Icke, https://www.bibliotecapleyades.net/biggestsecret/taltimloop/tales_timeloop10.htm.

Here's her observation of Queen Elizabeth during a ritual:

I have seen her sacrifice people and eat their flesh and drink their blood. One time she got so excited with blood-lust that she didn't cut the victim's throat from left to right in the normal ritual; she just went crazy, stabbing and ripping at the flesh after she had shape-shifted into a Reptilian... As far as enjoying the killing, enjoying the sacrifice, and eating the flesh; they're some of the worst of all of them. They don't care if you see it. Who are you going to tell, who is going to believe you? They feel that is their birthright and they love it. They love it.[434]

The British royals regularly practice satanic occult rituals that include torture, rape and child sacrifice in their own castles like Scotland's Balmoral, or in Belgium as well as other places in Europe, particularly around the satanic holidays. At some point during the summer months of 2001 ahead of 9/11, there was a major incident near Cagnes sur Mer in southern France close to the Riviera, part of the London-Amsterdam-Cannes-Cagnes sur Mer circuit within the larger satanic child trafficking network run by MI6 to serve their gluttonous, bloodthirsty global masters — the black nobility bloodlines. Recall that the British royals trace their family lineage back through the King David-Templar-Merovingian bloodline headquartered in 12th century southern France.[435] Except on this annual "Eyes Wide Shut" gathering, the sacrificial lambs happened to escape from the former Templar castle grounds. With child victims spilling out into the countryside, British intelligence and local police had their hands full scrambling frantically to ensure that leakage of the satanic powwow event didn't unravel to the point of attracting mass media attention. There were reports of royal family members hiding in potato sacks prior to being "rescued" and driven incognito out of the area in armored vehicles. How many victims were sacrificed before all hell broke loose is unknown.

These are the vile monstrous animals we're mind controlled to place on a pedestal and look up to. Again, because so many of these claims come off as scenes from a second-rate sci-fi blood and gore horror flick, so incredibly unbelievable, the villainous elite opportunistically utilize this fact to their advantage, knowing the masses will never accept this dark, grimmest of realities. The incredulous nature of these shocking accounts permits the queen's own 2016 confession on her website admitting she's not even human to be excused and quickly forgotten, a fleeting blip on a computer screen or just more unbelievable hoaxers from internet fringe attempting to pass off another conspiracy nut-job.

After the CIA's master stroke for Lucifer inventing that ever-useful label - "conspiracy theory" - to cast doubt on all those willing to question authority's false narratives,[436] every chance it gets, the CIA controlled Mockingbird MSM delights in taking potshots at conspiracy theorists,[437] particularly proponents of the reptilians from outer space. In 2009, in honor of the 40th anniversary of the lunar landing that the murdered film director Stanley Kubrick claimed was an

---

[434] David Icke, https://www.bibliotecapleyades.net/biggestsecret/taltimloop/tales_timeloop10.htm.
[435] "Child Abuse Timeline – Part 5," aangirfan.blogspot.com, February 1, 2014.
[436] "In 1967, the CIA Created the Label 'Conspiracy Theorists' ... to Attack Anyone Who Challenges the 'Official' Narrative," *Zero Hedge*, February 23, 2015.
[437] "Mockingbird: The Subversion of the Corporate Media by the CIA," *whatreallyhappened.com*..

insider hoax job, aside from that conspiracy theory,[438] *Time Magazine* examined, or more aptly mocked nine other high-profile cases including 9/11. Targeting David Icke's claim of the reptilian elite was its final 10th object of public ridicule and scorn:

They are among us. Blood-drinking, flesh-eating, shape-shifting extraterrestrial reptilian humanoids with only one objective in their cold-blooded little heads: to enslave the human race. They are our leaders, our corporate executives, our beloved Oscar-winning actors and Grammy-winning singers, and they're responsible for the Holocaust, the Oklahoma City bombings and the 9/11 attacks ... at least according to former BBC sports reporter David Icke, who became the poster human for the theory in 1998 after publishing his first book, The Biggest Secret, which contained interviews with two Brits who claimed members of the royal family are nothing more than reptiles with crowns.[439]

Fact: Multiple accounts of cannibalistic Illuminati satanic rituals involving adrenochrome drinking Luciferians, often in high places from bloodline families are known child sodomites and child sacrificing murderers. Both ancient occult and modern science know and confirm that:

Young blood counteracts and reverses pre-existing effects of brain aging at the molecular, structural, functional and cognitive level.[440]

Hence, the royals and Illuminati leaders have reversed the aging process by engaging in satanic blood sacrifice of children, cannibalism and blood drinking for millenniums. Two prime examples of our national leaders being pedophilic Luciferians are US President George H W Bush and UK Prime Minister Edward Heath, both allegedly also reptilian shapeshifters,[441] both to be repeatedly mentioned throughout this book series. And David Icke was hardly a fool for calling this pair of evil assholes out while they were still both alive, yet they never dared suing him because it was true. So it's Rothschild controlled publications like *Time Magazine* and *The New York Times* that are given crucial brainwashing roles disseminating falsehood and ridiculing truth and truthtellers because they are pedophilic bastions themselves.

Returning to further debunk *Time Magazine*'s feeble denying mockery: The Holocaust and both World War I and II were all financed and engineered by Black Nobility bloodlines like the Rothschilds in order to create the Jewish State, and the Bush family that helped finance Hitler was joined by plenty of others like the crypto-German "Windsors" who were fellow Nazi supporters. Prominent Zionist organizations worked in direct partnership with Adolf Hitler through their Haavara Agreement during the half dozen years leading up to WWII to facilitate German Jews to peacefully emigrate to Palestine.[442] But Victor Rothschild and his family turned

---

[438] T.S. Caladan, "Stanley Kubrick's Murder and the Moon Landings!" *blog.world-mysteries.com*, February 13, 2014.
[439] "Separating Fact from Fiction: The Reptilian Elite," *Time Magazine*, July 2009.
[440] Saul A Villeda, Kristopher E Plambeck, Jinte Middeldorp, Joseph M Castellano, Kira I Mosher, Jian Luo, Lucas K Smith, Gregor Bieri, Karin Lin, Daniela Berdnik, Rafael Wab, Joe Udeochu, Elizabeth G Wheatley, Bende Zou, Danielle A Simmons, Xinmin S Xie, Frank M Longo and Tony Wyss-Coray, "Young Blood Reverses Age-Related Impairments in Cognitive Function and Synaptic Plasticity in Mice," *Nature Medicine*.
[441] David Icke, https://www.bibliotecapleyades.net/biggestsecret/taltimloop/tales_timeloop10.htm.
[442] Mark Weber, "Zionism and the Third Reich," *Institute for Historical Review*, July-August 1993.

their backs on the hapless Jews remaining in Europe to become Holocaust victims, calculatingly written off as a forever source of sympathy, weaponized anti-Semitism silencer, but most of all as the necessary bargaining chips to establish the Rothschilds' very own Jewish State as King of the Jews. A separate chapter in Book 3 on the 20th century planetary overlord Victor Rothschild will further detail these documented facts and prove Rothschild was the British traitor in charge of the treasonous Cambridge Five.[443]

Hollywood titans behind the early major film studios were fellow Jewish Luciferians and much has been documented of the Hollywood pedo-gay mafia elite preying on children at sex orgies and belonging to satanic ritual cults (chapter to be covered in Book 4).[444] Both the 9/11 attack and the Oklahoma City bombing were planned false flags with the Clintons, Bushes and Cheney all known pedophiles involved in the plotting, execution and cover-up of both democide tragedies. *Time* goes on to list identified reptilian members – "Queen Elizabeth, George W. Bush, Henry Kissinger, Bill and Hillary Clinton and Bob Hope" and how they're linked to Freemasonry and Illuminati. Uh-hah, their crimes are all exposed in this book series.

After taking a hard look at reality, it's *Time Magazine* that's in fact the real fool for so blindly, blatantly protecting the pedo-crime cabal, of course all the while in total complicity. Its fascist Time-Life founder in 1923, Henry Luce, like the Bushes, a Yale Skull and Bones member initially financed by Rothschild agent JP Morgan, has proven to be linked to both CIA and its Mockingbird press.[445] And since 1923 it's all too obvious whose side *Time*'s been on. "Time is on my side," the hell it is Mick Jagger, only if you're one of them, which you've been reported to be.[446] If you're not, time is of the essence to drain this Luciferian pedo-cesspit of the world.

To those with an open enough mind to actually do their homework, researching history beyond the dogma of endless false narratives, it's not hard to find skeletons galore in the royal family closet. Queen Elizabeth's clan personify the most public face of the bloodline elite covertly up to no good like no other on this planet. Let's take a brief look at her consort, the queen's husband Prince Philip, Duke of Edinburgh. Behind the Malthusian overpopulation myth,[447] Philip shows his true eugenicist colors in a 1981 *People Magazine* interview explaining his wish to cull the human herd:

Human population growth is probably the single most serious long-term threat to survival. We're in for a major disaster if it isn't curbed - not just for the natural world, but for the human

[443] Mark Hackard, "Victor Rothschild, Soviet Spy," *espionagehistoryarchive.com*, March 27, 2018.

[444] "The Term Hollywood Derives from the Holly Tree," *thegreatwork208716197.wordpress.com,* March 9, 2020..

[445] Markab Algedi, "Father of Mainstream Media: Skull and Bones Member, Henry Luce," *humansarefree.com*, November 28, 2017.

[446] "Mick Jagger, Satanism and the CIA," *aangirfan.blogspot.com*, March 18, 2014.

[447] Kay Kiser, "Overpopulation – The Deadly Myth behind the Other Modern Myths," *wattsupwiththat.com*, May 25, 2019.

world... We have no option. If it isn't controlled voluntarily, it will be controlled involuntarily by an increase in disease, starvation and war.[448]

War, disease and starvation are the royal cabal's way of dealing with the falsehood of his so-called problem. What he truly thinks of humanity was next revealed both in a 1984 book and again reiterated in 1988:

In the event that I am reincarnated, I would like to return as a deadly virus, to contribute something to solving overpopulation.[449]

After the deaths of Princess Diana and her lover Dodi Fayed at the hands of the royals, at her 2008 inquest, Dodi's father claimed their assassination hit was ordered by the Prince of Edinburgh, calling Philip a "Nazi racist."[450] The owner of the Paris Ritz Hotel and Harrods stated that Diana had told him in July 1997 - two months prior to the Paris "accident," that she feared that Prince Philip and Prince Charles wanted to get rid of her. Also in 1995, she shared with her divorce attorney Lord Mishcon that the royals were plotting to murder her by way of a car accident. At the time of her death, Prime Minister Tony Blair "happened" to be staying with the royal family at Scotland's Balmoral Castle.[451] Strong evidence indicates that Diana's untimely death in the tunnel hitting the 13th pillar was both a planned occult blood satanic sacrifice as well as eliminating a growing threat to the royal family.[452] Diana had become increasingly aware of the "dark forces" lurking not only inside the family's palace and castle walls, but strong evidence exists that her phone calls were bugged and she was being closely monitored by security services in the final weeks of her life.[453] At her inquest, electronic surveillance expert Graham Harding testified that he'd discovered a bugging device in her Kensington apartment wall in 1994. So it appears definite in the last few weeks of her life she was being tracked. During a surge of IRA violence in the mid-1990s, Diana turned to her personal friend Rodney Turner and joked:

If it's not the IRA, it's my husband.[454]

It's extremely likely that Princess Diana had learned of the royal family's pedophilia involvement and, similar to BBC presenter Jill Dando's 1999 murder for intending to blow the whistle on Savile and the BBC pedophile network (addressed in Chapter 4 of this book), Britain's two most beloved goddesses paid for knowing too much with both their very lives violently snuffed out.

---

[448] Fred Hauptfuhrer, "Vanishing Breeds Worry Prince Philip, But Not as Much as Overpopulation," *People Magazine*, December 21, 1981.

[449] John Hind, "Did I Say That?" *The Guardian*, June 20, 2009.

[450] "Fayed's Rant: Prince Philip is 'Nazi Racist,'" *The Scotsman*, February 18, 2008.

[451] David Icke, https://www.bibliotecapleyades.net/biggestsecret/taltimloop/tales_timeloop10.htm.

[452] "Princess Diana's Death and Memorial: The Occult Meaning," *vigilantcitizen.com*, April 13, 2009.

[453] Nick Allen, "Diana 'Feared being Bugged by Dark Forces,'" *The Telegraph*, January 8, 2008.

[454] Nick Allen, https://www.telegraph.co.uk/news/uknews/1574893/Diana-feared-being-bugged-by-dark-forces.html.

Again, Diana confided that the royal family is not even human, calling them lizards. If Philip and Charles could have the mother of Charles' two supposed sons, a future King of England's own mother murdered, what does that say about Philip and Charles? Based on Prince Philip's wishful statement about his being reincarnated "a killer virus," the accused Nazi racist would just love nothing more than to wipe out 95% of the earth population, which is the unanimous wish and agenda amongst his fellow controllers - the world's 15th biggest landowner Ted Turner and 21st century's richest man Bill Gates,[455] who for years has been predicting sooner than later a killer virus would eliminate "over 30 million in six months."[456] At a TED2010 conference, Globalist Gates let the truth slip out:

First we got population. The world today has 6.8 billion people. That's headed up to about 9 billion. Now if we do a really great job on new vaccines, health care, reproductive health services, we lower that by perhaps 10 or 15 percent.[457][Boldface for EMPHASIS]

After matter-of-factly proclaiming a decade ago that he wanted more than a billion of us dead, and repeatedly predicting millions of us dying from a super-virus and ensuring Bill Gates owned the Coronavirus vaccine patent a few months **prior to** its worldwide outbreak,[458] it's now pretty obvious and certainly no accident that both the Deadly Virus King and the Deadly Vaccine King have all but made good on their bucket list promises with this "Corona" (Spanish word for "Crown") virus spreading rapidly across the globe.[459] The British Crown, Prince Philip as killer virus and Covid-19 itself are all traced back to Bill Gates funded Pirbright Institute.[460] No accident that the virus conveniently was ushered just in time for the Chinese New Year of the Rat to provide sleight-of-hand instant diversionary relief away from all the media's feeding frenzy headlines of the imploding royal family meltdown to the deadly bio-warfare disease,[461] said to have been contracted by humans from either reptillian snakes or vampire bats.[462]

Based on these facts and by both their past words and misdeeds, one can fairly surmise that both these admitted overpopulation eugenicists[463] are most likely behind this latest Crown Killer Virus. The Masonic Prince married to the Queen and bio-warmongering Billionaire Bill have us targeted in their crosshairs for elimination, both aligned with the infamous NWO Black

[455] "Billionaires," *Forbes*, March 5, 2019.

[456] Rachel O'Donoghue, "Over 30 Million will Die in 6 Months' Bill Gates Warns of Disease Pandemic," *Daily Star*, April 28, 2018.

[457] "Biological Attack on Humanity," *eyeopeningtruth.com*, January 26, 2020,.

[458] Ethan Huff, "Bill Gates Funded the Pirbright Institute, which Owns the Patent on Coronavirus," *DC Clothesline*, January 28, 2020.

[459] Helen Regan and Steve George, "China Warns Coronavirus Can Spread before Symptoms Show," *CNN*, January 27, 2020.

[460] "Coronavirus Traced to the British Crown," *americans4innovation.blogspot.com*, January 30, 2020.

[461] Shawn Paul Melville, "Bill Gates and the Coronavirus Conspiracy," *civilianintelligencenetwork.ca*, January 27, 2020.

[462] Gemma Mullin, "China Coronavirus: Fears Outbreak is Linked to Bat Soup Sold at Wuhan Market," *The Sun*, January 24, 2020.

[463] "Timeline of Depopulation Demanded by the British Rothschilds Crime Syndicate," *concisepolitics.com*, February 11, 2018.

Nobility bastion - the Club of Rome.[464] It has spearheaded the "green agenda" credo, hijacking the field of science, in recent years having turned it into nothing more or less than weaponized Orwellian junk science[465] [466]:

The common enemy of humanity is man. In searching for a new enemy to unite us, we came up with the idea that pollution, the threat of global warming, water shortages, famine and the like would fit the bill. All these dangers are caused by human intervention, and it is only through changed attitudes and behavior that they can be overcome. The real enemy then, is humanity itself.[467]

In the latest episode of the "like father, like son" "green agenda" hoax comes Prince Charles' obsession over climate change, kicking off the 2020 new year by introducing his 10-point climate plan at the global elite's annual Economic Forum soiree in Davos, Switzerland,[468] where he melodramatically declared:

Climate change the greatest threat mankind has ever faced.[469]

You mean it's not your daddy's killer virus going around causing lockdown fever? For the first time, the 2020 World Economic Forum (WEF) theme "tackled" climate change, highlighted by a photo-op when the future King met the Swedish showgirl, teenage climate change sensation herself Greta Thunberg.[470] The "green agenda" poster child is doubling down this year in her role as *Time Magazine's* "Person of the Year" and another of the elite's weaponized tools, fully exploited to promote the bogus CO2 bogie man agenda leading to carbon tax like Corona's leading to ID2020 biomed mandatory vaccination, all designed to strip away more of our disappearing individual rights – in Davos putty in the hands of the world's largest capital investment funds and the world's central banksters all in saluting attendance at this year's gala event.[471] Bad science[472] gives way to Big Business and global tyranny while control over the weather/climate and heavy metals ingested into the geoengineered lungs, brains and bloodstreams pissing on every earth inhabitant spells deadly prognosis for all of us.[473] Greta

---

[464] "The Club of Rome," *jeremiahproject.com*.

[465] Sean Martin, "Climate Change – The Real Inconvenient Truth: Scientist Claims Global Warming is Natural," *Express*, August 25, 2017.

[466] James Delingpole, "Man-Made Climate Catastrophe is a Myth, Studies Confirm," *Breitbart*, October 10, 2017.

[467] "The Green Agenda," *green-agenda.com*.

[468] Daniel Uria, "Prince Charles Introduces 10-Point Climate Plan at World economic forum," *UPI*, January 22, 2020.

[469] Tariq Tahir, "That's Rich Prince Charles Calls for Green Taxes as he Meets Greta Thunberg in Davos and Begs World Leaders to Tackle Climate Change," *The Sun*, January 22, 2020.

[470] Monica Showalter, "Swedish Child Climate Change Activist Reportedly a Tool of Al Gore-Linked Corporate Green Hucksters," *American Thinker*, August 19, 2019.

[471] F. William Engdahl, "Follow the 'Real Money' Behind the 'New Green Agenda,'" *Global Research*, January 28, 2020..

[472] Makia Freeman, "Guess How Much CO2 Humanity Contributes to Global Warming?" *thefreedomarticles.com*, October 4, 2018.

[473] Dane Wigington, "Global Weather Modification Assault Causing Climate Chaos and Environmental Catastrophe," *geoengineeringwatch.org*, March 14, 2018.

and Charles will never ever talk about the real climate-changer - the biggest elephant in the gas chamber room.

One more point on the Great Game changer, within a few weeks prior to the China coronavirus outbreak, the World Economic Forum and the Bill and Melinda Gates Foundation actually were running a simulation exercise on the same coronavirus that Bill secured the vaccine patent on a year earlier.[474] Whenever the elite decides to do another practice drill on anything, run for the hills because we now know a false flag's coming next. No doubt about it, the viral killer is here right on schedule, brought to you by our sponsors - the royals, the world's richest man and their WEF fat cats. The super-elites are not our friend.

In a related Windsor theme, if the new killer virus came to life from bat shit, the shapeshifting blood drinking Prince Charles once boasted "Transylvania is in my blood." The Prince of Cornwall is a proud direct descendant of one of the most murderous, sadistic figures in European history – Prince Vlad III, ruler of Wallachia.[475] Vlad made a practice of inviting dinner guests over, then impaling them as his prisoners-of-war and guests of honor, gleefully watching them flail about on wooden spikes to their agonizingly painful deaths in his war against Ottoman Muslims during the mid-to late 15th century. This very real historical vampire was the inspiration for Bram Stoker's Dracula character based on Vlad the Impaler's bloodthirsty lifestyle and dining practice. In his native Wallachian language, the modern connotation of Dracula means the devil and no one personifies the devil more than Vlad III. The meaning of Dracula in Vlad's day pertained to dragon, as he was born into the Order of the Dragon,[476] a secret society variation on the royal reptilian theme.

In as much as pedophiles are child-stealing energy vampires, and often literal vampires being cannibals seeking their next adrenochrome fix, it's hardly a stretch that an accused shapeshifting lizard prince from England directly related to Dracula would have as one of his closest friends, Britain's all-time most prolific predatory pedo-vampire devouring children and dead corpses alike - Sir Jimmy Savile. No wonder Charles would feel such profound affinity and identification pulsing through his bloody veins with his favorite ancestor of all-time - the bloodthirsty vampire prince, prompting England's future king to purchase not one but two 400-year old homes just to be close to his blood curdling grandpappy idol.[477] And to crown it off, in April 2017 the great-grandson 16 times removed was officially honored with the royal title of "Prince of Transylvania."

The queen relies upon a yearly government sovereign grant, for 2018-19 of £82 million (close to $100 million USD).[478] This absorbent cost of maintaining the ever-growing British royal family

---

[474] James Fetzer, "Bill Gates and World Economic Forum Ran Coronavirus Outbreak Simulation just 6 Weeks before the Real Outbreak," *jamesfetzer.org*, February 2, 2020.

[475] Marc Lallinilla, "The Real Dracula: Vlad the Impaler," *livescience.com*, September 14, 2017.

[476] Dylan Dominguez, "Dracula – Vlad the Impaler," *pcgs.com*, October 29, 2019.

[477] Camilla Tominey, "Prince of Transylvania: Charles Honoured as the Kin of Vlad the Impaler," *Express*, April 16, 2017.

[478] "Cost of UK Royals back in Spotlight after Queen's Year to Forget," *Agence France-Presse*, December 25, 2019.

has become an increasingly contentious boondoggle exploitatively fleecing overstretched UK taxpayers in footing their high-maintenance royal bill, and after their latest debacle of a year in 2019, the financial burden for their upkeep is wearing mighty thin with each unfolding scandal. With a protected pedophile for a disgraced favorite son, a grandson and wife suing British newspapers, and bitter internal disputes publicly boiling over, the gluttonous dysfunctional crime family is looking more like undeserving dead weight to overworked, stressed out Britons barely able to feed their own families. As early as nearly a decade ago during the queen's silver jubilee, the *Daily Telegraph* raised the same more salient point:

Bloated royal families are fine when you run a quarter of the world... not so good when you are in charge of a diminished, austere Britain, grappling with recession in the early 21st century.[479]

With 54 Commonwealth of Nations under Crown authority and a still bloated royal family in 2020, I'd say it's never "fine" to allow such nefarious theft, earthly rape and plunder. The argument that the Queen generates a huge surplus of tourist revenue falls flat as Buckingham Palace does not rank as Britain's top tourist attraction, that belongs to the British Museum.[480] Then when the well-known tourism agency VisitBritain was asked for details providing any impact the monarchy actually has on British tourism, it failed to give any evidence supporting the idea that the royals boost UK's tourism industry.[481] With the royals more than ever before exposed as a bad investment and unworthy high cost expenditure, add to the mix Prince Charles constantly writing letters to ministers flexing his muscle to push his own political agenda as typified by his Davos 10-point climate plan, and Harry and Meghan with last summer's *Vogue* magazine collaboration focusing on "forces for change," it's prompted a growing backlash of critics accusing the British royal family of far overstepping its boundaries. A *Sky News* interview of *Spiked Online* editor Brendan O'Neill just fired a shot across the bow:

Let's remember – we fought a civil war in this country and had a revolution in this country in the 1640s and the 1680s to get the royals out of political life and to make them this kind of decorative constitutional family... Once the Queen's reign is over, the future of the <u>Royal Family</u> will be called into question precisely because of the behaviour of people like Prince Charles and also Harry and Meghan.[482]

The recent development has royal historian Carolyn Harris pressing the alarm button, maintaining that the Meghan-Harry show spewing chaos and conflict is on the verge of inciting a larger revolt among Commonwealth nations against the royal family.[483] Both Canada and the queen have proclaimed they will not be footing the bill for the Windsor renegades' enormous

---

[479] Neil Tweedie, "Diamond Jubilee: A Stripped Down Royal Family Remodels Itself for an Age of Austerity," *The Telegraph*, June 5, 2012.

[480] "Fact Check: Do Tourists Visit Britain because of the Royal Family?" *The Conversation*, December 1, 2017..

[481] "Exclusive: No Royal Tourism Evidence Found by VisitBritain," *republic.org.uk*, May 16, 2018.

[482] Aurora Bosatti, "Prince Charles Warned 'Political Interference' to Put Future of Royal Family into Question," *Express*, January 28, 2020.

[483] Alice Scarsi, "Queen on the Brink: Royal Family Faces Commonwealth Rebellion – Meghan Markle will Spark Chaos," *Express*, February 29, 2020.

£20m security costs if they choose to live in Canada.[484] Dissension within the ranks may foment rejection of the Crown and monarchy altogether. Queen Elizabeth and Prince Charles are growing more nervous by the minute that their 1200-year reign of tax paid, freeloading gravy train ride may soon be over. God forbid they all pay their own way as it's looking like even God won't save the Queen. If anyone does, it's Lucifer his fallen angel.

Even prior to 2019's speed "bump" into royal oblivion, polls in Canada showed near 2 out of 3 citizens from that Commonwealth nation wanting out,[485] the majority wanting the monarchy to end once Elizabeth finishes her reign. As far back as 1999, Australians voted to shuck the monarchy,[486] but the then Prime Minister John Howard sabotaged the referendum.[487] Time is approaching for a new head of state in the Commonwealth nations.[488] With a whopping royal pay raise of 41% from the preceding year, Britons are growing tired of footing the bill on a bunch of royal derelicts sponging off cash-strapped taxpayers.[489] Indeed, Andrew's embarrassing criminal behavior alone is placing the royal family's future in jeopardy.[490]

Let's face it, in 2020 it's long overdue to pull the plug on the earth's most powerful and destructive feudal monarchy system that has no rhyme nor reason in this day and age to still be lording its burdensome parasitic authority, degenerate power and sinister control over its thoroughly exploited, constantly lied to subjugated subjects, especially considering the evildoing in totality that the royals have historically over so many centuries perpetrated and gotten away with. It's time to abolish this disgraceful predatory dinosaur from the Dark Ages that's been nothing short of a cancerous "killer virus" on not only the United Kingdom but Commonwealth of Nations and world at-large. It's time for the people to throw off their shackles of this archaic remnant to finally take humanity out of feudalism and slavery as an obsolete, corrosively corrupt, morally repugnant elitist institution at its Luciferian core - the Windsor clan, reputedly comprised of reptilian sodomites and baby killers disguised and propped up 24/7 as the benign do-gooders of the world when they in fact are among the prime destroyers of the world. Their dozen millennium run is finally reaching a bitter end.

---

[484] Oli Smith, "Queen Scold Harry and Meghan in Stunning Private Clash – 'Pay for Security Yourself,'" *Express*, February 29, 2020.

[485] Leslie Young, "How Canada could Break up with the Monarchy," *Global News*, June 28, 2017.

[486] Peter Harris, "Backwards Britain: Why I's Time to Abolish the Monarchy," National Interest, March 12, 2020.

[487] Jonathan Manthorpe, "Commonwealth Countries Consider Life after Queen Elizabeth," *ipolitics.ca*, April 18, 2018.

[488] Nalini Mohabir, "The Next Head of the Commonwealth must not be a Royal from Brexit Britain," *The Guardian*, February 15, 2018.

[489] Niall McCarthy, "The Royal Family is getting Increasingly Expensive for UK Taxpayers," *Forbes*, July 1, 2019.

[490] Martha Ross, "Prince Andrew's 'Toxic' Behavior Puts Family's Future into Doubt: 'Does the Monarchy have a Purpose?'" *The Mercury News*, November 22, 2019.

Chapter 2: Sir Jimmy Savile: British History's Biggest Pedophile, Sexual Blackmail Kingpin, BBC Pedo-Ringleader and the Massive Savile-BBC Cover-up

And the designated pedophilia monster of the world [conveniently for him discovered after he died] goes to… [Drumroll please] – Sir Jimmy Savile of Great Britain, the pedophilia epicenter of the earth! He epitomizes the sleazy "charismatic" psychopath who finagles his way into the innermost sanctum of the British royals and top United Kingdom politicians as not only their intimate confidante, but their longtime pimp as well. All the while, via the telly for over half a century recognized as a humanitarian fundraiser for children's charities, Sir Jimmy Savile played his dutifully deceptive public role of eccentric, clownish showman, masquerading as a saint for institutionalized, bedridden British children in order to cover up his hidden-in-plain-sight sick crimes as a twisted sexual predator from Hell, covertly getting his rocks off raping both dead corpses and thousands of the most vulnerable, defenseless kids trapped inside British group homes and hospitals with creepiest, unprecedented 24/7 access of any human alive.

A brief intro to James Wilson Vincent Savile (October 31, 1926-Ocober 29, 2011) offers some very telling clues. Savile was the youngest of seven children (with four sisters and two brothers) born on Halloween to working class Roman Catholic parents in Leeds in northern England. Fitting that he always promoted his Halloweenish, ghoulishly creepy image as the wildly unpredictable eccentric prankster-trickster while a not-so-secret lover of dead corpses, Satanist practitioner of ancient occult rituals at the same time pretending to be a devout Catholic would enter this world on Halloween, with its pagan origin the Celtic new year's eve as well as eve of the Day of the Dead and the later Catholic makeover All Saints Day.[491] His mother Agnes' birthday was the day after his on All Saints Day of the Dead.[492] The Celts believed that their favorite deity, the sun god, during the coming winter months was taken prisoner by Samhain, the Lord of the Dead and Prince of Darkness, no doubt something by misdeed that the shady, dark character Savile would secretly identify with and fashion himself after.

Though relatively little has been written about Savile's boyhood, as the seventh and final offspring born to a financially strapped, large family raised during the Great Depression era of

---

[491] "Legends and History of Halloween," *floramex.com*.

[492] Dan Davies, "The making of a Monster: Can Sordid Sexual Depravity run in a Family? In this Ground-Breaking Analysis, the Writer who has spent ten years Probing the Dark Twisted Mind of Jimmy Savile reveals the Most Deeply Disturbing Truths of all…," *Daily Mail*, July 5, 2014.

the 1930s, Savile has claimed that his arrival was unplanned and unwanted.[493] His father made meager earnings as a bookmaker clerk and insurance salesman.[494] At the age of two, it's been reported that Jimmy Savile nearly died of a life threatening illness, probably pneumonia, with the doctor fearing the worst, leaving a death certificate at his bedside.[495] But as Savile tells it, suddenly the toddler bounced back from the near dead, his sister calling it a miracle. Their mother had rushed off to pray at Leeds St. Anne's Cathedral where she found a pamphlet introducing the Scottish nun Margaret Sinclair who had died three years earlier at age 25, just over a half century prior to the pope in 1978 elevating her to Venerable status.[496] Per Savile, by the time Agnes returned home, little Jimmy had made a complete and instant recovery, attributing his mother's prayers invoking divine intervention from the Scottish factory girl nun as his lifesaver. Along with others, his testimonial was sent to Rome for review in efforts to enshrine nun Margaret Sinclair as a saint. Perhaps his love affair for would-be saint Margaret spilled over five decades later in his "love" for Margaret Thatcher. Their unholy pedophilia alliance is fully covered in this book in Chapter 4.

The Emergency Powers Act conscripted Savile as a teen during World War II to work as a Bevin Boy in the mines, but an alleged spinal back injury caused by a mine explosion apparently liberated him from the drudgery and hard labor of a coalminer.[497] He went on to try his hand as a pro athlete competing in bicycle racing and wrestling but soon gravitated to popular music and the burgeoning late 1940s dancehall scene. Jimmy Savile credits himself as the world's very first Disc Jockey in addition to pioneering the novel idea of placing dual turntables next to each other for nonstop record play, though his future employer the *BBC* had instructional documents dating back to the early 1930s, predating his self-credited "invention" long before he was even calling himself a DJ. But truth was never quite so important to Sir Jimmy as self-image enhancement and braggadocio for his grandiose self-promotion, feeding the bottomless pit of a highly-conceited ego to cover-up deep-rooted insecurity and impoverished depravation. As a brutally willful, extremely manipulative psychopath and brazen, in-your-face self-aggrandizer, the world seemed destined to revolve around him and his willfully diabolical whims and needs.

As Savile rose to fame throughout the 1960s and 1970s with such long running *BBC* standard fare as Top of the Pops making its broadcast debut on January 1, 1964 all the way to 2006 and later Jim'll Fix It from 1975 to 1994 granting children their dream requests come true, at the height of his popularity in the late 70s, the dream magician attracted 20 million viewers and

[493] Dan Davies, http://www.dailymail.co.uk/news/article-2681719/The-making-monster-Can-sordid-sexual-depravity-run-family-In-ground-breaking-analysis-writer-spent-ten-years-probing-dark-twisted-mind-Jimmy-Savile-reveals-deeply-disturbing-truths-all.html.
[494] "Sir Jimmy Savile," *The Telegraph*, October 29, 2011.
[495] "Sir Jimmy Savile," https://www.telegraph.co.uk/news/obituaries/8857428/Sir-Jimmy-Savile.html.
[496] "Sir Jimmy backs Saint Calls," *BBC*, July 11, 2003.
[497] "Sir Jimmy Savile," https://www.telegraph.co.uk/news/obituaries/8857428/Sir-Jimmy-Savile.html.

20,000 letters a week from hopeful kids across Great Britain.[498] Savile quickly became an enduring household name and TV icon in the UK for multiple generations of families. Then using his "tireless" philanthropy for various children's health causes as a deceitful cover while masquerading as the devoted Catholic saint receiving knighthoods from both the queen and the pope, in actuality all the while he was an evil imposter molesting his way to becoming Britain's most cruel, sadistic child sex maniac of all time, getting his rocks off gravely harming thousands among the most frail and defenseless population of all, the young, infirm and the dead. But he could never have done it without a supporting cast, platform and protective system. But more on that later.

Savile has been quoted casually proclaiming that women "equal brain damage."[499] The perennially unmarried misogynist and violently sexist predator took his hatred predominantly out on the fairer sex, forcing himself on his victims, constantly groping, molesting and raping females his entire adult life, mostly young girls with 82% of his victims reportedly female and 80% children.[500] But he targeted victims of all ages and genders, including boys and adult males as well. Doing Satan's work turned out to be his fulltime preoccupation while his "tireless" charity efforts took a backseat serving as his convenient part-time cover. Savile the sadistic Satanist mercilessly loved inflicting pain on less powerful individuals.

Jimmy Savile's relationship to his mother Agnes was a complicatedly twisted love-hate affair. On the one hand, he projected the image as the devoted son, loyally and faithfully living with and taking care of her at his flat in Scarborough until her death in 1972.[501] He described his mother "the Duchess" as the "only true love of his life, the only woman I ever loved," and the week he spent with her lying dead in open casket was "the best five days of my life," adding:

Once upon a time I had to share her with other people. We had marvelous times. When she was dead she was all mine, for me.[502]

As a necrophiliac, one can only imagine. For the next four decades right up to his own death in 2011, in bizarre, faithful homage, he left his mummy's bedroom unchanged, keeping all her clothes in her closet as is, other than religiously dry-cleaning them once a year.[503]

But on the other hand, in his final, never published interview just three months prior to his death, Savile revealed:

---

[498] "DJ and TV Presenter Jimmy Savile Dies, Age 84," *BBC*, October 29, 2011.
[499] Louis Theroux, "Louis Theroux: Looking back on Jimmy Savile," *BBC*, October 1, 2016..
[500] "Jimmy Savile Abuse: Number of Alleged Victims Reaches 450," *BBC*, December 12, 2012.
[501] "Savile was Devoted to his Mother the Duchess," *The Times*, October 19, 2012.
[502] Patrick Hill, "Paedophile Jimmy Savile believed his Mother 'never Trusted him' and expected he'd be Jailed," *Mirror*, February 6, 2016.
[503] Patrick Hill, https://www.mirror.co.uk/news/uk-news/paedophile-jimmy-savile-believed-mother-7277712.

My mother never got round to being proud. If anyone said, 'What is Jimmy like?' she would say, 'I don't know what he's up to, but he's up to something.' She never trusted me as she thought I was going to get nicked and end up in the pokey.[504]

"The Duchess" couldn't get behind gushing over how proud she was because her mother's intuition knew full well that Sir Jimmy was actually a total fraud and pathological criminal psychopath who deserved to be in jail. She saw past his phony saintly façade, belying his truly dark and sick nature at his core. It also bears noting that Agnes Savile raised three sons who all three became sexual predators.[505]

While Sir James Savile became the single, most prolific charity fundraiser[506] at £45million in his country's history,[507] he also degenerated into Britain's most prolific child rapist of all time.[508] By official tally of the UK's largest children's protection charity,[509] the National Society for Prevention of Cruelty to Children (NSPCC), at least 500 victims reportedly suffered at the hands of Jimmy Savile.[510] But other accounts project at least 1,000 victims sexually assaulted on *BBC* premises alone.[511] Considering these numbers include only registered abuse complaints to authorities on record, the actual total of wounded can never be precisely known but undoubtedly reaches into the thousands.

Incredibly for 60 years (1951-2011) while a volunteer porter at Leeds General Infirmary, Savile bragged about volunteering to have unconsented sex with dead corpses and how he made jewelry from glass eyes removed from their bodies.[512] We're talking one extremely demented sick fuck here. More than any other single figure in the history of humankind, Sir Jimmy's six-decade long crime spree cavalcade connects all the demonic dots like no other, from the Luciferian royals to the top government movers and shakers to the most infamous serial killers to his far-reaching *BBC* entertainment pedophile ring.

---

[504] Patrick Hill, https://www.mirror.co.uk/news/uk-news/paedophile-jimmy-savile-believed-mother-7277712.

[505] Dan Davies, http://www.dailymail.co.uk/news/article-2681719/The-making-monster-Can-sordid-sexual-depravity-run-family-In-ground-breaking-analysis-writer-spent-ten-years-probing-dark-twisted-mind-Jimmy-Savile-reveals-deeply-disturbing-truths-all.html.

[506] Anorak, "David Beckham, Jimmy Savile, Ronnie Irani, Maggie Thatcher and Jeffrey Archer: The Five Biggest Charity Boasters," *Flashback*, February 7, 2013.

[507] Paul Jeeves, "Ow's about that! Sir Jimmy Savile Raised £45m for Charity and left another £5m in his Will," *Express*, December 16, 2011.

[508] Tom Pettifor, "'He Groomed the Nation': Jimmy Savile was UK's Most Prolific Paedophile, Police Report Reveals," *Mirror*, January 11, 2013.

[509] "Exploring the Case for Mandatory Reporting: A Summary of a Roundtable Hosted by the NSPCC," *nspcc.org*, July 2014.

[510] Antonia Malloy, "Jimmy Savile Abused 'at least 500 Victims,'" *Independent*, June 2, 2014.

[511] Daniel Boffey, "Revealed: How Jimmy Savile Abused up to 1,000 Victims on BBC Premises," *The Guardian*, January 18, 2014.

[512] Chris Greenwood and Martin Robinson, "Jimmy Savile got Rape Victim, 16, Pregnant and told her to Threaten Suicide if she was Denied an Abortion," *Daily Mail*, June 26, 2014.

But on more than a half dozen occasions police actually questioned Sir Jimmy Savile as a repeated child abusing suspect but each and every time let him go. The first incident recorded by police occurred in 1955 in Manchester where Savile managed a dance hall.[513] In 1958 in his hometown of Leeds, while employed still as a nightclub manager, a police inquiry had Savile facing jail time for sexual assault charges.[514] Eight years ago according to Dennis Lemmon, a now 88-year old former Savile bodyguard and club bouncer at the time, Savile was in an especially agitated and foul mood one night before he was scheduled to appear in court the next day for "interfering with young girls."[515] But as it turned out, soon afterwards Lemmon was informed that the worried derelict had apparently bribed crooked police officers at the last minute into dropping the case. Other reports say he paid off the girls' families. Another early incident of Savile sex abuse involved an underage victim dating back to 1959 when Savile as a Luxembourg Radio DJ raped a 13-year old girl at Lime Grove Studios in London.[516]

Savile would have been 28 or 29 in 1955 with his first known criminal offense. With such a prolific, uninterrupted history of serial offending, there is near 100% certainty that the sexual predator began molesting children well before the mid-1950s. If he was performing sexual acts on corpses soon after he began working as a porter at Leeds Infirmary in 1951 at age 25, then it's almost certain he was sexually assaulting live underage kids up to a decade prior to his first known case. The bottom line, had English law enforcement done its job way back in either 1955 or 1958, over six decades ago, thousands of lives and undoubtedly dozens of suicides would have been spared the permanent scars from his sadistic marathon of abuse committed nonstop over the next half century. But illegal payoffs to corrupt police, aggressive intimidation, thuggish threats and manipulative blackmail as well as protection from elite living above the law in the corrupt British system kept the flaming maniac out of jail his entire life.

As far back as 1965 his entire hometown police force apparently was well aware of Savile's pedophilic predilections. A young constable on bicycle patrol one night spotted one of the DJ's trademark Rolls Royce parked in a secluded spot near Roundhay golf course, fairly close to Savile's penthouse in Leeds overlooking Roundhay Park.[517] The policeman observed Savile in the driver's seat sitting next to a very young girl. When the constable approached asking, "What's the matter?" Wisecracking Savile responded:

---

[513] Gordon Rayner and Stephen Swinford, "Jimmy Savile spent 'every Waking Minute' Thinking about Abusing Boys and Girls," The Telegraph, January 11, 2013..

[514] Robert Mendick, "Jimmy Savile: Police Officers Repeatedly Failed Sex Victims," *The Telegraph*, October 13, 2012.

[515] Robert Mendick, "Jimmy Savile: Police Officers Repeatedly Failed Sex Victims," *The Telegraph,* October 12, 2012.

[516] Jamie Grierson, "Atmosphere of Fear still exists at BBC, Savile Abuse Report Concludes," *The Guardian*, February 25, 2016.

[517] David Collins, "Cop who Caught Jimmy Savile with a girl was told to 'Clear off, she turns 16 at Midnight,'" *Mirror*, October 17, 2013.

I'm waiting for midnight when she turns 16.

It was 11:45PM and at first the young cop appeared bewildered until Jimmy winked at him. The policeman then turned to the girl and asked if she was alright, but she only smiled in silence. The cop realized he had just interrupted Jimmy Savile seducing an underage girl and it obviously did not set very well with the Leeds' leading pedo-kingpin who snapped back irritably:

Piss off. If you want to keep your job I suggest you get on your bike and fuck off.

When at the end of his shift, the patrolman began relaying the bizarre encounter to his sergeant, he was cut off:

Shut up, son, he's got friends in high places. If you know what's good for you, you'll leave it there.[518]

Savile was free to continue sexually assaulting children for almost the next half century.

The serial pedophile brags about his illicit exploits from cover to cover in his 184 page 1978 autobiography.[519] In one such lurid tale also in the 1960s, Savile explained he was visited by a senior female police officer in Leeds who asked him if he'd seen a young juvenile runaway, showing him her photo.[520] His answer was, "no but if I run into her, I'll keep her all night first as my reward," then be sure to turn her in the next morning. That night he did run into her at one of his dancehalls and then did exactly what he said he would do. Upon arrival at the station the next day, the policewoman wanted to book him with a sex crime but according to Savile:

The officeress was dissuaded from bringing charges against me by her colleagues for it was well known that were I to go, I would probably take half the station with me.[521]

Already in the 1960s Mr. Big Stuff knew all the crooked cops in town, and as a "local hero," was a major player in the blackmail game.

Savile's media career started at Radio Luxembourg in 1958 followed two years later at Tyne Tees Television with his *BBC* professional run commencing in late 1963. His criminal career path as a serial sexual child predator went wherever his career in public life catapulted him. Meanwhile, the more famous he became, the more brazen he acted out sexually. Throughout the late 1960s and 1970s, police probes into child sex abuse repeatedly had Savile and other

---

[518] David Collins, https://www.mirror.co.uk/news/uk-news/audio-jimmy-savile-told-police-2460910.

[519] Jimmy Savile, Love Is an Uphill Battle (London: Hodder & Stoughton, 1978)..

[520] James Moncur, "Jimmy Savile's Autobiography Shock as Pages Reveal Orgies, Naked Groupies and Furious Parents," *Daily Record*, October 4, 2012.

[521] James Moncur, https://www.dailyrecord.co.uk/news/uk-world-news/jimmy-saviles-autobiography-shock-as-pages-1359536.

BBC employees' names coming up again and again.[522] For two weeks in 1969, police interviewed dozens of *BBC* staff and musicians over complaints that on a consistent basis underage victims were routinely being sexually assaulted in dressing rooms at all the *BBC* studios. Yet no charges were ever filed against any suspects - as guilty as Savile and his pals were.

Then came the sad tragic case in 1971 of 15-year old Top of the Pops dancer Claire McAlpine, who via her diary alleged that a number of well-known public figures had taken sexual advantage of her, among them Jimmy Savile, longtime fellow *BBC* DJ Tony Blackburn, the legendary Frank Sinatra and alleged others.[523] Apparently in early 1971 no one believed Claire, and terrified that she may become pregnant, several weeks after reporting abuse falling on deaf ears, she allegedly committed suicide from a drug overdose.

Among the over dozen investigations into Savile's criminal past launched a year after his 2011 death, *BBC*'s whopping £10 million whitewash conducted by retired magistrate judge Dame Janet Smith failed to pursue Claire's accusations knowing some of her alleged perpetrators are still alive. So 60-year old former fellow dancer and friend of Claire's, Kelly Gold, claimed in 2016 she is ready to name names and work with police to bring belated justice for her fallen comrade.[524] In addition to stating that Savile had groped her as well, after their March 1971 Top of the Pops performance, Kelly Gold also maintains that a "world famous" superstar singer allegedly ended up at a hotel having sex with Claire (aforementioned Ol' Blue Eyes no doubt). To this day Kelly feels guilty because that night she lied to Claire's mother stating that Claire was staying at her place. Claire McAlpine was the first in a litany of strange and untimely deaths surrounding *BBC* employees as apparent casualties in the Savile-*BBC* pedophile scandal.

Yet more controversial fallout from this unsolved, unresolved McAlpine case was stirred over the February 2016 firing of DJ Tony Blackburn.[525] For the Janet Smith inquiry, *BBC* dug up a memo indicating Blackburn was interviewed over allegedly assaulting Claire in 1971. But Blackburn insists he is both innocent and that no one ever spoke to him about any accusations or improprieties with any underage girls. Dame Smith believed *BBC*'s contention and after 49 years on the job as a top *BBC* DJ, the *British Broadcasting Corporation* abruptly terminated Blackburn's employment.

---

[522] Robert Mendick, https://www.telegraph.co.uk/news/uknews/crime/jimmy-savile/9606494/Jimmy-Savile-police-officers-repeatedly-failed-sex-victims.html.

[523] Joseph Curtis and Josh White, "'World Famous' Singer Seduced Savile Victim, 15, at Centre of Tony Blackburn Sacking Scandal, says her Friend who Vows she'll name him," *Daily Mail*, February 28, 2016.

[524] Joseph Curtis and Josh White, http://www.dailymail.co.uk/news/article-3467609/World-famous-singer-seduced-Savile-victim-15-centre-Tony-Blackburn-sacking-scandal-says-friend-vows-ll-him.html.

[525] Joseph Curtis and Josh White, http://www.dailymail.co.uk/news/article-3467609/World-famous-singer-seduced-Savile-victim-15-centre-Tony-Blackburn-sacking-scandal-says-friend-vows-ll-him.html.

From a February 2016 *RT* article covering the *BBC* response to the Dame Smith's whitewashed report:

On Thursday afternoon, Director General of the BBC Tony Hall apologized to the survivors of abuse, saying the broadcaster had 'parted company' with DJ Tony Blackburn after his evidence given to the inquiry had been below standard,[526] [falling] short of the standards of evidence that such an inquiry demanded.[527]

The *BBC* had the audacity to think that axing one employee never arrested or charged for what he flatly denies, for allegedly lying that he never was questioned on abuse claims put forth by one underage *BBC* employee near a half century earlier should help absolve this criminal corporation from its mountains of past sins while this same underage *BBC* employee it failed to protect also accused the most prolific child abuser in Britain's history but the *BBC* elected to keep looking the other way for four straight decades has to be the height of hubris and hypocrisy.

In a newspaper interview shortly following Claire McAlpine's death, Jimmy Savile publicly denied ever seeing or knowing her.[528] Yet a photo clearly shows both Claire McAlpine and Kelly Gold with Savile and others on the March 1971 set. So when blood is on your hands for permitting thousands of the most horrific crimes imaginable against children on *BBC* premises (up to 1,000 by Sir Jimmy alone),[529] and then firing an employee apparently always in good standing for the past 49-years over possibly not being truthful (but perhaps is) about being questioned on a matter occurring 45 years earlier is then opportunely used by the *BBC* director general as evidence the company is proactively taking corrective measures to make up for all its past complicit crimes and cover-up is the most profoundly absurd line of bullshit for any sane, rational person to swallow.

With Savile signing off from Top of the Pops (TOTP) in 2006 after a 42-year *BBC* run and 35 years after Savile abused Claire McAlpine, obviously the *BBC* was still choosing to stand by its #1 pedophile. Former appeals court Judge Dame Janet Smith's February 2016 report focusing on Jimmy Savile crimes at the *BBC* proved to be a half-truth whitewash with its covert agenda to let those *BBC* senior executives guilty of horrendous crimes off the hook.

---

[526] "BBC Missed Multiple Opportunities to Stop Savile Abuse – Report," *RT*, February 25, 2016.

[527] Cole Moreton, "Top of the Pops: How BBC Show was a Breeding Ground for Sexual Abusers including Jimmy Savile," *Independent*, February 27, 2016.

[528] Paul Bracchi and Sam Greenhill, "A 15-year-old who Killed herself after leaving a Diary naming DJs as Abusers. Disturbing Questions about John Peel. So how many stars were involved?" *Daily Mail*, October 5, 2012.

[529] Daniel Boffey, "Revealed: How Jimmy Savile Abused up to 1,000 Victims on BBC Premises," *The Guardian/The Observer*, January 18, 2014.

Minimally there is more than enough evidence to prove senior *BBC* officers up and down the corporate ranks are guilty of criminal complicity, knowing rampant abuse was ongoing for years and decades but failed to act to stop it. Moreover, there is plenty of evidence that for years the *BBC* higher-ups are guilty of attempting to cover-up the scandal in order to preserve its reputation and own criminality. And thirdly, Jimmy Savile and his ragtag crew of fellow pedo-DJs and musicians weren't the only pedophiles committing sexual assault on children. Very powerful *BBC* VIPs along with MPs, PMs, high court judges, police chiefs, MI5 and MI6 heads, famous entertainers and royalty were and still are all active pedophiles participating in their still flourishing child raping network.[530] But mum's the word on all that.

Not one of these VIP scumbags have ever been arrested, prosecuted or brought to justice. With a growing number of citizens around the world very aware of this fact, it's the pink elephant in the UK's world pedo-epicenter war room that needs to be blown up with truth-bomb indictments and arrests. This is why the entire dozen after-the-fact Savile child abuse investigations are an outrageous hoax and insult put upon all good people of Britain as an over-the-top assault on their intelligence. The fact is the most vile evildoers alive are still in control, still doing the most vile evil to innocent victims. And as long as they remain in control, justice will never be served and children will never be safe. The remainder of this chapter and others to follow will clearly demonstrate the ugly truth about these pedophiles still in power still successfully evading justice.

Where it was "safe" to do so, that Dame Smith report did accurately disclose the sleazy breeding ground for sexual assault of underage girls at the TOTP studio,[531] "in the corridors, canteens, staircases and dressing rooms of every *BBC* premises."[532] Though led by prolific Savile, he was never acting alone. Rape and assault were commonly committed by many of the *BBC* performing musicians, presenters, roadies, photographers, you name it, this longtime cultural norm routinely practiced at the *BBC* studios particularly in dressing rooms allowed criminals to repeatedly get away with child sex abuse on an industrial scale. As alluded to earlier, it grew so out of hand in both 1969 and again in the early 1970s that it even drew half-assed police responses interviewing victims and perps though zero arrests or indictments were ever made. That's clearly criminal neglect and obstruction of justice by both *BBC* and the police. For over half a century, the *British Broadcasting Corporation* kept a lock on routinely ignoring victim complaints that extended to multiple intentionally failed police probes.

Then when an occasional whistleblowing celebrity happened to speak out against Savile crimes, even his shocking disclosure was routinely ignored and negatively consequenced. In the Radio 1

---

[530] Liam-Michael Roberts, "Jimmy Savile and British Establishment's Paedophile Ring," *conspiracytruths.co.uk*.
[531] Cole Moreton, https://www.independent.co.uk/news/uk/crime/top-of-the-pops-how-bbc-show-was-a-breeding-ground-for-sexual-abusers-including-jimmy-savile-a6900816.html.
[532] "Jimmy Savile Pictured on day of his last Attack," *NZ Herald/Daily Mail*, February 26, 2016.

BBC studio during a 1978 interview subsequently suppressed and never aired, John Lyden, otherwise known at the time as Johnny Rotten from the punk rock band the Sex Pistols, having heard enough substantiated rumors about Savile, called him out:

A hypocrite... into all kinds of seediness... that we're not allowed to talk about.[533]

Instead of being taken seriously to warrant investigating the derelict DJ over 40 years ago, Lyden claims *BBC* punished him for trying to honestly do the right thing:

If you said anything you'd be off playlists, but that didn't bother me as I was doing a good job of that independently. But firsthand experiences were reiterated to me by young girls who went to Top of the Pops and said he was touchy, feely, creepy, urgh... Doctor Death. I told them to report it but it would have been seen as grassing then. I knew all about it and said so and got myself banned from the BBC. Family values, eh? Turns out I was the only one who had any.[534]

Also in the late 1970s, a Stoke-Mandeville Hospital nurse also spoke up doing right by her patients suffering from spinal injuries who were being sexually attacked by longtime volunteer Savile, reporting his abuse to detective John Lindsey. But according to Lindsey, his police commander responded that there was "insufficient evidence" to proceed with a case against such a major VIP as Savile.[535] Like the *BBC*, police consistently looked the other way because they were ordered by higher-ups to give the famous pervert a free pass.

West Yorkshire Police detectives working the Ripper murder cases in the late 1970s also brought Savile in for questioning.[536] He was implicated by members of the public, his Leeds residence was in close proximity to where bodies were found with bite marks on them, thus leading to an order of Savile's teeth imprints to determine if they matched,[537] and during interviews with the prime suspect-turned-convicted serial killer Peter Sutcliffe, Savile's name and activity in proximity to murder did come up.[538]

Then many years later in 2007 Surrey police investigated Savile in response to a claim of sexual assault during the 1970s by a former resident of Duncroft Approved School for Girls. Though at least five girls had made claims that Savile abused them while attending the school under

---

[533] Linda Das, "'The BBC Blacklisted me over Savile': Sex Pistol John Lydon tells what happened when he tried to Blow the Whistle on 'Creepy' Jimmy Savile in the 70s," *Daily Mail*, May 27, 2016.

[534] Linda Das, http://www.dailymail.co.uk/femail/article-3612935/The-BBC-blacklisted-Savile-Sex-Pistol-John-Lydon-tells-happened-tried-blow-whistle-creepy-Jimmy-Savile-70s.html.

[535] Robert Mendick, https://www.telegraph.co.uk/news/uknews/crime/jimmy-savile/9606494/Jimmy-Savile-police-officers-repeatedly-failed-sex-victims.html.

[536] Anna Edwards, "Former Detective makes Shock Claims that Jimmy Savile was Quizzed over Yorkshire Ripper Murders," *Daily Mail*, November 6, 2012.

[537] Emma Reynolds and Anna Edwards, "Detectives 'had a Cast made of Savile's Teeth' to Check against Bite-Marks left on Bodies of Yorkshire Ripper Victims," *Daily Mail*, November 8, 2012.

[538] "The Trial: Week One, *execulink.com*, May 5, 1981.

government Home Office control until 1973, an eventual total of 23 Savile victims surfaced from that student body comprised of intelligent teenage girls with emotional problems claiming that Savile molested them.[539] Yet Crown Prosecution Service (CPS) insists that even with all those alleged victims, not enough evidence ever existed to charge either the perpetrator or the headmistress Margaret Jones. Jones gave the predator his own flat as the only male allowed overnights on the premises (similar to his other NHS' home away from home - Broadmoor and Stoke-Mandeville).

One of Savile's abuse victims told the press:

Jimmy treated Duncroft like a pedophile sweet shop.[540]

Yet every time police ever investigated Savile, between them and the CPS, never was there sufficient cause to indict the serial offender, which again only shows that he was repeatedly shielded in total whitewashed cover-ups his entire life.

A year after Surrey opened an investigation against Savile abuse charges that led nowhere, in 2008 Sussex Police followed suit questioning Savile over a complaint stemming from a 1970 incident, only to lead to the same abysmally poor excuse - not enough evidence. Whenever constables interviewed Savile as late as January 2009 over past abuse allegations, Savile's intimidating threats and megalomaniacal power put police on the defensive[541] with never enough evidence to dare charge him.[542] Savile called an old West Yorkshire detective buddy of his to arrange for the Surrey police to interview the 82-year old at his living quarters on the grounds of Stoke-Mandeville Hospital, a total breach of standard police protocol. Yet if he wasn't Sir Jimmy, he would've been locked away for life a half century earlier.

In the more than half dozen times that police actually did question the famous entertainer as a possible suspect, the arrogant Savile defiantly mocked his supposed interrogators, knowing full well he was above the law, protected by his loyal royal friends and prime minister allies who always had his back. Even honest cops trying to do their job to protect children were given the cold shoulder by their superiors. Just like the mafia, Savile the child procurer was "a made man" operating freely within the evil cabal system of organized crime called the British Establishment.

---

[539] Chris Greenwood and Richard Spillett, "Girls' School Head won't be Charged over Savile: Headmistress won't be Prosecuted despite Claims she turned a Blind Eye to late DJ using Establishment as a 'Paedophile Sweet Shop.'" *Daily Mail*, April 29, 2015.

[540] "Jimmy Savile treated School like 'Paedophile Sweetshop,'" *The Telegraph*, October 17, 2012.

[541] David Barrett and Robert Mendick, "Did Jimmy Savile Fix his Interrogation?" The Telegraph, January 13, 2013.

[542] "Savile Interview Part 1," *scribd.com*, January 10, 2009.

Right up to this very day, UK law enforcement is notorious for neither ever having the balls nor the will to follow through on any serious pedo-investigations of VIPs, invariably failing to find "hard" evidence to indict whenever members of the Establishment are suspects. This pervasive police pattern of indifference towards victims while demonstrating total deference towards protected powerful perps, combined with covert orders and instructions from MI5 or government heads to cease and desist from any further inquiry is the consistent historical pattern in both North America as well as Europe when the pedophilic higher-ups cherry-pick their pedo-enabling foxes to be in charge of investigations, centrally controlled in Britain by an always pedo-enabling occupant at Home Secretary office.

For over six decades this kind of criminal collusion by submissive, order-following UK law enforcement allowed the demented lunatic Savile to roam freely throughout the Isles, granted carte blanche from the National Health Service (NHS), with the sex savage completely on the loose, he was able to select virtually any criminal insane asylum, mortuary, children's hospital, children's group home or school of his choice, along with the sprawling safe haven confines of his *BBC* conglomerate. Sir Jimmy Savile uniquely possessed at his literal personal disposal an unlimited supply of readymade victims. Dead corpses, debilitated children and adults alike as well as adoring underage fans, mostly girls but boys too, both young and old, as an equal opportunity rapist, no-body was off limits to king predator Sir Jimmy. All were exploited, expendable sex objects filling his ruthless, insatiable need for cruelly satanic dominance and sadistic control, serving his necrophilia-loving, pedophilic carnal desires while fully shielded by diabolical intimate ties to queens, princes and prime ministers, all granting gatekeeper keys to Lucifer's earthly pedophilia kingdom.

Why? Because Savile supplied child victims to VIPs while working, in his own words, "deep cover" with British and foreign intelligence.[543] As demonstrated in the last chapter, Sir Jimmy was intimate with the royals.[544] The DJ opportunistically used his quirky, eccentric, philanthropic celebrity image and persona to amass immense influence and power primarily through ingratiation to royalty and prime ministers, and intimidation, threats and blackmail to everyone else that stood in his way, at will brazenly violating and raping the entire British Kingdom whose ruling masters in return guaranteed him lifetime insurance policy protection and impunity.

The next several chapters unravel the so-vile Sa-vile story in terms of its connecting implications, unmasking his ties to the larger global pedophilia network. As the pimping

---

[543] "Cover-up; CIA, Mossad, MI5, MI6; Savile and Jaconelli; Amsterdam Sex," *aangirfan.com*, November 7, 2014.
[544] Richard Kay, "How Savile Seduced the Royals: As it's Claimed he nearly became Godfather to Harry, how the Predatory DJ Wormed his way into the very Heart of Palace Life," *Daily Mail*, June 12, 2015.

procurer of child sex slaves,[545] raped and murdered by the queen and her princes,[546] prime ministers[547] and parliament members, elite media and entertainment figures, it didn't take long for the rising fame of the Top of the Pops DJ to morph into being a pivotal fixture within the ruling elite's sexual blackmail system. Not unlike the Mossad-made financier-cabalist Jeffrey Epstein, as long as Sir Jimmy continued delivering the sacrificial lambs of UK's throwaway population of institutionalized children to the earth controlling Luciferian puppet masters, they in turn would guarantee his protection for as long as he lived - to the ripe old age of just two days shy of his 85th birthday.

With Savile's super creepy close relationship to royalty specifically addressed in Chapter 1, his relations with London government VIPs, security services and taxpayer sponsored *British Broadcasting Company* as his longtime pedophile enabling employer are exposed in this chapter. But because pedophilia is the central binding nexus between the Windsor family, the 10 Downing Street-Westminster government and the *BBC* as the UK's false propaganda machine, separate chapters apart from Savile will follow to unveil the still unfolding, tip-of-the-iceberg royalty and government scandals while the crime cabal flounders desperately in vain to keep them covered-up. But as the elite's Achilles heel, fortunately enough of the ugly dark truth's already permanently out of the bag and there's no going back.

Despite the day after Savile's October 29, 2011 death when the famous "larger than life" entertainer was being widely heralded as a beloved "national treasure"[548] with sanctimonious tributes led by Prince Charles, celebrities and the media alike,[549] within months afterwards in response to a plethora of accusations emerging from his victims across the nation, multiple police investigations reactively sprang up ostensibly to look more closely into his "hidden" monstrous past. A horrified Britain was shocked to learn of Savile's countless crimes carried out at 41 National Health Service (NHS) medical institutions,[550] half at children's hospitals,[551] along with countless children's homes and schools, a highest security mental institution, even a hospice for the terminally ill[552] and in every *BBC* backstage dressing room, victimizing thousands of his defenseless prey ranging from age two to 75.[553] Again, underage girls were his preference with 80% of his victims children and 82% female. In 1976 nearing the height of his fame, with

[545] "Paedophile Pimp for the Royals," *helpfreetheearth.com*, October 31, 2012..

[546] "The Royals, Pedophilia & Murder," SGT Report interview of Jay Myers, YouTube video, posted on July 5, 2017..

[547] David Icke, "The British Establishment… Pedophiles Everywhere," *bibliotacapleyades.net*, January 18, 2013.

[548] David Marsh, "How to Become a National Treasure," *The Guardian*, July 26, 2013.

[549] "Jimmy Savile Dead: Prince Charles leads Tributes to TV Legend," *Mirror*, October 30, 2011.

[550] Tom McTague and Martin Robinson, "Why did NHS stay Silent on Savile? 177 Victims aged from five to 75 at 41 Hospitals after Bosses Missed TEN Chances to Stop Predatory Paedophile… and NO ONE will be held Responsible," *Daily Mail*, February 26, 2015.

[551] Josh Halliday, "Jimmy Savile: Timeline of his Sexual Abuse and its Uncovering, *The Guardian*, June 26, 2014.

[552] Martin Evans, "Jimmy Savile: Abuse extended to Hospice for the Terminally Ill," *The Telegraph*, January 6, 2013.

[553] Sarah Knapton, "Jimmy Savile's Youngest Victim was aged two," *The Telegraph*, June 2, 2014.

television cameras rolling before a national audience into the millions, Jimmy Savile was allowed to brazenly molest a teenager on-the-air, flagrantly violating the law without drawing any notice or criticism whatsoever, other than the poor victim's shocked, flailing on-camera reaction.[554] What does that tell you?

At the 1973 Top of the Pops pre-Christmas show, within minutes after walking off stage, still dressed in his Womble costume, back in the dressing room Savile's entourage had just dropped off two of his latest victims excitedly waiting to meet the star. With a sentinel guarding his dressing room door, the pedophile Womble proceeded to savagely rape a 10-year old boy while making a stunned 12-year old girl watch, then the petrified, frozen-in-trauma sodomized boy was forced to witness the girl's turn being sexually assaulted, at the end Uncle Jimmy turned to his prey to say it's "our little secret."[555] After countless episodes like this at *BBC* studios and confirmed evidence of having sex with corpses or infirmed hospital patients of all ages, it's also been revealed that Savile was very likely a not-so-closeted Satanist,[556] engaging in satanic murder rituals as an accomplice or co-participant, if not on his own, befriending the most notorious, coldblooded serial killers in British history.

Beyond the 1980s and long past Jimmy Savile's prime as a regular weekly *BBC* entertainer, his numerous homes across the British Isles and three or four Rolls Royces and all his accoutrements of wealth supporting his lavishly opulent lifestyle always remained ostentatiously evident throughout Sir Jimmy's life. As a pimp to royalty, prime ministers, MPs and rock stars, and a centrally embedded figure in Britain's sexual blackmail scheme, his lavish lifestyle right up to his end can best be explained by his sordid, highly lucrative criminal enterprise inside the thriving global pedophilia network. Otherwise, whatever legit income he may have still had as a senior citizen during the final two decades of his sicko life could never have afforded living so high-off-the-hog as he'd long been accustomed for six decades. In short, pedophilia was good to Sir Jimmy, "good while it lasted" as his now removed epitaph once briefly displayed on his desecrated gravesite. Despite some members of his family wanting his body exhumed from his huge triple plot overlooking the sea to be reburied in an unmarked pauper's grave, the £20,000 cost and his estate funds tied up in litigation settlements has kept his body in his original burial place though in an unmarked grave at a Scarborough cemetery.[557]

---

[554] Tom Evans, "Horrific Footage of Jimmy Savile Molesting a Woman Live on TOTP," Daily Record, January 22, 2016.

[555] Amanda Williams and Sam Tonkin, "Revealed: Jimmy Savile Dressed as a Womble to Rape a 10-year-old Boy and Sexually Assault Girl, 12, in his Dressing Room after Filming 1973 Top of the Pops Christmas Special, *Daily Mail*, February 26, 2016.

[556] James Fielding, "Jimmy Savile was part of Satanic Ring," *Express*, January 13, 2013.

[557] Chris Greenwood, "Fight to move Jimmy Savile's Grave to Cemetery is Sunk by £20,000 Cost: Paedophile's Body will Remain in his Huge Triple Plot Overlooking the Sea – and two local Schools," *Daily Mail*, October 29, 2016.

In the end Savile still possessed his prized £160,000 Rolls Royce that he called "the Beast" where he defiled many young girls, plus five other luxury cars including a Bentley Turbo and Mercedes 500 SL along with his reported eight homes[558] and a will leaving £5 million in two charitable trusts.[559] His estate at the time of his death was worth £4m but £2.5m of it went to both his and his plaintiffs' lawyers, leaving only about £1m to be divvied up amongst 78 victims seeking damages exclusively from the Savile estate.[560]

The raw, naked, despicable reality that a UK "national treasure" has turned out to be both a satanic murdering corpse fucker and biggest child rapist of all-time in Great Britain's long "glorious" history[561] speaks volumes in revealing the true nature of this world as it actually is, in contrast to the totally deceitful brainwashing bullshit we've all been led, taught and subjected to. The Jimmy Savile lesson runs deep to the very core of what's gone most wrong on this planet, teaching us that absolutely nothing in this world is as it seems, that the complete betrayal of truth and morality is more than evident everywhere we look, be it by outward appearance, accepted conventional wisdom, so called good deeds, or so called science, religion or revisionist human history, it's all one humongous pack of sinister lies carefully designed and packaged to effectively dupe and control the increasingly dumbed down masses.[562]

Over the millenniums the same bloodline planetary controllers have maintained humanity's truth-suppressing juggernaut by cunning deception, willful manipulation and calculated malevolence.[563] But through the Jimmy Savile saga, the emperor without his clothes can be fully unveiled, exposing the grotesquely vile, pedophilic evil of this still played out cautionary tale turned urgent wakeup call nightmare for the ages.

Just like every other pedophilia scandal covered in this 5-book series, virtually all the media, government and police inquiries conclude that one deranged beast, in this case Jimmy Savile, acted alone in "grooming the nation" as Metropolitan Police lead investigator Peter Spindler claimed.[564] On January 11, 2013, among the largest ever investigations conducted by the Metro Police in conjunction with UK's National Police Chief's Council (NPCC), based on their Operation Yewtree findings released a joint report entitled "Giving Victims a Voice."[565] But only voices of

[558] David Icke, "Pedophile and Child Killing," *bibliotecapleyades.org,* January 17, 2013.

[559] Paul Byrne, "Sir Jimmy Savile Leaves £5m to Charity in his Will," *Mirror*, December 16, 2011.

[560] Ekin Karasin, "Lawyers get £2.5million of Jimmy Savile's Estate leaving just £1million for the Paedophile DJ's Victims," *Daily Mail*, July 24, 2016.

[561] Paul Peachey, "Savile used Celebrity Status to become Britain's most Prolific Sexual Predator, Report says," *Independent*, January 12, 2013.

[562] Joachim Hagopian, "The Dumbing down of America – by Design," *Global Research*, August 18, 2014.

[563] Rishabh Banerje, "These are the 13 Families in the World that apparently Control Everything - From Politics to Terrorism," *India Times*, March 9, 2018.

[564] Martin Robinson, "Jimmy Savile Scandal: Report Reveals he Raped 34 Women and Girls and Sexually Assaulted up to 450," *Daily Mail*, January 11, 2013.

[565] Peter Walker, "Jimmy Savile Report: Key Findings," The Guardian, January 11, 2013.

carefully selected victims got heard, generally revealing only tip of the iceberg, lower levels of abuse. This calculated strategy was geared to protect the self-serving interest of the larger pedophilia cabal that Savile freely operated within, comprised of royalty, the national government, the security apparatus and the MSM *BBC* giant that carefully, collectively shielded him from having to answer for his mountain of heinous crimes while still alive.

As in all pedophilia scandals, by methodically disclosing an incomplete whitewash of half-truths, the elite's pedo-network always remains intact and well-preserved while temporarily appeasing the public's outrage and so called "right to know." This same overly contrived, overused damage control tactic is consistently deployed by the Luciferian planetary controllers who ritualistically torture, sodomize, butcher, drain and drink adrenochrome-filled blood,[566] and eat cut-out hearts of their sacrificial child lamb prey. By satanic design, these pedo-cabal victims never had a chance to either live or have a voice. They were surgically removed from Operation Yewtree-NSPCC's sanitized, incomplete, grossly distorted version of what actually transpired.

As an illustration of Sir Jimmy's power and fame to suppress his ugly sins, in 1994 the editor of the *Sunday Mirror*, Paul Connew, had two Savile abuse survivors in their mid-30s who were former residents victimized at Duncroft Approved School for girls in the 1970s, ready and willing to go public with their accusations.[567] Knowing firsthand what a monster Savile was, they were both tired and appalled seeing their abuser receiving such praise and honors from the likes of Margaret Thatcher, the queen and pope, each taking turns bestowing knighthood on their serial rapist. The former editor was certain they were not motivated to seek money as the pair just wanted to set the record straight and see if some semblance of justice could be achieved.

But Paul Connew felt compelled to compassionately warn the two women what they would be up against should their story be published - the ensuing, most certain, highly publicized scandal would result in a contentious libel lawsuit against them, and both a likely non-response from the police as well as a star-struck jury that tends to avoid conviction of enamored celebrities. The husband of one of the accusers convinced his wife to not pursue such public exposure, both to protect her and their children. And with that development, not wanting to move forward alone, for very good reason the other survivor lamented this incisively accurate scenario:

---

[566] Adrenochrome – Why Child Ritual Sacrifice is Used by Hollywood, Politicians and the Elite," Jay Myers documentary, 2018, YouTube video, 10:55, posted August 31, 2018.
[567] Paul Connew, "What Prevented me Exposing Jimmy Savile's Crimes to the World - former Sunday Mirror Editor Paul Connew," *The Drum*, February 27, 2015.

Who will believe me against Jimmy Savile with all his connections to Charles and Diana and Mrs. Thatcher and the Pope? They'll destroy me, even though I'd be telling the truth.[568]

So way back in 1994, a full decade and a half prior to Savile's final known sexual assault, unfortunately the story of his pedophilic abuse never went forward in the press when it came ever so close.

When it was all said and done after six decades of uninterrupted predation against thousands of victims, the detective superintendent from Metropolitan Police's pedophile unit - David Gray, emphasized how Savile must have been mentally preoccupied and obsessed with plotting his next sex offense "every minute of every waking day."[569] But Savile was never operating alone because every 3 minutes of every single day another British child goes missing, totaling 140,000 each year,[570] many of whom wind up in the global pedo-pipeline of enslaved, abused and ritualistically murdered children. And all that cannot be a one-man operation.

Yet David Gray went on to bogusly claim that no evidence exists suggesting that the "lone wolf" was ever part of a larger pedophile sex ring,[571] making it out like Savile the pedovore was some anomalous freak show oddity operating 24/7 365 days a year for well over a half century, completely within his own neatly spun cocoon-like vacuum. Nothing could be further from the truth! This willfully deceitful statement again promotes the constant false narrative of the "lone gunman" syndrome as the standard prototypical cover-up feature, present in every single pedophilia scandal as well as virtually every major assassination and false flag "terrorism" event,[572] a favorite tool used in all state-sponsored false flags.

Among the pedophilia scandals, think Lawrence E. King, Jeffrey Epstein, Coach Jerry Sandusky, Dr. Larry Nassar and Coach Barry Bennell (all expounded on in Book 4 chapters), or Lee Harvey Oswald, Sirhan Sirhan and James Earl Ray, all portrayed as the "lone gunman" by the mainstream media. In every single case, the press dutifully reports all these high profiled, most prolific pedophiles and assassins as always acting alone in order to sweep under the rug the far bigger reality of a massively globalized, interlocking pedophilia crime cabal network. Without exception, every one of their false narratives calls for reading off the same MSM Mockingbird script, just to keep you, me and John Q Public in the dark from ever knowing the far more disturbing, sinister truth.

---

[568] Paul Connew, https://www.thedrum.com/opinion/2015/02/27/what-prevented-me-exposing-jimmy-saviles-crimes-world-former-sunday-mirror-editor.

[569] Alexandra Topping, "Jimmy Savile Reports Published," *The Guardian*, January 11, 2013.

[570] Abi Wilkinson, "A Child is Reported Missing in UK every 3 Minutes," *Mirror*, September 24, 2014.

[571] Gordon Rayner and Stephen Swinford, https://www.telegraph.co.uk/news/uknews/crime/jimmy-savile/9795252/Jimmy-Savile-spent-every-waking-minute-thinking-about-abusing-boys-and-girls.html.

[572] Gary G. Kohls, "The Assassination of JFK, the 'Lone Gunman' Mythology and the CIA's Weaponizing of 'Conspiracy Theories,'" *Global Research*, November 4, 2017.

From the no-brainer file comes the *BBC* launched £10 million "self-investigation" boondoggle into the Savile debauchery, with a specific focus of determining if any *BBC* culpability accompanied Savile's crime spree. Led by "respected" former magistrate judge Dame Janet Smith, her inquiry insists that beyond widespread rumor and gossip, no one at *BBC* definitely knew Savile was committing sex crimes,[573] in one fell swoop clearing both all corporate executives and all company personnel that participated in the *BBC* pedophile sex ring as well as the *BBC* criminal cover-up, adding salt to the re-traumatized wounds suffered by thousands of Savile, *BBC* and cabal victims.[574]

Over a dozen major Savile investigations from the Metro-Scotland Yard police to the *BBC*[575] to the NHS,[576] Stoke-Mandeville,[577] Leeds General Infirmary,[578] to Crown Prosecution Service (CPS),[579] Department of Education, House of Commons, a so called national Independent Inquiry into Child Sexual Abuse[580] and on and on they go,[581] all designed to place zero blame, zero responsibility, zero complicity and zero criminal cover-up on the real pedo-network kingpins. By falsely depicting a virtual one-man operation, the most powerful pedovores systemically supporting and shielding Jimmy Savile, are allowed to get away with their ongoing brutal crimes. The elephant in all their rooms is the global pedophilia cabal. None will dare speak of this truth. But then what else is new? That's simply the way this Luciferian system works. But a considerable body of largely overlooked facts totally refuting their feeble claims and bogus conclusions about Savile's reign of terror is presented here in Book 2.

We'll start with the serial predator's own nephew, Guy Marsden, who supplies irrefutable firsthand evidence that from relatively early on in Savile's career, he was operating within a larger pedophile ring:

[573] Martin Robinson, Emma Glanfield, Katherine Rushton, Claire Elliott and Tom Kelly, "BBC's £10m Whitewash of Savile Scandal: Report 'Clears' TV Chiefs who were Warned about Years of Sick Abuse," *Daily Mail*, January 20, 2016.

[574] Dame Janet Smith, "An Independent Review into the BBC's Culture and Practices during the Jimmy Savile and Stuart Hall Years," *The Dame Janet Smith Review*, February 25, 2016, THE DAME JANET SMITH REVIEW REPORT

[575] Roy Greenslade, "National Press Rounds on the BBC, calling Savile Report a Whitewash," *The Guardian*, February 26, 2016.

[576] Martin Evans, "Jimmy Savile Scandal: Anger as no one is Blamed for allowing Abuse in Hospitals," *The Telegraph*, February 26, 2015.

[577] Josh Halliday and Sandra Laville, "Jimmy Savile Abused 60 People at Stoke Mandeville Hospital, Inquiry finds," *The Guardian*, February 26, 2015.

[578] Caroline Davies, "Jimmy Savile's Victims were Aged Five to 75 at Leeds hospital, Inquiry finds, *The Guardian*, June 26, 2014.

[579] Alexandra Topping, "Jimmy Savile Reports Published," *The Guardian*, January 11, 2013.

[580] Lizzie Dearden, "British Institutions 'Prioritise Reputation of Political Leaders over Children', Warns Child Sex Abuse Inquiry, Independent, April 25, 2018.

[581] Corinne Purtill, "The Child Sex Abuse Scandals Engulfing Britain," *PRI/Global Post*, August 4, 2015..

Uncle Jimmy took me to his sick parties, (Marsden specifically calling them) *paedophile parties*.[582]

After running away with three friends from their family homes in Leeds when Guy was just 13, Jimmy Savile walked in on a London dive where the runaways were staying. Initially Guy figured his parents put his uncle up to busting him in order to send the local boys straight back home. But much to Guy's surprise, in 1967 Uncle Jimmy began taking his nephew and buddies to wealthy celebrity mansions where Guy believes that men attending the parties were sexually abusing boys and girls as young as 10. For the next year and a half Marsden witnessed his uncle regularly showing up at these depraved soirees in fancy settings, often accompanied by a priest and children from nearby orphanages and group homes.

Eight years ago the now 66-year old Guy Marsden explicitly described how back in the 60s, Savile the pimp was already operating within an extensive elitist pedophile network amongst members of London's high society from the British entertainment industry:

The group of runaways ended up in a fabulous house - believed to belong to a famous pop impresario - with a big indoor swimming pool. The celebrity home was one of the party venues. At night you would get about 15 or 20 people turning up. There would be music and tables full of food, we couldn't believe it. There was everything we needed and we just hung around. At first we automatically assumed the children lived there, but we soon realized they didn't. They would be brought there, sometimes by Uncle Jimmy, and would stay for six or seven hours until 3 or 4AM. They were just little kids, boys and girls.[583]

With Savile the procurer working behind the scenes as well as openly with church clergy, funneling child victims from care homes into the pedo-elite way back in the swinging sixties while the DJ's influence and power were still on the rise, soon enough the big TV star was pimping kids off to the royal family, UK prime ministers and their Westminster minions, working undercover with British intelligence agencies. On behalf of the Luciferian worshipping pedophile cult consisting of English royalty, top politicians and entertainers, assisted by the British MI5 and MI6 security services, (just like their US and Israeli counterparts), all have long been steeped in the business of sexual blackmail operations and pedo-pipeline procurement, using the most vulnerable population of expendable, throwaway orphan children from group home charities, misused as sacrificial bait and prey consumed by the pedophilic elite.[584]

Sir Jimmy once told *Esquire*:

---

[582] Chris Brooke, "Uncle Jimmy took me to his Sick Parties: Nephew tells how his Childhood was Stolen at 13," *Daily Mail*, October 5, 2012.

[583] Chris Brooke, http://www.dailymail.co.uk/news/article-2213636/Uncle-Jimmy-took-sick-parties-Nephew-tells-childhood-stolen-13.html.

[584] "The Children's Homes Organized Pedophile Rings," *The UK and Ireland Database*.

The thing about me is I get things done and I work deep cover. I've known the Royal Family for a million years.[585]

That about says it all. Working "deep cover" with the royals and MI5, he pimped British kids to UK's VIPs - royalty, politicians and entertainers.[586] It's been reported as early as the late 1950s at the height of the Cold War, Jimmy Savile visited Moscow.[587] So did Lee Harvey Oswald in 1959 as uncovered evidence links the JFK assassin patsy as an employ of the CIA,[588] not unlike Sir Jimmy the MI5 stooge, but instead of deployment as a false flag spook, Savile's mission was expanding UK pedo-operations. Savile's name has come up in virtually every British care home scandal where pedophile MPs have regularly committed sex abuse on predominantly underage boys across the nation. A list of some of these scandals further fleshed out in later chapters are the Elm Guest Home (Chapter 7), Jersey's Haut de la Garenne covered in this chapter, Northern Ireland's Kincora boys home (Book 3's Chapter 3), and North Wales' Bryn Estyn care home (Book 3's Chapter 4) where Sir Jimmy would show up in his chauffeured limousine with his older brother.[589] MI5 has long been linked to running honey trap boy brothel blackmail operations out of the Kincora home in East Belfast, Northern Ireland, often escorted to parties at nearby mansions to be abused by politicos on both sides of the IRA conflict.[590] Jimmy Savile as much as admitted working as an undercover agent for the security services linked to Kincora as well.[591] So have his fellow pedo-buddies Prime Minister Ted Heath and per last chapter, the royal Lord Mountbatten, credited with introducing Savile to the Windsor family in 1966.

Typically, the global intelligence community acts as fellow handlers along with the Vatican, its secret societies like the Jesuits and Malta Knights, along with the Freemasons, Illuminati, and "deep cover" Satanists like Savile (covered in next chapter). A North Wales abuse survivor, now a barrister, has claimed that many of his perpetrators are Freemasons.[592] Infiltrating secret society members among top tier government (from national to local), law enforcement, the courts, big business, medicine, academia and entertainment media typically comprise the VIP pedophile network. The global intelligence community of course also functions as the ruling elite's private army of international mercenary assassins and bully boys to protect and serve cabal interests as well as coordinate the global child sex trafficking network.[593]

---

[585] Simon Edge, "How Jim really did Fix it," *Express*, May 8, 2008.
[586] "Paedophile Pimp for the Royals," *helpfreetheearth.com*, October 31, 2012..
[587] "The CIA Runs the Paedophile Rings," *aangirfan.blogspot.com*, November 17, 2014.
[588] "Top Secret Papers Reveal Oswald Was CIA Agent," *jfk.hood.edu*, July 5, 1976, .
[589] "Jimmy Savile Linked to North Wales Child Abuse Scandal," *The Telegraph*, November 7, 2012.
[590] Leslie-Ann McKeown, MI5 'used Sexual Abuse of Children at Kincora to Blackmail the Politician Paedophiles," *Independent*, May 31, 2016..
[591] CIA, Mossad, MI5 and Kincora Boys Home," *aangirfan.blogspot.com*, July 8, 2014.
[592] Jerry Lawton, "'Care Home Paedophiles were Masons," *Daily Star*, November 2, 2012.
[593] "The CIA Runs the Paedophile Rings," http://aanirfan.blogspot.com/2014/11/the-cia-runs-pedophile-rings.html.

Still another scandal reputed to have connections to procuring pedophile Savile involve group home kids from Islington transported to parties where VIPs abused them.[594] In the 1990s in an effort to cover-up the pervasive abuse, the head of the Islington Council - Lady Margaret Hodge (nee Oppenheimer[595]) tried to silence an outspoken victim-survivor turned attorney Demetrius Panton, calling him "extremely disturbed" in a *BBC* interview. Panton later forced her in a high court to apologize for her slanderous lie. In 1992 when the *Evening Standard* broke the story behind a hard-hitting series, exposing evidence of extensive pedophilia in a number of Islington children's homes, Hodge went on the offensive once again calling the article "a sensationalist piece of gutter journalism," for which she again later had to issue an apology. But evil deeds don't go unrewarded by fellow evildoers in power, so in 2003 Margaret Hodge was appointed henhouse guard as minister over all UK children by yet another pedo-enabling, war criminal prime minister Tony Blair,[596] whose government was also heavily infiltrated by pedophiles. And of course Blair was also a friend of both Sir Savile as well as British singing sensation Sir Cliff Richard, and using his convenient D-notices, he protected all his pedophile buddies.[597] But I'm getting ahead of myself as all this is taken up in future chapters of this book. But most importantly, as both British history's worst perpetrator and VIP child procurer, Savile's tied to all major pedo-scandals in the United Kingdom.

Incredibly for six long decades, Jimmy Savile's direct linkage, unlawfully procuring victims from group homes for British Establishment VIPs, made him privy to the elite's deplorable inside crimes, thus automatically guaranteeing his lifelong protection and impunity to recklessly and arrogantly live above the law, often right out in the open, constantly boasting about his powerful protectors.

Savile's explanation on how he was able to acquire documentarian Louis Theroux's home address speaks to his cocksure infallibility:

I can get anything. There's nothing I can't get, and there's nothing I can't do.[598]

After spending the last two weeks with Sir Jimmy filming his documentary in 2000, when Theroux finally led up to pressing him for an answer over the decades of pedophile rumors that had followed him, Theroux began with:

So why do you say in interviews that you hate children when, I've seen you with kids, and you clearly enjoy their company and you have a good rapport with them?[599]

---

[594] Eileen Fairweather, "Jimmy Savile Sex Abuse: 'Islington is still Covering up,'" *The Telegraph*, April 6, 2014.

[595] Kufara Gwenzi, "The Oppenheimer Dynasty,"*kufaragwenzi.blogspot.com*, March 21, 2008.

[596] Eileen Fairweather, https://www.telegraph.co.uk/news/uknews/crime/jimmy-savile/10746412/Jimmy-Savile-sex-abuse-Islington-is-still-covering-up.html.

[597] "Blair Protected Savile," *tapnewswire.com*, October 24, 2012.

[598] "Quotes" from "When Louis Met... Jimmy," 2000 TV Special documentary, *IMDb*..

After denying he hates them, Savile remarked:

We live in a very funny world. And it's easier for me, as a single man, to say 'I don't like children,' because that puts a lot of salacious tabloid people off the hunt.

With the door open, Theroux then asked:

Is that basically so the tabloids don't pursue this whole 'is he or isn't he a paedophile' line?

Saville's response:

Oh, aye, how do they know whether I am not? How does anybody know whether I am? Nobody knows whether I am or not. I know I'm not.

Savile's thousands of victims sure know, so does the *BBC* and a number of police departments, not to mention his customers in government and royalty. But a more tactful Theroux countered with:

To me that sounds more, sort of suspicious in a way.

A defensive, irritated yet still cocksure of himself Savile retorts:

Alright look, that's my policy, that's the way it goes and it's worked a dream. Ho, ho, ho.

In plain sight the infamous predator defied his victims, fans, law enforcement and entire nation, devilishly outfoxing his detractors with his brash, thinly-veiled word games of denial and mockery.

But as the crime cabal's go-to pedo-blackmail specialist, like his American counterpart Jeffrey Epstein, Jimmy Savile always remained confident knowing he was able to live above the law as an untouchable, fully protected by royalty, governments, courts, security apparatus (both law enforcement and MI5/6/CIA/Mossad) and the MSM propaganda machine, insulated and immune to any and all allegations from abuse victims, whistleblowers and muckraking journalists. After all, his litigious aggression, intimidating threats and thuggish brutishness had his victims rendered invisible, never really believed nor heard. Would-be truth-tellers are typically smeared, vilified, ridiculed, harassed, or otherwise silenced, even neutralized by either overt or covert assassination. Then there's the ultra-popular method of "being suicided." That part of the Savile saga is explored in detail in the next chapter.

So there exists bountiful proof that as far back as the sixties, Savile was a card-carrying member of a vast pedophilia network preying on underage girls and boys. Aside from the group home-

---

599 Louis Theroux, https://www.bbc.com/news/magazine-37517619.

orphanage pipeline, well-known disc jockeys of the day enjoyed free and easy access to legions of British minors, both male and female, willing to innocently and not so innocently, place themselves and their nubile young bodies in harm's way. Diehard fans, groupies or fledgling band members in the 60s and 70s would literally fall into the laps of sexual degenerates working in the music, radio and television industry, willing to do anything for an autograph, hug, positive attention or coveted airplay time to seek fame or simply "rub shoulders" with the rich and famous. The rock & roll age spawned generations of enamored lost souls, blindly engaging in idolatry worship of creepy celebrities like Sir Jimmy, his fellow *BBC* and rock star friends all eagerly frothing at the mouth to take full advantage. Apologists for child sexual abuse then chalk it up to the times, an era of sexual liberation on all fronts, the promiscuous, hedonistic "swinging 60s and 70s." Though some teenagers may have been willing, nonetheless they were still kids sexually mauled by a prolific procurer and voracious consumer, forcibly devouring children of every size, gender and age without consent, with a honing preference for the most vulnerable females between 13 and 15.

A man who was once an 11-year old victim of brutal rape perpetrated by Savile and his fellow *BBC* DJ colleague Alan Freeman in 1964, explained to Scotland Yard a year after Savile died during the 2012 Operation Yewtree probe, how German actor Victor Beaumont had lured the boy to the celebrity's ritzy Northwest London home.[600] Once locked in the bedroom, Beaumont called the two *BBC* tunesmen and the three sodomizing savages in a gangbang pounced on their defenseless trapped prey. Beaumont died 13 years later at age 64 while Australian born Al "Fuzzy" Freeman kicked the bucket in 2006 at age 79. After years of therapy, the traumatized victim-turned-survivor eventually married, emerging from his boyhood trauma to become a successful businessman, garnering the strength to speak out publicly and anonymously for the first time to protect his family as well as other potential victims in September 2013:

[Beaumont, Savile and Freeman] *showed me no pity and arrogantly thought they could get away with anything...* [Because they could and did].[601]

The Metro Police's half-assed cover-up-their-ass attempt called Operation Yewtree was ostensibly set up to investigate Savile's six-decade reign of terror, searching out other pedophiles in the Savile *BBC* network of horrors. Yet it has offered up only a handful of relatively low level, mostly low life pedophiles for the sole purpose of placating national public outrage, than actually busting wide open the elite's globalized network that Savile belonged to as any real effort to actually bring down the pedophile planetary controllers. The idea is to put

---

[600] Matthew Drake, "Man tells of Agony at the Hands of BBC Paedo Ring involving DJ Alan Freeman and Evil Pal Jimmy Savile," *Mirror*, September 22, 2013.
[601] Matthew Drake, https://www.mirror.co.uk/news/uk-news/man-tells-agony-hands-bbc-2292125.

behind bars a minimal few, semi-notable, rotten fruit hanging lowest on the pedo-vine food chain in order to save and protect the child raping elite atop this demonic child killing cabal.

That Savile was so well-connected, in his words, working "deep cover" as an operative with international intelligence agencies, high level politicians and royalty, supplying the most vulnerable group home children for the sickest members of the elite in a major blackmail operation that was global is never mentioned by mainstream media. But it's the elephant in the room that every inquiry purposely omits.

Canadian intelligence insider Roderick Russell, analyzing Savile's relationship with British security services, draws this conclusion in the *Daily Kos*:

With these cozy friendships with top politicians and royalty, no wonder Sir Jimmy Savile felt himself to be above the law in England - and the truth is that he was above the law.... Increasingly it seems that Savile was a protected man. One senses that the real question should be the role of the Intelligence/ Security services [MI5/MI6 in the UK] *and establishment elites in the cover-up.*[602]

A commenter on *aagirfan.com* wrote in to recount his experience as a 12-year old schoolboy when Jimmy Savile came to talk about himself and his charity work, but extemporaneously veered off topic to mention his other line of work:

He [Savile] *said it was great cover for his real work as a spy. He said spies have to have deep cover and England would be part of a grand plan and it was so exciting to be part of this and all of us children must help to bring England and Israel closer together.*[603]

Hence Savile's many trips to Israel as a security advisor working closely with Mossad-CIA chum Uri Geller.[604] Describing himself, Jimmy Savile once claimed to be:

… The most Jewish Catholic you will ever meet.[605]

His most publicized visit to the Jewish State was in 1975 when the Jim'll Fix It star brought along his television crew and an English boy wanting to see the land where Jesus was born.[606] But that was just a cover as Savile was steeped in British and Israeli intelligence. The 10-day trip was organized by Lord John Levy, director of the Friends of Israel Educational Trust. Levy is close

---

[602] Roderick Russell, "Jimmy Savile – Pedophile, Friend of Royalty – and the Cover-up to Pervert Justice," *Daily Kos*, October 18, 2012,.
[603] "Savile the Spy," *aangirfan.com*, October 18, 2012.
[604] "Yuri Geller and Mossad-CIA Mind Control, Obama, Michael Jackson, Savile, Elvis," *aangirfan.com*, June 14, 2013.
[605] Gordon Rayner, "Jimmy Savile Confessed to Reporter that he would be seen as 'Crooked' after his Death," *The Telegraph*, October 18, 2012.
[606] Jessica Elgot, "Jimmy Savile came to my Batmitzvah," The Jewish Chronicle, November 3, 2011.

friends with former Israeli Prime Minister Ehud Barak, who is a known houseguest[607] and Lolita Express flyer,[608] compliments of Israeli intelligence sexual blackmailer-pedo Jeffrey Epstein as well as a listee in his infamous little black book.[609]

Sir Jimmy would later boast how he came to be an Israeli security advisor to the then President Ephraim Katzir (from 1973 to 1978):

I arrived at this reception. The president came to me and asked how I was enjoying my visit. I said I was very disappointed: the Israelis had won the Six Day War but they had given back all the land, including the only oil well in the region, and were now paying the Egyptians more for oil than if they had bought it from Saudi Arabia. I said: 'You have forgotten to be Jewish.' He said: 'Would you like to tell my cabinet that?' Next morning, I went to the Knesset; they interrupted a cabinet meeting and I told them the same as I had told him.[610]

As expounded on in the next chapter, an intelligence insider commented how after Savile's death, the police in Leeds confiscated massive amounts of paperwork from his home and burned it, reportedly because much of it was correspondence from the twice elected former Israeli Prime Minister during the early 1980s Menachem Begin, rumored to be his main protector.[611]

As an undercover agent with ties to royalty and government, it's easy to understand why Savile's brutal 60-year crime spree was so thoroughly protected by the British Establishment and international crime cabal. And only after a year had elapsed since he quietly passed away in his sleep, was it finally deemed permissible to begin making public his "open secret" career as a vicious serial sexual predator. Ever since October 2012, when Savile's posthumously unraveled darker life as an evildoer-on-steroids, created such national shockwaves and public uproar, decent people from the United Kingdom began demanding justice for his countless victims as well as the countless other unpunished pedophiles from *BBC* entertainment and the British Establishment. And as a result of Operation Yewtree's investigation of a pedophile network hiding in plain sight, while insulated within the safe confines of the government sponsored *BBC* criminal enterprise, a trickling handful of suspected fellow pedophiles were arrested and a measly fewer actually convicted and imprisoned. But the media coverage of Savile's pervasive abuse, revealing that the entire nation was groomed by the most prolific pedophile in its history, remained the exclusive focus, by design to obscure and deflect from the real truth, that

[607] Sharon Churcher and Polly Dunbar, "Teenage Girl Recruited by Paedophile Jeffrey Epstein Reveals how she twice met Bill Clinton," *Daily Mail*, March 6, 2011.

[608] "Billionaire Jeffrey Epstein Shells out more Money in latest Sex Abuse Lawsuit," *New York Daily News*, December 19, 2009..

[609] Nick Bryant, "Here is Pedophile Billionaire Jeffrey Epstein's Little Black Book," *Gawker*, January 23, 2015.

[610] Jessica Elgot, https://www.thejc.com/news/uk-news/jimmy-savile-came-to-my-batmitzvah-1.28748.

[611] "Mossad's Links to Filthy Britain," *whale.to*.

he was merely a significant cog in the earthly demonic wheel that is the globalized pedophilia network run by the ruling elite. This full exposure becomes the focus of this entire book series and in this and coming chapters, through unveiling the curtain hiding the world's pedophilia epicenter of Britain, the horror of the elite's Achilles heel can finally be laid bare once and for all.

Within days after the Savile bombshell hitting the United Kingdom in the form of an *ITV* production called Exposure – The Other Side of Jimmy Savile, that aired on October 3rd, 2012,[612] in its immediate aftermath and fallout, Operation Yewtree was rapidly launched seeking a first round of ready-made suspects from the Savile-*BBC* pedo-ring, featuring the highly publicized arrests of glam rock star Gary Glitter, comedian Freddie Starr, and former *BBC* producer Wilfred De'ath.[613]

The parade of ensuing arrests by UK police's Operation Yewtree was meant to send the message that the nation's law enforcement was making up for allowing so many decades of Savile abuse to go unpunished. As part of the joint Metropolitan Police probe, coordinating efforts from multiple police departments across the nation, investigating Savile's connection to the larger *BBC* pedophilia network, rock n' roll glitter man himself Gary Glitter was the first, most infamous and obvious suspect arrested in late October 2012,[614] although despite several pedo-convictions prior, Glitter was not charged until June 2014. For years Paul Gadd (aka Gary Glitter) had been more than chummy with Sir Jimmy, appearing on television with him a number of times. And Glitter was no stranger to pedophilia, having done jail time in 1999 for possessing thousands of child pornography photos, spent Christmas 2002 in a Cambodian jail after being caught assaulting young boys,[615] and deported only to then be rearrested again in 2005 in Vietnam, another Southeast Asian sex tourist paradise, engaging in obscene acts with 10- and 11-year old girls, jailed and deported once again back home three years later in 2008. So, no surprise for that that pervert would be selected by UK law enforcement as Savile's lowest hanging, rotten fruit.

Paul Gadd's 2012 arrest arose within a few weeks after Savile was exposed, prompting thousands of child sex abuse victims to begin coming forth to report not only Savile, but pedophiles associated with him and his *BBC* sex ring. One key witness and abuse survivor, Karin Ward, maintains she observed Glitter sexually assaulting a 13-year old schoolgirl in pedo-pal Savile's *BBC* dressing room, while Sir Jimmy groped a 14-year old and another entertainer

[612] Mark Lawson, "Exposure: The Other Side of Jimmy Savile – Review," *The Guardian*, October 4, 2012.

[613] Martin Evans, "Operation Yewtree: The Successes and Failures," *The Telegraph*, February 5, 2015.

[614] Sam Greenhill, "Gary Glitter Released on Bail after Ten Hours of Questioning as Savile Probe Police Prepare to Swoop on more Celebrities," *Daily Mail*, October 28, 2012.

[615] Hugh Davies, "Cambodia Throw out Gary Glitter," *The Telegraph*, January 8, 2003.

reportedly still working today was abusing yet another schoolgirl.[616] The crime scene where most of the abuse took place was in the *BBC* dressing rooms where sickos indulged themselves at the expense of their in-over-their-head, adoring child fans. In February 2015, the then 71-year old Paul Gadd's lurid past finally caught up to him for good.[617] He was convicted on one count of attempted rape of an 8-year old, unlawful sexual intercourse with a 12-year old, and four counts of indecent assault against three girls at the height of his fame during the 1970s, and sentenced to 16 more years in prison.[618] Though he never stood trial for it, the beast is alleged to have repeatedly raped his own daughter's best friend, starting when she was just 8.[619] Two years prior to his death, Savile actually had the gall to publicly defend his child porn collecting, glittery Gadd-fly pedo-friend during an interview, insisting "he did nothing wrong."[620]

Second Yewtree arrestee - Freddie Starr, was at one time an English singer, a very popular comic as well as actor who rose to fame during the 1970s with Jimmy Savile, also often featured as a regular performer on his programs.[621] The incident that caused his charmed life to come crashing down, also was alleged to occur in Jimmy Savile's dressing room after he was a guest on Savile's Clunk Click show. According to alleged victim Karin Ward, who was 15 at the time, Freddie Starr's "wandering hands" went up her skirt and pinched her buttocks in what she described as "being goosed." Karin has stated that she would never have even bothered reporting the incident to police, had it not been for the Savile revelations and Starr humiliating her immediately following his ass groping, calling her a "titless wonder" in front of a bunch of hangers-on laughing and mocking her in the Savile dressing room.[622]

Decades after the humiliating incident, Karin Ward was interviewed for two different documentaries that were produced exposing Savile, one by *ITV* that opened the reporting floodgate in October 2012, and another by the *BBC* that was never shown, pulled by *BBC* senior executives at the last minute in favor of airing two holiday tributes to the dead degenerate.[623] Soon after the *ITV* doc aired, Karin found herself interviewed by the police, as Freddie Starr subsequently became Yewtree's second celebrity suspect arrested and released on bail. As to be expected, Freddie denied ever seeing or knowing this girl Karin but film footage of the

---

[616] Sam Greenhill and Claire Ellicott, "Gary Glitter 'raped girl, 13, in Savile's BBC dressing room'... as Jimmy and a third star 'abused two 14-year-olds,'" *Daily Mail*, October 3, 2012..

[617] Rebecca Camber, Inderdeep Bains and Chris Greenwood, "Glitter will Die behind Bars: Final Shaming of Glam Rocker Found Guilty of Sex with 12-year-old Girl," *Daily Mail*, February 6, 2015.

[618] Adrian Shaw, "Gary Glitter 'Crept into Bed and tried to Rape Girl, Eight', Court told," *Mirror*, January 19, 2015.

[619] Justine Ackroyd, "I Was Eight when Gary Glitter Abused me. I've carried his Shame for 24 Years, but I'm not Prepared to any longer," *Mail on Sunday/highbeam.com*, November 14, 1999.

[620] John Hall, "Sir Jimmy Savile Defended Paedophile Pop Star Gary Glitter saying 'he did nothing Wrong' and calling Child Porn just 'Dodgy Films,'" *Independent*, October 1, 2012..

[621] "Operation Yewtree: Freddie Starr held over new Sex Abuse Claims," *BBC*, February 12, 2014.

[622] "Freddie Starr Loses Libel case against Groping Accuser Karin Ward," *The Telegraph*, July 10, 2015.

[623] Ian Burrell, "Revealed: Newsnight Emails that Accuse BBC of Jimmy Savile Cover-up," *Independent*, October 20, 2012.

program episode in question soon emerged, confirming that the victim was present in the audience. Incidentally, Karin also testified that while on a camping trip from her Norfolk children's home to the notorious island of Jersey, where kids were regularly used and abused by British VIPs, she reported that savage Savile molested her there as well.[624]

Though Operation Yewtree ultimately concluded that insufficient evidence to prosecute comedian Freddie Starr resulted in no formal charges ever filed against him, based on testimony from other alleged victims, a year later in 2013, Starr was rearrested and again a third time, yet strangely never charged.[625] After his fourth arrest, Freddie Starr vowed to bring Operation Yewtree "down on its knees."[626] Though he successfully evaded prosecution, his reputation was completely tattered. Knowing he couldn't take on and expect to win in court against the Met Police behind Yewtree, a vengeful Starr went on the offensive, filing a suit against his prime accuser Karin Ward for libel and defamation of character. But in 2015 the presiding judge ruled in the victim's favor, and Starr was stuck with a million pound legal bill to cover Karin's attorney fees.[627] Still claiming his innocence with his career and life torn asunder and his health allegedly failing, Starr promptly sold his English property and moved to Spain without paying his debt. In the end, Crown Prosecution Service decided against charging Starr for any crime at all.

It appears the farcical, on again, off again arrest antics were all for show, amounting to a colossal waste of time and manpower at exorbitant taxpayer expense, not to mention causing further despair to already damaged lives. The question lingers, was Starr ultimately spared from standing trial because he could wreak damage on others higher up on the pedophilia food chain?

After skipping out, Freddie Starr reported to *The Sun* that at times he felt like taking his own life:

I was trapped like a dog. So I thought I'm just going to get on a plane and go to Spain. And this is where I'm going to die... Freddie Starr the entertainer is dead.[628]

In late 2016, an unshaven, pudgy Freddie rose from the dead to come out of hiding to entertain again, this time singing Elvis songs at his favorite local karaoke bar in Costa del Sol[629]... speaking

---

[624] Eileen Fairweather, "Jimmy Savile: 'He was the Tip of the Iceberg,'" *The Telegraph*, October 19, 2012.

[625] Josh Halliday, "Freddie Starr will not be Prosecuted over Sex Offence Allegations, says CPS," *The Guardian*, May 6, 2014.

[626] Frank Furedi, "Yewtree: More Propaganda than Police Investigation," *Spiked*, February 19, 2014.

[627] "Freddie Starr Loses Libel case against Groping Accuser Karin Ward.."

[628] "Freddie Starr Filmed Singing Elvis Presley during Karaoke Session at a Bar in the Costa del Sol," *Mirror*, November 24, 2016.

[629] Ryan Kisiel, "Disgraced Comedian Freddie Starr Resorts to Performing Clumsy Elvis Presley Karaoke for a Handful of Punters close to Costa del Sol Home," *The Sun*, November 24, 2016.

of pedophiles named Elvis,[630] apparently Starr reinvented himself a white-haired version of another bloated Elvis sighting. Though he claimed to be broke and unable to pay his legal fees back home, he had enough cash to plunk down £133,500 for his swanky pad on the Iberian Peninsula pleasure seeking paradise. Less than three years after the once popular comedian declared himself dead, the expatriated visionary this time really did die at his home in Spain at the age of 76 in May 2019.[631]

Also arrested during the first week of November 2012 was Wilfred De'ath, a *BBC* producer through the 1960s and 1970s who worked with Jimmy Savile on the radio program *Teen Scene*.[632] De'ath would later be interviewed in the explosive *ITV* documentary "Exposure - The Other Side of Jimmy Savile," stating that in phone contact as well as an in-person meeting in 1964, he saw firsthand evidence that Savile was engaging in unlawful sex with an underage girl, estimated between 12 and 14, but leaning towards 12.[633] In October 2012 as part of the Operation Yewtree witch hunt, De'ath found himself accused of sexual assault, but the alleged teenage victim as an adult would later withdraw her complaint and, as with Starr, the police never charged De'ath with any pedophilia crime.

As a fresh grad out of Oxford at age 23, the *BBC* hired Wilfred De'Ath as its youngest ever producer. But in the 1970s the acerbic whiz kid was sued for libel, writing that nine of his contemporaries were "intellectual pygmies." He lost not only a costly legal battle but his two-decade long career at *BBC* as well, sending him in a downward spiral for the next many years living in France as a homeless person, moving back and forth from the streets to jail cells over a series of petty crimes. Self-admittedly leading a riches-to-rags scoundrel's life, that is until he died in February 2020,[634] the 82-year oldie managed to still write a column for *The Oldie* about his up and down, colorfully checkered life.[635]

Dave Lee Travis and Jimmy Savile were both highly popular *BBC* DJ colleagues and Top of the Pops presenters, apparently affiliated with the same *BBC* child sex club from the late 1960s into the 1980s. The irony of Travis' statement paying tribute to his friend Sir Jimmy proved especially accurate for him:

---

[630] Iman Khan, "Stop Romanticizing Elvis Presley and start Acknowledging him for what he was," *Affinity Magazine*, August 21, 2017.

[631] Mattha Busby, "Freddie Starr: Comedian Found Dead at Home in Spain Aged 76," *The Guardian*, May 10, 2019.

[632] Ginny Dougary, "I've led a very Wicked Life: Wilfred De'Ath, BBC Producer, Thief and Vagrant on going from Riches to Rags," *Evening Standard*, April 3, 2013.

[633] "Exposure - The Other Side of Jimmy Savile," *ITV*, October 3, 2012.

[634] Wilfred De'Ath, Former BBC Producer who in his Oldie Column Chronicled his Scurrilous Adventures Thieving and Sleeping Rough – Obituary," *The Telegraph*, February 20, 2020.

[635] "Wilfred De'Ath," *The Oldie*..

We are all going to be worse off without him around.[636]

As the fourth Operation Yewtree suspect, the former *BBC* Radio 1 morning show DJ host Travis was arrested on pedophilia charges and taken into custody for 12 hours after an early morning raid at his home before his release on bail in November 2012.[637] Travis was eventually acquitted of a dozen charges in a first trial in 2014 as alleged underage victims' claims that he groped them decades earlier were not persuasive enough for the jury to convict.[638]

However in a second separate trial in September 2014, Travis was found guilty of indecent assault on a young researcher in her early 20s, working on the *BBC* production of the Mrs. Merton Show in 1995, receiving a three month suspended sentence.[639] In December 2015 a three judge appeals court panel upheld his conviction,[640] unconvinced that the 1995 victim had lied about her accusation. His victim has explained that the veteran DJ saw her smoking a cigarette in a *BBC* corridor, and jokingly admonished her, "You shouldn't be smoking. Think about your poor little lungs." She testified in court that he then walked up to her and proceeded to grab and squeeze her breasts for 10-15 seconds, adding that she was frozen in total bewilderment before retreating to safety.[641]

While the 1995 assault victim - comedienne Lucy Porter - who has worked Travis' "groping my tits" incident into her standup comic routine after becoming a television personality in her own right,[642] all along the aging DJ has claimed he's been a wrongfully accused innocent man and victim of a post-Savile witch hunt leaving him in financial ruin. But as of March 2018 a half decade after his initial arrest, the 72-year old Travis was once again back to work hosting a two hour weekend spot with the new digital station United DJs Radio.[643] Maintaining all along that he's the one who's been a victim, the former *BBC* shock jock can't hide his bitterness:

[636] Cole Moreton, "Jimmy Savile, the Big Fixer," *The Telegraph*, October 30, 2011.
[637] Chris Greenwood and Tom Kelly, "Dave Lee Travis Arrested over Allegations of Sexual Abuse as Jimmy Savile Probe Widens," *Daily Mail*, November 15, 2012.
[638] Josh Halliday, "Dave Lee Travis Cleared of String of Indecent Assaults," *The Guardian*, February 13, 2014.
[639] Mark Tran, "Dave Lee Travis found Guilty of Indecent Assault," *The Guardian*, September 23, 2014.
[640] Tom Pettifor, "DJ Dave Lee Travis Fails in Bid to have his Sex Attack Conviction Thrown out," *Mirror*, December 8, 2015.
[641] "Dave Lee Travis 'Squeezed my Breasts' Alleges TV Personality in Former DJ's Trial, *Huffington Post*, September 9, 2014.
[642] Sarah Ryan, "Lucy Porter - Northern Soul," *Nerve*, October 24, 2013.
[643] Patrick Hill and Alex Belfield, "Dave Lee Travis making Shock Radio Comeback - Four Years after Operation Yewtree Conviction," *Mirror*, January 27, 2018.

I do have pretty negative and strong feelings about things people have done that have been totally wrong. The unfortunate thing is that nowadays someone only has to say something and that's enough to stop a person's career.[644]

Again, Travis supporters believe the former *BBC* star has been unfairly maligned as a martyr for what they consider trumped up charges in a mockery of justice, succumbing to pressures to justify Operation Yewtree by finding so called pedophiles to pay for Savile's crimes in a feeble PR campaign to placate a shocked, incensed public... in effect, hanging from the gallows both innocent victims as well as a few low level offenders in order to shield guilty pedophilia kingpins at the top of the British Establishment. Fellow television presenter Noel Edmonds maintains that the royal family and the Thatcher government have been just as guilty for the Jimmy Savile scourge as the *BBC*.[645] Facts backing up his claim will be addressed in the next few chapters.

If Travis did grope, and he may well have, clearly grabbing a woman's breasts he didn't know without her consent is rightfully a reprehensible act and legitimate crime. But brutally raping thousands of victims - both young and old in hospitals or on *BBC* premises including sex with dead corpses in the morgue, all with fully complicit knowledge and protection from fellow pedophile top politicians, royalty, MI5/6 and *BBC* executives, in 180 degree contrast, based on this single incident - even if guilty, Dave Lee Travis' behavior isn't even remotely comparable to Savile and others unpunished atop United Kingdom's predatory pedophilia network. And to that degree, he and others like him in the post-Savile witch hunt are victims. Meanwhile, above-the-law unreachables atop government and royalty continue satanically raping and murdering kids in droves. This is a total mockery of justice for all humans on earth. Yet nothing changes.

It's obvious the British police targeted Travis as a designated sacrificial victim to doggedly pursue in order to safeguard the bigger pedo-operation of sodomizing Luciferian cannibals that own the pedo-cabal so that they remain free to continue slaughtering both our innocents and humanity. Rather than bring the planetary ruling monsters responsible for this egregious global crisis to true justice, throwing a few minor "victims" under the bus as a convenient, wag-the-dog, stop-gap measure to cover-up its own complicity is nothing short of an insult to our intelligence. The lap dogging Scotland Yard/Metro Police in their Operation Yewtree cover-up are puppet-controlled whores, proverbial gatekeeping foxes guarding the elite's satanic henhouse, in obedient protective service to their beastly masters - the earth's real pedophile rapists and murderers that continue destroying countless children with complete impunity.

---

[644] Patrick Hill and Alex Belfield, https://www.mirror.co.uk/3am/celebrity-news/dave-lee-travis-making-shock-11924525.
[645] Rosa Silverman, "Royals and Thatcher to Blame for Jimmy Savile Scandal, says Noel Edmonds," *The Telegraph*, November 16, 2014.

Without exception, the top tier of criminal power on the planet has always been allowed to live above the law.

Whereas Travis may be a victimized scapegoat, plenty of other *BBC* Radio 1 DJs and longtime presenters clearly are not, and aside from Savile, at 77 years old Chris Denning is currently serving a 13 year sentence for his plethora of pedophilia crimes.[646] Police and court records show that during his marathon DJ-pedo-career from the 1960s through the 1980s, Denning groomed boys as young as 8 and savagely abused dozens of underage victims in his home, even in Savile's home,[647] at *BBC* studios, on the road, in hotels, even offering his boys to fellow DJs and introducing others to fellow pedophile rocker Gary Glitter, and on and on it goes.

Get the picture? Savile was never a lone operator as portrayed by mainstream media but a procurer amongst an entire brigade operating within a vast ring of fellow *BBC* and British Establishment pedophiles. Just like Hollywood pedophilia, for decades the *BBC* has been an open secret cesspit. Inside bystanders within the corporation have long known and said nothing because countless *BBC* powerbrokers were also actively involved within the larger British Establishment's pedo-network that of course includes prime ministers, cabinet ministers and parliament members as well as Black Nobility royal bloodlines. More on their crimes in coming chapters.

Speaking of royalty, aside from Savile and his horde of *BBC* pedo-pals, another mainstay *BBC* pedophile employee that the corporation long protected is none other than Queen Elizabeth's 2005 official portrait painting artist, the Aussie born "Tie Me Kangaroo Down Sport" singer-child rapist himself Rolf Harris.[648] After a couple dozen complaints surfaced during the post-Savile stampede identifying him as their sexual predator, in 2013 Harris was arrested and in 2014 convicted and sentenced to almost six years imprisonment for committing a dozen indecent assaults against four underage girls as young as 7 from 1968 to 1986.[649] His most frequently abused victim was his own young daughter's best friend starting when she was only 13, amounting to 7 of 12 counts against him, similar to the other *BBC* musician derelict Gary Glitter.[650] But unlike fellow *BBC* pervert Savile, despite a lenient sentence at least this monster was forced to start paying for his disgusting, shameful sins in this world prior to the next. In the mid-1970s his buddy Savile invited his fellow *BBC* pervert for a pre-bedtime tour at Broadmoor, the country's most notorious maximum-security mental-health facility just so the lechers could

[646] Richard Spillett, "BBC Radio One DJ Chris Denning is Jailed for 13 Years for Sex Attacks on Children as Young as Eight as it is Revealed he took a 14-Year-old to Meet Gary Glitter," *Daily Mail*, October 7, 2016.
[647] "Former DJ Chris Denning Jailed for 13 years over Sexual Abuse of 24 Boys," *The Guardian*, December 16, 2014.
[648] Abe Hawken, "Paedophile Rolf Harris is seen for the first time since his Release Wearing Paint Spattered Trousers outside a Police Station," *Daily Mail*, June 18, 2017.
[649] Peter Walker, "Rolf Harris Jailed for Five Years Nine Months for Indecently Assaulting Girls," *The Guardian*, July 4, 2015.
[650] "Rolf Harris case: Daughter's Former Best Friend gives Victim Impact Statement," *The Guardian*, July 4, 2014.

gawk at the women having to undress in the hallway in front of male and female staff.[651] To make it more bizarrely Fellini-esque, Harris went into an impromptu version of his Tie Me Kangaroo Down Sport.

No doubt as a damage control, PR gesture to distance herself and her royal family from the disgraced convicted child sex offender, in 2015 the queen stripped the 84-year old Harris of his coveted CBE award - the Commander of the Civil Division of the Most Excellent Order of the British Empire.[652] Here's a dot connecting observation – every time the crown bestows knighthood and excellent order memberships on her loyal subjects, you can almost bet they're pedophiles or pedophile enablers as part of their illicit deviant club. Pedophiles reward their own kind. The queen took her OBE back from Harris immediately after it went public that the vile, remorseless pig sitting in jail had written a vindictive letter containing demented lyrics to a composed song calling his victims whose lives he destroyed "woodworms" crawling out of the woodwork 40 years after the fact to lay claim to his millions.[653] After decades of Rolf Harris also taking devilish delight exploitatively ravaging admiring underage female fans, crawling out from underneath the same *BBC* predator rock as Sir Jimmy, in May 2017 at age 87, the serial pedophile was released from prison.[654]

With all of Great Britain watching, by 2014 Operation Yewtree was growing desperate and needed convictions in the Savile aftermath following a series of high profile arrests resulting in either no charges or trial acquittals for a number of early suspects. The police scam operation finally struck gold, nabbing its first conviction to bring down UK's biggest publicist kingpin when Max Clifford was found guilty in May 2014 on 8 of 11 counts of indecent assault against seven teenage girls aged 14 to 19 from 1966 to 1984.[655] Ironically early into Yewtree, it was Clifford who was telling the press that dozens of stars were contacting him right and left for protection and advice, fearing they'd be arrested next over their past child abuse crimes. Little did the PR spin master know that it would be him who would be next, and the first conviction to boot.[656]

Then once incarcerated, many of those same famous predators worried Clifford would use his plethora of dark secrets to write a tell-all book in prison to pay for his legal fees that would expose all his former pal pervs. But instead, the once PR kingpin used his prison time to purposely bankrupt himself in order to deny victim compensations, liquidating his wealth by

[651] Matthew Weaver, "Jimmy Savile gave Rolf Harris Guided Tour of Broadmoor," The Guardian, July 1, 2014.
[652] Mark Tran, "Rolf Harris is Stripped of CBE," *The Guardian*, March 3, 2015.
[653] Olga Craig, "Rolf Harris's Vile Jail Song: In Shock Letter from Cell, Shamed Star Reveals 'Country Rock' Lyrics that Damn his Sex Victims as Greedy 'Wenches' – then Brags about Cushy Prison Life," *Daily Mail*, June 13, 2015.
[654] Abe Hawken, http://www.dailymail.co.uk/news/article-4615556/Paedophile-Rolf-Harris-seen-time.html.
[655] Simon Hattenstone, "Max Clifford: The Rise and Fall of the UK's King of Spin," *The Guardian*, May 2, 2014..
[656] Jerry Lawton, "Stars Fear PR guru Max Clifford will Spill Sex Secrets after Indecent Assault Convictions," *Daily Star*, April 29, 2014.

June 2017.[657] Though he planned to appeal his case in 2018, he never got that far, as his 8-year sentence was abruptly cut short when he apparently suffered a fatal heart attack in his jail cell in December 2017.[658] A mini-version of the Epstein outcome?

Critics of the 2014 verdict in the post-Savile era insist that Clifford's relative "minor improprieties" haplessly turned him also into a witch hunted scapegoat paying for mountains of unpunished sins of Savile and others. The man who once boasted Sinatra, Muhammad Ali and the Chelsea Football Club as his clients[659] and who current music industry mogul Simon Cowell once attributed "hiring Max Clifford" as the best career decision he ever made,[660] the publicity guru must have also held so much inside dirt on Establishment VIPs from the royals to Westminster that with his sudden passing at 74, Max Clifford may have been the pedo-elite's sacrificial fall guy used as political grist for the damage control mill in yet another installment of "dead men tell no tales."

Another big UK media star disgraced from what he figured was his untouchable *BBC* throne is longtime host and presenter Stuart Hall who turns 91 on Christmas Day 2020. Arrested as a result of Operation Yewtree in December 2012, Hall pled guilty in May 2013 to sexually assaulting 13 girls, one as young as 9, from 1967 to 1991.[661] He was then convicted and sentenced to a paltry 15 months in prison in 2013 before appeals court judges tacked on another 15 months. This unremorseful pedophile was released from prison in December 2015 and prevented from moving to Spain (unlike unprosecuted other ex-*BBC* fallen star Freddie Starr). And to further demonstrate the aforementioned nexus between Queen Elizabeth and pedophilia, shortly before the perv's arrest, the queen also rewarded yet another "national treasure" turned disgraced *BBC* pedophile with The Most Excellent Order of the British Empire (OBE).[662] From last chapter, Prince Andrew also maintained a cordial relationship with this pedophile.

Yet another low life errand boy in this never-ending saga of filth and perversion comes one of Savile's own chauffeurs - Ray Teret, at 73 sentenced in December 2014 to another 25 years behind bars for luring at least 11 underage girls with alcohol and drugs along with his relative

[657] Matthew Steeple, "Maxed Out," *The Steeple Times*, June 13, 2017.

[658] Samantha Bartlett, "Danniella Westbrook Sparks Outrage as she Defends Max Clifford over Sex Crimes," *Daily Star*, December 11, 2017.

[659] Andy Rice, "You're (In)famous and in Trouble? Call Max. Max Clifford," Daily Maverick, December 9, 2010.

[660] Simon Hattenstone, https://www.theguardian.com/media/2014/may/02/max-clifford-sex-politics-tabloids-simon-hattenstone.

[661] Tom Rawle, "Stuart Hall's 15-Month Prison term Doubled after Initial Sentence Considered 'Inadequate,'" *Express*, July 26, 2013.

[662] "Stuart Hall Case: National Treasure who had a Guilty Secret," *The Telegraph*, May 2, 2013.

mini-celebrity status to brutally rape victims between 13 and 15 years old from 1963 to 1979.[663] Teret was already convicted of sexual assault of a minor back in 1999, and risked further prosecution for sexual attacks alleged by yet more victims coming forth during the Savile aftermath. As of late March 2020, the 78-year old inmate was reported to be isolation after prison staff disclosed that he had tested positive for Covid-19.[664]

In October 2013 two years after Savile's death, longtime *BBC* Norwich broadcaster and presenter, 60-year old Michael Souter, was convicted and sentenced to 22 years in prison resulting from 26 child sex crimes against seven boys (though many more victims have emerged), committed from the late 1970s to 1999.[665] Not only did the sexual predator exploit his public position as a TV celebrity, he also entrenched himself in the Norwich community as a Boy Scout leader and social services mentor. Right to the end the serial child abuser denied his guilt, feebly blaming it on a conspiracy to maliciously smear his good name.

Another Yewtree semi-notable suspect whose home was raided in December 2012 is 68-year old Fred Talbot, the *ITV* This Morning weatherman for sexually assaulting boys while a biology teacher back in the 1970s and 1980s.[666] As the number of victims kept growing to at least ten, eight more months were tacked on in November 2017 to his already 4-year sentence in Scotland in May 2017 for abusing seven more schoolboys on top of an original 5-year prison term received from Manchester Crown Court for molesting two more underage victims. In January 2020 the 70-year old disgraced ex-weatherman was seen appearing very gaunt after his December release from prison, serving only half his sentence after just four years.[667]

But other than this handful of relatively little known low-lifes on the lowest rung of the elite's predator food chain, for all its alleged efforts, Operation Yewtree has been an utter waste and complete failure at placing the most powerful guilty pedophiles in the United Kingdom behind bars. To add insult to injury, more than a few of the identified suspects that were publicly arrested for pedophilia were never prosecuted for lack of evidence. To name a few... A month after Wilfred De'ath's arrest, in December 2012 another former fellow *BBC* Radio 1 producer that worked with Savile in the 1960s and 70s, the then 76-year old Ted Beston was arrested but

[663] Kim Pilling, "Jimmy Savile Chauffeur Ray Teret Jailed for 25 Years for String of Sex Attacks," *Mirror*, December 11, 2014.

[664] Tom Wells, "Paedo Gets Corona Jimmy Savile's Paedo Pal Driver Tests Positive for Coronavirus in Prison," *The Sun*, March 26, 2020.

[665] William Turvill and Dan Bloom, "Former BBC Presenter Michael Souter Jailed for 22 years for Sexually Abusing Seven Boys over two Decades," *Daily Mail*, October 31, 2013.

[666] Kelly McLaughlin, "Paedophile Weatherman Fred Talbot Moans his Convictions have Cost him his Career, Savings and four Stone in Weight as he's Jailed for a further eight months for Molesting a Tenth Victim," *Daily Mail*, November 29, 2017.

[667] Sabastian Murphy-Bates, "Paedophile TV Weatherman Fred Talbot, 70, Reveals Dramatic Weight Loss after Spending Four Years in Prison as he is Seen in Cheshire Village Weeks after his Release," *Daily Mail*, January 5, 2020.

told in May 2013 he would not face charges.[668] Beston and Savile were close friends collaborating on a series of *BBC* shows - Savile's Travels, the Jimmy Savile Old Record Club and the Double Top Ten Show. Beston is said to have procured underage girls and young women for Savile and was questioned again by police in November 2015 under "Savile related" crimes.[669] Is it another case of Yewtree scapegoating harassment against a more or less innocent man in order to make up for Savile sins or an accomplice guilty of complicit aiding and abetting unlawful sex crimes with minors?[670] We'll never know because the now 84 year old was never charged with a crime.

59-year old comedian Jim Davidson and 53-year old radio DJ Mike Osman were arrested in January 2013 but after nine months were neither charged nor prosecuted.[671] Next came 73-year old comedian Jimmy Tarbuck arrested in April 2013 and cleared a year later.[672] 65-year old *BBC* broadcaster Paul Gambaccini was arrested in October 2013 but after a year on bail was also not charged for alleged lack of evidence.

These men's lives and reputations were harmed and if they committed no crimes, justice was not served even with their investigations clearing them of wrongdoing. But if they did engage in sexual assault of underage minors or aided and abetted those who did, and for whatever reason, dodged the prosecution bullet for "lack of evidence," the UK justice system once again failed the victims… which leads to the next question. Are British police investigators that incompetent? Outside of the one case with Wilfred De'ath's alleged accuser backing out on her earlier complaint, no other alleged victims were reported to follow suit as the reason to not prosecute all those initially arrested.

Either these onetime suspects are innocent and wrongly arrested or police are grossly incompetent in putting together solid enough cases that warrant charges that stick, or perhaps they were spared, granted reprieves by the ruling elite for staying tightlipped under pressure in not implicating their criminal masters, as Savile did his whole life, loyally never outing or biting the pedo-hands that fed him such as royalty, PMs, MPs and *BBC* heads. In any event, Yewtree's been a horrendous debacle and tremendously shameful waste of time, taxpayer money and

[668] Martin Evans, "Savile's former Producer Ted Beston told he will not face Historic Sex Abuse Charges," *The Telegraph*, May 14, 2013.

[669] James Dunn, "Operation Yewtree Detectives Re-interview Jimmy Savile's Former Producer on Suspicion of Sexual Offences," *Daily Mail*, November 13, 2015.

[670] Moor Larkin, "The Killing of Uncle Ted," The Death of the Life of Jimmy Savile, *jimcannotfixthis.blogspot.com*, March 12, 2016.

[671] Rob Cooper, "'It's been nine Months of Murder': Jim Davidson tells Audience of his Relief in first Live Show since Assault Probe was Halted… and Reveals he turned down £150,000 to go into Celebrity Big Brother House," *Daily Mail*, August 21, 2013.

[672] "Jimmy Tarbuck Cleared after Police Investigation into Historic Sex Abuse," Daily Mail, March 24, 2014.

personnel, unjustifiably damaging too many people's lives and denying justice for thousands of victims.

In its fourth year alone in 2015 at a hefty price tag of £5m,[673] when police budgets across Britain were being cut by 20%, 63 separate police inquiries were probing historic child sex abuse in response to 2,100 victim claims, astoundingly more than half at over 1,200 committed at one youth detention institution alone at Medomsley.[674] That statistic reflects how the UK authoritarian state treats its "throwaway" youth as pure expendables, used and abused by sickos in its corrosively corrupt child welfare penal system. The massive police operation as a self-serving, face-saving, damage control exercise was nothing more than a grandstanding spectacle and show of force put on by British law enforcement to make up for permitting Savile to freely roam the countryside, committing 60 years of, according to *BBC*'s account:

... Over 600 crimes of sexual abuse recorded against Savile in 28 police force areas across the UK.[675]

The National Society for Prevention of Cruelty to Children (NSPCC), "the UK's leading children's charity,"[676] claimed an increase of 128% in child sexual abuse reporting from 2009/10 to 2014/15.[677] As of February 2015, a 71% increase in reported abuse cases since the Savile dam broke in October 2012 was cited by the National Police Chiefs' Council (NPCC) as part of Yewtree, released under its own codename Operation Hydrant.[678] The more investigative codenamed operations they have going, the more police chiefs get to stroke their self-inflated importance as empty gestures overcompensating for their gargantuan failures. In that February press conference, the NPCC boasted that 1433 suspects had been investigated, breaking down their numbers to reveal that 261 were classified as "prominent public persons."[679] Of those 261 so called "bigtime" pedo-suspects from the 1433 total, 135 were in TV, film or radio, 76 were politicians, 43 were in the music industry and 7 in sports. No doubt because so few of these 1433 suspects were ever arrested - only 19 in all,[680] much less prosecuted, much less convicted

---

[673] Josh Halliday, "Scotland Yard spent nearly £5m on three Child Abuse Inquiries in 2015," *The Guardian*, December 27, 2015.

[674] Martin Beckford, "63 Police Inquiries, 2,100 victims... the Child Abuse Dossier that Shames Britain after Horrific Explosion of Historic Sex Cases since Savile," *Daily Mail*, April 5, 2015.

[675] "BBC Charter Review," Media Policy Project Planner, *The London School of Economics and Political Science*, February 25, 2014.

[676] NSPCC website, https://www.nspcc.org.uk/.

[677] "Britain's Uncomfortable Extremes in Dealing with past Sexual Abuse," *The Economist*, March 28, 2016.

[678] Sandra Laville, "1,400 Investigated in Child Sex Abuse Inquiry, including Politicians," *The Guardian*, May 20, 2015.

[679] Kate Ferguson, "More than 1400 VIP Child Sex Abuse Suspects Investigated by Police Including Politicians and Celebrities," *Daily Record*, May 20, 2015.

[680] Martin Evans, "Operation Yewtree: Essex man, 79, Arrested on Suspicion of Sex Offences, *The Telegraph*, October 6, 2015.

- 6 in all,[681] much less imprisoned for any length of time, the UK police have little to show for all their failed efforts to put child abusers behind bars, all six of them, and make kids in Great Britain safe.

The fact that such a tiny pathetic handful of pedophiles were actually convicted by Yewtree, a few elderly degenerates caught up in Yewtree's umbrella comprising among the UK's largest national police operations ever,[682] is yet one more disgrace on top of the already unconsequenced Savile-*BBC* sex ring disgrace. Britain has merely demonstrated good reason to be called the pedophilia epicenter of the world. With rare exception, the tried, convicted and imprisoned pedophile few are minor in prominence and most were handed far too lenient sentences as well. Operations Yewtree and Hydrant proved to be merely a PR stunt turned propaganda circus intended to appease the shocked and outraged nation by dragging on for years at a time pissing in the wind, resulting in millions of wasted tax paid pounds paid in the flesh of thousands of damaged and destroyed lives still waiting for justice.

The Yewtree operations are one colossal scam of the highest order as UK's corrupt law enforcement[683] take orders directly from the so called national security apparatus - MI5/6 and Special Branch, which in turn take orders from royalty and government, which in turn take their orders from the Rothschilds and other subhuman bloodlines ruling the earth through a Luciferian pedo-blackmail control system while unencumbered throughout, they're still daily defiling children across the planet en masse.

Another glaring observation begs this unanswered question. Why has this massive all-nation police probe only yielded a few aging, doddering convicted derelicts who committed damage way back in the 1950s up to the 1980s, as if pedophilia suddenly stopped in the 1990s? Do the authorities think we're that stupid to believe that younger generations of pedophiles ceased abusing children in the 1990s or that pedophilia stopped altogether? Or have their global child raping operations only submerged deeper underground and in recent decades become more tightly insulated and protected? Meanwhile, there is plenty of contra-indicative evidence that child sexual abuse, child pornography and child sex trafficking in recent years have in fact been rising exponentially with an estimated 2 million kids a year being trafficked worldwide,[684]

---

[681] "Britain's Uncomfortable Extremes in Dealing with past Sexual Abuse," https://www.economist.com/britain/2016/03/28/britains-uncomfortable-extremes-in-dealing-with-past-sexual-abuse.

[682] Jamie Grierson, "Police Child Abuse Inquiries: Operation Yewtree to Operation Midland," *The Guardian*, August 4, 2015.

[683] Neil Darbyshire, "The Shocking Truth about Police Corruption in Britain," *The Spectator*, March 7, 2015.

[684] John DeGarmo, "The Shocking Truth of Child Sex Trafficking," *Huffington Post*, November 17, 2016.

amongst 8 million gone missing yearly.[685] Outside North America, the British Isles as a very small nation is the world's largest consumer of child pornography.[686]

It's gotten so out of hand clogging up the British court system that a pilot program has been launched with Sussex police knocking on doors and giving warnings to first-time offenders downloading child porn images so that the police can concentrate more resources on pedophiles posing immediate grave risk of physical contact with children.[687] One police chief is advocating that child porn should no longer be treated as a crime but as a deviant mental health condition meriting treatment. Critics of course slam this controversial approach warning that it may only promote more people turning to child pornography that in turn may set a certain percentage onto the slippery slope leading to physically acting out pedophilic urges and desires on victims. It reflects the current child abuse crisis that law enforcement is overwhelmed to adequately deal with during a digital age that's only contributing more to pedophilia crime.

So why aren't police busting current perps active in pedo-rings in larger numbers? Certainly not because they don't exist. Police will cite lack of resources. At the same time that humans today are being more electronically monitored and controlled than any time in history, one of the very few advantages of this advancing technology is that it should help police more rapidly identify and locate child rapists and murderers. Yet the powerful individuals behind the massive global pedophilia operations are not being arrested and brought to justice, and the reason is all too obvious – they simply are living above the law. That all these child abuse investigations have failed so miserably to catch the more "prominent" pedophiles most responsible in the UK who continue to criminally reoffend without disruption over the last three decades only says that they are all a scam, all for show to placate the angst-ridden public.

The pedophilia order-following gatekeepers masquerading in police uniform and priestly or high court robes are guarding and protecting current pedophile rings still flourishing within the global child trafficking network. Pedophiles and their enablers from the high courts, law enforcement, intelligence services, governments, secret societies, militaries, social services, large charities and MSM have simply walled off the currently entrenched malignancy with "out of sight, out of mind," sleight-of-hand mass deception. But despite MSM lies, with a growing awareness of Pizzagate turned PedoGate gaining traction in the last few years finally

---

[685] "Activities in more than 29 Countries around the Globe will Remember Missing Children on May 25," *International Centre for Missing and Exploited Children*.

[686] Lizzie Deardon, "Tech Companies 'must Stop Paedophiles Uploading Child Sex Abuse Images,' National Crime Agency says," *Independent*, June 21, 2018.

[687] Angela Wormald, "Online Paedophiles Avoid Arrest under Controversial new Police Warning Scheme," *Mirror*, February 7, 2016.

recognizing the global epidemic crisis,[688] as hard as the cabal tries to cover-up its crime tracks desperate to put the pedo-genie back in the bottle, enough realists with eyes wide open are now seeing through the continuous stream of lies and cover-up, and as a result, in the light of truth, the crumbling pedo-cabal will eventually come tumbling down sooner than later.

By bottom line design, Operation Yewtree was a monumental disaster in terms of exposing and bringing the ruling perps most guilty to justice and attacking the current scourge of worldwide pedophilia afflicting this planet. But then from the very start that was never the intended purpose of this controlled national police operation. Its actual objective was only to obscure and shield the much larger pedophilia network that only on a minor scale includes the *BBC* and is sadly still operating robustly as ever today.

Even then pedo-enabling Home Secretary Theresa May admitted in July 2014 that her office had previously covered up evidence that MPs and senior government officials committed child sex abuse.[689] But in the next breath May then insisted that the late MP Geoffrey Dickens never submitted a dossier to Home Office boss Leon Brittan in 1983 but only written letters. She also added that an earlier Home Office investigator found no evidence that the 114 missing sex abuse files allegedly lost were ever "removed or destroyed inappropriately." Again, placate a skeptical public by first openly admitting to covering up the truth but then follow immediately by defending and clearing her office and predecessors of all wrongdoing. Here's a loaded question - whose side is she really on? Be it her years as Home Secretary or Prime Minister, Theresa May's always been nothing more than sodomizer protector.

At the outbreak of the Savile bombshell during the first week of November 2012, Home Secretary May rejected a single overarching, super-inquest that would have possessed the necessary muscle to examine all links and tentacles of abuse to both the national and international pedo-cabal network. Instead she chose to endorse the already eight separate smaller investigations launched at the time.[690] While a slew of toothless, watered down, narrowly focused mini-inquiries are obviously aimed at protecting the global pedo-machine, the anti-pedophilia child victim advocate MP Tom Watson prophetically warned:

A narrowed-down investigation is the basic building block of [more] *cover-up. Many sickening crimes will remain uninvestigated, and some of the most despicable paedophiles will remain protected by the Establishment that has shielded them for 30 years.*[691]

---

[688] Joachim Hagopian, "Pizzagate turned PedoGate Leads to Momentum Surge in Busting Global Child Sex Trafficking Rings," *sott.net*, February 27, 2017.

[689] Andrew Gimson, "Top British Politicians Implicated in Child Sex Crimes," Newsweek, July 8, 2014.

[690] James Lyons, "'Sick Crimes will go Uninvestigated': Fears of Child Sex Abuse 'Cover-up' as Theresa May Rejects calls for Super Inquiry," *Mirror*, November 6, 2012.

[691] James Lyons, https://www.mirror.co.uk/news/uk-news/theresa-may-sparks-claims-of-child-sex-1421346.

May's pedo-enabling strategy has obviously worked, for years her supposed "independent" inquiry has been a cruel joke. Theresa May selected two female pedo-enablers in a row to head her so-called national inquiry into how UK government institutions responded to the massive child sexual abuse scandal as both of her choices were forced to resign over blatant conflicts of interest,[692] i.e., more evidence of foxes caught guarding the pedo-henhouse. Turned out former magistrate high court judge Baroness Butler-Sloss's brother - Sir Michael Havers - as UK's Justice Secretary for Thatcher's first eight years in office (1979-1986) knew the PM's senior diplomat Peter Hayman was abusing young boys, yet chose to do nothing but cover it up.[693] In fact, Havers did his best to ensure that pedophilia allegations were never aired in Parliament. Then May's Sloss replacement – Fiona Woolf, the Lord Mayor of London, was outed as a close friend and neighbor of pedophile Lord Brittan, Thatcher's notorious Home Secretary who, oops, lost the 1983 dossier on Westminster child abuse. Of course Theresa May claimed she didn't know about her two selections' biased backgrounds. Yet she and Woolf were caught colluding in a seven re-writes attempting to distance the Woolf from the pack she lived on the same street with, where she'd regularly attended the pedo-accused Sir Leon's dubious parties.[694]

Though the press called Theresa May "incompetent" for her pathetic selections to run an "open" and honest investigation into government pedophilia, May is not stupid and knew exactly what she was doing, trying to whitewash another inquiry by stacking the deck with yet more protectors like herself. To answer criticism stemming from her thinly veiled attempts to facilitate yet another government cover-up of past cover-ups, in February 2015 May ended up recruiting a foreign judge from New Zealand to lead the next "objective" attempt at "getting to the truth."[695]

Without explanation other than a feeble Dame Lowell Goddard claiming the investigation's "legacy of failure" was simply "too much" for her and she felt "lonely,"[696] so after a year and a half on the job, she abandoned ship and flew home to New Zealand. Obviously there's much more to the story than that. Perhaps she could no longer ethically take part in the Brits' habitual VIP cover-up. What does it say about a country when its chronically failed inquiries never cease failing? It says that Prime Minister May and now Prime Minister Boris Johnson are

---

[692] James Slack, "Theresa May under Fire as Baroness Butler-Sloss Quits Historic Child Abuse Inquiry over Alleged Cover-up of an Establishment Paedophile Ring," *Daily Mail*, July 14, 2014.

[693] David Barrett and Bill Gardner, "Margaret Thatcher Warned of Paedophile Scandal, Secret Documents Reveal," *The Telegraph*, January 30, 2015.

[694] Oliver Wright and Paul Peachey, "Theresa May Accused of 'Appalling Incompetence' over Fiona Woolf Affair," *Independent*, October 31, 2014.

[695] David Barrett, "New Zealand Judge Lowell Goddard to Chair Child Abuse Inquiry," *The Telegraph*, February 4, 2015.

[696] Ashley Cowburn, "Child Sexual Abuse Inquiry: Dame Lowell Goddard Resigned because it was 'too much,' says Amber Rudd," *Independent*, September 7, 2016.

never going to come clean, divulging their true crimes against children. It's called self-preservation. The cabal must survive at all costs to humanity.

A fourth chair, Professor Alexis Jay, took over in August 2016 but less than a year later by June 2017, the two biggest victims groups bowed out, asserting that the inquiry was "not fit for purpose," maintaining that victims from the get-go were "totally marginalized."[697] The largest victims group had already pulled out earlier, accusing May's "Independent" Inquiry into Child Sexual Abuse of being a "stage-managed event," like all the rest, all for show and no action. While the colossal £100million fleecing of Briton taxpayers in a fake probe lay in disastrous shambles, at this pathetic point in history, the not-so-great Britain knows only shameful shams and anything but the truth.[698] And in the course of empire rise and falls, currently also a has-been, historically America's right behind its mothership England just as mired in moral depravity and criminal cover-up.[699] No wonder, they're both part of the same global pedo-cabal.

The forever British stonewalling to shield powerful VIP child rapists at all cost has proven endlessly exhausting and nonproductive in the nation that's clearly the world's pedophilic epicenter. After a full half decade, as recently as October 2020, UK's "Independent" Inquiry is still dragging on with nothing new to show for itself. Per an October 7, 2020 piece from *The Guardian:*

The Church [of England] *had protected its own reputation and given abusers a place to hide.*[700]

Like the way the head of the Church of England, Queen Elizabeth and her heir Prince Charles, permitted their buddy Bishop Ball to rape boys with impunity for decades on end. IISCA, tell us something we don't already know years ago. The charade lumbers on year after year with the same old, same old, worn out rhetoric.

Let's face it. If you're a blood drinking sodomizer from a Black Nobility bloodline still wreaking havoc on children and this planet on a grand scale, for you Operation Yewtree and Britain's dirty dozen independent inquiries have been a smashing success designed to avoid the truth to keep you out of jail and the headlines. Inasmuch as the massive worldwide child raping, murdering network still remains fully operational and still flourishing, to the elite that only means that the IICSA and Yewtree et al have been a resounding success and triumph. To this day, top tier pedophiles continue to live above the law.

---

[697] "Inquiry into Child Sexual Abuse 'not fit for purpose,' claims Victims' Group," *The Guardian*, June 13, 2017.
[698] Rebecca Camber, Jack Doyle, Tim Skulthorpe and Matt Dathan, "Child Abuse Inquiry is in Crisis after a second Lawyer goes as Victims Warn of 'Devastating Blow' to the £100million Probe," *Daily Mail*, September 28, 2016.
[699] Jeremy Scahill, "Donald Trump and the Coming Fall of American Empire," *Intercept*, June 22, 2018.
[700] Harriet Sherwood, "Welby: C of E Must Do 'Whatever it Takes' to Redress Sexual Abuse Scandal," *The Guardian*, October 7, 2020.

But what the pedo-controllers fear the most is the fact that like never before, every single day more of us are learning about their massive criminal enterprise and ultra-destructive agenda targeting humanity for further abuse and sordid atrocities. Enough of a growing minority within the pliable masses are becoming more savvy, refusing to tolerate or accept the bullshit lies and excuses heaped on us daily.

Another huge farcical lie coming out of the wave of various Yewtree sub-operations was Operation Newgreen, conducted by Savile's very own West Yorkshire Police (WYP), tasked with policing Sir Jimmy's hometown of Leeds where 68 more of his victims emerged in the post-Savile era. Because psychopath Savile had long been cozy bedfellows with his likeminded local police buddies, establishing "the Friday morning club" where Savile regularly met socially for tea with his closest chums in blue at his penthouse home,[701] it came as no surprise that Operation Newgreen was a total cover-up, claiming "no evidence" that the most famous Leeds' resident was ever protected from arrest or prosecution.[702] Operation Newgreen insisted that the alleged 68 Savile victims never reported abuse to police while Sir Jimmy was still alive. I wonder why. Recall the earlier 1965 incident with pedophile and his underage victim sitting in his Rolls parked in Roundhay Park and the police sergeant's response. Ever since, that little episode served as a preview of what was to follow. Blindly loyal to their own prodigal son, West Yorkshire Police have always protected Britain's most prolific pedophile who, gladly paying his protection dues, relished running PR and public announcement campaigns for his local boys in blue - a win-win for morally corrupt depravity at its worst.

Another huge reason police have no record of victims reporting Savile crimes is West Yorkshire Police's nasty habit of "losing" [or more like destroying] their own records,[703] kind of like the Home Office does. This fact has come to light repeatedly. After an honest, retired WYP officer insisted that Leeds Vice Squad conducted an inquiry investigating indecent assault allegations made by two girls against Savile in the 1980s. But when no records were located on file to back it up, this discrepant matter was turned over to Metro Police to sort out, not that that did any good. Additionally, anonymous letters in 1998 sent to Metropolitan Police stating that Savile was "a deeply committed paedophile" were then forwarded on to West Yorkshire Police and again they too got lost in the shuffle. And perhaps the biggest reason West Yorkshire Police lag so far behind in reported sexual abuse cases and pedophile arrests is because more WYP cops turn out to be pedophiles than any other police force in the nation.[704]

The whitewashed Newgreen report also included this tidbit:

---

[701] David Jones, "Savile's Police Protectors: They were the Friday Morning Club - Police Friends who met weekly at the DJ's Flat," *Daily Mail*, October 18, 2013..
[702] "Jimmy Savile 'not Protected' from Arrest, West Yorkshire Police say," *BBC*, May 10, 2013.
[703] "Jimmy Savile 'not Protected' from Arrest, West Yorkshire Police say," *BBC*, May 10, 2013.
[704] "Police Paedophiles," *upd.co.uk*, July 17, 2014.

Savile offering his services as an intermediary for the police, should the 'Ripper' wish to make contact.[705]

My how neighborly of Savile considering he and Peter Sutcliffe, one of the deadliest serial killers in UK history, were actually pals who may have been partners-in-crime together. One of Ripper's victims' bodies was found at the edge of Savile's property and another attempted murder took place nearby.[706] The police knew Sir Jimmy used local hookers and even ordered an imprint of the pedophile's teeth since kinky Jimmy was a known biter and two Yorkshire Ripper victims had teeth marks on their bodies. But more on that dynamic duo from hell's incriminatingly intimate relationship and prison bonding in the next chapter.

As if not enough evidence has proven Savile was a known pimp and necrophilia Satanist involved in large scale pedophile rings, an October 2012 article in the *Express* entitled "Jimmy Savile Ruled Paedophile Ring" links Jimmy as the ringleader to the seashore resort town of North Yorkshire where at least two victims allege Savile assaulted them in the late 1960s and late 1980s.[707] Moreover, the article implicated that Savile was involved in a child sex ring in nearby Scarborough where the entertainer maintained intimate ties to the repeatedly accused, now dead prominent businessmen and onetime Scarborough mayor Peter Jaconelli.[708] Evidence shows on at least two occasions Savile the child procurer transported underage patients from Rampton without authorization to Scarborough where he and his mayor pal are believed to have sexually abused children.[709] Four years after Jaconelli's death, in 2003 the Scarborough Police were probing the same sex ring connected to Savile and Jaconelli that resulted in the conviction of at least one other offender for molesting two girls aged 9.

Perhaps the most egregiously compelling proof that Savile was a pimping procurer for VIPs is evidence confirming that former UK Prime Minister Edward Heath (1970-1974) sexually abused children from the Haut de la Garenne children's orphanage on the infamous island of Jersey. As the planet's top offshore tax haven at $2 trillion with a population of just 100,000 nestled in the Channel Islands just 14 miles off the French west coast,[710] Jersey is the repository of both the world's most hidden wealth and the most horrific pedophilia history of abuse and cover-up – the epicenter of the epicenter. Both Prime Minister Ted Heath and Jimmy Savile were frequent pleasure visitors to the famous tourist island. Heath was a committed pedophile to the extent that he risked his political career attending at least a half dozen meetings of the Paedophile

---

[705] "Jimmy Savile 'not Protected' from Arrest, West Yorkshire Police say."
[706] Emma Reynolds and Anna Edwards, http://www.dailymail.co.uk/news/article-2229786/Jimmy-Savile-Yorkshire-Ripper-Cast-DJs-teeth-check-bites-left-Peter-Sutcliffes-victims.html.
[707] James Murray and Mark Branagan, "Jimmy Savile Ruled Paedophile Ring," *Express*, October 28, 2012.
[708] James Murray and Mark Branagan, "Jimmy Savile Ruled Paedophile Ring," *Express*, October 28, 2012.
[709] Tim Hicks, "The Dangers of Misguided Loyalty," *The Real Whitby*, May 25, 2014.
[710] Leah McGrath Goodman, "Inside the World's Top Offshore Tax Shelter," *Newsweek*, January 16, 2014.

Information Exchange (PIE), the political group in the 1970s and 80s lobbying to eliminate age of sexual consent for children.[711]

Steeped in PIE, child torture, rape and murder, the cabal had Heath by the ca-balls by the time he was made PM in 1970. And within a year Heath was treasonously signing away Britain's sovereignty with a secret mandate kept hidden from British citizens for nearly a half century.[712] The sexually blackmailed Heath simply did what he was ordered by his masters that put him in power as a pedophile controlled puppet, usurping English law by subordinating it to the Treaty of Accession to the European Economic Union (EEC), the globalist forerunner evolving in 1993 into the unelected, undemocratic NWO monstrosity called the European Union, the same one that's bankrupting nations like Greece, Italy and Spain.[713] It wasn't until May 2018 that this subversive deception of the FCO30/1048 document was finally made public, illustrating how for the last 50 years so called national leaders are blackmail controllable pawns assigned to forward the totalitarian agenda of one world government.

Ted Heath's sodomy and killing of missing children that Savile escorted from Haut de la Garenne aboard the prime minister's yacht is supported by dock eyewitnesses that observed fewer boys returning.[714] Pedophilic child killers Savile and Heath have even been outed by a mainstream *Newsweek* article as raping murderers of ill-fated Jersey kids.[715] Other independent corroborating sources have emerged from abuse victims themselves as well as intelligence and national security consultant, barrister Michael Shrimpton, and investigative author-activist David Icke, a full dozen years ahead of Savile's death and over half dozen prior to Heath's demise.[716] Icke's shocking allegations against Heath went unchallenged in court while the powerful sicko was still alive because it was true. During the long decades of abuse that likely go back to the late 1930s on the island, whenever the abused children from Jersey care homes dared to complain, they were severely beaten, further abused and locked in cellars serving as barbaric dungeons.[717] And if they carried on too long about wealthy yachtsmen raping them during their group homes' "recreational outings" at sea, if not killed, they were even more severely beaten and punished.

---

[711] Nick Dorman and Don Hale, "Edward Heath Fixed it for Jimmy Savile to receive OBE and Attended Paedophile Information Exchange Meetings, *Mirror*, August 8, 2015.

[712] Lara Deauville, "We were lied to! Secret Document FCO 30/1048 kept Truth about EU from British for 30 years," *Express*, May 12, 2018.

[713] "Paul Craig Roberts! The Genocide of the Greek Nation," Paul Craig Roberts interview, YouTube video, posted on August 25, 2018, 10:36.

[714] Martin Robinson, "Mother Claims she had told Police a Child Vanished after going on Sir Edward Heath's Yacht but Officers were Warned not to Investigate by 'Someone above,'" *Daily Mail*, August 7, 2015.

[715] Leah McGrath Goodman, "Child Abuse Inquiry on Top Tax Shelter Jersey Island Delayed Again," *Newsweek*, April 6, 2017.

[716] David Icke, https://www.bibliotecapleyades.net/biggestsecret/esp_icke108.htm.

[717] "Jersey: Children were Loaned to Rich Paedophile Yachtsmen," *The UK and Ireland Database*.

Shrimpton maintains that the pedophile prime minister couldn't risk victims recognizing him as their abuser and thus had a number of his tortured, sodomized older victims 14 and 15-years of age murdered and thrown overboard.[718] After the *Sun* ran a series of articles linking Jimmy Savile to the Haut de la Garenne abuse then under investigation in 2008, Savile threatened to sue the newspaper, vehemently denying that he ever set foot on Jersey Island. The *Sun* then produced a photograph with the infamous sodomizer front and center surrounded by potential victims at Haut de la Garenne.[719] The pedo-kingpin then countered with a super-injunction prohibiting the *Sun* from publishing the incriminating photo. And to this day, the Rupert Murdock owned *Sun* has removed all its articles pertaining to the photos and court injunction.

Four years ago it also came to light that a *Jersey Evening Post* article dated July 29, 1967 quoted the disgraced entertainer boldly warning the island's parents to "lock up their daughters" during one of his many visits.[720] Savile had the audacity to boast he was "a villain" on the loose and that Jersey's "sun-bronzed daughters" need to be kept safely hidden away from his perverted evil clutches. Talk about a criminal brazenly not even hiding in plain sight.

Incidentally in a related side note, Jimmy Savile was also in Jersey in 1963, the same year that pedophile politician Lord Boothby thanked his gay lover crime boss Ronnie Kray in a letter dated June 6, 1963:

Thank you for your postcard. I very nearly went to Jersey myself, as I have never been there, and hear from so many people that it is quite delightful.[721]

Is it pure coincidence that two prolific pedophiles Ronnie Kray and Jimmy Savile were both on the same pedophilia infested little island at the same time, one procurer to the next? Back in 1963, aside from a little pedo-R&R, they may also have been expanding their mutual interests in Jersey as prime source for their child sex trafficking pipeline. Historically Jersey had already become Britain's offshore goldmine for VIP abuse. After all, Savile and the Kray brothers knew each other and were friends, attending the same sex parties with DJs, musicians and entertainers going back to the late 1950s.[722] Savile's ties to the mob originated a decade earlier during his dancehall days in northern England. A couple victims claiming to have been onetime girlfriends alluded to Sir Jimmy's underworld ties that even after his death kept them tightlipped.[723] His crude, ruffian Mafioso ways were reflected in his frequent self-reference as

[718] David Icke, https://www.bibliotecapleyades.net/biggestsecret/esp_icke108.htm.
[719] Richard Alleyne, "Sir Jimmy Savile: He Raped me as a Teenager Claims Woman," *The Telegraph*, October 3, 2012.
[720] Sam Christie, "'Lock up your Daughters': Jimmy Savile's Sick Warning to Parents as he Visited Jersey Revealed," *The Sun*, February 29, 2016.
[721] "Jimmy Savile, Edward Heath and the Kray Twins."
[722] Anthony T. Stokes, "Death of a Showman: Jimmy Savile 1926-2011," *The Truth Seeker*, November 1, 2011.
[723] Louis Theroux, https://www.bbc.com/news/magazine-37517619.

the Godfather,[724] and frequent reminders how with just a phone call, he could have enemies roughed up or worse.[725]

Despite being caught red-handed in a flagrant lie denying he was ever at the notorious Jersey Island crime scene of Haut de la Garenne, nothing further has ever come of the victims' allegations singling out both Savile as well as the murdering prime minister. And at the end of the day, incredulously not enough evidence to indict Savile and company was the false word put out by the corrupt Jersey authorities.[726] But the real reason is all too obvious - Sir Jimmy had far too much dirt on the royals and virtually all the pedophile-infiltrated prime minister governments from Ted Heath, Margaret Thatcher, Gordon Brown,[727] and Tony Blair to David Cameron (pedo-evidence on them primarily reserved for Chapter 6), more than enough to bring down the entire crime cabal in the UK if arrested. His life insurance policy bought his protection for over a half century from the pedos-on high, knowing they were supplied a constant flow of fresh victims enslaved in the Luciferian power pyramid blackmail machine.

Per barrister Shrimpton, another explanation as to why Heath was spared exposure and ruin prior to his death in 2005 was that his own Cabinet Secretary Baron Hunt of Tanworth, John Hunt was yet another alleged fellow pedophile whose job was to ensure the PM's high crimes were covered up.[728] That said, Hunt failed to stop David Icke in 1998 from outing the perverted onetime 10 Downing Street resident. But unfortunately back in 1998, not enough people paid any attention to Icke, unable to handle the shocking truth. Due to Hunt's pedo-gatekeeping diligence, like Savile the serial raping murderer Heath and Hunt were both permitted earthly escape in 2005 and 2008 respectively without paying their piper. And for performing his pedo-protecting duty, cabal movers and shakers the queen and pope each rewarded John Hunt the Knight Grand Cross of the British Order[729] and a papal knighthood,[730] as further testimony underscoring the unholy nexus of pedophilia and secret societies, Black Nobility royalty and the Catholic Church. Of course Catholic Zionist Sir Jimmy was also knighted by the queen in 1990, the same year pedo-enabling Pope John Paul II[731] bestowed papal knighthood on the Satanist as Knight Commander of Saint Gregory the Great.[732] At the height of all the commotion caused by

[724] Louis Theroux, https://www.bbc.com/news/magazine-37517619.

[725] James Saville, "Jimmy Savile and the IRA: Predator Boasted Terrorist Friends could have Enemies Hospitalised," *Mirror*, October 20, 2012.

[726] Richard Alleyne, https://www.telegraph.co.uk/news/uknews/crime/9583373/Sir-Jimmy-Savile-He-raped-me-as-a-teenager-claims-woman.html.

[727] Mike James, "Revealed: British Premier Gordon Brown is a Paedophile," *The Truth Seeker*, March 14, 2010.

[728] David Icke, https://www.bibliotecapleyades.net/biggestsecret/esp_icke108.htm.

[729] "John Hunt, Baron Hunt of Tanworth," *wikipedia.com*.

[730] "Association of Papal Knighthood in Great Britain," papalknights.org.uk.

[731] Maureen Dowd, "A Saint, he Ain't," *The New York Times*, April 23, 2014.

[732] Paul Crockerton, "The Dark Knight: Jimmy Savile could be first person ever to be Stripped of Papal Knighthood," *Mirror*, October 27, 2012.

Savile's posthumous 2012 dark side unveiling, talk of the exposed predator as the first ever to be stripped of papal knighthood turned out to be just talk once the initial shock blew over.

For six decades the poor defenseless children of the island of Jersey and Haut de la Garenne were unmercifully preyed upon by powerful Luciferian pedophiles. Because the Jersey government and law enforcement were among the worst offenders in the once WWII German occupied (and heavily influenced)[733] autonomous island nation, still a part of the queen's British Isles, ultimately the Jersey head constable Graham Power and deputy police chief Lenny Harper led a police investigation in 2007-08 to finally search for evidence of foul play at the infamous orphanage closed in 1986.[734]

But the local establishment largely consisting of threatened members from the island's pedophile ring hampered investigators' efforts at every turn, including a smear campaign from the *Jersey Evening Post*,[735] culminating in the island's then home affairs minister Andrew Lewis illegally suspending Powers in November 2008,[736] eventually running them both off the island,[737] but not before bones of five children had been dug up on the premises,[738] along with 65 teeth with roots attached and about 100 charred bone fragments once belonging to murdered missing kids.[739] The only reason more skeletal remains were not recovered at the site was many of the missing abused boys had been murdered at sea by prominent VIP yachtsmen Edward Heath and his procurer Sir Jimmy. If not directly murdered by their hands, it was at their orders, which is still coldblooded murder.

Among the many powerful men accused by former residents of Haut de la Garenne and other children's homes back in the 1960s and 70s was Jimmy Savile. They never reported the abuse to the Jersey constabulary before because they knew they couldn't trust those who were part of the systemic island pedophile ring. But in 2008 when investigators Power and Harper supported by Jersey senator, health minister and strong anti-child abuse advocate Stuart Syvret were finally listening to victims, a number reported that Jimmy Savile as well as Ted Heath were among their abusers. In addition to high crimes on the high seas, Sir Jimmy also attacked

---

[733] Vitali Vitaliev, "Channel Islanders Showing off their Sites of Shame," *The Guardian*, January 3, 1999.

[734] Helen Pidd, "Jersey's 'Secrecy Culture' led to my Suspension, says Former Police Chief," *The Guardian*, June 28, 2012.

[735] Leah McGrath Goodman, "Anarchy in the UK?" *leahmcgrathgoodman.com*, June 29, 2012.

[736] Graham Power, "Former Police Chief Statement to Wiltshire Constabulary," *voiceforchildren.blogspot.com*, September 7, 2017.

[737] Nigel Bunyan and Gordon Rayner, "Jersey Police Chief Suspended as Claims of Child Murders 'Ripped up,'" *The Telegraph*, November 12, 2008.

[738] Ian Cobain, "Jersey Abuse Inquiry: Remains of five Children Found, Police Reveal - but Murder Charges unlikely," *The Guardian*, August 1, 2008.

[739] "Jersey: Children were Loaned to Rich Paedophile Yachtsmen."

victims at both Haut de la Garenne as well as the Sacre Coeur orphanage run by French Catholic nuns.[740]

Two men also reported that actor Wilfrid Brambell who played "the dirty old man" on the *BBC* television series Steptoe and Son (American sitcom counterpart was Sanford and Son starring Redd Foxx) sexually molested them in a backstage room at the Jersey Opera House.[741] A notorious local pedo-procurer for visiting celebs fetched the group home victims to attend opera house performances as "a treat."[742] One was a child from the Haut de la Garenne and both were 12 and 13 years old at that time in the 1970s when Brambell in his sixties was at the height of his fame. Playing Paul McCartney's grandfather in the Beatles' Hard Day's Night, actor Brambell had a criminal record dating back to 1962 for soliciting underage boys in public restrooms. Apparently he was just playing himself as the dirty old man Albert Steptoe, dying friendless and near broke at age 72 in 1985. Both famous *BBC* entertainers were frequent island visiting pedophiles in the 70s, so chances are near 100% that Brambell and Savile knew each other. After all, the island has been a pedo-magnet since the WWII German Nazi occupation.

Renovation companies working on the Haut de la Garenne premises through the decades were always customarily instructed by orphanage staff to burn any bones they might encounter.[743] Traces of blood were discovered in the underground dungeon as well as detected in the drainage pipes. It became crystal clear that for many years children had been systematically tortured and killed in the "Jersey House of Horrors," their bodies incinerated in a large furnace in an effort to eliminate evidence. Yet with all this overwhelming incrimination corroborating well-documented firsthand accounts from nearly 200 victims, the Jersey minister was unconscionably able to shut down Graham Power's legitimate 2008 probe. Power's replacement promptly negated all earlier findings, contending that no evidence of abuse was ever found and proceeded to drag out the whitewash for another two years till December 2010 at a hefty taxpayer price tag amounting to a £20 million sham that led nowhere, like every "official" inquiry.[744]

The Jersey powers-that-shouldn't-be also harassed and effectively shut down any journalists attempting to uncover the horrific truth as well. Clearly protecting the child rapists, as soon as the Jersey authorities in September 2011 learned that respected American journalist Leah McGrath Goodman planned to write a book about the Haut de la Garenne abuse, they had her immediately deported, later detained at London's Heathrow Airport for 12 hours, in effect

---

[740] Steven Morris, "How 'House of Horror' Investigation brought Jersey Abuse to Light," *The Guardian*, July 3, 2017.
[741] Gordon Rayner and Eileen Fairweather, "Jimmy Savile: Steptoe and Son Actor Wilfrid Brambell 'Abused Boys in Jersey' Claims Whistleblower," *The Telegraph*, October 17, 2012.
[742] Stuart Syvret, "You Dirty Old Man," *Ex-Senator Stuart Syvret Blog*, July 17, 2008.
[743] "Jersey: Children were Loaned to Rich Paedophile Yachtsmen," *News of the World*.
[744] David Rose, "Bungled Jersey Child Abuse Probe Branded a '£20 Million Shambles,' Daily Mail, October 4, 2009.

under arrest while denying her right to a lawyer or notify family, subsequently banning her from returning to both the UK and Jersey.[745] It took nearly a year and a half later, a submitted petition and assistance from an MP before Leah was finally allowed back into the British Isles. Pretty pathetic, yet that's the sort of absurd extremes murderous regimes resort to when they have so much to hide.

Despite effectively quashing inquiries from both journalists and police alike, the 2008 probe did manage to take 1,776 statements from 192 alleged victims accusing 151 alleged abusers (121 of them still alive[746]), among the 30 dead Savile and Heath.[747] But because so many of the pedophiles are and were such influential wealthy figures high up in both the Jersey and London pedo-filled governments, to date only seven offenders have been successfully prosecuted.

Operation Whistle was the latest Jersey States Police investigation supposedly reexamining the historical abuse on the island,[748] including 13 famous still unnamed pedophile headliners that include celebrities, media personalities, politicians and sports stars.[749] We're still waiting on the outcome of those interested persons due for police questioning back in 2015. If like every other probe, "not enough evidence" and hence we will never hear of any of these high profile pedo-suspects, especially after the 2018 Sir Cliff Richard legal case covered in Chapter 4.

In a separate inquiry from 2014 to 2017, after compiling testimony of 200 witnesses describing 553 offenses uncovering island abuse from 1947 to 2004, another £20 million spent on the Independent Jersey Care Inquiry report was finally released after many delays in July 2017. It demanded that the Haut de la Garenne buildings be torn down and warned that children on the island even today are still at risk.[750]

Carrie Modral, the chair of the Jersey Care Leavers' Association, a charity devoted to those who've spent time in the so-called child welfare system, raised the poignant observation in October 2012, addressing why the Savile name finally resurfaced on Jersey after he died:

But why have the States of Jersey only admitted it about Savile now? Because he's dead and he can't talk or bring down all the other big names. Their view would be that we, the survivors,

---

[745] Camille Standen, "The Journalist who was Arrested for Investigating a Pedophile Orphanage," interview of Leah McGrath Goodman, *Vice*, February 27, 2013.

[746] Camille Standen, https://www.vice.com/en_us/article/xd4954/the-journalist-who-was-banned-from-investigating-jerseys-child-abuse.

[747] "Jersey: Children were Loaned to Rich Paedophile Yachtsmen."

[748] Sam Christie, https://www.thesun.co.uk/archives/news/272132/lock-up-your-daughters-jimmy-saviles-sick-warning-to-parents-as-he-visited-jersey-revealed/.

[749] "Operation Whistle," States of Jersey Police website, 2015.

[750] Lauren Fruen, "Tear It Down: Notorious Jersey Children's Home Haut de la Garenne must be Demolished as it Warns 'Kids are still at Risk,'" *The Sun*, July 3, 2017.

keep going on about celebrities abusing kids at Haut de la Garenne, so OK, 'Here's one, he's dead and he can't talk.' But Savile was just the tip of the iceberg.[751]

Never did hear about what happened to those 13 other prominent players under investigation. Will they all be dead before their names go public like Sir Jimmy's? Clearly there remains a powerful super wealthy elite group of pedophiles and complicit enablers on the island with high connections to fellow pedophiles atop the UK government and royalty that's controlled politics in the Jersey States for many generations, persecuting and destroying careers of children's advocates who've attempted to change the long-embedded culture of abuse. Courageous individuals challenging the status quo system in efforts to eradicate both the culture of abuse and its bookend twin Stuart Syvret calls "a culture of cover-up"[752] have had their reputations smeared by the government funded newspaper, were sued, gagged, terminated from jobs and even imprisoned.[753] The pedo-network at Jersey is just as alive and well as the one at Westminster, mainly because it's one and the same and its members all live above the law.

So, despite mountains of incontrovertible evidence on the infamous Jersey Island, well over 100 identified abusers are still out there roaming free, likely still abusing kids with - outside of the token seven, not a single pedophile more has been brought to justice. Of course, it's no different from America where known pedophile overlords like the Bushes, Clintons and Podestas are still on the loose, and until those British household names of top politicians, entertainers and royal princes go down in pedophilia flames, seeing is believing that anything substantial will ever change. As monstrous as the Sanduskys, Nassars, Bennells and even Saviles are, in the whole scheme of things, all are small fish within a global ocean of pedophile network sharks. The thoroughly corrupt, evil system has always been the protective buffer making the actual Luciferian kingpins behind the world's child raping machine unreachable and the sorry fact remains that not one dominant VIP pedovore from the political puppet establishment has ever been successfully prosecuted and brought to justice worldwide. And that's not even including the invisible, planet-controlling pedophiles pulling all the strings who own both this diabolical network and toxic planet.

After Savile had long become a permanent *BBC* fixture on British television throughout the 1970s and 80s, his growing circle of pedophile friends had expanded to popular soap opera stars from the *BBC* set of the longtime running series EastEnders ever since its 1985 debut.[754] In 2013 on the heels of the Savile bombshell, it was reported that the Scotland Yard Police began investigating *BBC* employees who misused their celebrity status to groom potential underage

---

[751] Eileen Fairweather, "Jimmy Savile: 'He was the Tip of the Iceberg,'" *The Telegraph*, October 19, 2012.
[752] Haroon Siddique, "Jersey Care Homs Covered up Abuse," *The Guardian*, February 26, 2008.
[753] Leah McGrath Goodman, https://www.newsweek.com/jersey-island-child-abuse-tax-shelter-uk-jimmy-savile-child-predators-rape-579698.
[754] Stephen Moyes, "EastEnders Paedo Probe," *The Sun*, March 24, 2013.

victims engaging in idol worship, seeking autographs at and around the studio. This post-Savile development uncovering an active pedophile ring systemically operating at *BBC* only further confirms that the media giant institution has been harboring a longstanding continuous history of organized child sexual abuse extending far beyond one designated ringleading monster or his handful of marginal fellow *BBC* players.

The Sun quoted an inside source in a 2013 article:

Police are shocked at what they have unearthed. Arrests are very likely. This is bigger than anyone imagined. A lot of work has been done over the last few months. Top police bosses have been shocked at what they have unearthed so far and are determined to finish the job.[755]

Again, all talk and no action, other than another silenced threat. A very suspicious *BBC* death among so many, taken up in depth in Chapter 3, is the convicted pedophile that worked as an extra on EastEnders. Due to be questioned over the *BBC* pedo-scandal involving the soap's cast and crew, he wound up dead along with his twin brother, both found asphyxiated with plastic bags over their heads in Spain.[756]

Speaking of EastEnders' derelict deaths, the latest deceased *BBC* actor - Leslie Grantham - like his *BBC* colleague Savile and former UK PM Heath - also escaped this world without arrest or prosecution for his pedophilic crimes to live out his lecherous life of 71 years.[757] But despite his TV stardom peaking in the 1980s, this guy was no stranger to police and criminal court. In 1967 while a young man serving in the British Army in Germany, Grantham was convicted of murder after shooting a taxi driver in a failed mugging attempt and did ten years of a life sentence for that serious crime. While in prison he took up acting and landed his popular role as an early EastEnders villain.

But his kinky lifestyle apparently began catching up to him again when in 2004 he was caught exposing himself on webcam in a lewd sex act.[758] It also was revealed he took drugs on the *BBC* set purchased from another *BBC* staffer, later arrested for dealing narcotics to fellow members of their *BBC* pedophile ring. Then in 2009, Grantham was accused of raping an underage girl less than 16 years old, culminating in his divorce in 2013 from his Australian actress wife, at which time the former star retreated to Bulgaria. But in recent years he developed lung cancer, and returned to Britain to die on June 15th, 2018.

---

[755] Stephen Moyes, https://www.thesun.co.uk/archives/news/612394/eastenders-paedo-probe/.

[756] Jonathon Corke, "Sick Jimmy Savile linked to five Mystery Deaths," *Daily Star*, June 29, 2014.

[757] Simon Boyle, "Last Picture Emerges of Leslie Grantham looking Frail as Dark New Claims Surface," *The Irish Sun*, June 15, 2018.

[758] Simon Boyle, https://www.thesun.ie/tvandshowbiz/tv/2720133/last-picture-emerges-of-leslie-grantham-looking-frail-as-dark-new-claims-surface/.

The former police officer behind the *ITV* Jimmy Savile Exposure documentary - Mark Williams Thomas - told the *Mirror* within hours after Grantham's death, that the actor back in 2012 as part of Yewtree was investigated over "compelling evidence" indicating Grantham repeatedly sexually abused a 14-turned 15-year old schoolgirl in 2009-10.[759] Thomas explained that after the girl contacted him "very, very scared," he informed Metro Police, but the girl eventually opted not to pursue the case.

Though that March 2013 *Sun* article claimed that pending *BBC* EastEnders arrests were pending at any time, as is so often the typical trademark of virtually every pedo-cover-up, no follow-up ever occurred on this notorious *BBC* cast and crew investigation, nor its never reported outcome in 7 years. But Leslie Grantham's death forced the *BBC* EastEnders pedophile ring once again to briefly resurface in the headlines before the story once again died. Never a follow through or any tangible results – always.

Apparently, the longstanding UK history of subservient, order-following police forces and an obedient pedo-controlled, state-owned media corporation, acting in cahoots with their higher-up handlers, have once again sealed off all information, shielding prominent pedophiles at the top as the same old, same old standard outcome in every pedophilia scandal throughout history. Despite the elite effectively burying the *BBC* pedo-scandal with Savile, in November 2012 *Esquire* editor-author Andrew O' Hagan took a longer pre-Savile view of *BBC* pedophilia in a piece published in the *London Review of Books*:

Paedophilia is an ethos and institutional disorder that's thrived in premier entertainment labyrinths.[760]

The *BBC* claimed that no pedophile ring ever existed at the corporation, concluding that Savile acted alone, claiming that other convicted *BBC* stars like Rolf Harris, Chris Denning and Stuart Hall committed their sex crimes completely independent of Sir Jimmy. Yet within seven months after the Savile bombshell broke, already 152 more allegations were made against 81 other *BBC* employees,[761] in part resulting in over 5 dozen known *BBC* pedophile convictions.[762] Of the over 80 accused, half are current *BBC* staff or contributors. If those numbers aren't indicative of a *BBC* pedophile ring cover-up, I don't know what is. On top of earlier evidence already presented, combined with these astounding statistics, all documented and publicly reported, how can any objective observer possibly conclude that Jimmy Savile sexually assaulted 1,000 victims at the *BBC* studios while operating completely alone without participating within the

[759] Tom Pettifor, "Leslie Grantham was Investigated over 'Evidence of Sexual Abuse against Girl', former Police Officer Claims," *Mirror*, June 15, 2018.

[760] Andrew O' Hagan, "Light Entertainment," *London Review of Books*, November 8, 2012.

[761] Victoria Ward and Jennifer O' Mahony, "More than 152 Allegations made at BBC in last seven months," *The Telegraph*, May 29, 2013.

[762] "BBC: Sex Offenders & Incidents Connected to the BBC," *skepticpeg.wordpress.com*, May 30, 2017.

obvious larger organized *BBC* network? Yet as the media corporation's lies of denial and cover-up continue to this day, police are still investigating *BBC* stars accused of child sex crimes, the latest announced in March 2018 for alleged sexual assault against a child under 16 in the late 1990s.[763]

The *BBC* director general from 2004 to 2012 was Mark Thompson, who began his career at the *BBC* employed as a production trainee in 1979,[764] right at the peak of prolific *BBC* abuser Savile's fame and power to harm. But just when the shit was hitting the fan bigtime at *BBC* over the October 2012 Savile pedophilia exposure, after more than three decades at the *British Broadcasting Corporation*, on November 12, 2012 Mark Thompson safely bailed for greener pastures, starting his new job as CEO of the *New York Times*.[765] After covering up crimes by Savile and the *BBC* pedophile ring committed under his watch during the previous 33 years he'd been a *BBC* rising star, he's rewarded with top job at one of the biggest newspapers in the world, no doubt to cover-up pedophilia in the US. When arriving at his first day of work in New York, Mark Thompson was asked if the pedophilia scandal exploding back home at his last workplace would impact his post at the *Times*, Thompson's arrogant, highly revealing reply:

It will not in any way affect my job.[766]

But a look back at how Mark Thompson ascended to the *BBC* throne is worth a peek. A major asset to his career has been his wife Jane Blumberg, like him an Oxford grad but also professor, writer, literary critic and daughter of super scientist Nobel Laureate, the late Dr. Baruch Blumberg, known for his pioneering work tackling Hepatitis B.[767] The year prior to Thompson's 8-year *BBC* reign, in 2003 Israel had furiously cut off all contact with the *BBC*, and Thompson's predecessor was terminated. *BBC* journalist Orla Guerin not only covered Israeli victims of the Israeli-Palestinian conflict but featured stories sympathetic to Palestinian victims as well. Yet the Israeli Government Press Office (GPO) called her on *BBC* coverage in general as "anti-Israeli," highly prejudicial reporting.[768] Mark Thompson was brought in to fix the growing tension. The highly secretive Balen report, released internally at the end of his first year in 2004, was never made public and privy only to the brand-new director general and a few of his top senior executives. Because the Balen report had found the *BBC* pro-biased favoring the Palestinians, to this day, it remains under lock and key. Hence, within months, director general

---

[763] Alex Green, BBC Radio Star 'is being Probed over Claim of Sex Offence against Child under 16,'" *Daily Mail*, March 11, 2018.

[764] "In Their Own Words," *Biased BBC*.

[765] Dominic Rushe, "Mark Thompson starts Work at New York Times as BBC Scandal Grows," *The Guardian*, November 12, 2012.

[766] Dominic Rushe, https://www.theguardian.com/media/2012/nov/12/mark-thompson-new-york-times-bbc.

[767] H. Roger Segelken, "Baruch Blumberg, who Discovered and Tackled Hepatitis B, Dies at 85, *The New York Times*, April 6, 2011.

[768] Keith Dovkants, "The Secret Report at Heart of BBC's Gaza Paranoia," *Evening Standard*, January 27, 2009.

Thompson and his Jewish wife headed off to Tel Aviv to smooth over relations with then Israeli Prime Minister Ariel Sharon, culminating with the resultant concession to boycott Gaza aid to Palestinians.

When Thompson met with war criminal Ariel Sharon in Israel in 2005,[769] pledging no longer to support Palestinian charities, as head of the British government-sponsored media corporation, that little controversy fomented criticism that he was a card-carrying Zionist. Order follower Thompson also promptly axed the fair-minded reporter Orla Guerin as *BBC* Middle East correspondent, reassigning her to Africa. And under Thompson's watch, the *BBC* has been relegated to being a mere mouthpiece for the Israeli lobby.[770] It's even been revealed that the *BBC* maintains a strict glossary of terms of euphemistic words and phrases acceptable to the Jewish State and taboo words and phrases that aren't.[771] The liberal *BBC* has a history of paranoia that its Middle Eastern coverage has been offensive to Israel and leans over backwards to placate the GPO's constant demands to alter and soften *BBC* headlines or incur more Jewish wrath.[772] In short, as with MSM and politics in the US, Israel regularly bullies and controls both its Zionist tool Mark Thompson as well as the wimpy, cabal order-following *BBC*. With spineless gatekeepers like this in charge, will truth and justice ever prevail? And with 2020's fake virus, draconian lockdown conditions worldwide, the masks, the distancing, the stay-at-home orders, people around the globe are finally reaching their limit, in the classic words of the 1976 film Network's Howard Beale:

I'm mad as hell and I'm not going to take this anymore![773]

That the exposure of the gargantuan *BBC* criminal cover-up of Savile and his *BBC* colleagues' multitude of child abuse crimes would "in no way" affect Thompson's new job at the *New York Times* is disconcerting to say the least. When word came down that Times Company owner Arthur Sulzberger Jr. picked the former *BBC* boss to be their new *NYT* boss, several veteran journalists boldly questioned whether Thompson was the right man for the job at the *New York Times*.[774] Two editors weren't going to take it anymore and quit in protest for bringing in what more than a few staffers concluded was a genuine pedophile enabler who actively covered up the dark criminal truth hounding the *BBC* for years.

Back in March 2012 director general Thompson was busily blowing smoke up his and his company's ass when he addressed the Royal Television Society in London:

[769] Richard Becker, "Serial War Criminal, Mass Murderer," *Global Research*, January 13, 2014.

[770] Robert Fiske, "Robert Fiske: How can you Trust the Cowardly BBC?" *Independent*, April 16, 2009.

[771] Keith Dovkants, https://www.standard.co.uk/news/the-secret-report-at-heart-of-bbc-s-gaza-paranoia-6870301.html.

[772] Amena Saleem, "How Israel Exerts its Influence on the BBC," *Palestine Solidarity Campaign*, November 20, 2015.

[773] Wayne Allyn Root, "I'm Mad as Hell and I'm not Going to Take This Anymore!" *townhll.com*, April 5, 2020.

[774] Yoichi Shimatsu, "Pedophile Savile Haunts the New York Times - PizzaGate 7," *Rense News*, January 3, 2017.

The modern BBC does everything possible to report on itself objectively.[775]

In view of his *BBC*'s massive pedo-cover-up, including the decision refusing to air the Savile Newsnight episode exposing Sir Jimmy just four months prior, the above statement is obviously a boldface lie. Despite being employed at *BBC* from 1979 to October 2012, and despite feeble contentions claiming he was never aware of any Savile abuse whatsoever, Mark Thompson was *BBC* director general when it canned that Newsnight exposé outing Savile in favor of two fluff pieces for Christmas 2011 shortly after the beast's death. Yet it was Thompson's successor George Entwistle who played the fall guy going down in flames less than two months after starting his new job.[776] Just as Thompson had no recall of Savile crimes during his marathon tenure at the *BBC*, when asked about the suppression of the Nightnews segment, initially he stated he had no knowledge of the program. Then realizing a flat denial might be construed as a lie, he later admitted he had "a chance meeting" about the *BBC* news program investigating the longtime *BBC* pedophile, though still hedging later when telling the *New York Times*:

I wasn't told any specific lines of inquiry and certainly not anything related to the BBC.[777]

Hard to fathom how the director general didn't even bother inquiring further about the nature of the Newsnight investigation when he first encountered *BBC* journalist Caroline Hawley at a holiday party in December 2011 telling him he must be worried about the Newsnight Savile story. Thompson maintains he told Caroline he was unaware of the Newsnight investigation. The next day he allegedly conferred with his senior management including head of *BBC* news Helen Boaden. Meanwhile, journalist Caroline Hawley asserts that she did explain to her boss that the Savile investigation was about child sexual abuse, directly contradicting Thompson's claim.[778] When pressed on why he allegedly failed to ask why Savile was being investigated by his own news team, he feebly responded:

You can say it's a lack of imagination.[779]

After coyly playing mindfuck games, in a letter from Thompson in New York in January 2013 addressed to Parliament, he unequivocally insisted that neither the Hawley nor the Boaden conversation:

...told me what the investigation had been about.[780]

---

[775] Matthew Purdy, "As Scandal Flared, BBC's Leaders Missed Red Flags," *The New York Times*, November 4, 2012.
[776] Christopher Hope and Gordon Rayner, "Jimmy Savile: BBC Scrapped Investigation after Newsnight came 'under Pressure' from Senior Managers," *The Telegraph*, October 21, 2012.
[777] Dominic Rushe, https://www.theguardian.com/media/2012/nov/12/mark-thompson-new-york-times-bbc.
[778] Mark Sweny and Adam Gabbatt, "Mark Thompson did not know Jimmy Savile was a 'Pressing Concern,'" *The Guardian*, October 24, 2012.
[779] Sam Marsden, "Jimmy Savile: Mark Thompson Admits 'lack of Imagination' over Newsnight Report," *The Telegraph*, November 5, 2012..

It's preposterous to actually believe Thompson was so blasé faire about the *BBC* Savile exposé that he "lacked imagination" to bother inquiring any further. Deceitfully playing dumb to save his own sorry ass, so he could successfully escape to New York, unscathed by all the messy flak that was his doing, subsequently unfairly dumped on his successor so he take over the *New York Times* free and clear only shows once again that Mark Thompson is a spineless worm, sheltered away just in time so he and his career could be rescued and protected by his pedo-cabal masters. In the words of the always inimitably incisive journalist Yoichi Shimatsu:

By hiring a bald-faced liar rather than a journalist of integrity, Sulzberger risked his own reputation against strong objections from veteran editors who understood the ethical liability of having a new boss who's in league with elite pedophile networks.[781]

In his rash of interviews at the time, the easily flustered and flighty Mark Thompson bounced shamelessly all over the landscape, scrambling to cover his own ass with what he claimed to not know, playing it unscrupulously safe and cagey, later backtracking to cover what he thought he'd said, granting himself just enough plausibility of denial to survive on his fresh feet in New York if and when his deception ever came back to bite him in his CYA ass:

That I might have formed the impression at the time of my conversations with Caroline and Helen that the investigation related to allegations of sexual abuse, this was speculation on my part in October 2012 about an impression I might or might not have formed after a pair of brief conversations nearly a year earlier.[782]

Incidentally, in addition to his "unimaginative" nature, (after all, by definition, order followers are always unimaginative, especially when struggling to express a thought of their own), before making his "great escape," also on record while still director general, his office was warned two more times in May and September 2012 about sexual predator Savile. But no doubt "unimaginative" Thompson deemed it too "irrelevant" as he wimpily sought his getaway transition to the *New York Times*.[783]

Also in September 2012, the London *Sunday Times Magazine* posed a series of probing questions to Thompson attempting to ascertain how much he knew and when.[784] On September 6 a letter from his lawyers outside the *BBC* legal department was sent aggressively threatening the *Sunday Times* with a libelous lawsuit should it even remotely suggest that Thompson and his *BBC* ever engaged in a cover-up. Clueless Thompson once again claimed he

---

[780] Maureen Orth, "The BBC Blame Game," *Vanity Fair*, February 15, 2013.
[781] Yoichi Shimatsu, https://rense.com/general96/savileNYT.htm.
[782] Maureen Orth, https://www.vanityfair.com/news/2013/02/bbc-chief-mark-thompson-jimmy-savile-scandal.
[783] Arthur Martin, "Former BBC Chief Mark Thompson's Office 'had Two Alerts about Savile Child Abuse Claims,'" *Daily Mail*, October 28, 2012.
[784] Maureen Orth, https://www.vanityfair.com/news/2013/02/bbc-chief-mark-thompson-jimmy-savile-scandal.

never even read the letter but a legal observer claimed if that's true, Thompson is "just as culpable." Of course, that same merry month of September was also when the New York Times Company was actively courting the pedo-enabler to fly the British coop for the *NYT* henhouse just in time to avoid the heat called accountability. And two months later, he fled.

When successor George Entwistle also came up with the same lame identical excuse, also claiming ignorance that he too was never responsible for canceling the Newsnight segment and did not even know the nature of the program, also refuted by others, back in London his lie didn't quite wash. With MPs hounding him at parliamentary hearings, a floundering Entwistle attempted in vain to pin the sole blame on Nightnews editor Peter Rippon, who apparently agreed to fall on the sword for his company, despite merely following his orders from above to cancel the broadcast.[785] Rippon was the first one fired. But as more deception plainly unfolded, somebody high up on the *BBC* food chain also had to pay the price and since Thompson had already been given his free pass to take flight, it had to be his successor.

When queried on this volatile issue in early November 2012, during his final week in the UK at an Oxford University lecture, Thompson was still playing his "ignorance is bliss" card:

Like many other people at the BBC and despite what you may have read, I had heard none of the stories about Jimmy Savile.[786]

Even when Thompson's extremely questionable word is taken at face value, he was the head honcho, the leader of a giant government funded news organization partially paid for by British citizens that's supposed to project an accurate account of what goes on in the world, much less his own company. Any decent leader or director general makes it his job and responsibility to know if criminal activity is being carried out or covered up under his or her watch. When it comes to facing the dark truth about one's corporation, oneself, or an infamous past company icon, it always was met with gross *BBC* failures to repeatedly report the truth when opportunities availed themselves before Savile's death, right after his death and far beyond to this very day. As the leader of the *BBC*, Thompson chose to consistently lie through his teeth to save his own skin. And with that kind of lame and weak leadership at the helm of *The New York Times* for almost a decade now until his late July 2020 departure,[787] of course he would be the cabal controllers' ideal choice as deliverer of fake news loyal to concealing the global pedophilia network.

---

[785] Lisa O' Carroll, "BBC Chief: Newsnight's Jimmy Savile Investigation should have Continued," *The Guardian*, October 23, 2012.

[786] Dominic Rushe, https://www.theguardian.com/media/2012/nov/12/mark-thompson-new-york-times-bbc.

[787] Jim Waterson, "Mark Thompson Steps Down as Chief Executive of New York Times," *The Guardian,* July 22, 2020.

Both Thompson and other senior *BBC* personnel chose to continue lying, pretending not to know that Savile and other *BBC* staff were committing the most egregious crimes against children decade after decade after decade. The Corporation's across-the-boards deception never ceased, culminating when they all lied about why they scrapped the Savile exposé pretending it was strictly for "editorial reasons."[788] Right to the end while director general Thompson was in charge, he and his management willfully buried the truth dug up by their own enterprisingly competent, brave journalists, then despicably hung them out to dry,[789] choosing to this day to continue living the *BBC* trademark lie.

Nine months after Mark Thompson began his new gig in New York, believing he'd finally shucked his shady past association with his *BBC* pedophile network, outside his luxury Manhattan apartment he was confronted by a Channel 4 news crew asking him about his part in the Jimmy Savile scandal and how much he knew that the Nightnews exposé was about child sex abuse. Because the CEO had already been outed as a liar trying to deny what it was about, apparently Thompson really lost his cool right then and there on the street with the camera rolling. A witness told the *New York Post*:

He was tense and angry and was talking very loudly. They followed him around the corner and he lost his temper and shouted at them. It really caused a scene.[790]

An honest man in his position would be far less apt to have a public meltdown especially with a camera rolling if he had nothing to hide. But a proven liar that can't escape his deceitful past certainly would.

Just as an organization's leadership can take credit for its accomplishments during the good times, during the rough times when losses, failures or scandals arise, a company's leader must also take responsibility for that too, even if not directly involved. But instead Thompson deceitfully played his constant denial card, slithered out of town just ahead of avoiding the runaway train wreck, only to seek safe refuge across the pond, rescued and rewarded $5 million during his first year alone,[791] working at another pedophile enabling media giant where he insists the enormous scandal exploding back home that he was in charge of will not affect him in the least at his new post. That has to be foreboding to any news organization with

[788] "Newsnight Investigation into Jimmy Savile was actually Shelved 'because it Clashed with Christmas Tributes to the Presenter,'" *Daily Mail*, October 19, 2012.

[789] Jasp Jackson, "BBC Forced out Team behind Savile Exposé, says ex-Newsnight Journalist," *The Guardian*, July 29, 2015.

[790] Tom Leonard, "Former BBC Director General 'involved in Angry Exchange outside Home with Channel 4 Crew who asked him about Savile Scandal,'" *Daily News*, August 11, 2013.

[791] Arthur Martin, http://www.dailymail.co.uk/news/article-2224236/Jimmy-Savile-rumours-Mark-Thompsons-BBC-office-TWO-alerts-child-abuse-claims.html.

integrity. But outside several ethical public protests and resignations, the *New York Times* demonstrated its lack of integrity.

And lo and behold, it didn't affect Thompson's *NYT* job performance at all. In the fall of 2016 in the lead-up to the November Trump election, WikiLeaks published Podesta emails online,[792] using a coded language commonly used by pedophiles per FBI documentation referring to sex with children,[793] incriminating the Podesta brothers as well as the Clintons and Obama as well.[794] Of course as previous Lolita Express frequent fliers, Bill and Hillary were already outed as pedophiles at Epstein's Orgy Island with incontrovertibly incriminating evidence reportedly in NYPD possession, stored inside convicted fellow pedophile Weiner's confiscated laptop.[795]

Thompson's *New York Times* along with all four other oligarch owned giant media conglomerates (down from 50 in 1983[796]) pumping out over 90% of the news propaganda frantically jumped to the immediate defense of one implicated pizza parlor owner, somehow ranked 49th on *GQ*'s DC VIP power list.[797] So when MSM called the ever-louder internet buzz actually exposing Pizzagate's Washington pedophile ring[798] on Reddit (soon shut down) "fake news,"[799] claiming it was inciting violence (i.e., enter the "lone gunman" stooge firing off a couple rounds inside pizza joint),[800] it became the perfectly contrived excuse to roll out the elite's oppressive agenda to crush 1st Amendment free press rights with McCarthy-esque blacklisted news sites to "justify" legislating increased censorship usurping internet control so that the mainstream fake news ultimately ends up the only news in town (or world for that matter).[801] Every totalitarian regime in history permits only state run propaganda (like the Soviet gulag era or perhaps *BBC* today) and, minus the internet, that's virtually where we're already at... less than a handful of major news outlets all reading off the same false narrative script. Welcome to today's Orwellian nightmare.

For once, Mark Thompson was true to his word, at the *NYT* he's been the same pedophile enabler engaging in pedophilia cover-up that he was at the *BBC*, continuing to pretend that top

---

[792] "The Podesta Emails," *WikiLeaks*.

[793] "FBI Pedophile Symbols," *WikiLeaks*.

[794] "John Podesta - #PizzaGate - Child Sex Trafficking - Satanic Occultism - The Deep State's Use of Pedophilia as a Means of Compromising Individuals and Controlling them," *kundaliniandcelltowers.com.*.

[795] Joachim Hagopian, "Breaking Sex Scandal from Weiner's Laptop may be the Smoking Gun that will bring down the Clintons for good," sott.net, November 4, 2016.

[796] Eric Sommer, "How Five American Companies Control what you Think," *RT*, May 14, 2014.

[797] Reid Cherlin, Rob Fischer, Jason Zengerle and Jason Horowitz, "The 50 Most Powerful People in Washington," *GQ*, January 18, 2012.

[798] Joachim Hagopian, "Pizzagate: Podesta Pedo Perps and Clinton's International Child Sex Trafficking Ring Exposed, *sott.net*, December 2, 2016.

[799] "'Pizzagate' shows how Fake News Hurts real People," *The Washington Post*, November 25, 2016.

[800] Joachim Hagopian, "Was the Pizzagate almost-Shooting a Deep State False Flag? If not, it sure was Conveniently Used to further Demonize Alt Media and 'Fake News,'" *sott.net*, December 6, 2016.

[801] Joachim Hagopian, "Deep State's Final Solution: The Death of Alternative News," *sott.net*, December 12, 2016.

echelons of government, the media, entertainment, the legal and economic system, charity and child welfare are not running a globalized pedophilia network. Thompson was the cherry-picked sentinel guarding the elite's pedophile henhouse, rescued from one cover-up scam in UK with valued cover-up experience evading that pedo-scandal to be tactically redeployed to do the same in the US. Remember that in the Luciferian world, the more deception and evil one commits, the more one is rewarded by the earthly powers-that-should-not-be.[802]

The ruling elite controlling this planet are largely comprised of pedophiles and pedophile enablers. Following the money explains why the world's deepest pockets are invariably linked to so much war, illegal trafficking of weapons, drugs, human organs, children and laundered trillions. Illuminati bloodline families like the Houses of Windsor and Rothschild are notoriously in deep in all of these most sordid criminal activities.

Meet the only non-executive director of the *BBC*'s new executive board – the Barclay Bank chairman until 2012 and current British Bankers Association head Marcus Agius, married to Edmond de Rothschild's daughter Katherine.[803] Barclays Bank is the most important shareholder in the NM Rothschild bank as well as the Lazard Brothers. Agius is also on the steering committee of the Bilderberg Group and on the advisory board of the City of London, where the queen's Rothschild money is secured. With his extended Illuminati family sharing connections to the Knights of Malta, the Jesuits Catholic Maltese lineage paternally and Jewish Cabbalist roots maternally, as *BBC*'s first non-executive director until 2012,[804] Marcus Agius was the Rothschild fixture controlling the *BBC* and all its director general pawns like Mark Thompson to ensure the pedo-web is covered-up and only nice things get said about Israel.[805]

Incidentally, in early 2012 when the crumbling cracks of the *BBC* scandal were rapidly spreading, Agius was caught fixing derivative rates in a separate fiasco of his own making called the Libor fixed rate scandal that led to his Barclays resignation.[806] Hypocrite *BBC* publishes a headline "Libor Scandal: Can we ever Trust Bankers Again?" while Agius was senior non-executive director on the *BBC* executive board.[807] The article actually quotes Agius who greedily violated the law but was never arrested. Yet to hear it from him, he was the long-suffering victim in all his pretentious moral outrage… unbelievable:

---

[802] Phillip D. Collins, "Luciferianism: The Religion of Apotheosis," *Conspiracy Archive*, January 10, 2006.
[803] Gearóid Ó Colmáin, "Rothschild's Slaughterships," *Dissident Voice*, January 24, 2016.
[804] "BBC Appoints its First Non-Executive Director," *BBC*, November 16, 2006.
[805] Yoichi Shimatsu, https://rense.com/general96/savileNYT.htm.
[806] Jill Treanor, "Barclays Scandal Forces out Chairman Marcus Agius," *The Guardian*, July 1, 2012.
[807] "Libor Scandal: Can we ever Trust Bankers again?" *BBC*, May 8, 2013.

I was sick to my stomach because I realised just what an appalling thing it was and I realised what a serious implication it would have for the bank[808].

A more apropos question is can we ever trust Agius or the *BBC* again, because based on their histories, the answer for both would be a definite no, never. After all, they not only represent the cabal, they are the cabal.

Speaking of untrustworthy and also unprosecuted, along with Agius, JP Morgan-Citibank's Jamie Dimon was also among the biggest Libor violating crooks but paid a $13 billion bribery fine to buy off his criminal probe.[809] As a tight-knit crony of both Obama and Rahm Emanuel, Rahm fixed JP Morgan's $16 billion bailout at taxpayer expense during the Wall Street 2008 housing bubble crisis. Compliments of Agius and Barclays "advisor" Jeb Bush, Lehman Brothers was taken over by Barclays Bank assisted by another $8.5 million US tax dollars padding the Barclays coffers.[810] Of course just like the Americans' near $29 billion bailout, the UK government had British taxpayers coughing up a staggering £850bn in its boondoggle bank bailout.[811]

You see where all this is going? With total impunity, a predatory inner less-than-human clique of pedo-vampires and cannibals get to both literally and financially feast off the lifeblood of humanity and our children. And it goes without saying that Mark Thompson and Marcus Agius as two powerful cabal agents serving their bloodline masters are in very tight with one another, not only sharing similar first names and prominent Jewish wives, but both are also Jesuit trained Catholics, thus in boldface connection with every demonic pedo-dot conceivable.[812] See why the cabal saved Thompson's ass from the *BBC* shitstorm?

The *BBC* rot at the top only continued with its Trust chairman Lord Chris Patten from 2011-2014. The former Conservative MP and minister in the pedo-saturated Thatcher cabinet threw his *BBC* line managers under the bus, describing their behavior amidst the Savile crisis as "frantic faffing about," claiming they misled him, thus strategically absolving himself of bearing any responsibility despite being Trust chairman since May 2011, a half year before Savile's death and a full 16 months ahead of the Savile fallout.[813]

The tax paid £3M Pollard report investigated the reasons why the Newsnight segment exposing Savile right after his death was pulled by *BBC* management (that Agius, Patten and Thompson

[808] "Libor Scandal: Can we ever Trust Bankers again?" https://www.bbc.com/news/business-22382932.
[809] Blair Erickson, "How is a Corrupt Criminal like Jamie Dimon, not in Prison for Fraud?" *Medium*, September 13, 2017.
[810] Christopher Bollyn, "Jeb Bush's Zionist Paymasters: Bloomberg and Rothschild," *bollyn.com*, July 8, 2015.
[811] Andrew Grice, "850bn: Official Cost of the Bank Bailout," *Independent*, December 4, 2009.
[812] Yoichi Shimatsu, https://rense.com/general96/savileNYT.htm.
[813] Peter Oborne, "The BBC rot starts at the top, with the elusive Lord Patten," *The Telegraph*, February 23, 2013.

all headed) from its December 2011 airing in favor of a pair of already planned holiday Savile tributes.[814] But the Pollard report was also a whitewash refusing to get to the bottom of who actually pulled the plug pretending it was for bogus editorial reasons when it clearly was not. Instead of revealing the truth, the Pollard report bogusly concluded the decision not to run the story was made "in good faith" and that no evidence indicated that *BBC* management attempted to suppress the story.[815] Rack up another VIP CYA LIE. Every inquiry into every scandal is a vehicle used to let the guilty off the hook while condescendingly pacifying the public.

But in a secretly taped phone conversation with former *Sky News* executive Nick Pollard who headed the inquiry, journalist Miles Goslett was told by Pollard that he purposely omitted evidence in his report protecting Mark Thompson.[816] What Pollard conveniently left out was the smoking gun, that *BBC* news director Helen Boaden in a phone conversation with Thompson in December 2011, 10 full months before Thompson's *BBC* resignation, Boaden explicitly informed the director general that the Newsnight piece exposed Jimmy Savile's longtime child sex abuse. Thus, in order to protect pedo-enabler Thompson, the Pollard report left out confirmation that golden boy kept lying to escape punishment to secure his CEO status at *The New York Times*, more evidence that the VIP pedo-club protects its own.

When Trust chairman Lord Chris Patten was informed by Pollard that he'd left out the smoking gun against Thompson from his report, Patten proceeded to dismiss it, hedging and even deceiving Parliament, still protecting Thompson and the BBC cover-up.[817] So taxpayers paid £3M for both Patten and Pollard to both withhold crucially incriminating evidence against Thompson and the *BBC*. As Miles Goslett put it:

If the BBC were an honest organisation, it would by now have insisted at the least that the Pollard report be amended accordingly. Until it does so, the cover-up continues.[818]

And predictably, to this very day the *BBC* cover-up continues.

With both the two top leaders of the *BBC* cover-up - Mark Thompson and Lord Patten - remaining unscathed from leading the biggest scandal in *BBC*'s history, Patten's appointed

---

[814] Miles Goslett, "My Bombshell Secret Tape... and a Cynical Cover-up by the Ducking and Diving BBC: Withering Broadside by Writer who Exposed Fatal Flaw in Savile Report," *Daily Mail*, December 15, 2013.

[815] Maureen Orth, https://www.vanityfair.com/news/2013/02/bbc-chief-mark-thompson-jimmy-savile-scandal.

[816] Miles Goslett, http://www.dailymail.co.uk/news/article-2523950/My-bombshell-secret-tape--cynical-cover-ducking-diving-BBC-Withering-broadside-writer-exposed-fatal-flaw-Savile-report.html.

[817] Miles Goslett, http://www.dailymail.co.uk/news/article-2523950/My-bombshell-secret-tape--cynical-cover-ducking-diving-BBC-Withering-broadside-writer-exposed-fatal-flaw-Savile-report.html.

[818] Miles Goslett, http://www.dailymail.co.uk/news/article-2523950/My-bombshell-secret-tape--cynical-cover-ducking-diving-BBC-Withering-broadside-writer-exposed-fatal-flaw-Savile-report.html.

director general and Thompson's successor, George Entwistle was forced to resign after only 54 days, though as chosen fall guy grossly overcompensated with an inflated severance package twice the amount specified in his contract at over £450,000.[819] Using taxpayer money to lavishly enrich outgoing senior management with overly generous parting gifts amidst *BBC* crisis cuts reflects the corporation's years of unchanged culture of greed. Throughout his 8 year run as director general, elitist Mark Thompson notoriously demonstrated total disregard for British taxpayers, again seriously undermining public trust by greedily signing off on excessive senior executive severances, bilking *BBC* license payers out of upwards of £369million, while flagrantly violating charter rules.[820] Thompson was the *BBC* director general during the first six years of an eight year National Audit Office review released in July 2013 specifying that ungodly £369million amount that might even be considered hush money payoffs. When you run with the ruling elite, as Thompson has for decades, you get used to living so high off the backs of the common people, all the while assured lifetime criminal protection from above.

While Patten's *BBC* Trust website vowed openness and transparency, the Lord's obscene severance packages were buried in lies and secrecy as was the creation of a new position never advertised in open competition that Patten filled with a former cabinet minister as a standardized cronyism appointment.[821]

After the likes of Mark Thompson and Lord Patten's gross mishandling of the Savile crisis, the UK government forced the *BBC* to make some fundamental changes in its governing structure.[822] After Patten stepped down for alleged health reasons in 2014, Prime Minister Cameron brought in *BBC*'s first woman to chair the Trust. Rona Fairhead was an overt ploy to distance the *BBC* from its scandalous, male-dominated, sexist past.[823] Though Cameron expected Fairhead to head the Trust over the next four years until 2018 during its restructuring into a unitary board that took over in April 2017, in September 2016 new Prime Minister Theresa May gave her fellow high-achieving female the heave-ho, selecting former Bank of England deputy governor Sir David Clementi in January 2017 to govern the new unitary board.[824] As anti-child abuse advocate MP Tom Watson said, PM May handed the job over to the very man she appointed to create that position. You can bet that with an alumnus from England's central bank now overseeing the queen's *BBC* charter, with Rothschild son-in-law Agius out after 2012 as senior executive board director, of course another Rothschild surrogate

---

[819] Peter Oborne, https://www.telegraph.co.uk/culture/tvandradio/bbc/9889137/The-BBC-rot-starts-at-the-top-with-the-elusive-Lord-Patten.html.

[820] Alasdair Glennie and Paul Revoir, "BBC's 'Outrageous Disregard' for the Licence Payers' Cash: Staff were handed £369m in Payoff Deals while TV Bosses Broke their own Rules says Watchdog," *Daily Mail*, July 1, 2013.

[821] Peter Oborne, https://www.telegraph.co.uk/culture/tvandradio/bbc/9889137/The-BBC-rot-starts-at-the-top-with-the-elusive-Lord-Patten.html.

[822] Yoichi Shimatsu, https://rense.com/general96/savileNYT.htm.

[823] "BBC Trust Chair Fiona Fairhead to Stand Down," *BBC*, September 14, 2016.

[824] Patrick Foster, "Sir David Clementi to Become new BBC Chairman," *The Telegraph*, January 10, 2017.

had to urgently fill the empty void making certain that *BBC* British government airwaves remain under firm Rothschild Zionist control.[825]

In summary, every single one of the dozens of so-called investigations associated with each and every pedophilia scandal covered throughout this book, including the plethora mushrooming from the Savile legacy alone, all amount to nothing more than just another systemic cover-up scam after the next. Infiltrating secret society cannibals atop this demonic food chain from government, security services, police, judges and the mainstream media acting as order-following gatekeepers guarding their satanic pedo-network never failing to always subvert justice, shut down police probes, lose incriminating evidence and otherwise conceal the truth, in order to ensure that their strings attached puppet masters controlling and protecting them are able to continue at will raping and cannibalizing children without fear of further exposure or consequence. That way every scandal to date - bar none - stays only tip-of-the-iceberg and the world's most powerful child sodomizers and murderers continue unimpeded and uninterrupted in their wholesale slaughter of our innocents on an unprecedented, massively globalized industrial scale.

The bottom line for these bottom feeding subhuman predators' very survival is that the cabal owning monsters must in turn feed their Luciferian masters – the demonic interdimensional forces summoned and released in satanic occult ritual that drive and possess the cabal pedovores to do their catastrophic bidding on the devil's earthly dominion, destroying what's left of our only planet we humans call home. We must fight the evil with the light of truth as our guide bringing justice, peace and planetary harmony.

The next Chapter 3 unveils Jimmy Savile as a satanic wizard and death cult practitioner, circulating as fluidly with royalty and prime ministers as Britain's most heinous serial killers in history and dead corpses, followed by Chapter 4 depicting how the *BBC*, British Establishment and their useful idiot stooge Sir Jimmy have gone to extreme criminal lengths to ensure that the cabal's pedophilia network avoids exposure. By historically ignoring or smearing victims, whistleblowers and muckraking journalists, and if need be, silencing perceived threats by numerous staged suicides, bizarrely suspicious "accidents" and both covert and overt assassination of more than a dozen *BBC* employees, they likely all paid the price for simply knowing too much. The powers-that-shouldn't be resort to no limits in order to prevent the ugly truth from ever coming to light that might threaten to bring down their international pedo-crime cabal.

---

[825] "Who Owns the Bank of England?" *tapnewswire.com*, February 27, 2010.

Chapter 3: Jimmy Savile - Occult Death Cult Practitioner of Satanic Ritual Abuse, Necrophiliac & Best Friend of Britain's Deadliest Serial Killers

Aside from a 1972 sensationalized book on pornography that two-time cabinet minister in the Harold Wilson government Lord Frank Longford authored, based on a just completed fact-finding mission with Jimmy Savile and Cliff Richard,[826] Lord Longford and Sir Jimmy also held in common another strange, obsessive fascination - their creepily close friendships with arguably British history's worst serial killers - Myra Hindley and her partner in crime Ian Brady.[827] Savile's close ties with Brady dating back to their killing spree were kept mostly on the low while Longford's public friendship with Hindley, once she was behind bars, included his "humanitarian" efforts to rescue her from state bondage that backfired with growing negative media coverage on both Longford and Hindley.[828] Unwittingly, Lord Longford singlehandedly torpedoed Myra Hindley's hope for parole, not that the coldblooded killer deserved it.

But revealed in 2017, back in 1985 accused but unprosecuted pedophile Leon Brittan, serving as Home Secretary in Margaret Thatcher's pedo-saturated government, approved the pedophilic serial killing duo's possible prison release as early as 1995 for Hindley and 2005 for Brady.[829] Looks like having so many pedophile friends in high places nearly paid off.

For over a half century the entire British nation has been fixated on the horror of how a young couple in Myra Hindley and boyfriend Ian Brady (who died in August 2017) carried out with such diabolical pleasure and bloodlust, the brutally sick Moors murders involving sexual assault, torture and death, mostly by strangling of at least two girls and three boys aged 10 to 17 between 1963 and 1965.[830] Through a recovered letter to a journalist, it's come to light that Brady boasted of killing five more children, and further research has uncovered the names of a total of seven additional victims tallying a dozen murders.[831] One of their victims, a little 10-year old desperately screaming for her mother, was stripped naked by Hindley while Brady took at least 9 photos of their traumatized defenseless naked prey, all the while tape recording her

---

[826] "Cliff Richard, Jimmy Savile, Myra Hindley" *aangirfan.com*, September 21, 2015.

[827] Tom Evans, "Moors murders: Jimmy Savile part of 'paedo ring with Ian Brady and Myra Hindley,'" *Daily Star*, September 21, 2017.

[828] Duncan Staff, "Dangerous Liaison," *The Guardian*, October 14, 2006.

[829] Tom Evans, "Revealed: Secret Government Plans to Release Moors Murderers Ian Brady and Myra Hindley," *Daily Star*, July 20, 2017.

[830] Cliodhna Russell, "The Stories of the Five Children Tortured and Murdered by Ian Brady and Myra Hindley," *The Journal*, May 20, 2017.

[831] David Trayner, "Ian Brady and Myra Hindley 'Killed Seven more — and these are their names,'" *Daily Star*, June 12, 2017.

last few minutes alive that was later replayed at their trial.[832] It was Lord Longford's friend Jimmy Savile who already knew and had bought Brady's child porn photos of young children that likely included their victims even prior to the serial killers' 1965 arrest.[833]

Yet leave it to devout Catholic Lord Longford to use his powerful contacts in government and high courts to tirelessly advocate for coldblooded Myra's prison release during the final 35 years of his life till death do him part in 2001 at age 95.[834] Their bizarre friendship is now the portrayed subject matter in a Golden Globe winning 2018 released film entitled "Longford."[835]

Lord Longford began collaborating with yet another powerful figure - journalist and *Observer* editor Lord David Astor (yep, from one of the world's most famous, wealthiest Illuminati bloodline families[836]) also an avid Myra Hindley freedom fighter. For 20 years Lord Astor and Hindley exchanged letters, and both lords conferred on strategizing ways to help the child killing satanic witch be set free.[837] Her sidekick Brady was the occult alchemist tied to Savile occult rituals at the Moors.[838] Why would two prominent Oxford grad Lords Longford and Astor, the upper crust of upper crust, take up such an unholy cause on behalf of what the press was calling "the most evil woman in Britain?" Like attracts like, that's why. Despite this odd disparity, the media simply passes it off as two misguided liberals in their senior years seeking redemption through saving one lost soul... hardly. Bottom line, these two serial killers and their beloved, famous, respected friends all likely belonged to the elites' not-so-secret crime cabal network.

As their loyal friend and supporter, Savile visited each murderer in prison and played songs on his radio show encoded in dedicated message as part of a secret occult system that the three utilized to communicate. A longtime Moors murder investigator has concluded that Brady and Hindley were part of Jimmy Savile's child sex ring.[839] When Savile was asked publicly about the Moors murders, his outlandishly truthful reply was, "I am the Myra Hindley story."

As another indicator Myra had friends in high places, her story took a bizarre twist in November 2002, when she likely did not die at age 60 as the media reported. Within a day or two of her so-called death, Myra Hindley was spotted and identified by a school nurse after Hindley's car

---

[832] Alan Keightly, "'If I said what she really did, she wouldn't get out of Prison in 100 years': Gloating over their Victim's Grave, the Picture Ian Brady said Proves Myra Hindley enjoyed Killing just as much as him," *Daily Mail*, May 17, 2017.

[833] Tom Evans, https://www.dailystar.co.uk/news/latest-news/624549/Moors-murders-Jimmy-Savile-Ian-Brady-Myra-Hindley-paedophile-child-killers-Saddleworth-BBC.

[834] Duncan Staff, https://www.theguardian.com/uk/2006/oct/14/ukcrime.weekend7.

[835] "Longford: Official Trailer," YouTube video, 01:47, posted July 20, 2018.

[836] Fritz Springmeier, *13 Bloodlines of the Illuminati*, (Ambassador House, 1998), "The Astor Bloodline," *bibliotecapleyades.net*.

[837] Robert McCrum, "Myra Hindley and David Astor: a Complex Relationship Revealed in Letters," *The Guardian*, October 28, 2012.

[838] Tom Evans, "Myra Hindley Exposed as a 'Practising Witch' whose Occult Links lead to Jimmy Savile," *Daily Star*, July 30, 2017.

[839] Tom Evans, https://www.dailystar.co.uk/news/latest-news/624549/Moors-murders-Jimmy-Savile-Ian-Brady-Myra-Hindley-paedophile-child-killers-Saddleworth-BBC.

accidentally bumped into hers.[840] When the nurse exclaimed, "You're Myra Hindley," the woman responded, "You can't say that! You can't say that!" and jumped back in her car and speedily drove off. Jotting down her license plate number, when the nurse reported the incident to the police, they told her to withdraw her accident report and that it if she knew what was best, it never happened. She went to the local paper and spoke to a journalist who then contacted Lord Longford's son who also alluded that Myra was still very much alive. No death certificate was ever published and her body was apparently "rushed" to cremation. Then location of her supposed "unknown" ashes several months later was reportedly "found" in - of all places - Saddleworth Moor where all her victims were buried.

Also the same year 2013 was when the Moor was implicated as a longtime satanic site where young boys and girls were ritualistically sacrificed and snuff films were recorded for secret distribution to wealthy Luciferian clientele.[841] Hindley and Brady were part of the earlier cult that was part of the larger satanic pedophile operation that Jimmy Savile, MP Cyril Smith and other British VIPs belonged to, which explains why the pedo-cabal might fake Hindley's death and assist her in assuming a new identity.

Evidence has also emerged that Jimmy Savile was well read in Aleister Crowley's Thelema philosophy that became the cornerstone of Crowley's sex cult OTO. Myra the witch, Ian the alchemist and Sir Jimmy the wizard are believed to have participated in black occult rituals together on Saddleworth Moor, the satanic location where most of their murders occurred and bodies lay buried.[842]

Back in the early 1970s Janie Jones was a singer who ran sex party orgies for *BBC* DJs and executives out of her home with schoolgirl dressed prostitutes supplied by record companies as bribes to entice DJs to play their records over the *BBC* airwaves, caught up in the "payola scandal."[843] The police investigation in an early *BBC* scandal in 1971 must have turned up some pretty explosive incrimination against Savile and others at the *BBC* because the investigative findings have been sealed for 50 years. With 49 years down and only one left to go, a few months away await more dirt on filthy Savile and his filthy *BBC*.

As part of that payola fiasco, in 1974 Janie Jones was arrested for controlling prostitutes and perverting justice, serving three years in prison where she met Myra Hindley and became another member of her twisted flock of devoted supporters.[844] Upon Janie's release, an angry Jimmy Savile demanded a meeting with her to chastise her favoring Myra over his boy Ian. Lord Longford, Lord Astor and Janie Jones and others were taken in by Myra's false contentions that

[840] "Spot the Paedo Child Killers and Myra Hindle is still Alive?" *spidercatweb.blog*, February 20, 2016.

[841] Andrew Dilks, "Satanic Paedophile Rings Linked to Government? Jim'll 666 it for you," *disinfo.com*, January 23, 2013.

[842] Jan Colley and Cathy Gordon, "Twisted Child Killer Ian Brady wanted Classical Music Piece 'full of Witches, Sorcerers and Monsters' at his Funeral," *Mirror*, October 13, 2017..

[843] Robert Mendick and Laura Donnelly, https://www.telegraph.co.uk/news/uknews/crime/jimmy-savile/9623109/Jimmy-Savile-Secret-of-BBCs-first-sex-scandal.html.

[844] Robert Mendick and Laura Donnelly, https://www.telegraph.co.uk/news/uknews/crime/jimmy-savile/9623109/Jimmy-Savile-Secret-of-BBCs-first-sex-scandal.html.

she inadvertently fell under Ian's demonic spell to blame him in her bid for freedom,[845] and Savile, who personally knew both serial murderers, realized Myra was just as wickedly guilty and evil, if not more than her boyfriend. But as a misogynist, Savile always favored friendships with male serial killers over female killers. But his bizarre response "I am the Myra Hindley story," suggests that Myra and Jimmy share the same "deep cover" capacity pretending to be someone they're not, hiding their dark occult powers as the wicked witch and wicked wizard. After carrying on about 13-year old girls actually "wanting" it in Savile's warped need to justify his raping young girls, Jones said that Savile then went into "bragging that he knew Ian Brady well" and that it was he who deserved her respect and favor.[846]

Yet more satanic linkage to Savile and his ties to the Moors has also surfaced. A man described as a High Priest of Satan named Michael Horgan regularly organized satanic ceremonies at Saddleworth Moor, where children 2 to 13 years of age were drugged, ritually tortured, sexually abused and sacrificed in the same satanic pedo-ring connected to Savile, Brady and Hindley.[847] Again, the ceremonial ritual abuse was often filmed for snuff distribution. Eventually Horgan was jailed in 1992 for 10 years. His own stepson, Michael Roberts, recounted the painful trauma that Michael Horgan sadistically put him through, recalling his molestation at the pudgy, filthy fingers of prominent MP pedophile fat boy himself - Sir Cyril Smith who was friends with Horgan, Savile and a bevy of other pedo-linked powerbrokers. Lots more on this obese, queen-knighted, scum-faced royal lieutenant tied closely to the Westminster pedophile abuse scandal-cover-up featured in Chapter 6.

Before leaving the Longford-Hindley-Saddleworth connection behind, one more telling fact - the porno-serial killer-infatuated Lord Longford's niece is none other than the child porn supporter, Paedophile Information Exchange (PIE) advocate, lower-the-age-of-consent-to-10 supporter Harriet Harman, the longtime Labour Party MP and deputy party leader. When Harman was legal officer for the National Council of Civil Liberties (NCCL now known as Liberty) from 1978 to 1982, she actively lobbied to legalize child pornography, unless it could be proven to harm a child.[848] The NCCL admitted PIE members allowing them to speak at its official functions and use the NCCL platform to promote legalization of incest. As the legal officer for four years, Harman signed documents promoting pedophilia and then when confronted in 2013, flatly denied it, refused to apologize, profusely defended herself against any wrongdoing, claiming to be a victim of a vicious smear campaign, and was willing only to regret PIE's status as an affiliate NCCL partner.[849] Moreover, her Labor MP hubby and party shadow police minister Jack Dromey was NCCL's chairman throughout this period in the late 1970s. Also

---

[845] Alan Keightly, http://www.dailymail.co.uk/news/article-4516340/Picture-Ian-Brady-said-PROVES-Myra-Hindley-enjoyed-killing.html.

[846] Robert Mendick and Laura Donnelly, https://www.telegraph.co.uk/news/uknews/crime/jimmy-savile/9623109/Jimmy-Savile-Secret-of-BBCs-first-sex-scandal.html.

[847] Patrick Hill, "Pervert MP Cyril Smith was Pals with Satanic Child Sex Monster," *Mirror*, January 19, 2013.

[848] James Murray and Jack Fielding, "'We can't Prove Sex with Children does them Harm' says Labour-linked NCCL," *Express*, March 2, 2014.

[849] Martin Robinson, "Letter from Paedophile Group links Harriet Harman and Patricia Hewitt to it AFTER they said it had been Marginalised," *Daily Mail*, March 7, 2014.

Harriet Harman is a cousin of pedo-enabling former Prime Minister David Cameron, who is a cousin of Queen Elizabeth.[850] Pedophilia enabling - if not pedophiles themselves - obviously runs rampantly in this cabal family.

Aside from the Moors abuse and killings and occasionally wearing the number 666 on his marathon runs, even more conclusive evidence indicating that Jimmy Savile was a Satanist is a 1975 incident in a candlelit basement room deep in the bowels of Stoke-Mandeville Hospital. Savile is alleged to have worn a hooded robe and mask during a secret satanic ritual ceremony that involved the beating and raping of a 12-year old girl patient.[851] She was led into an out of the way room where Savile and several other hooded, masked adults joined in to participate in the satanic ritual abuse, frequently repeating "Ave Satanas," Latin for "Hail Satan." The victim recognized Savile as the regular celebrity-hospital volunteer because of his distinctive voice and blondish white hair sticking out from the side of his mask.

Similar to arrangements at Broadmoor and Leeds Infirmary, Savile enjoyed his own living quarters at Stoke-Mandeville where he volunteered as a porter from 1965 to 1988 and sexually assaulted at least 60 known patients, volunteers and visitors with nine informal complaints and one formal complaint registered between 1972 and 1985.[852] Later testimony determined that an 8-year old brain damaged girl in a coma suffered abuse at the demon's hands. It was learned that another 8- or 9-year old whose relatives worked at the hospital was repeatedly raped 10 times at his "home away from home."

Five years after that satanic ritual abuse incident in 1980 another abuse victim at the time 21-years of age reported that Savile dressed in similar ceremonial wizardly garb this time played the leading role in another occult ceremony after an orgy party held at a wealthy private London residence.[853] The victim described her ordeal to the *Express*:

I was brought in to a dark cellar and made to stand in front of three men in a circle, with the man in the middle sitting on a throne-like chair in a bright gown with a cigar in his mouth. A man stood on either side in blue cloaks and masks… I was then taken by the man smoking the cigar, who I recognised as Jimmy Savile, to an altar table where I was stripped of my gown and tied to the altar. Savile then climbed on to the table and raped me. Others around him called out Satan's name and laughed hysterically and were worked up into a frenzy.[854]

Both young vulnerable females witnessing firsthand Savile's savage participation in satanic ritual torture went to the police afterwards but to no avail. UK's standard police policy has virtually always been to summarily dismiss all sex abuse complaints against VIPs. Years later each young woman independently contacted the same therapist in 1992 and 1993, both

---

[850] "Harriet Harman," *whale.to*..

[851] James Fielding, "Jimmy Savile was part of Satanic Ring," *Express*, January 13, 2013.

[852] Josh Halliday and Sandra Laville, "Jimmy Savile Abused 60 People at Stoke Mandeville Hospital, Inquiry finds," *The Guardian*, February 26, 2015,.

[853] James Fielding, https://www.express.co.uk/news/uk/370439/Jimmy-Savile-was-part-of-satanic-ring.

[854] James Fielding, https://www.express.co.uk/news/uk/370439/Jimmy-Savile-was-part-of-satanic-ring.

struggling with the long-term effects from such an emotionally jarring, scarring, eerily similar traumatic experience with Savile's active participation in his organized satanic ritual abuse ring.

Once famed pediatrician consultant at Stoke-Mandeville for two decades, Dr. Michael Salmon was also a charity organizer and chief medical director for Dreamflight, a charity renowned for annually sponsoring 300 disabled UK children on a flight to Florida's Disney World and Seaworld.[855] Dreamflight's maiden voyage was a 1985 Christmas flight with children on a jumbo jet accompanied by Sir Jimmy Savile. As a twice convicted pedophile guilty of indecent assaults, Dr. Michael Salmon also worked at the *BBC* and also sadistically abused at least 18 underage girls and one boy with the youngest victim only eight years old, also at Stoke-Mandeville and other hospitals from 1975 to 1989.[856] At 81 in December 2016 when already serving an 18-year sentence stemming from the two prior convictions dating back to 1990, the disgraced former celebrated doctor was convicted for a third and final time just two years after his last one. As a consequence, Michael Salmon will die in prison.

As is so common amongst youth charities, Dreamflight has attracted a number of child predators, including Savile, Salmon and another *BBC* entertainer and Savile pal Rolf Harris, who regularly attended the charity's pre-flight festivities. One of the doctor's victims specifically recalls a photo hanging on the wall in Salmon's office of his son and Savile posing together after the doctor took him to a Jim'll Fix It broadcast.[857] This confirms the doctor knew Jimmy Savile. Dr. Salmon and Savile shared too many overlapping parallels working at the same hospital during the same lengthy time, linked to the same charity while both were *BBC* employees and serial pedophiles victimizing underage hospital patients at the same place and time.

Additionally, one of Salmon's seriously ill victims at Stoke Mandeville confined to a wheelchair was drugged and gang raped by Salmon and two other men.[858] The girl remembers afterwards being wheeled back to her room by a hospital porter, more than likely Jimmy Savile. This incident with Savile's satanic ritual abuse involving other hospital staff victimizing yet another Stoke-Mandeville girl, point to Salmon most likely attending that satanic ritual abuse session. These recurring similar events involving both the DJ and the doctor indicate that for years they very likely participated in and belonged to the same sick satanic pedophile ring.

But these uncanny, striking parallels don't stop there. The female face of the *BBC*, news presenter Jill Dando, aware of the Savile-*BBC* pedophile ring, and both her and Jimmy Savile's longtime friend Sir Cliff Richard were also both Dreamflight patrons just months prior to Jill's

---

[855] "Stoke-Mandeville Hospital Paedophile Ring – Sir Jimmy Savile, Dr. Michael Salmon, Dreamflight Charity," *goodnessandharmony.wordpress.com*, January 3, 2017.

[856] Mark Duell, "Paedophile Consultant, 81, who believed he was 'Bomb Proof' is Jailed for four and half years for Sexually Assaulting Girls as young as eight in the same Hospital where Jimmy Saville Abused Children," *Daily Mail*, December 19, 2016.

[857] "Pervert Doctor Tried to Commit Suicide before 1990 Abuse Trial," *Berkhamsted & Tring Gazette*, February 6, 2015.

[858] Vicky Smith, "Michael Salmon Trial: Children's Doctor 'Drugged and Gang-Raped Seriously Ill Young Girl' in Hospital, *Mirror*, January 6, 2015.

tragic high-profile murder.[859] And Queen Elizabeth's dressmaker Lillian Joyce Burfield and the queen honored Dame Yvonne Trueman, sister of Dreamflight creator and British Airways pilot Derek Pereira, were also both Dreamflight fundraisers as well as Stoke-Mandeville volunteers, all running in the same circles both socially and professionally. So many common links appear more than coincidental, fueling high speculation and probability that connects all the dots between already established and confirmed nefarious relationships between the royals, Savile, Harris, Sir Cliff and Jill, child charity work and Stoke-Mandeville Hospital.

A final nail in the elite's dot connected coffin exposing the wider Savile-Salmon-*BBC*-Stoke Mandeville pedophile ring cult is the fact that the primary funder of Tavistock research on torture-induced mind control and dissociative disorder is none other than a Rothschild who also happened to be a close associate of the disgraced Michael Salmon.[860] Even after he was convicted of drugging and raping children, the late entomologist Miriam Rothschild wrote the introduction to Salmon's 2001 butterfly book. Apparently they both shared an acute interest in butterflies (no doubt over the well-being of children) that extends beyond the Monarch mind control developed at the Rothschild funded Tavistock.

A psychiatrist that studied art therapy practices at Tavistock, promoting a style of art depicting sex abused mind control victims called Art Brut happens to run the CrossCurrents Foundation, the major funding source for DC's 49th most powerful VIP Comet Pizza owner (of Pizzagate infamy) James Alefantes's Transformer Art Gallery that along with his pedo-pal lobbyist Tony Podesta collect and showcase this pathological "art."[861] An Art Brut favorite of theirs is former Tavistock abuse victim Kim Nobles whose artwork is prominently featured in both Alefantes' gallery, his notorious former Instagram account and Podesta's home depicting sexually traumatized children.[862] For decades the Savile-Salmon-Stoke-Mandeville-Rothschild-Tavistock-DC pedophile network has been globally interconnected through powerful bloodline families, their deep pocket foundations, elitist think tanks, university research centers, major research hospitals and large children's charities as a cherry picked gatekeeping pedo-system. And of course all these "benevolent," renowned institutions in turn work hand-in-hand with satanic rogue elements within the intelligence services, government institutions, law enforcement, military and mainstream media, all heavily infiltrated by secret society membership covertly operating unchallenged and thoroughly protected and insulated worldwide as the pedophilia webbed network.

In the 2001 Theroux documentary, Savile the satanic predator even refers to his bed at his Leeds home overlooking Roundhay Park as his "altar"[863] where sacrifices were frequently

---

[859] "Rothschild Worked Closely with Convicted Pedophile Doctor from Stoke Mandeville after he was Convicted," *svvordfish.blogspot.com*, August 20, 2018.

[860] "Rothschild Worked Closely with Convicted Pedophile Doctor from Stoke Mandeville after he was Convicted," http://svvordfish.blogspot.com/2018/08/rothschild-worked-closely-with.html.

[861] "Rothschild Worked Closely with Convicted Pedophile Doctor from Stoke Mandeville after he was Convicted," http://svvordfish.blogspot.com/2018/08/rothschild-worked-closely-with.html.

[862] Ken Ammi, "Kim Noble's Dissociative Identity Disorder Tortuous Pedophilia Paintings," *True Free Thinker*.

[863] "Quotes," https://www.imdb.com/title/tt0304938/quotes.

made.[864] If you view defiling pubescent virgins as sacrificing a child's innocence, then his crime scene bed could well be defined in his twisted, sordid mind as his designated satanic altar. No doubt the Satanist conducted ritual abuse there.

So vile Savile was always planting hide-in-plain-sight clues that only make sense in after-death exposure. He claimed to be Myra's story because they were key members within the same satanic death cult practicing the most egregious ritual abuse, torture and blood sacrifice that defy every decent human's sensibilities to even fathom much less grasp. There are those who believe Savile fashioned himself after another demonic wizard Aleister Crowley,[865] utilizing his black magick powers to cast spells on celebrities, *BBC* bosses, politicians, royalty, fans and the entire nation in order to successfully cheat fate and evade exposure.[866] He closely lived his life adhering to his idol Crowley's mantra "do what thou wilt." The megalomaniac valued freedom at all cost, and the power to be able to do, say and get away with anything that momentarily pleased his ego, whim or fancy, never worrying about paying the consequence. In his own words:

I am not constrained pretty well by anything. The tough thing in life is ultimate freedom. Ultimate freedom is the big challenge. Now, I've got it. And I can tell you that there's not many of us that's got ultimate freedom.[867]

Knowing full well all the evil misdeeds he remained so smugly confident he would continue getting away with protected by the power structure, his conquest for living his life with "ultimate freedom" so rarely attained by others takes on a whole new meaning.

During World War II as a teenager completing his rite of passage into adulthood, Jimmy Savile worked in the coalmines of northern England. But as an eventual Mensa member and avid reader of Crowley and the occult, he would marvel freaking out fellow miners. During a TV interview in the 1980s, he boasted:

No-one ever did eight hours down the pit and came back as immaculate as they set off with white shirt and everything like that. They were quite convinced I was a witch.[868]

Jimmy Savile was often photographed in public wearing a wizard's gown, complete with Crowley's 11-pointed star symbolizing his satanic cult. As standard accessory in every wizard's bag of tricks, Savile also possessed a crystal ball and a hexagram ring, among many other

---

[864] Kathryn Snowden, "Louis Theroux Speaks to Jimmy Savile's Victims in New Documentary 16 Years after Landmark Film," *Huffington Post*, February 10, 2016.

[865] "Was Jimmy Savile a Wizard? Full Documentary," YouTube video, 2014, 46:59, posted January 13, 2014.

[866] Patrick Knox, "Jimmy Savile 'Occultist Witch who Worshipped Satanist Aleister Crowley,'" *Daily Star*, September 17, 2016..

[867] Patrick Knox, https://www.dailystar.co.uk/news/latest-news/546207/conspiracy-theory-paedophile-jimmy-savile-wizard-satanist-new-aleister-crowley.

[868] Patrick Knox, https://www.dailystar.co.uk/news/latest-news/546207/conspiracy-theory-paedophile-jimmy-savile-wizard-satanist-new-aleister-crowley.

satanic themed paraphernalia.[869] In October 2012 the *Sunday Sport* ran an article addressing an incident that Savile wrote about indicating that he likely hypnotized a teenage girl.[870] He often repeated his catch phrases three times as in occult chants and incantations that use the power of words as hypnotic cues to mesmerize individuals and audiences alike.

Moreover, it's been documented that Savile's idol, the wizard known as the Great Beast 666 Aleister Crowley actually worked undercover for British Intelligence (just like Sir Jimmy), and during World War II was even involved in a spy plot to capture Nazi Rudolf Hess.[871] Wizards associated with British crowns can be traced back to the mythological Merlin in King Arthur's court and John Dee the astrologer and occult practitioner in Elizabeth I's court.[872] The incredibly intimate ties between Sir Jimmy Savile, British intelligence and the British royal family indicate that he, like Crowley, Dee and Merlin before him, also served the crown as their wildly eccentric, dark occult wizard.[873]

Yet more evidence that Sir Jimmy the queen's knight was a practicing Luciferian death cult practitioner comes from his activities in Scarborough not far from the Moors where he and the aforementioned former mayor Peter Jaconelli ran a local pedophile ring. Apparently not all satanic rituals involve the wearing of hooded robes and masks, at least not at the end of certain dalliance rituals that Savile allegedly participated in. With his likeminded pervs, in an underground chamber Savile is reported to have disrobed and danced naked around a flogging post as part of a secret satanic sex "club" in Whitby, Scarborough, where he lived for many years with his mother.[874] Along with a chamber flogging post, other reported features included a painted pentagram, black candles, restraining shackles and assorted S&M paraphernalia.[875] It's believed that fellow pedos Savile, Jaconelli and other prominent local figures regularly conducted occult ritual abuse in their subterranean chamber. A local insider stated:

Someone once made a recording of what unfolded and that film is still said to be in existence in DVD form. From what I understand this was not much serious Satanic ritual but celebrities and local dignitaries dancing around naked with a Satanic theme going on.[876]

Serious and hardcore or not, this Scarborough scene sounds awfully familiar, reminiscent of the infamous Bohemian Grove in northern California's Sonoma County where the elite run around naked in the redwoods at their exclusive, highly guarded summer camp for Luciferian puppet presidents and cohorts. Throughout the world the planetary controllers are bonded by their

---

[869] "Was Jimmy Savile a Wizard? Full Documentary," https://www.youtube.com/watch?v=-QUuCWNyvv8.

[870] "Was Jimmy Savile a Wizard? Full Documentary," https://www.youtube.com/watch?v=-QUuCWNyvv8.

[871] Richard B. Spence, "Secret Agent 666 - Aleister Crowley, British Intelligence and the Occult," *rense.com*, June 23, 2008..

[872] Riley Winters, "John Dee: Scholar, Astrologer, and Occult Practitioner that Captivated the Royal Court of 16th Century England," *Ancient Origins*, October 6, 2018.

[873] "Jimmy Savile: Illuminati Wizard," *5ocietyx.wordpress.com*, October 5, 2012.

[874] Dominic Gover, 'Satanic Jimmy Savile Wore Devil Robes at Scarborough Sex Club,' *International Business Times*, February 25, 2013.

[875] "Savile: North Yorks Police/Council Cover-up?" *Real Whitby*, November 5, 2012.

[876] Dominic Gover, https://ixquick-proxy.com/do/spg/proxy.

demonic occult rituals in the form of secret societies, ceremonial torture, rape and sacrificial murder of children, be it in Scarborough, the nearby Moors, or Scotland's royal Balmoral Castle,[877] Belgium's Mothers of Darkness castle,[878] Bohemian Grove,[879] Stoke-Mandeville Hospital or secret government underground milabs.[880]

Another related article from the local publication *Real Whitby* adds that Savile and "The Club" as the locals called it also partook in satanic ritual abuse ceremonies "on the edge of the moors" just outside Scarborough Borough,[881] not far from the notorious Saddleworth Moor. The four-decade run of South Yorkshire Police veteran who retired as acting police chief turned Scarborough Council Leader Tom Fox is accused of knowing of Savile's longtime pedo-satanic activities in the area yet turning a blind eye. Of course, everywhere the Crowley wannabe wizard went during his confirmed near six-decade long crime spree, law enforcement, the *BBC*, government and royalty always had his back because they're all as guilty as Sir Jimmy's sins in their demonic sexual blackmail cesspit.

Jimmy Savile's intimate encounters with satanic killer friends didn't end with Myra Hindley and Ian Brady. Long before he befriended them, he was close to the ruthless pair of pedophile gangsters - the Kray twins, who ran the Jewish mafia out of London's East End during the 1950s and 1960s.[882] Sir Jimmy also often bragged about having pals who were IRA assassins,[883] northern England mobsters and other paramilitary groups as an MI5/MI6 operative and Mossad asset. An insider Brian Palmer responding to an article on the *Coleman Experience* commented:

The police took away masses of paperwork after the death of Jimmy Savile, which was said to have been immediately incinerated, it has been said that a lot of correspondence was in the pile from the ex-Israeli prime minister Menachem Begin whom rumour has it was Savile's main protector.[884]

But a decade after Brady and Hindley were convicted, Savile may well have been a co-participant in the crimes of UK's biggest serial killer - the Yorkshire Ripper who murdered and left two of his victims' bodies on or near Savile's proverbial doorstep and another corpse discarded at Savile Park in Halifax.[885] Till the sicko's death, Savile maintained a longstanding,

---

[877] Mark Watts and Keir Mudie, "VIP Paedophile Ring 'Abused Boy Inside Buckingham Palace and Balmoral Castle," *Mirror*, November 29, 2014
.
[878] "The Illuminati Mothers of Darkness Castle: The Most Evil Place on Earth," YouTube video, 17:11, posted October 24, 2018.
[879] Richard Enos, "Why do the Elites Participate in Child Sacrifice at Bohemian Grove?" *Collective Evolution*, July 6, 2018.
[880] "MiLabs, Underground Bases, DNA Activation, The Unveiling," *augtellez.wordpress.com*.
[881] "Savile – And other Party Animals," *Real Whitby*, November 11, 2012.
[882] "Jimmy Savile, the Kray Twins, Ian Brady, Hampstead, Cliff Richard," *aangirfan.com*, November 5, 2015.
[883] James Saville, "Jimmy Savile and the IRA: Predator Boasted Terrorist Friends could have Enemies Hospitalised," *Mirror*, October 20, 2012.
[884] "Mossad's Links to Filthy Britain," *whale.to*.
[885] Emma Reynolds and Anna Edwards, *Daily Mail*, November 8, 2012.

publicized friendship with Peter Sutcliffe, the Yorkshire Ripper.[886] In northern England around Leeds from 1975 to 1980 Peter Sutcliffe killed at least 13 women, bludgeoned in failed attempts another 7, and was questioned in 17 other attacks on women involving hammers, his favorite lethal weapon aside from his trusty knife and occasional screwdriver.[887] This monster was reportedly once cheated out of some money by a prostitute and her pimp, setting him on his self-delusional Luciferian mission to eliminate as many prostitutes from the earth as possible. In 1981 he was convicted of the 13 murders and punished with 20 concurrent life sentences. A 2013 appeals court ruling dictated that he would never be eligible for parole as the now blind 73-year old paranoid schizophrenic is destined to die in prison as one of the worst all-time serial killers in British history.[888]

While Sutcliffe was serving time at Savile's own Broadmoor high-security psychiatric hospital, thanks to Sir Jimmy, the Ripper enjoyed a morosely twisted celebrity status, especially after Savile tricked former heavyweight boxing champion Frank Bruno into a surprise photo-op shaking hands with the serial killing devil himself as the cunning manipulator smugly looked on.[889]

After a suspended mismanagement of Broadmoor in 1987, the following year Britain's junior health minister Edwina Currie "selected" the totally unqualified volunteer Savile as the task force chairman of the nation's highest security criminal psychiatric hospital.[890] His formal Broadmoor documents included his false title "Dr. Jimmy Savile, OBE, KCSG, LLD."[891] For Britain's Health Minister, Kenneth Clarke, accused of sexually assaulting a teenager,[892] and confirmed pedophile protector,[893] to assign the serial predator in such official capacity demonstrates Savile's immense power and reach high up into Britain's Thatcher government (fully covered in Chapter 5),[894] further implicating that a national pedophile enabling network within the UK government was fully operational.

---

[886] George Clarke, "Ripper and Savile's afternoon Tea: Inside the Sick Pair's Weird Relationship," *Daily Star*, August 7, 2016.

[887] Josie Griffiths and Sofia Petkar, "Peter Sutcliffe, is the Yorkshire Ripper still in Prison, how old is he and how many Women did he Kill?" *The Sun*, March 25, 2018.

[888] Andrew Hough, "Britain's Worst Serial Killers," *The Telegraph*, July 16, 2010.

[889] Sanchez Manning, "Frank Bruno Reveals how Sick Jimmy Savile Tricked him into Shaking Hands with Serial Killer Peter Sutcliffe," *Mirror*, November 11, 2012.

[890] Claire Ellicott, "Jimmy Savile 'was given Key Position at Broadmoor and even personally Selected Hospital's bosses,'" *Daily Mail*, October 28, 2013.

[891] Vicky Smith, "Jimmy Savile: Broadmoor Gang's Sex Abuse Ring Linked to Former DJ as Arrests Expected, *Mirror*, June 8, 2014.

[892] "Ken Clarke 'Groping' Accuser found not Guilty of making a False Claim," *The Telegraph*, July 30, 2015.

[893] David Barrett, "Kenneth Clarke 'Failed to Act' over Lord Janner and Cyril Smith Child Abuse Tip-offs," *The Telegraph*, March 8, 2016.

[894] Stephen Moyes, Alex West and Leigh Holmwood, "Jimmy Savile given the Keys to Broadmoor under Ken Clarke," *The Sun*, October 13, 2012.

Calling himself "Governor," the celebrated predator Savile was awarded his own plush office at Broadmoor, his own sleeping quarters, gold plated keys, and full run of the institution.[895] Ensuring that his friend Sutcliffe's incarceration was a cushy accommodation, even after he killed and left for dead 20 women, Sir Jimmy immediately lobbied for coed access so his buddy could enjoy sex with female fellow inmates.[896] One of Sutcliffe's nearby cellmates for six years stated that Savile would regularly have tea with the Ripper inside his quarters, locked in spellbound conversation for hours on end.[897] Nurses commented that they heard Savile's belly laughs coming from Sutcliffe's room reacting to the Ripper's sick jokes as the likeminded dementos were obviously bonding.[898] The serial pedophile would often boast how he was such a big shot at Broadmoor, able to get 60 violent mentally ill patients, some convicted murderers released.[899] Fortunately, two years after Savile's death, the court made certain that was not going to happen for the Ripper.

But it turns out that Savile and Sutcliffe didn't just meet at Broadmoor. Just like the Moors murderers, back in Savile's hometown of Leeds when the Ripper was still a free man on the loose during his reign of terror, Sir Jimmy was already apparently friends with Sutcliffe.[900] When the murderer was questioned by police, Sutcliffe even mentioned Jimmy Savile by name.[901] Because Ripper victims sustained bite marks on their chests and bodies, the Leeds police even sent for Savile's dental imprint for analysis. With two of the victims' bodies discovered so close to Sir Jimmy's penthouse property and Savile known to have liaisons with local prostitutes, the most famous Leeds resident at one time was considered a suspect and possible accomplice.[902] Additionally, both whackos shared an unquenchable obsession for dead bodies.[903]

Former detective John Stainthorpe worked on the Yorkshire Ripper investigation. Based on tips from the public, the lawman not only confirmed Savile was briefly a suspect, but he also stated:

Child perverts soon become child killers.[904]

---

[895] Anna Edwards, "Former Detective makes Shock Claims that Jimmy Savile was Quizzed over Yorkshire Ripper Murders," *Daily Mail*, November 6, 2012.

[896] Aaron Tinney, "Jimmy Savile's Plea to get Sex for the Ripper," *The Sun*, November 9, 2012.

[897] George Clarke, "Ripper and Savile's Afternoon Tea: Inside the Sick Pair's Weird Relationship," *Daily Record*, August 7, 2016.

[898] Patrick Henningsen, "Savile's Travels: How Sir Jimmy was Fingered as Peter Sutcliffe's Accomplice," *21st Century Wire*, November 5, 2012.

[899] Vicky Smith, https://www.mirror.co.uk/news/uk-news/jimmy-savile-broadmoor-gangs-sex-3663459.

[900] George Clarke, https://www.dailystar.co.uk/news/latest-news/535953/Jimmy-Savile-Peter-Sutcliffe-Yorkshire-Ripper-Broadmoor-friends-Frank-Bruno-handshake.

[901] "Yorkshire Murders," *upsd.co.uk*, February 19, 2013.

[902] Patrick Henningsen, https://21stcenturywire.com/2012/11/05/saviles-travels-how-sir-jimmy-was-fingered-as-peter-sutcliffes-accomplice/.

[903] Patrick Henningsen, https://21stcenturywire.com/2012/11/05/saviles-travels-how-sir-jimmy-was-fingered-as-peter-sutcliffes-accomplice/.

[904] John Hall, "'Child Perverts soon become Child Killers': Jimmy Savile was Questioned by Police over Yorkshire Ripper Murders, *Independent*, November 7, 2012.

Professor David Wilson, head of criminology at Birmingham City University and former prison officer, draws a striking parallel between the known serial pedophile Savile and the known serial killer Sutcliffe:

Both inhabited a world where men were encouraged to take what they wanted by force and where girls and women were seen as things to be used and then discarded. They used sex and violence instead of intimacy to express their inner demons - the need to be powerful and to control girls and women.[905]

The prospect of Savile being a serial killer was so strong that a year after the pedophile's death another leading criminologist, Dr. Ian Stephen, urged police to investigate Savile as a suspect in cold case murders and missing persons investigations around the nation:

It is possible that he [Savile] upped the game, that he needed to get that buzz from getting away with it, and the question is does he increase it? There is always that risk with people who are sensation seekers, they sometimes get bored and raise it and the possibilities are there.[906]

In 2001 while agitated over documentarian Louis Theroux's questioning about his pedophile rumors and secretly recording Savile bragging about his criminal exploits as a nightclub boss in Leeds, Savile threateningly blurted out:

I mean, he was having a go to try and get a bit of salacious TV so of course I suddenly drop into Godfather mode. If he wants to die, he can die. He won't be the first that I've put away.[907]

This utterance is both an aggressive threat and outright boastful confession to murder. Yet there's more.

Alleged Savile victim, 46-year old Georgina Martin, maintains that Jimmy Savile began sexually assaulting her when she was just 13, and continued allegedly having his way at least 20 more times over the next three years.[908] Near certain that Savile impregnated her at 16, she contends that her now 31-year old daughter is Savile's. The mother and daughter requested a DNA test to confirm whether the daughter's father is Savile, neither claiming they seek financial compensation. Georgina stated that as soon as she told Savile she was pregnant, he angrily wanted nothing more to do with her. Another impregnated 16-year old victim was instructed by the infamous rapist to threaten suicide if not granted an abortion.[909]

---

[905] Aaron Tinney, "Savile and the Ripper," *The Sun*, November 4, 2012.
[906] Ben Borland, *Express*, October 28, 2012.
[907] Ben Borland, "Savile: Did he Admit Murder?" www.express.co.uk/news/uk/354874/Savile-Did-he-admit-murder.
[908] Matthew Drake, "Jimmy Savile's Secret Daughter: 'Mum was Abused by Monster - I Fear he is my Father,'" *Mirror*, February 21, 2015.
[909] Chris Greenwood and Martin Robinson, http://www.dailymail.co.uk/news/article-2670444/Jimmy-Savile-abused-corpses-boasted-jewellery-glass-eyes-NHS-report-reveals-shocking-new-details-paedophiles-crimes.html.

During Georgina's three year sexually abusive relationship, Georgina maintains that she learned extremely disturbing information about Savile that police would still find useful:

*He told me so many warped secrets and let me in on things I now realize are significant to detectives investigating what he did. I have tried to blot it out of my mind, but I can't. I know more about him than the police know. He was obsessed with death and with the Yorkshire Ripper, Peter Sutcliffe. He would always tell me how he had to be careful, especially with the 'birds.' When we went out in his car he would point out spots where dead bodies had been found and claim the Ripper had **not been working alone**. He told me he had been questioned by police after the body of a young girl was found near his home covered in **bite marks** [just like Georgina admitted he gave her]. Jimmy said they had made him hand over a sample bite mark. But he was always bragging about how **he was protected** and had people who looked after him.*[910] [Emboldened text added for emphasis]

His highly revealing personal disclosures come close to murder confessions.

In yet another possible slaying at the hands of Satan's "national treasure," in June 2014 a man claiming he was sexually abused by Sir Jimmy as a boy in the 1960s while living at Roecliffe Manor, a convalescent children's home in Leicestershire, stated that he saw Jimmy Savile dragging off a girl from the group home that turned up the following day dead.[911] Also two alleged suicides of female patients victimized by Savile at Broadmoor in part can be attributed to Britain's most prolific sadistic pedophile.[912]

As the Jimmy Savile scandal broke in late 2012, stories from firsthand accounts of the Satanist's love of dead bodies also began circulating. Just weeks after the bombshell of the *ITV* Savile Exposure doc, *BBC* DJ colleague Paul Gambaccini whose office in the 1970s was next door to Savile's, on a Radio 5 interview declared Sir Jimmy was a necrophiliac.[913] He said he'd heard about the claims in the 1980s. Paul citeed certain news outlets as hypocrites for bragging they knew of this disturbing side of his pathology ten years earlier but remained silent. Gambaccini then questioned how Savile was knighted by the queen when every sir gets vetted by MI5. That all these insiders were all too aware of Savile's despicably deviant crimes yet poured accolades on him right to the end only goes to show that the VIP pedos in power were simply protecting one of their own.

In his many decades as a porter at Leeds General Infirmary and Stoke-Mandeville Hospitals, Sir Jimmy maintained unsupervised free access to the morgues, at Leeds from the late 1970s to the

---

[910] Matthew Drake, https://www.mirror.co.uk/news/uk-news/jimmy-saviles-secret-daughter-mum-5207352.

[911] Richard Hartley-Parkinson, "Was Jimmy Savile involved in Death of Young Girl? New Police Probe into Pervert DJ," *Mirror*, June 27, 2014.

[912] Jonathon Corke, https://www.dailystar.co.uk/news/latest-news/386307/Sick-DJ-Jimmy-Savile-linked-to-five-mystery-deaths-and-calalogue-of-suicides.

[913] Larisa Brown, "Savile Sex Scandal Hits Horrific new Low as Former Colleague Paul Gambaccini Claims on Radio Five Live that DJ was a 'Necrophiliac,'" *Daily Mail*, October 23, 2012.

mid-1990s[914] and at Stoke-Mandeville as early as 1954, just three years into his volunteer position there.[915] His celebrity status and psychopathic nature ensured befriending the hospital chief mortician so that his inordinate amount of volunteer time spent down there hanging with the dead was never in question. It also came out that he bragged about his necro-exploits to other hospital staff. A former Broadmoor nurse maintains that Savile claimed he performed sex acts with the bodies, performing oral sex on them and placing fresh pre-rigor mortis corpses into lewd positions for sick pics. The nurse expounded:

He [Savile] *was saying that **they** used to put the bodies together, male and female, and he also said that **they** took photographs and also that he got involved in some of the photographs.*[916] (Emboldened for emphasis)

Note the plural pronoun "they," meaning that Savile engaged in these perversions with others, implicated again with distribution of photographs, the probability of a wider necrophilia ring. Another witness reported that Sir Jimmy noticed him peering at his bulbous rings on his hand and then boasted:

'D'you know what they are? They are glass eyes from dead bodies in Leeds mortuary where I work and I love working there, and I wheel the dead bodies around at night and I love that.'[917]

A night porter witnessed Savile wheeling a just deceased 4-year old's body into the Stoke-Mandeville morgue. A former therapist said that he had been told that sicko Savile was caught in the act:

Trying to have sexual intercourse with dead bodies in the hospital mortuary.

In a 1990 interview with *Q Magazine*, Savile spoke of his volunteer work as a Stoke-Mandeville porter:

One of my jobs is to take away the deceased. You can look after somebody, be alone with somebody, who has lived a whole lifetime, and I'm just saying goodbye and looking after him.

---

[914] Josh Halliday, "Savile told Hospital Staff he Performed Sex Acts on Corpses in Leeds Mortuary," *The Guardian*, June 26, 2014..

[915] Steve Robson and David Collins, "Jimmy Savile 'seen having Sex with Bodies and Wheeling Body of four-year-old in Pram into Hospital Mortuary,'" *Mirror*, February 26, 2015.

[916] Josh Halliday, https://www.theguardian.com/media/2014/jun/26/savile-bodies-sex-acts-corpses-glass-eyes-mortuary.

[917] Josh Halliday, https://www.theguardian.com/media/2014/jun/26/savile-bodies-sex-acts-corpses-glass-eyes-mortuary.

That is a privilege and an honour. Some people get hold of the fact that Jim likes looking after cadavers and say, 'Aha, Jim's a necrophiliac!' I'm not a necrophiliac.[918]

Famous last words… A vicious satanic ritual abuser of children and pimping procurer to the powerful, serial predator of anything that moves, and even the lifeless that can't move, big or small, young or old, male or female, it never mattered as long as his victims were the most vulnerable, infirm and defenseless. Ever on the prowl, he was always ready to pounce. Savile's rapturous best five days ever were admittedly spent alone with his rotting corpse of a mother he called Duchess.[919] Savile's penchant for partnership-in-crime with his best buddies Ian, Myra and Ripper, his multiple borderline confessions and their mutual fascination for making dead bodies makes him their likely accomplice and co-murderer.

With the binding thread that runs through Satanism, Luciferianism, 33 or higher degreed Freemasonry, the Illuminati, and the other numerous elite secret societies is systematic ritual child abuse, torture and sacrifice. Not surprising is a revealing photo at Sir Jimmy's funeral showing an inordinate number of freemasons in attendance.[920] Demonic infiltrators cherry picked to occupy enough top positions in government, military, media, law enforcement, judiciary, education, entertainment, religion, business, organized crime, social services and charities guarantee that VIP pedophiles continue getting away with child rape and murder. Jimmy Savile was a unique common link straddling every one of these interlocking institutional components to UK's pedophilia network. Also a British intelligence operative,[921] in his own creepy words:

I am like a sewing machine needle that goes in here and goes in there, but I am also the eminence grise: the grey, shadowy figure in the background. The thing about me is I get things done and I work under cover.[922]

Psychologist Oliver James points out that Sir Jimmy Savile possessed the dark triad of personality characteristics – psychopathy, Machiavellianism and narcissism.[923] Savile utilized his shrewdly keen intelligence to figure out others' weaknesses in his compulsive need to exploit, shock, control and hurt powerless victims. Devoid of emotion other than anger, he had no capacity to feel compassion or empathy toward others. His world revolved completely around him, and his grandiose need to inflate his own self-importance and ruthless power over others universally drove his every action motivated by a self-serving means to an end, using his "tireless" charity fundraising to predatorily access children buffered by a firewall façade of

---

[918] Larisa Brown, https://www.dailymail.co.uk/news/article-2221922/Jimmy-Savile-necrophiliac-says-colleague-Paul-Gambaccini.html

[919] Patrick Hill, "Paedophile Jimmy Savile Believed his Mother 'never Trusted him' and expected he'd be Jailed," *Mirror*, February 6, 2016.

[920] "Sir Jimmy Savile the Establishment's Favourite Paedophile," *The Truth*.

[921] "Cover-up; CIA, Mossad, MI5, MI6,; Savile and Jaconelli; Amsterdam Sex," *aangirfan.com*, November 7, 2014.

[922] Alison Boshoff, "Jim the Fixer: Is Jimmy Savile just a Fantasist... or is the Truth even Stranger than Fiction?" *Daily Mail*, May 9, 2008.

[923] Oliver James, "Inside the Mind of Jimmy Savile," *The Guardian*, June 26, 2014..

philanthropic benevolence. Savile's quirky "charm" ingratiated himself to VIP elite, facilitating alliances with prime ministers and future kings, predicated by a Luciferian pact based on sexual blackmail secrecy, a conditional, self-serving loyalty to Lucifer and self-preservation, and insulated, above-the-law firewall protection.[924]

The massive compilation of evidence of his "deep cover" damage and depravity that this monster got away with is incredible. His reign of terror was appalling, a nonstop incriminating history of circumstantial pieces to a nightmarish puzzle that together forms a composite whole - a lifetime substantiation that something wicked and foul this way came. His contribution to the British VIP pedophilia network has wreaked untold damage in the depraved business of torturing, abusing and murdering kids' souls and tortured lives, not to mention those ill-fated victims who crossed paths with UK's most infamous, bloodthirsty serial killers who invariably became Savile's best friends. This creepy court jester performer from hell had next to no real or close friends as many who knew him best admit they hardly knew him at all. The famous showboat, eccentric loner possessed far reaching social tentacles that afforded him unbridled access to the royal palaces, the halls of government, every entertainment stage, NHS hospital or school playground. But the more one digs into the demented, diabolically twisted Jimmy Savile, the more it appears by his closest company that the nation's most prolific serial pedophile was also a serial killer. As pathologically belligerent and destructive as he was in his psychopathically driven Luciferian marathon of a crime spree, consumed by dead corpses, killing and killers, and compulsively mauling young flesh galore, live or putrefying, from countless firsthand accounts, it's fair to conclude that Sir Jimmy, United Kingdom's national treasure, participated in murder with the Ripper on and around his Leeds home, as well as with the Moors duo and possibly on his own. After all, he himself proudly proclaimed to the world:

I am the Myra Hindley story.

Next comes what happens to those who know too much. Anyone inside the *BBC* [or out] that learned of Sir Jimmy's colossal crimes, the pervasive *BBC* cover-up and Savile's procuring child victims to princes and prime ministers, became a lethal liability threat to the cabal and were silenced one way or another. A deeper glimpse into murder and foul play via Jimmy Savile and his BBC syndicate continues in Chapter 4.[925]

---

[924] "Jimmy Savile: Who was Protecting him for Decades, and why?" *thedarknessmustend.blogspot.com*, March 28, 2013.
[925]

Chapter 4: The BBC, Sir Cliff Richard and Why Pedophilia Rules Britannia

Sir Cliff Richard, the always tanned, leather-skinned singing sensation, now 80-years old, (same as pedo-cabal friend Esther Rantzen) is not the Christian celibate he's faithfully claimed to be for well over half a century.[926] Sir Cliff was questioned several times by Metro Police pertaining to *BBC* broadcaster Jill Dando's April 1999 murder.[927] As longtime British intel-Mossad asset and Dando confidant, no doubt Cliff Richard knew a lot more than he let on with the police. But then this famous man is thoroughly protected, as of 2018 armed with Cliff's law, where no one can even associate him with pedophilia without risking a huge lawsuit.

All the more reason for a little bit of history on this UK legend in our time. He is reputed to have signed the Elm Guest Home ledger as "Kitty" in the early 1980s child sex abuse scandal (covered in Chapter 7),[928] reportedly accused by at least nine victims in their youth at the notorious Elm Guest House.[929] For several years running Elm Guest House was the pedo-party brothel of choice of prominent pedophile politicians, cabinet ministers, police and intelligence chiefs as well as entertainers, enjoying sex with young lads supplied from local group homes. Sir Jimmy Savile is known to have specialized in working "under cover" (Savile's words) as an MI5 operative and was reputedly well-acquainted with Elm Guest House owner Haroon Kasir.[930] Cliff was also accused of molesting an underage boy in 1985 at the Billy Graham crusade.[931]

Between 1979 and 1982, Carole Kasir and her husband Haroon were the Elm Guest House operators, who contracted with pedophiles from the Spartacus Club, run by a former Catholic priest, to provide their pad full of trafficked in "rent boys" from nearby Grafton Close children's home for all VIP regulars.[932] Haroon bragged about Savile being his best friend until Sir Jimmy stopped showing up and snubbed him.[933] Even the local head of Richmond social services was implicated as chief pipeline procurer and fellow Elm House club member. Solicitor for the Richmond Council responsible for the care [and abuse] at Grafton Close home at the time was

---

[926] "Cliff Richard," *whale.to*.

[927] Patty Dinham, "Ex-Flying Squad Boss calls for a new Probe into Jill Dando's Murder amid Claims Met Police Detectives Ignored 'Excellent Leads,'" *Daily Mail*, November 20, 2016.

[928] "The Mary Moss Elm Guest House VIP Paedophile Party List," *cigpapers.blog*, April 29, 2013.

[929] Katie Hodge, "Accuser Outrage Sir Cliff Richard Accused of Attacks by 'one of Britain's Worst Sex Offenders,'" *The Sun*, June 16, 2016.

[930] Simon Edge, "How Jim really did Fix it," *Express*, May 8, 2008.

[931] Rebecca Camber and Emily Davies, "'I'm Totally Innocent': Cliff Richard's Fury as Police Raid his £3m Home after Claims of Sex Assault on Boy at 1980s Christian Rally," *Daily Mail*, August 14, 2014.

[932] "The Mary Moss Elm Guest House VIP Paedophile Party List," https://cigpapers.blog/2013/04/29/the-elm-guest-house-vip-paedophile-party-list/.

[933] Fiona O' Clerigh and Mark Watts, "Haroon Kasir Boasted of Friendship with Jimmy Savile, and 'was odd after Star's Death,'" *Exaro News*, February 16, 2013.

none other than future MP power player Keith Vaz, a now disgraced outed pedophile and longtime pedo-enabler-protector. Until 2019 Vaz was shamelessly still holding the Leicester seat in Parliament.[934] During his 32 years as MP, he went from one scandal to the next, but the British political system is so corrupt, he remained a powerful fixture.

The Richmond council, police and social services were all in deep, protecting their pedophilia operations, caught ignoring victim complaints and losing files.[935] Police even gave the council a heads-up before conducting a notorious raid on the Elm Guest House in June 1982.[936] In 1990, 47-year old Carole Kasir suspiciously died of an insulin overdose while working with social worker Mary Moss, divulging explosive secrets as yet more alleged foul trying to desperately keep the lid tightly sealed on the VIP pedo-ring.[937] Despite corrupt subsequent police raids on Mary's home, confiscating and destroying incriminating evidence that would have been used to convict the powerful pedophile guests, subservient police following orders from their pedo-masters, were caught blatantly obstructing justice in order to shield VIPs from accountability. Fortunately, the raid did not prevent the social worker child advocates Mary Moss and Christopher Fay from securing and uploading records to show horrendous sexual abuse perpetrated by a who's who list of British VIPs that include famous cabinet ministers, MPs and lords along with heads of MI5, MI6 and police chiefs.[938] This notorious scandal will be covered in full detail in Chapter 7.

Once the bombshell news of Jimmy Savile's history of child sexual abuse was exposed in late 2012, it prompted retired whistleblowing child protection manager Peter McKelvie to submit a report to MP Tom Watson in October 2012 that included overwhelming evidence of pervasive child sex abuse over the previous 20 years. MP Watson then dramatically confronted Prime Minister David Cameron on the House floor, forcing him to launch what turned out to be a half-ass Westminster police probe into prominent UK politicians' historic child sexual abuse.[939] McKelvie estimated that up to 40 members of the House of Commons and Lords were either full blown pedophiles or confirmed pedophile protectors.[940]

Peter McKelvie, who has dedicated his entire adult professional life to protecting children and exposing those who harm them especially from high places, quickly became a target himself for character assassination by the pedophilia cabal. After being hired as a consultant by the national Independent Inquiry of Child Sexual Abuse (IICSA) formed in 2014, by October 2015 the *Daily Mail* ran a hit piece written by Stephen Wright and Sam Greenhill, launching a smear campaign intended to discredit McKelvie's integrity, accusing Peter of making false allegations

---

[934] Francis Carr Begbie, "Why did Keith Vaz Protect Greville Janner?" *Occidental Observer*, September 4, 2016.

[935] David Hencke and Mark Conrad, "Richmond Files Reveal Failure to Pursue Claim of Child Sex Abuse," *Exaro News*, April 27, 2013.

[936] Mark Conrad, "Richmond Council 'was Alerted to Allegations of Child Sexual Abuse,'" *Exaro News*, February 23.

[937] "The Mary Moss Elm Guest House VIP Paedophile Party List," https://cigpapers.blog/2013/04/29/the-elm-guest-house-vip-paedophile-party-list/.

[938] Rickeo, "The Elm Guest House List," *Free & Fearless*, July 27, 2017.

[939] Matt Chorleey and Tom McTague, Scotland Yard Dismissed Tom Watson's Claim of a 'Powerful Paedophile Network' Linked to Downing Street three years ago but never made it Public," *Daily Mail*, October 14, 2015.

[940] "At least 40 UK Politicians Complicit in Alleged Westminster 'Pedophile Ring' – Report," *RT*, July 5, 2014.

in an attempted "plot" to destroy the political career of a Tory cabinet minister, very likely Leon Brittan.[941]

For his career expertise in accessing and exposing the truth on behalf of child victims for so many years, McKelvie was recruited as a fully qualified consultant member of the Victims and Survivors Consultative Panel for the UK beleaguered Independent Inquiry into Child Sexual Abuse. But right after the *Daily Mail* article attacking his credibility, bogusly claiming his plot to ruin a Tory minister's career, in October 2015 Peter McKelvie resigned his IISCA position, maintaining he would soon be needed as an inquiry witness, stepping down to avoid conflict of interest.[942] But in actuality he was neutered by the destructive powers whose self-interest is to ensure that the full pedophilia truth never gets revealed to the public, and ridding McKelvie as a thorn in the cabal's side was chalked up as another victory for the VIP child rapists. Yet another child advocate was muzzled.

Several years earlier the West Mercia Police granted McKelvie full access to the diary belonging to prominent deceased civil servant-pedophile-PIE founder Peter Righton.[943] Peter McKelvie subsequently learned of Righton's child abuse dating back to 1957 along with group home roundups, procuring trafficked kids to VIP sex parties at locations like Dolphin Square and Elm Guest House. Though Righton died in 2007, thanks to McKelvie, at least the truth about his extensive serial crime history, supplying victims to VIPs ultimately emerged. One reason Peter took his 20 year criminal findings to MP Tom Watson in the 2012 post-Savile aftermath was the fact that the prolific pedophile-VIP pimp Righton had only been given a 1992 slap on the hand for possessing child pornography images.[944] This classic case of another predatory fox guarding the pedo-house consisting of UK's group homes, held top positions with Department of Health, National Children's Bureau and the National Institute of Social Work, and wrote national policy on childcare for UK social services. Yet McKelvie determined that Righton had a connection in Malta where they were trafficking child victims. Because Peter, the real child protection manager, had unearthed the international pedophilia network exposing a major player linked internationally, McKelvie's seminal investigative work was immediately shut down.

The biggest reason motivating Peter McKelvie to become a whistleblower was the fact that his investigative research and professional experience led him to realize that powerful, famous MPs, Lords and cabinet ministers were molesting and raping UK's throwaway kids for years, never investigated nor brought to justice. With Righton both a founding PIE member and UK's leading policymaking authority on protecting children, with key pedo-contacts in Malta, Sweden, Norway and Egypt and beyond, Peter McKelvie is actually a hero for following up on leads and uncovering widespread tentacles of the global pedo-network. He documented child

---

[941] Stephen Wright and Sam Greenhill, "Abuse Inquiry's Adviser Plotted to Smear Top Tory: Whistleblower made Baseless Claims MP was linked to Paedophiles, *Daily Mail*, October 15, 2015.

[942] "Child Sex Abuse Inquiry Advisor 'Plotted to Smear Top Tory,'" *The Telegraph*, October 16, 2015.

[943] "Heroes for Exposing Child Sexual Abuse - Part 1 - Peter McKelvie," *Cathy Fox Blog on Child Abuse*, March 8, 2017.

[944] "Heroes for Exposing Child Sexual Abuse - Part 1 - Peter McKelvie," https://cathyfox.wordpress.com/2017/03/08/heroes-for-exposing-child-sexual-abuse-part-1-peter-mckelvie/.

sex abuse committed by a couple of other, still living pedophile associates of Peter Righton, helping to convict Righton's longtime living partner Richard Alston, brother of diplomat Robert Alston and a former PIE Treasurer, and longtime schoolteacher Charles Napier, half-brother of MP John Whittingdale.[945] Napier wound up assistant head of studies at Cairo's British Council, implicating its sponsor Britain's Foreign Office in the child sex trafficking web. Yet for decades Napier was shielded and allowed to abuse at least 23 of his students in Britain between 1967 and 1983 that eventually led to his arrest and conviction in 2014. He accepted teaching posts in Europe, North Africa and Middle East before his criminal past finally caught up to him. But while in Egypt, in a letter to a friend, sexual predator Napier boasts:

[Cairo is] *full of boys, 98 per cent of them available.*[946]

Napier's half-sibling MP Whittendale more than likely was aware of his brother's sexual proclivities abusing young boys, and as Home Secretary Brittan's advisor, when Leon received the pedophile dossier from MP Geoffrey Dickens in 1983, Whittingdale also had to have been privy to known Westminster pedophiles.[947] In view of the MP's intimate ties with pedophiles, not deterring him from making grandstanding statements about *BBC's* cover-up of Savile's reign of terror,[948] Whittingdale needs to answer the same question about failing to safeguard children in harm's way of pedophiles in his own family and workplace. Where was he when his brother and boss were raping kids for decades?

In 1994 Peter McKelvie's valiant efforts to secure authorization for a proposal that his already established interdisciplinary team consisting of a senior police officer, two seasoned investigative journalists and child social workers from Peter's social services office were turned down in forming a joint task force with law enforcement, and then when his boss retired that same year, his office and team were disbanded.[949] Genuinely effective efforts to actually clean up pedophilia in the UK were systematically quashed. Due to so many abuse crimes committed outside his local jurisdiction, Peter McKelvie was forced to turn over his incriminating findings exposing the Westminster VIP pedophiles to various local authorities. And because orders to suppress evidence of child abuse always emanated from the top, the prime ministers' Home Office and/or intelligence agencies or higher, to this day police investigations throughout the nation never gotten off the ground. When victims' accusations were filed in the 1980s right up to today, it's always been the same old despicable story of next to no arrests and even fewer convictions.

---

[945] "Heroes for Exposing Child Sexual Abuse - Part 1 - Peter McKelvie," https://cathyfox.wordpress.com/2017/03/08/heroes-for-exposing-child-sexual-abuse-part-1-peter-mckelvie/.
[946] Keir Mudie, "Abuse Scandals Probe Widens: The Man who may Hold the Key to UK's Biggest Paedophile Network Ever," *Mirror*, November 11, 2012.
[947] "PIE: Charles Napier – No. 116," *goodnessandharmony.wordpress.com*, January 12, 2018.
[948] Mark Sweney, "Jimmy Savile's Cover-up Claims 'Damaging' for BBC, Says Whittingdale," *The Guardian*, October 22, 2012.
[949] "Heroes for Exposing Child Sexual Abuse - Part 1 - Peter McKelvie," https://cathyfox.wordpress.com/2017/03/08/heroes-for-exposing-child-sexual-abuse-part-1-peter-mckelvie/.

Out of the dozen or so post-Savile Scotland Yard spawned police investigations, from 2012's Operation Yewtree to 2013's Operation Fernbridge, launched specifically to probe both past and present allegations surfacing from Elm Guest House, not one VIP pedophile guest guilty of abusing boys was ever brought to justice, with Fernbridge was closed by March 2015.[950] While the still unscathed perpetrators with their stellar reputations still intact, die off from natural "old age" causes, their younger victims suffering lifelong effects directly from their abuse are dying in significant numbers at much earlier ages, either taking their own lives or under mysterious circumstances. Chapter 7 delves far deeper into this shameful Westminster marathon scandal with its ongoing cover-up, feeding off the lifeblood of innocent children with absolute impunity.

Famous pedophiles at Elm Guest House often used phony names to sign in on the guest list, like Cliff Richard aka "Kitty." Yet with authentic documents still in existence that include household names listed as guests, zero arrests or convictions have been made from the Elm Guest House of Horror.[951] A few years ago Sir Cliff exercised his legal clout and formidable VIP influence to secure a High Court super injunction, prohibiting his name from being associated with the notorious Elm Guest House scandal,[952] and that was before his 2018 landmark legal victory for the ever-popular, unreachable senior citizen.

The Crown Prosecution Service in June 2016 claimed not enough evidence was generated to forward Cliff Richard's case to trial. And the rest is history after the *BBC* and South Yorkshire police sensationalized their August 2014 raid on Richard's home and the July 2018 court decision granting Richard damages for violating his privacy, upwards of over four millions pounds and counting to ensure that in the future, famous people arrested for pedophilia (or any crime) never show up in either newspapers or on TV ever again without news companies risking a fortune. Only after formal criminal charges are brought against known powerful figures will they ever go public in the media. And with so many pedo-gatekeepers in government, law enforcement and courts, that will likely never happen.

Ultimately the 2018 legal development was designed to seal off protection and impunity for those at the top of the pedo-food chain from ever having to abide by manmade laws. After all, they delude themselves into believing they are gods, beyond all judgment and reproach, so they see it as their natural born Luciferian privilege and right to live on earth like gods, above all lowly manmade laws. In the United Kingdom, the ruling elite is now virtually unreachable, making certain that the pedo-epidemic raging at our planet's epicenter will only continue thriving to rage on indefinitely at vulnerable children's expense around the world. If you're an MP or a high court judge or royal family member or famous entertainer, you can rape, sodomize, cannibalize and murder children and adults at will until your cold heart's content. What they fail to realize is, if karma fails to catch up to them in this lifetime, then God most certainly will.

---

[950] "Elm Guest House Claims and Controversy," *revolvy.com*.
[951] Elm Guest House – Child Sexual Abuse – One Big Cover-up," *The UK & Ireland Database*.
[952] "The Mary Moss Elm Guest House VIP Paedophile Party List."

To see how we got to this unholy place and time with the beta tested, Teflon man himself, exploring sir pop legend's humble roots may be incisively useful. Cliff Richard arrived in this world in October 14, 1940 as Harry Rodger Webb in India, a top recruiting source for British intelligence.[953] Harry, his parents and three sisters moved to England in 1948 where his father secured a job with Thorn Electrical Industries (also known as EMI).[954] Electrical and Mechanical Instruments sold music in its heyday throughout the 1960s but was also a major producer of military electronics within UK's defense industry, establishing a crucial front for British military intelligence operations to covertly expand its cultural reach and influence among the younger British population.[955] Through Tavistock-developed mind control methods, UK's security services are notorious for recruiting and transforming cute little boys into future sex slaves, spies and assassins. That they are bred to evolve into iconic legendary singers only makes them more invaluable as a cabal-controlled tool for the UK-US-Israel axis-of-evil.

Satanic elements merged with military intelligence to transform the counterculture movement into an orgiastic youth drug-fest back in the swinging 1960s.[956] CIA's concocted mix of MK-Ultra mind control, international drug pushing[957] and satanic sex cults like Alistair Crowley's OTO, have been infused and embedded into popular culture through the globalized entertainment industry.[958] Deployment of mind controlled sex slaves in a grand social engineering experiment has been misusing humanity as guinea pigs, part of the false propaganda machine to brainwash and achieve mass mind control. Scientology founder L. Ron Hubbard[959] was once a naval intelligence operative who with Jack Parsons, a leading NASA rocket scientist, embraced Crowley's demonic sex occult teachings.[960] The subversively fascist and sinister dogma underpinning the CIA, manufactured the "peace, love and freedom" movement of the sixties also simultaneously promoted the burgeoning rise of modern art as a Cold War artifice used as an anti-Soviet psyops weapon,[961] just as the Cold War itself was also an internationalists' New World Order creation.[962]

From both sides of the Atlantic, the US-British intelligence apparatus launched the careers of many superstar artists from the 1950s, 60s and 70s right up to the present as a combined means of both social control and social engineering through promoting the lifestyle mantra of "sex, drugs and rock n' roll," in the short term to neutralize the antiwar movement in Vietnam, but in the long term to destroy family, nationalism and moral and spiritual values as barriers to

[953] "Cliff Richard; Crusaders; Military Intelligence."
[954] "Cliff Richard; Mind Control; Israel," *angirfana.blogspot.com*, April 2015..
[955] "The Manufactured Invention of the Beatles, Stones, Grateful Dead and the Birth of Rock n' Roll by the Tavistock Institute; A Jesuit Corporation," *tabublog.com*, December 26, 2015..
[956] Donald Phau, "The Satanic Roots of Rock," *100777.com.*
[957] "Dealing in Death – The CIA and the Drug Trade," *bibliotecapleyades.net*, 2005.
[958] David Livingstone, "Laurel Canyon: Sex, Drugs and Aliens," *Conspiracy School*, July 19, 2013.
[959] Erin Whitney, "16 Shocking Allegations in Scientology Documentary 'Going Clear,'" *Huffington Post*, March 29, 2015.
[960] Annalee Newitz, "The Strangely True Connection between Scientology, the Jet Propulsion Lab, and Occult Sorcery," *Gizmodo*, January 24, 2013.
[961] Frances Stonor Saunders, "Modern Art was a CIA 'Weapon,'" *Independent*, October 22, 1995.
[962] Servando Gonzalez, "The Cold War Hoax, Part 1," *News with Views*, August 15, 2014.

their New World Order.[963] Operation Paperclip and establishing MK-Ultra Monarch mind control through drugs, torture and child sexual abuse in order to mass produce sex slaves, assassins and spies was well underway by the 1950s (taken up in Book 4). NWO opponents in JFK, RFK and MLK were all systematically eliminated[964] and the "New Age" of Aquarius promoting rampant sexual promiscuity and hedonism in youth generations was ushered in to stay over the long haul. This socially engineered culture of "anything goes" paves the way for pedophilia as sexual deviance, perversion and predation to systematically and ritualistically be practiced by today's elites as an effective means to an end in order to gain increasing acceptance, power and control over the human race. And thus far, unfortunately for children and humanity alike, it's been working like a charm for them according to sinister plan.

In the same vein as drug and mind controlled Elvis Presley,[965] across the pond likewise Cliff Richard was selected and spawned in England as a covert intel operator for both the Mossad and MI5.[966] Thus, the meteoric rise of Cliff, the Beatles, the Rolling Stones and other British Invasion groups of the sixties were all bi-products of Tavistock and British secret service. In America such artists as John Phillips of the Mamas and the Papas, Jim Morrison of the Doors (whose father was an admiral in naval intelligence) and Jimmy Hendrix were all products of this same intelligence apparatchik. The late journalist and author Dave McGowan's treatise documenting the CIA's Laurel Canyon Hippie Movement incisively and graphically exposes this mass mind control phenomenon.[967]

And in the UK, it was intelligence services that co-opted the *BBC* and its hardcore pedophile DJs such as Alan Freeman, Jimmy Savile and Chris Dunning to name a few teamed up with pedo-notables from the music industry like producer Joe Meeks, manager Brian Epstein and impresario Jonathon King to corrupt, exploit and abuse British youth throughout the swinging 60s, spawning the age of "anything goes" into faithful practice reminiscent of Crowley's "do what thou wilt."[968] But the perversions that characterized the 1960s and 70s never faded, and if anything, have only grown both more pervasive and more perverse. As yet more confirmation of a wider pedophile network, both Savile and an unnamed "top 1960s pop group" (that some websites claim to be the Beatles[969]) have been exposed in a four page 1964 dossier discovered during Operation Yewtree as visitors to a teen brothel in Battersea, South London where runaway kids from group homes were being systemically pipelined and abused.[970]

During the 1950s and 1960s centered in the East End of London, infamous gay pedophile Jewish gangster twins – Reggie and Ronnie Kray - were busy running an extensive sexual pedo-

[963] "CIA Social Control Through Sex, Drugs and Rock 'n Roll," *21st Century Wire*, December 30, 2013.

[964] Dave Hodges, "JFK, RFK and MLK were all Killed by the same Forces," *biblioecapleyades.net*, November 17, 2013.

[965] "Mysterious Elvis Presley," *aangirfan.com*, November 7, 2013.

[966] "Tavistock and Cliff Richard: Mossad Control," *aanirfan.com*, August 15, 2004.

[967] Dave McGowan, "Inside the LC: The Strange but Mostly True Story of Laurel Canyon and the Birth of the Hippie Generation," *Illuminati News*, May 8, 2008.

[968] Greg Villepique, "'Do What Thou Wilt: A Life of Aleister Crowley,'" Salon, August 31, 2000.

[969] "Police Report: The Beatles Visited Paedophile Brothel with Savile," *humansarefree.com*, March 2017.

[970] Dominic Gover, "Which 1960s Pop Group was at Paedophile Brothel with Jimmy Savile?" *IB Times*, April 8, 2015.

blackmail operation,[971] similar to Donald Trump's mentor, CIA sanctioned Roy Cohn masterminding the New York City to Washington pedo-network during the exact same period.[972] Just as in America, mobsters, satanic cults and intelligence agencies all covertly work hand-in-hand in the increasingly lucrative child sex trafficking trade.[973] For years the Kray brothers regularly provided the conduit linkage between boy brothels funneled from group homes to service hundreds of entertainment luminaries, prime ministers, cabinet ministers, MPs, lords and more queen knighted sirs in one big flourishing underworld pedophilia network.

It was the Kray twins who identified Sir Cliff Richard as one of Lord Robert Boothby's "bum-boys."[974] One powerful central figure partaking services from the Kray syndicate was Lord Boothby, who had an unquenchable taste for little boy flesh like Harry Webb throughout the 1950s. As a prominent Oxford educated Conservative member in Parliament, Lord Boothby was also in tight with Sir Winton Churchill, his top tier government peers as well as the royal family. Lord Boothby is said to have had a sexual relationship with Ronnie Kray.[975] As birds of the same feather, veteran intel agent Anthony T. Stokes maintains that Churchill's original MI5 Sandhurst file described him as:

An idle layabout and a confirmed sodomite who was a menace to the younger boys.[976]

Pretty amazing but not surprising for the world's pedophilia haven Britain to have as its bulldog saint Sir Winston be another pedophile. Churchill's protégé bud Bobby Boothby was also an original founding member of the Bilderberg group in 1954. Truth activist *Abel Danger*'s Field McConnell alleges that the Krays, Boothby and the Bilderberg Steering Committee teamed up beginning in 1954 to operate pedo-entrapment rings at all the Bilderberg hosting hotels.[977] Boothby's linkage to the world's elite no doubt became one more reason why his kinky indiscretions were so often overlooked yet fiercely protected. Not only did Lord Boothby and the Kray twins share the same heinous predilection for "rent boys," and establishing VIP blackmail operations, they also assisted Cliff Richard as an initiate into their secret club's established inside connections that helped launch Cliff's musical career.[978] As a close friend of the Kray brothers, in the early days Cliff frequently performed at their nightclubs. Their relations went deep in a perverted "win-win" for all involved.

But not every kid made it out alive, much less become a superstar. The gruesome Tattingstone suitcase murder of 17-year old Bernard Oliver was suspected to be a victim of the Kray

[971] "Ronnie Kray's Pedophile Ring," *UK & Ireland Database.*

[972] Paul David Collins, "The Ghost of Roy Cohn," *Conspiracy Archive*, August 24, 2014.

[973] "Six Case Studies that point to Massive Pedophile Rings at the Highest Levels of Power," *The Last American Vagabond*, November 11, 2016.

[974] "Cliff Richard; Mind Control; Israel," https://angirfana.blogspot.com/2015/04/cliff-richard-mind-control-israel.html.

[975] David Barrett, "Letters Shed new Light on Kray Twins Scandal," The Telegraph, July 26, 2009.

[976] Anthony T. Stokes, "Death of a Showman: Jimmy Savile 1926-2011," *whale.to*, October 31, 2011.

[977] "Kelly 19 – Bilderberg Hotel Pedophile Steering, Clinton's Bin Laden Gyro, SERCO's Mentored Zulu Towers," Abel Danger, June 26, 2017.

[978] "Jimmy Savile, the Kray Twins, Cliff Richard…," *aangirfan.com*, October 6, 2012.

pedophile syndicate.[979] Ten days after leaving his North London home in January 1967, Bernard's dismembered body dissected into six pieces was found in two suitcases laying in a field[980] not far from property owned by the Krays in Suffolk where they trafficked group home rent boys to VIP sex parties. The dead boy's 15-year old brother recognized him from a gruesome newspaper photo of his brother's cut off head. Bernard's five siblings have been tormented by the grisly tragedy ever since. Two now deceased pedophile doctors, wanted for subsequent sex crimes and murders of other underage boys, who as fugitives fled the country, are believed to be Bernard's killers. Already interviewed by police shortly after Bernard's body was discovered, record producer Joe Meek, who frequented the Krays' Suffolk pedo-party scene with fellow attendees *BBC* DJs Savile and Al Freeman, went on a paranoid drug binge and fatally shot his landlady, then himself with a single gage shotgun.[981] The Kray twins are said to have sealed remaining loose ends with a couple more kills and over a half century later, the murder still sadly stays unsolved.

As a testimonial to the Kray-Sir Cliff friendship, even after Reggie and Ronnie were both locked away for life in 1969, Cliff Richard maintained his close ties with his old gangster buddies, signing one of his concert programs with a special nostalgic note to Ronnie.[982] Kray biographer John Pearson furnished a jailhouse letter written by Ronnie in 1969, expressing gratitude for Cliff sending him his support when other celebrity friends were fast disappearing from the recently convicted imprisoned killers, but not loyal Cliff. In Ronnie's own original misspelled words:

John, I had a verry nice letter from Cliff Ritchards. I thought it was marvoulas of him to write to me at a time like this. He must be a wonderfull person to go to the trouble at a time like this. Their are still a lot of nice people left around. [983]

David Litvinoff (Levy) was one of the Krays' prime procurers in their Jewish mob pedophile ring. In fact, as early as 1954 Litvinoff had a reputation as the go-to guy for delivering rent boys. Apparently his friend Lucian Freud thought so. Sigmund Freud's grandson and brother of fellow pedophile-writer-former MP Sir Clement (connected to the McCann abduction)[984] literally painted Litvinoff in a 1954 portrait he originally entitled "The Procurer," selling at Christie's the year Jill Dando died in 1999 for over a million pounds.[985] Another related tidbit - to capture the gritty real life reality of the Kray mafia scene, pedophile scum Litvinoff was hired as a film advisor on the 1968 Mick Jagger gangster flick "Performance," introducing the cast and crew to London's seedy underworld. As a crime boss lieutenant, especially once the Krays went to

---

[979] "Jimmy Savile, the Kray Twins, Cliff Richard…," *aangirfan.com*, October 6, 2012.

[980] Colin Adwent, "50 years on we remember Suffolk's Grisliest Crime - the Tattingstone Suitcase Murder," East Anglian Daily Times, January 6, 2017.

[981] Jake Arnott, "Jake Arnott: Joe Meek and Me," *Evening Standard*, June 12, 2009.

[982] Christian F. Simpson, Lost Youth Volume 2: London (London: Authorhouse UK, 2012, p. 429.

[983] "Kray Twins Memorabilia Sold at Auction," *The Telegraph*, October 20, 2010..

[984] Martin Evan and Gordon Rayner, "Sir Clement Freud Exposed as a Paedophile as Police Urged to Probe Madeleine McCann Links," *The Telegraph*, June 15, 2016.

[985] "Lucian Freud's Pregnant Teen Painting. Litvinoff, the Krays and anyone who was anyone!" *spidercatweb.blog*, February 19, 2016.

prison, for decades David Litvinoff was known to freely circulate socially amongst top British and American celebrities as the VIP pedo-pimp managing to accumulate enough wealth to live the last three years of his pathetic life in opulent style at Davington Priory in Kent before allegedly OD'ing on sleeping pills in 1975. Of all people, the current owner of Davington Priory is none other than the unsaintly Sir Bob Geldof, where silenced daughter Peaches married Cohen in the Priory estate gardens.[986]

Just like US pedo-operations in all these sordid affairs, drugs and alcohol are regularly used as standard sedating icebreakers to break children's hymens, anuses and souls as well as their capacity for trauma memory recall.[987] Like Savile, all the mayhem and suffering the Kray brothers, Litvinoff and Boothby and their ilk perpetrated against children were/are forgiven by the ruling elite, fully protected by the deep bonding glue of their systemic blackmail cesspool.

Boothby was a frequent aficionado at the Kray brother orgies and sex parties. The sex maniac even recklessly carried on a longstanding affair with the wife of the UK Prime Minister Harold MacMillan (their youngest daughter reportedly is his biologically).[988] Promiscuous Boothby even carried on a homosexual tryst with gangster Ronnie Kray,[989] amidst lots of masochistic sex with scores of underage boys like Harry Webb.[990] Kray biographer John Pearson accessed intimate accounts of some of Lord Boothby's favorite forms of kink, such as ordering rent boys to shit on a glass table while the aroused pervert below peered upwards, all boggled-eyed, lustily mouthwatering his chops.[991] Mind you these are the sick sort of perversions that the rulers of our planet customarily engage in for leisure when not participating in formal occult ritual torture and murderous sacrifice.

In 1964 the *Sunday Mirror* exposed the Boothby-Kray homosexual pedophilia operation.[992] But Labor Party's Harold Wilson sent in his legal fixer to do crisis damage control, and just like that, the paper had to eat their words on top of paying a £40,000 libel settlement for actually printing the truth, in effect scaring off the media from exposing any future scandals (not unlike 2018's Sir Cliff lawsuit). And despite opposing political parties (since pedos infiltrate all major political parties), Harold Wilson, by exercising restraint in saving Boothby's ass, was rewarded as the next elected prime minister. This little-known scandal provides graphic illustration of how the worst sins of the ruling class have always remained above the law. As untouchables, VIPs and gangsters alike can continue raping kids without the inconvenient truth getting in their way.

---

[986] Chloe Thomas, "She's never been Traditional! Peaches Geldof Marries Thomas Cohen Wearing three different Gowns throughout the day," *Daily Mail*, September 11, 2012.

[987] "Elm Guest House – Latest," *UK & Ireland Database*.

[988] Angela Lambert, "The Prime Minister, his Wife and her Lover Dorothy MacMillan had an Affair that lasted 30 Years," *Independent*, February 23, 1994.

[989] Cahal Milmo, "Ronnie Kray's Association with Tory Peer and Fellow 'Hunter of Young Men' led to MI5 Investigation and Government Panic," *Independent*, October 23, 2015.

[990] Claire Ellicott, "Ronnie Kray: Files Reveal Fears that Exposé Revealing Pair 'Hunted' for Men in the East End could bring down the Government," *Daily Mail*, October 23, 2015.

[991] John Pearson, "The Lords of the Underworld," *Independent*, June 15, 1997.

[992] John Pearson, https://www.independent.co.uk/arts-entertainment/the-lords-of-the-underworld-1256016.html.

With such high stakes of perverse power and protection granted the Kray mafia by the decadent British establishment, young group home lads never stand a chance. Ronnie Kray once threatened a boy:

You will go home with Lord Boothby. You will do exactly what Lord Boothby wants. Or I will hurt you.[993]

Ronnie boy also bought more protection for his "Firm" with a sexual dalliance with yet another prominent homosexual pedophile politician from the Krays' own district - Labor Party chairman and 30-year MP Tom Driberg. The KGB cashed in on Driberg's multiple affairs, blackmailing and enlisting him as a Soviet spy codenamed Lepage[994] while already a confirmed MI5 informer. At one point, Driberg was even cast out of the Communist party but remained a devout OTO "do what thou wilt" disciple. In his biography the question is raised:

Can the man who in the 1920s was anointed by Aleister Crowley to succeed him as the Great Beast be the man who in the 1960s tried to persuade Mick Jagger to become a Labour MP?[995]

It has recently come to light that the then British Director of Public Prosecutions Sir Norman Skelhorn blocked Driberg's pedo-espionage case from exposure and ever moving forward legally.[996] Again, another pedo-enabling "fox" knighted by the queen protecting VIPs inside their child raping network.

With such high-end protection, the Krays possessed sufficient muscle to pressure Metropolitan Police Commissioner Sir Joseph Simpson (yep, another knighted fox standing guard at the cabal's henhouse), to look the other way from 1958 to 1968.[997] An S&M dominatrix who ran with the Kray mob assured Ronnie she could handle Simpson because as one of her clients, he was her masochist whipping boy.[998]

The Krays underworld activities may have started out in the usual mafia domain - armed robbery, arson, protection racket extortion, gambling, drugs and prostitution, but in the pedo-epicenter of the world, it quickly expanded into sexual blackmail pimping children, especially the preferred Englishman's preference - 10-12-year old blue-eyed white boys. With Metro head Sir Simpson dying in 1968, the Krays' luck finally ran out as in 1969 they were tried, convicted

---

[993] "Jimmy Savile, Edward Heath and the Kray Twins," *google-law.blogspot.com*, November 2, 2012.

[994] Jonathon Owen, "Police Blocked from Charging Former Labour MP Tom Driberg with Sexually Abusing Boys, claims Simon Danczuk," *Independent*, December 3, 2015.

[995] Francis Wheen, *Tom Driberg, His Life and Indiscretions* (London: Chatto & Windus, 1990), Pg.11.

[996] Jonathon Owen, https://www.independent.co.uk/news/uk/crime/police-were-blocked-from-charging-labour-mp-tom-driberg-with-sexually-abusing-boys-claims-simon-a6759391.html.

[997] "Conservative Government Threatened by Sex Scandals," *aangirfan.com*, October 23, 2016.

[998] John Fleming, "Corrupt Cops, Sado Masochist Whippings and how Gangster Ronnie Kray Explained his own Dangerous, Psychotic Feelings," *thejohnfleming.wordpress.com*, October 29, 2013.

and each issued a lifetime sentence for their gangland murders, one victim shot in a pub for calling Ronnie "a fat poof" and Reggie fatally stabbing another in his flat.[999]

But even from their prison cells, the powerful Kray brothers, maintaining close ties with the American mob, were still in business providing security protection to VIP entertainers including Frank Sinatra, George Raft, Judy Garland (a child rape and mind control victim herself[1000]) as well as Saudi princes.[1001] With the media's longtime fascination romanticizing organized crime in both America and the UK, the press fielded stories of a 12-year old fatherless boy named Brad Lane becoming a mini-celebrity idolizing Reggie as his "adopted father" and the jailbird's #1 faithful prison visitor. Unfortunately, Brad died young, so in 2009 his mother had her son's collected memorabilia from the gangster twins auctioned off for a hefty £50,000.[1002]

Once sent to prison, Ronnie went increasingly psychotic and ended up at his old friend Jimmy Savile's Broadmoor, UK's maximum-security prison asylum till his death at 61, while a half decade later, brother Reggie stricken with cancer, was released a month before his death in 2000 at age 66. By the time Ronnie was shipped off to Savile's roost at Broadmoor, Sir Jimmy was already replacing the twins as UK's pimping kingpin, running the always profitable child procurement racket through his expanding MI5-*BBC*-group home pipeline, supplying the nonstop demand of kiddie fodder, devoured by those same voracious VIP pigs-in-power during the latter decades of the twentieth century.

As SOP spy world folklore, foreign espionage has long involved laying honey traps to gain control, targeting unsuspecting politicians and entertainers through sexual blackmail operations. Infiltrating CIA, Mossad, KGB and MI5/6 operatives have been deploying not just female seductresses to lure prominent husbands into adulterous affairs, but increasingly young men and children are regularly offered through Cohn-Kray-Savile-Epstein-spy service sex ring pipelines to own homosexual and pedo-leaning puppets in both high government and show biz.[1003]

In 1959 Cliff Richard signed a recording contract with EMI, the Tavistock mind control linked "Electronic Military Intelligence" corporation where his father began working a decade earlier. Ever since signing that 1959 contract on the dotted line and uniquely churning out hits in every decade since, for over sixty years as the pop sensation's handlers - the Mossad and MI5, have been taking full advantage of Sir Cliff's "goodwill" ambassadorship services for the Greater

[999] Charles Early, "March 4, 1969: Ronnie and Reggie Kray Found Guilty of Murder," *bt.com*, March 4, 2018.

[1000] Michael S. Rosenwald, "'I'll Ruin you': Judy Garland on being Groped and Harassed by Powerful Hollywood Men," *The Washington Post*, November 14, 2017.

[1001] Vanessa Allen, "How the Krays ran a Protection Business for Sinatra and Co behind Bars," *Daily Mail*, January 2, 2010.

[1002] "Reggie Kray's 'Adopted' Son: Letters show Close Bond between the Gangster and the Boy who Idolized him," *Daily Mail*, April 10, 2009.

[1003] Claire Ellicott, http://www.dailymail.co.uk/news/article-3285578/Tory-panic-kinky-peer-Ronnie-Kray-Files-reveal-fears-expose-revealing-pair-hunted-men-East-End-bring-Government.html.

Israel Project,[1004] no doubt in exchange for security protection against a long stint in prison for his alleged deviant pastime pleasures.

As an anecdotal inference of Cliff's mind control alters, from his own autobiographical account comes:

It was as if I was becoming a different character - almost like the mild mannered Clark Kent... The moment I put on the pink jacket... I was Cliff ... and when I came off the stage I went back to being a shy little boy...[1005]

Of course intelligence agencies have been pervasively deploying Monarch mind controlled superstars to the extent that it's become cliché today. From Beyoncé, Rihanna, Nicki Minaj, Madonna, Lady Gaga, Katy Perry, Britney Spears to Eminem and Lil Wayne, on and on New Babylon ad infinitum go the fashionably sheik, controlled pied piping sex slaves, mesmerizing and enslaving adoring global masses into unholy oblivion as the Luciferian elite's grand planned Trojan horse.[1006] Sir Cliff's simply a mind controlled prop hypnotizing the more conservative, Holy Roller geriatric crowd, still captivated by the borderline octogenarian's ass wiggling stage moves so that no one gets left out of this Illuminati cabal's mass mind control operation.

No matter his surface appearance and perennial "choir boy" banality, historic sordid truth just seems to keep haunting Sir Cliff. According to longtime British intelligence operative Anthony T. Stokes, an incident in the spring of 1970 implicated Cliff Richard, then still in his late 20s, as a reported pedophile. An unattended plastic carrier bag was discovered in a large London railway station. Inside the travel bag was a collection of letters and photographs apparently taken at pedophile parties with well-known entertainers and children present.[1007] Though Cliff Richard's name was not mentioned, enough is disclosed to leave no doubt as to whose identity was exposed:

One [photo] *in particular showed a pop singer who masquerades under a Christian persona; dressed in women's underwear he was pictured with young boys.*[1008]

No sooner was the travel bag picked up, while the railway worker was still filling out the lost and found form, two MI5 agents and a special branch officer suddenly barged in demanding the bag and all its contents.[1009] What does this tell us? It indicates that even back in 1970 [and earlier], British and foreign intelligence services were facilitating sexual blackmail schemes,

---

[1004] "Tavistock and Cliff Richard; Mossad Control," *aangirfan.com*, August 15, 2014.

[1005] "Cliff Richard; Mind Control," *aangirfan.com*, April 14, 2014.

[1006] David Gardner, "The Music Industry Exposed," *bibliotecapleyades.net*, November 29, 2014.

[1007] "Jimmy Savile, The Kray Twins, Cliff Richard…" http://aangirfan.blogspot.com/2012/10/jimmy-savile-kray-twins-cliff-richards.html.

[1008] "Jimmy Savile, The Kray Twins, Cliff Richard…" http://aangirfan.blogspot.com/2012/10/jimmy-savile-kray-twins-cliff-richards.html.

[1009] "Jimmy Savile, The Kray Twins, Cliff Richard…" http://aangirfan.blogspot.com/2012/10/jimmy-savile-kray-twins-cliff-richards.html.

utilizing underage children as honeytrap bait to target, compromise and control public figures in both entertainment as well as government.

Recall last chapter's blast-from-the past when Jimmy Savile and Cliff Richard back in the early 1970s were recruited and invited to join Lord Frank Longford's infamous fact-finding mission on pornography. With the former two-time cabinet minister in the Harold Wilson Labor government, Lord Longford's crew set out to learn all about the seedy world of porn (like they didn't already know firsthand), touring the UK to research the sleazy sex industry that included a brief stopover in Denmark to observe Copenhagen strip clubs.[1010] Now why would Longford choose a pop singer who claimed to be a devout Christian celibate and a single, never married radio DJ living at home with his mother unless he knew there was more to their seemingly uninitiated, "sheltered" lives than meets the eye. In any event, the factfinders came up with a best seller that flew off the shelves back in 1972 with the keyword title "pornography" strategically emboldened on its front cover. Hungry, sex-starved, sex-craving British citizens wanted to know what all the fuss was about with one in five male Brits at that time admitting to regularly buying (and jerking off to) porno rags[1011] sold at adult bookstores proliferating throughout the Isles in the early 70s.

The "porn trio experts" delivered some juicy, salacious tidbits of prep schoolboy spankings and a Danish transvestite's comical come-on to his Lordship, but otherwise never quite measured up to all the hype.[1012] Imagine if their perversions were actually unveiled, revealing their booming underground pedophile ring that would've blown the lid off the entire child raping cabal way back when. Instead of just the Kray brothers being stuck in prison in 1972, half the Parliamentary Houses would be joining them behind bars where demented child abusers belong.

In reality both Sir Jimmy and Sir Cliff were MI5/6 and Mossad tools used for many decades as undercover assets regularly paying homage to the Jewish State, making frequent trips in support of the Zionist government. In 2013 the pop legend was ready to dedicate his hit song "Living Doll" to Sara Netanyahu sitting in the audience at his Tel Aviv concert, till secret service nixed the plan not wanting the public to know the power couple was in attendance. Though Sir Cliff spent quality time schmoozing with the Netanyahus at their plush stately residence several days earlier,[1013] the Christian knight in Zionist armor also found time to visit the holy city of Nazareth a month earlier to attend a charity tennis fundraiser.[1014]

Richard was back again in 2017 for another concert performance and again having time to host another kumbaya PR tennis photo-op, this time bringing Jewish and Arab kids together,[1015]

[1010] Alwyn W. Turner, *Crisis? What Crisis?* (London: Aurum Press, 2008), Chapter 8: Obscenity.
[1011] Alwyn W. Turner, http://www.alwynwturner.com/crisis/extracts08.html.
[1012] Alwyn W. Turner, http://www.alwynwturner.com/crisis/extracts08.html.
[1013] Herb Keinon, "Shin Bet Nixed Cliff Richard Song Dedication to Sara Netanyahu," *Jerusalem Post*, August 8, 2013.
[1014] Ben Rosenfield, "Sir Cliff Richard's Tennis Trip to Nazareth," *Jerusalem Post*, July 11, 2013..
[1015] "Cliff Richard Supports Jewish-Arab Coexistence at Tennis Fundraiser," *Times of Israel*, October 10, 2017.

while on the West Bank, more Palestinian homes were being bulldozed.[1016] Like his friend Sir Jimmy, Cliff Richard devotes much time and energy to charitable causes, which of course is a good thing. But it's always used as leverage, along with his projected squeaky-clean image as a "martyred victim," to counter the disturbing claims and negative publicity that have lingered throughout his seven-decade long career.

Meanwhile, his cohort Sir Savile masquerading as a "saintly" Catholic pretender, the closeted Satanist-necrophiliac-child rapist-closeted serial killer also made certain to pay homage to Zionism, logging in a number of trips to the Jewish State. Referring to himself as "the most Jewish Catholic you will ever meet,"[1017] while knighted in 1990 by the queen[1018] and pope alike,[1019] in 1979 Sir Jimmy was also awarded a medal by Israel.[1020] The likes of Sir Jimmy and Sir Cliff are embraced and lauded as useful stooges by all three cabal powerhouse centers - the City of London, Rome and Israel.

According to Manchester businessman Benny Sandberg, because Savile was in tight with Egyptian President Anwar Sadat's wife Jehan and her family, Savile was approached by the Friends of Israel Trust to help forge a dialogue between Prime Minister Menachem Began and Sadat.[1021] Thus enlisted as an informal Israeli security advisor, in 1975 Savile accompanied his dispatched Jim'll Fix It crew to Israel on a 10 day visit to meet with the Jerusalem mayor as well as Israel President Ephraim Katzir. Fondly recalling his visit, Savile seized yet another boastful opportunity to plug his grandiose self-importance:

I arrived at this reception. The president came to me and asked how I was enjoying my visit. I said I was very disappointed: the Israelis had won the Six Day War but they had given back all the land, including the only oil well in the region, and were now paying the Egyptians more for oil than if they had bought it from Saudi Arabia. I said: 'You have forgotten to be Jewish.' He said: 'Would you like to tell my cabinet that?' Next morning, I went to the Knesset; they interrupted a cabinet meeting and I told them the same as I had told him.[1022]

Just another indicator that both pedophile Sir Jimmy and "alleged" pedophile Sir Cliff are Zionist pawns, working on behalf of the Greater Israel Project, is their mutual friendship with confirmed Mossad-CIA agent Uri Geller, the spoon bending phenom from the 1970s, endowed

---

[1016] Brennan Cusack, "Bulldozers in the West Bank: How Recent Israeli Settlement Expansion Jeopardizes the Peac Process," *Forbes*, July 13, 2018.
[1017] Gordon Rayner, "Jimmy Savile Confessed to Reporter that he would be Seen as 'Crooked' after his Death," *The Telegraph*, October 18, 2012.
[1018] Tara Brady, "Revealed: Bizarre Plan to give Jimmy Savile a second Knighthood so he can be Stripped of it Publicly," *Daily Mail*, January 13, 2013.
[1019] Patrick Counihan, "Catholic Church cannot Rescind Papal Knighthood Awarded to Pedophile Jimmy Savile," *Irish Central*, October 28, 2012.
[1020] "Jimmy Savile Scandal Exposes Pedophile Network at Heart of British Establishment," *sott.net*, October 1, 2012.
[1021] "Jimmy Savile Fixed it for Israel," *aangirfan.com*, October 1, 2012.
[1022] Jessica Elgot, "Jimmy Savile came to my Batmitzvah," *The Jewish Chronicle*, November 3, 2011.

with supposed supernatural New Age psychic powers.[1023] He was a natural to be recruited and deployed as an undercover intelligence operative for both Mossad and the CIA on overseas missions over a span of the next several decades. And of course, with both Geller and Richard steeped in mind control, as the Israeli-British go-between, Mossad handler Uri worked closely with both Lord Longford's "porno experts" Savile and Richard in support of their Greater Zionist causes, which by the way include the global pedophilia blackmail network[1024]

Tired of the constant tabloid rumors about his unorthodox personal lifestyle living with a parade of men under the pretense of plutonic relationships, 15 years after the queen knighted him, in 2010 Sir Cliff Richard renounced his British citizenship to become a permanent Barbados citizen where privacy allows him to indulge his prurient interests without nearly the interference and unwanted attention.[1025] No doubt he had to pull a few of his many political strings to pull that maneuver off as Barbados doesn't often grant outsiders citizenship. But then when Mossad both owns and owes you favors, and you're in tight with compromised British war criminal and Mossad operative Tony Blair, suddenly doors open while super court injunctions busily close the doors on inconvenient truths. With Tony Blair's alleged gay "cottaging" past,[1026] and Sir Cliff's likeminded proclivities, rumors of the unpopular Mr. former prime minister and the pop legend abound, stoked by the frequent visits Tony kept making to Cliff's humble abodes in Portugal and Barbados as shelter from his political shitstorm.[1027]

After a couple conscripted "PR girlfriends" briefly put on display a lifetime ago,[1028] since 1965 Cliff has steadfastly maintained that he found God, especially after hooking up with MK-Ultra operative, 33 degree Freemason and fellow pedo-club kingpin, the late Sir Billy Graham,[1029] fervently claiming Christ and celibacy despite that pesky accusation that wouldn't go away stemming from a 1985 incident at the Billy Graham crusade in Sheffield.[1030]

Speaking of which, in August 2014 Sir Richard's world crumbled in horrified shock. From his Portugal mansion, a stone's throw from pedophile neighbor Clement Freud's house and the McCann girl disappearance, a weeping Sir Richard watched on live television the *BBC* cameras rolling as South Yorkshire police invaded his Berkshire estate, searching for pedophilia evidence in response to allegations of child sexual abuse.[1031] An alleged victim while under the age of 16 at the time, was accusing the singer of molesting him at Rev. Billy Graham's 1985 evangelist

[1023] Geoffrey Macnab, "Uri Geller Psychic Spy? The Spoon-Bender's Secret life as a Mossad and CIA Agent Revealed," *Independent*, June 14, 2013.

[1024] "Cliff Richard; Mind Control," http://aanirfan.blogspot.com/2014/04/cliff-richard-mind-control.html.

[1025] Tim Walker, "Sir Cliff Richard: Why Barbados Beat Britain," *The Telegraph*, September 23, 2010.

[1026] Andrew Watt, "The Alleged "Cottaging" Conviction of Tony Blair - Submission to the Child Abuse Inquiry," *ukchildabuseinquiry.blogspot.com*, June 10, 2015.

[1027] Mark Brown, "Revealed: Why Sir Cliff gave Blair a Summer Holiday," *The Guardian*, August 24, 2006.

[1028] Alison Boshoff, "Homes around the World but never a lasting Love to Share them with - Sir Cliff Richard's Love Life, or apparent lack thereof," *Daily Mail*, August 14, 2014.

[1029] Caroline Davies, "Honorary Knighthood for Billy Graham," *The Telegraph*, December 7, 2001.

[1030] "Billy Graham and Cliff Richard," *aangirfan.com*, July 1, 2018.

[1031] Sam Greenhill, "Sir Cliff Richard was Eating Lunch at his Beloved Algarve Retreat when he Watched the TV in Horror as the Raid Unfolded at his Berkshire Apartment," *Daily Mail*, July 19, 2018.

rally,[1032] and in the aftermath of the Jimmy Savile-Operation Yewtree, police and *BBC* were zeroing in on Cliff's colorful past, like the underwear photo of Kitty posing with his underage boys. Six months after his home was raided, due to yet more claims of prior Cliff Richard sex assaults at Elm Guest House, the investigation widened as South Yorkshire Police Chief Constable David Crompton wrote in a February 10, 2015 letter to then chairman of the Commons Home Affairs Select Committee Keith Vaz:

This investigation has increased significantly in size since its inception.[1033]

As noted earlier, MP Vaz reining over the powerful parliamentary watchdog committee as a pedo-system gatekeeper, ended up in September 2016 forcibly retiring as committee chairman in disgrace after he was exposed as a pedophile and staunch pedo-protector of his mentor, serial pedophile Lord Greville Janner, each respectively high-up in the UK Muslim-Jewish VIP pedo-predator food chain.[1034] Back in 1991 when Janner was accused of chronically abusing two victims (that the presiding judge ruled out as incriminating testimony), it was his groomed young Indian protégé pedophile MP Keith Vaz on the House of Commons floor, vehemently defending his closest political ally, claiming Janner was "the victim of a cowardly and wicked attack."[1035] In that same deceitful speech, Vaz also made a case for **changing the existing law to prohibit prominent figures to be accused in open court** (emphasis added due to aforementioned "Cliff's law" resulting from Cliff's July 2018 court decision).

Despite voices of victims finally being heard (but mostly lip service heard) in the post-Savile aftermath, some of the ugly truth came out in the filthy wash when in 2014 dozens of Greville Janner victims came forth to report four decades of his reprehensible crime history violating young boys.[1036] But soon enough at the ripe old age of 87 in December 2015, similar to accused yet uncharged Lord Brittan's last remaining months alive, Janner died prior to facing formal indictment or even police inquiry. But in defense of their pedo-dad, his Jewish family in the coziest of relationships with British press circled wagons using the anti-Semitic card to successfully repress the overwhelming evidence that their patriarch was yet another longtime flaming VIP predator not unlike Jimmy Savile.[1037] More on the Lord Janner scandal in coming chapters.

[1032] "The Pop Star and Preacher who've been Friends for 48 years: How Cliff Richard and American Evangelist Billy Graham were United by a Shared Faith," *Daily Mail*, August 16, 2014.

[1033] Lucy Thornton, "Sir Cliff Richard Police Probe: Pop Star Facing more Allegations as Inquiry against him is 'Significantly Expanded,'" *Mirror*, February 25, 2015.

[1034] Francis Carr Begbie, https://www.theoccidentalobserver.net/2016/09/04/why-did-keith-vaz-protect-greville-janner/.

[1035] Francis Carr Begbie, https://www.theoccidentalobserver.net/2016/09/04/why-did-keith-vaz-protect-greville-janner/.

[1036] Francis Carr Begbie, https://www.theoccidentalobserver.net/2016/09/04/why-did-keith-vaz-protect-greville-janner/.

[1037] Francis Carr Begbie, https://www.theoccidentalobserver.net/2016/09/04/why-did-keith-vaz-protect-greville-janner/.

Is it any wonder that Cliff Richard's reversal of misfortune suddenly turned the tides in his favor? Though in 2015 it looked pretty bleak for Sir Cliff when growing evidence of his alleged past pedophilia crimes appeared to finally be catching up to him. But what a difference a year makes. In July 2016 Cliff Richard went on the offensive, suing both the South Yorkshire Police and the *BBC* for their collusion in the highly publicized police raid on his Berkshire home in 2014 after the Crown Prosecution Service the month prior somehow deemed not enough evidence to charge (which smacks of cover-up in and of itself).[1038] Then in May 2017 the police agreed to pay the singer a whopping sum of £400,000[1039] and another £300,000 for Sir Cliff's legal costs.[1040] Interesting that in June 2016 while Vaz still chaired the committee in charge of all pending UK legal cases, CPS chose not to formally charge Sir Cliff and then a mere month and a half later, news of Vaz's criminal child abuse history surfaced, forcing his resignation from his prominent political perch. See how the inner club constantly looks out for each other?

The question that begs answering is why can't the British "justice" system ever collect enough evidence to successfully get a VIP suspect charged, tried and convicted? Why are no child raping MPs or lords ever sent to prison for their crimes? In short, the system is corrosively and irreparably rigged and needs a complete overhaul of personnel, if not more. Another enormous reason is, as of the 1964 Police Act, all of the UK's chief constables heading the nation's city police forces have to answer to one centralized national source - the Home Secretary.[1041] And as long as the Home Secretary "fox" guarding the child henhouse is a pedophile or pedophile enabler in what's become a job prerequisite, no powerful pedophile in the UK will ever be convicted and brought to justice. Like in the US, it has yet to happen.

As of that 1964 structural policing change in Britain, no longer are independent law enforcement investigations permitted and thus a national policy of centralized control and cover-up has become the standard operating norm to suppress all police probes into British Establishment pedophile rings. This explains why top end politicians and entertainers who systematically rape children always - bar none - get away with it. The British legal system (and for that matter the US and virtually the entire world) is rigged to protect accused child rapists when members of the elite. This must change! Bring on the Truth and Reconciliation Commissions.

Sir Cliff and Queen Elizabeth's mutual admiration[1042] had her knighting him in 1995 while he was her only selected performer requested to sing at her 2012 Jubilee Celebration marking her 60 year reign.[1043] Upon learning from the Crown Prosecution Service that the police had dropped its pedophilia investigation against him in 2016, immediately after wiping his tears of

---

[1038] "Cliff Richard starts Legal Action against BBC and South Yorkshire Police," *BBC*, July 10, 2016..
[1039] "South Yorks Police Paid Sir Cliff Richard £400,000 Damages over Raid," *Belfast Telegraph*, April 17, 2018.
[1040] Martin Robinson, "BBC agrees to Pay Sir Cliff Richard £850,000 in Costs on top of his £210,000 in Damages - but Appeals Privacy Ruling over its Coverage of a Police Raid on his Home," *Daily Mail*, July 26, 2018.
[1041] George E. Berkley, "Centralization, Democracy, and the Police," *The Journal of Criminal Law, Criminology and Police Science*, 1970, Vol. .
[1042] "Sir Cliff Richard Diamond Jubilee Tribute: 'The Queen has been Dignified throughout her Reign,'" *The Telegraph*, June 1, 2012.
[1043] "Queen Elizabeth is a Huge Cliff Richard Fan," Celebretainment, March 22, 2018.

joy and relief, he then went to sing "God Save the Queen" for her birthday celebration at the Lisbon British Embassy.[1044] Fitting since she probably did save his ass. Of course it can't hurt to maintain super close ties with his global pedophilia handlers MI5, MI6 and Mossad,[1045] or war criminals Tony Blair and Benjamin Netanyahu, and all rest of the top tier puppet perps in the globalized pedo-network that made certain Sir Cliff remains immune from all consequence since his 2018 lawsuit represents their self-interest too.

In July 2018 it was *BBC*'s turn to lose in court. Ostensibly violating Sir Richard's right to privacy, broadcasting the August 2014 police fiasco on national live television, the multibillionaire was awarded another £210,000.[1046] £20,000 more was thrown into the plaintiff's lap as aggravated damages over the *BBC* arrogantly nominating itself for its coverage of the raid for the Royal Television Society's scoop of the year award. Still yet to be assessed are damages for Cliff's lost book deals and public appearances which will no doubt also be substantial.

The overkill of a *BBC* reporter staked out overnight waiting for the police to arrive and the *BBC* helicopter flying overhead was over-the-top sensationalism, raising the ante in full tilt damages. *BBC* journalist Dan Johnson had allegedly learned that South Yorkshire Police were investigating Cliff Richard's alleged pedophilic past and threatened to expose the investigation unless granted a front row seat tipoff so *BBC* cameras and helicopter could exclusively lie in wait for the massively staged morning police raid.[1047] Big media meets big law enforcement in the show of morning shows. And so far, the tally has cost *BBC* alone £1, 060,000 in compensation to "victim" Cliff,[1048] overcome with emotion in tearful relief for all the pain and anguish this poor little rich boy's been so grievously forced to endure.

The Sun editor Tony Gallagher's response to the High Court decision:

Arrests will go unpublicized. Suspects will assert privacy rights. Police probes impeded. Victory for (alleged) criminals and money-grabbing lawyers. Terrible for media.[1049]

BBC news director Fran Unsworth said even if the *BBC* low-keyed its coverage:

… The judge would still have found that the story was unlawful, despite ruling that what we broadcast about the search was accurate.[1050]

[1044] Jane Mathews, "Sir Cliff Richard: 'I Sang God Save the Queen when Historic Sex Abuse Investigation was Dropped,'" *The Telegraph*, November 5, 2016.

[1045] "Cliff Richard; Crusaders; Military Intelligence."

[1046] Jim Waterson, "Cliff Richard Wins £210,000 in Damages over BBC Privacy Case," *The Guardian*, July 18, 2018.

[1047] Martin Robinson, http://www.dailymail.co.uk/news/article-5993963/BBC-plans-appeal-Sir-Cliff-Richard-privacy-ruling-awarded-210-000.html.

[1048] "Cliff Richard – Victim," http://aanirfan.blogspot.com/2018/07/cliff-richard-victim.html.

[1049] Jim Waterson, https://www.theguardian.com/music/2018/jul/18/cliff-richard-wins-damages-from-bbc-over-police-raid-footage.

[1050] Jim Waterson, https://www.theguardian.com/music/2018/jul/18/cliff-richard-wins-damages-from-bbc-over-police-raid-footage.

Had Cliff Richard been charged and convicted, obviously his counter-lawsuit would never have been possible. But because the judicial process is so corrupted in the UK, with this court decision, the already rigged system just became even more stacked against truth and justice for the common people. This lawsuit and legal judgment are to ensure that the big wig pedophiles at the top of the power pyramid never get identified or arrested, much less ever brought to justice and serve prison time. This court ruling seals the deal for the most powerful on earth to continue living above the law. Rich and famous pedophiles had to be celebrating in their mansions over this one.

On the one hand, the pedophilia-saturated *BBC* that allowed its internal pedophile ring to flourish for numerous decades under Sir Jimmy and his gang running amok, along with the *BBC*'s continual criminal cover-up and nonstop denial of any wrongdoing, co-opted by a corrupted whitewashed investigation by its own appointed former judge as well as Operation Yewtree's police probe debacle, the *BBC* deserves to lose a whole lot more than just what amounts to chump change for the world's largest media organization[1051] with an annual income exceeding £5 billion.[1052] Its choice to deceitfully continue denying pedophilia within its own ranks for so many decades while, in the post-Savile witch hunt, relished in its co-opted police spectacle scoop, pouncing on and exploiting Cliff Richard (innocent or guilty) for cheap thrill ratings and accolades also serve this hypocritical, reprehensible, downright evil media giant right.

But on the other hand, this legal decision sets a dark, foreboding and dangerous precedent that muzzles, if not kills, what little freedom of speech and the press is still left. After initially maintaining the *BBC* would appeal the decision on "fundamental principle," a month later the government media giant changed its mind, not wanting to "prolong Sir Cliff's distress."[1053] More bullshit. This case is a huge setback for the people and children of the United Kingdom. From here on out this Cliff Richard judgment will cause news outlets to not dare pursue controversial stories for fear of incurring major damages for violating suspected public figures' right to privacy.

This 2018 case is not unlike the heavily retracted 1964 *Sunday Mirror* article mentioned earlier that accurately outed pedophiles Lord Boothby and gangster Ronnie Kray's joint government-organized crime operated child sex ring. And it was no accident that UK's 1964 Police Act centralizing all British law enforcement agencies under the pedo-friendly Home Secretary's control and the *Sunday Mirror* article being checkmated in court by a costly libel suit all went down at the exact same time. 1964 was a year the pedo-elite defeated truth and justice and now 2018 is another banner year for relieved VIP pedophiles. This Cliff Richard court decision is simply more of the same, the pedo-elite successfully pushing back after near exposure of its Achilles pedo-heel in recent years after the Savile scandal broke. The predatory elite's simply engaged now in successful damage control.

[1051] "BBC News," *Encyclo.*
[1052] "BBC," *wikipedia.*
[1053] George Bowden, "BBC will not Appeal Sir Cliff Richard Privacy Ruling," *Huffington Post*, August 15, 2018.

Super rich Sir Cliff Richard claims he spent £4 million defending his reputation to legally go after the *BBC* and police.[1054] With police already delivering its public apology and near a million pounds to the queen's singing knight and the *BBC* paying over a million so far, at the end of the day, they're expected to run up a tab of £5 million in damages to victim Cliff. As a result, this court decision now poses such enormous liability risk to every news corporation in the world, regardless of size, that extreme caution will be exercised before daring to expose the next super wealthy public figure turned pedophile or murder suspect caught in the act. In effect, this case silences the free press in the United Kingdom for good. Welcome to the totalitarian dystopian nightmare come true where evil planetary controllers get to live like gods above every manmade law while the rest of us condemned and shackled slaves wretch in purgatory made hell on earth, if not already genocided as part of their Agenda 21 eugenics depopulation plan.[1055]

The illusion of a free press that in reality no longer exists in the so called "free world" is today's manifestation of ruling psychopaths secretly bent on holding absolute power by any means necessary, deploying a number of deceitfully draconian methods to their end, one of which is concealing the truth from the public. It invariably occurs in every totalitarian regime-in-the-making,[1056] and when that regime is the current globalist precursor now underway promoting West versus East conflict and confrontation as a pathway to world war and one world government tyranny,[1057] writing-on-the-wall signs are everywhere.

Increasing censorship in the digital age, all in the name of "national security," combatting "extremism," legalized "rights" of the politically correct, and illegalized "fake news" decided by tech giant gatekeepers propagating official state-MSM lies are fueling battlefronts attacking freedom of press and freedom of speech.[1058] Consolidating globalized power and control over news outlets, outflow information and truth even on the internet are being centralized into fewer hands.[1059] And the censorship makers in China are working with Google Gestapo et al to make it worldwide.[1060] Add to this alarming backdrop of oppressive trends and developments the Cliff Richard case and its disturbing implications for exposing future pedophilia crimes - even when accurately reporting the truth, clearly the privileged pedophiles are increasingly armed with protection at the expense of their powerless victims and the public at large.

Additionally, not revealing the identity of an arrested suspect will foreclose any opportunity for other victims to feel empowered enough to brave the stress, liability and re-trauma of coming forth to report crimes against their powerful perps. Its effects are both sobering and grave, placing an enormous barrier now to exposing the crime cabal's ugliest sins and clearly is a

[1054] Martin Robinson, http://www.dailymail.co.uk/news/article-5993963/BBC-plans-appeal-Sir-Cliff-Richard-privacy-ruling-awarded-210-000.html.

[1055] K. Heidenreich, "Agenda 21: The Plan to Depopulate 95% of the World by 2030," *Disclose TV*, March 7, 2017.

[1056] Naomi Wolf, "Fascist America, in 10 easy Steps," *The Guardian*, April 24, 2007.

[1057] Michel Chossudovsky, "Global Warfare. Preparing for World War III? Targeting Iran," *Global Research*, July 29, 2018.

[1058] Mark Leonard, "The Illusion of Freedom in the Digital age," *The Strategist*, November 8, 2017.

[1059] Thomas Hughes, "Who will Protect Press Freedom now?" *The Guardian*, November 30, 2017.

[1060] Alex Hern, "Google 'Working on Censored Search Engine' for China," *The Guardian*, August 2, 2018.

landmark victory for the planet's most elitist criminals at the top of the predator food chain. Another consequence in-the-making is what's being referred to as "Cliff's law," where the mere reporting of arrested suspects in and of itself constitutes a criminal violation of their privacy rights.[1061] The Orwellian-like prediction that during a time of universal deceit, not only does telling the truth become a revolutionary act, it also becomes a crime.[1062]

So the rights of rich and famous criminals able to spend big bucks going after the media - however guilty of egregious crimes - are also able to trample over the public's right to know the truth and the rights of all victims seeking any semblance of justice. In the highly rigged economic legal system, the rich and powerful continue getting richer and more powerful at an unprecedented rate,[1063] reaping more control to rape and pillage our planet at an exponential, dishearteningly feverish pace. Humanity is in rapid descent, regressed into forcibly living in a current neo-feudal slave system compounded by nightmarish Artificial Intelligence-electronic techno control, surveilling every slave's move and thought, making Orwell's *1984* nostalgically appear a walk in the park.[1064] That's why sooner than later citizens of the world must unite in solidarity against the miniscule minority behind the global pedo-empire curtain.

Sir Cliff's landmark case is the beta test for the elite to finagle utilizing their so-called privacy rights excuse in order to secure their privileged lives forever to remain above the law. As common everyday citizens, where are our lost privacy rights?[1065] While we're living in history's most watched and controlled society ever on earth, the ruling elite's privacy rights are the only ones that apparently matter now. Sir Cliff utilized his legal clout after years of built up capital earned from all those trips to Israel as a lifetime Mossad pawn to first make libelous any reporting of "Kitty's" presence at the Elm Guest pedo-party lodge and now across-the-boards suppression of any of his alleged past criminal activity making him unreachable like all his fellow pedo-sirs and pedo-lords within an elitist aristocracy class guaranteed to continue living like gods above the law with complete impunity answering to no one... except God.

The ruling elite set up the *BBC* to take the fall for having gotten caught with its pants down vis-a-vis the Savile disgrace. So this monumental landmark decision was strategically orchestrated to add yet one more insurmountable buffered layer to seal off protection for the earth's top level pedophiles from all further accountability. With this legal triumph, "invincible" planetary controllers may be deluding themselves into actually believing their Achilles pedo-heel is now impenetrable. Lest they be reminded their war on truth is never over nor their defiance of karmic laws. In the end, only truth and justice prevail - not them.

[1061] Matthew Moore, "Cliff Richard's Court Victory over BBC Gags the Media," *The Sunday Times*, July 19, 2018.
[1062] Anders, "'During Times of Universal Deceit, Telling the Truth Becomes a Revolutionary Act" (Orwell) in Germany, EU, USA. "1984" in 2017," *new.euro-md.dk,* December 13, 2016.
[1063] Jim Puzzanghera, "Oxfam Report Highlights Widening Income Gap between Rich, Poor," *Los Angeles Times*, January 20, 2014.
[1064] Nate Brown, "Machine-Human Wars; US Army is Testing Mind Controlling, Brainwave Reading Technology, AI to Lead to New Arms Race," *The Christian Journal*, February 13, 2017.
[1065] Jean-Louis Gassée, "NSA Files show Privacy does not exist," *The Guardian*, August 5, 2013.

By design Operations Yewtree, Midlands, Fairbridge and a host of other police probes into alleged government pedophiles have all failed miserably to arrest the VIP pedo-establishment.[1066] While Sir Cliff celebrated his court victory, the alleged victim named "Nick" was hauled off to jail. Nick had claimed MPs and cabinet ministers tortured and sexually abused him for a decade in the 80s, while allegedly witnessing the murder of three underage boys. But in 2018 he was conveniently declared a public liar and slapped with charges of perverting course of justice with his so called false statements.[1067] The tide has once again turned against victims in the UK as their "unsubstantiated claims" have been blamed for lack of police operations' arrests resulting from all those post-Savile investigations. Thus, no members of the VIP establishment that we absolutely know have been raping children in droves have been arrested. The earth's pedo-epicenter is showing its true colors and true reason for its label in the latest round of intended death blows to truth and justice. Continuing unabated, the pedophilia cover-up in the United Kingdom reigns supreme.

In the summer of 2018, the UK elite has fought back, discrediting and silencing victims once again in order to retain impunity from any and all punishment. In a legal cesspool system, the power to declare victims liars not only lets the perps off the hook, it plants the seed of doubt in every abuse victim brave enough to come forth to file a complaint and endure the horrendous ordeal of re-traumatized hardship seeking systemically denied justice. These offensive, over-the-top moves by the Establishment are designed to thoroughly discourage future abuse victims from ever filing formal complaints, realizing their voices will never be heard in a morally depraved, fully bankrupted feudal system beyond repair.

In recent years the pedophilia elite have realized that a growing awareness of Pedogate scandals have been gaining momentum worldwide, influencing perceptions of an increasing number of people to accurately view the VIP establishment as a criminal sicko-infested cabal. This expanding base of informed citizenry has made them increasingly nervous and vulnerable to finally being made accountable.[1068] So they pushed back with a conjured up high profile pivotal court case under the guise of protecting privacy rights of the rich and powerful, killing a diminishing free press while rendering yet more VIP abuse victims unreliable false claimants. Meanwhile, the mired, "unfit for purpose" government-sanctioned child abuse inquiry dragging on impotently for years gets fined £200,000 in July 2018,[1069] the same month alleged VIP abuse victim Nick gets jailed and Sir Cliff wins in court. The inquiry is alleged to have inadvertently emailed out full names of child abuse victims, thus violating their privacy rights in the latest self-injuring blunder, seemingly intended to render the floundering charade completely impotent and ineffective at getting to the bottom of the British child raping epidemic. Of course, that too is the whole point by design as well.

[1066] Vikram Dodd and Matthew Taylor, "Operation Midland Police Fell for 'False Claims' of VIP Abuse, Report says, *The Guardian*, November 8, 2016.

[1067] Chris Baynes, "Westminster Paedophile Accuser 'Nick' Charged with Perverting Course of Justice over Sex Abuse Ring Claims," Independent, July 3, 2018.

[1068] Joachim Hagopian, "Pedogate Update: Global Elite's Pedophile Empire is Crumbling – But will it ever Crash?" *sott.net*, March 21, 2017.

[1069] "Child Sex Abuse Inquiry Fined £200,000 after Email Blunder," *The Guardian*, July 19, 2018.

All those repeatedly lost government pedo-dossiers,[1070] [1071] systemic failure by police to historically follow up hundreds of thousands of real abuse cases,[1072] and systemic historical failure by CPS to charge real criminals,[1073] or lose crucial evidence,[1074] and the multitudes of victims who've filed accusations in the post-Savile years,[1075] against both VIP perpetrators as well as the so called Muslim Asian community gangs unimpededly abusing thousands more underage girls in recent decades, all of these massive systemic failures have created an endemic national crisis[1076] in the United Kingdom like never before.[1077] Upward estimates nearing a half million UK abuse cases mounted up in a 2-year period between April 2012 and March 2014 alone.

By diabolical intentions, the world's worst pedophilia haven systemically protects powerful child rapists and killers while systematically silencing child victims, regardless of which brand of abuse - the VIP 10 Downing Street-Westminster type or the unchecked, out of control Telford, Rochdale and Rotherham debacle.[1078] Compounded by the globalist manufactured divide and conquer mass refugee crisis destroying Europe, the deteriorating conditions in the UK have been spreading virtually throughout the entire Western world with a ripple effect in Eastern nations as both a pedo-tourism magnet[1079] and ripe source for unbridled child abduction-sex trafficking.[1080] Until the citizens of the world come together in unified solidarity to fight this blight on humanity, the dire conditions for children worldwide are only crumbling from bleakly bad to bleaker worse.

History just keeps repeating itself in an endless recycle, ever-raising the ante with the world's puppet masters deploying their Mockingbird press propaganda to manipulate, shape, dumb down and blind public opinion,[1081] along with nonstop application of both their divide and conquer formula[1082] and the Hegelian dialectic (problem, reaction, solution) as their foolproof methods to increase authoritarian control over the masses while in one fell swoop snuff out

---

[1070] Roy Greenslade, "Editor Explains why he didn't Publish Barbara Castle's Paedophile Dossier," *The Guardian*, July 15, 2014.

[1071] Patrick Sawer and Tim Ross, "Whitehall Child Sex Inquiry: The 114 Files 'Lost,'" *The Telegraph*, July 5, 2014.

[1072] Alan Travis and Matthew Weaver, "Report Exposing Met Police Failings on Child Sex Abuse 'Shocking,'" *The Guardian*, November 25, 2016..

[1073] Ian Drury, "Britain's top Prosecutor Alison Saunders Denies being Pushed out her Job as QC who Criticised Police for Believing all Rape Victims is Tipped to Replace her," *Daily Mail*, April 2, 2018..

[1074] Lizzie Dearden, "DVDs of Child Sex Abuse Victims' Interviews Lost by CPS," *Independent*, May 17, 2018.

[1075] Randeep Ramesh, "NSPCC says Reports of Sexual Abuse have Soared after Jimmy Savile Scandal," *The Guardian*, August 31, 2013.

[1076] Joan Smith, "We've been Ignoring an Epidemic of Child Sex Abuse in Britain," *The Telegraph*, May 20, 2016.

[1077] Nick Sommerlad and Geraldine McKelvie, "Britain's 'Worst ever' Child Grooming Scandal Exposed: Hundreds of Young Girls Raped, Beaten, Sold for Sex and some even Killed," *Mirror*, March 11, 2018.

[1078] Mandy Duncan, "Child Protection Investigations Silence Children and Offer Impunity to Abusers," *The Conversation*, September 26, 2018.

[1079] "Pizzagate and the Western Pedophiles Lurking in Southeast Asia," *Thai Law Forum*, December 9, 2016.

[1080] "South Asian Nations Rank Poorly in US Trafficking Report," *UCA News*, June 29, 2017.

[1081] Kalee Brown, "8 Ways the Global Elite Manipulate our Perception of Reality," *Collective Evolution*, March 7, 2017,.

[1082] Joachim Hagopian, "How the New World Order 'Globalists' Are Dividing Americans," *Global Research*, October 28, 2015.

dissent, truth and justice.[1083] The current stakes are at an all-time high in recorded history as humanity is under an unprecedented, relentless homicidal assault. With the latest setbacks, exposing the unimpugnable, child raping monsters poses even more a formidable challenge. But living by the cherished tenet that the truth shall set us all free, armed with knowledge of the truth and vastly overwhelming numbers on our side, as sovereign members of the human race we possess the power to hold the subhuman handful of life destroyers fully accountable for all their crimes against our innocents and humanity.

The next chapter delves deeper in the British Broadcasting Corporation to explore so many suspicious deaths of its employees, tying it to the Savile-BBC pedophile web and its cover-up at all cost.

[1083] Joachim Hagopian, "Authoritarian Control and Mass Murder in America the Hegelian Dialectic Way," *Lew Rockwell*, June 16, 2016..

Chapter 5: BBC Pedo-Ring's Deadly Silencing of Those Who Knew Too Much: The Jill Dando Murder and over a Dozen Suspicious BBC Deaths

In addition to colluding police forces and the government's gross incompetence investigating Savile by intentional design, Savile's *BBC* sex ring, his VIP pedophilia network and UK police are also equally inept at solving over a dozen high profile murder cases and suspicious deaths surrounding *BBC* personnel. Of course that's also by sinister design. Again, the explanation is plain to see when heads of UK's largest police forces and *British Broadcasting Corporation* are controlled by the pedophile infiltrated British Establishment in government and royalty, secretly bound additionally by demonic brotherhood societies like Freemasonry, Knights of Malta, the Jesuits and Luciferian Illuminati.

The next important endeavor is to delve deeply into scrutinizing some of the mysterious deaths and unsolved murders at the *BBC* over recent decades that Britain's law enforcement just can't seem to crack. Here is a "short list" of the more than dozen known unexplained or highly questionable deaths and unsolved murders of *BBC* employees that repeatedly keep coming up. In addition to the aforementioned suicide of Claire McAlpine from Chapter 2, other more recent cases include Kevin Greening, Kristian Digby, David Smith, Paula Yates, Peaches Geldof, Natasha Collins, Mark Speight, Mike Smith, Rik Mayall, Terry Wogan, Jill Dando and Liz MacKean.

Kevin Greening was a former *BBC* Radio 1 breakfast DJ whose life was cut short on the eve of his 45th birthday on December 29, 2007.[1084] Westminster Coroner Dr. Paul Knapman ruled the cause of death the result of "sexual misadventure," involving drugs and bondage between Kevin and his homosexual partner. The press accounts did not elaborate beyond stating it included gaffer tape and cling film wrapped around Kevin's torso while wearing a rubber suit suspended in a black leather sling from bedroom scaffolding. It's either as purported a kinky gay sexual experiment, recklessly pushing the thrill envelope beyond the safety zone, or a concocted, bizarrely twisted tale of sinister cover-up, designed to offend all conventional sensibilities enough to not prompt further question or investigation.

We've seen this same scenario before of suspiciously "suicided" deaths frequently linked to intelligence service assassins. Recall the two cases that readily come to mind mentioned in a previous chapter, the controversial ex-MI6 agent turned anti-Establishment journalist-author James Rusbridger, bent on exposing the royal family's dirty secrets in his next book, and Tory

---

[1084] Anita Singh, "Radio 1 DJ Kevin Greening Died after Drugs and Bondage Session," *The Telegraph*, June 3, 2008.

MP Stephen Milligan,[1085] privy to both illegal arms deals and the Westminster pedo-network, both occurring just weeks apart in 1994.[1086] Professional MI5/6 hits purposely stage this kind of kinky sexually adventurous experimentation gone bad, followed by a sure-hand state medical examiner to explain it all away. Aside from the fact that it works like a charm every time, the threefold benefit for deploying this particular murder methodology is that it eliminates unwanted cabal threats, does it in a way that carries public shame, humiliation and dishonor to the deceased and his family and, the kinkier and more bizarre the "accident," the less public scrutiny and suspicion surrounding the death. Typical in these cases is a "sure-hand" coroner like Dr. Paul Knapman as the elite's go-to cause-of-death medical fabricator whose primary purpose is simply concealing British Establishment crime. But more dirt on Knapman later.

Yet another *BBC* presenter meeting a similar, equally disastrous fate in the realm of solo gay kink comes the alleged "sexual misadventures" of property development millionaire 32-year old Kristian Digby who died on March 1, 2010 of asphyxiation.[1087] He too was an alleged high flying thrill seeker but with his partner out of town, he fatally succumbed after wearing a plastic bag over his head when his apparent "sex game went wrong." If foul play was involved, again this is a favorite government assassination trick, easily passing it off as simply another careless joyride into hedonism gone awry.

Taking each so-called accidental misadventure at face value, it might be considered a stretch to attribute cause of death to the *BBC* pedophilia network or crime cabal. But when taken together, the odds of so many high profile, strange, anomalous, sudden deaths afflicting so many relatively young *BBC* employees seems beyond extremely remote. And knowing that the pedo-cabal has an agenda that reserves no limit to covering up its crimes at all cost, together they cast a long dark, nefarious shadow of suspicion hanging over all these mysterious deaths.

A strong case that fits both means and motive for foul play is another Savile pedophile chauffeur, most likely suicided the day before he was scheduled to face trial on sexual abuse charges in 2013.[1088] The 67-year old *BBC* chauffeur, David Smith, who drove for Jimmy Savile back in the 1980s was a definite liability to the pedo-cabal as a low rung lackey whose insider knowledge could potentially have brought some of the top rung pedo-monsters down… so it seems he was conveniently "suicided" on the eve of his court appearance in late October 2013.

This degenerate suddenly wound up dead on the one-year anniversary of Operation Yewtree's first suspect roundup. But then this is Standard Operating Procedure in high stakes Cloak and

---

[1085] Guy Adams, "Did MI5 Murder Orange in Mouth MP? Stephen Milligan Supposedly Died after a Bizarre Sex Game – But Chilling Investigation Raises an even more Sinister Possibility after Former Journalist 'Unearthed British Illegal Arms Sales,'" *Daily Mail,* October 5, 2018.

[1086] Crispin Black, "MI6 Dirty Secrets… Why do Sex Games Appear to Feature in so Many Spy Deaths," *Mirror*, May 5.

[1087] "Millionaire BBC TV Presenter Kristian Digby Suffocated to Death Accidentally 'when Sex Game went Wrong,'" *Daily Mail*, December 29, 2010.

[1088] Rebecca Camber and Lizzy Parry, "Jimmy Savile's Former BBC Driver David Smith Found Dead before Sex Crimes Trial," *Daily Mail*, October 28, 2013.

Daggery 101, eliminate any and all liability in order for the Luciferian child raping murderers to stay in power, to keep raping and murdering our children with impunity. Granted, there is a slim possibility that Smith acted alone, knowing he was facing more serious jail time, opting to snuff himself at the last minute. But the stronger means and motive slant towards execution-style suicide by the powers-that-shouldn't-be is more plausible.

Protecting the *BBC*'s criminality as part of the larger pedo-cabal network can't be emphasized enough, especially when the precedent has been repeatedly in place from time immemorial. It's already a well-established fact - an inordinate number of *BBC* employees suddenly drop dead who clearly pose a threat to the wider pedophilia network for knowing too much. By 2013, to silence perceived threats, Deep State political assassination by a "suicided" staged accident or artificially induced heart attack has become all too common.[1089] Smith's "suicide" by foul play is an extremely realistic explanation, after a long string of "too weird" deaths plaguing *BBC* staff. With 22 previous convictions dating as far back as 1966 under Smith's pedo-belt,[1090] and having driven Savile around London town for years, a sure bet is that this repeat offender took many dark secrets to his grave in another flimsily veiled case of "dead men don't tell tales."

But how can the UK legal system drop the ball, allowing a known relentless reoffender continue getting caught raping little boys nearly two dozen times? This creature should have been permanently removed and locked away from society to protect children after his second offence, not his 22nd. Of course, if he was protected by a VIP pedophilia network, 22 convictions suddenly make a lot more sense. Another anomaly, the *Daily Mail* suicide headline states that Smith was the very first pedophile charged out of the Yewtree Operation starting gate in October 2012.[1091]

But how could David Smith have been "the first pedophile" charged in October 2012? Despite his 22 convictions, Smith apparently remained a free man not taken into custody until April 2013. Stemming from an alleged sodomy incident involving a 12-year old boy in 1984,[1092] the adult victim happened to watch that *ITV* Savile exposé in October 2012, a full year ahead of Smith's "suicide," prompting the victim's partner to contact police, resulting in Smith's December 2012 arrest and posted bail. But if the Crown Prosecution Service receiving the case in late December 2012 didn't charge the prolific pedophile until early April 2013, how could this derelict end up the first suspect legally charged under Operation Yewtree? Recall that rocker Gary Glitter was arrested in October 2012 and was Yewtree's first suspect. Though a number of early suspects like Glitter were arrested a half year prior to Smith's April 2013 charge, unlike

---

[1089] The Obama's 'Dead Pool,'" *bibliotecapleyades.net*, December 12, 2013.

[1090] Rebecca Camber and Lizzy Parry, http://www.dailymail.co.uk/news/article-2478642/Jimmy-Saviles-BBC-driver-David-Smith-dead-sex-crimes-trial.html.

[1091] Rebecca Camber and Lizzy Parry, http://www.dailymail.co.uk/news/article-2478642/Jimmy-Saviles-BBC-driver-David-Smith-dead-sex-crimes-trial.html.

[1092] Rebecca Camber and Lizzy Parry, http://www.dailymail.co.uk/news/article-2478642/Jimmy-Saviles-BBC-driver-David-Smith-dead-sex-crimes-trial.html.

Glitter, most of those arrested were neither charged nor prosecuted, or later were acquitted at trial.

In 2002 Smith was apparently wanted by the police, but the left hand of UK's bungling legal system didn't know what the right hand was doing, failing to realize Smith was already in custody as a prison inmate and not a "fugitive" at all. Also, it was the *BBC* that revealed to the press that this low life had 22 prior convictions dating as far back as 1966. Yet the *BBC* apparently went ahead and hired Smith in the 1980s as one of its drivers anyway, very likely aware Smith had a reoffending sexual assault record a mile long while *BBC* insiders from top corporate executives on down either knew of or were active participants themselves in this out of control *BBC* pedophile ring. In fact, in 1984 after Smith met this victim at a local swimming pool and enticed him back to Smith's residence to sexually abuse the 12-year old, the pervert then allegedly assaulted this same victim a second time reportedly driving him home from touring the *BBC* studios at White City Television Centre in West London.[1093]

This chain of events demonstrates both police and *BBC*'s blatant criminal culpability. Yet there's no mention in this *Daily Mail* article of any of this police-*BBC* calamitous collusion that more than enabled this hardcore scumbag to do so much damage from age 20 to 67, nearly a half century of known legal convictions with a number of years operating within the *BBC*-Savile pedo-network. If you accept all these article statements as fact, then you know why the cabal system might want to eliminate this man before he could potentially blow the lid off the UK's VIP pedo-club.

Finally, the *Daily Mail* piece specifies Yewtree's three crime investigation categories reported by thousands of victims emerging since the October 3, 2012 airing of the *ITV* documentary, the first crime category involved Savile himself (three quarters of reported cases fell into this category), the second involved Savile and his associates, and the third, pedophilia crimes unrelated to Savile.[1094] But the *Daily Mail* then states that this particular case is filed under the third "unconnected to Savile" category. That's highly suspect since they were both *BBC* employees, both serial child rapists, both riding in the same limo for years at a time and no doubt committing the same pedo- crimes within the same *BBC* child sex ring, not unlike another one of Savile's chauffeurs Ray Teret.

Savile had chauffeurs who were hardened pedophiles like himself and no doubt for security sake, he only hired fellow criminals of the same deviant ilk. From the article we also learn that at least one of the assaults occurred shortly after the victim and the Savile chauffeur were together at the *BBC* studio where both Smith and his boss worked. So with both Smith and Savile enormously prolific pedophiles working together during the 1980s when many of Smith's said crimes took place, how could this be reported as a crime "unconnected to Savile?" Does

---

[1093] Rebecca Camber and Lizzy Parry, http://www.dailymail.co.uk/news/article-2478642/Jimmy-Saviles-BBC-driver-David-Smith-dead-sex-crimes-trial.html.
[1094] Rebecca Camber and Lizzy Parry, http://www.dailymail.co.uk/news/article-2478642/Jimmy-Saviles-BBC-driver-DavidSmith-dead-sex-crimes-trial.html.

the context "unconnected" mean that Savile's penis specifically did not sodomize the boy in the same way that Smith's did? Or perhaps it means they never sodomized the victim at the same time as in a threesome. As order followers, it appears the Yewtree boys in blue have gone out of their way to minimize the pedo-connection between S&S and their connection to the *BBC*. Hmmm, wonder why? Bet it has everything to do with the same reason that Smith never showed up for his scheduled trial.

In a *Mirror* article published five months after the *Daily Mail* post, David Smith's victim - 42-year old Jason Little - went public with a discrepant account from the earlier *Daily Mail* depiction of police and *BBC*. Where the *Daily Mail* version had both police and *BBC* attempting to distance David Smith abuse from both Savile and the *BBC* pedophile ring, Jason's disclosures in the *Mirror* are clearly at odds with the earlier rendition. Victim Jason Little maintains that his abuse lasted almost three years and that not only was David Smith a *BBC* employee chauffeuring Savile and a number of other *BBC* stars, but he also asserts that Smith took him on trips abroad to Israel and Amsterdam, provided him with a *BBC* pass and introduced him to scores of *BBC* stars at the Television Centre including Jimmy Savile.[1095] We also know that Sir Jimmy as an intelligence operative made a number of visits to the Jewish State.[1096] Jason also claimed that David Smith sexually assaulted him on a number of occasions inside the *BBC* studio premises as well. We also know that a favorite crime at *BBC* studios was Sir Jimmy's dressing room.

At the time of the *Mirror* article in April 2014, the coroner had just ruled Smith's death a suicide "beyond reasonable doubt" resulting from a drug overdose.[1097] Both Jason Little and his friend since childhood, 41-year old Lee Sullivan, another of Smith's alleged sex abuse victims, decided to waive their anonymity rights in an effort to both give hope to other victims and confront the *BBC* for covering up its own pedophile ring in its refusal to admit that David Smith as a *BBC* employee was part of it. Apparently David Smith even owned a vehicle with the license plate "372BBC."

Jason shared his angst over the whitewash:

It makes me sick that the BBC won't admit it. They haven't even bothered to speak to me about Smith.[1098]

Jason's friend Lee added:

He [Smith] *has cheated me of justice by killing himself.*

I'd venture to say that the UK Deep State and *BBC* in particular more accurately cheated Lee and Jason from any justice.

[1095] Tom Pettifor, "'I was Abused by Paedophile at BBC Television Centre': Victim's Anger at Jimmy Savile Friend's Drugs Suicide – Video," *Mirror*, April 3, 2014.

[1096] "Arch Paedophile Jimmy Savile was Israel Supporter and Devout Zionist," *21st Century Wire*, October 29, 2012.

[1097] Tom Pettifor, https://www.mirror.co.uk/news/uk-news/david-smith-suicide-victims-anger-3342513.

[1098] Tom Pettifor, https://www.mirror.co.uk/news/uk-news/david-smith-suicide-victims-anger-3342513.

Lending more credence that Savile operated within a larger pedophile network were reports from victims stating that they were abused by both Savile and other pedophiles together.[1099] Jason and his friend's account sound identical to other victims and witnesses such as Savile's nephew Guy Marsden as well as boys and girls taken from UK children's homes for weekend pedophilia parties at upscale London mansions:[1100]

He [Smith] *took me to parties with other men and kids. We were given drugs so they could attack us. Smith also took me to a big house outside Amsterdam where I was abused with other children. At the time I didn't know what was happening to me.*[1101]

Taking his victim on trips abroad and specifically to pedophilia parties in Amsterdam also implicates Smith and Savile operating within the larger international pedo-network, co-facilitated by intelligence agencies in cahoots with government social services and care home operators. The wider pedophilia network exchanging child pornography, child snuff films and sex trafficking of young boys between the UK and Amsterdam has been confirmed by both Dutch and British law enforcement.[1102]

The systematic use of drugs and alcohol given to children as grooming tools to pliably sedate them and blur abuse memories[1103] is identical with what routinely occurred like clockwork to trafficked in kids from Nebraska's Boys Town during the 1980s, including Dick Cheney's "meet and greet" escorting victims to plush Washington DC parties attended by the likes of pedophilia overlord President George HW Bush. Similarly, the history of exploitive, drug-induced seduction and rape of young boys by British pedophiles within government and *BBC* entertainment industry is pervasive from the 1960s to the present.

Not only did Jimmy Savile periodically molest underage boys (when not violating corpses and teenage girls), but other notorious *BBC* and music industry derelicts active in Savile's *BBC* pedophile ring,[1104] such as repeating offenders DJs Chris Denning and Alan Freeman, 1960s record producer-songwriter-murderer-suicider Joe Meek,[1105] and convicted pop maestro Jonathon King,[1106] all used drugs to entice their sexual prey. After all, for a very long time, predatory sexual grooming techniques as well as use of drugs for mind control abuse have remained the same the world over. Incidentally, Jonathon King has claimed that the late David Bowie had sex with more underage children than even Jimmy Savile and, as a pederast music

---

[1099] Tom Pettifor, https://www.mirror.co.uk/news/uk-news/david-smith-suicide-victims-anger-3342513.

[1100] "Care Home Abuse Victim tells of Sex Parties UK Government Pedo's," YouTube video, 11:49, posted on July 9, 2015..

[1101] Tom Pettifor, https://www.mirror.co.uk/news/uk-news/david-smith-suicide-victims-anger-3342513.

[1102] Mike Sullivan and Tom Morgan, "MP was at Snuff Film Lad's Murder," *The Sun*, December 6, 2014.

[1103] Charles Montaldo, "Profile of a Pedophile and Common Characteristics," *ThoughtCo.com*, December 14, 2017.

[1104] "All Finger in P.I.E.," *labour25.com*, March 3, 2014.

[1105] "The Kray Twins, Boys, Top People, Sex in Prisons," *whale.to*, June 1, 2009.

[1106] Robert Chalmers, "Jonathan King: 'The only Apology I have is to say that I was good at Seduction,'" *Independent*, April 22, 2012.

insider who likely knows, he accuses the *BBC*, the music industry and police for their sheer hypocrisy in protecting big name superstars like Bowie who also routinely broke the law.[1107]

Let's look at another suspicious death of yet another man employed by the *BBC* named Smith who was also privy to Savile's *BBC* pedophilia network - fellow Radio 1 DJ Mike Smith. If the 59-year old had health issues, he kept them tightly under wraps from even his closest friends, like fellow *BBC* Late, Late Breakfast Time co-presenter Noel Edmonds.[1108] As Princess Diana's favorite 1980s DJ, Mike Smith also, like Jimmy Savile, hosted Top of the Pops. In the wake of the Savile *BBC* scandal, Smith's unexpected, "mysterious" August 2014 passing was the third high profile *BBC* death that year alone, abruptly dying from so called "complications following heart surgery."[1109] Mike Smith admitted that while working at the *BBC*, he too was sexually hit on by other male DJs, alluding to the *BBC*'s out of control culture of sexual predation.

In 1988 Mike Smith was piloting a helicopter with his fellow *BBC* presenter soon-to-be wife Sarah Greene on board when it suddenly lost power for some unknown reason and went down, both barely surviving the crash.[1110] Their careers suffered after that and they were scarcely seen on television again. In 2002 Mike Smith became embroiled in a major legal battle with the showbiz agent of his wife's sister Laura Greene. The agent in question - Jon Roseman's biggest client was none other than murdered *BBC* presenter Jill Dando who knew all about the *BBC* pedophile ring. Like Jill's Crimewatch TV show partner Nick Ross, Roseman took to the *Daily Mail* platform to promote his version of events surrounding Jill's demise, buying into a bogus Serbian connection to explain her assassination.[1111] The question lingers, was Mike Smith's death the silencing of yet another *BBC* insider who may have known too much?

Then less than two months before Mike Smith was gone, the life of *BBC* Young Ones co-star and longtime popular comedian Rik Mayall came to a strange and sudden end at only 56 years of age. Both Rik's wife and everyone around him who knew him best maintain he was vibrant, happy and healthy right up to his death, with even a post-mortem report producing inconclusive results.[1112] His wife Barbara Robbin stated:

[1107] Tom Evans, "David Bowie had Sex 'with more young people than Jimmy Savile,' Disgraced Pop Mogul Claims," *Daily Star*, March 2, 2016.

[1108] Sam Marsden, "Mike Smith's Friends had no idea that DJ was Dying: Ex-Colleagues were kept in the Dark over Heart Condition and say he never Recovered from Death of Member of the Public on TV Show he Hosted with Noel Edmonds," *Daily Mail*, August 4, 2014.

[1109] Sam Marsden, http://www.dailymail.co.uk/news/article-2715085/Mike-Smiths-friends-no-idea-DJ-dying-Ex-colleagues-kept-dark.html.

[1110] "1988: BBC Presenters in Helicopter Crash," *BBC*, September 10, 2005.

[1111] Jon Roseman, "Why I believe Jill Dando was Killed by a Serbian Hitman," *Daily Mail*, March 5, 2012.

[1112] Anna Dubuis, "Cause of Rik Mayall's Death Remains a Mystery as Post-Mortem Result Inconclusive," *Evening Standard*, June 12, 2014.

We don't know yet what happened. He had a strong heart, so I don't think it was a heart attack...[1113] *At least we know it's not his heart as he's just had a check-up and been given the all-clear.*[1114]

Another young TV presenter, journalist and famous media personality who died tragically in 2014 under suspicious circumstance is 25-year old daughter of famed rock musician Sir Bob Geldof, Peaches Geldof. Having recently written just a few days prior to her death that she was happily married with 1- and 2-year old boys she adored, she also mentioned in her final interview how "heroin was such a bleak drug."[1115] The prospect seemed remote that she would suddenly snuff herself from an overdose with ten times the amount of heroin in her bloodstream that was alleged to have killed her *BBC* presenter mother Paula Yates in 2000.[1116] Without a suicide note, a scant 19 minutes prior to dying, Peaches Geldof posted two photos of her baby sons online. And just hours prior to that, loyal to her mother Paula to the end, Peaches tweeted a photo of Paula holding her shortly prior to her mother's untimely death. The biggest anomaly of all was the tweeted caption under Peaches' photo:

I have the heart of a 90-year old gangster.[1117]

Where would that incongruent remark come from?

Another major discrepancy - the police dispatched to the scene who found Peaches' lifeless body initially reported to the press that there was no evidence of drugs.[1118] But then police changed their story weeks later insisting that nearly 80 syringes were discovered laying around the house.[1119] Though police feebly claim "duty of care" compassionately protecting the family as the sole reason for falsifying the official narrative as an "unexplained death" for nearly a month,[1120] it seems far more apt to have been subsequently planted as after-the-fact evidence to protect those allegedly behind the decision to sinisterly have her silenced.

During the last several years of Peaches' life, she embraced love, marriage, family and especially motherhood. Also recently learning she was part Jewish through her paternal grandmother, and married to Jewish husband musician Tom Cohen whose parents met on a

---

[1113] Adam Withnall, "Rik Mayall Dead: 'We don't know what Killed him yet,' says Wife," *Independent*, June 10, 2014.

[1114] "Mysterious Deaths at BBC," *antioligarch.wordpress.com*, January 5, 2016.

[1115] "Peaches Geldof's last Interview: 'Heroin is such a Bleak Drug,'" *The Guardian*, June 20, 2014.

[1116] "Was Peaches Geldof Murdered by the BBC?" *sonarz.com*, March 1, 2016.

[1117] "Bob Geldof is Evil," *spikethenews.blogspot.com*, April 2014..

[1118] Hannah Ellis-Petersen, "Peaches Geldof: Weekend Plans and Posted Photos indicated 'Normal Self,'" *The Guardian*, May 1, 2014.

[1119] Harriet, Arkell, "Why did Police say Peaches' Death was 'Unexplained'? Force say 'Duty of Care' to Geldof Family was behind Decision to Withhold Details about her Death, *Daily Mail*, July 25, 2014.

[1120] Harriet Arkell, http://www.dailymail.co.uk/news/article-2705566/Why-did-police-say-Peaches-death-unexplained-Force-say-fear-upsetting-Geldof-family-decision-withhold-details-death.html.

kibbutz, Peaches was gravitating towards Judaism[1121] and away from her tendency toward cults like Ordo Templi Orientis (OTO) and scientology, leaving her fast lane, reckless drug lifestyle behind. Her past involvement in OTO, pedophile Alistair Crowley's satanic sex cult that Peaches had paid homage to having plastered an "O.T.O" tattoo on her arm, seemed in her latter days an increasingly remote if already nonexistent influence.[1122]

Many superstars like Jay Z, Beyoncé and Led Zeppelin's Jimmy Paige are said to be faithful OTO followers. A friend of Peaches, Marilyn Manson, has long admitted to be a hardcore, out of closet, proud Satanist.[1123] But then it's more than evident that the music industry is now overflowing with black occult satanic ritualism and in-our-face mind control.[1124] It's grown so bad that to be successful in the industry these days almost precludes one to swear allegiance to Lucifer.

In November 2013, just four months ahead of her death, Peaches tweeted the names of two deranged mothers that conspired to allow admitted pedophile rock star Ian Watkins from the band Lostprophets to sexually abuse their children, one just a year old baby.[1125] It's worth noting that Ian Watkins and his rock group were managed by a company called QPrime owned by Louis Mensch, husband of ex-Tory MP Louise Mensch.[1126] Louise used to work under a friend of Bob Geldof's at EMI, a record company linked to Satanism, mind control and military intelligence. Of course Peaches had a prior history to dabble, if not immerse herself into Satanism as a likely mind control victim. In 2012 Louise Mensch suddenly resigned from parliament, moved to New York while pedophile rocker Watkins was arrested in December 2012.

Having recently given birth to a six-month old son at the time of Peaches' controversial tweet outing Watkins and his sex ring, as a protective mother she had elected to expose pedophilia through her Twitter account. But due to a victim identity protection law, inadvertently she had potentially violated the confidentiality of the two child victims since she tweeted their mothers' last names. Despite Peaches' claim that the Welsh court had already publicly listed the names and that other websites had also posted them, as soon as she learned of the liability issue, she

[1121] Lauren Izso, "Peaches Geldof, British-Jewish Socialite and Daughter of Bob Geldof Dead at 25," *Jerusalem Post*, April 8, 2014.

[1122] Richard Price, "Forget Scientology, Celebs are now Falling for an even more Sinister 'Religion': Introducing the Satanic Sex Cult that's Snaring Stars such as Peaches Geldof," *Daily Mail*, April 21, 2013.

[1123] Leonie Cooper, "Marilyn Manson: The most Famous Satanist in the World talks Politics, Family and Collecting Human Skeletons," NME, September 22, 2017.

[1124] Shannon Lee, "10 Music Stars Tied to Satanic Worship," *The Richest*, July 4, 1014.

[1125] Martin Robinson, "'He'd have Sex with anyone': Ex-Girlfriend of Lostprophets Pervert Reveals his Sick Fantasies as it Emerges he 'Seduced Fan aged 15' before she Offered him her Baby to Abuse," *Daily Mail*, November 28, 2013.

[1126] "Peaches Geldof, Mind Control, Satanism, Israel," *aangirfan.com*, April 21, 2014..

removed her post from her Twitter account and apologized, though it failed to stop a legal inquiry looking further into the matter.[1127]

Peaches' close *BBC* Radio 1 DJ friend and fellow presenter Fearne Cotton once dated Ian Watkins back in 2005.[1128] Fearne's second cousin was longtime senior *BBC* executive and managing director Bill Cotton. And with both Peaches' mother, her father Hughie Green and maternal grandfather all career *BBC* employees who more than likely knew Savile and his *BBC* child sex ring, Peaches Geldof knew the secret pedo-history and publicly outing a high profile pedophile rocker on Twitter where she had over 161,000 followers demonstrated she was taking a bold stance against pedophilia, exposing the pervasive UK network she undoubtedly had firsthand encounters with in her past. Taking such conspicuous aim against the pedo-epidemic no doubt triggered fear and wrath amongst certain *BBC* and VIP pedophiles that such an outspoken, devoted young mother, popular celebrity and longtime entertainment industry insider could be launching a public crusade against their entire global pedo-cabal. Boxed into the corner, they likely concluded they had to get her before she got them. So just like Princess Diana and Jill Dando, Peaches Geldof prematurely met her Maker as another casualty in the earth's current war raging between the forces for good and evil.

Due to both Peaches and her mother's drug history, by many accounts her alleged murder could easily have been disguised to appear like just another typical fatal celeb overdose, not unlike her own mother Paula Yates's death. The pathologist in the Paula Yates case alluded to morphine depressing her brain and shutting down her respiratory system that killed her, not the heroin.[1129] But it was cabal coroner Dr. Knapman who insisted Paula Yates' death was the result of a "heroin overdose" due to "foolish and incautious" behavior after incongruently stating the amount of heroin she snorted wasn't enough to kill the average person.

Speculation immediately followed the breaking news of daughter Peaches' death, suggesting that imprisoned Ian Watkins was a powerful Illuminati member revengefully bent on silencing Peaches Geldof as retribution for publicly slamming him and his sordid, demented activities.[1130] Or more likely, similar to Jill and Diana, top echelons of the British pedo-establishment took notice and decided to silence another emerging potential threat for knowing too much.

Peaches' father, Sir Bob Geldof, is not the charity, "save the world" saint he's been cracked up to be in British high society and UK press. The triangular custody war between INXS lead singer Australian Michael Hutchence and Geldof's ex-wife Paula Yates versus rival Bob Geldof over Michael and Paula's own daughter Tiger Lily that Sir Bob used all his knightly power and

---

[1127] Matthew Weaver and Josh Halliday, "Peaches Geldof Apologizes for Ian Watkins Sex Abuse Tweet," *The Guardian*, November 29, 2014.

[1128] Hugo Gye, "Radio 1 DJ Fearne Cotton Slammed for using Paedophile Ian Watkins' Catchphrase 'Mega lolz' in a Jingle," *Daily Mail*, January 29, 2014.

[1129] Tania Branagan, "TV Star Killed by Heroin 'Bing,'" *The Guardian*, November 9, 2000.

[1130] Jerry Lawton, "Sick Satanic Website Claims that Peaches was Murdered as part of a Black Magic Plot," *Daily Mail*, April 12, 2014.

influence to win, led to such bad blood that many observers conclude that it resulted in murder by two staged suicides.[1131] First came Michael's alleged, highly anomalous suicide by hanging in November 1997, followed less than three years later by Paula's "accidental" heroin overdose. Just like Hutchence and Paula, as the outspoken rebellious daughter, Peaches also had a recent falling out in her increasingly strained relationship with Saint Bob in the months preceding her untimely death. See a pattern here?

Meanwhile, knighted by Queen Elizabeth back in 1985 and nominated for the Nobel Peace Prize by unprosecuted pedophile Lord Greville Janner in 1987,[1132] in the eyes of the ruling elite, Sir Bob Geldof could do no wrong. And ever since he's been running exclusively in Illuminati circles, surrounded by pedo-cabal presidents, crime-prime ministers and secret societies as a huge fan of war criminals George W Bush and Tony Blair.[1133] Even his acclaimed Band Aid, Live Aid and Live 8 series did not serve the poor in Third World Africa as advertised but largely himself as charity funds were misused on militant dictators engaged in genocidal forced migration policies and padding corporate coffers at debtor nations' expense,[1134] an earlier variation cut from the same grotesque cloth as the Clintons' Haitian rape and pillage plunder.[1135]

In another Clintonesque move, as the supposed antipoverty campaigner, in 2008 Geldof charged an incredible $100,000 for a single speech he made in Melbourne that included his first class airfare and hotel accommodations.[1136] With his "rock stardom" on the wane in 2012, when Bob Geldof arrived in Milan, Italy to perform a scheduled concert and found only 45 fans in his audience, the "saint" left the auditorium refusing to sing.[1137] Sir Bob's blatant self-opportunism, bloated self-importance, nouveau elitism, pugnacious, classless arrogance and shameless exploitation of the world's poor for his own personal gain made him an easy target leading to his eventual exposure and fall from knightly grace.[1138]

By the time Paula Yates and her rock n' roll bad-boy Michael Hutchence locked horns with Saint Bob, their doomed battle for child custody of Paula's three daughters sired by Geldof and the youngest belonging to Paula and Michael were already lost. As Saint Bob's enemies, they witnessed the dark side of the fallen "angel" emerge, each claiming that Sir Bob boastfully taunted and threatened them repeatedly with:

Don't forget, I am above the law.[1139]

[1131] Deborah Wilkes, "Bob Geldof's Cult of Mysterious Death," *Paranoid Magazine*, May 23, 2014.

[1132] "Geldof gets second Chance at Nobel," *LA Times/Reuters*, November 27, 1986.

[1133] George Monbiat, "Bono can't help Africans by Stealing their Voice," *The Guardian*, June 17, 2013.

[1134] Francis Carr Begbie, "The Tarnished Halo of 'Saint Bob' Geldof," *Occidental Observer*, July 28, 2016.

[1135] Ezili Dantò, "Hillary Clinton, Haiti Resources, US Thievery and the Female Butchers," *ezilidanto.com*, March 9, 2015.

[1136] "Sir Bob Geldof wants $100,000 for Antipoverty Speech," *Daily Telegraph*, November 14, 2008.

[1137] Barbara McMahon, "Geldof Cancels Italian Tour after only 45 Fans turn up for Milan Gig," *The Guardian*, July 24, 2006.

[1138] Nathalie Rothchild, "Bob Geldof: He's so Overrated," *Spiked*, November 11, 2010.v

[1139] Deborah Wilkes, http://www.paranoiamagazine.com/2014/05/bob-geldofs-cult-of-mysterious-death/

… a given privilege that makes for murder by fake suicide against vulnerable, perceived weaker enemies very plausible, fueling speculation suspecting foul play based on the elite's fact-based history, reinforced by the company one keeps.

Speaking of the company Sir Bob keeps, besides pedo- and war-friendly criminals Tony Blair[1140] and George W, Geldof is also in tight with his homies Lord Waheed Alli and Lord Peter Mandelson, both gay men linked to the VIP pedophilia ring. As the first openly gay lord and at 34 the youngest life peer compliments of PM Blair, Waheed Alli and his other half Charlie Parsons partnered with Geldof to make a fortune co-owning Planet 24 TV, UK's largest independent production company.[1141] Mandelson, a Rothschild steward, was caught downloading child pornography in 2002 under Operation Ore but Labor PM Blair sealed it with a D-notice to protect his two time cabinet secretary.[1142] After Parliament, the above-the-law pedophile became an EU Commissioner, a perennial Bilderberger and chief trustee to UK's largest child charity organization the NSPCC (yep, another gatekeeping pedo-fox).[1143]

Convicted US blackmailing pedophile felon Jeffrey Epstein listed Lord Mandelson 10 times in his infamous black book.[1144] According to British intelligence operative, French doctors leaked that Mandelson was hospitalized after indulging in the "gay sport" felching, where a cardboard tube is inserted into the rectum and a furry little hamster is inserted into the butthole for cheap sicko thrills.[1145] These are the type of compromised perverts the ruling elite places into power to run our planet. But more on these pedo-cabal puppets in Chapter 7's Westminster scandal. You now can understand why Sir Bob so freely and smugly throws his "I'm above the law" weight around.

Incredibly whenever Sir Jimmy felt threatened with exposure, he too would immediately resort to uttering this same weaponized line as his cruel reminder that he too reached the "untouchable" zone,[1146] as a fully knighted, impugned and protected member of the same planet plunderers club.[1147]

At the height of Michael Hutchence and Paula Yates' embattled custody faceoff against Geldof over Sir Bob's effort to steal their own biological daughter Tiger Lily, in his final interview just prior to his extremely suspicious death, Michael Hutchence prophetically warned:

[1140] "Tony Blair and the Paedophile Connection," *The Coleman Experience/whale.to*, April 28, 2014.

[1141] "Labour's TV Mogul Lord Alli with a new Fortune in his Sights," *Evening Standard*, June 30, 2010.

[1142] "Peter Mandelson," *whale.to*..

[1143] "Paedophile Politicians," *sites.google.com*.

[1144] Vanessa Allen, "Peter Mandelson stays Silent over his Contact with Prince Andrew's Disgraced Financier Friend," *Daily Mail*, March 7, 2011.

[1145] T Stokes, "Tony Blair as 'Miranda' he who Pay the Piper," *whale.to*.

[1146] Joe Shute, "How far did Police go to Protect Jimmy Savile?" *The Telegraph*, October 18, 2013.

[1147] "How Jimmy Savile Revealed all in the Psychiatrist's Chair," *Channel 4 News*, November 2, 2012.

Saint Bob, and Wild Boy Rock Star, you pick the one who people are going to believe. One day, the truth will be told.[1148]

For Michael Hutchence and wronged victims everywhere, it's time the truth finally be told. From his Sydney hotel room, Hutchence purportedly argued with Sir Bob over the phone about their impending custody decision, delayed several weeks until the following month of December 1997.[1149] Anxious to have Paula and her children including his baby daughter Tiger Lily joining him for Christmas in Australia, and increasingly distraught and exacerbated by drugs over Sir Bob reneging on an earlier agreement and putting the kibosh on Michael's big family holiday plans, the official narrative maintains that in a fit of alcohol-cocaine-Prozac enflamed depression, the reigning rock star took his own life using his belt and doorknob to hang himself.[1150] Paula Yates insisted her man did not commit suicide but died of asphyxiation playing an auto-eroticism game of the alleged David Carradine kind (though it too may be a disguised murder).[1151]

But others reminded of Geldof's repeated "above the law" threats, after a dozen doorknob hanging "suicides" in recent years, a growing number are questioning this implausible scenario as a staged pretext designed to conceal actual murder by strangulation,[1152] especially when a similar falling out pattern emerged later in the untimely supposed drug OD deaths of both Geldof's wife and daughter.[1153] Simultaneous celeb "suicides" by doorknob hanging of both designer Ann Spade and chef Anthony Bourdain in June 2018 shortly after Anthony called out sexual predator Harvey Weinstein in the face of increasing exposure of the global pedophilia crisis has given rise to speculation that the Deep State is leaving its cabal calling card assassinations as covert retaliation against truth tellers.[1154]

So on flimsy ground back in late 1997, the Sydney coroner refused an inquest or any further inquiry into the Hutchence doorknob hanging, rushing to judgment in favor of suicide and that was that.[1155] Grief-stricken Paula descended into self-medicating as no match for the saint to benevolently claim a loving home full of half-sisters for Tiger Lily, setting the stage for Paula's worldly exit less than three years later, by attrition leaving Saint Bob to snatch the youngest

[1148] "Bob Geldof is Evil," http://spikethenews.blogspot.com/2014/04/bob-geldof-is-evil.html.

[1149] Richard Shears, "Searching a Bin for Cocaine with Fingers covered in Cigarette Burns down to the Bone, Tawdry last hours of Rock Star Michael Hutchence: 17 years on, new Revelations from Police who Probed Death," *Daily Mail*, February 16, 2014..

[1150] Robert Milliken, "The Death of a Rock Star," *Independent*, April 5, 1998.

[1151] David Randall, "Suicide, Sex Game, or Murder? The Death of David Carradine could be a case for the FBI," *Independent*, June 7, 2009.

[1152] "12 Clinton Whistleblowers Found 'Hanging from Doorknobs,'" *NWO Report*, June 18, 2018.

[1153] "Bob Geldof is Evil," http://spikethenews.blogspot.com/2014/04/bob-geldof-is-evil.html.

[1154] "Death by Hanging from a Doorknob - The Signature of Pedophilia-Related Assassinations? Eleven People so far - Who Knew Doorknobs could be so Deadly?" *Stillness in the Storm*, June 12, 2018.

[1155] Derrick W. Hand, "Michael Hutchence Death explained: the Coroner's Account in his own words," *Herald Sun*, January 29, 2014.

daughter from her biological relatives in Australia.[1156] Once her mother was gone, 4-year old Tiger Lily's forced estrangement from her father's side of the family soon had her calling Sir Geldof "dad." And after a 5-day vacation in 2006 visiting her real father's family, Saint Bob cut Tiger Lily's grandparents and aunt completely out of his soon-to-be adopted daughter's life altogether. By 2010, unfortunately Tiger's Aussie grandparents were already dead, and Geldof forbid Tiger Lily from attending their funerals or have anything to do with the Hutchence family.[1157] But now that the grownup aspiring actress Tiger Lily Hutchence Geldof turned 21 in July 2018, Geldof's hold on her may be slipping just a bit. Much to his chagrin, Tiger Lily has already reestablished contact with her long-lost Aunt Tina,[1158] who referring to Sir Bob on Australian national television once stated:

I think he's Satan.[1159]

Turning to another ill-fated love affair between 42-year old *BBC* presenter Mark Speight and his 31-year old fiancé actress and fellow *BBC* presenter Natasha Collins, they died just months apart just over a decade ago in 2008.[1160] After meeting on the *BBC* TV children's show See It Saw It, they fell in love and were engaged to be married when their tragic fate intervened. When news of Natasha's untimely death surfaced just five days after *BBC* DJ Kevin Greening's bizarre, questionable demise, the media was all over the splashy, bizarre circumstance that led to Natasha's untimely end.

The story goes that the couple decided to indulge in an alleged end-of-holiday drug alcohol binge on January 3rd, 2008, sharing an alleged lethal cocktail of wine, vodka, sleeping pills and cocaine (with a suspicious five times the deadly dose found in her bloodstream).[1161] Mark testified they had retired for the night at around 4AM. But at some point, still in a drugged stupor, Natasha managed to get to the bathroom and into the bathtub, slipping into unconsciousness with the hot water still running with over 60% of her body scalded. Stupor or no stupor, one would think scalding water would be painful enough to wake up and get out of the bathtub.

By the time Mark discovered her lifeless body at 1PM the next day, it was too late. According to Westminster Coroner Dr. Paul Knapman, she died from a drug overdose.[1162] Police initially

[1156] David Graves and Geoffrey Lee Martin, "Geldof wins Custody of Paula Yates's Daughter," *The Telegraph*, December 18, 2000.

[1157] Matt Buchanan and Leesha McKenny, "No Tiger Lily at Gran's Funeral," *Sydney Morning Herald*, September 30, 2010.

[1158] Alison Boshoff, "Orphan who's Bob Geldof's Greatest Success: Tiger Lily whose Rock Star Father Killed himself when she was a Baby and Mum Paula Yates Died of a Drug Overdose Celebrates turning 21," *Daily Mail*, July 21, 2018.

[1159] Deborah Wilkes, "Bob Geldof's Cult of Mysterious Death…" *Paranoia Magazine*, May 23, 2014.

[1160] "Revealed: The Spot where Tragic TV Star Mark Speight's Body Hung Undiscovered for six days," *Evening Standard*, April 14, 2008.

[1161] "BBC Presenter Died in Scalding Bath after taking five times Lethal level of Cocaine with Fiancé Mark Speight," *Evening Standard*, April 2, 2008.

[1162] Gordon Raynor, "BBC Children's Host Died after Cocaine Binge," *The Telegraph*, April 2, 2008.

interrogated Speight as a possible murder suspect for allegedly supplying her with the illicit drugs that allegedly killed her, but ultimately opted not to charge him. Perhaps he knew too much about his employer's pedo-ring to risk him spilling the beans if charged with a crime.

But just five days after Natasha's inquest attended by a gaunt, depressed Mark Speight, and just three months after his betrothed's untimely death, the popular kids' show presenter of the *BBC* art program SMart was reported missing, then six days later also found dead. His body was reportedly discovered hanging at a strangely remote, unused, locked section within the Paddington Railway Station.[1163] Six days before his body was recovered by Paddington security, Mark was allegedly last spotted alive nearby by two police officers on patrol, claiming they briefly spoke to him, describing him as distraught and depressed. At the alleged suicide scene, police encountered a broken belt believed to have been first used before Speight allegedly turned to tying his shoelaces together to hang himself from a bannister. Hard to believe that his belt would break apart while two much thinner, much flimsier shoelaces from his shoes would somehow manage to hold the weight of a grown man's body until death without shredding or coming apart first. Thus, as reported in the media, his suicide method appears highly implausible. Also found in the deceased's pocket was an alleged scrawled suicide note and another one in his diary addressed to his parents.

A tragic Romeo and Juliet-ish ending of a doomed romance with no foul play involved was the official conclusion ruled by coroner Dr. Knapman... way too simplistic, smacking of an artificially scripted and delivered official narrative. But when viewed together after covering the slew of mysterious deaths all connected to the *BBC* pedophile ring, followed by a cursory look at the highly suspicious, nefarious career of Westminster coroner Dr. Knapman, who ruled over so many of the *BBC* and Westminster pedophile ring deaths, suddenly Natasha and Mark's cases loom much shadier, darker and increasingly suspect. So far Knapman has been official coroner in Kevin Greening, Paula Yates, Natasha Collins and Mark Speight's inquests. But then by close association, there's an entire cast of shady, supporting cabal characters to uncover.

First, we'll start with exploring Natasha Collins and her fiancé Mark Speight's link to the wider *BBC* pedo-network. Already mentioned was the Operation YewTree conviction of disgraced fellow *BBC* employee and now pedophile free bird Rolf Harris, who frequently worked side-by-side with Mark Speight on various *BBC* kids' projects and programs together. As such, Harris stated at Mark's 2008 memorial:

It was joyful to work with Mark. I realize that I never told him how much I appreciated his programs. You realize you should always tell people what you think, you should tell them that you love them because it might suddenly be too late.[1164]

[1163] Rebecca Evans, "TV Star Mark Speight Hanged himself with Shoelaces," *Mirror*, May 21, 2008.
[1164] Lizzie Smith, "Tearful Rolf Harris pays Tribute to Tragic TV Presenter Mark Speight at Memorial Service," *Daily Mail*, August 7, 2008.

As an admired *BBC* children's program host, Mark Speight also maintained very close ties with Esther Rantzen, longtime *BBC* fixture, presenter and producer of the two-decade running show That's Life and founder of the *BBC* ChildLine charity for abused children. Speight often volunteered his free time as an avid campaign fundraiser for ChildLine, Rantzen's 24-hour helpline organization providing a registry of child sexual abuse as well as counseling and support for reporting child abuse victims.[1165] However that said, ChildLine also has been openly accused of actually serving as a window-dressing front designed to protect the pedophiles instead of the children in another classic case of the fox guarded henhouse.[1166]

Esther Rantzen's helpline was concurrently launched back in 1986 when she and her cousin Sarah Caplan co-founded the ChildLine charity. Sarah's husband, Nick Ross, was the founder and 23-year presenter of *BBC*'s 33-year program staple Crimewatch (that ended in 2017).[1167] And his co-presenter from 1995 until her brutal murder in 1999 was broadcast journalist Jill Dando. Lots of evidence indicates that Jill had gathered evidence that was about to expose her own company's pedophile ring. But more on her tragic case along with her dubious cohost Nick Ross later.

The trustee and chief underwriter funding Rantzen's 1986 ChildLine with a half million pound contribution was entrepreneur and philanthropist Sir Ian Skipper,[1168] with links to Nathan M. Rothschild[1169] and Prince Charles.[1170] OBE appointed Skipper owned homes in notorious pedophile island of Jersey and Sir Cliff Richard's island nation of Barbados, both used as billionaires' tax haven write-offs.[1171] Interior decorator Conrad Jameson was hired by Skipper to perform work on his estate but soon found out that the trustee of the largest UK children's charity - the National Society for Prevention of Cruelty to Children (NSPCC), was a sexual pervert obsessed with pornography. Jameson threatened to expose Skipper, who then sued Jameson for sexual blackmail but lost the case in 1993.

Another suspicious listing in convicted pedophile blackmailer Jeffrey Epstein's address book was also a ChildLine director who worked with Esther Rantzen on That's Life, but also served as both an MP and Secretary of State for Northern Ireland - Shaun Woodward.[1172]

Under the familiar pretense of national security, D-notices forbid public access to governmental affairs deemed top secret as a favorite cabal device constantly misused by Blair's skeleton-filled closet in order to conceal VIP pedophilic perversions. Recall earlier that Tony Blair - aka crossdressing Miranda - issued a D-notice for 100 years based on a thick MI5 dossier collecting

[1165] "Childline Supporting Children for the past 30 Years," *nspcc.org.uk*.
[1166] "Esther Rantzen A Danger to Children," *scribd.com*.
[1167] "Mysterious Nick Ross," *Tap News Wire/ The Coleman Experience*, December 11, 2013.
[1168] "Esther Rantzen Reveals Childhood Abuse Secret," *The Telegraph*, August 30, 2011..
[1169] "Jorvik: The Vikings Return," 1984, *Yorkshire Film Archives*, at 7:38.
[1170] "Ian Skipper, Obituary," *Yorkshire Post*, July 31, 2009.
[1171] "Burnley Car Empire Boss Ian Skipper Dies," *Burnley Express*, August 14, 2009.
[1172] Vanessa Allen, "Peter Mandelson stays Silent over his Contact with Prince Andrew's Disgraced Financier Friend," *Daily Mail*, March 7, 2011.

blackmail evidence on Sir Peter Mandelson.[1173] Then there was the felching incident in France.[1174] A known Rothschild mole planted inside UK establishment to ensure political control and shield the global pedo-trade as director of UK's leading children's charity the NSPCC,[1175] Mandelson also enjoyed young boys vacationing at registered US child sex offender Jeffrey Epstein's Sex Slave Island. And Epstein listed on Mandelson no less than 10 different numbers and addresses belonging to fellow pedophile Sir Mandy,[1176] not to mention Tony Blair's address in Epstein's who's who as well.

Also key is VIP pedophile enabler Dame Rantzen's 2006 ChildLine-NSPCC merger securing her role as yet another charity pedo-gatekeeping trustee. One year later the NSPCC was busted using fake abuse stories to generate cash donations[1177] while its CEO was skimming a cool £162,000 off incoming gravy for his annual salary,[1178] that happens to be among the top dozen among all UK charities.[1179]

Meanwhile, NSPCC vice president multimillionaire Gerald Ronson's fundraiser wife Gail Ronson claimed "I've never, ever, met him [Epstein]. I swear," despite both their names also written in Epstein's now infamous black book.[1180] Gail is related to the late accused pedophile Home Secretary Sir Leon Brittan as is his other cousin foreign secretary under conservative PM John Major - Sir Malcolm Rifkind, who vehemently defended pedophile PM Heath's "besmirched reputation."[1181] The longtime resident of pedo-infested Dolphin Square and powerful head of the House of Commons intelligence and security committee, Rifkind falsely claimed in 2015 "nobody pays me a salary" despite officially earning £81,936 annually as an MP chair, forcing his resignation as part of a Channel 4 influence peddling sting.[1182] It's one very tightly knit Zionist network with the same infiltrating Jewish foxes all cherry picked as cabal pedo-guards protecting their child murdering Luciferian masters.

Now let's take a closer look at Nick Ross, husband of *BBC*'s ChildLine co-founder Sally Caplan (Esther's cousin) and TV partner of murdered Jill Dando. In 2013 a half dozen years after Ross left Crimewatch and 14 years after his co-presenter's assassination, the so-called crime expert actually came out with the following incriminatingly telling statement:

[1173] "Peter Mandelson," *whale.to*.

[1174] "Peter Mandelson," *whale.to*.

[1175] "About us what we do, who we are and how we're Fighting for every Childhood," *NSPCC*.org.

[1176] Vanessa Allen, http://www.dailymail.co.uk/news/article-1364001/Peter-Mandelson-silent-contact-Prince-Andrew-friend-Jeffrey-Epstein.html.

[1177] "How the NSPCC Faked Child Abuse Stories to Generate Cash," *Daily Mail*, September 11, 2011.

[1178] Melissa Kite, "Charities are the last Bastion of Corporate Greed," *The Spectator*, August 1, 2015,.

[1179] Jonathon Fagan, "Overpaid Charity CEOs – Top 20 of Highest Paid Employees," *legalrecruitment.blogspot.com*, December 6, 2014.

[1180] Angella Johnson, "How Prince Andrew shared a Room at Epstein's Caribbean Hideaway with a Busty Blonde who Claimed she was a Brain Surgeon," *Daily Mail*, March 13, 2011.

[1181] Matt Agorist, "Police Chief Confirms former UK Prime Minister Raped Dozens of Children and Government 'Covered it up,'" *The Free Thought Project,* February 19, 2017.

[1182] "Oh Dear! British Intelligence Chair Rifkind Caught in Influence Peddling Sting!" *Crimes of Empire*, February 23, 2015.

I'd probably watch child pornography to see what all the fuss is about...[1183]

Nick Ross was making a flagrant pitch to normalize this heinous sex crime exploiting children that in this computer age of dark web and snuff films, child porn and sex trafficking abuse have become the pedo-cabal's most lucrative, fastest growing illegal enterprise on the planet.[1184] The transparency of the pedo-cabal is at work through the *BBC* and disturbing, revealing comments like that from Nick Ross, who founded the Crimestopper helpline for the public to supposedly call in information to help law enforcement solve crimes. However, his Crimestopper helpline suddenly went dead right after his *BBC* partner's murder.[1185] More dot connecting to follow but back to Esther Rantzen's helpline organization.

Esther's choice as ChildLine's very first chief executive - Valerie Howarth - was the former head of social services in Brent when in 1984 a 4-year old girl under her department's supposed protection was tortured and brutally murdered by her parents.[1186] After learning the girl's social worker had only seen the child once in the 10 months leading up to the murder, Valerie forgot to pass this vitally crucial, life-saving information onto Brent's chief executive and social services committee and then conveniently failed to mention this gross if not criminal oversight when she later applied to head Cambridgeshire social services. But the dubious career of this unemployed, failed child protector was actually rescued by Esther Rantzen, placing her in a key position in charge of protecting all of United Kingdom's children, exactly like Blair appointed pedo-protecting, PIE connected Margaret (Oppenheimer) Hodge his minister of all UK children.[1187] This pervasive pattern permeates each interlocking cog invariably shielded by a pedophile sentinel guarding the pedo-pipeline henhouse.

If the largest children's charity in Britain - the NSPCC - whose very purpose is to protect its children colludes with UK law enforcement's Operation Yewtree endorsing the official lie that Sir Jimmy acted completely alone, with no evidence of an organized pedo-network and never any police corruption helping him,[1188] how can the National Society for Protection against Cruelty to Children really be a friend to UK children? The fact is, it isn't, not when it's run by the likes of pedophile Sir Peter Mandelson, pedo-lover Dame Esther Rantzen and accused child rapist Prince Andrew as its trustees and patrons.[1189]

Of course, Esther's celebrity status and popular acclaim as a famous TV personality and so-called child advocate pioneer has not gone unnoticed by the British establishment, earning her

---

[1183] Hannah Furness, "I'd probably Watch Child Porn, Admits former Crimewatch Presenter Nick Ross," *The Telegraph*, June 2, 2013.

[1184] Lori Handrahan, "Investigating the Trade in Child Rape," *Medium*, February 24, 2015.

[1185] "The Curious case of Nick Ross, VIP Child-Abuse, Filthy Comments, Operation Yewtree, Crimestoppers and the Death of Jill Dando," *whale.to/The Coleman Experience*, June 3, 2013.

[1186] Sally Baker, "'Twas the Night before Christmas and the Culprits were Named...," *drsallybaker.com*.

[1187] "Margaret Hodge – Children's Homes Abuse & Connections to PIE," *The UK & Ireland Database*.

[1188] Alexandra Topping, "Jimmy Savile Reports Published," *The Guardian*, January 11, 2013.

[1189] Jake Ryan, "NSPCC Distances Itself from Prince Andrew after Facing Backlash over its Historic Links to Scandal-Hit Royal," *Daily Mail,* August 24, 2019.

the most prominent position the last dozen years as an NSPCC trustee.[1190] Rantzen is also a patron of the National Association for People Abused in Childhood (NAPAC). Her accolades and awards are endless, an OBE for her services in broadcasting, and a CBE for her services for children. The queen appointed her Dame Commander of the Order of the British Empire (DBE) and on and on her honors go.[1191] For all her sterling awards and impeccable accolades, is it fair to conclude that Esther Rantzen is rewarded for protecting pedophilia empire interests more than protecting UK children? With the most vulnerable population inside the UK child welfare system the most targeted and accessible victims preyed upon historically by the British pedophile VIP crowd that Dame Esther runs with, I'd say just like her NSPCC, she's done a pretty horrible job protecting the very kids she pretends she cares most about. And her track record only proves it.

Immediately following an internal NSPCC audit, in August 2018 Dame Esther announced she was suddenly resigning her coveted trustee post that she was so paranoid of losing during the post-Savile aftermath. In a face saving move, the 78-year old claimed her three children sat her down for "a family intervention," pressuring her to slow down and take it easier in her golden years.[1192] But according to a recent smoke and *Mirror* fluff piece, while still ChildLine president and still active in her NSPCC fundraising role, with Sir Jimmy dead and gone, she's still the undisputed "charity champion" of the British Isles, flaunting her busier than ever schedule with talks of even reviving yet another run of her That's Life.[1193] Though her half century of being in the celebrity charity limelight may have helped some people, the number touted on her ChildLine is 3.2 million, too often outward appearances belie a much darker, hidden past as the Savile saga blatantly proves, especially when it comes to those so closely tied to the *BBC*, children's charities and British VIP pedophilia network.

Esther Rantzen's autobiography was released in 2001. As an adulterer for the second time in less than three years while in her mid to late twenties, her first as a mistress to a prominent married pedophile politician,[1194] Esther then began sleeping with her *BBC* producer in 1969, engaging in an 8-year extramarital affair that led to the breakup of a long-term marriage between her *BBC* boss Desmond Wilcox and his wife Patsy, who also worked in the same *BBC* department as Esther the homewrecker.[1195] Initially as Rantzen's co-worker and friend, Patsy brought her home to meet "this fantastic guy I'm married to."[1196] Rantzen spent so much time at Patsy's family home that Patsy's children called her "Aunty Esther." It took nearly eight years

[1190] "Dame Esther Rantzen DBE," *Avalon.com* website.

[1191] Steven Swinford, "Esther Rantzen to be made a Dame in New Year Honours List," The Telegraph, December 27, 2014.

[1192] Sebastian Shakespeare, "Dame Esther Rantzen is stepping down as a Trustee of the NSPCC after her Children 'Stage an Intervention and Asked her to do less,'" *Daily Mail*, August 8, 2018.

[1193] Patrick Hill and Alex Belfield, "Dame Esther Rantzen, 78, Refuses to Bow to her Kids' Demands to slow down with Work," *Mirror*, August 18, 2018.

[1194] Greg Christison, "Esther's Horror at Fairburn's Child Sex Allegations," *Express*, July 21, 2014.

[1195] Amy Oliver and Simon Trump, "That's Strife! Picture that Reveals the very Complex Saga of Esther Rantzen, her son Joshua and his Baby... by his Married Lover," *Daily Mail*, February 21, 2015.

[1196] Olga Craig, "That's Life: Esther Rantzen Broke my Mother's Heart," *The Telegraph*, February 18, 2001.

of Rantzin cheating behind her friend's back to eventually get pregnant and finally convince Patsy to give up on her 'fantastic guy" and lost cause marriage vows, to finally divorce Desmond so Esther and Desi could blissfully tie the knot and soon displace Patsy as the new matron living inside the large Wilcox family home.

But then like mother, like son. Years later it was Desmond and Esther's son's turn to carry on the family tradition, having an affair with a married woman in 2014, resulting in a pregnancy and her leaving her devastated high school sweetheart husband.[1197] When both parental role models commit adultery as an indelible family dynamic interwoven into the family history of both parents, it often becomes a common legacy that repeats itself inter-generationally. But let's skip over that little inconvenient truth and move on to more of Esther's do-gooder role in her real "that's life."

With absolutely zero remorse over destroying a family with three children, in Rantzen's 2001 book published a year after Desmond died, the homewrecker viciously attacked her onetime friend Patsy, a scorned woman unable to defend herself having died in 1999.[1198] One of Esther's stepchildren Cassandra Wilcox felt compelled to set the record straight in a *Daily Mail* article refuting what she considered Rantzen lies about her mother Patsy. When Desmond left his wife in 1977 to live with Esther at her place, Rantzen claims in her book that Patsy "wanted to live on her own," suggesting she abandoned her family when in actuality Patsy was so heartbroken by betrayal that she was literally suffering from a serious enough cardiac condition to warrant a two week stay in Charing Cross Hospital, which caused her younger 15-year old twins to temporarily have to move in with their father and Rantzen. Cassandra states that Rantzen misrepresented her mother as selfish, "virtually throwing them [her kids] out of the family house." But Rantzen's stepdaughter maintains that "nothing could be further from the truth." A brief examination of Esther's life will show that her self-serving, revisionist distortions of reality and less than honest liberties telling her skewed versions of "truth" reveal a lifelong characterological flaw of deception and hypocrisy.

After reading Esther Ranzen's autobiography, Victor Lewis-Smith's response had Rantzen accurately pegged back in 2001, long before the Savile scandal broke, writing in his *Evening Standard* book review:

Throughout Esther's career there's always been a yawning chasm between the image she presents to her public and what appears to me to be a deep-seated private contempt for them.[1199]

[1197] Amy Oliver and Simon Trump, "That's Strife! Picture that Reveals the very Complex Saga of Esther Rantzen, her Son Joshua and his Baby... by his Married Lover," *Daily Mail*, February 21, 2015.

[1198] Cassandra Wilcox, "Esther Rantzen's Stepdaughter Speaks out," *Daily Mail*, September 12, 2018.

[1199] "Esther Rantzen A Danger to Children," https://www.scribd.com/doc/256503576/ESTHER-RANTZEN-and-the-paedophiles.

While the British elite revere and fawn over Esther Rantzin as its legendary establishment darling and another queen honored "national treasure"[1200] (like Savile), serious charges have persistently plagued her ChildLine helpline alleged to systematically filter out callers reporting child abuse crimes perpetrated by British VIPs.[1201] Moreover, after chummily working side by side with Sir Jimmy at the *BBC* since the 1960s, incriminating accusations have also been levied against Rantzen for knowing about his and other *BBC* pedophiles, yet all the while doing nothing to stop them. What kind of true child abuse advocate would knowingly allow such widespread abuse to go on and then do nothing about it? After the Savile bombshell when called on the carpet in October 2012 for her years of inaction, no sooner did she admit to knowing about the "green room gossip," she then actually confessed that "green room gossip is always true."[1202]

But in the face of the Savile allegations, rather than take personal responsibility or show any personal regret as her nation's most famous and powerful child abuse advocate that did nothing to stop the nation's worst child rapist, she went from one interview to the next busily pontificating how all of Great Britain was fooled, attempting to assuage her own phony guilt (if she even has any) and criminal complicity by her concerted effort to spread the blame to the entire nation for being so bamboozled:

We as a whole nation were to blame.[1203]

No, she is to blame for helping herself to a celebrity career of fame and wealth at the expense of abused kids she refused to protect. She can't have it both ways, all chummy with Savile for decades, while knowing the green room "gossip" about the sicko was true. Meanwhile, anti-child abuse advocate Shy Keenan came forward in 2012 to disclose that she personally warned Rantzen way back in 1994 about Savile's widespread abuse, a full 15 years before his final known victim was abused.[1204] While Rantzen hosted her *BBC* series That's Life, a program boasting that it exposes corruption and criminality, she could have easily utilized her readymade broadcasting platform, her ChildLine hotline ostensibly set up for sexual abuse victims and her influential power and clout within the Establishment to unmask the disturbing truth behind the "open secret" rumors and suspicions she admits she knew about way back when. But instead, Rantzen chose not to look into Savile at all, despite acknowledging she'd been told about his abuse while a *BBC* intern all the way back to the 1960s.[1205] For many decades Dame Esther remained silently complicit, as a championing child advocate, she was

[1200] "Esther Rantzen: That's Life UK Tour Announced," Avalon Management website.
[1201] "Childline," *whale.to*.
[1202] Katy Brand, "Jimmy Savile Allegations: Esther Rantzen's Response Defies Belief," *The Telegraph*, October 5, 2012.
[1203] "Evidence Dame Esther Rantzen Lied about @ShyKeenan," YouTube video, 11:07, posted on November 21, 2017.
[1204] Antonella Lazzeri, "Abuse Campaigner: 'I told Esther Rantzen about Paedo Jimmy Savile 18 Years ago," *The Sun*, October 12, 2016.
[1205] "Esther Rantzen Lied about Knowing Shy Keenan," *Phoenix Post*, November 16, 2017.

Savile's accomplice, aiding and abetting his crimes, all the while failing to lift a finger to save hundreds, even thousands of Savile victims from abuse. But that's the way the system's designed, to protect the perps with gatekeepers like her.

And then when confronted with Shy Keenan's explosively incriminating revelation, Rantzen out and out lied, pretending she never heard of Keenan nor remembered their conversation.[1206] Then in the thick of it, when the press confronted her knowing about the Savile rumors and her total lack of response as a supposed child advocate, she was far more terrified and worried about losing her NSPCC trustee job[1207] and her "life's work" legacy being destroyed than any abused children. Her response in the *Daily Mail*:

Say what you like about me – just please don't destroy my life's work.[1208]

Instead of being honest and forthright, Esther Rantzen chose to hide behind her phony crocodile tears[1209] and such incredibly asinine explanations as the one below from an October 2012 *Telegraph* article:

... The fact that Savile had even been blessed by the Pope, and if the Pope can't tell someone's a paedophile, then how could they [we] possibly be expected to know?[1210]

Shy Keenan has pointed out that Rantzen even committed perjury while feigning lost charity revenue:

In 2015, Dame Rantzen claimed 'under oath' that a 2012 fundraising event was cancelled because of Shy, the evidence shows that the fundraising event took place and Dame Rantzen attended.[1211]

This woman has been caught up in her growing web of lies and deceit, virtually losing all credibility with the public. Yet Dame Esther still remains perched on her throne, insulated by the queen's bestowed honors. During former police investigator Mark Williams-Thomas' second *ITV* Exposure installment as a two-year follow-up probing how Savile's power allowed him to get away with his heinous half century crime spree, he lastly interviewed Rantzen. After mentioning a charity event that Savile contributed to her ChildLine (more than once she

[1206] Tom Bryant, "Esther Rantzen: 'No Memory' of being Contacted by Campaigner over Jimmy Savile Abuse Claims," *Mirror*, October 17, 2012..

[1207] Anna Edwards, Alex Ward and Larisa Brown, "'I'm Staying put': Esther Rantzen Claims she will remain Child Abuse Charity Patron after Claims she Ignored Warnings over Jimmy Savile," *Daily Mail*, October 13, 2012.

[1208] Emily Allen, "Esther Rantzen Fears the Savile Sex Scandal could Destroy her ChildLine Legacy," *Daily Mail*, October 16, 2012.

[1209] Esther Rantzen, "Jim Fooled us all into thinking he was a Saint. When I saw the Truth, I Wept," *Daily Mail*, October 1, 2012.

[1210] Katy Brand, https://www.telegraph.co.uk/women/womens-life/9587450/Jimmy-Savile-allegations-Esther-Rantzens-response-defies-belief.html.

[1211] "Esther Rantzen Lied about Knowing Shy Keenan," http://www.thephoenixpost.com/6444-2/.

appeared as a guest on his shows) and her thank you letter to the *BBC* pedophile kingpin, she had the audacity to lament:

If only a child had rung us [ChildLine helpline]... *and told us what he'd been doing to them, we could have passed that to the police and done so much good.*[1212]

In all the years from 1986 on with her ChildLine fully operational while Britain's worst pedophile in history was still extremely active abusing kids across the nation, of course her helpline got calls from Savile victims but they were all blown off because that was her gatekeeping job. Rantzen seriously expects us to believe her ludicrous statement - that not one of Savile's thousands of victims over his next quarter century crime spree ever contacted her helpline to report his abuse? The response to Rantzen's disingenuous "would've-should've-could've" from her army of critics would quickly counter-argue that whenever victims of abuse perpetrated by VIPs like Jimmy Savile did report crimes to her ChildLine workers, their complaints were methodically screened out and never heard again. Claiming to be a lifelong champion of child protection and safety, her half century actions speak far louder than her empty, feeble, fork-tongued words. She needs to be investigated as a child rape accomplice on the grandest scale.

Another little Rantzen inconsistency indicating what you see is clearly not what you get... former child actor Ben Fellows reported that in 1990 at age 15, he attended a party in New Forest hosted by *BBC* executives where Esther, the child advocate queen herself, was present and fully aware that lots of drugs and alcohol were being given to children while swarms of pedo partygoers, many of them *BBC* executives, producers, directors and stars, were propositioning 15-year old Ben and the other kids all night long as the party's forbidden fruit conquests.[1213] Rantzen again did nothing on behalf of the endangered children right before her eyes, witnessing youth being taken advantage of, sexually exploited and victimized. A drugged Ben Fellows recalled being sexually assaulted by a *BBC* employee who would later work in the children's entertainment department, perhaps manning her ChildLine. The *BBC* kids' department has always been a pedo-magnet within the Corporation's larger child sex ring.

Keep in mind that the *British Broadcasting Corporation* is a tax paid, government sponsored mega media giant, guilty of covering up both Savile's so-vile sins as well as its own inside pedophilia ring. Meanwhile, aside from Savile and the half dozen known *BBC* employed pedophiles Rolf Harris, Paul Gadd, Chris Denning, Jonathon King, Alan Freeman and Stuart Hall covered in Chapter 2, for several decades running, this same complicit company maintained a steady flow of *BBC* employed insiders privy to this massive criminal cover-up, suddenly winding up dead under highly suspicious circumstances. But more on the KIAs shortly. Back to Madam Dame Esther, the inside pedo-enabling fox masquerading as Britain's benign, saintly savior of children.

[1212] "Exposure Update - The Jimmy Savile Investigation," *ITV*, 2013, YouTube video, 24:56, posted on March 7, 2013.
[1213] "Esther Rantzen – Exposing Children directly to Drug and Sex Parties – Allegation," Ben Fellows interview, YouTube video, 2012, 02:42, posted May 14, 2013.

While working at a prep school, a teacher named Alex Standish provided testimony to crown court as well as an episode of Rantzen's That's Life that helped convict several teachers guilty of child sex abuse in 1991.[1214] That's all fine and dandy, but when that same tutor turned out to be a pedophile himself, as a favor to him, Rantzen kept that critical piece of information a secret between her and the child abuser, once again protecting yet another sexual predator (aside from her former MP lover, Savile and the rest of the BBC pedo-platoon), knowingly further placing innocent children at graver risk.

Turns out that Esther as well as the local police where Standish was teaching, both knew that he was a child molester but neither informed the school nor the parents of any eminent danger. Then when a newspaper exposed her dirty little secret, she sued the paper for libel and somehow won a court settlement despite the veracity of the article's claim that she had deceived the paper's editor in a phone conversation. Because the police also knew Standish was a child molester, she wiggled out of losing her case before a star-struck jury. But an appeals court lowered the overinflated damages from £250,000 to £150,000.[1215]

Though Esther Rantzen may not have been present at another social event held at her own residence in New Forest, Hampshire in August 1993, an invited guest, 63-year old former British Airways engineer Robert Gillings, sexually assaulted a 5-year old girl in Rantzen's swimming pool.[1216] At the time the victim and her parents were staying at Rantzen's estate. Culminating a series of yearlong abuse, the incident resulted in Gillings receiving an 18-month prison sentence in July 1994.

If the true nature of an individual is accurately reflected in the company one intimately keeps, then Rantzen may not love children as much as she purports. In 1966 at age 26 while a BBC researcher, Esther Rantzen began a two-year adulterous affair with married Scottish pedophile MP Sir Nichols Fairbairn.[1217] A year later the "saintly" serial adulterer embarked on yet another affair with her boss Desmond Wilcox.

NSPCC trustee Esther Rantzen and NSPCC chief executive since 2013 Peter Wanless have been the two highest profile figures atop UK's child protection system. Yet each has a history linked directly to pedophilia and pedophiles. For years prior to his current gig, Wanless was Principle Private Secretary to confirmed pedophile Tory MP and Cabinet Secretary Michael Portillo who was involved in the cover-up of the notorious Westminster child sex ring[1218] (fully taken up in Chapter 7). Despite his predatory exposure as a pedophile, the outed Portillo left politics only to reinvent himself at where else but BBC, the pedo-friendly broadcasting network as a television

[1214] "Esther Rantzen – Was she Ignorant to Child Abuse?" UK & Ireland Database.
[1215] Ying Hui Tan, "Law Report: Excessive Libel Damages Cut: Rantzen v Mirror Group Newspapers and others. Court of Appeal (Lord Justice Neill, Lord Justice Staughton and Lord Justice Roch)," Independent, April 1, 1993.
[1216] "Man Convicted of Sex Assault on Girl, 5, in Swimming Pool: Guest at Holiday Home of Child Abuse Campaigner Claimed Ideas were put into his Victim's Mind," Independent, July 19, 1994.
[1217] Marc Horne, "Esther Rantzen: My Shock over my MP Lover's Links to Elm House Paedophile Ring," Daily Mail, July 20, 2014.
[1218] "Wanless Linked to Portillo; Fake Investigation into Child Abuse?" aanirfan.blogspot.com, July 11, 2014.

presenter.[1219] When birds of a feather flock together, they inevitably morph into foxes guarding their child henhouse. Just as in America, all the top positions entrusted to protect children invariably protect the elite's pedophilia network cabal.

In March 2003 Esther Rantzen and Paedophile Information Exchange (PIE) founder Tom O'Carroll (see Chapter 2) appeared together as panelists on a *BBC* After Dark program discussing pedophilia and child protection,[1220] as if there's any common ground between the two when PIE organization advocates no age of consent for children at all.[1221] For someone who claims to dedicate her life to keeping children safe, why has her entire public and private life and record been so intertwined with the likes of those bent on violating and destroying children? Bottom line, Esther Rantzen's been sleeping with the enemy throughout her entire adulthood.

The *Coleman Experience* claims that a former British intelligence officer disclosed that Esther Rantzen's residence she calls Blood Oaks needs to be dug up for all the bloody dead child corpses literally buried in her backyard, allegedly murdered during satanic sex abuse rituals held at her estate.[1222] Rantzen's Jewish family with ties to a diamond fortune also has her making friends with Mossad-CIA agent Uri Geller, linked to running a mind control program for gifted children.[1223] The Sir Cliff-Sir Jimmy-Geller Zionist pedo-cabal has far reaching tentacles into both Europe and North America and Esther Rantzen and her charity organizations NSPCC and ChildLine appear to be UK's prime gatekeeping apparatus, shielding VIP pedophilia operations. And just like her longtime *BBC* friend and colleague Sir Jimmy, Dame Rantzen has utilized her lofty social position and "charity-minded" fame as a deceptive front, pretending to save the innocents. But to insiders who know her, her actions, like the VIP establishment she embodies, represent pure evil incarnate.

So what we have on the one hand are the Luciferian pedophile core at the *BBC* supported by the pedo-government and pedo-royalty and their loyal puppet enabling legions, and on the other hand, we have *BBC* staff who as insiders have come to know about their company's appalling pedophilia agenda as an open cesspit secret, but more than likely paid for their knowledge and moral conscience with their lives. Even after the smoke cleared from the post-Savile debacle, the culture of fear at the *BBC* is still running rampant.[1224] Those who offered testimony to the Dame Janet Smith report on the *BBC* did so strictly on an anonymous basis, selectively leaving out so much criminally sinister truth, especially about the wider *BBC*

[1219] "Michael Portillo Embarks on a new Adventure in Brand new BBC Two Series," *BBC*, June 20, 2017.

[1220] "Esther Rantzen: A Danger to Children," *scribd.com*.

[1221] Tom de Castella and Tom Heyden, "How did the Pro-Paedophile Group PIE exist openly for 10 years?" *BBC*, February 27, 2014.

[1222] "Why the Bloody Hell hasn't Esther Rantzen been Arrested yet?" *Coleman Experience*, January 27, 2016.

[1223] "Paris Jackson, Uri Geller and Mind Control," *aangirgan.com*, July 20, 2013.

[1224] Jamie Grierson, "Atmosphere of Fear still exists at BBC, Savile Abuse Report Concludes," *The Guardian*, February 25, 2016.

pedophile ring and senior management ignoring it. Few former *BBC* employees dare go public for the obvious reason that they wish to remain alive knowing too many individuals have met the same tragic, untimely fate for simply knowing too much ugly truth.

The closest to a *BBC* critic-ex-employee gone public may be the former *BBC* presenter Bill Oddie, who alluded to the longtime Savile abuse being "a running sick joke" within the *BBC*, according to Bill, covered up because of Sir Jimmy's close ties to Prince Charles.[1225] But no former or current *BBC* employee has ever gone public divulging the reality that the *BBC* possessed a wider, still active pedophile ring, much less connected to the even wider VIP establishment's pedo-network. Again, the risk of death is too grave and certain.

And likely a big part of that reason comes from Jill Dando. No single *BBC* death has carried more weighted impact and implications exposing this diabolical filth percolating for over a half century within the *British Broadcasting Company*, with its interlocking ties to both government and royalty than the brutal murder of Jill Dando in April 1999. Having worked her way up the *BBC* corporate ladder since her 1984 hiring, by the mid-1990s, Jill Dando had grown to be the most public face of women at the *BBC*, fronting the programs Crimewatch from 1995 to her death as well as Holiday and the Six O' Clock News.[1226] In recent years it was revealed that the ever-popular presenter and broadcaster had been approached by a number of her female colleagues at the Corporation complaining about sexual harassment that regularly included groping and sexual assault.[1227]

When fellow *BBC* presenter Sally Jones disclosed to the Crimewatch host that Jimmy Savile had attempted to kiss and grope her in an elevator in the late 1980s, Sally said that Jill's response was that "she had to fend off plenty of unwelcome advances herself," adding that Savile was "just a dirty old perv."[1228] Sexual harassment accusations in the 1980s had also been made by two other presenters Liz Kershaw and Miriam O'Reilly as well.[1229] Though a *BBC* spokesman said their allegations would be looked into, his next statement was the dead giveaway to indicate nothing would ever change at the *BBC*:

We have not seen anything to substantiate these claims.[1230]

That's forever been *BBC*'s spouted mantra excuse washing its filthy, blood-soaked hands from the pedophilia epidemic flourishing for decades within its ranks, conveniently claiming never to have any record of a single complaint against Savile or anyone else. Over time, Jill became not

---

[1225] "BBC Covered up Jimmy Savile's Child Abuse because he was Friends with Prince Charles, Claims Veteran Broadcaster Bill Oddie," *SWNS.com*, October 19, 2012.
[1226] Tara Conlan, "Profile: Jill Dando," *The Guardian*, November 15, 2007.
[1227] Don Hale, "Exclusive: Tragic Jill Dando Probed BBC Paedo Ring," *Daily Star*, July 21, 2014.
[1228] "BBC's Sally Jones: 'Pervert' Savile Groped me in Lift – and Jill Dando Warned me of 'Unwelcome Advances' at Breakfast Time Office," *Daily Mail*, October 27, 2012.
[1229] Miriam O'Reilly, "A BBC Executive Pinned me to a Wall and made a Crude Pass. But even other Women told me to Forget it - or Lose my Career," *Daily Mail*, October 18, 2012.
[1230] Don Hale, https://www.dailystar.co.uk/news/latest-news/389922/Tragic-Jill-Dando-probed-BBC-PAEDO-ring.

only increasingly aware of the prevailing sexist culture at the *BBC* promoting the hostile work environment for women, but came to realize it was far more pathologically sinister, foreboding and dangerous for children. According to a retired *BBC* worker who spoke to the *Daily News* in July 2014, Jill Dando was informed by her co-workers that many of the *BBC*'s "big name stars," DJs, directors, producers and executives were participating in a large organized child sex abuse ring.[1231] The anonymous source explained:

I think she was quite shocked when told about images of children and that information on how to join this horrible paedophile ring was freely available.[1232]

But when Jill tried to get her Crimewatch bosses to investigate, they completely blew her off, clearly not wanting to get involved in any effort to expose or stop it. While in her mid-30s as an ethically-minded, popular host of a program that was supposed to be all about stopping criminal activity, especially involving helpless, abused children, in the mid-1990s Jill went to *BBC*'s senior management with a dossier of identified perps to let the head honchos know what was going on under their noses (as if they didn't already know).[1233] A year before she was killed, as a committed child abuse advocate, Jill Dando began actively promoting a campaign program to educate children on how to identify potential pedophiles. Jill's onetime colleague stated:

She compiled a file of complaints but she was not really an investigative journalist, just a presenter. She passed the information to someone else and they gave it back. No one wanted to know. I do remember that she gave a file to senior management. I don't think she heard any more.[1234]

No one wanted to broach this alarmingly horrific reality because they placed their jobs and personal safety over the fate of abused children. Jill's friend concluded:

Nothing had been done and there seemed to be a policy of turning a blind eye.[1235]

And near two decades later in the Savile aftermath, the *BBC* was still turning a blind eye in October 2012, flagrantly still lying its ass off claiming that management was totally unaware of any allegations against Savile or anyone else because no formal complaints were ever registered against sexual predators at the *BBC*:

The BBC has conducted searches of the its files and has not found any record of allegations of misconduct by Jimmy Savile during his time at the BBC.[1236]

[1231] Don Hale, https://www.dailystar.co.uk/news/latest-news/389922/Tragic-Jill-Dando-probed-BBC-PAEDO-ring.
[1232] Don Hale, https://www.dailystar.co.uk/news/latest-news/389922/Tragic-Jill-Dando-probed-BBC-PAEDO-ring.
[1233] Don Hale, https://www.dailystar.co.uk/news/latest-news/389922/Tragic-Jill-Dando-probed-BBC-PAEDO-ring.
[1234] Don Hale, https://www.dailystar.co.uk/news/latest-news/389922/Tragic-Jill-Dando-probed-BBC-PAEDO-ring.
[1235] Don Hale, https://www.dailystar.co.uk/news/latest-news/389922/Tragic-Jill-Dando-probed-BBC-PAEDO-ring.
[1236] Steve Hayes, "Op-Ed: Jimmy Savile – The Real Scandal," *Digital Journal*, October 5, 2012.

Not only did Jill Dando inform top management in the mid-1990s, but the head of Radio 1 Douglas Muggeridge suspecting abuse way back in 1973, approached Radio 1 press officer Rodney Collins to request that he ascertain if any local newspaper reporters were investigating Savile for pedophilia crimes.[1237] To refute *BBC*'s October 2012 lie that no record of Savile abuse exists, Rodney Collins emerged to boldly state that he received feedback from all the major newspapers in 1973 that, though they were aware of rumors circulating around the *BBC* program Savile's Travels where the pedophile was abusing underage girls in his traveling caravan, the unanimous consensus was no newspaper had any intention of reporting on it. This means that not only the behemoth *BBC* knew about Savile's abuse back in 1973, but other major newspaper outlets in the UK were also privy to Savile's crimes, yet chose not to investigate or go public either. This fact - across-the-boards complicity, strongly suggests an existing wider pedophilia network extending far beyond Savile or the *BBC* existed, yet was protected.

Rodney Collins dutifully passed on his shamefully dubious findings to his higher-ups, urging them to launch a full-scale internal inquiry to determine who knew what and when, confirming as far back as the early 1970s that senior *BBC* management both knew and were covering up child sexual abuse within its ranks. Collins said that not only his boss was aware of allegations but he believes the *BBC*'s managing director, later promoted to *BBC's* top dog Director General Sir Ian Trethowan from 1977 to 1982, also knew.[1238] Hardly by accident that queen honored Sir Ian was running the *BBC* during Sir Jimmy's peak years as the most prolific pedophile in British history.

That the UK's so-called free press as well as the police refused to touch the organized pedophilia network with a 10 foot pole operating way back in the early 1970s, only proves that the world's epicenter has knowingly allowed it to flourish for a very long time. Keep in mind at that time the Luciferian child raping murderer Edward Heath was the British prime minister and his #1 child procurer was none other than Sir Jimmy Savile. One can easily see why the press tolerated and condoned the ongoing evil a near half century ago as the complicit MSM still tolerates it to this day, which in large part is why the worldwide child raping network has been permitted to reach epidemic proportions today.

A reminder worth noting here is the plethora of sexual complaints being filed with law enforcement that police were repeatedly having to investigate the *BBC* throughout the late 1960s and again in 1971 with the Claire McAlpine sexual allegations and suicide, and then also separately in 1971 over the so called "payola scandal."[1239] A News of the World undercover exposé implicated *BBC* executives, DJs and producers for rigging the pop charts based on cash giveaways and sexual favors at rampant orgies involving young prostitutes dressed as schoolgirls (some underage) sponsored by record companies, culminating in charges filed in

[1237] Josh Halliday, "Former BBC Radio 1 Boss 'Aware of Jimmy Savile Allegations in 1970s,'" The Guardian, October 3, 2012.

[1238] Josh Halliday, https://www.theguardian.com/media/2012/oct/03/bbc-jimmy-savile-abuse-claims.

[1239] Robert Mendick and Laura Donnelly, "Jimmy Savile: Secret of BBC's first Sex Scandal," *The Telegraph*, October 20, 2012,.

1973 against a record company executive, a *BBC* producer, a theatrical agent, several record promoters and the madam orgy hostess. All of this nefarious illegal activity at the *BBC* was happening more than two decades prior to Jill Dando alerting the *BBC* top brass in the mid-90s. These facts provide irrefutable evidence that the UK's largest media corporation sponsored by the national government has been consistently engaging in pedophilia while simultaneously waging a nonstop campaign of widespread deception, denial and criminal cover-up over a span of the last half century.

When Jill Dando was discreetly making waves at the *BBC*, the pedo-cabal establishment grew increasingly nervous over her plan to expose the pedophilia network on her live television program platform Crimewatch. Enter the pedo-plot thickener as two intimates were mysteriously sent to meet Jill Dando not long before she died, one the legendary pop star Sir Cliff Richard, whom she became very close friends with,[1240] and the other Doctor Alan Farthing, who ended up her fiancé less than three months prior to her murder. Their engagement was announced at a party attended by Sir Cliff Richard as well as her Crimewatch partner Nick Ross.[1241] A mere year and a half before her death, Alan and Jill were set up on a blind date to meet at a dinner party by a mutual friend,[1242] no doubt linked to intelligence services, **within mere weeks** after August 31, 1997, when the world lost Princess Diana, its most iconic British heroine possessing the integrity and will that was on the verge of exposing the royal pedophilia filth.[1243]

Born just four months apart in 1961, Diana and Jill were two of United Kingdom's most famous, highly recognizable, attractive, extremely popular women, both independently uncovering widespread pedophilia in the royal family, the *BBC* and government. It's quite conceivable, if not probable, that Jill and Diana came to know each other, conferred and compared notes on their explosive VIP pedophile findings.[1244] While Diana was ready to bring down the royal family, Jill was preparing to unveil and, if need be, bring down the *BBC* pedophilia network, both ultimately unearthing the same child raping murderous cabal. While Jill was making an unwanted ruckus attempting to alert senior *BBC* management of its internal pedo-ring, Diana's assassination was being plotted and carried out as a direct threat to the satanic royal order. With both high profile, well-intentioned do-gooders lined up in the fatal crosshairs of British intelligence, the pedo-establishment was growing terrified that if their bombshell of a secret got out to the public it would utterly destroy UK's rulers. Thus, each one was cold-bloodedly picked off and sacrificed little more than a year and a half apart.

No sooner was Diana's plan to bring down the British monarchy's pedo-network averted, the British intelligence agencies got busy again scheming to assess and potentially eliminate their

---

[1240] "Cliff Richard; Crusaders; Military Intelligence," *aangirfan.com*, June 16, 2016.

[1241] Joan Smith, "We Thought we knew her so well," *Independent*, May 2, 1999.

[1242] Geoffrey Levy, "Why the Murder of his ex-Fiancé Jill Dando still Haunts the Man who will Deliver Kate Middleton's Baby," *Daily Mail*, December 8, 2012.

[1243] Brandon Turbeville, "The Prince and the Pedophile: Charles' Connections to Pedophilia Networks," *Activist Post*, November 16, 2012.

[1244] "Princess Diana was Surrounded by Perverts," *TioS News Organization*.

next highly visible threat, the nationally adored *BBC* darling herself, stirring up a hornet's nest unraveling the same pedo-crime cabal Diana discovered. Enter veteran Mossad-MI5 asset-accused pedophile-mind controlled former rent boy superstar himself, Sir Cliff Richard,[1245] along with the "good doctor" Farthing to become Jill's fiancé and royal family's future gynecologist. Security services dispatched both Sir Cliff as her nearest and dearest confidante and compelled Alan Farthing to wine, dine and romance Jill in order to discern just how much dirt she'd dug up on the British pedo-Establishment.[1246] Cliff Richard was both feeding her selective information while pumping her for all she knew. Prime Minister Tony Blair tapped intelligence services to conjure up a dirty smear campaign on Jill Dando, the plan being to ruin her reputation providing sufficient grounds for her *BBC* termination. But MI5 couldn't locate any past boyfriends or contacts willing to badmouth Jill even for bribe money.

Meanwhile, Jill was alleged to be researching the massive sexual exploitation of young boys by British establishment VIPs, collecting a dossier containing a number of household names.[1247] As a cover, she told her *BBC* supervisors that her latest project was examining the sexual health and status of British adolescents. But shortly before Jill Dando's death, it's been reported that she'd heard that one of her intimate friends was implicated in the VIP pedophilia scandal involving *BBC* personnel, royals, MPs, PMs, high court judges, including top entertainers and influential doctors with VIP friends.[1248] A betrayed Jill may well have confronted her fiancé Dr. Farthing and/or her trusted confidant pal Sir Cliff, thus inadvertently sealing her own fate. It's been reported that Cliff Richard was caught in the middle, feeling pressured to leak to MI5 and Mossad all he'd learned from Jill, but under increasing conflict and stress over the inevitable consequences it would bring, allegedly checking himself into a health clinic over the next several days.[1249]

An alleged British insider, Brian Barrough, left a comment posted on the *Coleman Experience* blogsite:

My memory is beginning to slip but let me tell you what I know. Tony Blair received a phone call at approx 11.40am from Paul Condon who was in charge of the Met Police, the name Jill was mentioned as was becoming troublesome.[1250]

Within three days of the call, Jill Dando was dead. With thoroughly compromised, crossdressing[1251] war criminal, Masonic PM Blair[1252] officially alerted, knowing Jill had enough

---

[1245] "Cliff Richard – Victim," *aangirfan.com*, July 30, 2018.

[1246] Jill Dando Murdered by Britain's VIP Paedophiles," *Coleman Experience/Tap News Wire*, August 7, 2015.

[1247] Jill Dando Murdered by Britain's VIP Paedophiles," *Coleman Experience/Tap News Wire*, August 7, 2015.

[1248] "Royal Baby Scam : Jill Dando's Murder Link and Fiancé: In charge of the Scam : All you need to know : Kate was and has not been Pregnant : Why did they kill the Nurse : What a Right Royal Scam," *thecolemanexperience.wordpress.com*, July 9, 2013.

[1249] Jill Dando Murdered by Britain's VIP Paedophiles," *Coleman Experience/Tap News Wire*, August 7, 2015.

[1250] Jill Dando Murdered by Britain's VIP Paedophiles," *Coleman Experience/Tap News Wire*, August 7, 2015.

[1251] James Forsyth, "Does Mandelson remember that Blair thought Cross-Dressing was a good idea?" *The Spectator*, April 12, 2009.

[1252] John Wight, "If Tony Blair Can't Be Prosecuted for War Crimes then no one can," *Sputnik*, August 3, 2017.

goods on his New Labor pedo-cabinet that would inevitably destroy both his government and career, to save his own skin as well as the pedophilia empire, Brian Barrough believes that Blair had no other choice but to order a rushed hit on Jill Dando.[1253] So the criminal cabal sped into high gear to eliminate its latest threat since neutralizing and satanically sacrificing Diana and Dodi inside the Paris tunnel a year and a half earlier.[1254]

In March 2014 a former *BBC* staffer (unknown if the same July 2012 *Daily Star* source) also disclosed that Jill Dando had been investigating her friend Matthew Harding's death in a 1996 helicopter crash.[1255] Harding was the deputy chairman of the Chelsea Football Club and had confided in his Irish journalist friend Veronica Guerin about his concerns over rampant corruption and money laundering inside his popular sport football, and that was years ahead of the FIFA scandal. Guerin was then reportedly murdered while working on a Dublin drug probe just a few months before Harding's death. Only four months prior to his own death, in a panic Harding shared his growing fears with Jill that his life was in danger. Of course the accident was conveniently blamed on helicopter pilot error and "confusion."[1256] An inside UK government source leaked:

Matthew had been nosing around in something he shouldn't and Jill was trying to find out the results of a blood test on the pilot.[1257]

It's been said that Harding was close to Blair and Mandelson until he too learned of their Mossad controlled UK blackmail operation compromising so many British VIP pedophiles.[1258] While Harding died suspiciously under mysterious circumstances, his two journalist friends he confidentially confided in with his insider information - Veronica Guerin and Jill Dando - both wound up murder victims as well.

Jill Dando and fellow *BBC* presenter Alice Beer both received death threat letters sent four weeks prior to Jill's murder. Yet the police never bothered contacting Alice or Jill, failing to follow up on threats that vowed to kidnap, rape and murder them.[1259] Only a total inside job would "overlook" such blatant details.

By the time Jill was killed, she was basically living with her fiancé Alan Farthing in Chiswick. According to police records, on the morning of April 26th, 1999, after cooking breakfast for the doctor, Jill left his home for a brief shopping trip, afterwards traveling back to her own residence in South West London where the alerted killer lie in waiting.[1260] Only Farthing and perhaps one or two of Jill's closest friends (like Sir Cliff) would have known she'd be returning to her home at that particular time.

[1253] Jill Dando Murdered by Britain's VIP Paedophiles," *Coleman Experience/Tap News Wire*, August 7, 2015.
[1254] "What Princess Diana Knew," *The Event Chronicle*, December 17, 2015..
[1255] Ben Endley, "Fresh Clue in Jill Dando Murder case arises," *Daily Star*, March 24, 2014.
[1256] "Harding Helicopter Death Blamed on Pilot Confusion," *Independent*, February 25, 1998.
[1257] Don Hale, "Police: Hitman did Kill Crimewatch Presenter Jill Dando," *Express*, April 27, 2014.
[1258] The Mysterious Death of Mike Smith," *Tap News Wire/Coleman Experience*, November 29, 2014.
[1259] Nicola Harley, "Police Failed to act on Jill Dando Threats, says Colleague," *The Telegraph*, March 28, 2015.
[1260] "Jill Dando," *revolvy.com*..

A postal worker delivering mail at Jill's address noticed a man watching him about an hour and a half prior to the shooting. Less than an hour before Jill was dead, a window cleaner also noticed a man standing outside Jill's home talking on a cell phone.[1261] A number of witnesses recalled that a blue Range Rover was spotted repeatedly in the area prior to the killing and again leaving the crime scene at high speed afterwards. And despite the multitude of witnesses that caught a fair glimpse of a dark-haired man near 6 feet tall with a Mediterranean or Israeli looking appearance, estimated to be about 40 years old wearing a suit, periodically talking on his cellphone at or near Jill's address prior to the hit, the police apparently never followed up with questioning them or simply ignored eyewitness accounts in what clearly was an intentionally botched investigation ordered from the top never to be solved.

As Jill was about to place her key in the front door at 11:32AM, the professional assassin stealthily emerged to confront her on her doorstep.[1262] Grabbing her arm and pushing her to the ground with his right hand, with his left he placed the barrel of his handgun in direct contact with her head just above her left temple and swiftly fired off a 9mm single round killing her instantly. The entire deadly encounter lasted all of 20 seconds. Without a drop of blood on him, the well-dressed hitman calmly, briskly walked away.

More than one witness, including her neighbor Richard Hughes, heard her startled scream then saw her killer leaving her home.[1263] The automatic pistol placed against her head apparently was modified to muffle the gunshot sound. It wasn't for another 14 minutes that another neighbor noticed her slumped body in a pool of blood. The professional hitman, speculated to either be an intelligence operative or a hired contract mobster, was seen by others running down the street. Perhaps escaping in the Range Rover or slipping into the local underground subway station, the killer vanished, never to be seen again. With witnesses galore and London per capita possessing more installed closed-circuit TV cameras than any other city in the world, each Londoner caught on camera on average of 300 times a day,[1264] it's a shameful abomination and diabolical disgrace that Metro Police have not solved this near 21-year old murder mystery. The world's pedo-capital of the world goes unmatched in its overt contempt for justice.

Chief investigator Hamish Campbell and his team of detectives 20 days into the initial investigation concluded that the key to solving the murder case hinged on the phone contacts made with Jill on the morning of April 26th.[1265] The fact that in the last several months of her life, Jill spent next to no time at her own place, but was there that morning, could have only been known by a select few people, Farthing, Cliff Richard and perhaps one or two others that she may have spoken to just hours before her death. Crime expert John McVicar commented on the then 3-week old police investigation:

[1261] Richard Wheatstone and Jo-Anne Rowney, "What happened to Jill Dando? Five Unanswered Theories in Unsolved Crimewatch Star's Murder Case," *Mirror*, July 17, 2018.

[1262] Dominic Midgley, "Will Jill Dando's Killer be named at last?" *Express*, February 9, 2017,.

[1263] "Dando Trial: Friend 'Found Jill Slumped outside her Home,'" *Daily Mail*.

[1264] Ian Evans, "Report: London no Safer for all its CCTV Cameras," *Christian Science Monitor*, February 22, 2012.

[1265] "Jill Dando Murder," *David Icke Official Forum*, August 1, 2014.

Detectives are convinced that anyone who wanted to harm her needed to be in contact with Jill herself. And only someone close would be able to call Jill and casually inquire about her plans – as Jill was obviously unaware of what lay in store for her until that final scream.[1266]

Because the investigators appeared to be on track to swiftly solving what should have been an easy case to crack based on so much available evidence and eyewitness sightings, less than a month into the probe, after narrowing their focus to Jill's April 26 morning phone contacts, MI5 abruptly yanked Campbell off the investigation, replacing him with Detective Chief Superintendent Brian Edwards.[1267] Incredibly, just two weeks later the police inquiry was strangely halted until September. With Britain's biggest manhunt little more than a month into operation, the insane decision to shut down the investigation is pure self-sabotage, only demonstrating how corrupt and determined the British Establishment was to ensure that the ugly truth of the UK pedo-empire gets completely squashed. As if this overt obstruction of justice isn't brazenly criminal enough, DCS Edwards suddenly resigned the first week of December and Campbell was placed back "in command." Playing musical director chairs with one of the biggest probes in British history is yet one more blatant giveaway that the UK police were never actually in charge but totally manipulated and controlled from behind the scenes at every turn by intelligence services, determined to keep the case unsolved.

By this time the higher-ups had "reprogrammed" Campbell to toe the line as an obedient order follower and by March 2000, he was mouthing the lone gunman script,[1268] handed him as standard state protocol for virtually every false flag cover-up ever committed. Already a year into the butchered investigation, reacting to the mounting public pressure to find the killer, law enforcement honed in on their man Barry George, falsely arresting him in late May 2000 and little more than a year later the innocent man living just a half mile away with a 75 IQ, deemed an expendable target, was found guilty and facing a lifetime sentence for a crime he never committed.[1269]

Another anomaly was within an hour after Jill's death, Clarence Mitchell, the MI5-infiltrating *BBC* journalist,[1270] happened to be the first reporter on the crime scene.[1271] Later it was Mitchell recruited by Prime Minister Blair as director of his government's media monitoring unit, i.e., running a media operations campaign of propaganda disinformation, doing double duty as spin master first, unprecedentedly representing the Blair government in the Madeleine McCann disappearance, and then in 2007 representing Maddie's shady parents as their personal PR spokesman. No sooner did he abruptly leave the *BBC* for the Blair appointed civil service post, the UK was rocked by the 7/7 London bombings. Mitchell's remarkable meteoric rise from journalist to public media expert, smacks of British intelligence infiltration all the way

[1266] "Jill Dando Murder," https://forum.davidicke.com/showthread.php?t=198545.

[1267] "Jill Dando Murder," https://forum.davidicke.com/showthread.php?t=198545.

[1268] Kevin Scott King, "Anatomy of False Flag Events," *bibliotecapleyades.net*, December 2, 2015.

[1269] Gordon Rayner, "Jill Dando Murder: Only a matter of time until Barry George was Cleared," *The Telegraph*, August 1, 2008.

[1270] "Profile: Clarence Mitchell," BBC, September 24, 2007.

[1271] "Tony Blair and the Paedophile Connection," *whale.to/Coleman Experience*, April 28, 2014.

to the top. What are the odds as a *BBC* reporter of getting the scoop on the Jill Dando assassination[1272] a year and a half after being assigned two other huge murder cases - the Paris Princess Di aftermath, followed shortly by Sydney's Michael Hutchence fake hanging?[1273] Always the very first bloke dramatically on the scene at major state executed violent events wherever they are, no doubt as an intel mole assisted by security services. With a nose for "smelling out" state-sponsored assassinations and false flag terrorism as they occur, this guy is the "Johnny-come-early" on-the-spot for Britain's biggest news events, not so subtly leaving behind his undercover calling card.

Early on after Jill's murder, rumors began circulating that Alan Farthing may have had a conspiratorial hand or left fingerprints himself on Jill's murder, with claims he actually came face-to-face with the killer but "forgot" to tell police. Like so many squandered leads, after a few hours of questioning, law enforcement appeared to go through the motions taking direct orders from security forces to give the bereaved fiancé a free pass.[1274]

Again, consistent with the Jimmy Savile case, clearly following orders from above, the Metropolitan Police intentionally blundered the Dando murder probe from beginning to end. Detectives never bothered to interview Jill's neighbors who witnessed 11 potential suspects observed on her street that morning who were never identified.[1275] Nor did they even pay attention to two key witnesses who allegedly observed the killer in action, next door neighbor Hughes and the passer-by in a car Barry Lindsey. Barry happened to be driving by the crime scene literally as the shooting was taking place and saw a dark haired, olive complexioned man confronting a terrified Jill Dando standing at her doorstep, at the outset of a murder that took only seconds to complete.[1276] Lindsey told police that he even heard a muffled single gunshot as he was turning the corner off Dando's street not far away but, already driving away, it failed to register that he'd just witnessed a murder occurring right before his very eyes and ears. Months later, when he did report what he saw, Barry Lindsey said the police by that time were only interested in nailing their suspect Barry George. When they showed Lindsey a photo of George and he told them he was not the man he observed in front of Jill's home, the interview was over. The police had already targeted their framed suspect, and his guilt or innocence didn't matter in the least.

Meanwhile, Barry George languished in a jail cell, falsely imprisoned for eight long years before he won his freedom on a second appeal, a retrial that finally admitted lack of forensic evidence. He was released in early July 2008. One would think that Dr. Farthing and Jill's family would not rest until the real killer - obviously still at large - was brought to justice. Yet with no further

---

[1272] "Jill Dando Murdered by the State to keep Lid on Elite Paedo Ring," *google-law.blogspot.com*, July 28, 2013.

[1273] Mark Sweney, "A Veteran of Major Stories," *The Guardian*, September 18, 2007.

[1274] "Royal Baby Scam: Jill Dando's Murder Link and Fiancé: In charge of the Scam: All you need to know: Kate was and has not been Pregnant: Why did they Kill the Nurse: What a Right Royal Scam," *whale.to*, July 23, 2013.

[1275] Joshua Haigh, "This Morning's True Crime Series Discovers New Leads for Jill Dando's Shocking Murder," *Mirror*, February 8, 2017.

[1276] Nick Owens, "Jill Dando Murder Witness comes forward to Claim Detectives Ignored his Evidence, *Mirror*, July 21, 2013.

questions asked, they wanted the case immediately closed.[1277] Another gross miscarriage of justice resulted when George lost his formal requests for financial compensation for wrongly having eight long years stolen from his life. But the judge absurdly ruled he was not quite "innocent enough," only reinforcing the foregone conclusion that from start to finish, this was one royal government hit job, done on both Jill and Barry as well as every man, woman and child in Great Britain.

So predictably to this very day, the April 26th, 1999 assassination of Jill Dando remains conveniently "unsolved" for one obvious reason. Like Princess Diana who was ready to take down the British Establishment for its murderous, pedophilic ways, Jill was fatally gunned down, also deemed too much of a threat, knowing that Savile and the larger *BBC* sex ring were part of a vast gangster network for decades regularly procuring expendable children for the British VIP sickos.

The Scotland Yard insists that after interviewing over 5000 people,[1278] and amassing 2500 witness statements and 3700 exhibits within the first six months alone,[1279] the police exhausted every potential lead that after a year, incredulously led nowhere. With mounting pressure to solve this high-profile crime with all of Britain watching and waiting, after a year of nonstop fumbling and stonewalling, the investigators claimed that they had found their man and the rush to judgment was on. Based on a supposed speck of gunpowder residue invisible to the naked eye found (or planted) in Barry George's coat pocket, he was railroaded straight to murder conviction.[1280] Scarcely a year after his false arrest, Barry George was sentenced to life in prison. It mattered little that he was the wrong man as police purposely overlooked leads on at least 100 known suspects, along with dozens of significant witnesses never interviewed that would have led to solving Jill's murder.[1281] The government had the means to solve the crime but never the motive nor the will.

That was never part of the elite's agenda, so key witnesses were wholesale systematically screened out, dismissed or ignored,[1282] no doubt like the VIP child abuse victims calling in to Rantzen's ChildLine over the years. More than any other nation on earth, the insulated UK crime cabal system, thoroughly infiltrated by blackmail-controlled pedo-enabling puppets in government, law enforcement, high courts, the media, military, child welfare and charity

---

[1277] Christopher Leake, "Dando Family and Former Fiancé want her Murder Case Closed," Daily Mail, August 2, 2008.

[1278] Gordon Rayner, https://www.telegraph.co.uk/news/uknews/2484898/Jill-Dando-murder-Only-a-matter-of-time-until-Barry-George-was-cleared.html.

[1279] Andrew Alderson and Patrick Sawyer, "Jill Dando Murder: Cold Case Review as Feud Erupts over Verdict," *The Telegraph*, August 3, 2008.

[1280] Gordon Rayner, https://www.telegraph.co.uk/news/uknews/2484898/Jill-Dando-murder-Only-a-matter-of-time-until-Barry-George-was-cleared.html.

[1281] Martin Robinson, "How Police Failed to Trace 100 Suspects in the Jill Dando Murder - but Questioned Cliff Richard and Jeremy Paxman to find out about her life," *Daily Mail*, March 30, 2015.

[1282] Martin Robinson, http://www.dailymail.co.uk/news/article-3017544/How-police-failed-trace-100-suspects-Jill-Dando-murder-questioned-Cliff-Richard-Jeremy-Paxman-life.html.

services, ensure that all the puppet masters and their minions continue to live above the law while committing the most egregious, nonstop crimes on earth.

Adding insult to injury, the top cop in charge of investigating the Jill Dando murder, Hamish Campbell, because he'd proven himself such a loyal order follower, was duly rewarded for failing to find the real killer, and tactically redeployed to later head the Savile Operation Yewtree farce. In 2013, after a 40-year career, the last four capped as Scotland Yard's Detective Chief Superintendent at Homicide and Serious Crime Command, following his dictated script to the end, Hamish Campbell had the audacity to claim:

We, the Met police, did everything we could to understand that murder and bring the person responsible to court, and we did that, twice.[1283]

But before his retirement, DCS Campbell also ended up in May 2011 assigned as top cop investigating the biggest case in UK since Jill Dando - the Madeleine McCann disappearance in Portugal. After two Home Secretaries denied requests by the McCann parents calling for a review of their missing four-year old daughter's alleged abduction on May 3, 2007, PM David Cameron begrudgingly gave in to launch Operation Grange, a reexamination of the case. The same shady players like Hamish Campbell and Clarence Mitchell who were closely associated with the Dando murder investigation cover-up were repeatedly enlisted to do the same dirty bidding cover-up of the next British Establishment scandal.[1284] They were called to duty in the McCann case because it exposes the criminality of both British intelligence as well as the international pedophilia network, whitewashing the involvement of such pedophilia notables as pedo-MP Clement Freud whose estate was in such close proximity to Maddie's disappearance, Clement's pedo-buddies the Podesta brothers as guests in his home at the time,[1285] and accused-pedo-neighbor Sir Cliff who also lived nearby.

In recent years, ex-detective of *ITV* Savile Exposure fame, investigator Mark Williams-Thomas, has launched his own investigation into "operation kill Jill," commenting on Metro's shoddy probe:

I've never reviewed a case where there is so much information that was never followed up… There are eleven unidentified people still unaccounted for in the locality, there are over 100 potential suspects, there is other information naming people and specifically information on how this crime was carried out.[1286]

[1283] "We did all we could to Catch Jill Dando's Killer… and we did it Twice," *Evening Standard*, May 17, 2013.
[1284] "A Biography of Hamish Campbell, the man chosen to Head Operation Grange," *WhatHappenedtoMadeleineMcCann.blogspot.com*, April 28, 2014.
[1285] Ryan Christian, "The Podesta Brothers Revealed to be in Portugal the day of Madeleine McCann's Disappearance," *The Last Vagabond*, November 21, 2016.
[1286] Joshua Haigh, https://www.mirror.co.uk/tv/tv-news/mornings-true-crime-series-discovers-9773017.

Though as of August 2018, Thomas claims to know who the real killer is, we're still waiting on his full disclosure.[1287] Meanwhile, both he and law enforcement insist they are working together to solve among Britain's biggest unsolved murder mysteries. While Metro Police release statements assuring the public that if new information and leads emerge in the Jill Dando case, it will not hesitate to reopen a new investigation. That said, UK law enforcement's track record has only shown that it has done everything in its power to avoid capturing the real Dando killer, knowing if it does, British pedophilia's house of cards will undoubtedly come crashing down. No one's holding their breath waiting for that to happen.

Meanwhile, a hitman by trade surfaced, also insisting that he too knows who the professional hitman is among the suspect list in police possession, but refuses to publicly specify the killer's identity fearing for his own safety.[1288]

As fake news subterfuge, a number of other ongoing speculative explanations have been regularly peddled before Britons as sleight-of-hand decoys to answer why Britain's perennial girl-next-door and 1997 *BBC* TV Personality of the Year was shot dead at point blank range on her front doorstep in broad daylight. The most persistent theory is a mob hit over Jill Dando uncovering organized crime, but also an IRA revenge attack was circulated, and then there's the one that wouldn't go away - a Serbian warlord seeking revenge for the NATO war crime bombing of a Serbian radio station.[1289] A decade after Jill's co-presenter's Crimestopper helpline suddenly went dead perfectly co-timed during the critical hours seeking witnesses right after her murder, in January 2009 Crimestopper was at it again spewing more diversionary disinfo. Sounding almost like a joke – you here the one about the drunken Serbian in a West Midlands bar? It was reported that incoming Crimestopper calls were claiming a Serbian national in between downing shots of liquor in a West Midlands pub was bragging to his fellow barflies that he was the real Jill Dando murderer.[1290] Then after that preposterous lead went cold, suddenly it was back to the old Serbian connection all over again when a Belgrade widow began claiming that the same Serbian hitman 15 days prior to Jill's hit bumped off her journalist husband as well.[1291]

Another bizarre twist to this government plotted Jill Dando assassination chases the *BBC* rabbit hole even deeper into the conspiratorial realm. Crimewatch founder and Jill's co-presenter Nick Ross continued playing a suspicious role as a security services shill after her demise.[1292] One more recap seems in order. It was Nick Ross who went on record saying if given half a chance, he'd be checking out child pornography images on the web, alluding to actually doing so as part

[1287] Roxanne Hughes, "ITV This Morning: Ruth Langsford Stunned as Ex-Policeman Uncovers Jill Dando's 'Killer,'" *Express*, August 2, 2018.

[1288] Kathryn Cain, "Hitman Sensationally Claims on This Morning that he knows who Murdered Jill Dando – but won't name them for Fear of Reprisals," *The Sun*, February 7, 2017.

[1289] Patrick Sawer, "Jill Dando 'Murdered by Serbian Hitman,'" *The Telegraph*, March 3, 2012.

[1290] Victoria Richards, "New Police Probe as Serb Claims he Killed Jill Dando," *Express*, February 23, 2009.

[1291] Mario Ledwith and Chris Parsons, "Serbian Hitman Shot Dead Jill Dando and my Husband: Widow of Journalist Claims BBC Presenter was Killed for Attacking Milosevic's Regime just like her Partner," *Daily Mail*, March 3, 2012.

[1292] "The Curious Case of Nick Ross, VIP Child-Abuse, Filthy Comments, Operation Yewtree, Crimestoppers and the Death of Jill Dando," whale.to, June 3, 2013.

of his program Crimewatch. Again, his CrimeStopper helpline mysteriously went down right after news that Jill was murdered, an obvious sabotage attempt to prevent her killer from being identified. Then years later his CrimeStopper propaganda venue was the conduit source promoting the bogus Serbian connection again. And with her pedo-complicit cousin Dame Esther Rantzen, Nick Ross' wife Sarah Caplan co-founded *BBC*'s ChildLine accused of screening out called in reports of VIP pedophilia. A so-called friend and TV partner like Nick Ross begs the question, who needs enemies?

But there's more on this shady character. On the night of Jill's death, Nick Ross on Newsnight began reporting that retaliatory crimes against judges, lawyers and police are almost unknown,[1293] making readymade emphatic statements within hours of Jill's murder categorically denying Crimewatch had anything to do with Jill's bullet hole through her brain.[1294] From the get-go this in and of itself is a dead giveaway for planting deception and attempting to manipulate and interfere with both the ensuing investigation as well as public opinion. Every real crime expert knows that just hours after any murder, you cannot definitively rule anything out. Right away this unexpected, premature gesture proves, if not guarantees, Nick Ross is not a crime expert at all but simply a hired stooge implant working for state security services intent on hiding the truth in favor of pushing misleading, false information. In a blatantly transparent ploy, Ross attempted to willfully steer and manipulate both Jill's murder inquiry and public attention away from his own *BBC* program, away from any *BBC*-government linkage to intelligence agencies, and especially away from the *BBC*'s larger British VIP pedo-network to which he, his wife and cousin-in-law have all been longtime designated gatekeepers.

Fourteen years after Jill's death, in May 2013 Ross was still trying to shape, mold and control public opinion, writing a propagandist op-ed piece for the *Daily Mail*, desperately attempting to debunk various conspiracy theories surrounding the Dando murder that he himself played a role in, claiming none had any basis in fact, that it was far from a professional hit but a chance encounter with a bungling amateur,[1295] which is actually the furthest thing from the truth or established consensus. But as more people began considering the breaking news coming out that Jill knew about Britain's pedophilia epidemic and was violently silenced for it, the elitist plant Nick Ross was once again doing his order-following duty to frantically ward off the growing population from believing Jill was in fact murdered because his *BBC* network was so steeped in pedo-cabal ratlines extending from Sir Jimmy to PMs and MPs, the Queen, her hubby, their sons Charles and Andrew onto Jeffrey Epstein, the Mossad, the Clintons, Podestas and Bushes. And Nick - the "child porn's worth checking out" guy - as a cabal gatekeeping disinfo shill, pretending to be the Crimestopper "crime expert," was feebly trying to put out the spreading flames of truth threatening to burn down his cabal that he's no doubt sworn to protect.

[1293] "Jill Dando," *popflock.com*.

[1294] Peter Hyatt, "Nick Ross Statement Analysis," *Rich Planet TV*, December 21, 2017.

[1295] Nick Ross, "'How Jill Dando's Death Convinced me everything you know about Crime is Wrong': NICK ROSS tells the Shocking Truth about the Murder of his Friend and the real cause of Crime," *Daily Mail*, May 18, 2013.

Nick Ross even broke the law in an overt attempt to obstruct justice by interfering with the Barry George court outcome. In 2007 stakes to hide the truth were rising so high that Mr. "Crime Expert" took it upon himself to write an open letter to the appeals court judges in a last-ditch effort to sway them to deny a framed innocent man his long overdue justice. Ross claimed in his letter he "remains confident that Barry George killed Jill Dando" with his *Daily Mail* headline entitled, "I know Barry George killed my friend Jill."[1296] Again, with friends like Nick, Jill didn't need enemies because in her own TV co-host, she'd already met her Judas. Fortunately his desperate, extremist, illicit tactics failed as the innocent man was released the following year.[1297]

Still in another *Daily Mail* article written by Nick Ross in August 2015, in the wake of the Ted Heath pedophile allegations, the so called crime expert called for leaving investigations of past prime ministers from so many years ago to historians rather than risk fueling the rise of another satanic panic driven witch-hunt by the public, promoted by an over-reactive press.[1298] Once again voicing the pedo-apologist POV, Ross is clearly minimizing pedophilia as a public threat to children and clearly does not want the British to find out that their leaders, past and present, are pedophiles or pedo-enablers, again overtly attempting to shield the nation's VIP crime network from further scrutiny and public awareness.

Meanwhile, switching back to Jill's beloved Alan, less than a decade after her death and just days after his fiancé's accused's acquittal, Dr. Farthing's fast track medical career suddenly skyrocketed at the relative young age of 45, when in 2008 he was catapulted from virtual obscurity professionally to appointed next royal family head surgeon,[1299] the youngest to serve the royal kingdom in British history.[1300] Cherry picked to be Queen Elizabeth's official surgeon-gynecologist, 2008 proved to be a banner year for Dr. Farthing. Once he chose to not reopen the investigation of Jill's murder days after Barry George's prison release, with his role in the Dando affair completed, it appears that the royals duly rewarded him for his services rendered, vis-à-vis his silent complicity in his former fiancé's murder. At this juncture he was also free to enter into holy matrimony for a second time, marrying a fellow St. Mary's doctor with whom they share a child.[1301] The fateful events surrounding this mysterious, low key MD have fueled speculation that the British crown was paying him off, having already proven he could keep their murderous secrets intact.

But mysterious, highly suspicious deaths just seem to follow this doctor. As head medical surgeon for the royals, Farthing has overseen the births of Prince William and Kate Middleton's

---

[1296] Nick Ross, "Dando Murder: I know Barry George Killed my Friend Jill," Daily Mail, November 7, 2007.

[1297] Nick Dorman, "Barry George: I spent 8 years in Jail now Police must find Jill Dando's Real Killer," *Mirror*, April 1, 2015.

[1298] Nick Ross, "Why are we Prioritizing Crimes from 50 years ago over Crimes from the last 50 minutes? In Wake of Heath Scandal, BBC Star Nick Ross' Provocative View," *Daily Mail*, August 9, 2015.

[1299] Geoffrey Levy, http://www.dailymail.co.uk/news/article-2244910/Why-murder-ex-fianc-Jill-Dando-haunts-man-deliver-Kate-Middletons-baby.html.

[1300] Charlotte Bailey, "Jill Dando's Fiancé to be the Queen's Doctor," *The Telegraph*, September 26, 2008.

[1301] "Nine years later, Jill's Dando's Fiancé Enjoys a Quiet Wedding," *Daily Mail*, March 31, 2008.

three children, "delivered" at the Lindo Wing of his St. Mary's hospital in Paddington.[1302] But there's added reason the monarchy chose Farthing. The first week of December 2012, Kate Middleton entered King Edward VII Hospital under the phony pretense that she was suffering from morning sickness two months pregnant with Prince George.[1303] In actuality, Prince William and vanity-stricken Kate at 92 pounds arrived there to receive treatment for egg extraction and in vitro fertilization for a surrogate pregnancy to retain her slender delicate figure. As the future king's wife, she need not bother herself bearing the un-pleasantries of pregnancy by simply hiring a surrogate to bear the inconvenience of carrying Prince George to full term.

The day after William and Kate left the hospital, December 7th, 2012 should be a day of infamy and shame for the royal family because a nurse on Dr. Farthing's hospital staff, Jacintha Saldanha apparently became the next state-executed victim found in her hospital nursing quarters, "hanging" from her scarf in another staged suicide with her feet still touching the floor.[1304] A nurse with easy access to drugs would simply not choose to kill herself by such a violent, iffy method of hanging from her wardrobe, much less leave a husband, son and daughter she loved who loved her. It makes no sense at all. But the given reason for her so called suicide is too absurd to be believed: Jacintha committed suicide as a result of growing so humiliated and distraught after taking a phone call from a couple of idiot radio DJ imposters in Australia posing as the queen and Charles, Jacintha couldn't simply live with herself for shaming the royal family. Yet, if that was what drove her to kill herself, during her daily calls back home to India, the wife and mother made no mention of this silly, insignificant incident to her own family. Obviously, she was not distraught in the least over the minor buffoonery. The MI5 executioners sunk to an all-time low, slaying a nurse unwilling to play along with the royal game of deceitful charade of faking Kate's pregnancy. To once again avoid public scandal, the royals and their minions chose to violently silence another perceived threat as their Modus Operandi. But then the royals can be confident that with their good doctor Farthing in charge, mum's the word.

Regarding the royal surgeon's places of employment at St Mary's hospital in Paddington where he still remains a gynaecological consultant[1305] as well as the supervising physician of all royal births, along with the Royal Brompton hospital in Chelsea, he has been accused of participating in the unlawful removal of children's thymus glands. Until the year Jill was murdered, the British public and parents were completely unaware that the UK National Health Service maintained a clandestine nationwide policy across Britain's hospitals where, without family consent, removing ill-fated children's organs during major surgery was standard practice,[1306] not unlike Israel's standard practice of harvesting Palestinian young people's organs in their care and custody.[1307] Of course organ trafficking, especially when extracted from children, has

---

[1302] "Meet the Doctors who Delivered the Duchess of Cambridge's New Baby Boy, *The Telegraph*, April 23, 2018.

[1303] "Kate's Fake Pregnancy, Part 1," *helpfreetheearth.com*, June 27, 2013.

[1304] "It Got them Killed: Jacintha Saldanha," *Spike the News*.

[1305] "Consultant Directory," *imperialprivatehealthcare.co.uk*.

[1306] Cole Moreton, "Why did Professor Dick van Velzen think Butchering Babies was right?" *Independent*, December 5, 1999.

[1307] Alison Weir, "Israeli Organ Harvesting," *Counter Punch*, August 28, 2009.

become big business in both China[1308] and Israel as the cabal hub for illegal organ transplant operations,[1309] Big Pharma research[1310] as well as occult practice worldwide during satanic ritual child sex abuse and child sacrifice.[1311]

Speaking of Farthing's Royal Brompton hospital, the pioneering heart surgeon responsible for the world's first successful heart transplant in 1980, Dr. Magdo Yacoub, ran the children's cardiac unit at the Royal Brompton for decades and in 1995 founded the international children's charity Chain of Hearts. One of his charity's trustees, the once renowned Dr. Phillip Bonhoeffer, was charged with sexually abusing underage children while working as a Chain of Hearts physician in Kenya as well as abusing a 10-year old French boy with sex crimes committed against children from 1995 to 2008.[1312]

In 2007 17-year veteran *BBC* newsreader Anna Ford quit her pedophile saturated network in disgust, tired of *BBC*'s "atmosphere of fear" as her cited reason for departure.[1313] But in an interview just two days after Jill's 1999 murder, Anna Ford asked Dr. Farthing, "Does it worry you if it may remain unsolved?"[1314] That's an extremely odd, puzzling, telling question posed before the deceased even gets buried in the ground and the manhunt for her murderer and investigation among UK's largest barely get underway. As a *BBC* insider, did she know something the rest of us didn't? But then considering it was a state-executed assassination to urgently cover up the long infested pedo-epidemic raging atop Britain's diabolical elite, it's a no-brainer to conclude that by calculated design, Jill's murder will never be solved. No wonder Ford asked, she was merely reading from a script prepping the public to neither expect justice nor any closure - ever.

A year and a half prior to Jill Dando's murder, it appears intelligence agencies sent Dr. Alan Farthing to become her intimate fiancé and assigned asset Sir Cliff Richard as her intimate confidante. No doubt between them they were able to glean everything she learned about the Savile-*BBC*-British establishment pedophilia network for MI5 and Mossad to know and conclude that she simply posed too much risk to the crime cabal. It's been determined that she had to be eliminated because she likely felt betrayed upon learning of Sir Cliff and/or her fiancé's direct involvement in the pedo-crime network, using her to gather what knowledge she knew. Hence, on the fly the Mossad compromised Prime Minister Blair placed the hastily constructed hit on her life to prevent her from dropping the bombshell of all bombshells to the world via live national television.

[1308] Megan Palin, "The Reality of Human Organ Harvesting in China," *news.com.au*, September 19, 2016.
[1309] Noga Klein, "Israel Became Hub in International Organ Trade over past Decade," *Haaretz*, September 20, 2018.
[1310] Pamela Tsai, "Transplant Community Responds to Chinese Regime's Organ Harvesting," *Epoch Times*, May 3, 2011.
[1311] "Pedogate: A Special Report on the Washington, D.C. Pedophilia Scandal," *The Event Chronicle*, December 28, 2016..
[1312] Jeremy Laurance, "Revealed: Sex Abuse Charges for top Child Doctor," *Independent*, September 8, 2012.
[1313] Ben Clerkin, "Former Newsreader Anna Ford Quit the BBC because of an 'Atmosphere of Fear,'" *Daily Mail*, August 27, 2007.
[1314] Alan Farthing interviewed by Anna Ford, *ITV*, April 28, 1999, 01:12, *gettyimages.com*.

Clearly the Jill Dando murder was a conjoint Mossad-MI5-mob ordered contract on her life that originated from the highest-ranking British elite as a warning to any journalist or whistleblower who may also be entertaining ideas to expose the filthy truth. The shooting was one more tragic end in a seemingly never-ending series of strange and sudden deaths connected to so many *BBC* employees that were likely privy to the network's inner pedophilia ring. All the earlier theoretical conjecture explaining Jill's untimely tragic death was simply planting decoyed rabbit holes to muddle and obscure the actual truth and thereby protect the British pedophilia Establishment that is the ungodly trinity of the *BBC*, the UK government and the royal family.

And the British elite's "go-to" guy for propagating all these official false narratives on virtually every controversial death in the United Kingdom is the aforementioned West London-Westminster coroner Dr. Paul Knapman. For over 30 years from 1980 to 2011, Dr. Knapman ruled on over 85,000 deaths, 12,500 inquests and over 500 murders,[1315] explaining fake causes on a myriad of strange, unnatural deaths and assorted, undeclared murders of not only an inordinate number of *BBC* employees but others who also either knew too much or were sacrificed for propaganda purposes in false flag operations promoting the West's warmongering hegemony, spearheaded by the CIA and friends. Knapman's "work" was already cited in the suspicious deaths of Peaches Geldof's mother Paula Yates in 2000, the highly probable murders of Natasha Collins and Mark Speight in 2008 as well as *BBC* DJ Kevin Greening's gay bondage death just 5 days ahead of Natasha's.

Dr. Knapman has also repeatedly come under fire for his gross mishandling of a number of inquests involving casualties from major boating and railway accidents. His most grotesque publicized blunder was the Thames riverboat Marchioness collision with a dredger resulting in the deaths of 51 people in 1989. As an alleged convenient means of identifying victims, he simply cut off half the deceased's hands for easier fingerprint access, atrociously insensitive and arrogantly oblivious to the grieving needs of family members.[1316] Without even the families' consent, the creepy megalomaniac doctor removed body parts and tissues, not unlike Jill Dando's fiancé Dr. Alan Farthing's routine medical practice. The hands of one young woman were literally lost, misplaced and ultimately destroyed at the bottom of Knapman's morgue refrigerator for four long years prior to its rediscovery, prompting a victim's mother to respond:

Your mortuary is so dirty that it took four years to find a child's hands. You are a butcher.[1317]

Yet this "butcher" is the kind of unscrupulous, uncaring oaf the cabal system knows will carry out its orders with blind tunnel vision obedience.

As an example of how the global crime cabal system works to use Dr. Knapman's final "expert" word to further its destabilizing agenda for war and terrorism across the planet, comes the coldblooded murder of police constable Yvonne Fletcher in the so called Libyan Embassy siege

---

[1315] "Paul Knapman, Forensic and Medicolegal Consultant," *linkin.com*.
[1316] Richard Alleyne, "Coroner Decried as 'Butcher' in Marchioness Row," *The Telegraph*, December 9, 2000.
[1317] Richard Alleyne.

in April 1984 London.[1318] With a handful of Libyans protesting in front of the Libyan People's Bureau at St. James Square that day, shots rang out killing Yvonne instantly. Official conclusion purported by Knapman at the inquest pointed the finger at a Libyan gunman firing 9mm bullets from the embassy.

Yet the most respected senior ballistics expert in the British Army, a former Belfast hospital surgeon and a longtime Home Office pathologist - all three of the nation's foremost authorities on forensic firearm ballistics specified that the bullet that assassinated Yvonne Fletcher had to have come from the Enserch House, a building with known links to the CIA.[1319] Essentially the constable was most likely gunned down mercilessly as a sacrificial lamb, misused to incite anti-Gaddafi demonization the world over as prepping to justify the following year's 32,000 pounds of ordnance dropped in bombs over Tripoli by US warplanes based in the UK (i.e., all part of a prearranged election year Reagan-Thatcher deal).[1320] The cabal could always count on stooges like Knapman for his rubberstamp approval when needed.

Of course leave it to Hillary and company to finish the job offing Gaddafi in 2011 because he was busily uniting Africa behind his own gold-backed currency rather than continue paying subservient homage to the Empire's exploitive USD.[1321] Historically, the Zionist-Anglo-American Empire systematically demonizes and assassinates any and all national leaders around the world daring to operate independent of Rothschild imperialistic central bank control.[1322] That's why out of near 200 countries on earth, only the "pariah" nation North Korea doesn't have a central bank.[1323]

Little more than a half year before Princess Diana's life abruptly ended, another suspicious yet inconspicuous death occurred in the famous and mysterious Dolphin Square, the vast block of Pimlico flats in central London close to the House of Commons that's been home to "the famous, the infamous and the notorious" where MPs, lords, generals and foreign and British intelligence operatives frequently reside.[1324] VIP orgies at the Dolphin Square complex have always been notoriously common. An alleged eyewitness victim claimed that in the 1990s he and other children were picked up from various group homes and trafficked in by Peter Righton, the aforementioned British bigwig childcare specialist who wrote national policy on child abuse protection as former director of education at the National Institute of Social Work and consultant for the National Children's Bureau, also happened to be a co-founder of PIE (talk about a fox guarding the henhouse).[1325]

[1318] David Guyatt, "Target Libya," *plane-truth.com*, 1996.

[1319] David Guyatt, http://plane-truth.com/Aoude/geocities/target.html.

[1320] "Yvonne Fletcher Murdered by our Spooks," *aangirfan.com*, September 1, 2011.

[1321] "De-Dollarization: The Story of Gaddafi's Gold Backed Currency is not over," *Sputnik News*, March 17, 2016.

[1322] Steve Kangas, "A Timeline of CIA Atrocities," *Global Research*, August 6, 1997.

[1323] Michael Snyder, "Guess how many Nations in the World do not have a Central Bank?" *Zero Hedge*, June 10.

[1324] Michael Streeter, "Life and Death in Dolphin Square," *Independent*, February 28, 1997.

[1325] Frank Furedi, "What PIE and the NSPCC have in Common," *Spiked*, March 10, 2014.

Righton was a procuring pedophile with high-end connections who not only committed horrendous sexual abuse himself but trafficked kids to suffer even a worse fate by VIPs until he was eventually convicted of child pornography in 1992 and died in 2007.[1326] But over the years, victims and witnesses have reported four children were allegedly murdered at sex parties held at the notorious VIP pedo-haven Dolphin Square. One survivor states that when he was 15, Righton took him to a party where once the women left, about 15 adult men began sexually assaulting and torturing the group home children, among the attendees identified were a Tory minister, several MPs and a famous comedian.[1327] According to the victim, one of the trafficked children was a 15-year old girl with braces who was taken into one of the three torture chamber bedrooms and never seen again, suspected to have been murdered by a powerful Tory politician.

But in January 1997 another suspicious Dolphin Square death occurred, this time the 56-year old Conservative MP Iain Mills' body found a couple of days after dying, allegedly from acute alcohol poisoning according to coroner Knapman. Friends who knew Iain and Meridian residents who were his constituents for almost two decades insist that Iain never even drank alcohol but was only known to socially drink orange juice.[1328] Yet his body was surrounded by empty gin bottles. There are those who believe Iain Mills may well have learned firsthand about the widespread child abuse and alcohol-drug infested orgies going on all around him at Dolphin Square,[1329] frequented by his fellow MPs and lords as well as business, legal and military VIPs, violently acting out their sexual deviant criminal pathologies on underage children in the Westminster pedo-blackmail ring operating with impunity throughout the 1970s well into the 1990s.[1330] But in Iain's case both police and coroner alike appeared all too eager to brush his death aside, only fueling and reinforcing the speculation that probable foul play was involved.

Ten years later another bizarre twist in yet another Dolphin Square death misruled by Knapman, this one involving 64-year old High Court Judge Rodney McKinnon. Dr. "know-it-all" rigidly maintained that Rodney was suffering from depression due to high blood pressure medicine he'd been prescribed.[1331] At the inquest Knapman asserted that the judge just couldn't cope with life anymore and chose to end it, jumping off his Drake building in Dolphin Square and falling 50 feet to his intended death. With no suicide note, Rodney's brother Warwick McKinnon, who also happens to be a judge, claimed his brother made plans with his girlfriend just days prior to his untimely demise, adding:

[1326] "Peter Righton," Child Sexual Abuse in the British Establishment.

[1327] Kier Mudie and Mark Watts, "Westminster Paedophile Ring: Top Tory MP 'Murdered Girl at Vile Orgy' Claims New Witness," *Mirror*, January 10, 2015..

[1328] "Who are the Queen's Lord Lieutenants?" *whale.to*.

[1329] "Who are the Queen's Lord Lieutenants?" http://www.whale.to/c/who_are.html.

[1330] Amanda Williams, "I was Sexually Abused at Establishment Paedophile Parties: Victim of 1970s Dolphin Square Ring tells of being Forced to Perform Sex acts as senior Tories Celebrated Thatcher Victory," *Daily Mail*, May 5, 2015.

[1331] "Judge Killed in 50ft Fall from Flat 'was Suicide', Inquest hears," *Evening Standard*, September 5, 2007.

I don't believe it was suicide and neither does anyone in the family or any friends I have spoken to... He was a very tidy and literary man. He would have wanted to record the reason why if it was suicide... He would not have done this.[1332]

Yet the Svengali of death just knew it had to be suicide, obviously without sufficient cause, which in the case of a suicide verdict, by law must be "beyond all reasonable doubt." Bottom line, with the judge well aware his Dolphin Square community was historically rife with VIP pedophiles, some of whom he'd convicted in his own court, the plausibility remains strong that the pedo-crime network eliminated him for being a thorn in its side, and the suicide-on-the-brain doctor once again was simply following orders.[1333] The crime cabal's trail of those who get in the way in Britain is no different from the US trail traveled by the Bush[1334]-Clinton crime family[1335] because it's one and the same. Like everything else, it's global.

As a cabal tool, Knapman rubberstamped a number of other huge inquests like UK's own 9/11 inside job - the 2005 London 7/7 bombings,[1336] and the 2007 inquest of the 1997 Princess Diana-Dodi Fayed assassination.[1337] Again, demonic evil knows no earthly limit. Racking up so many unbelievably preposterous and highly suspect verdicts on his death track record involving so many suspicious, high profile, abrupt life endings, Dr. Paul Knapman was coming under increasing pressure and opposition from those who saw through his shady racket. Chris Pond, a Member of Parliament from 1997 to 2005 was the most vocal Knapman critic, raising serious and urgent red flag questions about the Westminster coroner's consistent misconduct over the years on the House of Commons floor that could no longer be sloughed off as mere incompetence.[1338] And during the debate, wouldn't you know it, accused pedophile MP turned *BBC* broadcaster Michael Portillo[1339] rushed to Dr. Knapman's defense.[1340] For being such an obedient crime cabal errand boy for over two decades, in 2008 Queen Elizabeth rewarded Dr. Knapman with the lofty title of the Queen's Deputy-Lieutenant for Greater London.[1341] As previously noted, bestowed honors from the queen are the dead giveaway revealing who the real pedo-cabal players are. The crown throws a bone to her designated puppets serving to protect her global pedophilia empire, after demonstrating an over and above zest for contributing to the malaise.

Britain's longtime *BBC* favorite Irish broadcaster - Sir Terry Wogan, less than three months prior to his January 31, 2016 passing, claimed he would "continue working another ten years" before retiring. Then suddenly the 77-year old, stricken with a remarkably fast spreading cancer,

[1332] "Judge Killed in 50ft Fall from Flat 'was Suicide', Inquest hears," *Evening Standard*, September 5, 2007.

[1333] Anne Wade, "Rochdale and Beyond – The Legacy of Child Abuse," *cathyfox.wordpress.com*, August 4, 2017.

[1334] "Bush Death List," *AttackOnAmerica.net*, September 29, 2003.

[1335] "The Clinton Body-Count," *What Really Happened*.

[1336] Joachim Hagopian, "Western State Sponsored Terrorism: False Flags Spreading Islamophobia, Race and Religious Wars and New World Disorder," *Lew Rockwell*, December 25, 2015.

[1337] "The Murder of Princess Diana," YouTube documentary by Jay Myers, 2017, 36:02, posted on July 8, 2017.

[1338] "Who are the Queen's Lord Lieutenants?" http://www.whale.to/c/who_are.html.

[1339] "BBC Broadcaster Michael Portillo; Alleged Child Sexual Abuse," *scribd.com*, January 27, 2016.

[1340] "Knapman," *spikethenews.blospot.com*, June 6, 2014.

[1341] "Who are the Queen's Lord Lieutenants?" http://www.whale.to/c/who_are.html.

learned he was dying a scant three weeks ahead of his death.[1342] Also just three weeks prior to Wogan's death, another longtime *BBC* employee, Savile colleague DJ at Radio 1 Ed "Stewpot" Stewart suddenly died shortly after suffering a stroke. The *BBC* deaths just keep piling up one after the other.

In 2014 Terry Wogan apologized for disrespecting David Icke for an on the air interview where he publicly ridiculed David for his unbelievable truth telling about the evildoers atop the power pyramid, coming to realize Icke was absolutely correct in so many of his earlier proclamations virtually no one took seriously,[1343] like years before the former prime minister's death, Icke asserted in 1998 that Edward Heath was a child murdering pedophile.[1344] Once the Savile scandal broke in October 2012, the host of the Children in Need telethon stated that he hated Jimmy Savile, blaming him for "poisoning" the *BBC*.[1345] In Wogan's words:

He [Savile] *always struck me as creepy. I've talked to people and not one of them has said: 'I really liked him.'[1346]*

Years before Savile's death, like so many others, the Jesuit educated and trained[1347] Terry Wogan also knew about the *BBC* serial pedophile, revealing at a celebrity luncheon that after Savile went to relieve himself in the bathroom, longtime journalist Jean Rook sitting nearby turned to Terry and asked:

When are they going to expose him?[1348]

"That's your job," Terry replied, passing the buck, waiting for an investigative journalist outside the *BBC* to uncover the filth. But Wogan was wrong, when so many insiders within the media entertainment industry knew Savile was abusing children but not one person at the *BBC* was bold or brave enough to step up and say anything except, of all people, Johnny Rotten. All the beloved queen honored *BBC* stars like Sir Terry Wogan and Dame Esther Rantzen knew full well what was going on, that the *BBC* was a pedophile haven, harboring not just one child rapist but many. The real reason not one *BBC* employee bothered making waves, other than Jill Dando and look where it got her, *BBC* personnel were afraid of not just losing their jobs, but their lives as well. For years they saw fellow colleagues dropping dead like flies left and right, and realized the deadly risk and consequence of standing up for what was right, protecting children just wasn't worth it to them.

[1342] Nicola Methven, "Terry Wogan only knew he was Dying three weeks before," *Mirror*, February 1, 2016.

[1343] Edward Richard, "Terry Wogan: 'Looks like David Icke was right all along,'" *Independent*, August 7, 2014.

[1344] David Icke, "What David Icke has said since 1998 about Paedophile and Child Killing Prime Minister Ted Heath is backed-up here by Barrister Michael Shrimpton, an Intelligence and National Security Consultant, from his own Contacts and inside experience," *davidicke.com*, January 17, 2013.

[1345] Karen Rockett, "Sir Terry Wogan Speaks of his Hatred of Jimmy Savile says his Crimes were Open Secret at BBC," *Mirror*, October 5, 2013.

[1346] Karen Rockett, https://www.mirror.co.uk/news/uk-news/terry-wogan-hatred-jimmy-savile-2341936.

[1347] Jonathan Wright, "Don't Blame the Jesuits for Dictators," *Catholic Herald*, December 8, 2016.

[1348] Karen Rockett, https://www.mirror.co.uk/news/uk-news/terry-wogan-hatred-jimmy-savile-2341936.

If you're still not convinced, former *BBC* personality Muz Murray literally feared for his life:

Everyone's a mason in the BBC. Masons are all over the place there. It was a frightening atmosphere and eventually I left, thinking someone was going to come after me and kill me. That's why I went into the Himalayan mountains, and I learned all the Tibetan yoga still frightened someone was going to come after me and kill me.[1349]

In addition to Jill Dando and the dozen *BBC* employees who met similarly bizarre, ill-fated deaths, a number of other *BBC* staff not mentioned in this chapter also died strange and untimely, questionable *BBC* deaths. They are featured in a website that links their deaths to a preponderance of Freemasons amongst senior *BBC* management, corroborating the firsthand observation of Muz Murray.[1350] The website author encountered a young woman whose father as a Mason and *BBC* employee had told her decades earlier that Jimmy Savile was a pedophile who was tricking top people in the television industry into compromising situations with children. The same article goes on to quote a senior insider running the government sponsored corporation from the shadows:

We're plotting to get Jimmy Saville to trick lots of TV stars and other high profile sorts into getting photographed with children, we're gonna angle the shots so they look like they're maybe fiddling around with the kids, we've sat down and thought of what the most unbelievable claim could conceivably be to say someone has done, we think the public would never believe we could fake child molestation, so that's exactly what we're doing, to cause the most total outrage and hatred of the public.[1351]

This confirms that the ruling elite placed Savile in charge of a major sexual blackmail operation not unlike the Mossad blackmailer Jeffrey Epstein in the US. The biggest pedophile in British history was an MI5 operative carrying out his diabolical duty as a blackmailing pimp for English royalty, the government and the Freemasons and Luciferians at the top of the predatory food chain. That's why he so arrogantly operated so brazenly in plain sight, knowing all the while he was fully protected and immune from all accountability.

This brings us to the final, most recent death covered in the *BBC* mysterious and suspicious demise file. As the second known *BBC* broadcaster since Jill Dando to prematurely leave this world exposing *BBC*'s culture of pedophilia and fear, longtime *BBC* journalist Liz MacKean suddenly suffered a fatal stroke at the age of only 52 in August 2017.[1352] After working her way up the corporate news ladder as a successful network correspondent from 1993 to 2013, her resignation arose under a flurry of conflict over a documentary she made that was actually the

---

[1349] "Part 6 Invitation to Join the Masons," *phonedupnshutup.com*.
[1350] "The Marconi Syndrome," *phonedupnshutup.com*.
[1351] "Part 6 Invitation to Join the Masons," http://phonedupnshutup.com/?page_id=86.
[1352] Simon Boyle, "Ex-BBC Reporter who Quit Corporation after Bosses Shelved her Investigation into Jimmy Savile Dies at 52." Mirror, August 18, 2017.

first to expose the Jimmy Savile crimes originally slated for broadcast just weeks after Savile's death.

BBC director James Harding described her as "remarkably tenacious and resourceful," especially commending Liz for her "insightful and hard-hitting reporting of the [Northern Ireland] conflict," adding:

It was as an investigative reporter that she really shone, shining a light on issues from the dumping of toxic waste off the African coast to Jimmy Savile, the story for which she is probably best known.[1353]

Blowing the lid off of Savile's reign of terror in a *BBC* Newsnight segment that never aired shortly after Savile's demise, Liz MacKean's producer was initially excited with the project, scheduled to broadcast weeks after the pedophile died. But overnight, succumbing to pressure from the big boys upstairs, the project was abruptly scrapped, put on an indefinite hold and the opportunity to expose Savile was lost for another year.[1354] *BBC*, the pedophile enabler, remained *BBC*, the pedo-cover-upper, canning Liz' groundbreaking work little more than a month after Savile's death in favor of broadcasting two fake holiday tributes glorifying the *BBC* beast.

The *British Broadcasting Corporation* disgraced itself yet again, cowardly shelving Liz MacKean's accurate and true indictment, fabricating the lame excuse that the 10-minute segment interviewing 10 Savile victims and witnesses was cut for "editorial reasons," citing that its claims "could not be substantiated," of course immediately recognized as a total boldface CYA lie.[1355] Consequently, the world had to wait nearly another full year before the *ITV* exposé dropped the "other side of Savile" bombshell. As small consolation, Liz's nixed Savile exposure garnered the London Press Club's scoop of the year award. While filming her Newsnight piece exposing the *BBC* cover-up, Liz MacKean's life was threatened. But unlike so many other *BBC* staff, her ethical duty to tell the truth was far more important. Though Liz's integrity remained intact, walking away in protest and pure disgust in 2013 for the *BBC*'s gutless decision, she expressed remorse and guilt to the Savile victims over her inability to deliver their timely truth, though certainly not from any lack of effort on her part:

I thought that that was a failure... I felt we had a responsibility towards them. We got them to talk to us, but above all, we did believe them. And so then, for their stories not to be heard, I felt very bad about that. I felt, very much, that I'd let them down. I was very unhappy the story didn't run because I felt we'd spoken to people who collectively deserved to be heard and they weren't heard.[1356]

[1353] Simon Boyle, https://www.mirror.co.uk/news/uk-news/jimmy-savile-bbc-documentary-panorama-11013587.
[1354] Simon Boyle, https://www.mirror.co.uk/news/uk-news/jimmy-savile-bbc-documentary-panorama-11013587.
[1355] Dan Sabbagh and Josh Halliday, "Jimmy Savile: Newsnight Staff were Furious after Abuse Report Dropped," *The Guardian*, October 1, 2012.
[1356] Simon Boyle, https://www.mirror.co.uk/news/uk-news/jimmy-savile-bbc-documentary-panorama-11013587/

The *BBC* also fired the Newsnight investigative producer Meirion Jones who worked with Liz for daring to tell the truth about Savile.[1357] From the day Meirion was a boy and his Aunt Margaret Jones was Duncroft School's headmistress in the 1970s when Savile allegedly abused 23 girls there,[1358] he witnessed Sir Jimmy driving off with soon-to-be victims in his Rolls. The *BBC* has gone out of its way to destroy careers of honest investigative journalists who value the truth and the moral conviction to tell it. In Meirion's words:

There is a small group of powerful people at the BBC who think it would have been better if the truth about Savile had not come out. And they aim to punish the reporters who revealed it.[1359]

Liz MacKean on how *BBC* treated her to the end:

When the Savile Scandal broke, the BBC tried to smear my reputation. They said they had banned the film because Meirion and I had produced shoddy journalism. I stayed to fight them, but I knew they would make me leave in the end. Managers would look through me as if I wasn't there. I went because I was never going to appear on screen again.[1360]

Meirion said that *BBC* creative director Alan Yentob called Meirion and Liz "traitors" after he saw the Panorama piece where the two explained how the *BBC* in chronic cover-up mode cancelled airing their Savile exposé.[1361]

After her two-decade tenure at *BBC*, Liz went on to make films for *Channel 4*'s Dispatch program. The bad blood that went down between Liz and her despicable former employer, then her sudden passing a short time later at a relatively young age leaving two daughters behind, ultimately joining the notorious *BBC* cemetery row of questionable, sad and highly suspicious deaths after exposing the *BBC* pedo-cover-up, leaves many still wondering... was she yet the latest brave KIA casualty in the war against truth?

The phenomenon of a plethora of highly suspicious deaths befalling employees at one particular company is nothing new. From 1982 to 1989 twenty-five scientists that worked at the UK defense contractor GEC-Marconi on the controversial US "Star Wars" project and the "Sting Ray" torpedo project were suddenly mysterious killed in an obvious cover-up of murder.[1362] And the obvious culprit was intelligences services just as they're undoubtedly involved in so many of the *BBC*-related deaths as well. One, the global intelligence community has both the means and motive to silence those endowed with valuable, highly-incriminating, top secret information and two, the CIA, Mossad and MI6 are never held accountable by either governments or law enforcement agencies.

[1357] Nick Cohen, "The Sinister Treatment of Dissent at the BBC," *The Guardian*, March 8, 2015.

[1358] Chris Greenwood and Richard Spillett, http://www.dailymail.co.uk/news/article-3060559/Jimmy-Savile-abused-23-youngsters-Duncroft-School-emotionally-disturbed-teenage-girls.html.

[1359] Nick Cohen, https://www.theguardian.com/commentisfree/2015/mar/08/bbc-whistleblowers-jimmy-savile.

[1360] Nick Cohen, https://www.theguardian.com/commentisfree/2015/mar/08/bbc-whistleblowers-jimmy-savile.

[1361] Camilla Turner, "Alan Yentob 'Branded BBC Journalists Traitors over Savile Exposé,'" *The Telegraph*, September 24, 2015.

[1362] "The Mysterious Deaths of Scientists," *think-about it.com*, February 4, 2015.

An identical parallel pattern has been unfolding with dozens of doctors paying the price for speaking out against the dangers of Big Pharma and vaccines.[1363] Then there's what commonly happens to muckraking journalists and activists who courageously uncover explosive evidence that could bring down crime cabal powerbrokers. Among the half-dozen short list are Gary Webb,[1364] artist Mark Lombardi,[1365] J.H. Hatfield,[1366] Danny Casolaro,[1367] Michael Hastings[1368] and Max Spiers,[1369] though many more around the world have been violently silenced making truth telling journalism as a profession an endangered species. One look at the Bush-Clinton crime family says it all for their never-ending list of "suicided" insiders that knew too much.

With so many nefarious forces all working together to conceal the truth from ever being revealed, it's no wonder the global pedophilia network has remained so fully intact, eliminating and silencing threats and constantly covering-up cabal criminality. Of course, after Jill Dando died, the Metropolitan Police were reported to have interviewed both Dr. Farthing and Sir Cliff Richard on a number of occasions. But because they were working with MI5 on behalf of the criminal British Establishment, nothing they could say or do would ever place them as suspects or accomplices. The Met always takes orders from British intelligence, or Special Branch, the UK's terrorism-counterterrorism unit. With all the massive, overwhelming evidence, it's flagrantly clear that the most powerful criminals in the United Kingdom murdered Jill Dando with complete impunity, and are determined at all cost to keep that ugly reality concealed from the public, no different from their deadly hit on Princess Diana, her unborn Muslim-to-be child and future Muslim husband little more than a year and a half earlier. For a very long time, the planetary controllers have been child raping murderers, millions if not billions of times over. It's high time we citizens of the world finally face this very grim and disturbing fact if we are ever to hold a handful of monsters fully accountable.

Because the government-funded *BBC* is part of the same interlocking pedophilia crime cabal as the Westminster government and British royalty, the giant media conglomerate has a long history shielding its VIP pedophiles and suppressing their heinous crimes. Case in point, the *BBC* is notorious for its atrocious track record, systematically attacking and smearing child abuse survivors along with journalists and the small minority of MPs, courageously attempting to expose the truth.[1370]

[1363] Samantha Debbie, "Doctors Murdered after Discovering Cancer Enzymes in Vaccines, September 19, 2016.

[1364] Tim Brown, "Journalist Gary Webb who Exposed CIA Cocaine Trafficking Allegedly 'Shot Himself' in the Head," Twice - Would Have Been 63 Today," *Freedom Outpost*, August 31, 2018.

[1365] "The Mysterious Death of an Artist whose Drawings were too Revealing," Patricia Gladstone interviewed by Jeff Schechtman, *Who, What, Why*, December 4, 2015.

[1366] David Cogswell, "The Death of Jim Hatfield," *davidcogswell.com*, May 15, 2003.

[1367] Dee McLachlan, "'The Octopus' and the 'Suicide' of Investigative Journalist Danny Casolaro," *Gumshoe News*, July 12, 2017.

[1368] "Was Michael Hastings Targeted by the CIA? WikiLeaks Reveals Agency's Covert Carjacking Ability," *MintPress News*, March 10, 2017.

[1369] Sara Kamouni, "UFO Expert found Dead after 'Vomiting Black Liquid,'" *New York Post*, October 17, 2016.

[1370] Mark Watts, "BBC Seeks to Discredit Police Witnesses and Supporters despite Scandal over Jimmy Savile," *Exaro*, October 1, 2015.

Let's face it, the pedo-cabal stops at no limit to punish and destroy those deemed a serious enough threat, from fellow criminals who know too much to morally strong souls, determined to expose the truth with their last breath. Knowing that the pedophilia scourge is the ruling elite's Achilles heel in the face of mounting overwhelming evidence unmasking the international pedo-crime cabal, elite pedophiles are growing more desperate, fearing their days are numbered, with critical mass amongst the global masses rapidly approaching. So as of late, they've been pushing back, winning in court, discounting and punishing victim allegations to silence the truth seekers. Their methods are many. The highest threats in recent times are targeted victims of both overt but, primarily covert assassination, through electronic weaponry, deployed as psychotronic warfare inducing untraceable, fast-spreading cancers, sudden heart attacks, aneurisms and strokes,[1371] perhaps exceeded only by the ever-so-popular standby – assassination by "suicide."[1372] The elite is currently engaged in genocidal war against humanity. But the truth will prevail. Spread it.

The next chapter exposes the "pedo-love affair" between the five-time nominated Queen's knight Sir Jimmy, and his insistent nominator Prime Minister Margaret Thatcher, featuring the undercover MI5 child pimping procurer, sexually blackmailing her saturated pedo-government.

[1371] Alan Yu, "Murder by Heart Attack," *fourwinds10.com*.
[1372] "Assassination by Suicide," *whale.to*.

Chapter 6: Sir Jimmy Savile and Margaret Thatcher's Pedo-Love Affair

Throughout his long public career Jimmy Savile curried favor with Britain's most powerful elite, from prime ministers to the royal family. As a social climbing Mensa member,[1373] he mastered the psychopathic game of ingratiation, invited to spend 11 consecutive New Year's holidays in a row with Prime Minister Margaret Thatcher at the British PM residence Chequers,[1374] just three miles from one of his favorite day or late night pedo-hunting grounds, the Stoke-Mandeville Hospital in Buckinghamshire where he raised near half (£20)[1375] of his total £45 million for charity[1376] in exchange for being able to freely sexually abuse over five dozen victims and screw dead corpses at Britain's National Spinal Injury Center alone.[1377] [1378]

One year the Chequers court jester showed up dressed head to toe in Christmas decorations with a large silver bell around his neck. Lady Thatcher turned to her rather uptight foreign secretary and proclaimed:

Jimmy can ring my bell any time.[1379]

Word has it that Savile went through every room at the prime minister's country estate that year writing on notepads his phone number with instruction that in case of emergency, the PM should ring his bell. Apparently such were the never a dull moment frivolities exchanged between these two intimates. Sir Jimmy fondly reminisced about his Christmases past with his Dame Maggie in an *Esquire* interview:

I knew the real woman and the real woman was something else. The times I spent up there [Chequers] - *Denis, me and her, shoes off in front of the fire.*[1380]

[1373] Paul Revoir, "BBC has to Apologise as Guest from Mensa Labels People with an IQ of 60 'Carrots' on live Breakfast Show," *Daily Mail*, December 21, 2012.

[1374] Cole Moreton, "Jimmy Savile, the Big Fixer," *The Telegraph*, October 30, 2012.

[1375] Peter Jukes, "Jimmy Savile Sex Abuse Scandal Taints Entire Era in Britain," *Daily Beast*, October 31, 2012.

[1376] Paul Jeeves, "Ow's about that! Sir Jimmy Savile Raised £45m for Charity and left another £5m in his Will," *Express*, December 16, 2011.

[1377] "Jimmy Savile: Report into Stoke Mandeville Hospital Abuse says Sex Abuse Victims included Spinal Injury Patients, Staff and Visitors," *ABC*, February 27, 2015.

[1378] "Jimmy Savile: Report into Stoke Mandeville Hospital Abuse says Sex Abuse Victims included Spinal Injury Patients, Staff and Visitors," *ABC*, February 27, 2015.

[1379] Jane Fryer, "Prince Charles, Saucy French Maids, and the Aphrodisiac Powers of a nice Chicken Sarnie. A very Bizarre Audience with the Eccentric Jimmy Savile," *Daily Mail*, November 13, 2010.

[1380] Alison Boshoff, "Jim the Fixer: Is Jimmy Savile just a Fantasist ... or is the Truth even Stranger than Fiction?" *Daily Mail,* May 9, 2008.

Early on in her ménage-e' tau, I mean 3-term premiership, a week after his last luncheon date with the Iron Lady in February 1981, a handwritten letter from Jimmy to Maggie says it all. His love note's nauseating lip-lock was unabashedly dripping off the page:

I waited a week before writing to thank you for my lunch invitation because I had such a superb time I didn't want to be too effusive. My girl patients pretended to be madly jealous and wanted to know what you wore and what you ate. All the paralysed lads called me 'Sir James' all week. They all love you. Me too!! Jimmy Savile OBE xxx O.B.E.[1381]

"Sir James" and Lady T would have to wait six more tries and almost a decade later before his knighthood was granted as Savile's creepy, uncouth nature had her honor committee staff protectively turning down her first five requests, deferring until she was safely out of office. This rather revealing love note was released in late December 2012 after being sealed for 30 years.

Savile closed his gushing confession sharing that all his patients love her, punctuated with "me too" next to his signature and attached OBE credential, the queen bestowed honor finagled back in 1972 through fellow pedophile-murderer the then Prime Minister Edward Heath.[1382] Jimmy Savile's cloying strategy always seemed to work like a charm on Thatcher, but less so on her staff. Per his request, Thatcher donated a half million pounds ($800,000 USD) on behalf of British taxpayers to his Stoke-Mandeville Hospital's new spinal unit. Her "generous" contribution to his cause, her determination to doggedly nominate him a half dozen times for knighthood and her re-inviting him back to Chequers on countless more occasions solidified their mutual love affair, probably motivated more by politics than sex. But with Savile, one never knows. What all this shows is how much weight and power he had over her.

The bulk of the Savile-Thatcher correspondence was withheld, rejecting Freedom of Information Act requests, fueling speculation over what dirty deeds must have transpired between them to cause it to be branded off limits to the public three decades later.[1383] But Jimmy and Maggie's crime cabal "fixed it" for the public not to know, having to wait until 2022 before another heavily redacted bundle gets released to the lowly plebeians.

Sir Jimmy's love for Dame Margaret (yep, queenie anointed her with an Order of Merit badge upon Lady Thatcher's resignation in December 1990[1384]) never went unrequited. As leader of the opposition party from 1975-1979, Maggie made a guest appearance on his Jim'll Fix It show broadcast on New Year's Day 1977 with Savile promising on the air to fix her election two years prior[1385] to her becoming Britain's first female prime minister (1979 to 1990) in exchange for

---

[1381] Cyril Dixon and Charlotte Meredith, "Jimmy Savile's 'Love' for Margaret Thatcher Revealed in Disturbing new Letters," *Express*, December 28, 2012.

[1382] Nick Dorman and Don Hale, *Mirror*, August 8, 2015.

[1383] Cyril Dixon and Charlotte Meredith.

[1384] Gilbert A. Lewthwaite," Queen Honors Thatcher with Order of Merit," *The Baltimore Sun*, December 8, 1990.

[1385] "Jimmy Savile and Margaret Thatcher," Jim'll Fix It episode, *BBC*, aired January 1, 1977, YouTube video, posted October 16, 2012, 01:56.

him being her favorite holiday guest the next near dozen years.[1386] Her loving tribute to him was expressed on a Savile episode of This Is Your Life:

So many Great Britons have had a touch of eccentricity about them and Jimmy is truly a Great Briton. Miner, wrestler, dance hall manager, disc jockey, hospital porter, fundraiser, performer of good works, Officer of the Most Excellent Order of the British Empire and Knight of the Realm, Jimmy, I and millions more salute you. God bless and thank you.[1387]

Thatcher selectively omitted his three biggest pastime passions that for years remained an open secret – serial necrophiliac, serial child rapist and most likely serial killer.

And it wasn't just Thatcher who was enamored with Sir Jimmy, every prime minister since has faithfully paid homage to Britain's "national treasure," his nauseating title repeatedly bandied about both before and after his October 2011 death. From John Major[1388] to Gordon Brown,[1389] Tony Blair[1390] [1391]and David Cameron,[1392] every prime minister after Thatcher also unswervingly kissed his ass. Perhaps that has everything to do with all of them being known pedophiles themselves or minimally known pedophile enablers.[1393] It was at PM John Major's invitation that Sir Jimmy spent the afternoon entertaining the G7 wives in 1991 while husbands carved up the geopolitical chessboard for more rape and pillage plunder.[1394]

Savile also spent time with Tony Blair at Chequers and made public appearances together.[1395] While war criminal dad Tony joined the Bush-Cheney Zionist gang lying to illegally invade and kill thousands of innocent Iraqi civilians, and mom Cherie was busy as president of Barnardos,[1396] a large children's anti-child abuse charity with a dubious reputation for child abuse[1397] (whose CEO urges more babies be taken away from parents[1398]) that operated

[1386] "Margaret Thatcher Speeches, Interviews and Other Statements," Margaret Thatcher Foundation, *margaretthatcher.org*.

[1387] "Margaret Thatcher Quotes," IMDb.

[1388] "North Wales Paedophile Ring," whale.to.

[1389] Michael James, "Revealed: British Premier Gordon Brown Is a Pedophile," *rense.com*, February 28, 2010.

[1390] Michael James, "Tony Blair Caught Protecting Elite Paedophile Ring," *whale.to*, March 5, 2003.

[1391] Martin Robinson, "Award-Winning Author Claims MP in Tony Blair's Government was part of Paedophile Ring which Infiltrated Council-run Children's Home," *Daily Mail*, July 14.

[1392] Chris Spivey, "Cameron's Closet," *Guerrilla Democracy News*, February 5, 2013.

[1393] Wayne Madsen, "The EU: A Powerhouse Pedophile Hierarchy," *Infowars/Madsen Report*, June 30, 2016.

[1394] Alison Boshoff, https://www.dailymail.co.uk/femail/article-565179/Jim-fixer-Is-Jimmy-Savile-just-fantasist---truth-stranger-fiction.html.

[1395] John Stevens, "Pervert DJ Jimmy Savile Harassed top Music Boss' Wife at a Dinner Party at Tony Blair's Chequers Country Retreat," *Daily Mail*, November 4, 2013.

[1396] Nicole Martin, "Barnardo's Role for Cherie," *The Telegraph*, September 18, 2001.

[1397] Peter Swindon, "Child Abuse 'Cover-up' claims after Barnardo's Admits Systematically Destroying Files," *The Herald*, June 4, 2017.

[1398] Tracy McVeigh, "Take more Babies away from Bad Parents, says Barnardo's Chief," *The Guardian*, September 6, 2009.

Duncroft School,[1399] Savile's "pedo-sweetshop" for underage girls,[1400] their own 16-year old daughter Kathryn in the spring of 2004 tried snuffing herself.[1401] Of course just like all his D-notices to suppress the outing of his pedo-filled government[1402] or his college cottage days as crossdressing Miranda picking up little boys in public toilets,[1403] a news blackout ensured that the people never learned their prime minister's teenage daughter was attempting suicide. What other skeletons does the Blair family hide in their closet besides being best friends with pedophiles (i.e., entertainers Sir "Kitty"[1404] and Sir Jimmy aside from Blair's own inside political pedo-pal circles)?

During the 9/11 era the child pimping undercover agent Savile dined with Admiral Sir Michael Boyce, the UK Chief of Defense Staff.[1405] Sir Jimmy's long association with the military began in 1966 when the most elite branch of service - the British Royal Marines - bestowed upon him their Green Beret honor, granted only to royals Prince Philip and Prince Charles.[1406] The degenerate DJ is said to have been buried clutching his coveted Green Beret cap.

So let's do a recap, Sir Jimmy Savile was more than chummy with elitist leaders from the military, media, entertainment, royalty, secret intelligence, religion, government, secret societies and the mob, covering every major player operating the globalized pedophilia network. That's rather telling.

Dame Margaret and Sir Jimmy's "love affair" was most definitely a royal match made in Lucifer's Hell. Hidden away in a page 23 opinion piece of the *Sunday Times*, journalist Janice Turner incisively summed up the essence of their true relationship, coalescing around his Stoke Mandeville Hospital:

But Stoke Mandeville is the most complex story. It is, of course, still about sexual abuse: the 60 reported victims, almost half of them children, the horror put in cool officialese that here his fondness for groping patients beneath bedclothes probably evaded detection 'as paralysed individuals would not have felt anything below . . . their spinal lesion.' **But this is also about**

[1399] Josh Halliday, "Jimmy Savile carried out 46 Sexual Assaults at Surrey Girls' School, say Police," *The Guardian*, April 29, 2015.
[1400] Richard Alleyne and Jowena Mason, "Jimmy Savile Treated School like 'Paedophile Sweetshop,'" *The Telegraph*, October 17, 2012.
[1401] Robert Henderson, "The Blair's Daughter's Attempted Suicide and the Public's Right to Know," *livinginamadhouse.wordprss.com*, October 2, 2010.
[1402] Mike James, "Are Pedophiles Running Blair's War Machine?" *Counter Punch*, January 29, 2003.
[1403] "Tony Blair has Links to Jimmy Savile," *neilscott1.wordpress.com*, November 9, 2013..
[1404] Mark Duell and Sam Greenhill, "Tony Blair called Sir Cliff Richard to Support him and Elton John told him to 'go for their Throat' over the Televised Police Raid of his Home on the BBC," *Daily Mail*, June 22, 2016.
[1405] Alison Boshoff, https://www.dailymail.co.uk/femail/article-565179/Jim-fixer-Is-Jimmy-Savile-just-fantasist---truth-stranger-fiction.html.
[1406] Becca Gliddon, "Royal Marines 'Erase' the Memory of Jimmy Savile," *Exmouth Journal*, October 19, 2012.

how politics and money gave him absolute power. Savile, the King. And it was Margaret Thatcher who crowned him.[1407] (Emboldened for emphasis)

Thatcher's Conservative Party in the early 1980s was looking for ways to drastically cut social services and healthcare expenditures from the national budget and using Jimmy Savile's "maverick" celebrity status to streamline privatization for funding National Health Services (NHS) was her party's preferred choice in a political marriage of self-serving convenience.[1408] Given carte blanche keys to the Kingdom's NHS institutions, Sir Jimmy was kept happy because he wielded ultimate power and freedom to do his predator thing while conjointly serving the queen's Commonwealth supplying sexual blackmail bait to British politicians and foreign dignitaries, while heartlessly and savagely destroying thousands of defenseless mentally and physically debilitated young lives in the process.

In return for Savile's services, PM Thatcher, her health minister Kenneth Clarke, assistant health minister Edwina Currie and their minions in September 1988 pressured Broadmoor civil servants at the nation's top security penal psychiatric institution to accept the *BBC* entertainer - like it or not - to head their hospital's taskforce after the Department of Health suspended Broadmoor trustees following a series of strikes leaving the Thatcher government firmly in control.[1409]

As a Broadmoor volunteer since the 1970s holding the title honorary entertainment officer, gradually the DJ assumed a higher profile and by the late 80s was anointed head honcho by Thatcher and her surrogates. That in and of itself is beyond ludicrous, strongly suggesting that he was granted a political favor in exchange for helping her slash her health and social services budget as well as for pimping kids to Lady T's pedophiles infiltrating her government.

In 1987 a career civil servant that ran the mental health division of the Department of Health and Social Services, the soon to be two time arrested but never charged accused pedophile Brian McGinnis,[1410] was instrumental in pushing for Savile's Broadmoor takeover.[1411] McGinnis was later hired as a high powered disabilities specialist despite allegedly sexually abusing disabled children as seemingly another protected predatory sentinel guarding the elite's pedo-clubhouse.

[1407] Janice Turner, "Savile, the King, and it was Margaret Thatcher who Crowned him," *The Times*, February 28, 2015.

[1408] Janice Turner, https://spotlightonabuse.wordpress.com/2015/03/03/money-and-politics-allowed-savile-to-molest-28-02-2015/.

[1409] Robert Mendick and Laura Donnelly, "Jimmy Savile: Questions for Edwina Currie and the BBC," *The Telegraph*, October 20, 2012.

[1410] "Mr. Brian McGinnis," *Zoom Info*.

[1411] "The Broadmoor Hospital, Jimmy Savile, and other Cover-ups," *Gumshoe News*, October 27, 2017.

Then years later when Savile was finally exposed, in chorus with so many complicit others, a defensive Edwina Currie said she always thought Sir Jimmy was "totally evil."[1412] If that's true, then why in the fuck did she go on public record in September 1988, fully complicit in Savile's criminality, and select an individual she was convinced was "totally evil," who neither held proper qualifications nor the moral character entrusted to seize control over the nation's top security asylum housing Britain's most violently insane criminals? What kind of moronic decision maker does that? But then immersed in a four year mutually adulterous affair with the then future PM John Major,[1413] perhaps Edwina's "moralist" outrage and judgment was already seriously compromised, contaminated and impaired. Or more likely her immediate supervisor, UK's health secretary Kenneth Clarke was morally impaired, a few years later accused himself of sexually assaulting a teenage child actor (covered in Chapter 20). Or for that matter, even Maggie the pedo-lover herself insisted that a totally unfit, "totally evil" yet thoroughly vetted and widely known pedophile should lead the Broadmoor taskforce.

Incidentally, Edwina's boss Kenneth Clarke under Thatcher was soon promoted by Edwina's lover John Major to the powerful position as UK's home secretary in 1992-93. And so like the Home Secretary Brittan a decade earlier, the not-so-great Britain had another gatekeeper fox guarding the pedo-henhouse, failing to act on knowledge that both MP Sir Cyril Smith and Lord Greville Janner were also sexually abusing children, choosing not to rock the boat, Clarke swiftly swept it under the rug.[1414] And it was while working his next job as Chancellor in 1994 that Clarke sexually assaulted former child actor Ben Fellows when he was 19.[1415] For making his accusation public as a journalist,[1416] Ben was subsequently charged with perverting justice but cleared in court,[1417] which in effect meant his accusation against Clarke could not be disproven, i.e., was true. But as always, when big wigs get caught committing crimes, they never get charged or serve time.

After reviewing her diary in October 2012, in the heat of the post-Savile uproar, Edwina Currie declared:

... When you look back, it does suggest he [Savile] was prepared to use blackmail to ensure people did what he wanted.[1418]

[1412] Robert Mendick and Laura Donnelly, https://www.telegraph.co.uk/news/uknews/crime/jimmy-savile/9623089/Jimmy-Savile-Questions-for-Edwina-Currie-and-the-BBC.html.

[1413] Richard Wheatstone, "When did Edwina Currie have an Affair with John Major and what's she said about the MPs Sex Scandal," *The Sun*, November 3, 2017.

[1414] David Barrett, "Kenneth Clarke 'Failed to act' over Lord Janner and Cyril Smith Child Abuse Tip-offs," *The Telegraph*, March 8, 2016.

[1415] Steph Cockroft, "Ex-chancellor Ken Clarke says the 'Nasty Allegation' he Molested a Young Actor in the 1990s was 'rather like the Martians Landing,'" *Daily Mail*, July 27, 2015.

[1416] Ben Fellows, "Ben Fellows Writes Direct to Ken Clarke," *The Tap Blog*, June 19, 2013.

[1417] Paul Cheston, "Former Child Actor who Accused ex-Chancellor Ken Clarke of Sexual Assault is Cleared of Perverting Course of Justice," *Evening Standard*, July 30, 2015.

[1418] Robert Mendick and Laura Donnelly, https://www.telegraph.co.uk/news/uknews/crime/jimmy-savile/9623089/Jimmy-Savile-Questions-for-Edwina-Currie-and-the-BBC.html.

Aided by hindsight, Currie's carefully chosen words are aimed at passing the buck in order to minimize her own criminal culpability. Her statement above reveals that as UK's pedo-pimp commander-in-chief, King Savile's M.O. was throwing his weight around using blackmail threats right and left to subdue, neutralize and silence perceived threats in order to ruthlessly grab whatever and literally whomever he wanted. For example, to silence his Broadmoor critics, he accused his adversaries of collecting undeserved overtime paychecks and allowing family members not employed at Broadmoor to sublet their housing.[1419]

MP Edwina Currie has herself been accused of sexually assaulting 13-year old Andrew Ash in Parliament no less.[1420] Her adulterous affair with Prime Minister John Major and silence knowing not only Savile was a monster but Thatcher minister Peter Morrison was a pederast committing sex crimes against pubescent minors under 16 while maintaining in her memoir it was common insiders' knowledge reveals that her Zionist Friend of Israel membership may have been at work for the Greater Israel Project spreading sexual blackmail ammo and contributing to Britain's pedophilia epidemic.

https://www.larouchepub.com/eiw/public/1983/eirv10n48-19831213/eirv10

Savile possessed the classic psychopath's instinctive knowhow for ferreting out others' weaknesses and liabilities. As Thatcher and the royal family's designated child procuring kingpin, Savile enjoyed a long successful history of aggressive intimidation and threat of blackmail. So arrogantly full of himself and his unbridled, unchecked power, by the late 1970s when Thatcher assumed Downing Street residency, Savile had become the public face of charity while the undercover saint was covertly running Britain's sexual blackmail operations. Pedo-loonies had not only officially taken over the asylum, but the nation's equally insanely pathological government as well. Throughout the Thatcher years sexual blackmail and Zionism reigned supreme.[1421]

The bottom line, for decades as UK's pimping child procurer working "deep-cover" with British intelligence services and police, setting up child pipelines across the nation under the cover of charity with care home operators, social services and city councils, Sir Jimmy possessed the dirty lowdown on every top government VIP pervert in both Thatcher's top-heavy pedo-cabinet as well as all the compromised and controlled Parliament members from all three major political parties. He was the macro-to-micro go-between national pedo-operative that made things happen, or as he loved bragging:

The thing about me is I get things done and I work undercover.[1422]

[1419] "Jimmy Savile Abuse Reports 'Reach 500,'" *BBC*, June 2, 2014.

[1420] "Friends of Israel," *aangirfan.com*, September 5, 2018.

[1421] "Friends of Israel," http://aanirfan.blogspot.com/2018/09/friends-of-israel.html/.

[1422] Jane Fryer, https://www.dailymail.co.uk/femail/article-1329332/Jimmy-Savile-Prince-Charles-saucy-French-maids.html.

Savile's guaranteed protection was fully secured because, under potential threat of mutual blackmail, the VIP child raping club goes to great lengths to protect its own. Additionally, as the loose cannon with loose lips capable of sinking some very powerful ships, Sir Jimmy virtually always got what he wanted. After all, through his blackmail services, the Luciferian Illuminati bloodline families were able to freely implement their Zionist-Anglo-American Axis-of-Evil agenda, making huge strides pushing towards absolute one world government control, so that all their compromised and controlled puppet-stringed public servants simply do whatever they're told in order to keep their high-end jobs safely enjoying their criminal, above-the-law, opulent lifestyles. If for whatever reason they don't, they know they or their careers will die sudden deaths like so many hapless *BBC* employees covered in the last chapter.

It wasn't just Savile currying favor with Thatcher and her Establishment pedophiles. The predator pecking order food chain has them all beholding to the British bloodline royal family. The *Daily Record* won on appeal its Freedom of Information Act request to reverse blocking the government's overt attempt to redact all mention of Savile and the royal family on the same official documents.[1423] Despite Britain's waning freedom of the press and public right to know, in 2013 while it still had a little left, it was learned that via a memo from a Thatcher aide to the PM dated March 1980 that Prince Charles had already agreed to sign on as the Patron of the Appeal backing Sir Jimmy's Stoke-Mandeville charity campaign, the same one Thatcher got behind. Savile's public and private liaisons with the royals go back to the late 1960s and early 70s when Prince Charles' childhood mentor and fellow pedophile Admiral of the Fleet Lord Mountbatten first introduced the *BBC* DJ to Prince Philip and Queen Elizabeth.[1424] The Windsors' unholy alliance and shared intimacies with Sir Jimmy, their nationally treasured derelict whose buffoonery made even the stoic royals appear more human and less coldblooded and scaly, their mutual romance will be addressed in Chapter 24.

At London's private highbrow Athenaeum Club in 1985, three years prior to heading the Broadmoor taskforce, Jimmy Savile and health minister Currie's assistant (and McGinnis' successor in 1988) - Cliff Graham, met with Alan Franey, the then NHS administrator at Leeds General Infirmary (1975-1985),[1425] where volunteer porter Savile remained at liberty for decades defiling underage girls, boys and dead corpses alike. At the posh Athenaeum where no doubt many shady VIP deals get hatched, Godfather Savile and sidekick Graham made Franey an offer he couldn't refuse, joining King Savile's Broadmoor and in short order leap-frogging him to "top dog" as Broadmoor's general manager. Just as Savile was totally unqualified to run Broadmoor, so was Franey who had no experience in security, the criminal justice nor mental health systems.[1426]

[1423] Jonathan Corke, Deborah Sherwood and Rick Lyons, "Charles' Links to Savile," *Daily Record*, May 12, 2013.
[1424] Brandon Turbeville, "The Prince and the Pedophile: Charles' Connections to Pedophilia Networks," *Activist Post*, November 16, 2012.
[1425] Claire Ellicott, "Jimmy Savile 'was given key Position at Broadmoor and even personally Selected Hospital's Bosses,'" *Daily Mail*, October 28, 2013.
[1426] Tim Hicks, "Savile and the Broadmoor Abuse Allegations, "*North Yorkshire Enquirer*, November 27, 2012.

With another cherry picked fox helping to guard Sir Jimmy's united pedo-kingdom, Savile was bringing Franey along at Broadmoor knowing he'd be beholding to him. Savile shrewdly figured wherever he went, it always helps to install an indebted subservient figurehead puppet implicitly vowing to protect and obey the hand that feeds him.

No sooner was Franey made a Broadmoor executive, in 1986 just two years before Thatcher's pedo-friendly ministers appointed Savile taskforce commander, a Broadmoor nurse was caught in a pedophile ring operating at the hospital and arrested for photographing pornographic images of children as young as 3 and 5 years of age on the high security premises...[1427] yet one more criminal Savile link never investigated. A longtime Broadmoor nurse who aptly described Savile as the lunatic taking over the asylum, also maintains that all the line staff knew the madman in charge was a pedophile and observed how as a pedo-magnet, he had dozens of fellow pedophiles gravitating to him both from within and out of the insane asylum.[1428] You'd best believe the king of all pedophiles had to be in deep with any pedo-nurse involved in a child porn business on the grounds where Sir Jimmy not only ruled the roost but also lived part-time.

So knowing a pedophile ring had recently been exposed at Broadmoor where insiders knew the most famous pedophile was a fixture, what does the pedo-infested Thatcher government do? It selects British history's biggest pedophile ever to become its next head honcho at its highest security criminal psych institution in the country. Makes sense only if with the most brazen impunity, the already existing VIP pedophilia network is intent on expanding its massive operations, signed off by royalty, the prime minister and British intel services.

In 1996 senior NHS executive Ray Rowden who was hired to oversee England's three top security hospitals claimed Franey bragged to him that back in the 1980s Franey drove Savile around Leeds to the DJ's old nightclub stomping grounds.[1429] Franey and Savile allegedly had met back in Leeds while running marathons together. Rowden added that when he first came to inspect Broadmoor, he confronted Franey over Savile's free, unlimited access anywhere inside the asylum, including the women's section where for prurient kicks, Savile brought along his fellow *BBC* pedophile pal Rolf Harris for a cheap thrill tour during their bedtime strip down inspection.[1430] Of course Franey insisted he never went to a nightclub in his entire life and that said conversation with Rowden never happened. Of course it also goes without saying that Franey claimed he had no clue his good old buddy since the 80s who "fixed" him his job happened to be Britain's worst serial pedophile preying for decades off Alan Franey's patients

---

[1427] Murun Buch, "There was Evidence of a Broadmoor Paedophile Ring in 1986," *spotlightonabuse.wordpress.com*, December 6, 2013.

[1428] "Broadmoor: Savile was 'a Lunatic in Charge of the Asylum,'" *Channel 4 News*, October 31, 2012.

[1429] Robert Mendick and Laura Donnelly, https://www.telegraph.co.uk/news/uknews/crime/jimmy-savile/9623089/Jimmy-Savile-Questions-for-Edwina-Currie-and-the-BBC.html.

[1430] Matthew Weaver, "Jimmy Savile gave Rolf Harris a Guided Tour of Broadmoor," *The Guardian*, July 1, 2014.

at both major medical institutions he ran as senior administrator for over two decades.[1431] Franey "ran" Broadmoor until resigning in 1997 amidst a police investigation over yet another possible child pornography ring allegedly operating inside the walls of his and Sir Jimmy's high security institution.[1432]

Returning to the Athenaeum Club, how did lecherous crude dude Savile ever gain membership at such an exclusive upper crust Establishment organization? He was nominated by the venerable former Archbishop of Westminster, Cardinal Basil Hume, who also introduced Savile in 1982 to Pope John Paul II to set the stage for Sir Jimmy's 1990 papal knighthood.[1433] Wouldn't you know it, UK's top pedo-enabling Church of England and Catholic leaders were also in tight with Savile and Prince Charles - particularly Bishop Peter Ball who also turned out to be a serial pedophile.[1434] Again, more on the royals' pedo-love affair in Chapter 24. With the infamous *BBC* court jester's incredible knack for social networking leading straight to the most powerful people in the world, his intimate ties to the pope, the queen, future king and every single prime minister for over a half century based on their mutual shared pedophilic self-interest, more than guaranteed Savile's untouchable lifetime free bird status.

And due to the entertainer's fundraising capabilities, Savile was granted unlimited authority and access at virtually any NHS institution, like Leeds General Infirmary and Stoke-Mandeville National Spinal Injury Center where he'd been a longtime volunteer at both facilities. After a roof cave-in, Stoke-Mandeville selected Jimmy as prime architect spearheading both the design and construction of the new spinal unit. Like Broadmoor, Stoke-Mandeville also provided a home away from home to the lecherous kiddie fondling midnight rambler to fully accommodate his insatiable predator needs. After all, he'd been granted carte blanche keys to the entire British pedo-Kingdom.

According to one child victim's claim, Sir Jimmy's personal assistant for 32 years, Janet Cope actually walked in on Savile while he was abusing her.[1435] But vehemently denying she ever knew of her boss's predatory sex habits, Janet Cope was apparently also too afraid to say anything, knowing up close and personal her boss's vindictive, petty and sheer cutthroat power:

Jimmy was untouchable... He controlled everything. He controlled me. Everybody was - I'm going to use the word frightened - of him.[1436]

According to Janet, after 32 years of loyal service to the psychopathic rapist, he selfishly used her up too, rewarding her loyalty and valuable service by firing her on the spot with no discernable explanation. But then without a conscience, that's what psychopaths do.

[1431] "Exposure Update – The Jimmy Savile Investigation," YouTube video, 2013, 54:56, posted March 7, 2013.
[1432] Matthew Brace, "Broadmoor Chief Resigns," *Independent*, June 4, 1997.
[1433] Tim Walker, "Sir Jimmy Savile causes anguish at the Athenaeum," *The Telegraph*, October 10, 2012.
[1434] "The Secret Connection between Pedophile Jimmy Savile and the British Royal Family," *humansarefree.com*, November 2017.
[1435] Janice Turner.
[1436] "Savile 'thought he was Untouchable,'" *ITV*, November 22, 2011.

As the powerful devil incarnate was granted increasing access, power and control over Britain's NHS institutions, the mutually self-serving Savile-Thatcher tradeoff helped facilitate Iron Lady's diversion of millions of taxpayer pounds away from providing much needed social services to financing a jingoistic war against Argentina. Attempting to reclaim imperialistic British Empire status, violently holding onto stolen South American islands,[1437] the prime minister seized the moment using a British submarine to sink an Argentine ship killing all 323 sailors aboard with the false excuse that it endangered British forces. Bottom line, her security advisor Lord Victor Rothschild possessed substantial investments in Falklands' vast mineral deposits that he didn't want shared with Argentina.[1438] The subservient, order following "Iron Lady" simply complied with his greedily selfish, coldblooded demand offering her a golden opportunity to bolster her tough woman persona and vainly resurrect lost empire glory. It was followed a year later with US Empire's turn to show off its saber rattling might - Reagan's bogus Grenada "invasion" in October 1983 against a few Cuban foot soldiers running loose on the island[1439] where a few American med students who couldn't get into stateside medical schools were studying.[1440]

These rah-rah military campaigns were analogous to the two neighborhood bullies boldly venturing outside their home turf in direct competition to see who was the biggest and baddest global oppressor. The US Empire couldn't pass up the chance to test out its emerging unipolar hegemony proving it was supreme world policemen and serial nation killer, doing one better than old has-been British Empire in their parasitic neocolonial juvenile jerkoff contest, all the while dutifully working as partners-in-crime as the Anglo-American-Zionist triumvirate, predatorily carving up the entire globe for the carnivorous, pedovore-loving elite's ravenous consumption.

Embracing her friendship with despotic bloodthirsty Chilean dictator General Pinochet who provided intelligence to Britain against Argentina during her Falkland War, then years later once indicted in 1999 for war crimes, Thatcher protected him while on house arrest in London. Taking tea with him long after out of office, Thatcher was still the best of friends with Pinochet, ever supportive and grateful for the mass murderer's assistance waging war against his old rival Argentina.[1441] Overnight Iron Lady cashed in, winning another war for British Empire bravado while concurrently jumpstarting UK's war machine industry at the expense of the British people, waging class warfare against them to drastically cut their vital health and social

---

[1437] John Goss, "Las Malvinas or the Falkland Islands? The Ugly Face of British Imperialism and Its Startling Cost," *News Junkie Post*, January 5, 2013.

[1438] Anthony T. Stokes, "Margaret Thatcher's Part in the Sinking of the General Belgrano," *whale.to*, December 24, 2011.

[1439] Eric Lormand, "Granada: How we continue to Believe the Hoaxes of our Military Establishment," *personal.michu.edu*.

[1440] Anemona Hartocollis, "Second-Chance Med School," *The New York Times*, July 31, 2014.

[1441] Palash Ghost, "Cold Warriors after the 1973 Coup: Why did Britain's Margaret Thatcher Support Chilean Dictator Augusto Pinochet?" *IBT*, September 11, 2013.

services,[1442] in part rescued by the likes of Sir Jimmy's public fundraising campaigns – in effect, a Luciferian win-win for the earth's baby raping killers.

While stiff upper lip Thatcher was eagerly cutting off free milk and school lunch programs for poor needy British kids, earning the label "Thatcher the milk snatcher,"[1443] the unholy Maggie-Jimmy partnership-in-crime was cemented by her regime that oozed blackmailed pedo-slime. The PM Dame and Sir Jimmy's convenient love affair on steroids bolstered Britain's sexual blackmail apparatchik, controlling government policymakers that Savile busily pumped kids to, ensuring that the international crime cabal debaucherously fed its own growing satanic pedophilic network.

After all, Margaret Thatcher's government was overloaded with pedophiles who couldn't keep their filthy hands off little boys, comprising upwards of nearly a third of her cabinet.[1444] Lady T and Savile mutually benefited, expanding Britain's sexual blackmail pedo-operation already long in place. Working "deep cover" for MI5, Savile the child pimp developed care home victim supply lines to an increasing number of her ministers and MPs just as he did a decade earlier under the fellow conservative pedophilic Heath government. As part of their disgustingly perverse "I'll scratch your back if you scratch mine" collusion, beginning in 1983 virtually every year Thatcher would feverishly and faithfully promote Savile for knighthood, the same year her fellow Tory MP Geoffrey Dickens provided a pedophile dossier to Thatcher's Home Office Secretary Sir Leon Brittan listing pedos in her regime.[1445] More on that caper later.

Per Thatcher's senior advisor, Savile's "strange and complex private life" posed a serious obstacle to knighthood. Her first five requests were repeatedly rejected by the honors committee chairman due to fear that the uncouth eccentric could bring dishonor to the British Commonwealth's highest royal tradition.[1446] In the AIDS crisis of the eighties, fear of his self-confessed "promiscuity" tainted Iron Lady's perennial bid for granting him the coveted accolade. But Thatcher's persistence along with Savile's nonstop ass kissing eventually paid off as Queen Elizabeth crowned Pimp King Savile his knighthood in 1990, safely waiting a month after Lady Thatcher left office.

Margaret Thatcher's 11 years at the British helm was a win-win for the Anglo-American Empire as the unholy Reagan/Bush-UK alliance and Apartheid South Africa (her calling Nelson Mandela a terrorist[1447]) were all part of the same diabolical cabal. With the universal principle of "like attracts like" operating, fresh out of office, Dame Maggie was also soon honored for her

---

[1442] "Thatcher, Pinochet and the Legacy of Class Warfare," *The Conversation*, April 10, 2013.

[1443] "From 'Margaret Thatcher, Milk Snatcher' to 'Theresa May, No Lunch Today': UK Conservatives Launch Manifesto," *Telesur*, May 18, 2017.

[1444] Matt Chorley, "Thatcher's former Bodyguard Reveals most of her 'Conservative' Ministers were regularly going to Ped-Parties," *sott.net/Daily Mail*, July 27, 2014.

[1445] "Tory MP Warned of Powerful Paedophile Ring 30 Years ago," *Independent*, February 22, 2013.

[1446] Vanessa Allen, "Revealed: Lady Thatcher's Five Attempts to Secure Knighthood for Jimmy Savile while her Aides Warned of his 'Strange and Complex' life," *Daily Mail*, July 17, 2013.

[1447] Gavin Evans, "Margaret Thatcher's Shameful Support for Apartheid," *Mail & Guardian*, April 19, 2013.

nefarious services rendered with both America and South Africa lavishing her with their highest achievement awards. In 1991 crime family overlord pedo Prez George HW Bush bestowed the Presidential Medal of Freedom honor on to Dame Maggie,[1448] followed just two months later by South Africa's racist President de Klerk's Grand Cross of the Order of Hope.[1449] The demonic pedo-love affair continued two months later when the queen stepped in to honor Lady T as Dame of the Order of St. John, an affiliate of the Knights of Malta,[1450] joining her Malta Knight Sir Jimmy whose Order is pro merito Melitensi of the Sovereign Military Order of Malta.[1451] Secret societies, knighthood and intelligence services are all guiltily synonymous with the global pedophilia network showing up repeatedly as the same critical players in virtually every pedo-scandal in the world.

Keep in mind that while Thatcher's pedophile-saturated government was embroiled in the Westminster scandal, with British VIP vultures feasting on freshly supplied pedo-pipelines compliments of Savile, MI5 and their procuring killer gangs abusing UK's expendable, most vulnerable population – children trapped in group "care" homes, at the exact same time America's own Boys Town orphanage pipeline funneled in boys for Reagan-Bush's White House midnight tours in the Franklin scandal (see Chapter 13), also flourishing as part of the same interconnected Luciferian cabal network. While constantly touting "family values," child rapists Reagan and Bush and pedo-lover Lady T were busily overseeing massive globalized pedophilia trafficking operations. If you don't believe she was part of it, a brief gander at her closest cabinet ministers and advisors speaks volumes.

Definitive evidence has emerged that the Iron Lady knew that her own Parliamentary Private Secretary Sir Peter Morrison, her own Home Secretary from 1983 to 1985 Sir Leon Brittan, her own Tory Party diplomat and former MI6 deputy director Sir Peter Hayman, leading Liberal Party MP Sir Cyril Smith as well as Northern Ireland Minister Sir William van Staubenzee were all knighted pedophiles of the royal pedo-order, not to mention her intel operative-goodwill ambassador Sir Jimmy.[1452] Archive records show handwritten notes written by Mrs. Thatcher insisting that known PIE member Peter Hayman should not be publicly outed.[1453]

In addition to his little boy diddling, multiple accused pedophile then 28-year old Sir Leon Brittan allegedly raped a 19-year old girl while on a 1967 blind date, questioned under caution

[1448] "Speech Receiving Presidential Medal of Freedom," Margaret Thatcher Foundation, *margaretthatcher.org*, March 7, 1991.

[1449] "Speech on Receiving the Order of Good Hope from President De Klerk," Margaret Thatcher Foundation, *margaretthatcher.org*, May 15, 1991.

[1450] "No. 52590," *The London Gazette*, July 1, 1991. p. 10029.

[1451] "Will Sir Jimmy Remain a Knight of Malta?" *maltastar.com*, October 27, 2012.

[1452] Jonathon Corke, "Margaret Thatcher Knew of Paedophile's Tory's Sick Secret but still Secured him a Knighthood," *Mirror*, May 9, 2015.

[1453] Peter Walker, "Thatcher Stopped Peter Hayman being named as Paedophile-Link Civil Servant," *The Guardian*, February 2, 2015.

by police in July 2014 not only about that but a plethora of child rape allegations.[1454] Sir Leon was also reportedly arrested by customs officials for attempting to smuggle child pornographic images in a suitcase but the elite's "hidden hand" ensured that story was suppressed as well.[1455] Recall that Mr. Brittan was also a VIP name on Mary Moss's infamous list at the rent boy brothel the Elm Guest House. Additionally from the *Daily Star* in October 2012:

Police sources in the minister's home region said there are other unsubstantiated allegations that he was once found trying to abuse the son of a friend.[1456]

Time and time again this pedo-cat was free to live out all nine of his lecherous lives. Though outed by multiple accusers in multiple settings, brought in for questioning in July 2014[1457] and in March 2015 his homes were raided six weeks after his death,[1458] Lord Brittan was never once arrested, prosecuted nor ever punished for his alleged series of sordid crimes. Though unnamed in the above quote from the 2012 *Daily Star* article, subsequent substantial documented evidence clearly indicates that the Tory minister referred to in both the *Star* and a February 2013 *Mirror* piece[1459] was Thatcher's Home Secretary Sir Leon Brittan.

Under police surveillance, in 1986 Brittan and a number of other VIPs were photographed attending Elm Guest House orgies and abusing rent boys dropped off by the notorious child raping and murdering Sidney Cooke gang.[1460] But since Brittan's office was in charge of MI5 and both his office and MI5 centrally control all UK police investigations, the serial child predator had nothing to fear, given ultimate control over the Great (Pedophilia) Kingdom additionally as the lost dossiers gatekeeper as well. This Lithuanian Jew was granted unlimited power as the kingpin fox guarding his own filthy pedo-house of ill-repute.

Per a police detective that worked on the Elm Guest House case, others frequenting the VIP brothel shindigs included the other untouchable "deep cover" procurer himself Sir Jimmy Savile and the other prolific serial child rapist kingpin that Thatcher also knew about - MP Sir Cyril Smith.[1461] Also recall from Chapter 20 that for years co-owner of the Elm Guest House Haroon Kasir had boasted that Sir Jimmy was his best friend.[1462] At least 16 VIP politicians, an entertainer (aka "Kitty"), Sir Peter Morrison, a high court judge, a high ranking policemen, an MI5 officer and royal art collector, double agent spy and British traitor Sir Anthony Blunt were

[1454] Vincent Moss and Dominic Herbert, "Ex-Home Secretary Leon Brittan Questioned by Police over Rape Claims," *Mirror*, July 5, 2014.

[1455] "Leon Brittan, Elm Guest House and Disappearing Children," *The Tap Blog*, November 3, 2014.

[1456] Jonathon Corke, Tony Bushby and Deborah Sherwood, *Daily Star*, October 28, 2012.

[1457] Daniel Boffey, "Leon Brittan 'Questioned by Police over Historical Rape Claim," *The Guardian*, July 6, 2014.

[1458] Keir Mudie and Mark Watts, "Leon Brittan Homes Raided in VIP Paedophile Child Abuse Probe six weeks after Tory Lord's Death," *Mirror*, March 8, 2015..

[1459] Justin Penrose, "The Net Closes: Ex-Tory Chief Faces Child Sex Arrest over Claims Girl was Raped and Boys were Abused," *Mirror*, February 16, 2013.

[1460] Justin Penrose, https://www.mirror.co.uk/news/uk-news/former-tory-faces-child-sex-1714162.

[1461] Justin Penrose, https://www.mirror.co.uk/news/uk-news/former-tory-faces-child-sex-1714162.

[1462] Fiona O'Clerigh and Mark Watts, "Met Detectives told of Jimmy Savile's Link to Elm Guest House," *Exaro News*, February 16, 2013.

all identified as avid partakers in this child sex ring bonanza where all the partying pervs knew each other well, knowing also that the bulk of their victims were supplied by Savile's procuring gang of brutal murderers led by Sidney Cooke.[1463]

Speaking of murder, files that the police had lied about, claiming they were destroyed, suddenly resurfaced in 2017 to indicate that the other Elm Guest House owner, Haroon's 47-year old wife Carole Kasir, may well have been murdered in 1990 to keep the dossiers she'd collected on VIP rapists hidden from the public.[1464] The so called insulin overdose explanation from her original inquest failed to examine the needles found next to her in bed. Standard toxicology tests were never performed on her body, her longtime GP believes she did not commit suicide and the pathologist maintains that she "did not die from natural causes." North West Leicestershire MP Andrew Brigden and others are calling for a fresh new inquest into Carole's suspected murder cover-up.

Child abuse advocates are also demanding a new investigation into evidence that young Irish boys from Northern Ireland's Kincora Boys Home were trafficked in as victims at both the Elm Guest House and Dolphin Square orgies as well as to cities in Europe,[1465] confirming a wider international pedophilia network that also corroborates claims that Savile pimped care home kids nationwide from England to Northern Ireland to Wales and beyond. Current PM Theresa May's farcical "independent national inquiry" refuses to even look at Northern Ireland's Kincora scandal, much less the UK pedo-network connections to global child trafficking.[1466] She and the elite she represents at the world's pedophilia epicenter have too much scum to hide, like the royal family's involvement at Kincora Boys Home scandal in both Prince Charles' boyhood mentor Lord Mountbatten[1467] and Sir Anthony Blunt.[1468]

This rabbit hole goes deeper as the Elm Guest House scandal also has yet more links to the international pedophilia network. Abuse victims claim that foreign VIP dignitaries were brought in from Belgium and other places in Europe, landing at Royal Air Force Northolt just outside London to violate the trafficked in British rent boys.[1469] This clearly implicates the British Royal Air Force as an accomplice to VIP high crimes as part of the major pedophilia operation run by the power-broking European pedo- Establishment.

[1463] Keir Mudie and David Hencke, "Was Owner of a Paedophile Palace who kept list of Secret VIP Visitors Murdered?" *Mirror*, November 11, 2017.

[1464] Keir Mudie and David Hencke, https://www.mirror.co.uk/news/uk-news/secret-files-prove-carole-kasir-11506791.

[1465] "Kincora Child Sex Abuse Victim Richard Kerr: I was Molested by Powerful People at Dolphin Square and Elm Guest House in London," *Belfast Telegraph*, April 7, 2015.

[1466] Gary Fennely, "Newton: Kincora's Exclusion from UK Child Abuse Inquiry is Unforgiveable," *Tap News Wire*, July 29, 2015.

[1467] Joe Oliver, "Mountbatten is Linked to Ulster Boy Sex Scandal," *The People/thefreelibrary.com*, December 8, 2002.

[1468] James Fielding, "MI6 Covered up Historic Child Sex Abuse Ring Discovered during Surveillance Operation," *Express*, April 12, 2015.

[1469] Jonathon Corke, Tony Bushby and Deborah Sherwood, https://www.dailystar.co.uk/news/latest-news/279380/TORY-PAEDO-COVER-UP.

On top of all his, the highly frustrated law enforcement insider maintains that his investigative team was about to arrest all the VIP sickos involved in the Elm House scandal when the day prior to the scheduled roundup, "superiors" ordered their police operation disbanded immediately,[1470] an overly familiar and consistent outcome whenever members of the pedophilic elite get caught red-handed. The detective said the original whistleblowing victim vanished right after reporting the abuse to the police, an equally common fate amongst those young people courageous enough to immediately reveal VIP crimes committed against them to the authorities.[1471] Powerful child rapists never fail to go free while their victims either disappear, commit suicide or suffer the lifelong effects from child abuse, especially when neither given a voice nor a shred of justice. So many precious, innocent lives lost and ruined by so many evildoers hiding behind fame, wealth and power held up on a false god pedestal clearly is Lucifer's way.

So the Elm Guest House police probe discovered links to 10 Downing Street, Parliament and even Buckingham Palace. For ten straight days in October 1982, even all the mainstream newspapers had a flurried field day - the *Daily Express, The Times, The Guardian* and *The Sun* - without naming names busily running story after story reporting the Savile-government connected VIP pedo-scandal.[1472] But soon enough it all came to an abrupt, squelching halt. After fellow pedo Attorney General Sir Michael Havers threatened a libel suit against the press protecting his own criminal ilk, the story died a week and a half later after just scratching the surface, exposing the VIP child raping network involving the most powerful figures in the British government. But the pedo-genie can never be put back in his bottle no matter the ironclad efforts sought by sickos in charge to suppress the ugly truth of the horrific crimes committed by the powerful pedo-cabal establishment. The anguished police officer working the investigation stated:

It wasn't that we ran out of leads but it reached a point where a warning to stop came. It was a case of 'get rid of everything, never say a word to anyone.' It was made very clear to me that to continue asking questions would jeopardise my career.[1473]

After his police operation was shot down, the former detective checked the file containing all their diligent work collecting the incriminating photos and carefully documented evidence on Brittan and his VIP pals.[1474] But the file was empty of both photos and all the high profile pedophiles' names were missing - proof that the establishment in cahoots with the lowly Metro Police were guilty of another major criminal cover-up.

[1470] Jonathon Corke, Tony Bushby and Deborah Sherwood, https://www.dailystar.co.uk/news/latest-news/279380/TORY-PAEDO-COVER-UP.

[1471] "100 Victims of VIP/Westminster Child Sexual Abuse," *scribd.com*.

[1472] Murun Buch, "Elm Guest House: The History of a Cover-up," *spotlightonabuse.wordpress.com*, February 13, 2013.

[1473] Jonathon Corke, Tony Bushby and Deborah Sherwood, https://www.dailystar.co.uk/news/latest-news/279380/TORY-PAEDO-COVER-UP.

[1474] Justin Penrose, https://www.mirror.co.uk/news/uk-news/former-tory-faces-child-sex-1714162.

Would-be jailbirds of a pedo-feather, never fail to flock together in the Savile-Thatcher VIP pedophilia network. Cases in point – Freemason PIE member clockmaker Keith Harding who appeared alongside Sir Jimmy on his Fix It Christmas episode would also entertain VIP pedophile guests regularly showing up at his London shop,[1475] among them Leon Brittan, Cyril Smith and fellow MP Liberal Party leader Jeremy Thorpe who became embroiled in a scandalous case of attempted murder of his former gay lover.[1476] But little boy lover Thorpe threatened to tell all he knew to the world, promptly securing his not guilty verdict.[1477]

It was former Liberal Party leader Jeremy Thorpe who kept showing up at the rent boy orgies sponsored by the gangster Kray twins back in the 60s that *BBC* DJs Savile, Freeman and Denning along with music maestros Jonathon King, Joe Meeks and Beatles manager Brian Epstein were regulars, that is until police chiefs caught wind of Thorpe and a few other prominent MPs' presence and shut it down as too high a risk.[1478] That was prior to the more flagrantly open days of Thatcher's 1980s when British intelligence and police chiefs along with the usual VIP suspects from government in both UK and Europe were all joining in on the kiddie gangbanging rapes at places like Elm Guest House and infamous Dolphin Square.

All these lecherous, treacherous VIP perverts belonged to the same pedo-club yet not one of them ever paid for their child abuse crimes that included occasional murder before dying of old age. And a few are still hiding out waiting to die after living their "good life." Only the low hanging predators like Denning is still in the slammer[1479] while King's been in and out.[1480] But the likes of Mr. Undercover and his MP Johns belonging to the VIP uppermost tier have always managed to successfully live like unholy gods above all the manmade laws they make for only us to abide by.

Yet another queen-knighted minister in Lady Thatcher's cabinet caught frequenting the Elm Guest House was Scottish Tory MP Sir Nicholas Fairburn who got away scot free after repeatedly molesting and raping his close friend's 4-year old daughter,[1481] in addition to raping Elm House kids and carrying on an adulterous affair with Dame Esther Rantzen, the notorious pedo-loving queen as *BBC* ChildLine-NSPCC pedo-cabal gatekeeper.[1482] It's no accident that the

---

[1475] James Fielding, "Clockmaker Keith Harding played vital role in Britain's Biggest Child Sex Ring," *Sunday Express/ spotlightonabuse.wordpress.com*, May 10, 2015.

[1476] Joe Dziemianowicz, "British Police Reopen Scandalous Gay Murder-for-Hire Case," *New York Daily News*, June 2, 2018..

[1477] Anthony T. Stokes, "The Wheel of Fortune," *whale.to*, September 6, 2011..

[1478] "Jimmy Savile, Edward Heath and the Kray Twins," *google-law.blogspot.com*, November 2, 2012.

[1479] Richard Spillett, "BBC Radio One DJ Chris Denning is Jailed for 13 years for Sex Attacks on Children as Young as Eight as it is Revealed he took a 14-year-old to Meet Gary Glitter," *Daily Mail*, October 7, 2016,.

[1480] Bob Woffinden, "Is this Proof that Jonathan King didn't do it? New Evidence Suggests Pop Mogul could have an Alibi which puts him in America when Teenage Boy was Abused in UK," *Daily Mail*, April 30, 2016.

[1481] Guy Adams and Andrew Malone, "Revealed: The Full Horrifying Truth about Sir Nicholas Fairbairn - the other Paedophile at Margaret Thatcher's Side," *Daily Mail*, August 22, 2014.

[1482] Marc Horne, "Esther Rantzen: My shock over my MP Lover's Links to Elm House Paedophile Ring, *Daily Mail*, July 20, 2014.

names from the same flock of pedo-foxes keep resurfacing again and again at the same crime scene network.

In 1986 (same year Rantzen started her ChildLine), Thatcher's bodyguard and former detective chief inspector Barry Streven told his prime minister straight out that many of her key cabinet members were full blown child abusers.[1483] Yet knowing her closest advisors and confidantes were harming innocent kids never stopped Lady T or Queen Elizabeth from shielding and rewarding knighthood to all the worst offenders - Savile (after 5 failed tries), Sir Cyril Smith, Sir Leon Brittan, Sir Nicholas Fairburn, Sir Peter Morrison, Sir Peter Hayman, Sir Jeremy Thorpe and on and on we go. Every one of Thatcher's incoming cabinet ministers as well as the queen's knighthood recipients are all thoroughly vetted by UK's security services whose job is to keep close running tabs on the who's who of VIP child molesters occupying high places within the nation's long established blackmail system. So ignorance is no excuse. It's an indisputable fact that royalty and political leaders favor their child rapist friends over the well-being of their nation's own children and aiding and abetting child rapists has always been their unprosecuted crime (among a litany of others). So by law Dame Maggie and Queen Lizzie were/are also criminals.

Moreover, it's also intelligence agencies' equally important task to ensure compromised and controlled pedophiles are guarding their United pedo-house Kingdom at every level - from the VIP politicians, to their senior civil servants, from law enforcement and high courts to the media. All are overpaid, totally controlled and protected criminals as long as they continue to stand vigil guarding their pedo-peer clubhouse.

Thatcher's home secretary Brittan at age 43 was the youngest UK law enforcement chief since fellow pedophile Sir Winston Churchill assumed the helm before WWI.[1484] Since numerous victims at sex parties held at Dolphin Square and Elm Guest House accused Sir Leon Brittan of being a child molester,[1485] in 1983 Brittan made sure that the 40-page dossier listing himself and his fellow minister peers and MPs as child rapists given him by Tory Party MP Geoffrey Dickens was intentionally "lost." Incredibly also in 1983 the Scotland Yard submitted to Brittan a separate second dossier exposing 15 prominent VIP PIE members and Sir Leon "misfiled" that one too.[1486] Brittan proceeded to "lose track" of (i.e., destroy) all evidence that would've sunk both him and the British Establishment once and for all. Thus Sir Leon became the principal presiding over the infamous Westminster pedophilia cover-up more fully detailed in Chapter 23.

Goes without saying that British intelligence services already had the lowdown on all of these dossier listed perverts but as child pimping handlers and blackmailers, many pedophiles

---

[1483] Matt Chorley, "Thatcher's Bodyguard says he Warned her about Underage Sex Rumours about Close Aide amid Claims Senior Ministers were named in Dossier," *Daily Mail*, July 27, 2014.

[1484] Nico Hines, "How Thatcher's Government Covered up a VIP Pedophile Ring," *The Daily Beast*, March 6, 2015.

[1485] Levi Winchester, "Leon Brittan 'Attended Paedophile Parties in Notorious Brothel,'" *Express*, January 25, 2015.

[1486] Steven Swinford, "Leon Brittan was given a second Paedophle Dossier," *The Telegraph*, July 7, 2014.

themselves, working "deep cover" with the likes of Sir Savile, for decades throughout the West the power business has always been about controlling top politicians through sexual blackmail,[1487] and with adultery and homosexuality gone mainstream, it's degenerated into misusing children as their cannon fodder kiddie bait on a massive scale. This cold hard fact speaks volumes as absolute proof that to reach the highest echelons of power in this world, be it in the UK, America, or the entire Western world and beyond, you must already be either a certifiable pedophile yourself or a thoroughly compromised, pedo-enabling, heartless, psychopathic, sniveling snake in the grass.

Savile's Mossad controlled US counterpart is Trilateral Commission and Council on Foreign Relations member Jeffrey Epstein (see Chapter 14).[1488] For purposes of maintaining their absolute impunity over the long haul, to be invited into this diabolical inner sanctum, pathetically it means you must already be one of them. Their earthly dominion controlling fallen angel Lucifer wouldn't have it any other way.

Still unconvinced that Prime Minister Thatcher and Sir Jimmy's love affair was a pedophilia front for the global cabal's pedo-network? In July 2014 a onetime Tory Party insider and little boy procurer himself for Tory VIPs became a pedophile namedropper outing yet more ministers from Thatcher's notorious cabinet.[1489] In addition to the aforementioned handful, former Tory activist Anthony Gilberthorpe said that Thatcher's Education Secretary Sir Keith Joseph, Minister of State Social Security Sir Rhodes Boyson, Attorney General Sir Michael Havers and another still serving as MP today were/are abusing rent boys that Gilberthorpe supplied at sex parties.[1490] Joseph and Boyson are even listed as PIE members in the second dossier given to Brittan in 1983.[1491] Yet with all this undeniable evidence, they either go to their graves unblemished or are still serving in government unblemished.

As illustration of the unbelievable hypocrisy exhibited by these elite pedophiles, the knighted Sir Rhodes Boyson was a raving homophobe claiming that being gay was "unnatural" and "biblically wrong." Yet privately it never stopped him from attending drug sexed orgies homosexually ravaging little boys while mouthing to the press such classic, ignorant, bigoted lines as:

If we could wipe out homosexual practices, AIDS would die out.[1492]

[1487] Philip Jenkins, "Sexual Blackmail's Long History," *The American Conservative*, January 16, 2017.

[1488] "About Jeffrey Epstein VI Foundation," *jeffreyepstein.org*.

[1489] Vincent Moss and Matthew Drake, "Tory Child Abuse Whistleblower: 'Margaret Thatcher Knew all about Underage Sex Ring among Ministers," *Mirror*, July 13, 2014.

[1490] Rebecca Lake, "Thatcher's Cabinet Minister Paedophile Cover-up," *Wessex Scene*, July 17, 2014.

[1491] Matthew Drake, "Margaret Thatcher's Cabinet Bigwigs named in Leon Brittan Paedo Files," *Mirror*, July 26, 2014.

[1492] Rebecca Lake, https://www.wessexscene.co.uk/politics/2014/07/17/thatchers-cabinet-minister-paedophile-cover-up/.

Eventually at 87 so did he in 2012, of course unpunished and unexposed for his lifelong sins "against nature."

Anthony Gilberthorpe went on to state that as a friend he also personally informed Margaret Thatcher that many of her closest right hand men were using more than their right hands to savagely violate underage boys at Conservative Party orgies. But Anthony the whistleblower naively failed to realize that Iron Lady was already well aware she was surrounded by carefully placed, thoroughly vetted sexual predators having received multiple "tips" from multiple other inside sources.

Gilberthorpe elaborates further:

I outlined exactly what I had witnessed and informed her I intended to expose it. I made it very clear to Mrs. Thatcher most trusted ministers had been at these parties with boys who were between 15 and 16. I also told her of the amount of illegal drugs like cocaine that were consumed.[1493]

But Gilberthorpe fails to mention to the prime minister **when** he planned to expose all those pedophiles, as apparently he safely chose to withhold this damaging information from the public until years later **after** Thatcher and virtually every one of his identified VIP sickos had already died off.

As if all this isn't incriminating enough, just a year later in July 2015 yet another "discovered" bone was thrown to the citizens for mass consumption to reveal that again in 1986 MI5 chief Sir Anthony Duff sent a letter "informing" the prime minister that prominent MP Cyril Smith was a pedophile.[1494] The notion that the head of British intelligence responsible for coordinating UK pedophilia blackmail operations would disclose in a letter that a single member of the House of Commons from an opposing party just happened to be a flaming pedophile is an affront to our intelligence when we know that the Thatcher government was by design swarming with meticulously infiltrated child molesters and rapists galore.

This is the British establishment's cunningly deceptive methodical strategy to minimize the pedo-scandal in the post-Savile era, unwilling to admit even half-truths, instead choosing to trickle it down to one-one thousandth truths in piecemeal fashion. But the far more significant bottom line issue here is that the Duff letter serves as yet one more among numerous sources unequivocally confirming that Maggie the pedophile lover knew all along that creepy crawling degenerates of the worst order had saturated her government. Based on Duff's written assessment below, it's made perfectly and assuredly clear to all involved that from both head of UK intelligence to prime minister and all her pedo-filled cabinet members:

[1493] Rebecca Lake, https://www.wessexscene.co.uk/politics/2014/07/17/thatchers-cabinet-minister-paedophile-cover-up/.
[1494] Corinne Purtell, *Global Post/pri.org*, July 23, 2015.

At the present stage... the risks of political embarrassment to the government is rather greater than the security danger.[1495]

In other words, the ongoing, unchecked grave risk to their nation's children being permanently scarred and damaged was never even part of the equation. In his warped mind, saving the government from public embarrassment was a much greater priority than either their welfare or national security's (i.e., foreign Zionist or Soviet interests controlling Britain's government through blackmail was deemed less risk). This telling disclosure reveals the pure evil and wickedness that guide all of these major power players' every move and why a satanic spook like Jimmy Savile was so usefully important to them. For a very long, long time, since the Babylonian Baal worshipping, satanically ritualized practices of pedophilia and child sacrifice (see Chapter 3) along with sexual blackmail have always been how this world has operated atop the subhuman pedo-food chain.

In another overt, incriminatingly explosive episode demonstrating that Thatcher engaged in a massive, widespread cover-up to conceal her hardcore pedophile ministers within her cabinet, in 1982 Maggie was joined by her then Home Secretary Willie Whitelaw, a senior policeman and an MI5 officer to discreetly meet with one of her top ministers, a rising Tory Party star being groomed at the time for higher office, to warn him to be more careful in his personal taste for little boys.[1496] But the press's watered down version includes this Thatcher quoted admonishment:

You have to clean up your sex act.[1497]

Give us a break! Like making sure her pedo-crew would ever stop raping little boys was ever really even close to a priority during her entire 11-year reign. Instead the "warned" minister, knowing full well he could safely continue acting out his sickness living above the law, he ignored his boss and was again observed four years later in a Scotland Yard sting operation still soliciting sex from underage lads at the Victoria Railway Station.[1498] Of course because Standard Operating Procedure for UK police has always protected and ignored pedophilia in its VIP ranks, police politely requested the serial child rapist to not hang out at railway station toilets anymore. This information came to light after an inside Scotland Yard source in 2014 disclosed the story to the *Sunday People*. Again, proof that by careful Luciferian design, Prime Minister Margaret Thatcher was surrounded by hardcore pedophiles, brazenly lurking in complete impunity inside her den of iniquity at the very heart of the British government. And you can bet

---

[1495] "MI5 Warned Thatcher about Westminster Pedophiles, no action taken," *RT*, July 25, 2015.

[1496] Nick Buckley and Kier Mudie, "Margaret Thatcher 'Personally Covered-up' Child Abuse Allegations against Senior Ministers," *Mirror*, July 12, 2014.

[1497] Nick Buckley and Kier Mudie, https://www.mirror.co.uk/news/uk-news/margaret-thatcher-personally-covered-up-3848836.

[1498] Nick Buckley and Kier Mudie, https://www.mirror.co.uk/news/uk-news/margaret-thatcher-personally-covered-up-3848836.

that nothing has changed since, except that in 2018 the pedo-cabal remains not only alive and well but bigger, more powerful and more protected than ever.[1499]

A brief glimpse into Thatcher's earlier life growing up raised by her strict Methodist lay preacher father Alf Roberts[1500] proves very illuminating. Little Maggie adored her neighborhood grocer patriarch, who also possessed quite a notorious reputation within the community as a pervert groping any underage girl he could get his paws on.[1501] While pitying her mother and older sister for their more maternal, traditional ways,[1502] Margaret admired the strong work ethic of her frugal, "puritanical," intellectual dad who instilled in her ambition, hard work and austerity alongside repressed inner conflict between self-righteous, holier than thou hypocrisy and arrogant pride overcompensating her closeted embrace of sexual deviance and wicked predation. As her father's favorite, perhaps she herself was a pedophile incest victim. Similar to Dame Rantzen who alleged being molested as a child by a family member,[1503] this dynamic goes far in explaining such strong attraction, affection and tolerance towards so many known child predators like Savile and all her gay pedophile gang atop her government. More gatekeeping female pedophile-loving dames standing guard for their pedo-cabal that's in turn treated them so well.

As a former MP hailing from Finchley, the one district containing the largest Jewish constituency[1504] in a nation with an overall population of less than half of 1% Jewish,[1505] Prime Minister Thatcher filled upwards of 25% of her cabinet with Jews.[1506] Several were accused pedophiles like Brittan and Joseph. Others like Sir Leon's foreign minister cousin Sir Malcolm Rifkind, later parliamentary committee chair presiding over Mossad run British intelligence[1507] [1508] and adulterous Jewish princess (more Rantzen echoes?) Edwina Currie who appointed known predator Savile to head Broadmoor are more pedophile enabling apologists. Another Jewish minister David Young whose proud Lithuanian father bragged:

One son deputy chairman of the government, another [Simon] *chairman of the BBC -- that's not bad for immigrants.*[1509]

[1499] Richard Enos, "Illuminati Pedophilia: What is the Role of the Awakening Community?" *Stillness in the Storm*, September 10, 2018.

[1500] Eliza Filby, "Margaret Thatcher: Her Unswerving Faith Shaped by her Father," *The Telegraph*, April 14, 2013.

[1501] Keith Nuthall, "Thatcher's Dad: Mayor, Preacher, Groper," *Independent*, June 22, 1997..

[1502] Robin Harris, "The Mother Maggie Pitied, and the Sister she left behind... and the Puritanical Father who wouldn't pay for an inside Loo and Banned her from Playing Snakes and Ladders on Sunday," *Daily Mail*, April 15, 2013.

[1503] Giles Sheldrick, "Esther Rantzen: I Suffered Sex Abuse as a Child," *Express*, August 31, 2011.

[1504] Jonathon Boyd, "Where Jewish Votes Matter the most," *Jewish Policy Research*, May 2015.

[1505] "Vital Statistics: Jewish Population of the World," *Jewish Virtual Library*, 2017.

[1506] Maayan Meir, "Margaret Thatcher and the Jews," *aish.com*, July 22, 2017.

[1507] Richard M. Bennett, "Assassination and the License to Kill," *Asia Times*, June 13, 2003.

[1508] "The British Establishment is Controlled by Israel's Mossad," *The Coleman Experience/gmmuk.com*, June 27, 2015.

[1509] "The Real Thatcher," *aangirfan.com*, April 9, 2013.

Yet another Jewish minister Michael Howard went on to become the Conservative Party leader but not before working with the Rothschild City of London shepherding through Thatcher's hated poll tax,[1510] leading to today's shameful inequality mess where the top 10% of British wage earners pay less of their income to taxes than the poorest 10%.[1511] Thanks to her and Howard's poll tax, outside one other among the world's developed nations, UK has suffered the worst inequality gap between the rich and poor.[1512]

Additionally, the most powerful Jew in the Thatcher government was Lord Victor Rothschild as her security advisor. Thatcher selected, or more likely Rothschild selected her as his puppet prime minister, and then the head of the bloodline family's banking dynasty controlling the Bank of England was entrenched throughout the 1980s as her closest security confidante.[1513] But Rothschild was also a Communist and the fifth and actual leader of the treasonous KGB Cambridge 5 spy ring consisting of gay pedophile Anthony Blunt, longtime British intelligence operative and art curator for the royals who were fully aware of both Blunt's treason[1514] and degenerate taste for little boys.[1515] Other Cambridge spies were the 1951 Soviet defectors Guy Burgess who introduced Blunt to the gay pedo-lifestyle along with fellow defector Donald MacLean and Kim Philby,[1516] who the Mossad helped flee to the Soviet Union in 1963.[1517]

After Blunt recruited Rothschild to the KGB while at Cambridge University in 1936,[1518] Rothschild wound up a very close friend to Prime Minister Churchill throughout WWII, providing updated intelligence to Stalin throughout. In 1940 it was Rothschild's turn to invite Blunt into MI5.[1519] Over the course of the next half century, until his death in 1990, Victor Rothschild and his four fellow KGB traitors working in MI5, MI6 and the British Foreign Office (that controls MI6) gave away critical allied atomic and nuclear secrets to the Soviets. During the 1980s along with Home Office Secretary Brittan, double agent Lord Rothschild used his immense influence to oversee MI5 and MI6 operations[1520] and is believed instrumental in leaking nuclear secrets to the Israelis as well.[1521]

Additionally, Savile and one of his early protectors Blunt were both pedophiles with enormous kiddie appetites, both intimate with the Windsor family, both worked undercover for MI5, both were instrumental in setting up blackmail operations throughout the British Isles extending

---

[1510] Colin Brown, "Howard Distances himself from the Thatcher Years," *Independent*, April 12, 2005.

[1511] Benjamin Kentish, "Poorest Pay Higher Taxes than Richest, New Figures show," *Independent*, April 26, 2017.

[1512] Malcolm Dean, "Margaret Thatcher's Policies Hit the Poor Hardest – and it's happening again," *The Guardian*, April 9, 2013.

[1513] Henry Makow, "Victor Rothschild was a Soviet Agent," *henrymakow.com*, April 19, 2017.

[1514] Andrew Alderson, "King George VI Suspected Blunt was Russian Spy," *The Telegraph*, March 2, 2003.

[1515] "Rothschild's Friend Blunt; International Child Abuse Ring," *aangirfan.com*, April 13, 2015.

[1516] Henry Makow, https://www.henrymakow.com/2017/04/Was-Victor-Rothschild-a-Soviet-Agent.html.

[1517] Rothschild; Philby; Angleton," *aangirfan.com*, March 24, 2013.

[1518] Henry Makow, https://www.henrymakow.com/2017/04/Was-Victor-Rothschild-a-Soviet-Agent.html.

[1519] "Cold War: Anthony Blunt," *Alpha History*, https://alphahistory.com/coldwar/anthony-blunt/.

[1520] "Leon Brittan, Elm Guest House and Disappearing Children," http://tapnewswire.com/2014/11/leon-brittan-elm-guest-house-and-disappearing-children/.

[1521] "Rothschilds," *aangirfan.com*, October 20, 2017.

blackmail pedo-rings to top establishment VIPs, and both maintained strong loyal ties to both Israel and Jewish banking family patriarch-spy-Thatcher security advisor Victor Rothschild.[1522] Sharing a mutual vested interest in the global pedo-blackmail-trafficking apparatchik, the links between Savile, Blunt, Rothschild and the royal British bloodline that feed both the parasitic pathology of pedophiles and the obvious control mechanism over compromised puppet politicians, these same sexually deviant Zionist traitors' names keep popping up all the time. It was definitely no accident the planetary controllers made certain their Dame Margaret Thatcher as Britain's first female prime minister stack the deck with controllable pedophiles fervently loyal to Zionism during Iron Lady's near dozen year premiership.

Still another from Thatcher's inner circle that stood accused of pedophilia crimes was her Chief of Defense from 1982-85 - Lord General Edwin Bramall, who served years earlier under royal pedophile Lord Mountbatten. Metro Police Detective Superintendent Kenny McDonald found Bramall's accuser Nick a highly credible source from 2014-2016, disclosing on record:

Nick has been spoken to by experienced officers from child abuse teams and experienced officers from murder investigations. They and I believe what Nick is saying is credible and true.[1523]

Still alive and kicking turning 95 in December 2018, as of 2016 the old accused pedophile soldier was no longer considered a suspect because suddenly the police did a 180 reversal and publicly concluded that Nick's (and undoubtedly others') allegations were somehow false.[1524] The Establishment rules dictate that only dead monsters can be accused and believed, but dare call out any famous still alive pedophiles and the system makes mincemeat of them. Why were Nick's allegations deemed so credible by the top cop for two years running and then abruptly declared false and discarded? Several police officers are also under investigation that worked on the failed £2.5 million fiasco Operation Midland that netted zero VIP pedophile arrests, based on compiled accuser Nick's allegedly bogus allegations,[1525] sending the loud and clear message to both accusers and police alike to not even think about going after the VIP child rapists.

This unsettling development is more pedo-Establishment pushback, a psyops designed to place doubt and second thoughts on future victim accusers.[1526] Lots of propaganda mileage to be gained here from making false allegations against one "innocent," distinguished, highly decorated famous old war hero, then declare the accuser dishonest and under arrest, vindicating the victimized VIP ala Sir Cliff. Like every other child sex abuse inquiry, investigation

---

[1522] "Jimmy Savile; Rothschild; Anthony Blunt; MI5," *aangirfan.com*, October 3, 2012.
[1523] "Nick Versus Lord Bramall," *aangirfan.com*, February 7, 2018.
[1524] "Nick Versus Lord Bramall," https://aanirfan.blogspot.com/2017/09/nick-versus-lord-bramall.html.
[1525] May Bulman, "Police Officers Linked to VIP Paedophile Ring to be Investigated," *Independent*, November 17, 2016.
[1526] Ian Greenhalgh, "Investigation of British Elite Child Sex Abuse Scandal continues to be Sidetracked," *Veterans Today*, February 5, 2016.

and police operation into historic UK child abuse, despite numerous victims implicating powerful VIPs as their abusers, always the outcomes remain the same – "not enough evidence."[1527] Not one minister, MP, military general or intelligence chief has ever been prosecuted, much less found guilty. Yet all accumulated evidence over the years is overwhelming.

Meanwhile, thousands of alleged victims and witnesses have emerged in recent post-Savile years providing incontrovertible evidence for arrest and prosecution sharing identical or similar corroborating accounts against the same identified VIP perps. Once the Savile scandal broke, both abuse that occurred recently as well as historic abuse reporting have soared, in just one year rising to over 31,000 reported cases, up by more than a third from the year before.[1528] Just based on media reports and police records alone, back in the 1980s thousands of British children in care homes were systematically trafficked around the UK and abroad, regularly abused by Britain and Europe's elite at many places, particularly Dolphin Square and Elm Guest House as well as dozens of other locations around the British Isles, Amsterdam and Brussels. Yet VIP convictions remain zero. The indisputable fact that the Establishment has historically shut down police investigations, wilfully destroyed or lost evidence, obstructed justice, chronically using the lie of never having enough evidence to prosecute every single powerful pedophile that's been accused (other than the minor *BBC* has-beens that can be counted on one hand), the fact that all the major politicians never go to jail proves beyond any question or doubt that the cover-up only continues.

It's sickening to know that so many victims have reported abuse to authorities yet UK's pedo-foxes infiltrated into key positions in government, police, Crown Protection Service, social services and the media have successfully closed ranks to tightly guard their pedo-henhouse, effectively blocking the truth from fully coming out, resulting in countless VIP perps never brought to justice. It's the same old despicably disgusting story - evildoers in high places abuse their power that allows them to forever get away with unimaginable, sordid perversions simply because it's their granted privilege as members of the pedo-elite. As the truth spreads amongst us citizens of the world who outnumber members of the VIP pedophilia club a zillion to one, our message is we're coming after you and your days of impunity are numbered.

Just like Jimmy Savile, Ted Heath, Cyril Smith and all the rest, virtually every accused VIP pedophile is permitted to safely live out their lives to the end, rotting away in their graves, or better yet, roasting in eternal hell, after never spending a single day in prison for all their heinous crimes. By design, overly stringent UK libel laws protect VIP criminals[1529] - made even more pedo-friendlier with Sir Cliff's July 2018 court victory[1530] (covered in last chapter), striking a major blow against both freedom of press and freedom of speech. And now morphing into

---

[1527] "British Police end VIP Child Abuse Investigation with no Arrests," *Sputnik*, March 23, 2016.
[1528] "Reports of Child Abuse Rising Sharply, NSPCC says," *BBC*, June 17, 2015.
[1529] Henry Williams, "How English Libel Laws Dent Free Speech across the Globe," *Spiked*, July 30, 2015.
[1530] Richard Spillett, "A British Weinstein would have got away with it: Experts say Mogul may never have Faced Justice if Sir Cliff Privacy Ruling was in place," *Daily Mail*, July 19, 2018.

Cliff's law, interchangeably synonymous with LIVING ABOVE THE LAW, it's designed to further seal off protection for perpetrators at the top. It delays if not eliminates unwanted exposure of prominent pedo-monsters until they're all safely buried in the ground from natural causes despite a lifetime of committing the most debaucherously unnatural transgressions.

Back in the 1980s when even mainstream newspapers dared to cover pedophilia ring arrests, after four ringleaders were caught and convicted, the *Daily Telegraph* crime correspondent admitted in a February 1989 piece:

Despite the convictions, police believe there is still a flourishing pedophile network in Britain, with a sophistication said to resemble the Mafia.[1531]

Of the four men convicted and sentenced, the one considered highest in rank was Colin Peters, an Oxford trained former senior advisor at the British Foreign Office,[1532] which exercises control over MI6 operations.[1533] For sodomizing young boys and pimping them to VIPs, he received only a 6-year sentence. Interrogated during the pedo-ring investigation was at least one senior member in the House of Lords, a West London vicar and a number of other government officials. Like always, VIPs at the higher levels avoid prosecution with the overly familiar excuse specified in *The Telegraph*:

But the police did not have sufficient evidence or manpower to pursue their suspicions.[1534]

Code word: VIPs are high enough on the British Establishment food chain to be immune from arrest. The pipeline procurers that did go to jail were/are bottom dwellers feeding off runaways, junior soccer league players as a probable MI6-Savile-Barry Bennell (see Chapter 18) link. Another source was one of the convicted pedo-ring operators owned a cleaning company business and would regularly advertise want ads in local newspapers for potential recruits. *The Telegraph* article went on to explain a familiar theme found throughout the global child abuse trafficking network on how boys as young as 9 get:

Passed around its [pedophile] *members for sexual degradation and, when the attraction faded, abandoned to a life of prostitution, drugs, and petty crime... The boys were tempted off the unfamiliar London streets with promises of food, accommodation, money, and a sympathetic ear. Some were plied with drugs, including cocaine, and sexually assaulted while under their influence.*[1535]

[1531] Mark Burdman, "Pedophiles Arrested in Britain more Powerful than the Mafia," *EIR*, February 17, 1989.

[1532] Mark Burdman, https://larouchepub.com/eiw/public/1989/eirv16n08-19890217/eirv16n08-19890217_042-pedophiles_arrested_in_britain_m.pdf.

[1533] Joseph Fitsanakis, "MI6 Chiefs used Secret Slush Fund to Finance Operations, Document Shows," *IntelNews.org*, November 22, 2017.

[1534] Mark Burdman, https://larouchepub.com/eiw/public/1989/eirv16n08-19890217/eirv16n08-19890217_042-pedophiles_arrested_in_britain_m.pdf.

[1535] Mark Burdman, https://larouchepub.com/eiw/public/1989/eirv16n08-19890217/eirv16n08-19890217_042-pedophiles_arrested_in_britain_m.pdf.

Police in Italy, UK and the US found links between Colin Peters' UK pedo-ring and the international network.[1536] A wealthy businessman in Italy, Allesandro Moncini, arrested in the US in 1988 for attempting to procure an underage girl for satanic ritual abuse served just three months in prison for smuggling child pornography.[1537] Italian investigators working in America believe they uncovered "a most exclusive ring of international pedophiles." Recall that the Vatican secret societies and P1 Masons work hand-in-hand together with bankers and organized crime in Italy, Europe and far beyond.[1538]

The satanic ritual abuse of trafficked children around the globe is perpetrated on victims of what experts maintain is a highly organized, sophisticated, interlocking network run by Illuminati, Freemasons, Malta Knights and Jesuits among other infiltrators operating at the highest levels of national governments, the intelligence community, law enforcement, the court system, organized crime, the military, charity organizations and mainstream media.

A mind control-child abuse victim turned courageous survivor-activist, Australian Fiona Barnett who as a child was passed around globally and raped by presidents, prime ministers, Reverend Billy Graham and a number of the world's most powerful men, has this to say in her International Tribunal of Natural Justice (ITNJ) testimony[1539] recalling her firsthand experience and direct observation:

Child trafficking is run as a **single integrated world operation**. *This operation is coordinated by the* **CIA** *in collaboration with British and Australian intelligence services. Retired NYPD Detective James Rothstein was appointed to the first US taskforce to investigate this child trafficking operation which, he found, went all the way up to the White House. Detective Rothstein found that the CIA were behind a blackmail operation in which child prostitutes were used to honeytrap and compromise politicians, military brass, top businessmen, and key government officials...* **Luciferianism** *is arranged according to a hierarchical structure which vaguely resembles a caste system. At the very top sit* **13 family dynasties** *including the* **Rothschilds** *and the* **British Royal Family**. *These are recognised by the cult as demi-gods. Below these sit approximately 300 Luciferian bloodlines who are generally high IQ, although this tends to have been watered down in some families due to intermarriage. Below this group sit the commoners who can never attain higher status because they lack the desired bloodline.*[1540] (Boldface for emphasis)

[1536] Mark Burdman, https://larouchepub.com/eiw/public/1989/eirv16n08-19890217/eirv16n08-19890217_042-pedophiles_arrested_in_britain_m.pdf.

[1537] Mark Burdman, https://larouchepub.com/eiw/public/1989/eirv16n08-19890217/eirv16n08-19890217_042-pedophiles_arrested_in_britain_m.pdf.

[1538] Conrad Goeringer, "Murder, Banking, Strategy – The Vatican," *voxfux.com*.

[1539] "Eye Opening ITNJ Testimony from Fiona Bartlett," YouTube video, 2018, 1:24:42, posted on September 7, 2018.

[1540] Fiona Barnett, "Witness Statement by Satanic Ritual Abuse Survivor, Fiona Barnett – Calling out her Pedophile Abusers," *prepareforchange.net*, September 3, 2018.

Other than her oversight not mentioning the Mossad-Zionist slant in the global pedo-operation, her insider insights are spot on accurately explaining how the Luciferian pedo-cabal works.

It's important to note again that Thatcher's Westminster scandal was flourishing at the same exact time that George Bush's CIA Finders Cult (Chapter 12) and his Nebraska to Washington Franklin scandals (Chapter 13) were also in high gear. The UK branch of this vast interconnected worldwide pedo-network was fronted by Prime Minister Thatcher, ravenously participated in by her derelict political cronies she fiercely protected and largely run by Savile and his British intelligence services coordinating procuring gangs like Colin Peter, Peter Righton and Sidney Cooke's recruiting from the streets and group homes. But only this lowest rung of pedophile traffickers are ever subject to busts and actual jail time. The rest of the low-lifes in this heinous operation remain insulated and unreachable from their elitist, thus far impenetrable perch.

Even before she became PM, no doubt Thatcher had accepted as a precondition to her storied rise to historic glory that it was her cabal duty to "appoint" her heavily MI5 vetted cabinet intentionally flooded with flaming pedophiles. After all, her biggest holiday guest was Britain's biggest pedophile ever. In the UK the precedent had already been set a full decade earlier with Savile as "deep cover" pimp supplying victims for another compromised Tory Party prime minister who happened to be a PIE linked brutal child rapist and coldblooded child murderer.[1541] Edward Heath had been strategically planted by his Luciferian puppet masters to secretly strip Britain of its national sovereignty, coercing it into what would become the European Union monstrosity.[1542] As saber rattling warmongers on steroids, both the Reagan/Bush and Thatcher role was to facilitate transference of Western oligarchic wealth out of UK/Europe/US as foreign investment largely into Asia, ushering in the next wave of neocolonialist theft in the longtime overexploited, conquered Third World, while introducing permanent austerity and hardship to the everyday British/US household trying to eke out daily survival in an increasingly hostile world on the brink of economic disaster.[1543]

From across the pond back in the 1980s, Maggie's chosen counterpart cutout Ronnie Reagan, for all intents and purposes, was replaced a little more than a month into office by a "wayward" bullet[1544] when his opportunistic CIA directing VP, crime family pedophile-drug overlord Daddy Bush moved in.[1545] Once the Luciferian controllers had their perfect US-UK-Zionist puppets in place, using their old divide and conquer standby, they heightened tensions in the Middle East, engineered the bloody Iraq-Iran War selling arms to both sides, promoted jingoistic expansion wars abroad, and created an emerging enemy called "war on terror" using Islam as

---

[1541] Laura Burnip, "Edward Heath 'Linked to a Murderous Paedophile Ring that Killed 16 Kids,'" *The Sun*, February 20, 2017..

[1542] Alan Sked, "How a Secretive Elite Created the EU to Build a World Government," *The Telegraph*, November 27, 2015.

[1543] Martin Sieff, "The Death of US and UK Neo-Colonialism," *Zero Hedge*, August 6, 2018.

[1544] Tony Bonn, "Did Bush Assassinate Reagan?" *The American Chronicle*, February 7, 2012.

[1545] David Malmo-Levine, "George H.W. Bush: Biggest Drug Lord Ever," *Cannabis Culture*, May 16, 2017.

scapegoat.[1546] Finally, they set the stage for the military industrial complex to become the driving force behind imperialistic Anglo-American-Zionist Empire aggression that's been ravaging the planet ever since.[1547]

Maggie, Ronnie and George simultaneously ushered in the death of the US[1548] and UK middle classes[1549] to deliver austerity and hardship overseeing a Fortune 500 exodus overseas for cheap Third World slave labor in order to gut the domestic manufacturing sectors. One in four manufacturing jobs disappeared within Thatcher's first term alone.[1550] And to ensure the undoing of America and UK proceeded as planned, sexual pedo-blackmail reigned supreme, producing treasonous compromised robots who smile on cue for the camera while their puppet masters celebrate in orgiastic satanic ritualized gluttony their New World Order fast closing in on absolute control over the masses during the home stretch of their depopulation plan called human genocide.[1551] Pretty despairing picture unless we stop the Luciferian sodomizers from raping and destroying our entire planet, now in the 11th hour and 59th minute.

Years after Bush senior and Iron Lady did their damage decimating US-UK middle class affluence and national sovereignty in favor of the ever-widening rich-poor inequality gap[1552] and predatory globalization,[1553] the NWO architects then installed their two bisexual cottage boys "Miranda" Blair and George W[1554] for their turn to drive the world closer to the edge. Bush-Cheney's treasonously masterminded, neo-conned "new Pearl Harbor" vis-a-vis 9/11 false flag was more dirty bidding for Netanyahu's Greater Israel Project.[1555] By elite design, the Anglo-American-Zionist axis-of-evil then launched its ambitious, willfully destructive 7 nation in 5 year takedown plan,[1556] demolishing Iraq, Libya, Sudan, Somalia, Lebanon and Afghanistan into failed states. A decade and a half later unfinished wars are still raging in Syria and the Afghan "empire graveyard" for illicit heroin production[1557] at the precipice gateway to the 7th and final

[1546] Arjun Walia, "How False Flag Terrorism and Religion are being used as a Means of Control," *bibliotecapleyades.net/Collective Evolution*, September 11, 2016.

[1547] Mika Freeman, "Has the US-Israel-UK war with Iran Officially started?" *Sleuth Journal*, January 25, 2018.

[1548] Wes Williams, "This Chart Shows how Reaganomics has Destroyed the Middle Class," *The Daily Banter*, August 8, 2017.

[1549] Owen Jones, "Class War: Thatcher's Attack on Trade Unions, Industry and Working-Class Identity," *versobooks.com*, April 8, 2013.

[1550] Aditya Chakrabortty, "Why doesn't Britain make things anymore?" *The Guardian*, November 16, 2011.

[1551] Steve Jones, "NOW Plans to Depopulate the Earth," *rense.com*, April 13, 2005.

[1552] Jason Beattie, "Inequality Gap between Rich and Poor in UK to be at Biggest since Margaret Thatcher was in Power," *Mirror*, February 1, 2017.

[1553] "Global Establishment Aspects of the Reagan Administration," *News of Interest.TV*, September 15, 2018.

[1554] Kevin Barrett, "Bush & Blair: Blackmailed Pedophiles or just War Criminals?" *Veterans Today*, June 21, 2014.

[1555] Christopher Bollyn, "9/11 and the War on Terror: Israel's History of False Flag Operations against the U.S.A.," *American Herald Tribune*, July 7, 2018.

[1556] Wesley Clark and Amy Goodman interview, "Global Warfare: 'We're Going to take out 7 Countries in 5 Years: Iraq, Syria, Lebanon, Libya, Somalia, Sudan & Iran...'", *Global Research/Democracy Now*, March 2, 2007.

[1557] Eric Margolis, "Afghanistan, Graveyard of Empires," *Lew Rockwell*, August 18, 2018.

vowed to vanquish nation prize Iran. The elite's diabolically twisted suicide pact is now plunging humanity off the Armageddon cliff.[1558]

Once the Anglo-American-Zionist pedo-axis manufactured its perpetual state of war in the Middle East and North Africa,[1559] the NWO architects engineered[1560] the earth's largest displaced population in history as of 2014 and in Europe a year later the worst refugee crisis since WWII.[1561] Flooding millions of Muslims into Europe and North America under the euphemistic Trojan horse guise of "multiculturalism," just to jack up the cultural, racial, religious divide and conquer violence and upheaval, bankrupting the euro[1562] and EU[1563] with Italy now at the breaking point,[1564] like dominos ultimately crashing the global economy just as elitist controllers trigger the West versus East WWIII showdown,[1565] the crime cabal is closing in on destroying the West and creating such dire, turbulent, desperate global conditions that offer the excuse to bring on the long awaited one world government as humanity's only "salvation" for survival. This is the child fuckers' nearly accomplished endgame as its sleight-of-hand answer to growing Achilles pedo-heel exposure.

In recent years the post-Savile revelations once again placed unwanted spotlight on that Achilles heel, especially the notorious Thatcher government and her Westminster scandal cover-up, featured partially in a book co-written by Labor MP Simon Danczuk exposing one larger-than-life, villainous character, the over 400 pound (29 stone, 12 pounds or 190kg[1566]) gluttonous pedophile Sir Cyril Smith.[1567] Hailing from the same Rochdale district, Simon Danczuk was elected the same year the rotund Sir Cyril died in 2010. In July 2014 Danczuk asked the doddering Leon Brittan what happened to those missing dossiers from the 1980s.[1568] Unfortunately exercising a gross lapse of moral judgment in 2015, the 50-year old married Danczuk was caught sexting a 17-year old girl a-la Weiner style,[1569] completely self-sabotaging whatever legitimate voice he had to further expose the pedophilia network. The Labor Party promptly suspended him and the same day he defiantly announced he'd run as an independent

---

[1558] Key Pieces on the Global Geopolitical Chessboard Are Being Stealthily Rearranged for the Hot Phase of World War III," *State of the Nation*, April 3, 2018.

[1559] "Stratfor Chief Reveals Zio-Anglo-American Plot for World Domination," *State of the Nation*, September 11, 2015.

[1560] Alex Newman, "Globalists who Created Refugee Crisis now Exploiting it," *The New American*, September 8, 2015.

[1561] Griff Witte, "New U.N. Report says World Refugee Crisis is Worse than anyone expected," *Washington Post*, .

[1562] Joseph Stiglitz, "The Euro could be nearing a Crisis – can it be saved?" *The Guardian*, June 13, 2018.

[1563] "Migration Crisis 'could be the Undoing of the EU,'" *Straits Times*, September 3, 2018.

[1564] Markos Kounalakis, "How Italy is Threatening the World Economy," *Washington Monthly*, October 21, 2018.

[1565] "Are we on the Brink of World War III?" *The Week*, September 4, 2018.

[1566] Paul Vallely, "Rochdale makes its mark at last, to the Regret of Mr Brown," *Independent*, April 30, 2010.

[1567] Nicholas Blincoe, "Smile for the Camera: The Double Life of Cyril Smith by Simon Danczuk and Matthew Baker, Review," *The Telegraph*, May 1, 2014.

[1568] Georgia Graham, "Simon Danczuk: I was Warned not to Challenge Leon Brittan over Paedophile Dossier," *The Telegraph*, July 6, 2014.

[1569] Nick Parker and Mile Sullivan, "MP Simon Danczuk Accused of Raping Young Woman in Westminster – but Insists he'll still stand in General Election despite Police Probe," *The Sun*, May 9, 2017..

in the 2017 general election, a young woman accused him of rape. Chalk up another victory for the pedophilia cabal subduing yet another potential threat who turned into little more than a historical footnote and another hypocritical perv.

The October 2012 Savile exposure inspired Labor Party leader MP Tom Watson to take up the cause that MP Geoffrey Dickens initiated three decades earlier to once again call for an a real police investigation looking into the pedo-infested British Parliament and prime minister office, forcing the then pedo-enabler Prime Minister David Cameron to begrudgingly initiate the latest "pseudo-probe" to placate public interest. With his dramatic October 24th, 2012 confrontation on the House of Commons floor, MP Watson demanded UK's prime minister and police:

Investigate clear intelligence suggesting a powerful pedophile network linked to Parliament and Number 10.[1570]

Dramatically caught off guard, Cameron halfheartedly pledged to look into the matter after pretending he didn't grasp which 10 Downing occupant Watson was referring to, knowing full well it was Margaret Thatcher.[1571] Of course technically it could've been Edward Heath, Gordon Brown or Tony Blair or even himself, as Cameron knew every UK prime minister over the last half century was/is a pedophile or pedophile protector. And as a cousin of PIE supporting Harriet Harman and 5th cousin to Queen Elizabeth herself,[1572] a loyal pedo-enabler to the end, three years later in October 2015 it was David Cameron self-righteously striking back, imploring anti-pedophile crusader Tom Watson to "examine his conscience."[1573]

After Watson dared to mention Lord Leon Brittan's alleged pedophilia (without even bringing up his infamous "lost" pair of pedo-dossiers), instantly Watson became an easy target having the nerve to call for a new investigation nine months after accused pedophile Brittan's death.[1574] The ensuing drama played out once again before the House with Cameron and his indignant fellow pro-Brittan-pro-pedo-defenders demanding Watson's resignation, yelling "shame, shame" after Watson reiterated the need to revisit investigating government pedophilia on behalf of the thousands of victims never heard nor ever given any true justice. The UK pedo-Establishment never fails to jump on the political bandwagon to demonize every rare MP who's ever been bold enough to try and hold their powerful pedo-peer majority accountable. Watson's righteous proposal obviously hit way too close to home for the untold number of VIP child rapists in his audience.

[1570] Martin Hickman, "England: Land of Royals, Tea and Horrific Pedophilia Coverups," *Time Magazine*, July 10, 2014.

[1571] Tim Wilkinson, "Paedo Files: A Look at the UK Establishment Child Abuse Network," *Lobster Magazine*.

[1572] Stuart Heritage, "Please don't say I'm Related to David Cameron," *The Guardian*, January 29, 2014.

[1573] Rajeev Syal, "David Cameron: Tom Watson should Examine his Conscience," *The Guardian*, October 12, 2015.

[1574] "Tom Watson's Defiant Response to Cameron's Leon Brittan Statement is Perfect, YouTube video, posted on October 12, 2015, 9:32.

In 2014 Home Office then under current Prime Minister Theresa May admitted to 114 pedo-related files gone missing or destroyed.[1575] With so much "lost" evidence bolstering their "never enough evidence" mantra, by design the pedophilia epicenter of the world appears totally incapable or more apt totally unwilling to honestly hold establishment pedophiles accountable. Hence, Operation Midland ostensibly set up in late 2014 to investigate the alleged Westminster MP pedophilia scandal collapsed for "lack of evidence."[1576] Though both Operations Midland and Fairbridge were specifically set up after Savile died to investigate government VIP abuse, both probes shamefully failed to arrest a single Elm Guest House or Dolphin Square VIP... some things never change.

Then Metro Police's onetime key witness "Nick" whose accusations (along with unnamed others) between 2012 and 2014 of widespread abuse and alleged witnessing three boys murdered deemed "credible and true,"[1577] by top cop himself, suddenly was charged with the crime of perverting justice with so called "made up" lies.[1578] This latest legal development is meant to frighten off victims from ever coming forth. So the government pedophiles once again remain fully protected and unreachable. And with Theresa May's floundering national "independent" Inquiry hoax into child sexual abuse refusing to include Northern Ireland's MI5-Savile-Mountbatten-Heath-Blunt linked Kincora Boys Home scandal,[1579] nothing ever changes.[1580] Because all these biggest VIP names in British pedophilia all directly linked to royalty striking at the heart of the UK pedo-cover-up, Prime Minister May will never dare allow the Kincora scandal enter her pathetic whitewash.

Incidentally, a former detective probing early Jimmy Savile crimes angrily maintained that fellow pedophile, royal historian, MI5 double spy and traitor Sir Anthony Blunt successfully blocked police investigations into the infamous *BBC* DJ,[1581] just one more indicator that Savile was an employed MI5 operative. Of course for Soviet spy Blunt's confession of treason, as a member of the "hidden elite," in 1964 Blunt was granted full immunity from prosecution as both a pedophile and national traitor, and protection from public exposure for another fifteen years.[1582] This allowed Blunt to freely travel to Northern Ireland often to sodomize yet more

[1575] "British Government expected to Launch Child Sex Abuse Investigation," *Associated Press/The Journal ie*, July 7, 2014.

[1576] Sandra Laville and Rajev Syal, "Operation Midland: Inquiry into Alleged VIP Paedophile Ring Collapses," *The Guardian*, March 21, 2016.

[1577] Dan MacGuill, "UK Police: We believe Witness who says an MP Murdered a Boy during an 'Abuse Party,'" *The Journal.ie*, December 18, 2014.

[1578] Vikram Dodd, "Man who said he was Victim of VIP Child Sexual Abuse Ring Charged," *The Guardian*, July 3, 2018.

[1579] "International Network – Whistleblower Kerr," *aangirfan.com*, December 4, 2017.

[1580] Anne St. Claire, "Rothschild's Friend Sir Anthony Blunt & their International Child Abuse Ring," *1776 Again*, January 10, 2018.

[1581] Anne St. Claire, http://www.1776again.com/2018/01/10/rothchilds-friend-sir-anthony-blunt-their-international-child-abuse-ring/.

[1582] John Burns, "Memoirs of British Spy offer no Apology," *The New York Times*, July 23, 2009.

boys from Kincora and other group homes in the area, again with impunity and without fear of exposure or arrest.

According to the late British intelligence insider Anthony T. Stokes, Victor Rothschild, Anthony Blunt and many other Establishment VIPs practiced satanic ritual abuse and murder at their black magick orgies, specifying that Blunt asphyxiated child victims causing their bodies to contract to heighten the orgasm for the sodomizer.[1583] Jimmy Savile was right at home in this top of the predator food chain element, the above the law club of monsters ruling our planet that ensures protection of their own.

A former MI6 agent assigned to surveillance of right wing loyalist extremist groups in Northern Ireland has reported that British intelligence was fully aware of both illegal arms trafficking as well as child sex trafficking but looked the other way not wanting to blow its cover or "tread on the toes" of the Ulster Constabulary.[1584] The ex-spy claimed a sophisticated international pedophile ring trafficked boys from Kincora Home to London, Brighton, and abroad to Amsterdam and Vienna. The simple reason nothing was done to intervene to save the exposable children being sodomized wholesale is that it was a British intelligence operation to traffic children to gain sexual blackmail control over politicians both domestic and foreign.[1585] For many, many decades now, multiple child sex slaves have been moved around the globe through the massive worldwide pedophilia network primarily coordinated through the international intelligence community, particularly the CIA, Mossad and both MI5 and MI6.

Just like the Vatican and Catholic Church, the royal crown, the UK government, the *BBC* and entire British Establishment's long been completely taken over by Luciferian demons. For the pedophilia crisis endemic inside the putrefying United Kingdom to ever effectively be ameliorated, much less eradicated, the entire government needs to be scrapped and totally replaced from ground zero up. The US and virtually the entire Western world are in the same pathetically depraved dire straits. But since we know that will likely not happen any time soon, a good place to start would be to at least replace Britain's antiquated, grossly unfair, abominable family court system.

As it's existed, the UK's secret closed court system has been in the diabolical business of systematically breaking up and destroying British families, removing children en masse from parents without justifiable or due cause, and unmercifully sending them to be further abused in institutionalized "care"[1586] that serves as the child raping pipeline for the international sex trafficking trade. By sinister design, this enormous systemic flaw in Britain has allowed the vitally fundamental social institution of family to be obliterated, literally killing both children

[1583] Anthony T. Stokes, "One World Government Coming Soon," *Illuminati Archives*, March 3, 2010.
[1584] James Fielding, "MI6 Covered up Historic Child Sex Abuse Ring Discovered during Surveillance Operation," *Independent*, April 12, 2015.
[1585] Lesley-Anne McKeown, "MI5 'used Sexual Abuse of Children at Kincora to Blackmail the Politician Paedophiles,'" *Independent*, May 31, 2016.
[1586] Lara Prendergast, "The Sinister Power of Britain's Family Courts," *The Spectator*, September 9, 2017.

and parents alike, customarily placing kids in peril within the very broken system set up to protect them, just as my own direct experience as a child therapist in America confirmed.[1587] In keeping children safe, like the one in America, the British child welfare system has only proven to be a failed abomination that like its larger government needs drastic overhaul.

This same diabolical dysfunction and process currently gripping both the US and UK's child welfare systems is largely replicated worldwide. But then for a very long time the international cabal has also insidiously been at war with the basic family institution, particularly the diminishing nuclear family unit as an impediment to the cultural Marxism inherently behind today's entrenched neoliberal movement embracing one world government totalitarianism.[1588] On May Day in 1776 Illuminati funder Baron Rothschild and founder Adam Weishaupt concurred, the basic family unit along with religion and national sovereignty were identified as the primary enemies obstructing their path to centrally controlled tyranny and coveted prize of one world government.[1589] Weishaupt also articulated the key value of strategically deploying sexual blackmail as the Illuminati's "ends always justify the means" Modus Operandi.[1590]

In 2013 newly appointed President of the High Court Family Division Judge James Munby went public stating that the most drastic legal matter that British judges deal with today is the pervasive removal of UK children from their families.[1591] Judge Munby has called for a more transparent and open family court system that doesn't systemically place gag orders on parents from being able to speak to the press. Munby also wants to reform the system to make both the court decisions available to the public as well as the identity of judges, social workers, attorneys and expert witnesses known. In the past too many parents with legitimate grievous complaints have been unjustly imprisoned for calling for public scrutiny in family court cases where gross miscarriage of justice is regularly perpetrated. But the wall of resistance to Sir Munby's proposed changes that supports the status quo of institutionalized child abuse and the prevailing pedophilia epidemic still rigidly persists.[1592] Paradoxically, family court has used strict confidentiality laws to ostensibly "protect" the anonymity of children as its primary justification for secrecy when in fact it's been tearing the institution of family apart for systematically placing children at far greater risk of harm.

Another despicable misdeed willfully imposed by Justice Secretary Jack Straw in April 2009 intended to strengthen the blight of British pedophilia impunity was his unilaterally changing British law to prohibit children in group home care to the basic human right of speaking out

[1587] Joachim Hagopian, "The Failures of America's Foster Care System," *Global Research*, July 19, 2014.

[1588] Anthony Mueller, "Is Cultural Marxism America's New Mainline Ideology?" *Mises Wire*, October 10, 2018.

[1589] William H. McIlhaney, "A Primer on the Illuminati," *New American*, June 12, 2009.

[1590] Sonny René Stermole, *America's Subversion The Enemy Within,* Chapter 2, "The Plan is Hatched," *bibliotecapleyades.net*.

[1591] Steve Doughty, "Top Judge's War on Secret Courts: Family Hearings must be Exposed to 'Glare of Publicity,'" *Daily Mail*, September 5, 2013.

[1592] Nicholas Watt, "Family Court must Open up to Avoid 'Outrageous Injustices,' warns Ukip," *The Guardian*, October 26, 2015.

against abuse or maltreatment received while trapped in the closed off, insulated child welfare system.[1593] Step by step in the face of increasing exposure of the ongoing Savile-Westminster scandal, the elite has closed ranks to busily construct systemic barriers designed to muzzle and frighten victims and seal off the no longer free press from unveiling the filthy truth.

Because of the proliferating exposure of Savile related abuse along with so many other high profile pedo-scandals like Pizzagate/Pedogate in recent years gaining traction in growing citizens' awareness of the ruling elite's global child sex trafficking epidemic,[1594] as mentioned previously the pedo-cabal in the UK has aggressively pushed back with two enormous court victories culminating in the same month of July 2018. The prospect of placing alleged abuse victim "Nick" behind bars for so called false allegations of a murderous Westminster pedophile ring lends the pretext for officially proclaiming the entire British VIP scandal an exaggerated myth and total hoax.[1595] Then days later Sir Cliffy destroys what little freedom of the press is left, rendering its future capacity to report on and investigate high profile pedo-suspects impotent.[1596] No doubt these days UK's pedo-elite are celebrating in their mansions as these recent relatively unknown monumental setbacks validating VIP pedophiles' above-the-law immunity from justice only embolden the powerful British Establishment to commit yet more crimes against innocent children.

This sad reality must change and we the people as protectors of our children must make it happen. A good place to start is advocating for truth and reconciliation commissions, supporting organizations like the International Tribunal for Natural Justice (ITNJ), presently gathering testimony from victim-turned-survivors[1597]

With the cabal's designated blackmail "specialists" Jimmy Savile and Jeffrey Epstein working in cahoots with the global intelligence community, joined by popes, corrupt churches, royalty, organized crime and their infiltrating satanic secret society allies, each dutifully play out their respective roles facilitating sexual blackmail pedophilia operations to gain absolute control over puppet politicians worldwide.[1598] Figureheads like Maggie, Blair and Cameron along with their US counterparts the Bushes, Clintons and Obamas serve as chosen (not elected[1599]) public face pedophile overlords while behind the scenes their Luciferian bloodline masters quietly pull their order-following strings.[1600]

[1593] "Justice Ministry to Bar Parents from telling their own Stories," *Independent*, February 15, 2009.
[1594] Joachim Hagopian, "Pizzagate turned PedoGate Leads to Momentum Surge in Busting Global Child Sex Trafficking Rings," *sott.net*, February 27, 2017.
[1595] Chris Baynes, "Westminster Paedophile Accuser 'Nick' Charged with Perverting Course of Justice over Sex Abuse Ring Claims," *Independent*, July 3, 2018.
[1596] Roy Greenslade, "The Cliff Richard Ruling is a Chilling Blow to Press Freedom," *The Guardian*, July 18, 2018.
[1597] "International Tribunal for Natural Justice," *itnj.org*.
[1598] Roger Landry, "Ultimate Control: Politicians, Pedophilia & Blackmail," *The Liberty Beacon*, October 8, 2018.
[1599] Tyler S. Bloyer, "Presidents are Selected – not Elected," *steemit.com*, 2017.
[1600] Joachim Hagopian, "As Treasonous Bush-Clinton-Obama Pedo Cabal Dynasty gets Exposed, Desperate Elite Steps up War against Humanity," *sott.net*, March 31, 2017.

Sir Jimmy Savile is linked to both abusing and pimping kids at virtually every major group home scandal in Britain. From Jersey Island's Haut de la Garenne[1601] to Elm Guest House,[1602] he was there. From Islington[1603] to North Wales Bryn Estyn[1604] where 650 children from a total of 40 group homes were sexually assaulted,[1605] from Northern Ireland's Kincora Boys Home[1606] to Surrey's Duncroft School for Girls, Sir Jimmy was there doing his satanic thing for queen and country.[1607]

And now after violating more victims in Britain, including dead bodies, than any other known sexual predator, alive or dead, the government-sponsored broadcast company that while knowing his savagery, paid him big bucks to use its expansive facilities as convenient crime scenes, the BBC has announced that it will showcase a miniseries on Sir Jimmy Savile called "The Reckoning." [1608] What this series is guaranteed to not show is how the BBC's top management as well as the British government signed off on his lifetime of despicable perversions, all the while protecting him from all accountability. It only adds insult to injury to have this BBC criminal accomplice that aided and abetted the monster for decades on end now create yet another whitewash that will never reveal the truth that Savile was the British Establishment's go-to pimp, satanically procuring children for prime ministers and royalty. For the BBC to parade this rehash before the public when the scourge of pedophilia rages more out of control than ever before is an insult to every child in this world who's ever been sexually abused.

One big orgiastic demonic death cult dance uses the elite's flourishing child sex trade booming larger than ever today[1609] to own and control the planet and their minions through sexual blackmail[1610] carried out with an accompanying permanent war against humanity agenda[1611] that includes spreading global destabilization, deploying military wars around the world, using a

---

[1601] Josh Halliday, Katharine Viner and Lisa O'Carroll, "Jimmy Savile linked with Haut de la Garenne Children's Home Scandal," *The Guardian*, October 9, 2012.

[1602] Fiona O'Cleirigh and Mark Watt, https://www.exaronews.com/met-detectives-told-of-jimmy-savile-s-link-to-elm-guest-house.

[1603] Robert Mendick and Eileen Fairweather, "Margaret Hodge 'Sorry' as Council she led told to Investigate Savile Abuse Allegations," *The Telegraph*, April 26, 2014.

[1604] "Jimmy Savile linked to North Wales Child Abuse Scandal," *The Telegraph*, November 7, 2012.

[1605] Clare Hutchinson, "Investigation into Child Abuse in North Wales Care Homes finds new Evidence of 'Systematic and Serious Sexual and Physical Abuse,'" *Wales Online*, April 29, 2013.

[1606] "Kincora – CIA, Mossad, MI5, MI6 – The Bigger Picture," *aangirfan.com*, March 22, 2017.

[1607] Chris Greenwood and Richard Spillett, "Jimmy Savile Abused 23 Girls at Duncroft for Disturbed Teenage Girls," *Daily Mail*, April 29, 2015.

[1608] Chris Sweeney, "The BBC is Reviving the Life and Crimes of its Former Star Jimmy Savile with an Ill-Conceived Drama Nobody Wants to See," *RT*, October 15, 2020.

[1609] Allison Chawla, "The Disturbing Reality of Human Trafficking and Children, in Today's World…," *Huffington Post*, February 25, 2017.

[1610] Fiona Barnett, "Watergate was Pedogate," *The Millennium Report*, July 30, 2018.

[1611] Ajamu Baraka, "The Responsibility to Protect the World… from the United States," *Counter Punch*, January 12, 2018.

litany of both fast and soft kill eugenic methods,[1612] increasing unregulated covert psychotronic warfare,[1613] nonstop disinfo propaganda and mass mind control.[1614]

All this while the planetary controllers' collapsing, unsustainable global economy now shuddering in death throe implosion,[1615] has been orchestrated to tighten the neo-feudal grip of their debtor slavery system[1616] along with unprecedented global habitat destruction[1617] that's fast leading to earth's sixth mass life extinction and first by a demonically executed agenda of human genocide.[1618] Meanwhile, depopulation doomsday globalist Bill Gates has recently been at it again, frothing at the mouth to raise alarm over the impending "30 million dead" pandemic from infectious diseases,[1619] doing his nefarious duty to prep humanity for forced vaccination[1620] amidst false flag biological warfare terrorism,[1621] like AIDS[1622] and Ebola[1623] launched out of a Fort Detrick Petri dish.

Just in case it somehow escaped your attention, it appears that to even be considered qualified for such regal honors as British royal knighthood, you must already be a card carrying member of the VIP pedophilia club first. That way, every compromised politician holding higher office is subject to sexual blackmail and control by elite fascist Anglo-American-Zionist interest.[1624] To the pedophilic puppet masters and their sexually blackmailed politician pawns throughout the world, it's never been about sworn oaths of loyalty to any one country or one's country of citizenship, not with Israeli first dual citizens comprising the embedded neocon core still running Washington, or when a handful of Luciferian families from a few nations (most notably yet not exclusively from the West)[1625] are pulling international cabal strings rapidly bringing

[1612] Joachim Hagopian, "The Globalists' New World Order: Soft and Hard Kill Methods. An Unknown and Uncertain Future," *Global Research*, May 23, 2015.

[1613] Deb Chakraborty, "What is Mind Control / Psychotronic Torture?" *geeldon.wordpress.com*, September 6, 2011.

[1614] Dave Ratcliffe, "Mind Control, Psychological Operations, Propaganda and Disinformation," *Hidden History Center*, August 24, 2016.

[1615] Thomas Peter, "Asian Stock Markets pick up where Plunging Wall Street left off," *Reuters/CBS News*, October 11, 2018.

[1616] Ghasson Kadi, "The Fallacy of Western Economics; Slavery in Disguise," *The Saker*, September 7, 2018.

[1617] James Allan, "Half the World's Ecosystems at Risk from Habitat Loss, and Australia is one of the Worst," *The Conversation*, December 14, 2016.

[1618] Doyle Rice, "'Biological Annihilation:' Earth's 6th Mass Extinction is Underway," *USA Today*, July 10, 2017.

[1619] Meghan Bartels, "Bill Gates: Pandemic Disease Threat could Kill 30 Million People in just 6 months," *Newsweek*, April 28, 2018.

[1620] Rima Laibow, "Forced Vaccination is a Crime against Humanity," *Dr. Rima Reports*.

[1621] Zachary Crockett, "Geoengineering Is Biological Warfare," *Geoengineering Watch*, May 21, 2015.

[1622] Alan Cantwell, "More Evidence HIV was made at Ft. Detrick," *rense.com*, June 2, 2007.

[1623] Fabríz'zio Txavarría Velázquez, "The Ebola Virus was Handled Biologically by USA at Fort Detrick as a Weapon," *Progresismo Humano*, August 17, 2014.

[1624] Ghali Hasson, "Stand up to Anglo-Zionist Fascism," *Counter Currents*, July 14, 2017.

[1625] Richard Enos, "Why we need to stand up to the Illuminati together right now," *Collective Evolution*, August 24, 2018.

mounting geopolitical conflict, polarization, destabilization, uninterrupted war, financial hardship, economic disparity[1626] and psychological trauma worldwide.[1627]

In the meantime, widespread battlefields of war and overcrowded migrant camps caused by all the manufactured global conflict provide the ideal cover and setting for trafficking illegal arms,[1628] illegal drugs,[1629] illegal child sex slaves,[1630] illegal body parts[1631] and illegally laundered trillions into the pedophilic elite's international crime coffers,[1632] which in turn are misused to finance the deep underground military bases,[1633] secret deep space program and limitless, deep pocketed CIA-DARPA black budgets[1634] and black ops[1635] that include Frankensteinian research into genetic engineering across species interbreeding,[1636] Artificial Intelligence,[1637] transhumanism,[1638] robotics,[1639] mass mind control,[1640] advanced technological warfare[1641] amongst numerous other completely unknown, dangerously destructive, nightmarish developments. As Luciferian masters of secrecy and deceit, all participants involved are betrayers of their constitutions, their governments, their nations, the entire human race, our planet and our One Creator.[1642]

In recent years the NWO movement towards the coveted one world government and Luciferian one world religion has accelerated its collision course in a race against time[1643] while the ruling elite's hourglass to materialize such dire, deplorable and extreme conditions risks running out

[1626] Helene D. Gayle, "Top 10 Trends of 2014: 2. Widening Income Disparities," *World Economic Forum Report*, 2014.

[1627] Kevin Zeese and Margaret Flowers, "New U.S. Focus on Great Power Conflict and Nuclear Supremacy," *Consortium News*, February 5, 2018.

[1628] "Arms Trafficking," *havocscope.com*.

[1629] Frank Dux," American Made: CIA Drug and Sex Trafficking in the National Interest," *artvoice.com*, October 27, 2017..

[1630] Ewelina U. Ochab, "Human Trafficking is a Pandemic of the 21st Century," *Forbes*, July 26, 2018.

[1631] Joachim Hagopian, "Israel is the Organ Harvesting and Human Trafficking Global Ringleader, with Complicit Help from US and Turkey," *sott.net*, May 14, 2016.

[1632] "Transnational Crimes are Crimes that occur across National Borders," *scribd.com*..

[1633] Preston James, "Developing, Mastering and Weaponizing New Technology to Control you," *Veterans Today*, August 6, 2018.

[1634] Arjun Walia, "'The Black Budget.' This is what the 'Secret Government' doesn't want you to know," *Collective Evolution*, June 29, 2016.

[1635] James Casbolt, "MI6 are the Lords of the Global Drug Trade," *bibliotecapleyades.net*.

[1636] Fritz Springmeir, "Clones, Synthetics, Organic Robotoids and Doubles," *bibliotecapleyades.net*.

[1637] John Naughton, "Don't Worry about AI going bad – the Minds behind it are the Danger," *The Guardian*, February 25, 2018.

[1638] Alexander Thomas, "Super-Intelligence and Eternal Life: Transhumanism's Faithful follow it Blindly into a Future for the Elite," *The Conversation*, July 31, 2017.

[1639] Robert Hackett, "Leaked Video Reveals 'Nightmare Inducing' Google Robot," *Fortune*, February 2, 2017.

[1640] Steve Jacobson, "Mind Control Theories and Techniques used by Mass Media," *Vigilant Citizen*, April 28, 2010.

[1641] Thomas Macaulay and Tamlin Magee, "The Future of Technology in Warfare: From Drone Swarms to VR Torture," *Tech World*, April 18, 2018.

[1642] Peter B. Meyer, "The Truly Most Evil Enemy: The Deep State's Traitors," *finalwakeupcall.info*, August 8, 2018.

[1643] Michael Snyder, "Moving toward a One World Government, a One World Economy and a One World Religion," *Zero Hedge*, October 19, 2015.

of time before the slumbering masses wake up. The elites' desperate timetabled mission through increasing geopolitical instability, global earth surface turmoil, massive censorship (especially targeting the worldwide web), draconian oppression and tyranny[1644] is intended to thwart critical mass from taking hold when enough informed, educated and empowered, pissed off citizens around the globe ultimately unite in solidarity[1645] to demand the planetary controlling pedophiles finally be held fully accountable for all their crimes against both children and humanity. That day is soon approaching… if the enemy elite doesn't unleash their Armageddon and nuclear winter agenda first.[1646]

Chapter 23 exposes the full gamut of the widespread UK government pedophilia scandal and its never-ending cover-up that's been allowed to flourish for far too many decades. By self-serving design, the criminal concealment of pedophilic crimes has enabled Establishment VIPs to always live above the law due to designated pedophile foxes always guarding their pedo-henhouse through centrally controlled, fully sabotaged police investigations and totally bogus "independent" child sex abuse Inquiries never leading anywhere, co-opted by the pedophile-infiltrated, thoroughly corrupted government, high courts, security intelligence, social services and mainstream media. Sadly, the pedo-cabal at the earth's epicenter - not so Great Britain - remains a fully operational, thriving criminal enterprise to this very day.

[1644] Thomas Scripps, "European Union Announces Draconian Internet Censorship Measures," *wsws.org*, September 20, 2018.
[1645] Nozomi Hayase, "Why Americans Need to Defend Julian Assange's Freedom," *Common Dreams*, July 27, 2018.
[1646] Steven Starr, "Turning a Blind Eye towards Armageddon - U.S. Leaders Reject Nuclear Winter Studies," *Federation of American Students*, January 9, 2017.

Chapter 7: Tony Blair, his Pedo-Infested Ministers and how Zionism and Pedophilia Reign Supreme

This section will chronicle in full detail the systematic child abuse and nonstop cover-up of the British government protecting its own army of hardcore pedophiles who for over a half century have been free to act out their child raping pathology against UK's most vulnerable population – children in group home care. The massive evidence is overwhelming yet to this very day not one politician in the UK Parliament or prime minister cabinet has ever been brought to justice. Britain is a disgrace to the entire world, serving as just the tip of the iceberg permitting hundreds, if not thousands over the years of prominent serial child sexual predators shielded in high places to permanently wound as well as murder millions of their own innocents without paying for their scourge of diabolical violent crimes. They have gotten away with it forever because pedophiles and their enablers who've long saturated government, high courts, police, civil servants, British intelligence, the media and royal family have all made certain this out of control epidemic is kept hidden from exposure and accountability.

Though Sir Jimmy may have been one central connecting hub within this despicable national operation, with or without him, the UK government is still guilty of perpetrating the sickest perversions against its own defenseless children living throughout the British Isles and beyond. The heinously pervasive practice sodomizing this nation's little boys in particular, since violating young males appears to be the overwhelming sexual preference amongst so many of UK's pedophile politicians, earns the not-at-all-great Britain the dubious distinction as the pedophilia epicenter of this entire world, with Belgium, Netherlands, North America and Australia not far behind.

This section will methodically begin by covering various major scandals around England with later chapters focusing on those in Wales, Northern Ireland and Scotland (along with connections to the wider international pedophilia network) involving sexual crimes committed by prominent Westminster and Downing Street politicians against targeted child victims from mostly group homes, special schools and the pedophile "home" away from home - railway station public toilets frequented by predatory PMs and MPs on the prowl for underage runaways and rent boys.

After interviewing scores of abuse victims over the years who identified powerful VIPs atop the British government as their perpetrators, longtime child activist-journalist Sonia Poulton has turned over her findings to the police. In an article written for *Express* in March 2014, she asks why not one of the accused pedophiles has ever been arrested or prosecuted.[1647] She cites the sheer hypocrisy of the mini-scandal making headlines at the time involving prominent Labor politicians Harriet Harmon, husband Jack Dromey and Patricia Hewitt's past NCCL-PIE association in comparison with the glaring avoidance of the real tragedy - that household names of those who remain unscathed after having committed the most heinous acts imaginable are still walking free:

I have heard stories of satanic ritual abuse, a significant factor in many paedophile rings, at the hands of household-name parliamentarians past and present.[1648]

Sonia interviewed whistleblowing former British intelligence officer Andrea Davison who confirms what we've already come to know:

Paedophiles are a staple of parliamentary life and have been for some decades. She [Andrea Davison] *claimed that MPs have been filmed abusing children and this footage is used to blackmail parliamentarians into acquiescing on issues of global importance.[1649]*

And those issues of "global importance" you can bet have everything to do with the Anglo-American-Zionist Axis-of-Evil's agenda to eugenically depopulate the planet through war and manmade disease,[1650] make pedophilia legal (Chapter 2) and gain absolute tyrannical control through one world government as humanity's false savior promoting UN Agendas 21 and 2030 and the UN's star-studded "Global Goals."[1651]

In an interview for a 1995 TV documentary, UK Conservative Party Whip Tim Fortescue (1970-73) demonstrated a rare display of matter-of-fact honesty:

Anyone with any sense, who was in trouble, would come to the whips and tell them the truth, and say, 'Now I'm in a jam. Can you help?' It might be debt, it might be ... a scandal involving small boys, or any kind of scandal in which ... a member seemed likely to be mixed up. They'd come and ask if we could help, and if we could, we did. We would do everything we can because we would store up brownie points. That sounds a pretty nasty reason but one of the reasons is, if we can get a chap out of trouble, he'll do as we ask forever more.[1652]

Strings are always attached once MPs are helped out of a jam, thereafter remaining beholding to the party whip or risk exposure, a variation of the familiar blackmail theme. With this reality the standardized norm and unwritten rule etched in stone, coercion politics through "owed

---

[1647] Sonia Poulton, "Paedophile MPs are Mocking British Law," *Express*, March 2, 2014.

[1648] Sonia Poulton, "Paedophile MPs are Mocking British Law," *Express*, March 2, 2014.

[1649] Sonia Poulton, "Paedophile MPs are Mocking British Law," *Express*, March 2, 2014.

[1650] Colin Todhunter, "Poisoned Agriculture: Depopulation and Human Extinction," *CounterPunch*, November 10, 2015.

[1651] Michael Snyder, "One World Government: How The Elite Dominate The World – Part 5: The Endgame Is Complete And Utter Global Domination," *theeconomiccollapseblog.com*, 2015.

[1652] Toby Helm, "Black Books, Threats and Rumour: Secrets of the Whips may be laid Bare," *The Guardian/The Observer*, July 12, 2014.

favors" and sexual blackmail become the primary control mechanism by which puppet politicians dutifully dance to their masters' tunes.

Since this chapter focuses on the role that Tony Blair and his ministers have played in promulgating government VIP pedophilia and its cover-up, prior to addressing his heavily infiltrated pedophile and pedo-enabling cabinet, a cursory examination of Anthony Charles Lynton Blair's pedo-tendencies himself provide a broader contextual background and linkage leading to today's pedophilia pandemic. Former Prime Minister Tony Blair's past includes sexual deviance with a predilection for crossdressing, frequenting public toilets in lustful search of young boys, a pair of college mentors who were confirmed pedophiles, and his subsequent blackmail at the hands of the Mossad and Zionist Israel to join his equally compromised American counterpart George W. Bush Jr similarly possessing the same proclivities.[1653] 9/11, the War on Terror and invasions of Afghanistan and Iraq were all machinations reflecting Zionism's far-reaching global reach and control through sexual blackmail manipulating the United States and Great Britain to fight Greater Israel Project wars, forcing them into Israel's bloody bidding.[1654]

A highly significant, telling fact and certainly no accident, during Blair's 10-years as prime minister from 1997 to 2007, the number of missing children in the United Kingdom nearly doubled, rising from 570 in 1997 to 950 in 2007.[1655] Knowing his perverted history of lies and deception and scandalous misconduct throughout both his life and decade in power, the disturbing reality that missing kids nearly doubled on his watch alone is in accordance with his evil misdeeds providing a boom for both Zionism and the globalized child raping network, two related entities that later in the chapter will be further elaborated.

While attending the Edinburgh boys' boarding school Fettes, the type taken up with homoerotic spanking rituals as typical subject matter in Lord Longford, Sir Jimmy and Sir Cliff's 1972 bestseller *Pornography* (covered in Chapter 20), "Miranda" the crossdressing collegiate was regularly visited by Irish loyalist Sir Knox Cunningham, a confirmed lover of boys.[1656] Cunningham was part of a pedophile ring that ran in the same circles as royal family curator and treasonous pedo-Russian spy Sir Anthony Blunt and William McGrath, an MI5 operative-right wing loyalist-housemaster-convicted pedophile at Northern Ireland's Kincora boys' home in 1981 (fully addressed in Chapter 26).[1657] The onetime MP and PM Macmillan cabinet secretary, Knox Cunningham was also friends with other Cambridge spies, fellow pedophile traitor Guy Burgess and Lord Victor Rothschild (Thatcher's foreign adviser),[1658] and additionally financed William McGrath's Protestant paramilitaries that also maintained close ties with Zionist

[1653] Kevin Barrett, "Bush and Blair: Blackmailed Pedophiles or just War Criminals?" *Veterans Today*, June 21, 2014.
[1654] Kevin Barrett, https://www.veteranstoday.com/2014/06/21/bushnblair/.
[1655] "Top UK Paedophile Rings," *aangirfan.com*, September 1, 2011.
[1656] Tony Blair and Child Abusers," *aangirfan.com*, February 12, 2010.
[1657] "Top UK Paedophile Rings," https://aangirfan.blogspot.com/2011/08/top-uk-pedophile-rings.html.
[1658] Joseph De Burca, "Sex Abuse Musical Chairs," *Village Magazine*, June 12, 2017.

gangsters' illegally supplying Israeli weapons... again confirming another of many Zionist-pedophilia-Blair connections.

Moreover, during Tony Blair's years at Fettes (1966-1971) prior to his Oxford education, "Miranda" had befriended his spiritual mentor the school chaplain, Rev. Ronald Selby Wright, a popular Church of Scotland minister with links to both the military and boys clubs.[1659] Wright reputedly preyed on Fettes students and in his final summer at the Scottish boarding school, Blair ran a summer camp for Wright's kids. From age 13 to 18, possessing such close relationships with significantly older male role models who were known pedophiles strongly suggests he himself may have been victimized. With disgraced alt-right poster boy Milo Yiannopoulis, a fine line exists between victim and predator when it comes to his own pederast relationships.[1660] If truth be known, Blair might admit he too enjoyed his relationships with older, powerful mentoring males he so much admired as they groomed him for bigger and better things.

Former British intelligence operative Anthony T. Stokes has written that in 1983 Tony Blair was caught soliciting sex from underage boys in a police surveilled London public restroom, "importuning in public toilets."[1661] Required to appear at the Bow Street Magistrate Court where he used his two middle names "Charles Lynton," Blair thereby avoided a career ending scandal as a brand new elected Member of Parliament. Court records, police notes and evidence of several prior verbal warnings were later "disappeared."[1662] With a past history of sexual deviance, the protected Tony Blair became the perfect candidate to be groomed for higher office as an easily blackmail-able, thoroughly compromised puppet for Mossad-Zionist control to commit British soldiers and nation against the people's will to disaster dying on Middle Eastern battlefields using deadly WMD lies to sell more wars for Israel killing over a million Muslims in Iraq alone.

Former Prime Minister Tony Blair worked for the MI5 prior to becoming Labor Party leader.[1663] This chapter will show that virtually every major Labor Party politician at an early age started out as left leaning communists yet at some point early in their career they undergo a fundamental ideological paradigm shift as they ascend the political cesspit ladder, carrying out marching orders of the Luciferian elite. In Blair's case, he was employed as an MI5 spy to infiltrate radical left circles as an informer for British intelligence. David Shayler, ex-MI5 counterterrorism officer, disclosed that during his entire political career, Blair was a controlled puppet, his strings attached to both MI5 and Mossad as his political handlers.

[1659] Marcello Mega, "Blair's School Mentor was Sex Abuser," *Sunday Times/Spotlight on Abuse*, May 25, 1997.
[1660] Hannah Perry, "Alt-Right Poster boy Milo Yiannopoulos gets Married in Hawaii - but Crops out his new Husband's Face from all Social Media Pics," *Daily Mail*, October 1, 2017..
[1661] Anthony T. Stokes, "Tony Blair as 'Miranda' He who Pays the Piper," *whale.to*.
[1662] Anthony T. Stokes, http://whale.to/c/tony_blair4.html.
[1663] Tony Gosling, "Shayler: 'Blair was an MI5 Agent,'" *aangirfan.blogspot.com*, October 19, 2005.

That explains Blair's meteoric rise from obscurity as a 30-year old opportuning public toilet occupant and newly elected MP to only a decade later his Labor party leader and three more years to claim his anointment as prime minister. From the get-go, Tony Blair was the elite's choice as their infiltrating order following mole, cut from the same puppet-making mold as the Bushes, Clintons and Obama. FDR's once slip of the pen admitted that presidents (and prime ministers) are never actually elected by the people but are simply chosen, most often at a young age by the planetary controllers using intelligence services as their chosen ones' primary handlers and protectors.

Between his Zionist top backers Lord Levy and Friends of Israel, and his perverted habits targeted for sexual blackmail by Mossad and MI5, Tony Blair was Israel's whore. His primary handler was "Lord Cashpoint" – Committee of 300 player Michael Levy, who financed Tony Blair's ascendancy to the world stage along with his New Labor Party from 1994 to 2007.[1664] In return, Lord Levy headed Blair's special envoy to the Middle East. Levy was in deep with the "Cash for Honors" scandal, brazenly selling wealthy Jewish businessmen appointments to the House of Lords.[1665] His son David Levy is an Israeli citizen who's often held top level positons in the Israeli government. A month after becoming former PM, Tony and his wife Cherie attended David's plush wedding on the heels of the Blair-Levy cash for honors fiasco.[1666] Scandal or no scandal, the Anglo-Zionist cabal remains one big happily-ever-after controlling family.

The Blairs didn't stay long at the wedding celebration as they were due to fly out first thing the next morning to the Caribbean to vacation at Sir Cliff's £3 million villa in Barbados again. Sir Kitty's crash pad had become Miranda's home away from home, his shelter from the storm during his decade long bruised and battering as such an unpopular war criminal. It was the fifth summer in a row that Tony chose to lick his wounds compliments of his nurturing good buddy.[1667] Of course it was only eight years earlier that Blair was alleged to put the professional hit on Cliff's dear friend Jill Dando for knowing too much, just like Princess Diana little more than a year and a half earlier, both murders committed on Blair's watch of two of Britain's most beloved women for threatening to bring down the VIP pedo-cabal.

Another key Jewish Blair handler of the Zionist persuasion, or so called chief foreign policy/national security advisor from 2001 to 2003 coordinating the US-British Iraq invasion was Committee of 300 VIP,[1668] Sir David Manning. Prior to that, he was UK ambassador to Israel and from 2003-07 was ambassador to US. At the time of 9/11, Manning was flying over New York

[1664] Christopher Bollyn, "Zionists Subjugate Nations by Controlling their Political Parties," *therearenosunglasses.blogspot.com*, November 23, 2008.

[1665] Tobias Langdon, "A Very Jewish Scandal: The Newmark Affair as Paradigm of Jewish Corruption," *Occidental Observer,* March 15, 2018.

[1666] Rebecca Camber and Sam Greenhill, "Levy Welcomes Blair, Wedding Guest of Honor," *Daily Mail*, July 30, 2007.

[1667] Rebecca Camber and Sam Greenhill, https://www.dailymail.co.uk/news/article-471689/Levy-welcomes-Blair-wedding-guest-honour.html.

[1668] "World Dictatorship-Committee of 300 Led by British-Swiss-Rothschilds Crime Syndicate," *Concise Politics*, October 29, 2017.

City watching the twin towers come tumbling down, ostensibly in America to meet the day before with neocon 9/11 co-conspirator Richard Armitage.[1669] The CIA appointed head of Pakistani Intelligence Services General Mahmoud also just happened to be meeting in Washington that same day is on record making payments to the lead 9/11 "terrorist" stooge Mohammad Atta,[1670] the one whose untarnished passport just happened to be found near the fallen rubble a few days later.[1671]

Within a year after Sir David was US ambassador he was paid £50,000 per year as part-time advisor to giant permanent war contractor Lockheed Martin.[1672] Similar to Sir Jimmy, Sir David Manning also appears to be éminence grise for the royal family. In 2009 the queen appointed Manning advisor to Princes William and Harry for all their foreign travel expeditions. As recently as June 2018 the monarchy's employ of the Jewish Middle East controller continued as the future British king visited Israel and Israeli Occupied Palestinian Territories, a royal first.[1673] To this day the Zionist grip continues ruling over both the UK and US.[1674]

And now for a look at Tony Blair's prime minister record as a pedophile enabler, if not pedophile as well, although his embarrassing public toilet episode at the same time he entered Parliament is said to have taught him a lesson to be more discreet indulging in his favorite perversions. But like Thatcher, it didn't stop him from saturating his government with pedophiles. But prior to uncovering the identities of Blair's child abusing ministers and aides, an accounting of how they wound up on law enforcement radar in the first place sets the stage for this cast of criminal characters in the Blair pedo-lineup.

In 1999, the same year Blair more than likely had Jill Dando murdered, Britain's National Criminal Intelligence Service working under the codename Operation Ore put together an exhaustive list of child pornographers and pedophiles identified to be offending in Britain alone, totaling 7,250 suspects of which 1850 were charged with child sex crimes and 1451 were convicted.[1675] Police interviewed nearly 500 suspects under caution and 900 remained under ongoing investigation in the United Kingdom's most thorough and comprehensive police probe into crimes against children.[1676]

A January 19, 2003 *Sunday Herald* article quoted a recently retired Scotland Yard police officer accusing the Operation Ore probe of intentionally sabotaging the arrest and prosecution of high

[1669] "Prince William's Jewish Mentor, who has Links to 9/11," *aangirfan.com*, January 18, 2010.

[1670] "Britain and 9 11 : Sir David Manning was in Washington on 9 11," *aangirfan.com*, April 6, 2005.

[1671] Ann Karpf, "Uncle Sam's Lucky Finds," *The Guardian*, March 19, 2002.

[1672] "Tony Blair's Iraq Advisor wins £50,000 US Defence Job," *Daily Mail*, November 17, 2008.

[1673] Raf Sanchez and Hannah Furness, "Prince William's Middle East Tour Causes Controversy as Palestinians claim it is 'Indirect Apology,'" *The Telegraph*, June 22, 2018.

[1674] Christopher Bollyn, "Exposing the Zionist Hidden Hand that Rules Britain and the United States," *whale.to*, December 20, 2007.

[1675] Wayne Madsen, "Tony Blair Declares News Black-out on Pedophilia Investigations," *OpEd News/WMR*, April 5, 2007.

[1676] Mike James, "Are Paedophiles running Blair's War Machine?" *CounterPunch*, January 29, 2003.

profile Labor politicians that included Blair cabinet ministers as well as MPs caught downloading child pornographic material.[1677] No doubt by design, the police inaction allowed guilty parties the opportunity to delete and destroy evidence. The detective from the Operation Ore investigation blamed both law enforcement and the Blair government for not following through on their vow to make the crime of pedophilia a top priority, calling it "smoke and mirrors." Had Blair not willfully obstructed justice, covering up the scandal by issuing a D-notice blackout on all subsequent press coverage, the final line in the *Herald* article relays the bold claim destined never to come to pass:

Police say that the list of rich and famous Operation Ore suspects would fill newspaper front pages for an entire year.[1678]

Only one entertainment luminary's name was not spared from press headlines, disgraced rock star Pete Townshend of the legendary band the Who, given a caution and placed on a sex registry for five years.[1679] As in post-Jimmy Savile Operation Yewtree, the powers-that-should-not-be will gladly sacrifice a token entertainer or two long before bringing pedophile MPs and ministers to proper justice.

Operation Ore was part of a larger police investigation stemming from Operation Avalanche in America involving the FBI, US Postal Inspection Service and Dallas police originally unearthing a landslide of files from a company called Landslide Productions in Fort Worth, Texas.[1680] This outfit serviced thousands of international customers busily downloading its child pornography. Despite 35,000 perverts investigated as suspects in the US, only 100 were charged.[1681] For the same reason so few in Britain were indicted, the derelict-filled Bush 2 administration (same as daddy Bush and Blair's) was also caught red-handed neck deep in pedophilia. Also guilty were child pornography and sex abuse rings found operating throughout the US armed forces, including the Pentagon, at military prisons like Abu Ghraib and Guantanamo, and amongst private military contractors like DynCorp[1682] and Halliburton in places like Bosnia, Kosovo, Afghanistan, Ethiopia and Thailand (see Section 3, Chapters 8-11).[1683] In effect, deep links to the entire global pedophilia network were accidentally uncovered and then quickly covered up.

By January 2003 the police inquiry known in Britain as Operation Ore was the largest child abuse online investigation in British history to date,[1684] honing in on a number of high ranking

---

[1677] "Child Porn Arrests 'too slow,'" *The Sunday Herald/cigpapers.files.wordpress.com*, January 19, 2003.

[1678] "Child Porn Arrests 'too slow,'" *The Sunday Herald/cigpapers.files.wordpress.com*, January 19, 2003.

[1679] Neil Sears, "'What I did was Insane': The Who's Pete Townshend breaks nine year Silence on Child Pornography Scandal," *Daily Mail*, September 28, 2012.

[1680] "Did PM Tony Blair Cover up Paedophile Scandal? List of Child Sex Offenders in British Government," *sott.net*, October 10, 2012.

[1681] Wayne Madsen, https://www.opednews.com/articles/opedne_wayne_ma_070405_tony_blair_declares_.htm.

[1682] David Isenberg, "It's Déjà Vu for DynCorp all over again," *Huffington Post*, December 6, 2010.

[1683] Wayne Madsen, https://www.opednews.com/articles/opedne_wayne_ma_070405_tony_blair_declares_.htm.

[1684] "Child Porn Suspects Blame Fraud," *BBC*, May 10, 2007.

pedophiles within the Blair government, including at least two senior ministers.[1685] But because Blair was busily lying through his teeth following the marching orders of his Anglo-American-Zionist puppet masters, on the verge of launching the infamous US-UK "shock and awe" Iraq invasion, the pedo-protecting PM issued his D-notices under the pretense of national security interests in order to prohibit the press from covering the pedophilia scandal that would have overnight destroyed Blair's career, his and Bush's war-making regimes and their bloody, costly, protracted catastrophe in Iraq. The large scale police investigation had uncovered links between child sex abusers in Blair's Labor Party cabinet and a massive pedophilia trafficking network moving children across the Euro-continent between the UK, Netherlands, Belgium, Austria[1686] and Portugal involving dignitaries and VIPs in every nation.[1687]

Of course Tony Blair was far from the first UK prime minister to be sexually blackmailed into fighting wars for Israel. Zionist sexual blackmail controlling top UK politicians has gone on for a century now. For instance, the political marriage of convenience between Tory Prime Minister Harold Macmillan (1957-1963), reportedly expelled for "homosexual perversions" at age 16 from the exclusive private Eton College in 1910, and his wife Dorothy, who maintained a 30-year extramarital affair with promiscuous pedophile gay-Lord Boothby, provided ample opportunity for sexual blackmail.[1688] Enter Cambridge UK-KGB-Mossad superspy Lord Victor Rothschild,[1689] later Thatcher's security advisor, who likely blackmailed Macmillan on behalf of Israel to initiate the 1956 attack on Egypt's Suez Canal.[1690]

To avoid sexual scandal, blackmailed prime ministers eager to retain their power and impunity resort to great lengths to protect VIP pedophilia operations which through intelligence services over the course of time have expanded internationally, especially by the late 1970s. Such notable UK operatives as Sir Jimmy Savile (MI5), Sir Anthony Blunt (MI5-KGB), Peter Righton (National Children's Bureau; National Council of Social Work) and Colin Peters (British foreign office)[1691] to name just a few, all hardcore pedo-pimps (covered in previous chapters) were busily supplying children for VIP sickos in both Britain and Europe. Yet another pimping culprit to emerge in the 1980s (whose crimes will be detailed in the next chapter) is Tory Party Thatcher "advisor" and speechwriter Derek Laud, a son from a broken home of Jamaican immigrant parents.[1692]

[1685] "Did PM Tony Blair Cover up Paedophile Scandal? List of Child Sex Offenders in British Government," https://www.sott.net/article/253318-Did-PM-Tony-Blair-cover-up-paedophile-scandal-List-of-child-sex-offenders-in-British-government.

[1686] Ann St. Claire, "Rothschild's Friend Sir Anthony Blunt and their International Child Abuse Ring," *1776again.com*, January 10, 2018.

[1687] Wayne Madsen, https://www.opednews.com/articles/opedne_wayne_ma_070405_tony_blair_declares_.htm.

[1688] Anthony T. Stokes, "Did Rothschild Blackmail UK to Aid Israel in 1956?" *henrymakow.com*, October 8, 2011.

[1689] "Rothschild and the Gay Cambridge Apostles," *aangirfan.com*, June 25, 2013.

[1690] Anthony T. Stokes, "Did Rothschild Blackmail UK to Aid Israel in 1956?" *henrymakow.com*, October 8, 2011.

[1691] Paul Cahalan and James Hanning, "Paedophile Ring Leader, Colin Peters, Linked to Barnes Scandal," *Independent*, March 3, 2013.

[1692] "Mysterious Derek Laud," *aangirfan.com*, October 25, 2012.

Keep in mind that the pedophile ring pimps that indulge the sick demented needs of powerful untouchable Britons are nearly always just as covered up and concealed as the identities of the famous VIP pedophiles involved, because they are the connected bread crumb ratlines running straight to the royal palaces, 10 Downing Street and Westminster. Yet despite such heavy-handed protection and impenetrable concealment furnished by intelligence services, law enforcement agencies, Crown Prosecution Services, the controlled media and all levels of government from national to local that invariably lose and destroy massive amounts of crucial criminal evidence,[1693] together they still provide more than enough proof that the aforementioned named procurers funneling victims to powerful, largely unnamed, still unpunished VIP pedophiles demonstrate beyond all question or doubt that a highly sophisticated, highly insulated, interlocking international child raping network has in fact been in existence for a very long time. And what else is perfectly clear is that all this tangible, irrefutable evidence amounts to "only the tip of the iceberg."[1694] That said, even with a handful of known and publicly identified powerful pedophile suspects being shielded in the House of Commons and Lords, not one politician at the national level has ever been convicted or served time in prison, **not one**. And undoubtedly a partial list of over 100 convicted British pedophile politicians at local council, mayoral and party levels posted online as of April 2012 is but a proverbial "tip of the iceberg."[1695]

Though influential homosexual-pedophile-pimp Derek Laud's been legally protected, another black Englishman who made history as Britain's first black cabinet minister appears even more powerfully connected. Paul Boateng, son of a Ghanaian minister and Scottish mother, in the 1980s was an ambitious young attorney and NCCL executive member intimately allied with PIE,[1696] embarking on a long career in politics as a Labor MP from Brent South (1987-2005).[1697] Selected as Tony Blair's home minister from 1998 to 2001 overseeing UK police investigations, in 2001 until 2005 Boateng was treasury secretary and then the British High Commissioner to South Africa from 2005 to 2009. As of 2010 he's been elevated to the House of the Lords as Baron Boateng.

But this high profile British slickster of a politician has also been implicated in murderous pedophilia that Blair ensured stayed protected and covered up. However, far too many loose ends refusing to go away can be traced back to his scandalous-prone past and are long overdue to catch up to this highly shielded, still acclaimed VIP lord.[1698] But before diving into his part in the Blair pedophilia cover-up, a little background info on his neck of the woods is critically important to comprehending the bigger picture.

[1693] "UK Government Document Confirms over 2,000 Child Sex Abuse Files Destroyed," *whale.to*, February 3, 2015.
[1694] "Keywords: Pedophilia "tip of the iceberg," *duckduckgo.com*.
[1695] "Partial List of Convicted British Paedo Politicians," *cuttingthroughthematrix.com*.
[1696] Leo McKinstry, "The Left's Web of Shame: It's not just Harman, Dromey and Hewitt. As we Reveal, many other members of Britain's Ruling Liberal Elite held Senior Posts at the NCCL when it was closely Linked to Paedophiles," *Daily Mail*, March 1, 2014.
[1697] "Paul Boateng," *rovolvy.com*, https://www.revolvy.com/topic/Paul%20Boateng.
[1698] "Paul Boateng," *100greatblackbritons.com*.

In 1983 when MP Geoffrey Dickens was first learning of a pedo-ring involving MPs and cabinet ministers engaging in sexual abuse of British children, compiling his dossier to be given Home Secretary Leon Brittan, social workers across the nation went on strike for better pay and improved work conditions. As a consequence, local children in the UK care system were uprooted and separated by hundreds of miles apart from their hometown family and friends. In 1983 it was reported that social services from the South London borough of Lambeth were sending 124 kids as far away as North Wales,[1699] straight to notorious care homes like Bryn Estyn where one of UK's most deadly abuse scandals and cover-ups was occurring from the 1970s through the 1990s. The rampant child abuse in North Wales will be thoroughly covered in Chapter 26.

But while Lambeth children were being placed in harm's way in Wales, they were perhaps even more endangered as residents in any one of 25 care homes in their own home district. With Lambeth also the home headquarters of Britain's notorious foreign intelligence services the MI6,[1700] and the proven nexus between worldwide pedophilia operations and global intelligence services (see Chapters 9-11),[1701] is it purely by coincidence that for so many decades Lambeth has been such a safe haven for pedophile beasts to prolifically prey upon the borough's defenseless group home children?

That was then and this is now. As far as kids in the UK Care System being placed far from home, though it grew very bad in the 1980s, right now it's at a record high. Despite the British government's pledge to not send children in its care system hundreds of miles away from their homes, knowing they are at far more risk of abuse, the 2018 Education Department report reveals that the rate at which British children are being sent to placements lengthy distances from home has risen by 64% from 2,250 in 2012 to 3,680 in March 2017.[1702]

Even more alarming is the number of children in the UK "care" system gone missing in the past two years alone, having skyrocketed to more than double from 4,380 in 2015 to 9,190 in 2017. What does it say when the latest numbers show that more than 10,000 kids in the system disappear for weeks or longer at a time[1703] out of the total Care System population of over 90,000?[1704] With record numbers entering the care system at 90 a day in 2017[1705] and already over 11% missing from their placements, it means that children are being mistreated and abused both in and out of their care homes, compounded and exacerbated by the rising record

[1699] "Anguish of Care Kids," *News of the World/spotlightonabuse.com,* October 23, 1983.

[1700] "Paul Boateng; Godfather: Sex Ring," *aangirfan.com*, March 3, 2016.

[1701] Fiona Barnett, "Connections between CIA Child Trafficking, Ritual Abuse and MK-Ultra Mind Control," *fionabarnett.org*, August 2, 2018.

[1702] Eleanor Busby, "Hundreds more Children 'Farmed out' to Care Homes Miles from where they live despite Pledge to cut number," *Independent*, May 8, 2018.

[1703] Tim Stickings, "More than 10,000 Children in Care went Missing last year amid Fears of Exploitation by Child Grooming Gangs," *Daily Mail*, April 21, 2018.

[1704] "Children in Care Numbers 'Rise to 90,000,'" *ITV News*, January 13, 2014..

[1705] May Bulman, "Record Number of Children in Care as Social Services Reach 'Tipping Point,'" *Independent*, October 12, 2017.

numbers being sinisterly placed hundreds of miles from home. The dire consequences of an already broken system are breaking even farther apart at the seams.

In May 2018 MP Ann Coffey accurately stated:

Despite the [government's] *pledge, record numbers of children are being sent away to places where they are more vulnerable to exploitation. The farming out of children to areas where they have no friends or family circles or local social workers has created a perfect storm where it is increasingly difficult to protect children. These children* [far from home and especially gone missing] *are **being targeted and preyed upon by paedophiles and criminals who know they are vulnerable.***[1706] [**Emphasis** added]

Essentially what appears to be happening is that a brazenly criminal decision was made at the top of the British government to substantially increase the flow of throwaway children into a well-established nationwide pedo-pipeline operating on an industrial scale to feed the growing perverse demands of a pathological international elite that's behind the biggest ever global child raping and trafficking network. The agenda of the UK family court system's been to tear families apart, remove children from non-abusive parents and tragically destroy the nation's most basic, most vital social institution providing a bedrock of stability for eons of time, placing its most defenseless, vulnerable population into the predatory jaws of the UK Care System that's systemically destroying them in unprecedented numbers.

The bottom line - the Anglo-American-Zionist agenda rooted in Luciferianism is determined to obliterate families around the world while establishing one world government tyranny. The diabolical larger plan is to export this same wholesale destruction of family as humanity's foremost institutional life-force presently being deconstructed in the UK to every nation in the world. The endgame of this collectivist Marxist agenda is to globally replace family (along with religion, national sovereignty and private ownership) with the state.[1707] The totalitarian gulag state of Stalin and Mao's oppressive Communist democide dictatorships is right around the corner if the planetary controllers are allowed to achieve their dystopian globalist objective.

Examining how this demonic grand plan strategy from hell unfolded at the local micro-level and spread rapidly nationally in Britain is illustrated by how Labor politician Margaret Hodge saturated her district's youth care homes with infiltrating pedophiles back in the 1980s. The Islington council leader in 1982 began her 10-year reign of terror against group home kids, promoting a highly publicized invitation to hire gays into her Islington council, its social services and group home facilities.[1708] Using the LGBT agenda of fairness to all as her deceptive Trojan horse, she cunningly flooded group homes with child rapists proudly claiming they were gay to

---

[1706] Eleanor Busby, https://www.independent.co.uk/news/uk/politics/children-in-care-residential-homes-missing-paedophiles-drugs-gangs-adoption-a8340006.html.

[1707] "Cultural Marxism: The Hidden Agenda Destroying America," *The Millennium Report*, July 29, 2018.

[1708] Murun Buchstansangur, "How Margaret Hodge's Policies Allowed Paedophiiles to Infiltrate Islington's Children's Homes," *spotlightonabuse.wordpress.com*, April 30, 2013..

work with children in all dozen of her Islington group homes. No one would dare risk challenging the "Political Correctness," much less "violate" the rights of homosexuals, even if they're masquerading as parasitic kiddie killers. Following Islington's lead just a stone's throw away, in parallel process also waving the gay rights' banner, the Labor dominant Lambeth council coalition also flooded its social services and care homes with child predators claiming to be exercising their gay and lesbian rights.

In a very much related move, under the leadership of Margaret Hodge's husband Henry Hodge as chairman of the National Council for Civil Liberties (now known as Liberty), in 1975 he openly partnered with the Paedophile Information Exchange (PIE), fully embracing the rights of UK pedophiles.[1709] Thus through both his and her interventions in the 1970s and 80s, virtually all the London districts became interconnecting, highly embedded safe havens for hardcore child rapists deceptively wearing the LGBT label. Higher-ups at councils and social services alike invited likeminded perverts to infiltrate, network and seal off virtual safe zones to establish a thriving secret network of predators serving their own sick lustful compulsions at the expense of Britain's most defenseless population, while also providing easy access for UK's establishment VIPs sworn to safeguard their pedo-club impunity for survival. Even the British government's Home Office became infiltrated with likeminded child pedophiles.[1710]

For Margaret Hodge to pretend she didn't know her 1983 open advertisement for gays to work with her care home children as a thinly veiled invitation for co-opting pedos under the "gay rights" movement that her own hubby championed is preposterous. Of course both she and her Lambeth Labor counterpart Ted Knight knew they were saturating their 37 care homes with child sexual predators.[1711] With the Islington beta test underway making it super easy for pedos to access care home children while guaranteed protection under gay rights, by September 1983 Islington's next door neighbor Lambeth was pushing Hodge's same Trojan horse policy. Thus it seems from the very get-go, her assigned mission from the UK pedophilia establishment was to expand the child raping network nationwide. It certainly was no accident that as a brand new MP in 1994 Hodge nominated her Islington neighbor Tony Blair to be the next Labor Party leader[1712] and he in turn made her Britain and his first minister of children - all sanctified by Lucifer's design.

[1709] Leo McKinstry, https://www.dailymail.co.uk/news/article-2570675/The-Lefts-web-shame-Its-not-just-Harman-Dromey-Hewitt-As-reveal-members-Britains-ruling-liberal-elite-held-senior-posts-NCCL-closely-linked-paedophiles.html.

[1710] Murun Buchstansangur, "Strange Days: How Paedophile Pressure Groups were Allowed to Lobby and Infiltrate the Home Office," *spotlightonabuse.wordpress.com*, November 10, 2014.

[1711] Murun Buchstansangur, https://spotlightonabuse.wordpress.com/2013/04/30/how-margaret-hodges-policies-helped-paedophiles-infiltrate-islington-childrens-homes/.

[1712] Tim Walker, "Margaret Hodge has told Gordon Brown she wants to leave, say Friends," *The Telegraph*, September 27, 2008.

The Islington and Lambeth borders are separated by a scant two mile stretch of the City of London, the Illuminati Rothschild independent enclave that funds global child sex trafficking.[1713] While Labor politician Margaret Hodge ruled over Islington with an iron fist, her friend in Lambeth Knight,[1714] often referred to as the "Godfather," ran his council like the Mafia. By intended design, both London districts were notoriously swimming with infiltrated pedo-sharks reportedly swapping children between boroughs and outward in all directions among the Isles. To maintain impunity, it wasn't long before the massive amount of incriminating files and records establishing direct links between Islington-Lambeth to all other pedophile rings operating throughout the nation were systematically destroyed.

In the words of award winning reporter Eileen Fairweather who originally broke the Hodge story:

Islington shredded every incriminating file, sacked whistleblowers and smeared victims as mentally ill.[1715]

Abraham Jacob, a pedophile social worker employed at a Lambeth group home prior to employment at Islington social services, was busted in 1986 and imprisoned for his involvement in a Piccadilly Circus pedo-ring. He specialized in picking up runaway rent boys off the street and supplying them to Labor Party politicians and *BBC* executives.[1716] He would also pimp his underage boys, showcasing them in a window of a gay bar to attract johns.[1717] Abraham Jacob was very familiar to Labor council leaders Ted Knight, Margaret Hodge and Jack Straw. Of course Hodge and Straw went on to rarefied heights in the Blair government holding key ministerial posts. What's been proven by their actions throughout long political careers is that they all are ultra-pedophilia-friendly.

Recall from Chapter 19 that a few social workers originally from the Channel Island of Jersey who moved to Islington were both voracious pedophiles as well as child traffickers.[1718] The Jersey-Islington connection exchanged child victims and pedo-pimps posing as both social service workers and traffickers servicing Westminster VIPs in both locations, and of course aided by Sir Jimmy Savile's pimping exploits. Throughout the 1970s and 1980s a nationalized pedophile ring network was developed and expanded under Margaret Thatcher's watch to every corner of the UK through the likes of Savile, Anthony Blunt, Peter Righton, Derek Laud and a host of other prominent pimping players networking and interfacing with intelligence

---

[1713] Murun Buchstansangur, "Were Islington and Lambeth Paedophile Rings Connected?" *spotlightonabuse.wordpress.com*, March 23, 2013.

[1714] "Lambeth Police Station Paedo Sex Ring Dungeon Scandal," *tapnewswire.com*, May 29, 2014.

[1715] Eileen Fairweather, "Jimmy Savile Sex Abuse: 'Islington is still Covering up,'" *The Telegraph*, April 6, 2014.

[1716] "Lambeth Police Station Paedo Sex Ring Dungeon Scandal," http://tapnewswire.com/2014/05/lambeth-police-station-paedo-sex-ring/.

[1717] Shan Lancaster, "Boys in Wimpy Bar 'Sold for Gay Sex,'" *The Sun/spotlightonabuse.wordpress.com*, May 3, 1986.

[1718] Eileen Fairweather, "'I have known about Jersey Paedophiles for 15 years,' says Award-Winning Journalist," *Daily Mail*, March 2, 2008.

services, law enforcement, the National Health Service, local social services, charity organizations, the family court system and dozens of district councils.

From the lower levels of group home employees and operators to the top Westminster and Downing Street powerbrokers, by the 1980s infiltrating pedophiles were thoroughly entrenched throughout Britain, maintaining a close-knit, highly organized secret "sex club" network providing sealed off protection for their collective survival. An August 1st, 1993 *Sunday Times* article observed:

For the past five months officers from the squad have secretly liaised with directors of social services in more than half a dozen London boroughs amid fears that organised gangs have targeted vulnerable children in their areas. Several of the most prominent offenders under surveillance are wealthy businessmen [and other establishment VIPs conspicuously omitted].[1719]

More than a half dozen years later a February 2000 headline in the *Daily Mail* read "Even Worse," reflecting that this same operational pedo-network had grown to industrial strength size, far worse than expected, and this is over a decade prior to the Jimmy Savile bombshell. The article reported that:

Detectives believe a nationwide network of paedophiles has claimed as many as 11,000 victims over 20 years.[1720]

Keep in mind that police estimates tend to always be on the conservative low side. That said, British law enforcement discovered that hundreds of pedophiles were able to roam freely about the country and beyond to continental Europe,[1721] often dispersed with sterling job recommendations and referrals from infiltrated fellow pedophiles embedded as gatekeepers in the UK power structure, from national to local, granting carte blanche license and protection to further harm defenseless underage victims. Even in the 1980s and 1990s the abuse had reached an unprecedented industrial scale.[1722] Historically in the UK, prior to police investigations implicating and potentially exposing VIP perpetrators, British intelligence, Scotland Yard's Special Branch and police commissioners have always stepped in to swiftly shut down probes as soon as identities of government higher-ups are involved.

The above statement is backed up by serving and former Metro Police officers on an anonymous Scotland Yard online forum. A transcript was leaked to investigative journalists at *Exaro News*. One said:

[1719] Richard Palmer, "Child Abuse Sex Ring Found," *Sunday Times/spotlightonabuse.wordpress.com*, August 1, 1993.
[1720] Peter Rose and Stephen Wright, "Even Worse," *Daily Mail/spotlightonabuse.wordpress.com*, February 18, 2000.
[1721] Nick Davies, "The Epidemic in our Midst that went Unnoticed," *The Guardian/spotlightonabuse.wordpress.com*, June 2, 1998.
[1722] Christian Wolmar, "Home Truths," *Independent/spotlightonabuse.wordpress.com*, October 8, 2000.

This is about kids being raped by those in power that included politicians of all sorts. It goes to the very heart of our establishment. There is very clear evidence that the general nature of the allegations are true. There are enough officers on this site who have mentioned paedophile ops involving high profile politicians being stopped at the eleventh hour.[1723]

Two retired Special Branch officers came forth in 2014 to disclose to the half dozen detectives assigned to work Operation Fairbank launched in 2013 in response to MP Watson's assertion that historic child sexual abuse committed by Westminster VIPs still needs investigating. A source close to Fairbank alleged that the retirees claim:

There was a significant paedophile group in Parliament who were untouchable to the police.[1724]

This of course explains why no past or current member of Parliament or the prime minister's office has ever been arrested, much less convicted or imprisoned, confirming what's become at this point common knowledge - government VIPs live above the law. And true to form, Operation Fairbank was shut down as yet another abysmal, costly failure netting not one politician's arrest despite police surveillance videos reportedly catching MPs, ministers and celebs in action partying with and abusing trafficked children at the Elm Guest House.

Yet occasionally back in 2000, the alarming truth gets leaked out to the public by a then far less controlled press. The abuse that had been shielded for several decades in Lambeth grew so blatantly out of control that in 1995 all 25 care homes were closed.[1725] In 1998 and 1999 Operations Trawler and Middleton were launched, initially to investigate John Carroll, then uncover pedophilia crimes in Lambeth from 1974 to 1994 and in 1999 expanded into a nationwide inquiry, recognizing the overwhelming presence of an extensive, flourishing network of deranged sickos preying on UK's throwaway kids, "even worse" than previously imagined.[1726] Coincidence that Metro Police investigated the rampant Lambeth abuse from 1974 to 1994, the exact same years that the Blair minister's wife served on the corrupt Lambeth council?

Despite Operation Middleton lasting four years into 2003, unfortunately only a miniscule number among the legions of criminals were ever brought to justice, all three low level employees granted overly lenient short prison sentences. The central figure in this scandal - John Carroll - did only five years. Hundreds of hardened child sodomizers have been granted full impunity by the rotten to the core system, including the high profile Blair minister that the

---

[1723] Alex Varley-Winter, "Police Privately Admit 'Cover-up' for Paedophile MPs and VIPs," *Exaro News*, December 13, 2014.

[1724] Mark Conrad, "MP Paedophiles were 'Untouchables' – Ex-Special Branch Officer," *Exaro News*, November 22, 2014.

[1725] Jason Bennetto, "Paedophile Network Abused 200 Children," *Independent/spotlightonabuse.wordpress.com*, February 19, 2000..

[1726] "Operation Trawler and Operation Middleton: Blair Ministers and the Lambeth Care Home," *sceptiicpeg.wordpress.com*, September 15, 2017.

media has largely avoided naming,[1727] but anyone who knows anything about the Lambeth scandal knows it's Lord Paul Boateng, in 1998 a home office minister in charge of UK police investigations.[1728]

For a half century or more, the British pedophilia network has been firmly controlled by gatekeeping degenerates from social services, borough councils, law enforcement, high courts to top echelons of governmental power in Westminster and Downing Street. In all this time, absolutely nothing has changed... except over time passage, more and more truth has leaked out in little bits and pieces.

By 1999, even the compromised and controlled Scotland Yard was reporting that up to 50 suspected pedophiles were involved in Lambeth group home abuse during the preceding 20 years.[1729] 16 of the identified perpetrators were already deceased prior to the outset of Scotland Yard's Operation Middleton, strongly indicating murder was treacherously used as a silencing weapon against any would-be informers and whistleblowers.[1730] 50 children who entered Lambeth care homes were never seen again by their families.[1731]

Shirley Oaks Children's Home, another notorious Lambeth group home complex bearing a tragic history of rampant abuse from its 1903 founding to its 1983 closure, was comprised of 52 Victorian cottage "care" homes on 80 acres,[1732] reputedly the world's largest single children's care home.[1733] The Shirley Oaks Survivors Association (SOSA) is made up of over 700 members, all purported child abuse victims at Lambeth care homes from the 1950s to the 1990s.[1734] SOSA maintains that the pedophile ring operating in Lambeth in actuality was far greater in number than the 50 admitted by the police, more like well into the hundreds.

In March 2016 Raymond Stevenson, the SOSA founder and abuse survivor, testified at the IICSA that:

What took place at Shirley Oaks and other children's homes in Lambeth was physical and sexual abuse on an industrial scale which remained unchecked for decades. The damage done was irreversible. Lambeth council itself has had many inquiries in the past. For whatever reason,

[1727] Tom Pettifor, "Minister in Tony Blair's Government among a Group of Men Suspected of Abusing Children at a Home run by Paedophile," *Mirror*, April 27, 2014.

[1728] "Paul Boateng; Godfather: Sex Ring," http://aanirfan.blogspot.com/2014/05/child-abuse-ring-godfather.html.

[1729] James Tapsfield, "Go now! MP Demands Alexis Jay Quits as Chair of Government's Embattled Child Sex Abuse Inquiry as Victims Withdraw Support," *Daily Mail*, November 18, 2016.

[1730] Nick Hopkins and Jake Morris, "The Council that Employed an Abuser to look after Children," *BBC*, March 1, 2016.

[1731] "Lambeth Police Station Paedophile Sex Ring Dungeon Scandal," *cigpapers.blog*, April 2, 2013.

[1732] Sam Christie, "Where is Shirley Oaks Children's Home, when did the Sexual Abuse take place there and how much Compensation will they Receive?" *The Sun*, December 16, 2016.

[1733] "Shirley Oaks Abuse Campaign Finds '32 Paedophiles,'" *BBC*, December 10, 2015.

[1734] Arthur Martin, Emily Kent Smith and Tom Kelly, "Every Child in Care Home at the Centre of Sexual Abuse on an 'Industrial Scale' to get a Share of £40million Payout," *Daily Mail*, December 15, 2016.

including council cover-ups and institutional cover-ups ... we now see they were whitewashes.[1735]

Only eight months after Stevenson's testimony, it was all too evident that Theresa May's so called "Independent" Inquiry is just another futile exercise staged and controlled by Home Office designed to whitewash the real truth and never bring justice for the victims against the perpetrators. As a panel member for the first two years, the Shirley Oaks Association quit in November 2016 when it became painfully clear that May's inquiry was merely another hoax. SOSA had this to say about its official pullout:

Having watched the IICSA unpalatable circus stumble and lurch from crisis to crisis with multiple resignations and claims of racial and sexual abuse thrown into the mix, it no longer matters whether we think the inquiry is just another stitch-up because it's clearly a botch job that needs a drastic overhaul if it is ever to achieve its initial objectives.[1736]

Unfortunately with the IICSA, it was déjà vu. With the disturbing reality that Britain's ruling elite will never come clean in its deplorable institutional crime history against children, as much effort it exerts to block the truth, courageous abuse survivors will ensure that the colossal concealment of atrocities is made public. Media coverage of the abuse epidemic has burst forth in waves, starting over three decades ago, then two decades ago, and then came the most recent 2012 avalanche exposing the Savile abuse that resulted in thousands more allegations against powerful elite pedophiles, echoed in MP Tom Watson's October 2012 House of Commons confrontation with former Prime Minister Cameron.[1737]

But even after a near half decade of the IICSA, not one MP or cabinet minister has ever gone to jail for raping, much less murdering children at will from orphanages and care homes over the last half century. With the national inquiry a cruel joke and the pedophilia cabal's 2018 pushback via Sir Cliff Richard's court victory (see Chapter 21), in so many words warning "don't mess with the privacy rights of the rich and famous," it effectively silences both the media and victims, vis-a-vis indicted accuser "Nick" due to stand trial in March 2019.[1738] So don't hold your breath waiting for the first VIP rapist to go down any time soon, not as long as he's still alive anyway. Before the elite pedophiles can ever be brought to justice, so smugly secure are they inside their fortified pedo-epicenter of the earth mansions, the waking masses will need to revolt first. What's more than clear is nothing short of that will change the shameful and pathetic status quo in Britain.

[1735] Tom Marshall, "Children 'Abused on an Industrial Scale' at South London Care Homes," *Evening Standard*, March 24, 2016.

[1736] "Sex Abuse Inquiry Suffers Fresh Setback as Survivors Group Quits," *ITV News*, November 18, 2016.

[1737] Martin Hickman, "Was there a Paedophile Ring in No 10? MP Tom Watson Demands Probe," *Independent/21st Century Wire*, October 24, 2012.

[1738] Martin Evans, "VIP Paedophile Accuser 'Nick' to Stand Trial Accused of Perverting the Course of Justice, and Fraud," *The Telegraph*, November 19, 2018.

That said, one encouraging sign as a significant shining example of taking bold successful action toward achieving some modicum of justice is the story behind the Shirley Oaks Survivors Association (SOSA).[1739] Though seeking justice against perps obviously can never give back victims' stolen childhoods and many decades of pain and struggle since, the published SOSA report has singlehandedly compelled the Lambeth council to allocate £100m in compensation to its tens of thousands of past abuse victims (at least £10,000 each estimated for 3,000 expected claims).[1740] Once victims united as empowered survivors led by Raymond Stevenson, they have been able to identify abusers where police have failed (no doubt intentionally), resulting in arrests and financial compensation for victims. SOSA serves as a model of inspiration and courage for child abuse victims and citizens for justice everywhere.

In 1967 the UK family court system decided that Raymond Stevenson's father was unable to properly care for his son and sent him to Shirley Oaks Children's Home near Croydon where Raymond lived for the next eleven years, drugged and physically abused the entire decade.[1741] During his final year at Shirley Oaks in 1977, a 15-year old friend of his named Peter Davis was found hanging by a cord in a bathroom of one of the cottages. Though evidence indicated he'd been abused by at least two staff members that went on to abuse others,[1742] the court ruled his death a "misadventure," a favorite scenario for murder cover-up by staged foul play.[1743] Two years earlier Peter Davis had testified as a court witness in a rape trial. When in 2003, documents from the trial were suddenly sealed for the next 100 years,[1744] music producer and abuse survivor Raymond Stevenson realized that "Peter's voice was the first of many to be silenced."[1745] He vowed to expose the horrific truth once and for all and within a month coordinated a reunion of Shirley Oaks survivors and SOSA was spawned.

Raymond and his business partner Lucia Hinton interviewed over 400 former resident survivors and published their own report of documented evidence in December 2016.[1746] This comes after much of the Shirley Oaks records of abuse crimes and documents confirming gross miscarriage of justice have been "lost" or destroyed by the Lambeth council.[1747] The SOSA

[1739] "Shirley Oaks Survivors," *shirleyoakssurvivorsassociation.co.uk.*

[1740] Pippa Crerer, "Council Proposes Paying out £100m to Victims of Abuse at Shirley Oaks Children's Home," *Evening Standard*, December 8, 2017.

[1741] Ros Wynne Jones, "Drugged and Abused for a Decade in 'Paedophiles' Paradise' – the Extraordinary Story how one man Fought back and Won for many Victims," *Mirror*, March 1, 2018.

[1742] Sandra Laville, "Lambeth Council to Pay Tens of Millions to Child Abuse Survivors," *The Guardian*, December 15, 2016.

[1743] Nick Beake and Josephine McDermott, "Shirley Oaks Abuse: Calls for Case of Hanged Boy to be Reopened," *BBC*, October 27, 2015.

[1744] Nick Beake and Josephine McDermott, https://www.bbc.com/news/uk-england-london-34648935.

[1745] Ros Wynne Jones, https://www.mirror.co.uk/news/uk-news/drugged-abused-decade-paedophiles-paradise-12111109.

[1746] Arthur Martin, Emily Kent Smith and Tom Kelly, https://www.dailymail.co.uk/news/article-4037852/700-former-residents-children-s-home-centre-sexual-abuse-industrial-scale-set-multi-million-pound-payout-carrying-investigation-scandal.html.

[1747] Nick Hopkins and Jake Morris, https://www.bbc.com/news/magazine-35686482.

report has led to the naming of up to 60 suspected pedophiles, 10 more than the final number all the failed police investigations and Lambeth council inquiries had ever come up with.

It's also been reported that Jimmy Savile visited three cottages designated to house children with various disabilities, was friends with a Shirley Oaks superintendent back in the 1950s and 60s and DJ'd events at the Shirley Oaks Community Centre.[1748] As both a knight of the queen and pope and also a prime pedo-pipeline architect laying ratlines for UK's trafficking network, Sir Jimmy not only was his nation's most prolific abuser and VIP procurer, he also enjoyed unequalled access to both Britain's children as well as inside elitist contacts with royalty, government, intel services, law enforcement, National Health Services, entertainment, media and religion. So of course it'd be more than a safe bet he victimized children living at the world's biggest care home complex in a district proven to be among the most notorious pedophile havens.

After escaping justice twice in court trials in the 1990s, in August 2016 the conviction of former Catholic priest Philip Temple jailed for a dozen years after admitting to abusing a dozen boys and one girl dating back to the 1970s was vindication.[1749] With SOSA's assistance, police have since charged a couple more pedophiles. Prior to Raymond and his association's heroic efforts, only one Shirley Oaks child rapist, a swimming instructor named William Hook was ever convicted for the thousands of sex crimes against children at Shirley Oaks during the 80 years of appalling abuse.[1750] In 2001 63-year old Hook was sentenced to 10 years' imprisonment after admitting to 26 charges of indecency and sexual assault on a half dozen boys, though he may have abused hundreds since the 1970s.[1751]

In 1983 Shirley Oaks was finally forced to close its doors after eight straight decades of horror. But by the mid-1980s, living conditions for children placed in all 25 Lambeth group home facilities were growing intolerable. A flurry of sexual abuse allegations perpetrated by childcare workers toward handicapped children began surfacing in the media at several group homes where Lambeth social services placed youngsters. In late December 1985 into 1986 it was publicly reported that several children were being sexually abused. A 12-year old boy with an alleged intellectual capacity of a four-year old just released from a care home disclosed to his mother that a male staff working at the home had sexually assaulted him after she noticed

[1748] Arthur Martin, Emily Kent Smith and Tom Kelly, https://www.dailymail.co.uk/news/article-4037852/700-former-residents-children-s-home-centre-sexual-abuse-industrial-scale-set-multi-million-pound-payout-carrying-investigation-scandal.html.

[1749] Harriet Sherwood, "Catholic Priest Jailed for 12 Years for Sexually Abusing 13 Children," *The Guardian*, August 10, 2016.

[1750] Ros Wynne Jones, https://www.mirror.co.uk/news/uk-news/drugged-abused-decade-paedophiles-paradise-12111109.

[1751] Ian Cobain, "Paedophile Jailed for Ten Years may have Abused Hundreds," The Times/spotlightonabuse.wordpress.com, April 12, 2001.

severe anal bruises.[1752] The police soon suspected that all six children at the group home had been abused.

Another incident involved a care home's senior social worker forcing a 15-year old handicapped girl to give him oral sex.[1753] Four separate cases went public at different homes operated and supervised by Lambeth council, all surfacing within 13 months apart. Yet ultimately no action by either police or social services' investigations was subsequently taken against alleged abusers despite in some cases medical evidence supplied by police doctors.[1754] Due to the limited cognitive functioning of alleged victims rendering their testimony "unbelievable," despite physical evidence, the lame Crown Prosecution Services claimed all cases were too weak to deliver convictions and were summarily dismissed.[1755] Both Scotland Yard police and Lambeth council failed these abused children in the worst way, unconscionably sending them right back to their abusers allowed to continue working in the homes harming children.

Moreover, a tit-for-tat petty turf war emerged between the Lambeth council and the local police, both refusing to share and exchange critical information and evidence,[1756] resulting in even grosser child endangerment that predators took full advantage of.[1757] In 1987 even the whistleblowing child advocate MP Geoffrey Dickens called upon Attorney General Michael Havers, himself later an accused pedophile, to reopen the horrendously unjust Lambeth abuse cases.[1758]

Lambeth's deadly CYA culture of intimidation and fear permeated a rigidly enforced policy of inaction characterizing the borough's systemic failure to protect and care for vulnerable children, much less bringing scores of perpetrators to justice. Just as in districts like Islington and countless other cities and towns across the British Isles, looking the other way was becoming a given policy and national norm. Pedophiles fully exploited the fact that back in the 1980s in their fervor to recruit "gays" to work with kids, places like Islington and Lambeth never required background checks, nor were childcare workers required to report suspected child abuse to police. Time and time again, councils in these "liberal" London boroughs ignored the fact that they had unleashed predatory pedophiles on abusive rampage against their children. Moreover, as is common in virtually all cover-ups, during the subsequent so called inquiries one

---

[1752] David Mitchell, "Inquiries into Alleged Sex Assault on Child in Care," *Community Care/spotlightonabuse.wordpress.com*, July 31, 1986..

[1753] David Mitchell, https://spotlightonabuse.wordpress.com/2014/04/29/lambeth-councils-monkton-street-nursing-home-timeline/.

[1754] Peter Burden, avid Williams and Gill Swain, "Police Quiz on Child Sex at Council Home," *Daily Mail/spotlightonabuse.wordpress.wordpress.com*, September 1, 1986.

[1755] Robert Galvin, "No Charges in Kids' Home Sex Row," *South London Press/spotlightonabuse.wordpress.com*, November 25, 1986.

[1756] Robert Galvin, "Cops Rapped in Sex Abuse Row," *South London Press/spotlightonabuse.wordpress.com*, December 5, 1986.

[1757] Robert Galvin, "Council Curb on Help for Police," *South London Press/spotlightonabuse.wordpress.com*, December 19, 1986.

[1758] David Williams and Peter Buren, "Evil Men in Child Sex case 'must not go free,'" *Daily Mail/spotlightonabuse.com*, December 3, 1986.

after the other by either police or social services, it became increasingly clear that hundreds of incriminating files from offices were either lost or destroyed, not from incompetence but a calculated, sinister decision to obstruct justice to protect the guilty.[1759]

Where you find pedophiles and pimps, you also find child pornographers. In October 1992 police found thousands of photos of naked boys and many pornographic videos at the private home of an arrested childcare worker employed at one of several care homes involving hundreds of abused victims.[1760] As the offenders were rarely if ever consequenced, the magnitude of abuse soared to the extent that by 1995, Lambeth was eventually forced to close all 25 of its care homes.

Child sexual predators like Lambeth care home operator Michael John Carroll, a previous convicted pedophile for abusing a boy in Merceyside in 1966, were systemically permitted to continue committing serial sex crimes against children.[1761] During the decade Carroll ran his Angell Road boy brothel from 1981 to 1991, even midway through his tenure in 1986 when his past conviction record became known to the Lambeth council, apparently due to his connections with VIPs like the Boatengs, his license to operate was continually renewed.[1762]

For years in the 1980s Paul Boateng's attorney wife Janet served as council chair on Lambeth's social services committee directly responsible for group home care[1763] as well as a Lambeth councillor for 20 years coinciding with the borough's worst decades of pedophile ring abuse.[1764] Even when the Lambeth council finally terminated Carroll's employment in 1991, it wasn't even over his flagrant sexual assaults, but in comparison, a relatively minor financial impropriety, using public funds to buy cigarettes and liquor.[1765]

Once the Lambeth council finally terminated Carroll's employment contract, after his criminal habit had forced exits from Merceyside and then eventually Lambeth, John Carroll and his wife began looking to relocate to set up shop in the next location, this time on the border of England and Wales. In January 1991 the serial pedophile bought an antique shop as well as plunked down £725,000 in cash on a hotel near Wrexham in North Wales, the center of another horrendous UK child abuse scandal.[1766]

Since for years Carroll was part of the Lambeth brothel system pimping kids out for a price to VIPs, no doubt lots of dirty money exchanged hands in his rent boy operations along with

[1759] Nick Hopkins and Jake Morris, https://www.bbc.com/news/magazine-35686482.

[1760] Niall Hickman, "Scandal of Vile Child Sex Ring," *South London Press/spotlightonabuse.wordpress.com*, October 20, 1992.

[1761] Kim Sengupta, "Care Worker had Paedophile Record," *Independent*, July 6, 1999.

[1762] Kim Sengupta, https://www.independent.co.uk/news/care-worker-had-paedophile-record-1104540.html.

[1763] Murul Buchstansangur, "Janet Boateng: Former Chair of Lambeth Social Services Committee," *spotlightonabuse.wordpress.com*, October 20, 2013.

[1764] "Lambeth: Operations Trawler and Middleton: Blair Ministers and Lambeth Home Care Scandal," *scepticpeg.wordpress.com*, September 15, 2017.

[1765] Nick Hopkins and Jake Morris, https://www.bbc.com/news/magazine-35686482.

[1766] "A North Wales Timeline," *secretofbrynesyn.wordpress.com*.

Lambeth's prospering child pornography business, affording his near three quarters of a million pound property in an area where boy brothels in North Wales were attracting even more top government VIPs. Carroll's confirmed social networking links to prominent fellow child abusers have fueled speculation that he turned his Wales acquisition into yet another lucrative brothel business.

For a number of decades Michael John Carroll was allowed to continue abusing kids entrusted in his care - since Lambeth council failed to ever initiate corrective or disciplinary action against him to protect their children, chronicling an identical parallel process that unfolded during the exact same years in the borough next door at Hodge's pedo-lodge as an interconnected twin sanctuary. Investigating police during Operation Middleton concluded that at least seven abusers of the dozen potential suspects at Angell Road were from outside the boy brothel. The huge unanswered question remains - was Lord Boateng one of them?

Back in the 1980s, attorney Boateng was spotted by several credible witnesses making evening visits at Carroll's home a regular thing. Teresa Johnson, a former social worker employed at the Angell Road facility went public before a national audience on a *BBC* Newsnight broadcast maintaining that she spoke to Paul Boateng requesting him to sign the facility guestbook and observing him frequently visiting the home on about a half dozen occasions.[1767] A youth worker also claiming that John Carroll boasted of his ties with the rising political Labor star, also maintains he witnessed Boateng attending a holiday camp that Carroll ran as well as often seeing Boateng in Carroll's company.[1768]

And still another witness reported that Boateng contacted him on behalf of the pedophile after three neighboring social services turned down Carroll's request to foster a couple more kids, deemed potential victims by Croydon, Southwark and Wandsworth.[1769] When seeking foster approval, Lambeth also withheld that Carroll was rejected by other councils, including the fact Carroll was named in a 1993 independent inquiry into child sexual abuse. For Lambeth to go to such extreme, deceitful measures on behalf of a known pedophile shows just how much power of corruption was behind John Carroll. And the prime source of that power according to a number of witnesses appears to be Lord Paul Boateng.

Former assistant director of social services on Lambeth council Dr. Nigel Goldie stated in 2014:

There was a cover-up to protect politicians' reputations following allegations of abuse at a children's home.[1770]

[1767] Louise Sassoon, "Cop Axed from case after bid to Quiz Labour Peer Lord Boateng about Paedophilia," *Mirror*, March 2, 2016.

[1768] "Lambeth: Operations Trawler and Middleton: Blair Ministers and Lambeth Home Care Scandal."

[1769] Tom Pettifor, "Tony Blair's Minister Accused of Helping Convicted Paedophile to Foster Young Boys," *Mirror*, July 7, 2014.

[1770] Ross Hawkins, "'Cover-up to Protect Politicians after Abuse Claims,'" *BBC*, July 25, 2014.

Yet when asked in March 2016 about John Carroll at Prime Minister May's laughable farce of an "Independent" Inquiry on Child Sexual Abuse, the former Blair minister came prepared, adamantly denying he ever met or knew John Carroll. Again, keep in mind that Boateng in the 1980s was an executive member of NCCL, the human rights lobbying organization that embraced in partnership PIE, the outfit publicly pushing pedophilia as a natural birthright:

As a campaigning youth justice lawyer I acted for many young people in care and visited many youth facilities in the course of my work. I didn't know Mr Carroll personally and have no recollection of meeting him professionally or visiting the Angell Road children's home or anywhere else where he was present. I'm unaware how the investigation into Mr Carroll was conducted. I therefore cannot comment on why the police did not seek my assistance.[1771]

Here the head honcho ruling over all of Britain's police investigations in 1998 is claiming 20 years later that he knew nothing of the Metro Police probe into pedophilia at a care home in his neighborhood that his wife was legally in charge of. So as Home Secretary at the time, he has the audacity to pretend he knows nothing? That's the same kind of absurd, preposterous claim that Margaret Hodge offers when she insists she had no clue her district was infested with child rapists. These highly implausible statements only demonstrate that by simply using denial as their feeble defense, MPs and ministers guilty as sin of criminal misconduct are always granted a free pass to live above the law. In Boateng's case, it's at least three people's word against his, all having far more to lose than gain by their claims. Shortly after Teresa Johnson's 2016 *BBC* interview, she was dead. In contrast, who in this case possesses both motive and means to lie? Politicians bent on saving their own ass and who lie because they get away with it. In England apparently a lord's word is taken as "the gospel" and is deemed truer than lowly common folk.

Prime Minister Theresa May's fake inquiry must have swallowed Boateng's fish story hook, line and sinker, trusting "the good lord's word" since the baron to this day remains in good standing as esteemed member of the House of Lords. So much for May's promise of an "independent" investigation of institutional wrongdoing she admitted while placing her Home Office fully in control to "get to the bottom" of the British government pedophilia cesspit. For us to actually think that criminals in charge of investigating their own crimes are ever going to come clean is an insult to our intelligence and complete sham. But it's the British way, or more apt, the Luciferian way.

Rendering the savvy politician's 2015 IICSA public performance even more suspect, the clincher to this smoldering crime drama arrived in November 1998 when Clive Driscoll, Scotland Yard's lead detective heading up Metro's Operation Trawler was investigating Carroll and closing in on questioning Boateng regarding his possible role in the Lambeth scandal. Meanwhile, amidst the post-Savile uproar in 2014, liar Tony Blair who conned Britain a decade earlier into the bloody mess in Iraq claimed he had "no recollection" of ever learning that one of his ministers was a

---

[1771] Louise Sassoon, https://www.mirror.co.uk/news/uk-news/cop-axed-case-after-bid-7475713.

child abuse suspect.[1772] We know that's another Pinocchio lie since Blair's D-notice is the only reason his minister Peter Mandelson didn't go to jail after Operation Ore caught him purchasing child pornography.[1773]

111 pages of documents and memos released through Freedom of Information requests show that in 1998 prior to Detective Driscoll being relieved of his Operation Trawler duties, both Blair's Home Office Minister Boateng and Health Minister Frank Dobson were both briefed on Scotland Yard's ongoing investigation into Angell Road home abuse identifying a dirty dozen suspects that included Boateng.[1774] This absolutely proves that between Blairite disciples Sir Peter and Lord Paul, the prime minister was well aware that at least two of his ministers were/are extremely probable pedophiles. Yet in a feebly indignant gesture attempting to demonstrate he has nothing to hide, in 2014 Blair self-righteously demanded yet another investigation into multiple claims suggesting his buddy Boateng was a child abuse suspect.[1775] Once a liar, always a liar. Of course order follower Dobson also maintained he has no recall of ever being briefed on the case either.

In a related theme, in March 2015 another brick in the crumbling cover-up wall of deception came loose when it was reported that Britain's top cop - Metropolitan Police Chief Sir Bernard Hogan-Howe, was being questioned by his own detectives in his role in the Lambeth pedophilia scandal.[1776] It's standard operating procedure in the UK that even the nation's "top cop" is an order follower when higher-ups in British Intelligence or national government are giving the orders. And as soon as Home Office Minister Paul Boateng's name came up as a possible suspect amidst the widespread Lambeth abuse, the pedo-investigation leading to him was soon enough halted. At that time in 1998, Hogan-Howe was the Merceyside assistant chief constable leading the Carroll criminal investigation. Again in 1966 back in Merceyside, John Carroll was convicted of his first child abuse offense, only to become years later the pivotal central stooge in the Lambeth scandal/cover-up. The borough council employing Carroll was well aware of his status as a Level-1 convicted child sex offender running one of its care homes doubling as a VIP boy brothel.

Politicians and top cops simply lie their way out of trouble every time. In 2015 the *Mirror* reported the 111 documents were handed over to the Metro anticorruption unit.[1777] But with Boateng's IICSU appearance in March 2016 and nothing more ever heard since from either that inquiry or the police anticorruption inquiry, you can bet that no further action has been or will

---

[1772] Tom Pettifor, "Tony Blair Demands Investigation into Claims one of his Ministers Sexually Abused Children," *Mirror*, May 1, 2014..

[1773] "Cover-up of Blair Minister Child Abuse," *aangirfan.com*, November 14, 2014.

[1774] Tom Pettifor, "Blair Government was Briefed about Paedophile Probe Involving Labour Minister before it was Halted," *Mirror*, July 23, 2015.

[1775] Tom Pettifor, https://www.mirror.co.uk/news/uk-news/blair-government-briefed-police-paedophile-6123122.

[1776] Jason Silverstein, "Top Cop in Britain Questioned by his own Detectives for Role in Alleged Cover-up of Sex Abuse Claims against Tony Blair Minister," *New York Daily News*, March 18, 2015.

[1777] Tom Pettifor, https://www.mirror.co.uk/news/uk-news/blair-government-briefed-police-paedophile-6123122.

be taken despite irrefutable evidence strongly indicating that senior members of the Blair government are unpunished hardcore pedophiles.

With over 200 abused children in Lambeth care homes according to Operation Middleton,[1778] in 1998 the highly skilled investigator Driscoll, who later cracked the notorious Stephen Lawrence murder,[1779] was making headway uncovering the pedo-ring involving VIP politicians when he was abruptly removed and disciplined for committing "serious indiscretions,"[1780] simply for "confidentially" naming the powerful players involved during an August meeting with Lambeth officials.[1781] Three months later Driscoll's boss apologetically notified him that he was off the case and told the "orders come from on high,"[1782] indicating 10 Downing Street as the probable source in order to protect Home Office Minister Boateng who was not only briefed but in charge of the very UK police operation making him a suspect...[1783] déjà vu Leon Brittan receiving the Dickens dossier fifteen years earlier. See why cabinet ministers from the British Home Office are always pedophiles or minimally pedophile enablers? UK's nonstop cover-up would be impossible otherwise.

In 2014 it also came out in the *Mirror* that when Lambeth assistant social services director Dr. Nigel Goldie as the council boss in charge of child protection working in 1998 directly with Clive Driscoll mentioned Boateng's alleged evening visits at Carroll's Angell Road "brothel" back in the early 1980's, Det. Driscoll's Operation Trawler investigation was soon enough shut down.[1784] When politicians so close to a nation's leader are implicated, without exception in every single case, any ongoing police inquiry becomes past tense as standard operating cover-up procedure. Whenever a major pedophilia scandal risks VIP exposure, the self-preservation mode always kicks in no matter the country or abuse location.

Detective Clive Driscoll ultimately wrote a 2015 autobiography entitled *In Pursuit of the Truth* based on his many years with the Scotland Yard, specifically devoting two lengthy chapters to the Lambeth child abuse case involving his unjustified termination as Operation Trawler Chief Detective Inspector (CDI).[1785] In August 1998 Clive met with Lambeth officials to explain that his investigative team had already come up with a dozen suspects whose names were "confidentially" revealed, among them several VIP politicians that included headliner Boateng

---

[1778] Jason Bennetto, https://spotlightonabuse.wordpress.com/2013/02/26/paedophile-network-abused-200-children-19-2-00/.

[1779] Rose Hill, "Stephen Lawrence Murder Detective Clive Driscoll Reveals Catalyst for 'Solving entire Case,'" *Mirror*, April 20, 2018.

[1780] Lauren Probert and Holly Christodoulou, "Lord Boateng in Paedo Link Quiz after Detective 'Axed from Abuse Probe over bid to speak to Labour Minister,'" *The Sun*, March 2, 2016.

[1781] Tom Pettifor, "Paedo MP Cover-up Claim: Top Cop Removed from Sex Abuse Probe after Naming Politicians as Suspects," *Mirror*, March 26, 2013.

[1782] Guy Adams, "Crack Scotland Yard Detective says Top Brass Sabotaged his Bid to Expose Blair Minister in Establishment Paedophile Ring," *Daily Mail*, July 24, 2015.

[1783] Louise Sassoon, https://www.mirror.co.uk/news/uk-news/cop-axed-case-after-bid-7475713.

[1784] Tom Pettifor, https://www.mirror.co.uk/news/uk-news/tony-blair-minister-former-pms-3468050.

[1785] Clive Driscoll, *In Pursuit of the Truth* (London: Ebury Press, 2015).

as well as a council member and a popular entertainer. All hell broke loose after that. The Lambeth council stonewalled the investigation. Clive Driscoll's probe had stirred up a hornets' nest, making instant enemies amongst guilty parties, subsequently resulting in anonymous phone call threats to Clive and his family's safety.

Social worker Steve Forrest had raped a 6-year old boy at Carroll's Angell Road home in 1987. Forrest died of AIDS five years later.[1786] In a tumultuous November 1998 meeting Driscoll confronted the Lambeth senior officials, stating it was unconscionable that the then 11-year old victim was never informed that his rapist had died six years earlier from AIDS. But the Lambeth council refused to disclose the truth to the boy on the grounds that it was deemed "not in the boy's best interest." During the heated showdown, Driscoll was even threatened with removal as DCI from his own police probe.

Early on in the Lambeth investigation, social worker Libby Blake employed at Lambeth social services from 1992-2005, approached Det. Clive Driscoll, informing him that Lambeth council in 1986 had become aware of John Carroll's previous 1966 conviction. Though the statement below was reportedly denied by the former Lambeth social worker, in his book Clive maintains that Libby also stated:

Carroll was only the tip of the iceberg, the children's homes have been the playground for the rich and powerful for years.[1787]

Speaking of the rich, powerful and famous, for his 51st birthday in 2002, four years after Det. Driscoll was removed from investigating the Blair minister, the now 67-year old VIP Lord Boateng had his superstar pal Michael Jackson fly in special to sing happy birthday in the House of Commons, merrily joining his "birds of a feather friends" in a photo-op with not only the accused pedo-King of Pop but also Uri Geller, the infamous Zionist double agent spy, MK Ultra handler and multiple pedophile friend,[1788] and the well-known pedophile fellow Labor Zionist Lord Greville Janner.[1789] The photo alone raises a thousand words worth of suspicion that collusion was taking place between high profile figures within the international pedophilia community.

Libby Blake recommended that Detective Driscoll talk to former Lambeth council chairwoman Anna Tapsell. According to Driscoll, Libby said Anna is "the only one in Lambeth who'll tell you the truth."[1790] At one time Anna headed the Lambeth social services committee (same post held earlier by Janet Boateng), and for two decades Tapsell vigorously campaigned to expose

[1786] Cathy Fox, "Lambeth Part 4 – Clive Driscoll the Truth about Child Sexual Abuse in Lambeth," *cathyfox.wordpress.blog*, September 10, 2015.
[1787] Guy Adams, https://www.dailymail.co.uk/news/article-3173883/Crack-Scotland-Yard-detective-says-brass-sabotaged-bid-expose-Blair-minister-Establishment-paedophile-ring.html.
[1788] "What Links Michael Jackson, Jimmy Savile and Mr. X?" *aangirfan.com*, March 1, 2014.
[1789] Keily Oakes, "Jackson's Visit Raises Eyebrows," *BBC*, June 14, 2002.
[1790] Guy Adams, https://www.dailymail.co.uk/news/article-3173883/Crack-Scotland-Yard-detective-says-brass-sabotaged-bid-expose-Blair-minister-Establishment-paedophile-ring.html.

the horrendous abuse at considerable risk to herself. Anna was visited by several intimidating senior officers from Special Branch,[1791] known for shutting down police probes, disappearing evidence and protecting the pedo-network at all cost, demanding she leave the Lambeth affair alone. Threatened and harassed on numerous occasions by other nameless intimidators, the undaunted Anna Tapsell persisted in telling the truth, stating to the press:

When I learned that Clive was being removed, not only from the case but also from Lambeth, I realised that the Met were caving in to political pressure that was far more powerful than Lambeth Council.[1792]

Referring to John Carroll and other protected child abusers in the Lambeth pedo-ring, Anna added:

At the same time alleged perpetrators were moved or allowed to leave for financial misconduct or other misdemeanours, instead of for the abuse.[1793]

As a courageous insider, Anna states the obvious conclusion:

I have no doubt Angell Road may have been used for organized child abuse which involved adults other than staff. This view is reinforced by the strong investment that officers and politicians have in blocking any effective investigation.[1794]

Prior to being yanked off the case and reassigned, CDI Clive Driscoll uncovered lots of dirt:

I found someone who admitted they'd seen pornography changing hands on council property, which led to someone else saying there was a video doing the rounds featuring 'prominent' people engaged in sexual activities with minors.[1795]

Because higher ups at Scotland Yard were clearly in cahoots with the corrupt Blair government as well as the corrupt Lambeth council criminals abusing children, despite admitting there were over 200 victims, in four years Operation Middleton netted a total of three measly convictions, one being John Carroll.[1796] Though Metro Police claimed 19 suspects remained unidentified, indicating they likely operated outside the UK Care System,[1797] scores if not hundreds of infiltrated child rapists that were/are part of the British pedophilia network got off scot free,

---

[1791] Guy Adams, https://www.dailymail.co.uk/news/article-3173883/Crack-Scotland-Yard-detective-says-brass-sabotaged-bid-expose-Blair-minister-Establishment-paedophile-ring.html.

[1792] Tom Pettifor, https://www.mirror.co.uk/news/uk-news/paedophile-mp-cover-up-claim-detective-1785273.

[1793] Tom Pettifor, https://www.mirror.co.uk/news/uk-news/paedophile-mp-cover-up-claim-detective-1785273.

[1794] Tom Pettifor, https://www.mirror.co.uk/news/uk-news/paedophile-mp-cover-up-claim-detective-1785273.

[1795] Guy Adams, https://www.dailymail.co.uk/news/article-3173883/Crack-Scotland-Yard-detective-says-brass-sabotaged-bid-expose-Blair-minister-Establishment-paedophile-ring.html.

[1796] Tom Pettifor, https://www.mirror.co.uk/news/uk-news/paedophile-mp-cover-up-claim-detective-1785273.

[1797] Tom Pettifor, https://www.mirror.co.uk/news/uk-news/paedophile-mp-cover-up-claim-detective-1785273.

free to move on to abuse more kids elsewhere, exactly like the legions of Catholic priests around the world.[1798]

As if all this incriminating circumstantial evidence and oddly suspicious anomalies aren't enough, there is also the plethora of suspicious deaths and murders of victims and potential whistleblowers. Onetime Lambeth council member turned MP John Mann has stated publicly that two murders of would-be whistleblowers were committed to keep the lid on the VIP pedophile ring operating in his borough.[1799] In 1989 a social worker planning to expose the rampant abuse in care homes was allegedly killed in an arson fire.

Another unsolved murder mystery that took place in 1993 involves the sudden death of veteran Lambeth council insider, the district housing manager Bulic Forsythe who shared with a colleague that he was about to "spill the beans" on the Lambeth scandal.[1800] As housing manager Bulic had discovered photos of children abused by members of Lambeth council[1801] and learned that both women and children were being systematically raped on Lambeth city property, including the basement of his own housing office headquarters. He was determined to blow the whistle to stop such abusive shenanigans being committed right under his nose. But just three days later, he was found murdered, bludgeoned to death, with three men sited leaving the crime scene of his flat carrying files shortly before it was set on fire.[1802] And predictably to this day, his murder remains unsolved... an all too common fate among truth tellers.

Moreover, in December 2014, MP John Mann submitted critical information contained in a dossier to police, naming 22 MPs, including a half dozen still serving at Westminster, implicated in pedo-parties at the notorious Dolphin Square flats.[1803] Mann maintains the evidence shows that boys from Lambeth group homes were being trafficked to nearby Pimlico for abuse as part of a wider pedophile ring. But as always, there's been no follow-up on this highly significant development, only indicating it too has been buried. But the main point remains, government VIP pedophiles are and were fed trafficked kids from care homes from virtually every surrounding borough in the greater London area, Lambeth and Islington being just two of the most guilty. The Westminster scandal that includes orgies at both Dolphin Square and Elm Guest House will be blown wide open in the next chapter.

[1798] Brian Clites, "The Catholic Church's Grim History of Ignoring Priestly Pedophilia – and Silencing would-be Whistleblowers," October 9, 2018.

[1799] Rebecca Camber, "VIP Child Abuse Whistleblowers were 'Murdered': MP says Men were Poised to Lift Lid on Scandal," *Daily News*, December 23, 2014.

[1800] Tom Pettifor, "Was Bulic Forsythe Killed to Protect Paedophile Ring 'Linked to Future Minister in Tony Blair's Government?'" *Mirror*, May 21, 2014.

[1801] Cathy Fox, https://cathyfox.wordpress.com/2015/09/10/lambeth-part-4-clive-driscoll-in-pursuit-of-the-truth/.

[1802] Tom Pettifor, https://www.mirror.co.uk/news/uk-news/bulic-forsythe-killed-protect-paedophile-3578788.

[1803] Rebecca Camber, https://www.dailymail.co.uk/news/article-2884471/VIP-child-abuse-whistleblowers-murdered-MP-says-men-poised-lift-lid-scandal.html.

Another inquiry report disclosed that underneath the Lambeth police station, part of Metro Police Service, existed a secret sex chamber involving both local council members as well as at least one known MP.[1804] FYI as of 1987, Boateng was an MP. The creepy sex den was discovered with a red light, chains, manacle and bedding, linked to the widespread child sex abuse and the making of more kiddie porn, confirmed by a large volume of pornographic material discovered at the station. It became obvious that children from the group homes were taken to the Lambeth police station sex dungeon for abuse and pornography by group home staff, police, social services and council staff including both local and national politicians. The two Lambeth civilian staff members who bravely leaked the information to the Scotland Yard were suspended. In a corrupt criminal system where the bad guys are in charge, good deeds never go unpunished and evil deeds are always loyally protected with lies to the bitter end.

A police report emerging in March 2015 specified that senior Lambeth council members were recording "homemade" porno films on borough premises while committing acts of brutal sexual assault, bestiality and pedophilia.[1805] Known politicians were reportedly wearing animal masks, robes and chanting while children and animals were also present. Lambeth criminals appeared to be engaging in satanic ritual abuse.

In another incident on Lambeth property, a female staff member maintains that she was drugged and then savagely raped by her council manager.[1806] When she bravely filed a complaint and pursued a civil lawsuit against him, an intruder entered her home, dousing her with gasoline, but the match went out. The victim also had acid thrown in her face. A month later the she was still suffering from "serious injuries" sustained in the attacks. Reportedly the "Godfather" of the Lambeth council subverted justice and harassed witnesses in a flagrant attempt to stop the rape investigation.[1807] Rape, murder, destroyed evidence and public denial are the four standard trademarks spelling massive criminal cover-up.

Moreover in January 2011, 38-year old Lambeth Police Constable Jordan Janssen was caught distributing online indecent images of young teenage boys, jailed for 12 months after resigning from Met Police in disgrace.[1808] It begs the question whether he was connected to the Lambeth police officers involved in the production of child pornography in their underground police headquarters dungeon where the council operated its makeshift pornography studio.

Entering the crime scene in the early 1980s, a soon-to-be MP frequently shows up as Carroll's evening guest at his Angell Road boy brothel. Britain's top cop no doubt had to play his order-follower role in the cover-up. But as always when a guilty accomplice is caught red-handed, the

---

[1804] Lee Brown, "Sex Den Found in Cop Shop," *South London Press/spotlightonabuse.wordpress.com*, November 1997.

[1805] Afua Hirsch, "Was Man Murdered for Exposing Paedophile Ring? *Sky News*, March 11, 2015.

[1806] Louise Garrett, Petrol Attack to Silence Rape Victim, *South London Press/spotlightonabuse.wordpress.com*, June 2, 1995.

[1807] Louise Garrett, "'Godfather Tried to Block Rape Investigation," *South London Press/spotlightonabuse.wordpress.com*, June 2, 1995.

[1808] "Shame-Faced Ex-Cop Jailed for Child Porn Pics," *Square Mile News*, January 31, 2011.

standard response is deny, deny, and more deny. So of course in 2015 when his subordinates were asking him questions, a most obvious blatant conflict of interest in and of itself, Metro Chief Sir Bernard claimed he "does not recall details about the [1998] investigation" nor of any suspects. You see a consistent pattern of cover-up here? The guy was second in charge of the lead police agency investigating the notorious pedophile John Carroll with direct links to a VIP Blair minister, and he feebly claims he knows nothing about it. How convenient that another queen-knighted pedo-gatekeeper would suddenly come down with a timely case of amnesia. A source close to the 2015 investigation in so many words tactfully called Hogan-Howe a liar, explaining to the *Mirror* that it was "inconceivable" he would not have been aware:

The senior investigating officer at the time would have been expected to have reported to his senior officers the fact a serving government minister [Boateng] *had come under suspicion.*[1809]

One more note of relevant passing interest on Lord Paul Boateng conjures up the old adage - "like father, like son." Paul's son Benjamin Boateng is a convicted rapist and registered sex offender. After charges of raping a 17-year old girl in South Africa were dropped in 2006 while daddy was British High Commissioner,[1810] the serial rapist struck again a few years later back in London, smiling for his mug shot, smugly confident his father's VIP status would once again get him off.[1811] But this time he was found guilty in October 2011 and sentenced to two months shy of four years in prison.[1812]

For those not high enough on the pedo-predator food chain, the mounting evidence against Boateng's alleged buddy that he claims he never knew just kept piling up to the point that in 1998, long past the point of protection by even the VIP establishment, John Carroll couldn't evade the law any longer. With alleged interest in tapping his wealth of inside pedo-knowledge of the North Wales scandal as a hotelier, Merceyside-Metro Police finally took the serial predator-VIP child procurer into custody after he admitted to 35 sexual assaults against a dozen boys, receiving a 10 year prison sentence for over two decades worth of mostly unpunished crimes. After serving only half his sentence, a mere five years, John Carroll was once again a free man in 2004 to get back to his "hotel" business in North Wales.

Should Carroll ever come forth to provide evidence against Lord Boateng and his VIP pedo-network, he realizes he would obviously go the same way of Bulic Forsythe and a bunch of others. John Carroll was again charged with yet more crimes committed back in the 1970s in Merseyside in North West England and once again was scheduled to face another trial in a Liverpool court in April 2018. But the elite's hidden hand, known to reward fellow pedophiles

[1809] Jason Silverstein, http://www.nydailynews.com/news/world/top-uk-questioned-role-sex-abuse-coverup-article-1.2153329.

[1810] Jonathan Clayton, "Boateng Rape Charge is Dropped," *The Times*, January 21, 2006.

[1811] Sarah Oliver, "Boateng thought he was Untouchable... the Son of Privilege who could get away with anything," *Daily Mail*, December 3, 2011.

[1812] Rebecca Camber and Jessica Satherley, "Seen for the first time: Lord Boateng's Sex Attacker Son Grins for his Mugshot after Assault Arrest," *Daily Mail*, October 26, 2011.

who keep their mouths shut, perhaps intervened as the three charges the 70-year old was facing were suddenly dropped mysteriously in January 2018.[1813]

Another bizarrely suspicious Lambeth case involves 38-year old youth worker Jason Hoyte, convicted and sentenced to nine years in 2009 for sexually abusing a half dozen girls over a 20-year period, one as young as four.[1814] The musician was also reportedly grooming children for *BBC* executives as well as joined a London Pentecostal Church to prey on vulnerable victims' trust. The married father actually sued Lambeth council for wrongful dismissal after he was arrested for sexual abuse. Perhaps his arrogance was based on not having to submit a criminal background check despite a 1989 charge of sexual assault. Or maybe it was Hoyte's *BBC* connections that led Appeals Court Judge Mark Bishop to out of the blue order a retrial in May 2013 that in turn five months later led to Hoyte's acquittal of all charges.[1815] Another common pattern - lower level pedophiles serving higher level pedophiles often receive little or no punishment for their heinous crimes as reward for keeping what they know to themselves.

As strong evidence in recent years that sick pedophile rings are still operating in Lambeth and London vicinity still frequently preying on care home children comes the bizarre twisted case of 28-year old pedophile Gihan Muthukumarana.[1816] For several months in 2015 this derelict attempted to recruit his hired female escort to join him sexually abusing, torturing and murdering 10 girls from local care homes in a business proposal offered as part of a snuff film deal the plotted ending the victims' bodies being disposed of in vats of acid, all for the perverted viewing pleasure of elite politicians. He promised his would-be accomplice "millions of pounds," boasting that VIPs are willing to pay £10 million for the film. Fortunately the alarmed woman took this information to the police and a sting operation was set up to get the creep on tape pitching the same business proposition to an undercover cop calling herself "Donna." The case was heard in a Southwark court in February 2018. But here's the clincher - this guy walks after he too was acquitted.[1817]

So apparently the British court has seen fit to render this man free to carry out his hideous plan. Even if he's a complete crackpot, conspiring to commit mass murder renders him a free man? Oh yeah, I forgot, his alleged victims were only expendable, throwaway kids from UK care homes. If this sicko is for real, and evidence that snuff films shared amongst the most whacko of the rich and powerful does exist, depicting the most deplorable crimes imaginable, blood sacrificing children on camera do draw top dollar.[1818] So why hasn't mainstream press bothered

---

[1813] Lynda Roughley, "Former Wirral Children's Care Home Boss Michael John Carroll Cleared of Historic Sex Abuse Charges," *Wirral, Globe*, January 18, 2018.

[1814] "Lambeth Police Station Paedophile Sex Ring Dungeon Scandal," *cigpapers.blog*, April 2, 2013.

[1815] Matt Watts, "Sacked Paedophile Sues Lambeth for Wrongful Dismissal," *Your Local Guardian*, December 10, 2009.

[1816] Virginia Hale, "UK Court Hears of Plot to Rape, Dissolve in Acid Children for Pleasure of Unnamed 'Top Politicians,'" *Breitbart*, February 14, 2018.

[1817] "VIP Plot has been heard, says Court," *researchingreform.net*, March 2, 2018.

[1818] Lasha Darkmoon, "Snuff Porn Pedophilia: Killing Children for Sexual Pleasure," *fourwinds10.com*, May 20, 2017.

with this strange and highly disturbing story? And why is this dude not behind bars? The most likely answers are because he really does have links to actual VIPs who are protecting him in order to protect themselves and as a bigtime accomplice, MSM is also shielding the elite from unwanted damaging publicity.

Sadly this atrocious and despicable track record of total abuse against group home children as UK's expendable, throwaway population is far too commonplace in and around London, be it Lambeth, Islington, Richmond or Westminster. Or outside England in Jersey, Wales, Ireland and Scotland, the legally protected abuse is everywhere inside the United pedo-Kingdom and queen's Commonwealth. And for that matter, inside England over the last couple decades it's rampantly grown out of control in places like Rochdale, Rotherham, Telford or Bradford as well, where abused underage girls don't have to be plucked from care homes to be forcibly conscripted into child-raping-murder rings belonging to brutal pedo-pimping gangs (taken up fully in Chapter 25).[1819] Be it abuse by non-VIP or VIP rapists alike, it doesn't much matter who, where, what, how or when, the sad story's endgame is always the same. The cold hard fact is Britain's tortuously long, vile history of pedophilia and accompanied state cover-up demonstrates that the world's epicenter doesn't give two shits about its own child population, whether trapped inside or outside its abominable pedo-matrix of a Luciferian child care system or not.

And what's even more sobering, the UK is the ruling elite's mere beta test for having maintained to this very day such an impenetrably sealed cover-up guaranteeing impunity as the beta test model being presently exported, eventually coming to a neighborhood near you... that is if the Luciferian planetary controllers are allowed to continue their crime spree against humanity unchecked and unstopped. Our only way out of this ungodly nightmare requires citizens of the world to finally rise up from their shackles in solidarity and begin holding these evil, sodomizing planet killers fully accountable. They've scorched and destroyed enough of our earth, us and our children to successfully reach the critical point of no return. Now on the brink of total self-destruction, it's do or die time for the human race. Stand up and be counted as part of the million to one majority committed to doing what's right and necessary to save and protect both our children and future.

Speaking of NWO sodomizing destroyers, let's revisit another familiar character in this UK pedo-house of horror, the overly protected, pedophilic Rothschild surrogate in the Tony Blair and Gordon Brown Labor governments – the hamster "felching" Sir Peter Mandelson (see Chapter 21). Peter's Jewish father worked as advertising manager at the *Jewish Chronicle* and his maternal grandfather had been a Labor cabinet minister.[1820] As a young political neophyte, "Mandy" started out a Communist Party member but soon switched over to the CIA/MI6

[1819] "Pakistani Paedophile Rings in the UK – Why and How?" *theukdatabase.com*.
[1820] "Peter Mandelson," *revolvy.com*.

inspired Socialist International youth fest that morphed into the Labor Party,[1821] on his way to becoming another rising star first launched from - where else but of all places - the Lambeth council (1979-82), ascending to the title of architect of the New Labor Party while riding the coattails of the 1997 Tony Blair landslide.[1822] Similar to Mandelson, Tony Blair too was inspired by Marxist revolutionary Leon Trotsky.[1823] Like fellow Labor leftists Harman, Dromey, Hewitt and the Hodges, Lord Baron Mandelson (lord since 2008) also lobbied for lowering the age of sexual consent, prioritizing his first order of business to press brand new prime minister Blair to make fellow Jewish pedophile Greville Janner a lord peer in 1997, a half dozen years **after** Janner was publicly accused of child sexual abuse in a British high court of law.[1824] Infiltrated pedophiles don't care if voiceless, powerless kids from care homes accuse them of wrecking their lives, after all, once they reach Parliament, their "life insurance" automatically kicks in entitling them to living the remainder of it above the law.

Lest we not forget how they're able to do this. Because child rapists are often strategically cherry-picked as gatekeeping foxes in the pedo-Kingdom henhouse, Sir Peter Mandelson served as vice chairman of the largest UK child charity, the National Society for the Prevention of Cruelty to Children (NSPCC)[1825] as well as chairman of the British Youth Council (1978-80).[1826] With 10 phone listings in Jeffrey Epstein's pedophile who's who of a black book,[1827] openly gay-closeted pedo Peter the perennial Bilderberger guest, former EU Commissioner and queen-knighted New World Order Zionist was also Tony Blair's chief fixer for every scandal. Mandelson has been accused of kidnapping children while in Brussels for pedo-consumption by his fellow EU derelicts.[1828] And of course it was Blair's D-notices that fixed it for Mandy to stay a free man despite ordering child pornography online in 2002 during Operation Ore.[1829] With all his known perversions, Mandelson fits the ideal blackmail-able mold to run the country behind the scenes as a Rothschild implant,[1830] and by 2009, he'd already held a record 35 cabinet committee posts.[1831] As the unelected power behind the PM throne of both the Tony Blair and Gordon Brown governments from 1997 to 2010, an opposition Tory party leader astutely commented:

[1821] Mike James, "Blair's Protection of Elite Paedophile Rings Spells the End for his Career," *Illuminati News*, July 20, 2006.

[1822] Jon Swaine, "Peter Mandelson: Timeline of his Career," *The Telegraph*, October 3, 2008.

[1823] Anushka Asthana, "Blair reveals he 'Toyed with Marxism' after reading Book on Trotsky," *The Guardian*, August 10, 2017.

[1824] Sam Marsden, "Mandy Lobbied Blair to give Janner a Peerage after Sex Abuse Claims: Grandee said to have asked then-Labour Leader about Ennobling him ahead of 1997 Election," *Daily Mail*, May 17, 2015.

[1825] "Peter Mandelson," *whale.to*.

[1826] "Peter Benjamin Mandelson," *Prabook*.

[1827] Vanessa Allen, "Peter Mandelson Stays Silent over his Contact with Prince Andrew's Disgraced Financier Friend," *Daily Mail*, March 7, 2011.

[1828] "Peter Mandelson," http://whale.to/c/peter_mandelson.html.

[1829] Mike James, "Revealed: British Prime Minister Gordon Brown is a Paedophile," *The Truth Seeker*, March 14, 2010.

[1830] Peter Walker, "Nat Rothschild Loses Libel Case against Daily Mail over Mandelson Trip," *The Guardian*, February 10, 2012.

[1831] Murray Wardrop, "Lord Mandelson's Empire: 35 Cabinet Committee Posts," *The Telegraph*, July 22, 2009..

It is quite obvious that Peter Mandelson is the real unelected prime minister pulling the strings from No 10.[1832]

Speaking of string-pulling power, Nathaniel Rothschild fondly reflected in a 2012 London courtroom on his 2005 male-bonding sauna experience in Siberia with then EU trade commissioner Peter Mandelson and Russian oligarch Oleg Deripaska as pure pleasure, adamantly denying any conflict of interest backroom business deal ever took place.[1833] Cabal central bankster Rothschild insisted that he flew his buddy Mandy in on a Siberian one-day jet set turnaround as purely recreational and was in court in 2012 suing the *Daily Mail* for libelously implicating shady business, misusing Mandelson's political position to smooth over a big aluminum deal with the very same Russian magnate the US denied granting visas to, branding Oleg a criminal with ties to organized crime.[1834] Thankfully Nat's bromance angle lost in court.[1835]

As the earth's aluminum king, despite being on Washington's shit list, Nat and Mandy hastily dispatched fellow Lord Gregory Barker to DC to clear the way for Oleg to sell off some of his alum assets in exchange for lobbying/bribing cash to remove all his sanctions, freeing him up to make deals with US Empire like never before.[1836] Since aluminum by volume is the most common geoengineering metal in the cabal's global aerosol lethal cocktail spraying,[1837] and vast amounts are consumed in the sinister agenda to poison our planet with heavy toxic metals for waging warfare on multiple fronts - weather modification, electrical brainwave conductor for mass mind control and of course slow kill eugenics depopulation,[1838] Oleg now stands to regain his status he lost to China in 2015 as the world's number one aluminum producer. Of course since Rothschild and Mandelson are used to living like gods far above any human laws [or sanctions], globalist "lackey" Mandy and his Rothschild master Nathaniel could care less, since they're megalomaniacally in it destroying our planet solely for the pure hell of it and of course for taking in a little globetrotting, sheer bromanctic pleasure.

Yet another one of Blair's perverts caught up in Operation Ore that the prime minister's D-notices didn't quite save in time was his less senior aide and confidante Phillip Lyon who was arrested for both downloading as well as creating pornographic images of children on his work

---

[1832] Murray Wardrop, https://www.telegraph.co.uk/news/politics/5882622/Lord-Mandelsons-empire-35-Cabinet-committee-posts.html.

[1833] Martin Evans, "Nathaniel Rothschild says Sauna with Lord Mandelson was Purely Pleasure, not Business," *The Telegraph*, January 25, 2012.

[1834] Misha Glenny, Robert Booth and Tom Parfitt, "US Refused Oligarch Visa over Alleged Criminal Associations," *The Guardian*, October 31, 2008.

[1835] Peter Walker, https://www.theguardian.com/politics/2012/feb/10/nat-rothschild-loses-libel-daily-mail.

[1836] Andrew Higgins and Kenneth P. Vogel, "Two Capitals, One Russian Oligarch: How Oleg Deripaska is trying to Escape U.S. Sanctions," *The New York Times*, November 4, 2018.

[1837] John P. Thomas, "Artificial Clouds and Geoengineering: Public Exposed to Toxic Chemicals," *Health Impact News*, 2015.

[1838] Alfred Lambremont-Webre, "HAARP/Chemtrails WMD," *Exopolitics*, August 13, 2014.

computer at the House of Commons.[1839] The up and coming 37-year old's career suddenly took a nosedive when Scotland Yard arrested the Blair advisor on "10 counts of making indecent images of children."[1840] In August 2003 the father of two was found guilty downloading almost daily his growing collection of thousands of images of children, some of them toddlers forced to engage in sexual acts of perversion. When officers arrested him, the sicko confessed:

It is like a drug - you try one and you want to try something harder and it has a snowball effect.[1841]

For possessing his drug of choice that ruins young children's lives, Phillip Lyon served only five months of a one year prison sentence. One more pedo-connection, Lyon began his career in politics as an Islington council member.[1842] Why are so many of these Lambeth-Islington alums ending up hardcore pedophiles?

Not to be outdone a decade later from the same 10 Downing Street sleaze file comes another pedo-friendly prime minister named David Cameron who had a similar rude awakening learning his longtime close friend and senior aide, 62-year old Patrick Rock, up for peerage at the time, was intercepted and arrested for his child porn collection.[1843] No surprise that the perverted bureaucrat from European aristocratic stock was once a Margaret Thatcher protégé. The sick irony is that Cameron's Rock was responsible for the conservative government's policy on cleaning up the internet to prevent child pornography and child abuse imagery. Guess he too caught that highly contagious, nasty Downing Street "snowball effect" going around. Another fitting reminder that pedophilia rules every political party and persuasion... and per the old last NWO guru still alive Henry Kissinger and his pithy observation that "power is the ultimate aphrodisiac,"[1844] especially when derived from literally getting your rocks off on traumatized, adrenochrome-filled children.

So what's the pedo-enabling war criminal Tony Blair been up to in the dozen years since his prime minister days? First thing the ex-PM did was declare himself Roman Catholic after 30 years' pretense and political expediency as a closeted Catholic and official Anglican in name only.[1845] In October 2012 right when the most Jewish Catholic's so-vile sins were shocking the nation, Blair's priest Friar Michael Seed was caught selling papal knighthoods to the highest bidders that paid up to £50,000.[1846] The disgraced senior Catholic, often a 10 Downing Street

---

[1839] "Did PM Tony Blair Cover up Paedophile Scandal? List of Child Sex Offenders in British Government."

[1840] "UK Parliamentary Clerk Charged," *BBC*, August 2, 2002.

[1841] "Commons Clerk Jailed over Child Porn," *BBC*, August 19, 2003.

[1842] "Paedophile Politicians," *sites.google.com*.

[1843] Matt Chorley, "No 10 Aide Arrested in Child Porn Probe had been subject of Staff Complaint about 'Inappropriate Behaviour,'" *Daily Mail*, March 4, 2014.

[1844] "The World According to Kissinger," *The Telegraph*, May 21, 2011.

[1845] Stephen Bates, "After 30 years as a Closet Catholic, Blair finally puts Faith before Politics," *The Guardian*, June 22, 2007.

[1846] Ian Gallagher, "Tony Blair's Priest Fixed Papal Knighthoods for Cash: Senior Catholic took up to £50k Donations for Honours," *Daily Mail*, October 12, 2012.

guest, celebrated his 25th ordination ceremony putting on a posh champagne shindig with entertainment provided by men in drag wearing nun costumes prancing around a racy London club. The unpriestly Seed of decadence lives like a king in a Dolphin Square flat, rent-free compliments of one of his wealthy papal knight donors... more evidence illustrating the unholy marriage between politics and the Church as the dual driving pedo-forces behind today's globalized child raping crisis.

At the same time Tony Blair became Catholic, in a move straight out of Lucifer's playbook, immediately following his resignation, President George W. Bush made his partner-in-love-and-war crimes his Middle East "peace" envoy in 2007. Blair then proceeded to utilize all his accumulated war contacts fresh off the spilled blood of dead British soldiers to rack up a record breaking fortune of over £60 billion in blood money since leaving office,[1847] fully exploiting his illicit conflict of interest between Tony Blair Associates consultancy firm and his "pro bono" gig in peace diplomacy, greedily signing up all the world's worst dictatorial human rights offenders his war crimes could buy, including Gulf State monarchies as exclusive clients.[1848] His shameless cashing in his chips of criminal infamy for gobs of easy money puts even the pay-to-play Clintons in the minor leagues. But then once Charles Lynton aka Miranda the cottaging sleazebag whore, right into his multi-billionaire golden years, always the cottaging sleazebagging whore.

But as hard as it is to think it could get any more diabolical, Gordon Brown as Blair's Labor Party successor from 2007 to 2010 has even more overwhelming incriminating evidence that for decades he's been engaging in satanic ritual sexual abuse of children.[1849] Twenty-one years prior to his becoming prime minister, at a private party in 1986 veteran journalist Mike James learned that Gordon Brown was a serial pedophile, per Norman Lamont, the future Chancellor of Exchequer under PM John Major. Mike James continued investigating the Zionist blackmail controlled Gordon Brown, writing during Brown's final year in office:

Gordon Brown, the current British prime minister, is a practicing pedophile whose activities are known not only to the British, American and Israeli intelligence services, but also by Rupert Murdoch and his senior editor at the Sunday Times.[1850]

To add insult to injury, in July 2017, Theresa May's farcical IICSA cover-up charade brought both former prime ministers Gordon Brown and Sir John Major in for questioning about what they know (wink, wink) of UK institutional child sex abuse[1851]... like known pedophiles and their enablers would ever incriminate themselves by telling the truth for once.

[1847] Luke Heighton, "Revealed: Tony Blair Worth a Staggering £60m," *The Telegraph*, June 12, 2015.

[1848] Kate Ferguson, "Tony Blair was 'Paid Millions' by a Wealthy Arab State while Working as Middle East Peace Envoy, Emails Reveal," *Daily Mail*, August 14, 2017.

[1849] Mike James, "Revealed: British Premier Gordon Brown is a Pedophile," *rense.com*, February 28, 2010.

[1850] Mike James, http://www.the"truthseeker.co.uk/?p=12346.

[1851] Sean O'Neill, "Sir John Major and Gordon Brown will give Evidence to Child Sex Abuse Inquiry," *The Times*, July 11, 2017.

And now onto the star of this chapter's horror show, Margaret Hodge. The Islington pedophilia scandal involves all dozen group homes supervised by the district council leader, longtime Blair cabinet minister and even longer MP Dame Margaret Hodge from Barking since 1994. Among the worst pedophilia rings in southern England is the one that thrived for many years in Hodge's Islington borough, a district just north of the City of London, where the Rothschild controlled central Bank of England is located.[1852] At the heart of this scandal is yet another Anglo-Jewish princess - 74-year old Dame Margaret Hodge (nee Oppenheimer). She can be referred to as the Islington abuse ringleader by virtue of the fact that for two decades while serving on the Islington council, she was well aware of the widespread abuse of children in her borough's care homes, yet chose to ignore and go out of her way to cover up her crimes against children and their desperate cries for help. Similar to two aforementioned fellow Jewish female pedophile enablers - 78-year old Dame Esther Rantzen (Chapter 21) and 72-year old Tory minister-MP Edwina Currie (Chapter 22), this aging trio represents the old guard Zionist pedophilia foxes, all assigned critical gatekeeping duties guarding the elite's United-pedo-Kingdom.

But prior to covering Margaret Hodge's enormously significant role in the British pedo-epidemic, according to *13 Illuminati Bloodlines* author Fritz Springmeier, the family she was born into:

The Oppenheimers were early members of the Bavarian Illuminati [with Rothschild money the same Illuminati order that Adam Weishaupt founded in 1776.]... *The Oppenheimers apparently are close to the Rothschilds.* ["Father of the Atomic bomb"] *J. Robert Oppenheimer of the Council on Foreign Relations was exposed as a communist.*[1853] *Harry Oppenheimer* [1908-2000], *an international banker, is chairman of the Jewish De Beers world-wide diamond monopoly, and chairman of the Anglo-American Corp.*[1854]

Born a year after Margaret Oppenheimer in 1945, Harry's son Nicholas took over DeBeers in 1998 and is the third richest man in Africa, living off his family's rape and pillage of his African slave labor diamond industry for a reported net worth of $6.6 billion...[1855] a drop in the blood bucket to Tony Blair's 60 billion.

Turning to Margaret's Oppenheimer's immediate family background, from her traceable Illuminati bloodline roots, Margaret's multimillionaire father Hans was originally from Stuttgart, Germany, just a two hour drive from his Bavarian bloodline stomping grounds. In the mid-1930s young Hans answered his uncle's call in Africa as an employ of the booming Oppenheimer family mining monopoly.[1856] During the final year of World War II, Margaret was born in

[1852] David Nova, "The Control of Central Banks Worldwide by Rothschild," *bibliotecapleyades.net*, January 26, 2017..

[1853] John Earl Haynes and Harvey Klehr, "J. Robert Oppenheimer: A Spy? No. But a Communist once? Yes." *The Washington Post/historrynewsnetwork.org*, February 12, 2012.

[1854] Fritz Springmeier, "The Power of the Rothschilds," *rense.com*, August 12, 2007.

[1855] Veli Mbele, "The Fall of Cecil Rhodes and the Rise of Black Power in Africa," *Counter Punch*, April 3, 2015.

[1856] "Margaret Hodge," *revolvy.com*.

September 1944 in Cairo, Egypt. But with the State of Israel's 1948 grand opening bloodbath "cleansing" Arabs from Palestine in the first Arab-Israeli War, as Jews living in the Middle East, patriarch Hans with wife and five children in tow headed for safer ground in London.

A half dozen years later at 10-years old, Margaret lost her mother to stomach cancer. With paucity of maternal influence suffering such a major loss at a relative early age, circumstances in young Margaret's life brought out her fierce competitive drive and burning ambition to prove herself to both her highly successful father and the entire world, living up to her prominent Oppenheimer family name. The five Oppenheimer children were raised in opulence not only from the family's booming African mining interests but once in England, daddy Oppenheimer founded Stemcor, the world's largest privately owned steel-trading corporation and Britain's six largest company overall.[1857] Her only brother Ralph took over the family business three years before Hans' death in 1985 until three years prior to his own passing in 2016 when Stemcor for the first time had a non-Oppenheimer chief executive though Margaret's family ensured they still retain controlling interest. Growing up in one of the world's wealthiest, most powerful families on earth, silver-spooned Margaret always attended the finest schools, ultimately graduating from the London School of Economics, the elitist university founded in 1895 by the Fabian Society.[1858]

While still in her mid-20s not long out of college, Margaret Eve Oppenheimer married Andrew Watson in 1968 but divorced him a decade later after having a son and daughter by her first marriage. 1978 proved to be one busy year for Margaret, divorcing one husband and marrying another in a turnstile turnaround the same year Queen Elizabeth gifted the Jewish rising star not even 34 yet with her first royal honor, the most Excellent Order of the British Empire (MBE).[1859] Her Labor seat on the Islington council and famous Jewish surname must have enhanced her worthiness as a royal chosen one freshly paired with her up and coming new husband Henry Hodge, a future royal knight and high court judge. Henry and Margaret had first met when she was Mrs. Watson back in 1973 as fellow Labor Party councillors on the Islington council. But her rapid ascendancy had her elected as council leader by 1982. Meanwhile, a mere year after joining Henry on the Islington council, in 1974 Henry Hodge took a new job as chairman of the infamous National Council for Civil Liberties (the civil rights lobby now known as Liberty) and within a year it was Henry who made the NCCL an affiliate partner with the notorious Paedophile Information Exchange (PIE) in 1975.[1860] In 1977 the NCCL invited convicted pedophile PIE leader Tom O'Carroll as a platform speaker at its spring conference.[1861]

[1857] "The Story of Stemcor," *Financial Times/steelguru.com*, July 28, 2013.

[1858] Tunde Folawiyo, "The History of the London School of Economics," *tundefolawiyo.org*, April 21, 2014.

[1859] "Margaret Hodge," https://www.revolvy.com/topic/Margaret%20Hodge.

[1860] Leo McKinstry, https://www.dailymail.co.uk/news/article-2570675/The-Lefts-web-shame-Its-not-just-Harman-Dromey-Hewitt-As-reveal-members-Britains-ruling-liberal-elite-held-senior-posts-NCCL-closely-linked-paedophiles.html.

[1861] Andrew Gilligan, "The 'Right' to Sleep with Children was one 'Civil Liberty' that NCCL Supported," *The Telegraph*, February 21, 2014.

So in 1978 when Hodge and Oppenheimer were formalizing their marital partnership, Henry already had forged a cozy working partnership with UK's publicly known pedophile organization lobbying to abolish all age of consent so British adults could legally enjoy having sex with children of all ages. Do you really think it was purely by accident that just four years later under Margaret Oppenheimer-Hodge's Islington council leadership that Britain's biggest VIP pedophile ring became fully and safely operational, flourishing over the next 10 years all the while guarded feverishly by the Illuminati bloodline hawk and pedo-gatekeeper-in-charge - Oppenheimer-Hodge?

And do you think it mere coincidence that in 1976, the same year Margaret's future hubby turned his NCCL chairmanship over to his fellow Labor Party, PIE-loving faithful Jack Dromey (NCCL chairman 1976-1983), an official NCCL report signed by the organization's general secretary Patricia Hewitt (1974-1983) stated:

Childhood sexual experiences, willingly engaged in, with an adult result in no identifiable damage.[1862]

And more coincidence that pedo-enabler Prime Minister Tony Blair would later make his Islington next door neighbor Margaret Oppenheimer-Hodge his minister of children and Patricia Hewitt his health secretary and Jack Dromey's wife Harriet Harman former NCCL legal officer New Labor's deputy leader?

Oppenheimer husband Henry Hodge left NCCL just in time to escape public scrutiny for making PIE its sleazy bedfellow in 1975 and was only the third non-barrister elevated to high court judge, then knighted by the queen in 2004 before dying in 2009.[1863] But a few years after Hodge's death, it was Harman, Dromey and Hewitt, all still active Labor Party leaders, who were left answering for their shameful PIE affiliated past when records revealed that they, along with Henry Hodge, publicly advocated for laxer child pornography laws, legalized incest and lowering the age of consent to ten.[1864] As longtime fellow Labor Party MPs each sharing an ultra-cozy pedophilia past together, Harriet Harman once revealed that Dame Margaret Hodge is her best friend in Parliament.[1865] The pedo-wheel just keeps spinning round and round with the same incestual cast of high profile pedo-lovers as the usual suspects.

It's also more than coincidental that until 1978, Margaret Hodge served alongside fellow counsellor Jack Straw for his last five of seven years on the same Islington council together.[1866] As yet another Jewish Labor politician possessing a pedophilia enabling record, before Straw man was Blair's foreign "war crime" minister (2001-06), he was home secretary (1997-2001).

[1862] James Murray and James Fielding, "'We can't Prove Sex with Children does them Harm' says Labour-linked NCCL," *The Telegraph*, March 2, 2014.

[1863] "Sir Henry Hodge," *The Telegraph*, June 22, 2009.

[1864] Andrew Gilligan, https://www.telegraph.co.uk/comment/10653944/The-right-to-sleep-with-children-was-one-civil-liberty-that-NCCL-supported.html.

[1865] Eileen Fairweather, "Jimmy Savile Sex Abuse: 'Islington is still Covering up,'" *The Telegraph*, April 6, 2014.

[1866] Colin Hughes, "Jack Straw: Jack of all Tirades," *The Guardian*, July 24, 1999

While infiltrated pedophiles were still rampantly abusing kids in his old home district Islington and all around Britain, Straw was in charge of UK law enforcement and CPS, responsible for shutting down so many police investigations into VIP pedo-crimes and pedo-cases. Then it was Jack Straw as Justice Secretary in 2009 who prohibited children in UK care homes from speaking out when abused.[1867] Straw also gagged parents from being able to talk to the press about family court injustices as UK's mainline pedo-pipeline feeder, eerily similar to America's disastrous child welfare system.[1868] That's because a global Anglo-American-Zionist pedophile elite controls and enslaves both countries as well as Israel, Europe, Canada, Australia, New Zealand and virtually the entire globe. But the old Rothschild bloodline system is crumbling and losing its grip on humanity.

Why would Great Britain as a nation willfully tear apart its families, funneling so many of its children into its residential care system that renders them six times more likely to be assessed for abuse while living in government care homes than children in the general population?[1869]... **unless** the nation already has a longtime historical policy allowing its most powerful elite wealthy class - including politicians and entertainers - to systematically rape its most vulnerable population - the throwaway kids from residential care homes on such an immense industrial scale.[1870]

Tony Blair, Jack Straw, Margaret Hodge, Henry Hodge, Paul Boateng, Peter Mandelson, Greville Janner, Harriet Harman, Jack Dromey and Patricia Hewitt are but a handful sampling of 10 prominent pedophilia protectors who've been atop Britain's Labor Party. The British VIP pedophilia incest network extends literally into the personal lives of Margaret Oppenheimer and Jack Straw's spouses from their first marriages, both ending up as husband and wife on their next marital go-round. What are the odds of that? It's almost as if they all come from the same Jewish Illuminati bloodlines... perhaps that's because they actually do.[1871]

Jack Straw's brother was found guilty of committing indecent assault on a 16-year old girl. Jack Straw's son William was caught dealing drugs but given only a caution due to his Home Secretary father.[1872] What is it with all these pedo-loving Labor politicians' sons? Aside from Jack Straw's, Patricia Hewitt's was arrested and fined £350 for possession of cocaine[1873] and Tony Blair's was arrested for being "drunk and incapable,"[1874] of course none serving any jail time. A given perk that comes with the turf is the elite's family privilege to live like gods above

---

[1867] "Justice Ministry to Bar Parents from telling their own Stories," *Independent*, February 15, 2009.

[1868] Brian Shilhavy, "Child Sex Trafficking through Child 'Protection' Services Exposed – Kidnapping Children for Sex," *Health Impact News*, 2015..

[1869] GF Hobbs, CJ Hobbs and JM Wayne, (1999), "Abuse of Children in Foster and Residential Care," *Child Abuse & Neglect*, 23 (12), p.1239–52.

[1870] Beatrix Campbell, "The Scale of Historical Sexual Abuse in the UK is a Catastrophe. We need Catharsis," *The Guardian*, September 12, 2016.

[1871] "Straw's Brother on Sex Register," *BBC*, September 8, 2000.

[1872] Chris Irvine, "Russell Brand Jokes about Jack Straw's Son's Drug use on Twitter," *The Telegraph*, April 7, 2009.

[1873] "Patricia Hewitt's Son Fined for Cocaine," *The Guardian*, September 30, 2009.

[1874] "Blair's Son 'Drunk and Incapable," *BBC*, July 6, 2000.

manmade laws as protected members of an inner club in charge of the pedo-crime cabal network.

Of course from last chapter we learned the Conservative Party is just as bad. The Thatcher regime was crawling with Zionist pedophiles as well. VIP sodomizers from all political parties in virtually all Western nations hungrily devour and spit out the used and abused remains of victimized children everywhere on earth. That's why at this point we've reached such an acute crisis stage, because abuse has gone totally unchecked for so very long.

For more than a century Britain's ruling elite has systematically separated its male youth at a very early age from their families, for multiple generations customarily sending them to the same private upper-class boarding schools where both homosexuality and pedophilia have flourished in isolated infested entrenchment.[1875] This age old practice in the UK as well as Europe and, to some extent North America, has long been a familial, cultural norm for boys to be victimized by teachers, headmasters or older students,[1876] and in turn all too often become perpetrators themselves, resulting in a cultivation of inbred pedophilia as a historical, traditional way of life amongst the elite, a young man's twisted, not-so-secret rite of passage anymore in recent years with all the VIP pedo-scandals... another open secret exposed.

The uppermost stratosphere of royal and aristocratic family bloodlines have been vetting, grooming and controlling their men this way for centuries. In the US an example would be accepting an invitation to join the exclusive secret society Skull and Bones at Yale University where degrading sexual ritual is embedded in the traditional all male initiation ceremony as a transitional steppingstone of what's likely to come.[1877] They share a tradition of "elite deviance," a sense of built-in superiority that grants them the protected privilege to live above the law. Through sexual blackmail, pedophilia has been increasingly utilized by the pathological, psychopathic control system to groom, mold and manipulate "powerful" puppet males into assuming lofty prominent positions as compromised and controlled national leaders who do the filthy bidding of their pedophilic masters.[1878]

Secret occult knowledge and pedophilic ritual often play a central grooming role in conditioning "chosen" by birthright males into accepting and engaging in pedophilia through the social conditioning process in both elite families and elite educational institutions.[1879] In the UK the most powerful have been permitted methodically to indulge and perversely nurture their most

---

[1875] Alex Renton, "Abuse in Britain's Boarding Schools: Why I Decided to Confront my Demons," *The Guardian*, May 4, 2014.

[1876] Natalie Corner, "Paedophile Teacher Insists 'Intimate Relationships' with young Pupils is Normal at British Boarding Schools - as Documentary Lifts the Lid on the Shocking Scale of Sexual Abuse," *Daily Mail*, February 19, 2018.

[1877] Kevin Barrett, "FBI Child Pimp Raid Ignores the Elite," *Veterans Today*, August 1, 2013.

[1878] Ben Madigan, "Vile Bodies – Mutual Secrets, Mutual Blackmail," *eurofree3.wordpress.com*, September 23, 2015.

[1879] Makia Freeman, "Black Magic: Satanists Rule the World, not Politicians, Bankers or Military Heads," *The Freedom Articles*, August 20, 2015.

demented, inbred pathology, embracing a vampiric, tribal elitism as part of an inner club at the top of the predator food chain. Created by this diabolically decadent and depraved system, British homosexual VIP pedophiles regularly prey on the weakest and most defenseless humans, systemically kidnapped and trapped in the morally bankrupt, overloaded, thoroughly broken UK Care System,[1880] thus allowing unchecked pedophilia at the earth's epicenter to spread like a cancer to morph into the modern scourge of humanity currently plaguing our entire planet. This historical macro-analysis transcends the pitfalls of the micro-ephemeral approach to examining the phenomenon of rising pedophilia as a mere sociological outgrowth of the prevailing societal trends of the times.

In a July 2015 article, the *Daily Mail* explains how throughout the 1970s and 1980s, homosexuals masquerading as pedophiles were fiercely protected and how any staff in the London borough councils, the social services and group homes that attempted to protect abused children by exposing the pedophiles were punitively dealt with in very harsh terms:

Staff who raised concerns were accused of racism and homophobia, and often hounded out of their jobs. Some… received death threats. Almost 30 council employees accused of child abuse crimes were allowed to take early retirement (on generous pensions) instead of being subjected to formal investigations or referred to the police.[1881]

According to a *Daily Mail* article just a year prior in 2014, the rationale given to explain the widespread abuse in Islington was that child care home operators and line staff who were the alleged perpetrators were:

… convincing Labour-run Islington's political elite that anyone who attempted to blow the whistle on their crimes was motivated by homophobia.[1882]

But this is merely surface level, superficial explanation that overlooks the far deeper, darker reality that a vast pedophilia sexual blackmail network in Britain had long been operating for at least two decades prior to the 1970s, orchestrated primarily by British intelligence with full approval from countless government VIP pedophiles consisting of prime ministers, cabinet members and both the House of Lords and Commons extending down to countless local councils throughout the UK.[1883] It was never a matter of low level care home operators "convincing" their council politician bosses like Oppenheimer and Straw that in the sexually liberated 70s and 80s, it was hip for homosexual pedophiles to "liberate" their youth residing in

[1880] May Bulman, https://www.independent.co.uk/news/uk/home-news/social-care-crisis-uk-children-figures-per-day-a7995101.html.

[1881] Guy Adams, "A Blind Eye to Child Abuse: Whistleblowers Warned Labour Leadership Favourite Jeremy Corbyn of Paedophiles Preying on Children on his Doorstep - but claim he did nothing," *Daily Mail*, July 31, 2015.

[1882] Guy Adams, "Apologists for Paedophilia: As the Mail Exposes more links between Senior Labour Figures and a Vile Paedophile Group, one Man who was Abused as a Child asks them: why won't you Admit you were Wrong?," *Daily Mail*, February 22, 2014.

[1883] "The Mountain of Evidence for a Massive International Pedophile Ring Protected by Police and Intelligence Agencies," *The Millennium Report*, December 13, 2016.

Britain's care homes, and if you dare object, you were labeled "a homophobe." Though it may have been true, it's a convenient lame excuse to try and pass off the pedo-scandal in the 1980s as a mere sign of the "crazy" times - when the liberal left allowed itself to "momentarily" be blind-sighted, co-opted and hoodwinked by a few wacky hardcore PIE perverts.

Both the Labor and Tory governments misused taxpayers' money to help finance PIE between 1977 and 1980,[1884] Prime Minister Edward Heath attended PIE meetings[1885] and MI6 Chief Peter Hayman was a card carrying member[1886] as well as the aforementioned Labor notables aligned and fully supporting pedo-rights. These facts relegate this notion of UK pedophilia as a passing fad or mere byproduct of the wild 70s and 80s sexual liberation movement as preposterous and false. Yet this heavily promoted, historical revisionist argument heavily promulgated by pedo-apologists is intended to eliminate culpability and obscure the true reality that a highly organized, insulated, massive pedophilia network was covertly expanding and becoming further entrenched throughout the UK and beyond. And it never left.

It was just four years earlier that yet another piece in the *Daily Mail* completely refutes its own above quote. The ruling elite had long been building UK's national child abuse trafficking network, preying on care home kids since the straight-laced, "unhip" 1950s. The 2010 *Daily Mail* article expounds on the unsavory affairs of such child raping luminaries as Labor Party leader, Communist spy, MP traitor Lord Tom Driberg, his pal longtime Conservative Party minister, Bilderberger Lord Bob Boothby and their Jewish mafia, pimping killer pals the Kray twins,[1887] joined in the early 1960s by none other than the undercover intel operative himself Sir Jimmy Savile. Clearly a highly organized pedophilia network in Britain was operating long before the so called sexually liberated 1970s and 1980s. Cold hard fact - the UK pedophilic elite has been indulging nonstop in systemically destroying expendable British children's lives with total impunity for over six decades.

Back to this chapter's headliner, with her MBE secured way back in 1978, one of Britain's major pedo-players for the last four decades is Margaret Oppenheimer-Hodge, again honored by the queen in 2004 as Lady Hodge when her high court judge hubby Henry was knighted while she was Minister of Children under Blair's newly created cabinet position.[1888] Her royal Dame Commander trophy came in 2015. The children's ministry post served as ideal cover for an Oppenheimer to oversee the entire British nation's covert pedophilia operations. Also worth noting is that in 1998 and 1999, busy MP Margaret served in her spare time as chair of the

---

[1884] Paul Bentley, "Home Office 'gave Paedophile Information Exchange £70,000': Group allegedly given Taxpayers' Money between 1977 and 1980," *Daily Mail*, March 2, 2014..

[1885] Nick Gutteridge, "Ted Heath 'Fixed it for Jimmy Savile to get OBE and Attended Paedophile Group Meetings,'" *Express*, August 9, 2015.

[1886] Jennifer Smith, "Peter Hayman Named as VIP who Sexually Abused Boys at Dolphin Square apartment Complex near Parliament," *Daily Mail*, November 9, 2014.

[1887] John Pearson, "Sex, Lies, Downing Street and the Cover-up that left the Krays Free to Kill," *Daily Mail*, August 20, 2010.

[1888] Matthew Steeples, "The Rt. Hon. Margaret Hodge MBE MP (also known as Lady Hodge)," *The Steeple Times*, July 4, 2012.

infamous Fabian Society that for over a century as an elitist front for communism has been subversively pushing for one world totalitarian government. Sweet lady heading a sweet society.

Thee Fabians have openly supported eugenics and forced sterilization in their scientifically planned utopian society run by the superior "elite," certainly not by "lowly" working stiffs from a Marxist labor class.[1889] Until recently the Fabian logo was literally a wolf in sheep's clothing.[1890] Joining her as fellow Fabian Society members are two of her prominent Islington VIP Labor Party neighbors - Tony Blair and Jack Straw, and, as of 2001, just four years into Blair's decade long premiership, the elite Fabian Society boasted 200 MPs in the House of Commons.[1891] War criminal Tony Blair, both a Fabian and Malta Knight,[1892] loyal to both Zionism and Rome, both major contributors to the pedo-epidemic, if anything suggests Blair's deeper commitment to globalization of the international pedophilia trade. Right after his 2007 resignation as prime minister, the Malta Knight officially declared himself a Roman Catholic.

The common threaded nexus of pedo-lineage runs throughout virtually all elitist secret societies as well as all major political parties. Blair and Hodge's very own Labor Party was in fact founded by Fabians in the early 20th century and the pedo-infil-traitors rose to power in the Zionist controlled British government,[1893] reaching its zenith perhaps during Tony Blair's war crime pedo-regime when virtually his entire cabinet were card carrying Fabian members.[1894]

Similar (if not one and the same) with the Illuminati, Fabians believe that religion and family should be usurped and replaced by the expanding power of the centralized state through that familiar operative word "collectivism," whereby individuals' worth is derived and defined solely and strictly by their collective contribution to the group that is the supreme state. While the collectivist goal remains much the same as Marxism, rather than gain power and control through a proletariat working class rising up to wage revolutionary, violent revolt against the elite class, Fabians as the bourgeoisie prefer subversively, sneakily seizing control through slithering infiltration, hence their iconic, deceitfully cunning "wolf in sheep's clothing" methodology pretty much says it all.[1895]

Far beyond conjecture the British historical record demonstrates a pattern of prime ministers seeking to appoint fellow party politicians as proven experienced protectors of the ruling elite's international child sex abuse trafficking cabal. The key point is just as Thatcher's Tory government was stacked with flaming pedophiles and enablers galore throughout the 1980s, so

---

[1889] Diane Paul, "Fabians, Progressives and Eugenics," *blog.fair-use.org*, September 11, 2007.
[1890] "The Fabian Society – Creeping Communism," *fourwinds10.com*, September 3, 2009.
[1891] "The Fabian Society: A Brief History," *The Guardian*, August 13, 2001.
[1892] Evgeny Lebedev, "Caped Crusaders: What really goes on at the Knights of Malta's Secretive Headquarters?" *Independent*, March 29, 2014.
[1893] "Israel/Zionist Control of UK Government," *whale.to*.
[1894] "The Fabian Society: A Brief History," https://www.theguardian.com/politics/2001/aug/13/thinktanks.uk.
[1895] "The Fabian Society – Creeping Communism," http://www.fourwinds10.com/siterun_data/religion_cults/news.php?q=1252088437.

was Blair's turn during his turn of the century decade. And with nothing changing under yet another pro-Zionist prime minister currently in office, already having declared herself a Jew,[1896] Theresa May is carrying out her puppet duty holding a shameless sham of an Independent Inquiry for Child Sexual Abuse (IICSA), designed from the outset to protect status quo by keeping VIP pedophiles unnamed and out of both the headlines and prisons.[1897] And so far, unfortunately her "floundering-on-purpose" IICSA debacle has succeeded… never a living MP charged much less ever jailed for pedophilia.

Recall from last chapter that Theresa May is yet another self-professed Zionist with neighborly ties to Mossad agent Uri Geller. May has much to hide as prime minister in both protecting the pedophilia network at the world epicenter as well as her own family's paternal links that minimally suggest a nefarious past by association with the mass murdering Doctor John Bodkin Adams, a homosexual very likely protected by his lover Lord Roland Gwynne, former Eastbourne mayor in Sussex and knighted by the queen during his lover's infamous trial in 1957.[1898] Additionally like Sir Cliff Richard, May's father was born in India to a British soldier, a favorite common breeding ground for UK military intelligence.[1899]

For six years in the 1950s chronologically bisected by Theresa's birth in 1956, May's father Hubert Brasier was the Anglican-Catholic chaplain of Eastbourne Hospital in Sussex where the general practitioner Dr. Adams worked, suspected of killing over 165 of his elderly patients, over 130 mostly widows leaving a sizeable inheritance for their killer shortly prior drug overdoses administered by Adams.[1900] Though nurses had complained about Dr. Adams for months, similar to Jimmy Savile, the hospital management ignored their accusations. However, eventually the notorious doctor was prosecuted on a murder charge of just one of his patients. But in a blatant cover-up engineered by well-connected Sir Lord Gwynne who called upon his ex-attorney general friend to run interference, a year after Theresa's birth Dr. Adams was acquitted of murder and only found guilty of three minor offenses that led briefly to his revoked medical license before resuming his medical practice as if murdering over 160 people meant nothing…[1901] echoes of yet more sinister protection from the top of the food chain.

Though there appears no direct criminal evidence connecting May's father as an accomplice sharing the same workplace crime scene, yet another strange anomaly again by association is the fact that Rev. Brasier worked within the same small Chichester Diocese in Sussex that produced an inordinate number of pedophile priests caught running a longstanding Eastbourne

---

[1896] Gilad Atzmon, "At Last, a Jewish Prime Minister," *gilad.co.uk*, July 11, 2016.

[1897] Amy Southall, "Child Abuse Inquiry Member: 'I was Silenced in 2015 to Ensure Theresa May could become Prime Minister,'" *talkradio.co.uk*, August 11, 2017.

[1898] "Roland Gwynne Explained," *everything.explained.today*.

[1899] Mary W. Maxwell, "Theresa May's Father and his Death in a Car Crash," *Gumshoe News*, October 10, 2017.

[1900] "Theresa May, Gordon Rideout, Bodkin Adams – Famous Eastbourne People," *aangirfan.com*, July 2, 2016.

[1901] "Roland Gwynne Explained," http://everything.explained.today/Roland_Gwynne/.

pedo-ring.[1902] It was so blatant that in March 2018 even May's IICSA fiasco was pressured to look into the chronic abuse.

By some stroke of luck, just in time May's father was promoted and reassigned elsewhere as 1st Vicar of Enstone in the Oxford Diocese, almost as if he (like Dr. Adams) was protected by the elite's invisible hand.[1903] Then when Theresa had just turned 25, her father's good luck ran out as he was mysteriously killed in a car accident, a common pattern amongst future leaders groomed by their handlers, making loss of a parent while still young easier to control their puppet. As one who should know, FDR once admitted, presidents (and prime ministers) are chosen, never elected.[1904] Only adding suspicion to indicate that the current PM clearly does not want information about her family history available to the public, as soon as she became prime minister in 2016, all references regarding her father were suddenly removed from the internet.[1905] But fortunately plenty was already captured prior to her overt censorship.

For her Illuminati lineage, the true essence of one Dame Margaret Oppenheimer-Hodge emerges while she presided over the Islington council between 1982 and 1992, the direct overseer in charge of her district's social services for children. During her decade long leadership, all dozen Islington group homes she governed became overrun by infiltrating pedophiles on staff throughout her "care" homes, her council run schools, her social services offices, her own Islington council that as foxes guarding the pedo-henhouse were also at liberty to farm out their susceptible kids to VIPs for yet more systematic abuse.[1906] Under her watch a major pedophile ring was booming between her Islington and the queen's Commonwealth's Channel Islands of Jersey and Guernsey branching out further across the Isles to Northern Ireland's Kincora, North Wales Bryn Estyn as well as closer to home in and around London, like Haringey to the north and Lambeth to the south, but also nearby Richmond, Birmingham to Northern England's Savile country Leeds and Scarborough. Additionally, the tentacles of the London based pedophilia network reach abroad to continental cities in Europe such as Amsterdam, Brussels, Copenhagen, Vienna and Portugal's Casa Pia. All will be uncovered in detail in later chapters.

Another pedophilic link between the United Kingdom and Amsterdam was exposed over three and a half decades ago by the *Daily Star* back in August 1983. Norman K. Walker misappropriated government funds through his bogus children's foundation owning two British care homes for handicapped children located in Suffolk and Norfolk.[1907] Social services from those two counties did not place children at those homes but districts like Lambeth, Islington and other London boroughs did. With public social services funding, Walker financed a string of

[1902] Andreas Whittam-Smith, "Chichester Child Abuse: How did one small Church of England Diocese Produce so many Paedophile Reverends?" *Independent*, March 25, 2018.

[1903] Mary W. Maxwell, https://gumshoenews.com/2017/10/10/theresa-mays-father-death-car-crash/.

[1904] Tyler S. Bloyer, "Presidents are Selected, not Elected," *steemit.com*, 2017..

[1905] Matt Taylor, "Theresa May: Leadership of Lunacy," *Guerilla Democracy News*, June 8, 2017.

[1906] Emily Finch, "Claim Council Workers 'Helped Paedophiles,'" *Islington Tribune*, October 6, 2017.

[1907] Tony Sapiano, "Mr Nasty," *Daily Star/spotlightonabuse.wordpress.com*, August 1, 1983.

pedophilia rent boy bars and sex businesses in Amsterdam, among them a notorious waterhole called Why Not that included upstairs room accommodations for pedos. Seedy establishments like Walker's in Holland were/are part of the international child trafficking network, with British rent boys recruited to cater to sex tourism pedophiles and child pornographers that produce and distribute murderous snuff films.[1908]

Warwick Spinks, the most wanted British pedophile criminal and international fugitive for decades was allowed to infamously engage in sexually and commercially exploiting and even murdering underage boys in his sex slave business. In November 2012 Spinks, who at one time managed the Why Not bar, was finally apprehended in Prague after 15 years on the run.[1909] More on this sleaziest violent kingpin in the next chapter on his Elm Guest House-Westminster connection. One of the reasons speculated that this so called "pied piper of pedophiles" successfully evaded police for so long and has been awarded such light sentences is his connections to VIP pedophile clients. Chapter 24 fully covers Spinks' London to continental Europe pedo-network featuring his Dutch snuff film production as well as trafficking victims from both Britain and Eastern Europe to Amsterdam as well as Prague, Brussels, Munich and Berlin.

Meanwhile in 1983 while Dame Margaret recruited pedophiles posing as gay men to do damage to children in her dozen care homes, horrific tragedies struck Islington group home children year in and year out under her leadership and care. In September 1983 a 13-year old boy was abducted and brought to France by his group home childcare worker where he allegedly sexually abused the victim for nearly two months before his rescue.[1910] In 1985 a far more tragic fate befell 14-year old Jason Swift who was kidnapped, sexually passed around a notorious pedophile ring, repeatedly raped, tortured and savagely killed by the Sidney Cooke gang. These sickos murdered up to 17 boys while procuring and trafficking victims to the Elm Guest House for the likes of Sir Jimmy Savile, Home Secretary Sir Leon Brittan and MP Sir Cyril Smith among other "distinguished" VIP guests both domestic and foreign.[1911] A year later in 1986 13-year old Tony McGrane was bludgeoned to death with multiple stab wounds by another teenager.[1912] Both Jason and Tony were residents at one of the Islington care homes Margaret presided over - Conewood Street Assessment Centre.[1913]

[1908] Nick Davies, "When Sex Abuse can lead to Murder," *The Guardian*, November 27, 2000.

[1909] Amanda Williams, "The 'Pied Piper of Paedophiles' Caught after 15 years on the run: Britain's most Wanted Child Abuser who Kidnapped and Sold Young Boys is Arrested at Heathrow," *Daily Mail*, November 18, 2012.

[1910] Julie Isherwood, "Runaway Boy Found in France," *Islington Gazette/spotlightonabuse.wordpress.com*, November 11, 1983.

[1911] Steph Cockroft, "Notorious Paedophile Gang 'could have Covered up 17 Child Murders and be Linked to VIP Guest House,'" *Daily Mail*, November 20, 2014.

[1912] James Morris, "This Week 30 Years Ago: Man on Trial for Stabbing Tony McGrane to Death," *Islington Gazette*, May 22, 2017.

[1913] Conman Jeremy Corbyn?" *aangirfan.com*, June 10, 2015.

When Margaret Hodge was selected by Blair to be Britain's first minister of children, a stampede of social workers, whistleblowers and victims stepped forward in loud protest to set the record straight. In her defense, Hodge claimed:

All that happened when we didn't really understand child abuse in the way that we understand it now. This was the early 90s...[1914]

Wrong! Years prior to her Islington debacle pedophilia scandals splashed across UK's headlines and TV news broadcasts – for starters the 1984 Dickens' accusations from the infamous "lost" dossier maintaining a Westminster VIP pedophile ring at the heart of the British government.[1915] Dickens even went so far as to expose child abuse in Islington while Hodge was council leader.[1916] Then there were numerous earlier scandals reported at care homes in places like Newcastle's Tyneside children's home in 1976,[1917] Northern Ireland's Kincora in 1980[1918] and Piccadilly Circus' Leeways children's home in 1985,[1919] plus many high profile cases of pedophiles working with children as priests, teachers and scoutmasters were also being widely reported long before the 1990s. Hodge again pretended pedophiles preying on UK's most vulnerable population was a completely unknown, new phenomenon... total bullshit to cover her own ass. But in her feeble, lame self-defense, she uttered these words:

This was the early 90s... it was only beginning to emerge that paedophiles were working with children, in children's homes and elsewhere, and so I think my great regret there was believing without question the advice that I was given by the social services managers.[1920]

Typically, weak leaders never fail to pass the buck, always blaming subordinates for feeding them erroneous information and advice. Again, another lie as senior social workers alerted her two and a half years prior to the story finally breaking in the press in early October 1992,[1921] the year she slipped out the council backdoor in a vain attempt to avoid the heat. The fact remains that by early 1990, social worker university lecturer Dr. Liz Davies and her social services manager David Cofie reported to Margaret Hodge an infiltrated pedophile ring was rampantly

---

[1914] Aida Edemariam, Margaret Hodge: "'The Tax you owe is a Duty. It's an Obligation,'" *The Guardian*, April 27, 2013.

[1915] Tom Symonds and Daniel De Simone, "Police to Investigate Geoffrey Dickens Sex Abuse Dossier," *BBC*, October 21, 2015.

[1916] Steven Swinford, "Jeremy Corbyn Accused of Inaction over Paedophile Scandal," *The Telegraph*, July 23, 2015.

[1917] Murun Buchstansangur, "Brian Roycroft and the Tynside Children's Home Scandal," *spotlightonabuse.wordpress.com*, December 6, 2013.

[1918] Peter McKenna, "Kincora: How Scandal was first Reported in 1980," *Belfast Telegraph*, January 24, 1980.

[1919] Alex Marauchak, Scandal of Top Cop and Rent Boys," *News of the World/spotlightonabuse.wordpress.com*, May 11, 1986.

[1920] Aida Edemariam, https://www.theguardian.com/politics/2013/apr/27/margaret-hodge-tax-duty-interview?INTCMP=SRCH.

[1921] Eileen Fairweather and Stewart Payne, "The Scandal at the Heart of Child Care," *Evening Standard/spotlightonabuse.wordpress.com*, October 6, 1992.

operating throughout all her Islington care homes but their warnings went unheeded by arrogant Hodge, condescendingly calling their warnings "hysterical" and "obsessional."[1922]

Overwhelmed by the ever-widening scope of abuse in their outlying community, upon learning it was systemic throughout the district involving child pornography and trafficking, when David Cofie urgently requested increased staff and funding to adequately meet the demand of investigating the major scandal brewing, Hodge severely chastised him, insisting a sound manager should be resourceful enough to work within a budget in the face of social services cutbacks.[1923] David Cofie has in effect said she ruined his career. Bent on burying evidence, Hodge actively squelched proven widespread abuse that Liz and David had discovered and painstakingly presented to her.

Dazed and distraught 12 to 15-year old children kept showing up at Liz and David's social services office in droves, having clearly been abused the night before, sometimes perpetrated by group home staff, sometimes by Islington council staff, and sometimes abused after being trafficked to wealthy private mansions around London.[1924] Liz found out that not only was her district overflowing with child molesters but that PIE's international office was a mere few hundred yards away from her desk.[1925] Links that Islington kids were being transported to Elm Guest House and Dolphin Square parties were found. Britain's director of education at the National Institute of Social Work, PIE founder, sadistic child rapist and pedo-pipeline VIP pimp Peter Righton is known to have picked up children at group homes in Islington.[1926]

Recall that big wheel procurer Righton himself was arrested in 1992 for attempting to smuggle in as well as possess child pornography but like Savile for years the pipeline pimp was permitted to freely operate as a key protected player within the Westminster VIP network.[1927] Considered the foremost expert on group home care of Britain's near 100,000 children in the UK Care System (same number of UK kids slipping into poverty in the last year alone[1928] and same number of 14-year olds in UK harming themselves, including one in four girls[1929] – talk about a broken system and nation), like Savile, Righton freely roamed the Isles with access to hundreds of residential care homes and special schools, brazenly boasting:

[1922] Liz Davies, "Open Letter to Margaret Hodge MP," *lizdavies.net*, August 3, 2014.

[1923] David Cohen, Yes Minister, you were told about Child Abuse in the Care Homes, yet you Refused to Listen," *Evening Standard/spotlightonabuse.wordpress.com*, June 30, 200.

[1924] David Cohen, https://spotlightonabuse.wordpress.com/2013/02/28/yes-minister-you-were-told-about-child-abuse-in-the-care-homes-yet-you-refused-to-listen-30-6-03/.

[1925] Nico Hines, "How Thatcher's Government Covered up a VIP Pedophile Ring," *Daily Beast*, June 3, 2015.

[1926] Guy Adams, https://www.dailymail.co.uk/news/article-3181783/Did-Jeremy-Corbyn-try-protect-fellow-Left-wingers-implicated-paedophile-scandal.html.

[1927] John Hall, "Officer involved in 1992 Child Porn Arrest said five Suitcases Stuffed with Letters suggested links to Establishment and Senior Clergy," *Daily Mail*, July 9, 2014..

[1928] May Bulman, "Number of Children in Poverty Surges by 100,000 in a Year, Figures show," Independent, March 22, 2018.

[1929] Sarah Marsh and Amanda Boateng, "Quarter of 14-year-old Girls in UK have Self-Harmed, Report finds," *The Guardian*, August 29, 2018.

Every Islington care home manager knows I like boys from 12 [1930][on up].

Just like the Hollywood and Savile pedophilia scandals, founding PIE member Peter Righton was yet another "open secret" where his guilt was sworn to "open" secrecy amongst a select insider group in order to protect the larger national and global pedo-network. After his arrest for importing child pornography and his home raided in 1992, he was simply given a £900 fine and never served jail time, in spite of tons of evidence he was a serial predator and major pimping trafficking ringleader for the VIP establishment.[1931] In addition to pornographic images of children found at his residence, a prolific amount of letters, documents and diary entries exposed Righton's exchange of child sex slaves with fellow criminal collaborators in other locations in Europe, such as the Mediterranean islands of Gozo and Malta, a known sex trafficking haven.[1932]

In 1993 Department of Health Minister Virginia Bottomley received a report from Hereford and Worcester social services outing the alarming state of betrayal from UK's Care System sworn to protect children, singling out mastermind Righton as the nation's prime pedo-networker with full access to all of Britain's children's homes and schools.[1933] But Bottomley ignored that report and though the police investigation continued into 1994 as more incriminating evidence was amassed, the probe was suddenly, prematurely shut down. In charge of all UK police investigations, Tory Home Secretary (1993-97) Michael Howard likely ordered the probe closed in order to protect Britain's VIPs and involvement in the international child trafficking network.[1934]

Right after his initial arrest, Peter Righton and his 40-year lover Richard Alston were granted safe refuge by Lord John Henniker to live comfortably at his sprawling country estate in Suffolk for the next four years.[1935] But Lord Henniker's estate was also being used by Islington and other London borough social services as a designated children's activities center for day trips and holidays.[1936] In the same way Dunsmore school for girls was used as Savile's "sweet shop," Thornham Magna had to be Righton, Alston and their fellow pedophile buddy Charles Napier's sodomizer-paradise. Surrounded by kids in the UK Care System, the Suffolk chief constable even went so far as to pay a visit explicitly warning Henniker that he was housing two pedophiles with national connections on his estate. Lord Henniker, a longtime diplomat and director general of the British Council from 1968 to 1972, maintained close ties with the queen's hubby

---

[1930] Guy Adams, https://www.dailymail.co.uk/news/article-3181783/Did-Jeremy-Corbyn-try-protect-fellow-Left-wingers-implicated-paedophile-scandal.html.
[1931] Vanessa Allen, "Paedophile at Centre of Historical Abuse Inquiry 'Visited Children's Homes around Britain and took Boys out' before Advising Home Office on Child Care System," *Daily Mail*, August 18, 2014.
[1932] Sarah Carabott, "Malta again Fails to take Action to Fight Human Trafficking - US State Department," *Times of Malta*, July 6, 2018.
[1933] Peter Rose, "An Abuse of Trust," *Daily Mail/spotlightonabuse.wordpress.com*, February 24, 1994.
[1934] "Evidence of 'Organised Abuse' and 'Trade' of Young Boys in Gozo Resurfaces," *Independent*, August 17, 2014..
[1935] "Policeman Cleared of Child Rape; Righton, Napier, Henniker, Islington," *aangirfan.com*, February 14, 2013.
[1936] Stewart Payne and Eileen Fairweather, "Country House Hideaway of Disgraced Care Chief," *Evening Standard/spotlightonabuse.wordpress.com*, May 6. 1993.

Prince Philip who is the godfather to Lord Henniker's firstborn son, his heir and later to become the current 9th Lord Henniker.[1937] The current lord's son, age 10-13 at the time Righton and his lover lived there, ended up committing suicide by age 21, leaving speculation whether he was a victim.

Protected by the top of the predator food chain, Peter Righton appeared immune from accountability and granted unrestricted access to children right up until his death in 2007 at the age of 81. The full extent of his pivotal role as a major cog in the UK pedo-wheel has been carefully concealed to shield his pedo elite masters he faithfully served from further scrutiny and justice... another illustration of how pedophilia overlords close rank to protect their own criminal self-interest by protecting their suppliers.

Despite being Righton's longtime partner-in-crime and brother to notable diplomat Robert Alston, especially without his deceased lover's impunity, former teacher and headmaster Richard Alston wasn't deemed high enough on the pedo-pecking order to be completely immune from prosecution. In 2015, the 70-year old PIE member was convicted of repeatedly sexually molesting an 11-year old boy in the 1970s, receiving 21 months in prison.[1938] The Alston brothers and Peter Righton all attended Ardingly College,[1939] a higher educational institution sponsoring its own Freemasonry lodge.[1940]

Another serial pedophile who often joined Righton and Alston in incidents abusing boys is British Council teacher and PIE treasurer, the previously mentioned Charles Napier, half-brother to longtime Tory MP John Whittingdale.[1941] Napier bragged about using diplomatic privileges to smuggle child pornography into the UK from a British Council school in Cairo. As Napier's friend and British Council chief, Lord Henniker allowed Napier to work with children despite an earlier pedo-conviction that banned him from teaching in UK.[1942] No wonder the boy abusing trio was so welcomed at the country kiddie sweet shop.

In December 2014 the 67-year old Napier was sentenced to 13 years for committing hundreds of sexual assaults on rent boys and schoolboys over a span of numerous decades. As a PIE officer within an organization publicly advocating sex with children of all ages, Napier knows much more than he has let on regarding the crimes of other PIE members, many of whom happened to be VIP establishment in politics, the church and law enforcement. As alluded to earlier, one of those VIPs was MI6 chief and diplomat Peter Hayman married to Charles Napier's cousin. Released files prove that not only was Sir Peter Hayman a PIE member, he

---

[1937] Christopher Wilson, "A Suicide, a Bankrupt and an Adulterer: The Perils of being one of Prince Philip's 50+ Godchildren as the Duke becomes a Godfather again at 97," *Daily Mail*, August 1, 2018.

[1938] Corey Charlton, Former School Teacher and Partner of Paedophile Information Exchange Founder is Sentenced to 21 Months in Prison for Molesting an 11-year-old Boy in the 70s," *Daily Mail*, September 28, 2015.

[1939] "Richard Alston," *loucollins.uk*.

[1940] "Ardingly College Lodge No 4410," *ardinglycollegelodge.org.uk*.

[1941] Paul Peachey, "Tory MP's Half-Brother Charles Napier Sentenced to 13 years over 'Prolific' Child Sex Abuse," *Independent*, December 23, 2014.

[1942] "Policeman Cleared of Child Rape; Righton, Napier, Henniker, Islington."

carried on lengthy correspondence with other sickos indicating that he shared a deranged obsession for sexual torture and murder of children.[1943]

To keep a lid on these international implications, Zionist Home Office puppet Michael Howard and Health Minister Virginia Bottomley were no doubt ordered to pass the word down to cease and desist two simultaneous probes by West Mercia and Metro police looking into VIP pimp Righton, the nationally recognized "expert" on child residential care. And it was Tory leader Howard who awarded Virginia Bottomley her peerage in the House of Lords in 2005.[1944]

At just 12-years old Virginia (née Garnett) met her then 16-year old future husband, was impregnated by 18 and married by 19 to Sir Peter Bottomley (knighted in 2010), a Thatcher minister-MP since 1974 to present.[1945] Peter Bottomley was a member of the Conservative Monday Club linked to pedophile trips to Amsterdam as well as Elm Guest House.[1946] Peter's brother Henry was a member on Hodge's pedo-enabling Islington council from 1986 to 1990.[1947] Are these reasons why Sir Peter's so touchy about any pedophilic affiliation that he has gone on record threatening to sue any publication linking him to "untrue" child abuse?[1948] But more on him and the notorious Monday Club in the next chapter.

As a related aside, Baroness Virginia Bottomley's cousin Jeremy Hunt seemingly owes his political career to her nepotism, following her same career footsteps as South West Surrey MP turned Cameron's Tory health minister,[1949] quoted worldwide reacting to the Savile bombshell, declaring So-vile's actions have "shaken our country to the core."[1950] Profusely apologizing to Savile victims, Hunt indignantly issued the following stern warning:

If there is evidence that people have criminally neglected claims at the time, behaved inappropriately... in a way that could make them subject to disciplinary procedures, that should happen and we will urge all NHS organisations to look carefully at anyone mentioned in these reports, and of course the police will look at the evidence against any individuals.[1951]

We're still waiting Jeremy... Meanwhile, while his cousin was health secretary in 1993 learning of Peter Righton's near four decade long history of horrific child abuse, international trafficking and Virginia's subsequent part in halting an ongoing police investigation, Hunt's tough talk extended to the "Savile greenlight" health ministers' Edwina Currie and Kenneth Clarke was

---

[1943] "UK Government Document Confirms over 2,000 Child Sex Abuse Files Destroyed, *whale.to*, February 3, 2015.
[1944] Joe Murphy, "Tony's Cronies to give Labour Lords Majority; Blair Risks Row as Army of Retiring MPs are made Peers," *Evening Standard/questia.com*, 2005.
[1945] "The Peerage: Virginia Hilda Brunette Maxwell Garnett, Baroness Bottomley of Nettlestone," *peerage.com*.
[1946] "Spooks Versus Cameron; Daily Mail Psyops," *aangirfan.com*, September 22, 2015..
[1947] "Peter Bottomley," *revolvy.com*.
[1948] Jason Groves, "I'll Sue if anyone Links me to Untrue Paedophile Claims, says Tory Grandee Sir Peter Bottomley," *Daily Mail*, July 7, 2014.
[1949] John Ward, "Revealed at last: The Hunt-Bottomley Link," *The Slog*, October 10, 2012.
[1950] Rowena Mason, "NHS Staff and Ex-Ministers should Face Action over Savile, says Jeremy Hunt," *The Guardian*, June 26, 2014.
[1951] Rowena Mason, https://www.theguardian.com/society/2014/jun/26/nhs-staff-jimmy-savile-jeremy-hunt.

conspicuously absent applied to his own cousin's obstruction of justice shutting down a police inquiry to allow a known serial abuser and VIP pimp to continue committing crimes. But then the theatrics of high-minded tough talk indignation with cameras rolling comes with the territory of all whorish puppet politicians.

Speaking of Sir Jimmy damage, as an intelligence operative and another national VIP pimp, his name invariably comes up in every single United pedo-Kingdom scandal, the Islington debauchery no exception. One abused girl said that a fleet of procuring "Jimmy Savile taxis" would show up regularly at her group home to whisk away children for waiting VIP predators.[1952] Victims maintain that they were not only trafficked around London but other locations inside the UK as well, and even abroad, indicating yet more evidence of a well-organized international pedophilia network. Another child victim recalls being driven around by abuser Savile in a taxi.[1953]

According to the *Express*, another noteworthy Islington resident "playing a vital role in Britain's biggest child sex ring" was convicted pedophile, active PIE member, clockmaker and antique shop owner Keith Harding who, like Cyril Smith, was a Savile featured fellow pedo-guest on a Jim'll Fix It's Christmas show.[1954] Harding was also known to run with such infamous VIP pedo-politicians as Sir Leon, Sir Cyril and Sir Jeremy Thorpe who were reported to frequent his Islington shop.

Two and a half years after personally informing Dame Margaret Hodge about the out-of-control abuse, turning to the press in October 1992, whistleblowing duo Liz Davies and David Cofie ultimately found receptive reporters in Eileen Fairweather and Stewart Payne from the *Evening Standard* whose articles finally began publicly exposing the pervasive child sex abuse raging throughout the Islington borough and beyond. But council leader Hodge's response this time turned even more aggressive and insulting libelously accusing the highly respected, award winning journalists of "a sensationalist piece of gutter journalism."[1955] Hodge was later forced to apologize once she could no longer pretend that she didn't permit a humongous murderous pedophile ring to not only freely operate but flourish like never before throughout her ten year reign of child terror atop the Islington council.

In 2008 during the height of the police investigation on Jersey Island's Haut de la Garenne, veteran journalist Eileen Fairweather was dispatched to meet secretly with Detective Constable Peter Cook who told her he had uncovered major links between the pervasive abuse at Jersey

---

[1952] Robert Mendick and Eileen Fairweather, "Margaret Hodge 'Sorry' as Council she led told to Investigate Savile Abuse Allegations," *The Telegraph*, April 6, 2014.

[1953] Jon Dean, "Fresh Savile Link to Islington Child Abuse Scandal," *Islington Gazette*, November 20, 2014.

[1954] James Fielding, "Exclusive: Clockmaker Keith Harding Played Vital Role in Britain's Biggest Child Sex Ring," *Express*, May 10, 2015.

[1955] Andrew Johnson, "Islington Child Abuse Scandal that Haunts Margaret Hodge, Politician Poised to Run for Mayor of London," *Islington Tribune*, September 19, 2014.

and Islington.[1956] Cook said his superior officers on Jersey prohibited him from reporting his findings directly to London police abuse specialists as part of the larger cover-up, pathetically forcing him to use Eileen as his go-between. Pedophile social workers from Jersey ended up working at the Islington social services offices and arranged unofficial trips trafficking children from both Islington group homes and Channel Island group homes where they were further abused by establishment VIPs. Keep in mind that Jimmy Savile as Britain's main VIP procurer also is linked extensively to both Islington and Jersey child abuse rings. The major VIP pedophile ring operating between Channel Islands Jersey and Guernsey and Islington-North London involving prominent politicians in both Jersey and London also included a famous diplomat (likely Peter Hayman), prominent clerics (among them Prince Charles bud Anglican bishop Peter Ball), a social services chief (allegedly Richmond's Louis Minster) and senior police officers (too many to name).

As an illustration of how the pedophilia-system rewards its own foxes guarding the henhouse, the Islington head of the police Child Protection Team at the height of the scandal in the 1990s - Sue Akers, refused to meet or talk to reporter Eileen Fairweather, despite Eileen begging her to look into a brothel after a 13-year old victim (and relative of Baby P discussed shortly) had reported he recruited dozens of other victims for three pimps.[1957] His evidence was suppressed and Sue Akers went on to be promoted as the deputy assistant commander responsible for all of the child abuse investigations for Britain's largest police force Metro. You can easily see why VIPs never get arrested or go to trial and that police probes always lead nowhere.

While investigating abuse at the dozen Islington group homes and special schools in the early 1990s, honest lower level detectives had informed Eileen Fairweather that children's home operators and employees served as "networkers" working the pedophile supply line with child pornographers and hooking up VIPs. Years later while in Jersey conferring with Peter Cook, Eileen was startled by the number of eerie similarities between the two abuse operations, the "recreational outings" often at sea where victims were isolated and easily abused while trafficked considerable distances to awaiting VIP customers and child pornographers in other cities for further abuse.[1958] Also identical is the pattern of dismissing and smearing whistleblowers and victims initially coming forth to report the crimes and then the repeated crime of "misplaced" missing records, all standard earmarks of major cover-up at the highest levels, and aborted police investigations. The cumulative evidence clearly points to sophisticated abuse rings consisting of pedophile operatives running Britain's child trafficking network, from the likes of Jimmy Savile, his friends at MI5, the Kray brothers, Sidney Cooke, Peter Righton and Colin Peters among numerous others as primary child procurers for VIP

[1956] Eileen Fairweather, "'I have known about Jersey Paedophiles for 15 years,' says Award-Winning Journalist," *Daily Mail*, March 2, 2008.
[1957] Eileen Fairweather, https://www.telegraph.co.uk/news/uknews/crime/jimmy-savile/10746412/Jimmy-Savile-sex-abuse-Islington-is-still-covering-up.html.
[1958] Eileen Fairweather, https://www.mailonsunday.co.uk/news/article-523706/I-known-Jersey-paedophiles-15-years-says-award-winning-journalist.html.

politicians like Heath, Thatcher, Brown, Blair and Hodge as either pedophiles themselves or pedophile-protecting overlords.

In addition to whistleblowing senior social workers and newspaper journalists sounding the Islington alarm that Margaret Hodge continued only to scoff at, yet another scandal tipoff occurred in 1991 when boarding school sports instructor Roy Caterer was arrested, convicted and sentenced to seven and a half years in prison for sexually abusing seven boys and two girls.[1959] Though this case garnered brief local headlines treating it as an isolated anomaly, the coverage either concealed or completely overlooked its linkage to the much wider pedophilia operation that had been thriving in Islington since the 1970s when the likes of Margaret Oppenheimer, Henry Hodge and Jack Straw were leading council members.

A couple of high profile child murder cases in adjacent Haringey in 2000 and 2007 highlight a link to the Islington pedophile ring. Eight year old Victoria Climbié from Ivory Coast was sent by her parents hopeful for a better life for their daughter to live in North London with her aunt and her boyfriend who tortured and murdered the little girl in 2000, bringing much needed scrutiny and pressure on the negligent borough's social services to become more responsive in placing at risk children on the services register to prevent or stop severe abuse and death.[1960] But rather than rectify glaring deficits that caused the young girl's murder, seven years later Haringey's reputation failed to improve as the same serious problems of incompetence and poor management still plagued its social services department, setting the stage for the next tragedy.

The same extreme dysfunction and endangerment caused the death of a blue eyed blonde haired toddler known only as Baby P at the sadistic hands of the mother's husband and his friend in 2007. The three relentlessly injured the child, ripping his fingernails out, breaking his ribs, soon his back, paralyzing him from the waist down.[1961] Fifty injuries despite sixty social worker visits later, the mother persistently lied to incompetent, negligent social workers about his nonstop injuries blindly accepted without question or suspicion. A week prior to his death social services legal department ruled that there remained insufficient grounds to remove the child from his mother and four days before he died a welfare officer was the last outsider to see the 17 month old still alive. No one paid attention to the poor kid's rapidly deteriorating health. The one social worker who did desperately attempt to alert authorities of increasing dangers six months ahead of Baby P's death became subsequently targeted as the blame game victim of abuse by Haringey CYA social services, nearly taking her child away.[1962]

[1959] Paul Waugh, "Another Minister under Fire: Call for Hodge to Quit over Child Abuse Scandal," *Independent*, July 1, 2003.

[1960] David Batty, "Timeline for the Climbié Case," *The Guardian*, September 24, 2001.

[1961] "Teenager Reveals full Horror of Shocking Ordeal Suffered by Baby P at the Hands of his Tormentors," *Daily Mail*, November 16.

[1962] Eileen Fairweather, "Baby P Council Falsely Accused me of Abusing a Child, Reveals Whistleblower who Feared she'd Lose her Daughter," *Daily Mail*, November 16, 2008..

An older unnamed close relative to Baby P who apparently had no contact with the murdered toddler had been placed in a care home in Islington at the age of 12 in the early 1990s.[1963] A child protection expert commented:

The family should have been subjected to forensic examination. Even cursory checks would have rung alarm bells. Social workers might then have removed the baby, as a paediatrician and police pleaded.[1964]

The Baby P relative was sexually abused and recruited by local pimps in Islington through money, drugs and coercive threats to procure more boys from local care homes for the larger VIP ring operating in Hodge's domain.[1965] The boy tried to get help, confiding in his social worker. Baby P's relative even furnished social services and police with a list of abuse victims and known perpetrators, reporting that he and other children were being trafficked from Islington care homes to Manor Park, Tottenham, Soho and Westminster where they were further abused by pedophiles, some of whom were members of the British VIP establishment.[1966]

Neville Mighty, the social services unit superintendent in charge of the boy's placement was eager to intervene on the boy's behalf as the hazardous living conditions for children at the borough's group homes he directly supervised had pimps flagrantly shacking up overnight in care homes openly abusing preyed upon children.[1967] As outrageous and unacceptable as it had become in Islington, Neville Mighty's boss called him "a prude" for repressing the sexuality of the group home residents, insisting the pimps were simply the children's "boyfriends." When Neville presented this insanely perverse, out of control situation to then Islington's social services director Lyn Cusack, the Hodge lackey whose husband was a local senior police superintendent, incredibly threatened to write him up on disciplinary action for being "rude."

In June 1992 social worker Neville Mighty was fired. At this point senior social worker Liz Davies encouraged and supported Neville to blow the whistle going public to expose the scandal. As is so typical, neither the Baby P relative, nor Neville, nor Liz, nor supervisor David Cofie were ever listened to by their higher-ups in social services, the borough council or the co-opted, thoroughly controlled local police as they refused to place the identified VIP child rapists under surveillance or even call them in for questioning. That's how evilly corrupt Islington under

---

[1963] Eileen Fairweather, "Revealed: How a Close Male Relative of Baby P is Linked to a Big Paedophile Network," *Daily Mail*, November 16, 2008..

[1964] Eileen Fairweather, https://www.dailymail.co.uk/news/article-1086200/Revealed-How-close-male-relative-Baby-P-linked-big-paedophile-network.html.

[1965] Eileen Fairweather, https://www.dailymail.co.uk/news/article-1086200/Revealed-How-close-male-relative-Baby-P-linked-big-paedophile-network.html.

[1966] Eileen Fairweather, https://www.dailymail.co.uk/news/article-1086200/Revealed-How-close-male-relative-Baby-P-linked-big-paedophile-network.html.

[1967] Eileen Fairweather, https://www.dailymail.co.uk/news/article-1086200/Revealed-How-close-male-relative-Baby-P-linked-big-paedophile-network.html.

Margaret Oppenheimer-Hodge's leadership was. Liz Davies explained to journalist Eileen Fairweather:

We got too close. There were too many powerful people involved. Child sex, pornography and sadism are extremely lucrative industries.[1968]

As Neville, Liz and David became increasingly aware and frustrated over the horrific crime network operating in their neighborhoods they were supposed to be protecting, Hodge's hostile suppression and overt criminal cover-up successfully shielded the perpetrators as she and her lackey Cusack summarily dismissed the courageous whistleblowers as "hysterical" troublemakers, ordering them to cease and desist their underfunded, understaffed internal investigation interviewing dozens of key abuse witnesses, victims and parents. Fortunately Nevile, Liz and David's whistleblowing persisted at grave risk to themselves, all being bodily threatened with harm and death threats. Through their brave, persistent efforts, finally a 1995 independent fact-finding report was compiled and released by Oxfordshire social services director Ian White. It vindicated their heroic efforts, but confirmed the deplorable prevailing conditions of blatant widespread abuse that also included child pornography, trafficking and pimping victims to VIPs both domestically and internationally, allowing the network to grow and thrive unimpeded for decades. The White report was based on the 112-page dossier supplied by the series of *Evening Standard* articles written over the 3-year preceding period, charging Margaret Hodge and her council with permitting at least 26 accused identified child sex abusers working at Islington care facilities to leave its employ without investigation, many even with positive job references.[1969]

One such vile pedophile who was a former Islington employee granted a free pass was Nick Rabet, a deputy children's homes superintendent until his 1989 resignation.[1970] Having originally come from Jersey with a background in childcare, Rabet was a key figure linking child abuse in both Jersey and Islington. Under the auspices of providing recreational camping outings to the Channel Island resort, Rabet regularly escorted, or more aptly trafficked children from Islington group homes to Jersey. Like Peter Righton, he developed a reputation as a known pedophile shielded by the system run by Margaret Oppenheimer-Hodge. After leaving Islington, he befriended a wealthy elderly widow who left him her estate in the East Sussex countryside, where he opened his own private children's activities center as a local retreat utilized by charities, schools, families and social services.

Though Rabet had been placed on a consultancy register barring him from working with children in government facilities, his loophole was working in a private sector setting. At his

---

[1968] Eileen Fairweather, https://www.dailymail.co.uk/news/article-1086200/Revealed-How-close-male-relative-Baby-P-linked-big-paedophile-network.html.
[1969] Eileen Fairweather, https://www.telegraph.co.uk/news/uknews/crime/jimmy-savile/10746412/Jimmy-Savile-sex-abuse-Islington-is-still-covering-up.html.
[1970] Stewart Payne and Eileen Fairweather, "Country life of a Child Abuser; 'Rabet Recruited many young Boys to work at his Activity Centre,'" *Evening Standard/spotlightonabuse.wordpress.com*, August 7, 1995.

child activities center on his estate, Rabet was regularly still abusing boys from Islington group homes. The investigative work by journalists like Eileen Fairweather exposed Rabet's pedo-ring targeting both children and elderly predators in both Islington and Jersey that "befriended" wealthy elderly individuals, manipulated them into changing their wills, and all soon met similar fates, suddenly dying of heart attacks. Rabet and his crew of serial pedophiles appeared protected by Islington council as well as local police in Sussex, Cambridgeshire, London and Jersey.[1971] Through media accounts exposing Rabet's pedo-operations, he fled Britain for the pedophile haven Thailand. After being charged with abusing 30 boys as young as six with estimates of molested 300 children in the sex tourism capital Pattaya, the 57-year old committed suicide with a drug overdose in 2006 to avoid punishment.[1972] Another of his cronies found with hundreds of videos and photos of child pornography also OD'd though it's just as likely they were silenced because they knew too much about VIPs that for years they had supplied with child victims.

One severely abused boy in 1989 reported Rabet and others' sex crimes taking place at both his group home and school to his social worker who was committed to stopping the abuse.[1973] But as of Christmas Eve that year, that conscientious social worker was never seen again and neither were the victims' files. Thus when Islington council was asked in a police probe about placing a child at the school, the council falsely claimed no children under its care were ever sent to the school. Missing files lead to cover-up.

Speaking of which, the Ian White report could only draw from Fairweather's articles interviewing the named whistleblowers, victims and parents because literally hundreds of files were criminally removed from all the Islington borough social services offices in order to protect the countless guilty parties, which included personnel from group homes, social services, Hodge's Islington council, establishment VIP politicians, high court judges, entertainers, businessmen, religious leaders and senior police officers.[1974] Unable to enlist interest from the local police department because it took its marching orders from people like Hodge, Straw and Blair, Liz and David finally convinced the Scotland Yard to launch an investigation but sadly by that time, gross obstruction of justice had already been committed. And sadly as always, the Yard's police probe concluded "not enough evidence" justified charging even a single perpetrator.

No doubt to save both her own skin and career from prison along with all her prominent VIP friends, the-powers-that-shouldn't-be saw fit to destroy all the incriminating evidence, just as

---

[1971] Eileen Fairweather, "'I do not Doubt Men in Smart Cars Preyed on Boys – but Justice Requires Detective work not Hearsay,'" *The Telegraph*, November 9, 2012.

[1972] Eileen Fairweather, https://www.mailonsunday.co.uk/news/article-523706/I-known-Jersey-paedophiles-15-years-says-award-winning-journalist.html.

[1973] Eileen Fairweather, https://www.mailonsunday.co.uk/news/article-523706/I-known-Jersey-paedophiles-15-years-says-award-winning-journalist.html.

[1974] Eileen Fairweather, https://www.telegraph.co.uk/news/uknews/crime/jimmy-savile/10746412/Jimmy-Savile-sex-abuse-Islington-is-still-covering-up.html.

Sir Leon did a decade earlier. Law enforcement never seriously probed into the massive criminal operation because VIPs were too involved and few if any victims and witnesses were ever even interviewed. Demetrious Panton, an abuse victim who went on to become an outspoken child abuse advocate and barrister, maintains that during the 13 separate Islington child abuse investigations, not once was he ever contacted or interviewed by police.[1975]

The pattern of destroyed evidence and criminal cover-up never stops at the earth's pedophilia epicenter. The missing dossier files that would have completely exposed Islington, Downing Street and Westminster sickos will likely never be found in order to ensure their continued full protection. Over the decades, cover-up tactics have always remained the same, not once failing to deliver the same atrocious, predictable outcome, proving that through the impenetrable wall of nonstop cover-up, procurers and predators alike close to the VIP criminals are also shielded and manage to live above the law as well. That way as long as their lips stay sealed, they stay alive and the pedo-party continues unabated to this very day.

Despite the police investigation going nowhere due to so much destroyed records containing hard evidence of Islington's connections to the larger pedophilia network, a full quarter century ago in 1993 the biggest Scotland Yard probe into organized child sexual abuse in British history was launched. According to an August 1993 *Sunday Times* article:

The investigation into networks of paedophiles who have been paying for sex with boys and girls, has uncovered several groups across London and other parts of southern England who link up to swap information and abuse children. For the past five months officers from the squad have secretly liaised with directors of social services in more than half a dozen London boroughs amid fears that organised gangs have targeted vulnerable children in their areas.[1976]

As in the Righton inquiry, speculation prevails that in 1993 then Home Secretary Michael Howard again intervened to shut down Metro Police's largest child abuse investigation to date that would have likely incriminated Hodge's operation as the nation's connecting hub to all other pedophile rings thriving throughout the nation.[1977]

Unbelievably, during Oppenheimer-Hodge's decade long disastrous tenure as Islington council leader, allowing a pedophile ring to both infiltrate and flourish at all dozen of her district group homes, then defiantly denying, rebuking and ultimately having virtually all the insurmountable evidence" disappear," in 1992 Margaret Hodge fled the very crime scene she'd meticulously created and tried in vain to completely cover up, escaping temporarily for a few months to a cushy consultant job at Price-Waterhouse before selected in 1994 as Labor's next MP for Barking where she's been a permanent fixture ever since. Throughout this entire scandalously

---

[1975] Robert Mendick and Eileen Fairweather, https://www.telegraph.co.uk/news/uknews/crime/jimmy-savile/10747257/Margaret-Hodge-sorry-as-council-she-led-told-to-investigate-Savile-abuse-allegations.html.
[1976] Richard Palmer, "Child Abuse Sex Ring Found," *Sunday Times/spotlightonabuse.wordpress.com*, August 1, 1993.
[1977] Murun Buchstansangur, "Was Islington the Center of a Vast Paedophile Network?" *spotlightonabuse.wordpress.com*, March 19, 2013..

grotesque spectacle played out in plain sight within her Islington district, Hodge's neighbor in Richmond Crescent a few doors down was none other than fellow pedo-enabler-crossdresser-D notice provocateur Tony "Miranda" Blair, and unfortunately for the UK and world as of 1997, the next Labor prime minister.[1978]

In 2003 Tony Blair rewarded Oppenheimer-Hodge for building and successfully protecting the nation's largest, most blatant, "out-of-control" pedophile ring, selecting her as Britain's first Minister for Children, a new cabinet post within the Ministry of Education designed and created especially for her proven record. After all, she effectively shielded scores of VIP pedophiles routinely victimizing her expendable care home kids with complete impunity and then allowed them to escape, making her the ideal job candidate to go nationwide. Only at the pedophilia epicenter of the world would the nation's top leader, knowing full well his fellow Fabian neighbor living so close made it her priority to protect child rapists over the well-being of children under her care, ostensibly design a brand new cabinet position to "protect" all of Britain's children, confident that she'd do as magnificent a job protecting VIP pedophile rings operating throughout Britain at the tragic expense and grave suffering of UK's most defenseless, innocent population. You simply can't make up this kind of pure evil shit, nor can you get any more diabolically Luciferian.

Per Illuminati doctrine, as minister of children Hodge pushed for state authoritarianism usurping parental rights and increasing the secrecy of UK's infamous family court system to tear apart British families, separating children from their parents, swallowed up in a pipeline straight into the highly organized, insulated, well-oiled machine called the global pedophilia network. And what better candidate for the job than the unabashed Orwellian Big Brother Zionist aficionado who blatantly insisted:

For me it's not a question of whether we should intrude in family life, but how and when.[1979]

Oppenheimer-Hodge has always been known for her aggression while venomously lashing out, twice committing libel first against "gutter" journalist Eileen Fairweather for her shockingly truthful account of the pedophilia that the council leader did her vicious best to criminally cover-up. The second time she engaged in libelous revenge came after abuse survivor turned child advocate Demetrious Panton bravely went public with his own harrowing story of abuse after years earlier in 1985 sending a 6-page letter to Hodge detailing the torture he was forced to endure a few years earlier living at Islington group homes she supervised.[1980] Making unwanted publicity in 2003 for the freshly installed minister of children, in a letter to *BBC* chairman Gavyn Davis, the vengeful drama queen called Panton an "extremely disturbed

[1978] David Cohen, https://spotlightonabuse.wordpress.com/2013/02/28/yes-minister-you-were-told-about-child-abuse-in-the-care-homes-yet-you-refused-to-listen-30-6-03/.

[1979] John Carvel, "Nanny State knows best, Hodge tells Critics," *The Guardian*, November 27, 2004,.

[1980] Guy Adams, "Apologists for Paedophilia: As the Mail Exposes more Links between Senior Labour Figures and a Vile Paedophile Group, one man who was Abused as a Child Asks them: Why won't you Admit you were Wrong?" *Daily Mail*, February 23, 2014..

person."[1981] But in response to her libelous attack, the successful barrister and healthy survivor despite years of institutional abuse smartly consulted fellow lawyers. Metro Police Detective Superintendent John Sweeney countered Hodge's malicious slurs with a glowing public testimonial:

I found Demetrious to be very articulate... He had a very measured response to what had happened. I have no doubt that if it had got to court we would have had a very strong case. I wouldn't say he was disturbed at all. He certainly wanted justice and he wanted to see Mr Bain [his abuser] in the dock in a British court. That's perfectly understandable.[1982]

"Sour grapes" Hodge was forced to publicly apologize for her reprehensible smear in order to quash growing demands that she resign her abusive brand of "ministering" to all of UK's children. Further, in a transparent act of self-serving political expediency, Hodge was compelled to submit to Demetrious' demands that she publicly apologize, pay his legal bills and make a financial contribution to a charity of his choice. Both her atrocious past record and latest toxic antics produced an unprecedented flood of calls demanding her resignation from child rights activists, the opposition party and the public at large. In 2003 Tory shadow secretary for health and education Tim Yeo applied political pressure on Hodge to step down, providing a sound and reasonable explanation:

The biggest problem in cases of child abuse is to get the victims to have the confidence to come forward. If they feel that if they do come forward that they are going to be branded by the minister responsible as disturbed people, what does that do to the chances of us being able to uncover more cases of child abuse?[1983]

In spite of her slightly bruised ego, the politically weakened, thoroughly compromised minister still managed to barely survive the Islington abuse scandal. A powerful Oppenheimer lives nine lives and to this day at age 74, Hodge still remains a member of the House of Commons.

After all her afflicted damage, both Hodge and Blair continued catching nonstop flack for appointing her overseer of British children's welfare, barraged by relentless blowback and more than justified criticism for her ghastly pro-pedophilia career. Finally after less than two years as UK's first Minister of State for Children, no doubt exhausted from constantly having to feebly defend his appalling choice, Blair quietly transferred her to Ministry for Work and Pensions. But she put her foot in her mouth again, flippantly dismissing 6,000 displaced workers from a closed MG plant, telling them in so many words "go work at the grocery store chain Tesco, they're hiring" as reverberations of Marie Antoinette's "let them eat cake."[1984] So her Oppenheimer nine lives in politics were once again given new life as the Culture and Tourism Minister, eventually winding up both minister and parliamentary chair for the powerful Public Accounts

---

[1981] Roy Watkins, "Paedophile Investigation into Islington Council," *roywatkins.uk*, July 8, 2014.
[1982] Claire Cozens, "Minister tries to Halt Today Investigation," *The Guardian*, November 11, 2003.
[1983] "Hodge Apologizes to Abuse Victim," *BBC*, November 14, 2003.
[1984] Julie Bindel, "Overrated: Margaret Hodge," *Standpoint Magazine*, April 2014.

Office. In 2015 Hodge finally stepped down as a cabinet minister resuming her role as MP, the same year the queen promptly rewarded her with Dame-ship for her longtime service dedicated to doggedly promoting the global elite's pedophilia agenda. But her final ministry resignation was also prompted by more Hodge hubris and hypocrisy.

No accident that while in control over UK public accounting, for the first time in the nation's history, it was announced that the poorest 10% of British citizens end up paying higher taxes from earned income than the richest 10%.[1985] While Hodge railed against mega-corporations like Google for not paying its fair share, her Oppenheimer family controlled interest in the world's largest steel corporation Stemcor inherited from daddy pays just a sinful .01% of its colossal £2.1billion a year earnings.[1986] Her double standards know no limits as she blasts everyone else while she as the chosen one pays the least.[1987]

For a native-born Oppenheimer, money means power and power to her means honor, regardless of how scandalously criminal her behavior to reach it. Like her fellow Jewish pedo-gatekeeping sisters Esther and Edwina, Oppenheimer-Hodge's life has been full of hypocritical inconsistencies and drama queen fakery. On the one hand, she railed against corporate and government waste, but on the other hand, as recently as June 2018 she sought a volunteer job at the University of London that by statute is an unpaid position.[1988] Yet this superrich prima donna refused to "volunteer" without demanding an additional £20,000 annum as part of yet another deal cut especially for her, as if the over two billion pounds her family company rakes in yearly as a spoon fed Oppenheimer or the near £80,000 as MP for the last quarter century is never enough. For this greedy Jewish bloodline prima donna, time is money and money is power and be damned with the rest of us lowly goyim plebeians.

In the post-Savile Operation Midland when police were going through the motions pretending to investigate the VIP pedophiles in government, Savile was linked to Islington abuse and as a result, the local council was once again pressured to conduct yet another of its "objective" inquiries ad nauseam. And guess who was selected to lead this one in 2014? Margaret's very own son-in-law Joe Caluori. Even after this blatant conflict of interest was exposed, the Islington council insisted on keeping their man at the helm married to an Oppenheimer daughter.[1989] With or without all those missing files, it's no wonder no arrests have ever been made. So the never-ending saga of UK cover-up shamefully continues to trudge on forever.

[1985] Benjamin Kentish, "Poorest Pay Higher Taxes than Richest, New Figures Show," *Independent*, April 26, 2017.
[1986] Leon Watson, "Multi-Millionaire Labour MP's Family Business 'Paid just 0.25% Tax on its Profits,'" *Daily Mail*, November 10, 2012.
[1987] Aida Edemariam, https://www.theguardian.com/politics/2013/apr/27/margaret-hodge-tax-duty-interview?INTCMP=SRCH.
[1988] Camilla Turner, "Veteran Labour MP Dame Margaret Hodge seeks Salary for a Voluntary University Pot," *The Telegraph*, June 15, 2018.
[1989] Robert Mendick and Eileen Fairweather, https://www.telegraph.co.uk/news/uknews/crime/jimmy-savile/10747257/Margaret-Hodge-sorry-as-council-she-led-told-to-investigate-Savile-abuse-allegations.html.

Incidentally, in addition to being the Islington council attorney empowered to look into his mother-in-law's criminal cover-up, Joe Caluori is also very active in his community as Islington's current children and young people leader.[1990] Nothing like keeping it in the family. Joe also is reported to be working for a high-end consultancy firm called Britainthinks (globalized version Worldthinks) that advertises innovative solutions for success boasting such clients as McDonalds, the BBC, the Fabian Society and ebay, all great corporate sponsored covers for the NWO pedo-cabal. Again, nothing like keeping it in the family.[1991] Sitting on its advisory board is Baron Lord Daniel Finkelstein, *Times of London* editor and Savile-Cyril Smith pedo-apologist.[1992]

It was reported in 2017 that Sandy Marks, the Islington council member who chaired the social services committee during the years Margaret Hodge presided over the council, attended a conference back in 1980 with a pedophile group known as the Fallen Angels.[1993] After initially denying it, when presented with a photo busting her lie, Marks who went on to becoming the Islington mayor no less, finally admitted the error of her ways, claiming she was too easily influenced by the pro-pedophile crowd and culture back in the day immersed in Labor Party left wing politics that embraced homosexuality and sexual liberation for all, including predators pouncing on babies.

That a former popular mayor held views that sex with children was okay and saw her custodial role as social services committee leader making sure washing machines at the homes were in proper working order over protecting the well-being of children proved such a "shocking" revelation that yet another investigation into Islington abuse was initiated. But the 8-month "independent" review by Sarah Morgan QC recently released its finding that "no organized abuse" took place in the 1970s-1990s.[1994] The victims that provided their painful testimony to once again relive their traumas felt completely betrayed because they firsthand know it was highly organized and involved well known VIPs. Every so called "independent" inquiry in Britain, from the *BBC* Dame Smith report to Theresa May's national IICSA, all are one big whitewash, repeatedly throwing salt on the wounds that can never heal for the victims whose promised justice by conspired diabolical design is continually denied.

Back to drama queen Oppenheimer-Hodge, to this day she continues spewing out her toxic venom to the point of irreversibly fracturing her own embattled Labor Party, nastily turning against her Labor leader Jeremy Corbyn. As current MP from Barking, Dame Hodge just can't seem to keep her "good" name out of the scandalous headlines. A mere month after her fiasco

---

[1990] James Morris, "'Encouraging Steps' for Islington Youth Crime Scheme – which has worked with 76 Gang Members in past year," *Islington Gazette*, June 27, 2018.

[1991] Britainthinks website, *britainthinks.com*.

[1992] "Danny Finkelstein OBE," *britainthinks.com*.

[1993] Hannah Somerville, "Islington Child Abuse Survivors' Network Reacts Angrily to Claims of 'no Organized Abuse' in Sandy Marks Report," *Islington Gazette*, November 13, 2018.

[1994] Emily Finch, "Islington Survivors of Child Abuse: 'Review is a Massive Step back,'" *Islington Tribune*, November 9, 2018..

trying to gouge a salary out of a nonpaid volunteer job, in July 2018 she verbally accosted Corbyn on the House of Commons floor, in an out of control rage screaming:

You're a fucking anti-Semite and racist![1995]

Within hours, the foul-mouthed hothead felt compelled to double down, defending her cheap shot ambush of a false accusation with yet more melodrama grandstanding in a *Guardian* article:

My grandmother and my uncle were murdered by Hitler and many cousins and other relatives were slaughtered in the gas chambers.[1996]

True to Zionist form, she used the old Jewish Holocaust card. But in her next statement, Dame Oppenheimer shows her true racist colors:

It [Palestinian/Israeli conflict] *appears to have become a legitimate price that the* [Corbyn's Labour] *leadership is willing to pay for pursuing the longstanding cause of Palestinians in the Middle East.*[1997]

So the Dame's all for cracking down on free speech in favor of Political Correctness tyranny.[1998] In this neoliberal age of pampered crybaby feelings, if you dare hurt someone's fragile ego expressing your own opinion, especially about a Jew or Israel or Zionism, Dame Margaret and those like her wish to send you to prison. Under the burgeoning umbrella of "anti-hate speech laws," spreading their flimsily veiled cover for absolute authoritarian tyranny, more governments are seeking to criminalize the truth, in this case objecting to Israel's rampantly aggressive genocidal policies against the Palestinians.[1999] This double standard injustice was taken to task almost a decade and a half years ago in an incisively convincing essay written by Edgar J. Steele who foresaw the coming wave of Zionist led oppression and war on free speech:

Hate speech laws in action, ladies and gentlemen. They are coming to America next. Already, the imprisonments have begun, even in America, albeit by twisting and subverting other laws. Some people have died, too, but their deaths falsely are attributed to other causes. Truly, hate speech simply means anything that Jews hate to hear. That's why we have to have Jews to identify it for us.[2000]

[1995] Zoe Drewett, "Labour MP Turns on Jeremy Corbyn Calling him a 'f***ing anti-Semite and a Racist,'" *Metro*, July 18, 2018.

[1996] Margaret Hodge, "I was right to confront Jeremy Corbyn over Labour's Antisemitism," *The Guardian*, July 18, 2018.

[1997] Margaret Hodge, https://www.theguardian.com/commentisfree/2018/jul/18/jeremy-corbyn-labour-antisemitism-margaret-hodge.

[1998] Cathy Young, "Political Correctness: When Liberalism Stops being Liberal," *Medium*, June 22, 2017.

[1999] Glenn Greenwald, "Greatest Threat to Free Speech in the West: Criminalizing Activism against Israeli Occupation," *The Intercept*, February 27, 2016.

[2000] Edgar J. Steele, "Hate Speech: Anything Jews Hate to Hear," *rense.com*, January 10, 2004.

Zionism's current zeal to suppress free speech embodied by the likes of British Zionists like Oppenheimer-Hodge and Washington's Israeli First neocons and their ultra-friendly relationship to pedophilia are definitely not two mutually exclusive phenomena independent of each other. Just the opposite. Like Freemasonry and Illuminati, Zionism too is akin to the global pedophilia epidemic.[2001] That's why it's so important to briefly delve further into Zionism and its shady dark history in order to understand its full implication in the current global pedophilia crisis.

On September 4, 2018 the site *aangirfan.com* published a very revealing article entitled "Friends of Israel," succinctly tying Zionism and the international pedophilia network together:

The Zionist modus operandi for shaping UK politics, foreign policy, and public opinion includes the use of Organized Child Sexual Abuse and Child Trafficking – as a tool for rewarding, entrapping, removing or blackmailing parliamentarians and other prominent public office holders and VIPs.[2002]

Recall Sir Jimmy Savile's self-description as the "most Jewish Catholic,"[2003] concedes his status as a devoutly committed Zionist making numerous pilgrimages to Israel advising prime ministers and Knesset on security matters (covered in Chapter 19). As the British nation's primary child procurer for VIPs throughout the 1970s and 1980s, Savile the Zionist also made frequent trips to Jersey where he and the island's Jewish leader Senator Wilfred Krichefsky regularly abused, tortured and murdered children at Haut de la Garenne,[2004] that is when Zionist Jimmy wasn't supplying kids for treasonous Prime Minister Edward Heath on his Morning Star yacht murdering and throwing used up dead boys overboard.

Then there's Mossad-CIA double agent, the longtime Zionist UK resident Uri Geller who lived in the village of Sonning west of London for 35 years, all the while maintaining intimate ties with not only UK's "most Zionist Catholic," but also other Zionist aficionados sharing Savile's same pedo-predilection - Lord Greville Janner, Uri's distant cousin and McCann-linked MP Clement Freud and goyim-pedo MP Michael Portillo.[2005] Coincidentally, Uri and current UK PM Theresa May are apparently best buds both residing in Sonning,[2006] as mentioned earlier another staunch Jewish State supporter and cabal protector of the VIP pedo-epidemic.[2007] So you can see regardless of party or persuasion, Dame Margaret Oppenheimer possesses many likeminded allies in her pro-Zionist camp. By the way, nearby neighbors in the exclusive community of May and Geller (who recently sold his Sonning estate for $15 million) include

---

[2001] "President Adam's Law Prohibiting Freemasonry aka; Zionism," *politicalvelcraft.org*, December 8, 2011.

[2002] "Friends of Israel," *aagirfan.com/hollygreigjustice.blogspot.com*, September 4, 2018.

[2003] Gordon Rayner, "Jimmy Savile Confessed to Reporter that he would be seen as 'Crooked' after his Death, *The Telegraph*, October 18, 2012.

[2004] "Jersey Care Inquiry: Wilfred Krichefsky Accused of Rape," *BBC*, December 5, 2014,

[2005] "What Links Michael Jackson, Jimmy Savile and Mr. X?" *aangirfan.com*, March 1, 2014,

[2006] Graeme Culliford, "Psychic Uri Geller Bonded with Theresa May over Spoon-Bending and Predicted she'd be Prime Minister," *The Sun*, January 21, 2017.

[2007] "Theresa May, Uri Geller, Bodkin Adams, Gladio…," *aangirfan.com/tapnewswire.com*, July 13, 2016.

Crowley's OTO satanic cult disciple Zeppelin's Jimmy Page[2008] and by association pro-Israel elitists[2009] Lord George and Lady Amal Clooney.[2010]

Just as Zionist lobby groups completely dominate American politics, they also control the British government with "friends of Israel" camps firmly embedded in all major parties, bribing them both with hefty campaign contributions but offer more trips to Israel than all politicians from the US and continental Europe combined.[2011] Additionally, the British-Israeli Communication and Research Center is a monopolizing influence at the *BBC* and *Sky News* as well as the *Financial Times*. Zionism's power over Britain (and the world) is Incredible considering Jews make up less than half of one percent of the UK population. The Zionist agenda that includes global economic and political hegemony also plays a major role in global pedophilia operations.

A loyally steadfast Parliament member in both Blair's New Labor think tank Progress[2012] as well as current member and former chair of Friends of Israel comes the openly gay Zionist Jew Stephen Twigg, originally deputy leader and protégé under Margaret Hodge's Islington council in the 1990s where he was complicit in her pedophilia cover-up and "lost" evidence. As Hodge's surrogate deputy on the council in 1992, Twigg also met with abuse survivor Demetrius Panton but simply passed the buck, deflecting Demetrius's grievance by redirecting him to speak to Hodge herself, yet Twigg never even relayed to his mentor that a justifiably distressed abuse victim came a-calling.[2013] Knowing how testy and upset Margaret can be, apparently Twigg didn't want to rile her ire, aware she was taking the heat for allowing the scandal to get so out of control.

Following in Dame Margaret's footsteps and true to form, Stephen Twigg became secretary-general of the Fabian Society. After all, he was raised by Communist parents.[2014] Notice the recurring theme of Fabian-communist lineage amongst all the Zionist pedo-friendly Labor Party heavyweights? Twigg's biggest claim to fame was his 1997 upset victory against Conservative incumbent MP from Enfield, UK's standing defense secretary no less - fellow homosexual and reputed pedophile Michael Portillo.[2015] This charismatic political figure has quite a colorfully checkered past.

With Prime Minister John Major's defense secretary a flaming yet married homosexual pedophile, Portillo was an easy target for sexual blackmail by both British as well as foreign

---

[2008] Richard Price, "Forget Scientology, Celebs are now falling for an even more Sinister 'Religion': Introducing the Satanic Sex Cult that's Snaring Stars such as Peaches Geldof," *Daily Mail*, April 21, 2013.

[2009] "Guilty by Association: Do the Clooneys 'Heart' Israel?" *The New Arab*, April 8, 2016.

[2010] Laura House, "Sonning: A Picture-Perfect British Village Where Privacy is Protected," *Mansion Global News*, October 15, 2016.

[2011] Syarif Hidayat, "Zionists Control and Rule America and United Kingdom," *hshidayat.blogspot.com*, August 14, 2014.

[2012] Lee Harpin, "Corbyn-Sceptic Think Tank on Brink of Collapse," *Jewish Chronicle*, June 26, 2017.

[2013] "Timeline: Margaret Hodge Row," *The Guardian*, November 19, 2003.

[2014] Andrew Roth, https://www.theguardian.com/politics/2001/mar/25/profiles.parliament6.

[2015] John Ward, "The Paedophile: MI5 'gave Geoffrey Dickens Michael Portillo's Name' for his Dossier," *The Slog*, February 8, 2015.

intelligence. In 1996 private detectives of Egyptian born business magnate Mohamed Al-Fayad, father of Dodi Fayad allegedly murdered in Paris with Princess Diana by the royal family in 1997,[2016] reportedly obtained photos of then defense minister Michael Portillo with a young boy allegedly in North Wales.[2017] Al-Fayad had moved to Britain in the 1960s where he made a vast fortune as owner of Harrods, the Ritz Hotel Paris and Fulham Football Club. Even prior to his son's death, Al-Fayad had a personal interest in exposing certain British government scandals, and invested in *Scalawag*, a small satirical monthly magazine begun by a pair of half-brothers with a mission to uncover corruption and pedophilia in its run from 1991-98 before going bankrupt.[2018]

The compromising photos of Portillo were passed on to *Scalawag Magazine* editor and cofounder Angus James who took them on a business trip to northern Cyprus in September 1996.[2019] At the time, because *Scalawag* was going full bore exposing the Westminster VIP pedophile ring exploiting British care home children and even naming VIP names, it was increasingly targeted for litigation by the pedophile establishment and, in a David vs. Goliath battle, the publication was forced from the newsstands to an online site before going under in 1998. Angus James was starting up his second publication *Spiked* and took the controversial photos to Turkish controlled northern Cyprus to meet another *Scalawag* financial contributor - British fugitive Turkish Cypriot entrepreneur Asil Nadir.

Turns out the CIA and MI6 had used Nadir's Polly Peck International conglomerate as a cover for illegal British arms shipments to Iraq during the 1980s' Thatcher years.[2020] Nadir had fled Britain in 1993 seeking refuge in his Turkish Cyprus from UK prosecution for bogus fraud charges. James was reportedly there to close a deal with Nadir to finance *Spiked* with the photos likely providing a blackmail bargaining chip to negotiate a dismissal of charges against Nader back in England.[2021] In September 2010, after 17 years in exile, the flamboyant Nadir made his grand re-entrance in a London courtroom under much fanfare, only to be deferred, fitted with ankle bracelet and midnight curfew under virtual house arrest while prosecution re-prepared its fraud case with the trial scheduled the following year.[2022] During the trial, key evidence that would have proven Nadir's innocence was withheld, a CIA dossier[2023] prohibited under false pretense of "national security" was never included.[2024] Nadir was framed by the US-UK-Israel cabal syndicate. So in August 2012 the tycoon was convicted of "stealing" nearly £29m from his own company and at age 71 sentenced to 10 years.[2025]

[2016] Alex Naumov, "Royal Family Murdered Diana with the Help of MI6?" *Pravda,* December 15, 2006.
[2017] "Asil Nadir and the Secret Photographs," *asilnadirandthesecretphotographs.blogspot.com*, April 22, 2016.
[2018] "Asil Nadir and the Secret Photographs," http://asilnadirandthesecretphotographs.blogspot.com/.
[2019] "Asil Nadir and the Secret Photographs," http://asilnadirandthesecretphotographs.blogspot.com//
[2020] "Child Abuse, Arms Deals, Murder, Deep State, Cyprus, Iraq, Wales," *aangirfan.com*, November 23, 2012.
[2021] "Asil Nadir and the Secret Photographs," http://asilnadirandthesecretphotographs.blogspot.com/.
[2022] Paul Harris, Judge Orders Fugitive Tycoon Asil Nadir to be Tagged as he Faces Court 17 years after Fleeing Britain," *Daily Mail*, September 4, 2010.
[2023] "Secret CIA Report," *asilnadirstitchedupbymaggiethatcher.blogspot.com*, April 22, 2016.
[2024] "The Story of Project Babylon, British Spooks, Illegal Arms Deals, Murder and a Judicial State Conspiracy," *True Publica*, February 17, 2018.
[2025] Asil Nader Jailed for 10 Years for Polly Peck Thefts," *BBC*, August 23, 2012.

After attending a party at Nadir's home in 1996, while driving down a mountainous road 31-year old Angus James met a violent end in an auto accident with a truck.[2026] The driver of the car, Angus's colleague Simon Stander and the two women passengers all connected to the magazine survived. Simon suffered bruises and was hospitalized while arrangements were swiftly made to fly the two uninjured women back home to London. Nadir's fixer was Peter Diamond who placed Simon in hiding in an attempt to keep his boss's name out of the headlines. But a journalist friend of Angus writing for the *Independent* mentioned Angus's meeting with the multi-millionaire before being killed on the road.[2027] With Angus James's death, whatever deal was reached that night was immediately scrapped. Diamond confiscated James's files, the photos and his possessions. The featured exposé on Portillo scheduled in the following month's issue was never published. There was also an apparent break-in at the *Scalawag* London office, removing additional software and computers containing the edition that would have featured the story outing the top Tory cabinet minister in compromising photos with his abuse victim.[2028]

Within a year after Angus James' death, the UK defense minister Portillo lost his election to relative unknown, Zionist Hodge protégée Stephen Twigg. But just two years later in 1999, Portillo was back in Parliament representing Kensington and Chelsea for the next half dozen years. But just two months prior to the 1999 election, just when Tory MP Alan Clark keeled over to conveniently open up a safe seat, Michael Portillo announced in an interview his homosexual past,[2029] chalking it up to a phase he went through back in his gay old college days.[2030] But the LBGT community wasn't buying it, calling him a hypocrite for refusing to lower the age of consent for homosexuals and lesbians to 16 on par with the hetero crowd and still voting to kick gays out of the military.[2031]

Of course the real hypocrisy here is all the titillating soap opera uproar questioning his "phase," providing the smokescreen cover-up to his blackmailed puppet status as a pedophilic criminal. Through the politic apparatchik, the darling of the Conservative party as a still semi-closeted chameleon reinvented himself as a popular *BBC* broadcaster where homosexuals are most welcomed and pedophiles are most protected (covered in Chapter 21). That's the much bigger issue, along with the illegal arms deal, pedophilia and multiple murders including perhaps Angus James in northern Cyprus.

More death, scandal and intrigue seem to follow this Michael Portillo around like smell to shit. From his college days at Cambridge as 18 year old "Polly," he engaged in promiscuous sex on alternate days with his gay lover while dating his future wife for the next 8 years. With his male

---

[2026] Louise Jury, "Satirical Paper's Editor Killed," *Independent*, September 9, 1996.

[2027] Louise Jury, https://www.independent.co.uk/news/satirical-papers-editor-killed-1362529.html.

[2028] "Child Abuse, Arms Deals, Murder, Deep State, Cyprus, Iraq, Wales."

[2029] Tom Utley, "Who cares about Portillo's Past? Er, lots of us, actually," *The Telegraph*, June 20, 2001.

[2030] John Arledge, "'Many Wed after Gay Flings. They usually Relapse,'" *The Guardian*, September 12, 1999.

[2031] David Aaronovitch, "Michael Portillo's Sexual Past is Colourful - but it's his own Affair," *Independent*, September 10, 1999.

lover ending up HIV positive, Portillo was also rumored to have indulged in homosexual trysts with fellow Tory MP Minister Peter Lilley and the first and only professional footballer (soccer) to come out publicly as gay - Justin Fashanu in 1990.[2032] Another favorite Portillo activity was rendezvousing with pedo-pals at his favorite hotel in the world - La Gazelle d'Or in Morocco.[2033] And among his fave travel companions is fellow homosexual-pedophile-Tory pimp-sadist Derek Laud, lounging at La Gezelle d'Or together doing little Moroccan boys whenever Derek didn't bring along his rent boys from home.[2034] Considered to be a political mover and shaker amongst the elite throughout the 1980s and 1990s, with no formal higher education degree nor holding any elected public office, Derek Laud's claim to fame was writing speeches for Margaret Thatcher and suppling fresh little kids for elitist vultures. But more to come on this enigmatic boy supplier in the next chapter.

Turning to Justin Fashanu and his link to powerful politicians like Portillo, he was born to a Nigerian barrister and Guyanese nurse in Hackney in 1961. But when his parents' marriage broke up, Justin and his year younger brother John were placed in Barnardos children's home, the same pedo-scandal outfit that Tony Blair's wife Cherie became president of in 2001,[2035] no doubt reason enough a dozen years later the queen bestowed a CBE honor for her pedo-gatekeeping "charity" work.[2036] By the age of six, Justin with his brother were fortunate enough to move into a foster care home raised by an elderly white couple in rural England. Growing up as the only black kids in town, both were skilled athletes and went on to the pros.

As the only openly gay professional in football, Justin Fashanu paid a heavy price for his bold honesty coming out at age 29, and was never quite prepared for the backlash. Unlike the world of politics where gay men make up a significant percentage of MPs in government, in the world of football Justin stood alone. John Fashanu ultimately rejected his brother for being gay, even paying him £75,000 not to disclose his gayness to the world in order to spare him and his family from embarrassment.[2037] But in 1990 Justin took his brother's money and ran straight to *The Sun* for another £70,000 to declare his sexual preference to the world,[2038] creating an enduring rift between brothers that would last till Justin's death eight years later. John took his troubled brother's death very hard with a suicide note saying Justin did not wish to bring any more shame and despair on his family and friends.

But at only 19 playing for Norwich, Justin Fashanu appeared to have the world at the palm of his foot, scoring the famous goal of the decade against Liverpool, catapulting him to becoming

---

[2032] James McMahon, "The Life and Death of Football's first Openly Gay Player," *Vice*, October 10, 2017..

[2033] "Interview: Michael Portillo," *Five Star Magazine*.

[2034] "Wikipedia Page Alteration: Has Derek Laud been 'Unfriended' by Tory Elite?" *21st Century Wire*, December 2, 2012.

[2035] Nicole Martin, "*Barnardo's* Role for Cherie," *The Telegraph*, September 18, 2001.

[2036] "Cherie Blair made a CBE for Charity Work in New Year Honours," *BBC*, December 29, 2012.

[2037] Oliver Todd, "John Fashanu paid Brother Justin £75,000 to Stop him coming out as Gay after Begging him not to 'Embarrass me or my family,'" *Daily Mail*, October 31, 2015.

[2038] James McMahon, https://www.vice.com/en_uk/article/zm39e9/the-life-and-death-of-footballs-first-openly-gay-player.

the first black million-pound player. But soon after when his Nottingham coach learned he was gay, he was banned from training with the team and soon let go from the club.[2039] His confidence shattered, for many years Justin bounced around playing for a series of lesser leagues in England, Scotland, North America, never quite measuring up to all his early hype and promise. According to mainstream press, Justin acquired a reputation and habit as a compulsive liar, making up scandalous stories for some cheap thrill change.[2040]

Fashanu found himself mixing socially amongst fellow gays who were government VIPs that happened to get off on raping kids. While frequenting gay clubs around London, he met longtime Conservative MP from Bournemouth East (1977-2005) David Atkinson, the typical church going family man with wife, a son and daughter, and a big secret, his affair with a notorious black football star.[2041] But Justin soon learned that David Atkinson also indulged in another far more sinister secret - sex with rent boys. The Tory MP died in 2012 HIV positive suffering from bowel cancer. Two years later Atkinson's son Anthony came forward to also reveal that his father was a serial child sexual predator like Savile.[2042] Anthony stated that there is evidence that his MP father was sexually blackmailed by a Westminster Palace staff member threatening to sell details of his dad's sexual life to a newspaper.

Fate would have it that two very different lives, one belonging to an infamous black gay footballer and another highly respected, this time straight white Conservative MP would intersect and each tragically end four years apart. *Scalawag* wrote about the bizarre death of Tory MP Stephen Milligan in February 1994. At the time the former journalist Milligan was Parliamentary Private Secretary to defense procurement minister Jonathan Aitken,[2043] and his day-to-day work no doubt brought him in contact with British intelligence services making Milligan privy to illegal arms deals.

Scalawag suggested that Stephen was approached by MI5, pressing him to intervene as the go-between in an urgent matter regarding Justin Fashanu.[2044] Apparently in early 1994 with Justin Fashanu's career on the downswing, in search of another quick cash windfall, the fading athletic star had already gone to the *Daily Express* ready to tell all he knew about the Westminster VIP pedophile ring based on his alleged intimate encounters with high profile MPs and senior cabinet ministers.[2045] MI5 pressured the MP Milligan to convince the footballer to stay quiet. When Stephen approached Justin to inform him that his life was in danger should he persist in disclosing the sleaze atop the British government, Fashanu naively couldn't believe it. After

[2039] James McMahon, https://www.vice.com/en_uk/article/zm39e9/the-life-and-death-of-footballs-first-openly-gay-player.

[2040] "Profile: The Striker who didn't Score: Justin Fashanu, Dribbling round Westminster," *Independent*, February 12, 1994.

[2041] "Gay Conservative and Rent Boys," *aangirfan.com*, July 19, 2014.

[2042] Robert Mendick, "My Dad was a Predator like Savile, Claims Tory MP's Son, *Independent*, July 21, 2014.

[2043] Guy Adams, "Did MI5 Murder Orange-in-Mouth Tory MP? Stephen Milligan supposedly Died after a Bizarre Sex Game - but Chilling Investigation Raises an even more Sinister Possibility after the Former Journalist 'Unearthed British Illegal Arms Sales,'" *Daily Mail*, October 5, 2018.

[2044] "Fashanu, Cabinet Ministers, Whistleblowers," *aangirfan.com*, November 4, 2013.

[2045] Tony Gosling, "Child Abuse Scandal Raises Disturbing Questions about UK Establishment," *RT*, August 15, 2014.

failing to convince Justin to back off from trying to sell the scandalous story to the media, MI5 told Stephen that Justin Fashanu would be killed and made to appear a suicide.[2046]

Already appalled by all the suspected pedophilia perpetrated by his colleagues in conjunction amidst a flood of breaking Tory sex scandals at the time coming from the political party that went out of its way espousing family values,[2047] MP Milligan also grew increasingly disgustedly upset that a branch of his own government would go so far as to assassinate someone willing to take measures to clean up the filth in high places.[2048] Under mounting pressure, the former *BBC* journalist panicked, making the fatal error of threatening MI5, that should anything happen to Justin, he would go to his former employer at *The Sunday Times* and blow the whistle.[2049] Similar to the impromptu hit on Jill Dando ready to drop the cesspit bombshell just three years later, either Downing Street or senior intelligence very likely made the decision to eliminate Stephen Milligan, leaving him naked laying roped on top of his kitchen table with a bag over his head wearing women's nylon stockings and an orange fruit segment in his mouth to come off as yet another kinky "sexual misadventure," a favorite kill method security services notoriously utilize to avoid major investigations.[2050] Recall in Chapter 21 during this same time period of the 1990s, several other *BBC* employees met similar fates engaging in this so called bizarre sex play gone awry.

But a leading pathologist concluded Stephen Milligan was a murder victim as he had never heard of both a bag over the head and ligature in the mouth as suicides always involve one or the other. Even initial police reports indicated the MP's death appeared suspicious, very likely involving foul play,[2051] backed up by all who knew Stephen best, including past girlfriends unanimously certain he was murdered.[2052] Stephen's former editor friend from the *Sunday Times* Andrew Neil checked with his previous intimates and all concurred:

There was nothing about his private life that would make you think the way he died was possible.[2053]

Justin Fashanu's security guard Bobby Munro has stated that Stephen made a rash of calls to Fashanu hours before his death, but Justin refused to take the calls. Also a few years later, the

[2046] "Fashanu, Cabinet Ministers, Whistleblowers," https://aangirfan.blogspot.com/2013/11/fashanu-cabinet-ministers-whistleblowers.html.

[2047] William Tuohy, "Britain: Sex Scandals Contradict Tory Moralizing: Prime Minister John Major can't seem to Plug all the Leaks in his 'back to basics' Policy," *Los Angeles Times*, January 15, 1994.

[2048] Tony Gosling, https://www.rt.com/op-ed/180616-british-home-secretary-child-abuse/.

[2049] "Fashanu, Cabinet Ministers, Whistleblowers," https://aangirfan.blogspot.com/2013/11/fashanu-cabinet-ministers-whistleblowers.html.

[2050] Kevin Garside, "Forbidden Games: the Justin Fashanu Documentary that Exposes Sport's Gay Taboo," *i News*, October 5, 2017.

[2051] "The Late Stephen Milligan MP," *scribd.com*.

[2052] Guy Adams, https://www.dailymail.co.uk/news/article-6245607/Did-MI5-murder-Stephen-Milligan-Investigation-raises-sinister-possibility.html.

[2053] "The Late Stephen Milligan MP," https://www.scribd.com/document/256327891/The-late-Stephen-Milligan-MP-9-FACTS.

same police investigator - Brian Edwards – responsible for the unsolved, botched-on-purpose Jill Dando murder case in May 1999 was also the lead police investigator in Stephen Milligan's death.[2054] It's no wonder the rushed inquest was unwilling to look at any other evidence not leading to the conclusion of a self-induced "sexual misadventure."

It was then that an MI5 agent allegedly paid a visit to Justin Fashanu, threatening that he would be next should he proceed with telling the world about top food chain pedophiles. Instead Justin reportedly decided to accept the hush money offered. The mainstream press reported Justin's agent contacted police detectives urging them to interview Fashanu about Milligan's death, but the police claimed his input was just more pathetic, made up lies.[2055] His negative publicity prompted Justin's football club to terminate his contract and Fashanu took the next plane out to America where he played a couple more seasons, bouncing from one league down to the next, 22 teams in a 20 year career including a stopover in New Zealand.[2056]

After a 17-year old boy in Maryland accused Justin of rape, he was questioned and then released, escaping back to England before being charged though he maintained the sex was consensual.[2057] A short time later the first and only pro footballer bold enough to disclose his homosexuality to the world wound up hanging from a beam in a garage at age 37 in 1998.[2058] Since British police and mainstream press both have a very long history of covering up the murderous VIP Westminster pedo-scandal, it comes as no surprise that Justin Fashanu would be portrayed as a pathological lying desprado compulsively seeking money and attention for his so called sordid tall tale stories. Another convenient tactic the state deploys to silence would-be truth tellers and victims is to discredit and smear their credibility and reputation. So the legitimate question lingers on two decades after his death, did Justin Fashanu become yet another murder victim for knowing too much?

A related angle to this sad ending episode is that MP Milligan as Parliamentary Private Secretary to a defense minister would provide him with access to sensitive information involving covert British illegal arms trafficking to Iraq.[2059] The CIA and MI6 commonly use front companies like Asil Nader's and Gerald James' arms company called Astra in their booming illegal international gun running trade, right along with drugs, small children and human organs. Gerald James wrote a memoir about his experience that included exposing unusually suspicious deaths of eight individuals such as a former MI6 agent and a journalist who were both very likely

[2054] "The Late Stephen Milligan MP," https://www.scribd.com/document/256327891/The-late-Stephen-Milligan-MP-9-FACTS.

[2055] "Profile: The Striker who didn't Score: Justin Fashanu, Dribbling round Westminster," https://www.independent.co.uk/voices/profile-the-striker-who-didnt-score-justin-fashanu-dribbling-round-westminster-1393543.html.

[2056] Claire Toureille, "20 years after his Death, why Justin Fashanu is still so Influential to LGBT History," *Pink News*, May 2, 2018..

[2057] Kevin Garside, https://inews.co.uk/culture/film/justin-fashanu-documentary-lays-bare-sports-enduring-gay-taboo/.

[2058] Kate Watson-Smyth, "Justin Fashanu Found Hanged in Lock-up Garage," *Independent*, May 4, 1998.

[2059] Guy Adams, https://www.dailymail.co.uk/news/article-6245607/Did-MI5-murder-Stephen-Milligan-Investigation-raises-sinister-possibility.html.

murdered/suicided by the familiarly bizarre asphyxiation method for their independent pursuit to uncover the full truth about Britain's illegal arms sales.[2060]

Back during the Iraq-Iran war in the 1980s, Reagan/Bush and Thatcher used US and British intelligence to secretly violate their own arms embargos and weapons bans exporting their war machine to warring enemy camps in the Middle East,[2061] just as the Rothschilds and more recently the Harrimans and Bushes have been financing both sides to every elite orchestrated war for centuries.[2062] Mark Thatcher, the prime minister's son, got 12 million pounds richer selling warplanes to the Saudis in British history's biggest arms deal,[2063] so more innocent civilians in Yemen can be massacred with full US-UK complicity.[2064] Similar to how Angus James may have died for potentially exposing pedo-Portillo and the British government's illicit arms shipment to Saddam Hussein, two years earlier Stephen Milligan may have been murdered by the Deep State for the exact same reason(s).

Returning to the fellow pro-pedo MP originally from Islington chosen to bring down UK's secretary of defense Portillo in 1997, Stephen Twigg entered Parliament at just 30-years old. But he'd already impressed the newly elected British Prime Minister Tony Blair, then moving from Islington to Downing Street. In 1996 the two fellow Fabians from Islington co-wrote and published through the Foreign Policy Centre their 35-page *A Global Alliance for Global Values*,[2065] outlining their pathway to dystopia through elitist globalization. But eight years later Blair's unpopular war in Iraq had Labor party losing seats in 2005, Twigg's historically conservative Enfield district among the casualties. That same year while dancing the night away in a London gay nightclub, Twigg was attacked by an Islington child abuse survivor accusing him of direct involvement in Hodge's Islington-Jersey child abuse-pornography-murder scandal.[2066]

While still licking his wounds from his last election smack-down and forcibly delivered smack-down reminder of his pedophilia culpability, Twigg was rescued by his close ties to Prime Ministers Blair and Brown. In 2010 their New Labor party pressured a 27-year Labor MP veteran to give up his Liverpool West Derby seat 200 miles away from Enfield for big Twigg's relaunch into Parliament.[2067] And just a year later the rising star was awarded the post of Labor shadow minister of education. But just two years on after his lackluster performance failing to challenge Tory education minister Michael Gove,[2068] in 2013 Labor party leader Ed Miliband fired Twigg.[2069] Ed and brother David Miliband were raised as Marxist Jews, with Ed on record

---

[2060] Guy Adams, https://www.dailymail.co.uk/news/article-6245607/Did-MI5-murder-Stephen-Milligan-Investigation-raises-sinister-possibility.html.

[2061] Peter Eyre, "The Illegal Arms Trade: Iraq-Iran War 1980-1988," *vijayvaani.com*, October 3, 2012.

[2062] Michael Collins Piper, "Bush, Rockefeller, Rothschiild and Hitler," *American Free Press*, January 23, 2013.

[2063] David Leigh, "Mark Thatcher's Return to the Spotlight," *The Guardian*, April 11, 2013.

[2064] Marjorie Cohn, "Khashoggi's Murder and Saudi War Crimes in Yemen were Facilitated by US," *truthout.org*, October 19, 2018.

[2065] Tony Blair and Stephen Twigg, *A Global* Alliance *for Global Values* (London: Foreign Policy Centre, 2006.)

[2066] "Paedophile Politicians," *sites.google.com*.

[2067] Marc Waddington, "Labour's Stephen Twigg Wins West Derby Seat," *Liverpool Echo*, May 7, 2010.

[2068] Francis Beckett, "Why Tristam Hunt is the man to Teach Gove a Lesson," *New Statesman*, October 24, 2013.

[2069] Daniel Hewitt, "Liverpool MP Stephen Twigg Sacked from Shadow Government," *ITV News*, October 7, 2013.

looking up to fellow Jew Jack Straw as a "father figure,"[2070] yet another former Islington council deputy under Hodge. Ed Miliband worked in 1993 for PIE linked pro-pedo deputy Labor leader Harriet Harman. Note the same ties that bind - Labor-Marxist-Zionist-pedophilia recirculating ad infinitum.

In 2015 two old guard Zionist Jew former foreign secretaries Jack Straw and Malcolm Rifkind, Sir Malcolm still in charge of Mossad infiltrated British intelligence services,[2071] were both thrown out of government after getting caught greedily boasting of their corrupt omnipotence before hidden Channel 4 cameras in the "cash-for-access" sting[2072] (British variation of the Clintons' "pay-to-play" racketeering), and as a result, the brass ring of House of Lords peerage eluded them.[2073]

But rest assure there's always the next generation of Zionist Jews controlling UK politics despite Jewish people comprising a miniscule .04% of the total UK pop. Jew or no Jew, what all Zionists share in common is the elephant in the room – Rothschild control over Britain (and much of the world).[2074] The next wave of Zionist Rothschild plants in British government are represented by the likes of Stephen Twigg and the Miliband brothers with Polish-Russian connections,[2075] their deceased Marxist father a possible KGB asset.[2076]

In 2010 Ed Miliband beat his pissed off older brother David out for a half decade of failed Labor leadership, in 2015 upended by the present party leader - non-Jew Jeremy Corbyn. No doubt seething inside, initially Ed Miliband pretended graciously to accept Corbyn, but he seized on the divisive Brexit issue to show his fangs demanding Jeremy's resignation.[2077] The reality of Corbyn's populist appeal has Israel and their London Zionist minions frothing at the mouth to depose the non-Jew who actually recognizes the rights of Palestinians.[2078] But remaining loyal to the Blair-Hodge-Straw-Rifkind-Mandelson "old" New Labor-pro-pedophilia-Zionist-Rothschild camp, MP Stephen Twigg is on record staunchly opposing Corbyn.[2079] Though hostile to his leadership, it's Twigg's old mentor MP Oppenheimer-Hodge who's leading the mutinous party coup. Because Corbyn is not a Zionist, forces in pro-Zionist UK have been hard at work for three

---

[2070] "Paedophile Politicians," https://sites.google.com/site/paedophilepoliticians/home.

[2071] "Israeli Secret Service (Mossad) and Tory Government – Friendly Relations Re-established – But what a Can of Worms," *caltonjock.com*, May 22, 2015.

[2072] Claire Newell, Edward Malnick, Luke Heighton and Lyndsey Telford, "Jack Straw and Sir Malcolm Rifkind in latest 'Cash for Access' Scandal," *The Telegraph*, February 22, 2015.

[2073] Jason Groves, "Labour Grandee Jack Straw is Denied a Peerage over Lobbying Sting which saw him 'Boast about Political Connections,'" *Daily Mail*, June 20, 2015.

[2074] David Icke, "David Icke on Rothschild Zionism," *rense.com*, September 24, 2013.

[2075] "The Milibands' Soviet and US Connections," *aangirfan.com*, December 3, 2012.

[2076] Tobias Langdon, https://www.theoccidentalobserver.net/2018/03/15/a-very-jewish-scandal-the-newmark-affair-as-paradigm-of-jewish-corruption/.

[2077] Heather Stewart and Mark Tran, "Ed Miliband calls for Jeremy Corbyn to Resign as Labour Leader over Brexit," *The Guardian*, June 29, 2016.

[2078] Gilad Atzmon, "Jeremy Corbyn and the Jews," *gilad.co.uk*, August 17, 2015.

[2079] Matt Dathan, "'We cannot go on like this!' Labour MP openly calls on his Colleagues to Kick Jeremy Corbyn out of Power 'for the sake of people being Bled Dry by the Tory Government," *Daily Mail*, March 25, 2016.

years to depose the Labor Party leader. Results of a supposed unbiased poll by BMG Research just released in January 2019 making headlines are touting older brother pro-Zionist David Miliband as the most popular choice among 1,514 adult Britons to replace Corbyn.[2080] Britain just can't seem to live without Jews for Israel running the country. Or is it the planetary controllers?

Last July Margaret Oppenheimer-Hodge was caught once again treasonously and vulgarly acting out on behalf of her favorite foreign power, attempting to incite a leadership revolt for a second time to rid Jeremy Corbyn for supporting the Palestinians' right to exist.[2081] The current political squabble in the UK over Zionism warrants a deeper look within the broader historical context since Zionism and pedophilia go hand-in-hand together. That's why Luciferian planetary controllers thrive and literally get their rocks off waging permanent war and bloody carnage around the world because it provides fertile unlimited ground and opportunity for trafficking guns, drugs, laundered money, children and body parts, financing black ops projects that benefit only the monster squad in control.

The specific reason why Oppenheimer-Hodge threw her public tantrum on the world stage was over her Labor Party recently modifying its definition of anti-Semitism, which only deleted a couple of small examples from the previous definition, from the word-for-word extraction taken directly from the International Holocaust Remembrance Alliance (IHRA). The IHRA definition clearly conflates anti-Semitism with any and all criticism towards Israel. The aging Dame had a cow over Labor's recent changes under Corbyn that declawed the "anti-Semitic" label applied to disagreement with Israel's racist apartheid genocidal policy toward Palestinians.

Margaret needs to grow up and recognize the party's over - her Jewish State can't continue throwing its "anti-Semitic" weight around to keep its growing number of critics silently at bay with its weaponized victim card anymore. For years the IHRA has dictated to the world what constitutes anti-Semitism based on anyone calling out Israel's longtime policy towards Palestinians as "racist," inhumane and unfair.

But just when you think the dog days are finally over, Zionist pushback arrives in the form of tantrums, harassment and censorship by the likes of Hodge and the Anti-Defamation League's latest collusions with the Google Gestapo and Facebook Nazis.[2082] Like it or not Oppenheimer and the rest of you Zionists, the world is beyond fed up with the whining prima donna Jewish State for all its duplicitous double standards, now caught desperately still trying to use its worn-out victim card forever. It's not going to work any longer and if you don't want to be called Nazis, then stop acting like them.

[2080] Lizzy Buchan, "David Miliband most Popular Choice for next Labour Leader, Poll shows," Independent, January 12, 2019.

[2081] Ian Greenhalgh, "Margaret Hodge leads Israeli Plot to Overthrow Corbyn," Veterans Today, July 23, 2018.

[2082] Philip Giraldi, "Shutting down Free Speech in America: Government and Lobbyists Work Together to Destroy the First Amendment," American Herald Tribune, September 24, 2018.

Another chicken bone of contention caught in Dame's turkey gobbler throat, the IHRA labels us anti-Semitic if we accuse people like her to be an Israeli firster or Zionista. Oppenheimer, all your past bad behavior including your treasonous blind loyalty to that foreign power you represent neither qualifies you or "your people" as God's chosen ones. You're definitely not. In the Creator's eyes, no one group of humans is more favored over another, regardless of race or religion. And IMHO, it's another flawed human distortion and abomination of God's true essence to believe otherwise. Nope Dame Margaret, even Lucifer can't help you now.

The 2018 Pittsburgh synagogue shooting as a weaponized false flag leading up to the November mid-term election is just more rollout of this same nefarious acted out, multi-purposed agenda, desperately attempting to mold and control public opinion by casting broad-stroke dispersions, lumping in those critical of Zionist Israel with the violent, anti-Semitic, racist, extremist nutjobs.[2083] Truth be told, that synagogue attack would not be the first time Zionists sacrifice their own kind for their so called "worthy" causes, as in the WWII Holocaust itself,[2084] or the blown up S.S. Patria murdering 252 Jewish refugees off the Haifa coast in 1940,[2085] or the 1950-51 Baghdad bombings killing Iraqi Jews,[2086] or Argentina's 1992 Israeli embassy bombing or the 1994 Buenos Aires Jewish community center attack.[2087] And that's just the shortlist of Zionist Jews killing innocent, decent Jews. At the 1958 Patria memorial service mourning 252 innocent Jewish refugees' lives assassinated by Zionists that have never represented the vast majority of Jews, former Israeli Prime Minister Zionist Moshe Sharett came right out and said it, giving away the Zionist MO:

Sometimes it is necessary to sacrifice the few in order to save the many.[2088]

252 murdered people can hardly be considered a "few." Nor is the inflated Holocaust sacred number of 6 million a few.[2089] If you believe all the propaganda, you'd never realize estimates of 5 million non-Jews also died in the Nazi Holocaust, but as goyim, their lost lives don't matter, just like the Palestinians. For many decades Jews killing Jews has been at work by the terrorist organization known as the Mossad, the Israeli government's own intelligence service. The Mossad is crawling with veteran masters of false flag terrorism[2090] (9/11 a prime example),[2091] falsely blaming "Islam" in the form of al Qaeda/ISIS mercenary stooges as well as providing the

[2083] Robert David Steele, "Synagogue False Flag - Bullshit - FEMA Legalized Lies UPDATE 17: Synagogue Business as Usual... No Bio-Hazards?" *phibetaiota.net*, October 27, 2018.

[2084] Henry Makow, "The Reason for Israel's Moral Failure," *rense.com*, April 7, 2007.

[2085] Henry Makow, "Nazi Collaborators, Zionists don't Represent Jews," *henrymakow.com*, August 27, 2018.

[2086] Naeim Giladi, "The Jews of Iraq," *bintbeil.com*.

[2087] Adrian Salbuchi and James Fetzer, "False Flag Attacks in Argentina: 1992 and 1994," *Voltairenet,org*, October 13, 2009.

[2088] Henry Makow, https://www.henrymakow.com/091202.html.

[2089] J.S. Chiappalone, "Holocause – Fact or fiction," *bibliotcapleyades.net*, 1997.

[2090] Michael Collins Piper, "Israel's Use of False Flags in Global Terrorism," *American Free Press*, September 14, 2013.

[2091] Christopher Bollyn, "9/11 and the War on Terror: Israel's History of False Flag Operations against the U.S.A.," *American Herald Tribune*, July 7, 2018.

pretext for the neocons' fake "war on terror" as yet more Mossad-CIA-MI6 inventions[2092] stripping away our Constitution.

The most dangerous extremists out there today placing our free speech rights in such serious jeopardy are the fanatical brigade belonging to the Political Correctness armies largely occupying college campuses around the world.[2093] These days they are the neo-Nazis imposing absolute absurdity without limits on free speech rights. The PC gestapo police are banning gender pronoun usage[2094] and sarcasm on college campuses in Australia.[2095] So called "anti-hate laws" that are spreading worldwide ostensibly designed to protect the rights and feelings of both Jews and Muslims alike are the Luciferian master stroke in censorship and the silencing of free speech and the brain capacity of critical thinking.[2096] [2097]

We are living in a time when the control system's draconian strategy applies the Hegelian Dialectics in an indefinite, repetitive cycle whereby Western governments identify a self-created **problem**, then engineer a destructive **reaction** immediately linked to that **problem**, virtually always in the form of violent false flags thus providing ample excuse and opportunity for the government's proposed **solution** that never fails to facilitate tighter authoritarian control.[2098] This endless do-loop cycle is the state's ticket leading to rising oppression and despotism exploited to the point of demolishing our freedom guaranteed under the Constitution. So called Western democracies are fast turning into the Communist Soviet gulag era of the 1940s and 50s.

Oppenheimer's House of Commons outburst last July and the October Jewish synagogue shooting are merely staged events designed to identify a **problem** that major political leaders labeled as "anti-Semitic racists" are leading to a **reaction** inspiring anti-Semitic racist reactionaries worldwide to violently act out, as in the synagogue shooting. **Solution** – create more "anti-hate laws" locking up truth with the realists who speak it. Another illustrative example would be pronouncing the 2016 internet Pizzagate hype as "fake news" to be a **problem** that "dangerously" inspired the Comet pizza shooter's **reaction**,[2099] necessitating the immediate rollout within two weeks of Obama's pre-written "fake news" censorship legislation as the state **solution**. Round and round the dialectic gyroscope goes, our Orwellian descent spiraling humanity into despotic oblivion, everyone whose eyes are wide open knows.

[2092] Garikai Chengu, "How the US Helped Create Al Qaeda and ISIS," *Counter Punch*, September 19, 2014.

[2093] Joachim Hagopian, "'Politically Correct': The War on Free Speech, Free Press, Free Internet and the Truth. What is the Endgame?" *Global Research*, October 2016.

[2094] Caroline Marcus, "The Politically Correct Purge on our Language," *The Daily Telegraph*, August 6, 2018.

[2095] Mahesh CK, "Australian Universities Ban Sarcasm from Campus," *recentlyheard.com*, November 18, 2018.

[2096] "European Hate Speech Laws," *The Legal Project*.

[2097] Johanna Markind, "Freedom of Speech Is under Assault in America: Book Review of The Silencing: How the Left Is Killing Free Speech, by Kirsten Power," *The Legal Project*, January 5, 2016.

[2098] Joachim Hagopian, "Authoritarian Control and Mass Murder in America the Hegelian Dialectic Way," *Lew Rockwell*, June 16, 2016.

[2099] Joachim Hagopian, "Was the Pizzagate almost-Shooting a Deep State False Flag? If not, it sure was Conveniently used to further Demonize alt Media and 'Fake News,'" *sott.net*, December 6, 2016.

The immediate first choice Dialectic **solution** for Hodge would be materialization of her intended leadership coup to depose Corbyn, but fortunately that failed. Also her Plan B **solution** would be for the Labor Party to return to its original, more inclusive IHRA definition of anti-Semitism. That failed as well. A longer term **solution** for Hodge and her beloved Jewish State would be to enact more laws around the globe outlawing "anti-Semitic hate" that under the older Labor Party definition would facilitate the arrests of anyone criticizing Israel or calling it a Zionist racist nation. An extremist **reaction** to the **problem** of a so called "racist" party leader that inspires and incites violent racist extremists to shoot Jews then provides the excuse to pass anti-hate legislation to silence truth and opposition to state tyranny as the cabal's "final **solution**." Using this incredibly revealing lens to filter and process today's world events and unfolding developments, it becomes far easier to figure out the real truth of how the corrupt, morally crumbling international pedo-crime cabal operates day in and day out.

PC tyranny plays a pivotal key role offering a convenient cover for totalitarian censorship and oppression where speakers of the truth such as independent journalists and citizen activists exposing government crimes are slated for incarceration. With US Congress controlled by pro-Israel lobby groups like AIPAC and the ADL,[2100] the US Senate is seeking to pass legislation to redefine anti-Semitism to include conflating Israel criticism with anti-Semitism. Under the catch-all category of a "hate crime," in May 2018 South Carolina became the first state to make it illegal to criticize Israeli occupation.[2101] With a concentration of Zionist evangelicals voting in South Carolina, they're anxiously awaiting Armageddon and the Second Coming.

To demonstrate just how powerful the Jewish State, its Zionist Nazis and Israel's lobbying power are in the United States of Israel, I mean America, it's coming down to if you wish to remain gainfully employed, you must be willing to forego all your First Amendment rights. An American citizen in Austin, Texas who for decades has worked as a professional school speech pathologist in good standing was recently terminated from her job because she refused to sign a required oath stating she will not engage in a boycott of Israel.[2102] We can boycott products from states or all United States for that matter, but refusing to buy from Israel and you lose your job. These kind of laws against free choice and freedom are already in effect now in many states as well as in the UK and Europe.

Several decades ago back in the 1980s the boycott movement proved successful against apartheid South Africa as an effective catalyst pressuring that racist nation to change.[2103] But when the same movement is applied to Israel, suddenly the right to organize and engage in economic boycott against this present criminal regime as a just and viable option is being systematically criminalized around the globe. We are currently living under increasing Anglo-

---

[2100] Wayne Madsen, "US Congress is 'Occupied Territory,'" *Wayne Madsen Report/The Ugly Truth*, January 3, 2016.
[2101] Whitney Webb, "South Carolina's New Hate Speech Law Outlaws Criticism of the Israeli Occupation," *Mint Press News*, May 1, 2018.
[2102] Glenn Greenwald, "A Texas Elementary School Speech Pathologist Refused to Sign a Pro-Israel Oath, now Mandatory in many States — so she Lost her Job," *The Intercept*, December 17, 2018.
[2103] Megan Hanna, "BDS Movement: Lessons from the South Africa Boycott," Aljazeera, February 23, 2016.

American-Zionist oppression and tyranny that will soon rival the worst of times from the Soviet gulag era. What's even worse is that the loss of our fundamental human rights and freedoms are being spread through globalized fascism by planetary controllers bent on one world governance sooner than later.

Using the "hate crime" lynchpin to tighten the noose, the cabal is fast killing off what's left of our First Amendment rights to free speech and free press.[2104] Telling the truth and activism are fast becoming a crime. In a related development, as of June 2018 Trump's new Assistant Secretary of Education for Civil Rights Kenneth Marcus is pro-Zionist zealot that equates anti-Semitism with any criticism of the Jewish State and has targeted Boycott, Divest, Sanctions (BDS) activism against Israel as his enemy vowing to instill "fear" on college campuses with a plan to shut the movement down nationally. Like Dame Oppenheimer-Hodge, he too conflates support for Palestinians' rights as anti-Semitic. With the Jewish lobby Zionists so powerful yet desperate, expect more states to follow suit with South Carolina.

To counteract worldwide criticism against Israel's genocidal crimes and appalling human rights violations against Palestinians, Zionists are pushing back with the agenda to coerce nations around the world into passing laws criminalizing criticism of Israel as a hate crime by meeting the broader definition of anti-Semitism to include any Israeli form of criticism.[2105] First they came for all those who stood up for the Palestinians...[2106]

Through decades of social engineering emasculating men while promoting fanatical male bashing PC feminist extremists exercising increasing Marxist power in campus witch hunts, the ruling elite's man-eating attack dogs are actually attacking and undermining man-woman relations and ultimately marriage and family as the fundamental social institutions that for eons of time have provided societies a foundation for stability and cohesion.[2107] Recall that centuries ago Illuminati "founder" Adam Weishaupt identified the destruction/abolition of family to be among the primary objectives toward achieving one world government tyranny.[2108]

Meanwhile, on another nefariously related front, the ruling elite has an overt, insidious, constant agenda attempting to normalize pedophilia (see Chapter 2). The media propaganda machine utilizing the PC-protected LGBT agenda armed with militant social justice warriors ready on demand to robotically pounce on their next designated target, which in some twisted circles may apparently be the "pedo-basher." NAMBLA, the North American counterpart to PIE, the North American Man/Boy Love Association in 2017 was tied to the AntiFa radical left's riots

[2104] Glenn Greenwald, https://theintercept.com/2016/02/16/greatest-threat-to-free-speech-in-the-west-criminalizing-activism-against-israeli-occupation/.

[2105] Alison Weir, "International Campaign is Criminalizing Criticism of Israel as 'Antisemitism,'" *israelpalestinenews.org*, May 17, 2017.

[2106] Martin Niemöller, "First They Came for Me," *veni.com*.

[2107] Joachim Hagopian, "The Elite's Social Engineering Endgame: A Battle between the Sexes where Humanity Loses," *sott.net*, May 30, 2016.

[2108] Joseph Trainor, "Adam Weishaupt- The New World Order and Utopian Globalism," *Illuminati-news.com*.

at Berkeley in violent protest of right wing speakers based on uncovered documents.[2109] Then at a Columbia University speaking engagement featuring rightwing provocateur Mike Cernovich, a banner clearly displaying AntiFa, NAMBLA and "no pedo bashing" made headlines that the left-leaning press immediately accused alt-right of staging a hoax.[2110] Hoax or no hoax, it would come as no shock if misguided social justice warriors looking for their next "cause" would come after pedo-bashers like Cernovich or his writer for that matter. Elitist puppet masters have already hoodwinked America and have too many right where they want them - cluelessly divided and conquered.[2111] Fortunately the not so hoodwinked in America now growing in numbers see through their lies and manipulations.

Predatory pedophile scum are lurking just beneath LGBT's more palatable, socially acceptable cover so en vogue in today's prurient saturated mass media, now calling themselves Minor Attracted Persons (MAPs), as if a name change makes it okay or normal to have sex with kids.[2112] It's déjà vu of PIE in the 1970s and 80s all over again, when the sickos co-opted the liberal left's sexual liberation/gay movement, insisting that kids have sexuality too, needing liberation right into the waiting perverted grasp of hungry sexual predators. From today's warped POV dictating blind adherence to moral and cultural relativism in an "anything goes," hipster world[2113] comes the progressive left's latest battlefield front, defending against "pedo-bashing," excusing predatory child rapists simply by renaming them MAPs as just another misunderstood, persecuted, oppressed minority. After all, one man's sin is another man's pleasure girl or boy-toy.

Chapter 2 mentioned that the progressive left's rag *Salon* in 2015 actually ran a series of articles penned by an alleged celibate pedophile (that *Salon* abruptly removed from the internet in 2017) as a sympathetic inside glimpse into the distraught, complicated world of society's most hated sexual pariah for simply being born with a biological predisposition for attraction to children, not by volitional choice (though the author admits he was molested at age 7).[2114] *The New York Times* published a controversial piece in 2014 by a professor asserting pedophilia may be a mental disorder but not a crime,[2115] while other accounts are promoting it as a mere sexual orientation or lifestyle preference.[2116] For decades the Hollywood A list has made no bones about its unwavering loyal support for such acclaimed aging unprosecuted pedophile directors as Roman Polanski and Woody Allen; and Chapter 15 features how much the Hollywood cesspit is a pedophilia-infested and controlled haven for Luciferian predators.

[2109] Peter Hasson, "Documents Tie Berkeley Riot Organizers to Pro-Pedophilia Group NAMBLA," *Daily Caller*, April 28, 2017.

[2110] Kelly Weill, "Alt-Right Frames Protesters as Pedophiles with Fake NAMBLA Sign," *Daily Beast*, October 31, 2017.

[2111] Joachim Hagopian, "How to Overcome the Elite's Divide and Rule Control over a Divided Nation and World," *Lew Rockwell*, February 7, 2017.

[2112] Jessica Jenkins, "Pedophiles believe they should be part of the LGBT Community," *The Daily Caller*, July 9, 2018.

[2113] Sean McDowell, "Are There Absolute Moral Truths?" *allaboutphilosophy.org*.

[2114] Todd Nickerson, "I'm a Pedophile, but not a Monster, *Salon*, September 21, 2015.

[2115] Margo Kaplan, "Pedophilia: A Disorder, not a Crime," *The New York Times*, October 4, 2014.

[2116] Ian Johnston, "Paedophilia a 'Sexual Orientation – like being Straight or Gay," *Independent*, April 3, 2016.

From professional mental health to academia, and media to entertainment on multi-pronged fronts, be they subliminal or overt, the recurrent, in-our-face message and theme is that like LGBT, society should learn tolerance and acceptance towards pedophiles. Bottom line, only the sexual offenders at the top of the predator food chain possess both the most motive with the most means at their disposal more than any other single group to relentlessly push this over-the-top, highly manipulative, diabolical agenda. Once legal and normalized, all child rapists are home free.

We're living in an upside down, Luciferian ruled, extremist, polarized world right now where deception is the pedo-elite's most effectively deployed globalized weapon of mass destruction. The late author Michael Ellner sized it up succinctly:

Just look at us. Everything is backwards; everything is upside down. Doctors destroy health, lawyers destroy justice, universities destroy knowledge, governments destroy freedom, the major media destroy information and religions destroy spirituality.[2117]

It's been the sinister agenda of Illuminati bloodline families like the Rothschilds and Oppenheimers that have deceitfully turned and twisted this world upside down. Controversial but incisive Canadian Jew Henry Makow offers his take on the Rothschild reach into every human's life on the planet:

The Rothschilds are Cabalist Jews who represent their own demented megalomania that jeopardizes the destiny of mankind. They are imposing their occult tyranny by virtue of their worldwide monopoly over the medium of exchange. They produce credit and currency from nothing in the form of a debt to themselves, something our government could do itself, interest-and-debt-free. Organized Jewry and Freemasonry are accomplices in this scam. Alas, our 'money' is just coupons, virtual chips in their digital casino. They can manipulate or void these chips any time they want. Their agenda is to protect their money monopoly by extending it into a monopoly over everything – power, knowledge, culture, religion - by re-engineering humanity to serve them. This is the real meaning of Communism.[2118]

Only by spreading this dark secret truth can more of us see through the Rothschilds and their minions' thinly veiled endgame of nonstop lies spewing out daily from their puppet governments and MSM propaganda ministries as well as from the wide spectrum of today's bloodline controlled, morally bankrupt, corrosive institutions. Too many poisoned, dumbed down sheep are too gullible and blinded to reject the spoon-fed bullshit. But urgent, concentrated dissemination of truth to inform, educate and empower the masses is our best hope, chance and weapon for mobilizing a worldwide grassroots level movement to fully expose and overthrow the not-so-hidden shackles by holding the ruling demons fully accountable for all their egregious crimes against our children, adults and all life forms on this

---

[2117] Michael Ellner, "Michael Ellner," *whale.to*.

[2118] Jonas E. Alexis and Henry Makow, "Communism, the Rothschilds, and the Central Banking Cartel," *Veterans Today*, July 3, 2018.

earth. That's what the controllers are most afraid of, that we band together in recognition of the true enemy.

Returning to Jeremy Corbyn's stance on Israel and why militant fanatics like Hodge are going berserk. Jeremy's conspicuously laudable refusal to entertain, wine and dine a Zionist war criminal, Corbyn publicly snubbed blowhard Netanyahu on his November 2017 visit to Britain to celebrate the Balfour centennial fiasco.[2119] 100 years ago the then UK foreign minister Arthur Balfour pleased his Rothschild overlord by making it official, Great Britain was paving the way for a future Jewish State.[2120] In effect, the long reigning imperialistic British Empire gave the greenlight for 60,000 Jews then living in Palestine to assume rule over the 600,000 disenfranchised Arabs who had zero say in their grand theft homeland despite their 10 to 1 majority.

But then that's how oligarchies are. For some time now numerous Western governments pretending to be democracies are actually oligarchies,[2121] never representing the majority's interests but only the small powerful elite minority.[2122] Another reason VIP pedos get away with raping and murdering children. As owners of the world central banking cartel, the Rothschilds have exploited this reality for centuries.[2123]

Since Jews are lighter-skinned than Arabs, once the Balfour declaration was out, the rest is history. Down through the ages, people with darker skin complexions have nearly always been the prime targets of the worst racist atrocities and inhumane persecution. The historic murderous Balfour proclamation set the stage for the true Semite Palestinians to be illegally run off their land, homes bulldozed and torched and people genocided to make room for wave after wave of non-Semite Khazars known as the Ashkenazi Jews emigrating from Eastern Europe and Western Russia whose ancestors never stepped foot on Middle Eastern soil.[2124]

The Balfour Declaration unleashed a 70-year bloody violent reign of terror of nonstop divide and conquer rule over Arab and Muslim states throughout the region, always with totally complicit US and UK support. Hence, with the British crown globally dominant for several hundred years, the Anglo-American-Zio agenda has virtually controlled mankind's fate over the last several centuries. Crimes against humanity remain unpunished because this axis-of-evil has always been a master manipulator in deception, rewriting history, faking science, creating and twisting religion as yet another control mechanism, hiding the real truth from the masses for

---

[2119] Joachim Hagopian, "'Jeremy Corbyn is taking a Courageous stand against Netanyahu and Apartheid Israel,'" *Muslim Press*, October 31, 2017.

[2120] Avi Shlaim, "The Balfour Declaration: A Study in British Duplicity," *Middle East Eye*, November 1, 2017.

[2121] Natalie Jones and Alastair Gee, "America's Super Rich: six things to know," *The Guardian*, September 26, 2018.

[2122] Michael Hudson, "Europe's Transition from Social Democracy to Oligarchy," *michael-hudson.com*, December 6, 2011.

[2123] Liam Michael Roberts, "Rothschild Zionism: The Gods of Money and War," *The Event Chronicle*, February 10, 2016.

[2124] Stuart Littlefield, "Who are the True Semites in the Topsy-Turvy World of Anti-Semitism?" *Veterans Today*, April 2, 2018.

millenniums. The old world order in fact is the New World Order but with the naked, ugly truth exposed, the jig's about up.

Founder Theodor Herzl's Zionist Movement credited with securing the birth of Israel in 1948 (again through Rothschild support and power) as an independent sovereign nation, having actively co-opted with Hitler's National Socialist Party in 1933 right up to wartime with their mutually cooperative plan to utilize World War II death camp Jews as sacrificial pawns, essentially punished for failing to join the 60,000 that freely immigrated from Nazi Germany to Palestine.[2125] The exodus additionally involved over 300,000 other fleeing Jews heavily relocating to the US but also South America and Europe as well.[2126] The Zionists shared with Hitler that an Aryan Germany free of Jews and a Jewish State in Palestine full of immigrating Jews from around the world was both the answer and solution to the Jewish question.[2127]

The tragedy of the death camp Jews was viewed by the handful of Zionists that bargained their fate with the Nazi devil himself as simply a necessary cost or collateral damage required to whip up the obligatory, undying postwar sympathy worldwide that would then provide the bargaining chip to secure the UN endorsed national Jewish State in Palestine.[2128] After all, from the very get-go, Zionism's Modus Operandi has always been that the ends justify the means.[2129] Zionists opportunely used the horror of the Holocaust to readily brand and silence critics with the "anti-Semitic" label should they disagree with the Jewish State's brutally aggressive policies towards Arabs in the Middle East. Orthodox and traditional Jews never wanted anything to do with Zionism,[2130] recognizing that the suffering of Jews has benefited only the Zionists as a subversive political movement having zero to do with their Jewish religion and that clearly Zionists never had the Jews' interests at heart in their ruthless quest for global power, domination and control.[2131]

Both the World Zionist Organization (WZO) and American Jewish Congress during World War II literally turned their backs on fellow Jews dying in the concentration camps.[2132] With WZO's full approval, Zionist head of Jewish Rescue and Relief Committee Rudolph Kasztner negotiated with the Nazi architect of the Holocaust Adolf Eichmann in 1944, paying over $1.6 billion for 1,685 of his fellow Zionist friends and the Budapest Jewish elite a safe passage on a train to neutral Switzerland in exchange for helping to round up 460,000 non-Zionist, common Jews

[2125] Rehmat, "Zionist-Hitler Haavara (Transfer) Agreement 1933," *rehmat1.com*, February 25, 2012.

[2126] Henry Makow, "How Zionists Deliberately Sacrificed Jews in the Holocaust and otherwise to Chase them to Rothschild's Palestine. Is Israel their next Victim?" *new.euro-med.dk*, November 30, 2017.

[2127] Mark Weber, "Zionism and the Third Reich," *The Journal of Historical Review*, July-August 1993, (Vol. 13, No. 4), pages 29-37.

[2128] Henry Makow, https://rense.com/general76/maak.htm.

[2129] Henry Makow, "Zionism: Compulsory Suicide are Americans next?" *Ether Zone*, 2002.

[2130] Michael F. Blume, "Jews against Zionism," *rightlydividingtheword.com*, 2008.

[2131] Robert David Steele, "Eradicating Zionism with Truth – A Plan for Peace and Prosperity for All," *American Herald Tribune*, May 6, 2018.

[2132] Reuben Samuels, "Zionism Betrayed Holocaust Victims, Jewish Refugees," *Workers Vanguard*, May 31, 2013.

headed for Auschwitz and certain death.[2133] The story was kept secret until word slipped out while Kasztner was living in Israel and reportedly a Mossad operative murdered him in 1957 in order to keep another dark page in Zionist history hidden.[2134]

For well over a century the Zionist Movement established deep roots in both the British as well as the American Empires through robust infiltration politically, culturally and economically. Zionist control over centralized world banking[2135] and the mass media propaganda machine[2136] along with Zionist government operatives as permanent fixtures still occupying halls of power in Washington[2137] and London[2138] (like Dame Oppenheimer-Hodge) represent today's Anglo-American-Zionist Axis-of-Evil, still readily sending naïve, patriotic young Americans and British off to fight and die on foreign soil for Greater Israel Project wars, Big Oil and the ever-Bigger Military Industrial Complex, psychopathically killing over four million innocent Muslims in the process just since 1990.[2139]

As a bona fide globalist, Margaret Hodge's position on migration is disingenuous at best:

Migration is a feature of globalization. You can't stop it; so every time a political party says it is going to be tough on immigration, it fails to deliver and loses trust.[2140]

Hodge emphatically rationalizes the elite's manufactured migration crisis in Britain and Europe as a mere fact of life, pretending that flooding millions of Muslim migrants from Greater Israel Project wars of her Zionist making is not part of the Axis-of-Evil agenda to destroy the West.[2141] It is, and her last statement is a boldface lie and she knows it. While hypocritically accepting open border migration as a "get used to it" NWO reality for the nation she supposedly serves, her own beloved Jewish State as the actual nation she loyally serves has always steadfastly maintained a rigid policy completely refusing to accept ethnic and religious diversity of any kind at and within its borders.

Let's look at the effects of her Anglo-American-Zionist Empire. Jewish usury moneylenders triggered Jesus' temple tantrum and paper credit introduced fractional reserve banking out of thin air,[2142] traced back to cabbalist-rooted, anti-Jesus Knights of Templar during the Crusades (see Chapter 4). From that lineage the unholy trinity of Anglo-American-Zionism now holds

---

[2133] Henry Makow, https://www.henrymakow.com/091202.html.

[2134] Adam LeBor, "Eichmann's List: a Pact with the Devil," *Independent*, August 23, 2000.

[2135] "The Federal Reserve - Zionist Jewish Private Bankers," *rense.com*, March 28, 2009.

[2136] Joel Stein, "Who runs Hollywood? C'mon," *Los Angeles Times*, December 19, 2008.

[2137] Dick Fojut, "Zionist Control of America Virtually Complete," *rense.com*, July 23, 2006.

[2138] Evan Jones, "Zionism in Britain: a Neglected Chronicle," *CounterPunch*, August 28, 2015.

[2139] Kit O'Connell, "4 Million Muslims Killed in Western Wars: Should we call it Genocide?" *Mint Press News*, August 18, 2015.

[2140] Robert Shrimsley, "Lunch with the FT: Margaret Hodge," *Financial Times*, December 7, 2013.

[2141] "Unmasked: The Mastermind behind the Mass Invasion of Europe and His Plan in 8 Steps," *new.euro-md.dk*, November 6, 2015.

[2142] "The Hidden History of Money and the Feudal Order Usury Secrets." *Scribd.com*, June 25, 2008.

humanity hostage, drowning in insurmountable debt slavery with an embedded pedophilia blackmail-bribery system controlling compromised puppets to do Empire's dirty bidding.

The crime cabal outrageously extorts $40 billion from American taxpayers alone as military aid supporting the Jewish State's "final solution" - its genocidal policy against Arabs.[2143] Both the US and UK governments' carte blanche loyalty to Israel has as much to do with sexual blackmail extortion as embracing Zionism's apartheid ethnic purge of an already decimated Palestinian population.[2144] US President Trump's moving the US embassy to Jerusalem was simply the Anglo-American-Zionist cabal setting the stage for its ticking time bomb to Armageddon.[2145]

Zionists like Oppenheimer can't face the fact that if Jeremy Corbyn ends up prime minister in favor of a sovereign state of Palestine, Israel may no longer rule the roost as it has for seven straight decades now. That's also why Israeli firsters from North America, Europe and Tel Aviv have had Iran in their crosshairs for nearly just as long. The evil controllers would prefer Armageddon over restructured balance of power in the Middle East where a sovereign Palestine, Iran and Syria emerge vibrantly independent from the death clutches of the Anglo-America-Zionist Empire in freefall hegemonic decline, relegating both Israel and Saudi Arabia to minor regional players. That's the real reason behind all the childish hissy fits, acted out temper tantrums and escalating tensions recently.

Rational, peace-loving citizens around the globe have long seen through this most nightmarishly insane, satanic endgame. But as long as aging British foul-mouthpieces like Oppenheimer-Hodge keep spouting off their own duplicitous hate with their worn-out, weaponized "anti-Semite" PC control card, rehashing Nazi Jewish death camps ad nauseam, calculatedly intent on turning free speech and inconvenient truths into codified hate crimes bent on imprisoning anyone daring to criticize their totalitarian Zionist-Marxist fascist agenda, make no mistake, in actuality they are openly, desperately promoting their long-awaited Luciferian-Illuminati-Fabian inspired pedo-cabal of one world governance.

Today's Labor Party leader Jeremy Corbyn may be much maligned when it comes to Israel,[2146] but when it comes to protecting British care home children from chronic sexual abuse in his own Islington-North London district, sad to say, it's the children who remain most maligned as his record isn't much different from Hodge's. As longtime Islington MP, Jeremy has also apparently failed miserably to help abused children. Way back in 1992 and 1993, the good folks Liz Davies, David Cofie, Eileen Fairweather and articulate victim-survivor Demetrious Panton (among others) all had individual meetings with the House of Commons rising star Corbyn, and

[2143] Ed Adamczyk, "$40 Billion Aid to Israel is 'Largest ever' to any Country, says Susan Rice," *UPI*, June 14, 2016..

[2144] Miko Peled, "De-Arabizing Jerusalem: Biblical 'History' Underwrites Israel's Ethnic Cleansing," *Mint Press News*, August 20, 2018.

[2145] Allison Kaplan Sommer, "Analysis Armageddon? Bring It On: The Evangelical Force behind Trump's Jerusalem Speech," *Haaretz/The Muslim Times*, December 10, 2017.

[2146] Stuart Littlewood, https://www.veteranstoday.com/2018/04/02/who-are-the-true-semites-in-the-topsy-turvy-world-of-anti-semitism/.

all report that to their face, he appeared supportive and sympathetic to their cause, claiming he would inquire further to assist stopping the widespread cancer of child sex abuse rocking his and their community (especially after the Dame seized control over the Islington council in 1982). But all the anti-abuse whistleblowers and advocates who met with Jeremy, to a person were gravely disappointed, maintaining that he never once contacted them again, never mentioning the scandal publicly, nor thanking them for courageously putting their lives on the line presenting and exposing the irrefutable evidence to him and the public. Their unanimous verdict - **Corbyn was of no help at all**.[2147]

Moreover, back in the mid-1980s and 90s, after Tory MP Geoffrey Dickens first accused Westminster-Downing Street VIPs of pedophilia, even drawing specific attention to an alleged child brothel operating at Islington's Elthorne housing state, Corbyn registered a formal complaint with the House Speaker, angry that without informing Jeremy, Dickens had gone to his constituency, Corbyn territorially called the snooping Dickens "irresponsible" on February 17, 1986.[2148] Think how many lives could have been saved from the horror of abuse had Corbyn actually taken urgent measures to help protect children by joining forces with the one brave whistleblowing MP who first brought the Westminster scandal to the public's attention in 1984 with the infamous dossier that pedophile Sir Leon Brittan lost. But instead MP Jeremy Corbyn accused Dickens in the press of "getting cheap publicity at the expense of innocent children."[2149] Unfortunately, like so many of his colleagues, Corbyn denigrated Geoffrey Dickens, ridiculing him for his "wild antics," and wrongly dismissing all his truthful accusations as unwarranted fuss, melodrama and "cheap publicity" stunts over nothing.

When asked to comment on the July 2015 *Daily Mail* story exposing Corbyn's apparent failure to act on what he'd learned in the early 1990s from all the insiders he'd met face-to-face with, his office released the following statement:

*Jeremy Corbyn has a long record of standing up for his constituents. He called for an **independent inquiry into child abuse in Islington at the time, and has taken this strong line ever since**.*[2150][**Bold** for emphasis]

Really? Other than the single one line statement below in reply to Eileen Fairweather's piece in the *Evening Standard* in 1992 that broke the horrendous abuse story:

These allegations are extremely serious and must be properly investigated.[2151]

[2147] Guy Adams, https://www.dailymail.co.uk/news/article-3181783/Did-Jeremy-Corbyn-try-protect-fellow-Left-wingers-implicated-paedophile-scandal.html.

[2148] Guy Adams, https://www.dailymail.co.uk/news/article-3181783/Did-Jeremy-Corbyn-try-protect-fellow-Left-wingers-implicated-paedophile-scandal.html.

[2149] Guy Adams, https://www.dailymail.co.uk/news/article-3181783/Did-Jeremy-Corbyn-try-protect-fellow-Left-wingers-implicated-paedophile-scandal.html.

[2150] Guy Adams, https://www.dailymail.co.uk/news/article-3181783/Did-Jeremy-Corbyn-try-protect-fellow-Left-wingers-implicated-paedophile-scandal.html.

No other words or actions by Corbyn can be found, nor is there any public record of Corbyn's alleged "inquiry" "at the time." Too bad he apparently never put any of his words or promises "at the time" when first confronted with the truth into any observable action on behalf of so many of his abused children suffering in his district's group homes. Only when Corbyn was presented with indisputable evidence in person did he ever respond at all, and then merely paying lip service, never backing up his vowed support with any further actions or acknowledgement of any public crisis. Astute anti-abuse advocate Demetrious Panton poignantly points out:

I am aware that Mr Corbyn is an active campaigner for the protection of human rights of a range of people, including those who have never been his constituents. I am not aware that he ever deployed his obvious zeal and effort to ensure that the human rights of his constituents who were abused while in the care of the London borough of Islington, were protected.[2152]

It then seems a fair and accurate conclusion to draw that political expediency during Jeremy's early career not to rock the boat won out over his acting on the moral and legal imperative to protect his own constituent children being horribly abused "at the time."

In 2014 Jeremy Corbyn made the following statement in the House of Commons:

There have been complaints about Islington children's homes in the past and the council has investigated them.[2153]

Corbyn's latter contention is totally false. Islington council has only pretended to investigate the widespread abuse while overtly and aggressively obstructing justice by losing and destroying evidence at every turn, and either ignored, rejected or suppressed claims by victims, social workers, witnesses and whistleblowers. Any so called internal investigations by the council are nothing but thinly veiled cover-ups. Virtually all the child abusers have been allowed to go free with almost none ever charged for their crimes and brought to justice. And the complicit Jeremy Corbyn knows this.

Another blemish filed under the crowded meme, "oops, I didn't know," is the fact that Jeremy Corbyn's constituency agent was Derek Sawyer, the Hodge successor as Islington council leader presiding over the borough for a total of seven years. Derek Sawyer has been a permanent political heavyweight in the local government, first becoming a Labor party council member when Margaret Hodge assumed her position as council leader in 1982 and taking over for her a decade later in 1992 in the thick of the erupting scandal.[2154] With his years leading the council

---

[2151] Guy Adams, https://www.dailymail.co.uk/news/article-3181783/Did-Jeremy-Corbyn-try-protect-fellow-Left-wingers-implicated-paedophile-scandal.html.
[2152] Guy Adams, https://www.dailymail.co.uk/news/article-3181783/Did-Jeremy-Corbyn-try-protect-fellow-Left-wingers-implicated-paedophile-scandal.html.
[2153] Steven Swinford, "Jeremy Corbyn Accused of Inaction over Paedophile Scandal," *The Telegraph*, July 23, 2015.
[2154] Jeremy Corbyn and Mr Vazeline," *aangirfan.blogspot.com*, April 18, 2017.

in 1992-94 and again in 1997 to 2002,[2155] his lengthy span on the Islington council dates from 1982 all the way to 2006. For a quarter century Derek Sawyer held top positions overseeing Islington police operations and probation services as well as the London magistrate courts.[2156] He worked under and with not only Hodge but two other Blairites Jack Straw and Stephen Twigg.

The same year that Hodge resigned and Sawyer took over was also the same year that whistleblowers Liz Davies and David Cofie sat in Corbyn's office sharing the horrific child abuse scandal with the MP who publicly did nothing to assist endangered and abused children. If there ever was a key witness to the nefarious goings-on in Islington for three decades it would be Derek Sawyer. Yet he too claims he never knew abuse was running rampant in all dozen care homes and defended both his own as well as Margaret Hodge's record and reputation, insisting they did everything legally proper in protecting children on their watch.[2157] That in and of itself is simply not true or the abuse would neither have been so pervasive or long lasting. That kind of double talk renders Sawyer even less credible. But the kicker is his super close association with one of Britain's most notorious, three-time convicted child beating pedophiles.

Derek Sawyer maintained a 40-year friendship with Derek Slade going back to their college days as well as maintained an enduring business partnership involving four different organizations. Boasting he was the best man at Sawyer's wedding, for many decades the brutally sadistic serial child abusing headmaster Derek Slade beat and sodomized boys as young as 8 at St. George's School in Suffolk and numerous others to follow.[2158] In 1986 when Slade was arrested for violently assaulting one of his students, Sawyer was the character witness who kept Slade out of jail. Slade's abuse fit the same familiar pattern as Catholic priests allowed to move from church to church to continue abusing. Slade went on from Suffolk to damage more kids at a school in Sussex, where he was arrested and convicted yet again, somehow managing to avoid prison.

Four days prior to the 1995 Ian White report that Sawyer was forced to commission exposing the Islington abuse, Derek Sawyer and Derek Slade cofounded International British Education Projects (IBEP) together, raising money for building international schools in Swaziland and India.[2159] Again, Sawyer was complicit, assisting his business partner to change his name (using a dead kid's name Slade picked from a graveyard) and as chairman of IBEP, supported Slade in assuming a new identity as director of education of an IBEP school in Swaziland where Slade abused yet more boys in Africa. From 1978 right up to his 2010 conviction and 21-year prison sentence (based solely on abuse crimes committed in Britain from 1978 to 1983), Derek Slade

---

[2155] "Key Individuals," *islingtonsurvivors.co.uk*.

[2156] "Derek Sawyer – Leader of Islington Council 1992-1994," *islingtonsurvivors.co.uk*.

[2157] Paul Harris and Martin Bright, "The Whistleblower's Story," *The Observer/spotlightonabuse.wordpress.com*, July 6, 2003.

[2158] "'Corruption,'" *The UK & Ireland Database*.

[2159] "'Corruption,'" https://theukdatabase.com/uk-child-abusers-named-and-shamed/calls-for-change-in-law/corruption/.

physically and sexually assaulted hundreds of victims on three continents for over 30 years. A lawsuit representing abused boys in India was somehow quashed. Again, through his contacts with prominent established figures like best bud Derek Sawyer, Slade's reign of terror over children entrusted in his care committing over 50 convicted offenses of child sexual abuse, child pornography and child physical assault, all the while supported and seemingly protected by Sawyer and friends.

Roger Cook's half-hour *BBC* documentary entitled "An Abuse of Trust" succinctly chronicles Derek Slade's marathon crime spree,[2160] reminiscent of such despicable creeps as Jimmy Savile and Cyril Smith. Though predictably, Jeremy Corbyn's onetime constituency agent Derek Sawyer claims he never knew his friend and partner was a habitual child sex fiend, Sawyer remains neck deep in complicity in both Margaret Hodge's gross mishandling and abuse cover-up as well as enabling a monster on the loose to ruin so many lives for so long. In March 2016, after serving the first half dozen of his 21 year sentence, Derek Slade died at age 66.[2161] Sawyer's feeble excuse "I never knew" is a stretch for all but the brain dead.

Though no one can accuse either Derek Sawyer or Jeremy Corbyn of child abuse per se, both their poor judgment and enabling of sex crimes through inaction certainly can and should be called into question. The potential future prime minister of the United Kingdom has seemingly been given a free pass by the press on his culpability in Britain's child sexual abuse epidemic, at its worst in his own backyard. No one in government except MP John Mann has directly confronted Corbyn on his dereliction of duty to protect his child constituents.[2162] And what appears most troubling is a statement made in the House of Commons by Corbyn to then Home Secretary May on November 3, 2014:

Finally in my own borough of Islington there have been complaints about Islington children's homes in the past and the council has investigated them.[2163]

If he is claiming Islington council ever actually investigated its own abuse, he's dead wrong. The council sat on and withheld the 1995 White report conducted by an outsider for 20 years before releasing a heavily redacted version in 2014.[2164] And the White report lambasted Islington council for its abject failure to protect its children. At no time has Islington council on its own effort ever produced anything but a whitewash in the countless go rounds it calls investigations. MP Mann wrote an open letter to his Labor leader colleague:

Your carefully worded excusing of Islington Council in the House of Commons equally demonstrates why it is inappropriate for you to attempt to lead the Labour Party at the critical

[2160] Roger Cook, "An Abuse of Trust," *BBC*, 2013, YouTube video, 29:56, posted on Jun 11, 2013.
[2161] "Jailed Sex Abuse Headmaster Derek Slade Dies," *BBC*, March 3, 2016.
[2162] Guy Adams, https://www.dailymail.co.uk/news/article-3181783/Did-Jeremy-Corbyn-try-protect-fellow-Left-wingers-implicated-paedophile-scandal.html.
[2163] Matt Chorley, "'A new low for Labour Leadership Race': Jeremy Corbyn Hits back at Rival's Attempt to Accuse him of 'non-action' on Child Abuse," *Daily Mail*, July 23, 2015.
[2164] Michael Patrick O'Leary, "Ad Hominem, Mr Corbyn," *Ceylon Today/pcolman.wordpress.com*, August 4, 2015.

time of the Goddard Enquiry [IICSA]*, as child abuse is the issue that will haunt this Parliament.*[2165]

Though Mann was seemingly the only odd man out faulting Corbyn on his shoddy child abuse record, the Labor Party leader has managed to retain his position for over three years now despite formidable challenges and opposition, led by Hodge blasting him for his so called "anti-Semitism" because he insists on standing up for the rights of the Palestinians.

At this point as an anti-abuse child advocate, here's what I would say to Mr. Corbyn as a means of redemption for his failing children in the past.

As the UK Labor Party leader, it's never too late to make up for past mistakes by uniting with your fellow party peer Mr. Watson to finally do something real about your country's most shameful and disgraceful blight neglecting and damaging your own children, no longer allowing your powerful degenerate peers to forever live above the law without consequence. For that matter, I implore you to use your position and considerable power and influence to unite the world in leading humanity to finally begin protecting the earth's children as our most precious resource from the godless evildoers who've been in control, as no more worthy a human rights cause exists than saving our most innocent, defenseless and vulnerable human population.

If you champion this most worthy cause, you will go far in restoring integrity to the world of politics and faith to millions of skeptical, wary citizens proving that there still does exist at least one public servant and leader who actually does care about the people he's taken sworn oaths to represent and protect. Fighting for children to bring justice against the VIP criminals would generate such a sweeping, massive groundswell of populist appeal and support that it could easily carry you to becoming the next British prime minister. And perhaps with other major world leaders like Vladimir Putin and Donald Trump, who have both publicly recognized the global epidemic scourge of pedophilia for what it is, together you three could take the lead in making this your urgent priority, ultimately creating a far safer world for our children, humanity and our collective future.

Before closing this long winding road of a chapter, it's fitting to come full circle with more Tony Blair crimes. The hidden hand of MI5 and MI6 left visible fingerprints all over Scotland's tragic 1996 Dunblane Massacre, murdering in cold blood 16 schoolchildren and their teacher by a notorious pedophile Thomas Hamilton who ran a VIP pedo-ring involving NATO director-general Lord George Robertson.[2166] The sticky loose ends prompting the trigger-happy D-notice kid Blair to immediately slap a press blackout for the next 100 years on the truth shall be given its full due in Chapter 25 covering Scotland's pedophilia cover-ups. Again, British intel services and Tony Blair's subversive role in the Madeleine McCann disappearance and murder, covering up the international pedo-network will be detailed in Chapter 26. And finally, the next Chapter 24 addresses the heart of the government pedophilia epidemic unveiling the crimes in

---

[2165] Steven Swinford, "Jeremy Corbyn Accused of Inaction over Paedophile Scandal," *The Telegraph*, July 23, 2015.
[2166] Frederick Forsyth, "Dunblane Cover-up Needs Investigating, says Frederick Forsyth," *Express*, May 6, 2016.

Westminster and Richmond committed at the favorite VIP haunts - the Elm Guest House and Dolphin Square.

Chapter 8: Heart of the Westminster VIP Scandal and Cover-up: Elm Guest House and Dolphin Square

Outspoken rabblerousing author, activist and lecturer David Icke articulately frames the elementary function that pedophilia serves for the Luciferian planetary controllers:

Paedophilia is a fundamental 'cement' that holds the networks of manipulation together across all political persuasions and allows those in the shadows to blackmail politicians into introducing legislation that advances the agenda of human control.

This agenda of human control is their New World Order propagating one world centralized government dictatorship through a so called anti-Christ, one world Luciferian religion, and cashless one world digital microchipped one world currency. The ruling elite has been planning and pushing for this endgame scenario for centuries. The next quote comes from Britain's national Independent Inquiry for Child Sexual Abuse (IICSA).

There was no evidence of any kind of organised 'Westminster paedophile network' in which persons of prominence conspired to pass children amongst themselves for the purpose of sexual abuse... Similarly, no evidence of any attempts to cover up or suppress information about the existence of such a ring was found at MI5, SIS, GCHQ or in Metropolitan Police Special Branch records now held by Metropolitan Police Counter Terrorism Command.[2167]

Lies, lies and more lies. The above first sentence comprises the second sentence from the United Kingdom's official Independent Inquiry for Child Sexual Abuse, succinctly specifying its conclusive findings of unrelated instances of pedophilia committed by members of the Westminster government, but clear absence of any organized network. The fact that it's a colossal lie perpetrated on the citizens of Britain, and particularly on its victims who've consistently been trafficked across the British Isles and beyond for over a half century only proves that the entire "inquiry" is but a scam designed to continue its governmental policy of denial and cover-up of what Chapters 18 through 32 of this book have already definitively flushed out thoroughly documented, completely refuting and debunking these bogus claims. To deny that either the Home Office or its MI5, Metropolitan Police and Special Branch never aborted police inquiries or covered up pedophilia by destroying or losing evidence, implementing up to 100-year blackouts on all records as desperate measures to maintain its criminal cover-up policy is yet another preposterous lie. To pretend that members of the British Parliament, ministers, prime ministers, senior civil servants, the judiciary, law enforcement, security services, entertainment, military, mainstream media and royalty have never conspired to coordinate, operate, perpetrate and cover-up the mountains of overwhelming evidence of

---

[2167] "Allegations of Child Sexual Abuse Linked to Westminster Investigation Report Part K1: Conclusions," *iicsa.org.uk*, February 2020.

their highly organized pedo-network blatantly proving that it's all very real tells those of us interested in the truth that the British taxpayers financing the Home Office controlled IICSA have for the last half decade been criminally fleeced, bamboozled and willfully deceived through both criminal subversion and criminal perversion of justice.

Let's jump in to one of the most suppressed British pedophilia scandals of all time. Married couple Haroon Kasir (aka "Harry" originally from India) and Carole Kasir (recently learned not from Germany but England) opened up their Elm Guest House initially as a bed and breakfast for gays in Barnes, South West London in the mid-1970s, less than a decade after adult homosexuality was decriminalized in the UK. As part of the sexual liberation of the 1970s, the Elm Guest House that has since been converted into flats, began as a meeting place for gay men to hook up and comfortably enjoy sex with an adult consensual partner. But a group of evil men had other nefarious plans. Enter South African transplant out of Amsterdam Peter Glencross, commercial manager for the international Spartacus Club, who convinced Carole Kasir of the opportunity to make gobs of money catering to the sick whimsical perversions of homosexual pedophiles. Queen Elizabeth's 1977 silver jubilee was considered the turning point. The Elm Guest House used the queen's celebration to transition towards a boy brothel for demented child abusers, throwing the first of many King and Queen Balls where powerful VIPs, some dressed in drag, marked the occasion indulging in their deviant sexual appetites with delivered boy toys at what quickly morphed into a house of horror assembly line for trafficked in hapless care home residents.

Defiling children was the main course on the menu, mostly rent boy runaways and care home youth brought in for orgies and regularly plied with drugs and alcohol by UK establishment figures, rich and famous predators lustily seeking gratification through molestation, rape, torture, and perhaps even murder,[2168] paralleling the eerily identical goings-on at VIP sex parties held at the notorious Dolphin Square complex in nearby Pimlico (covered later in the chapter). A short list of household political names identified as perpetrating heavy hitters at the Elm Guest House are Leon Brittan, Cyril Smith, Anthony Blunt, Nicholas Fairbairn, Peter Hayman, Peter Morrison and Jimmy Savile, every single one of them high-powered, queen honored knights celebrated as Very Important Persons within the British Empire.[2169]

The earliest victim to come forth and divulge his shocking, sad story to the *Sunday People* in February 2013, just four months into learning about Jimmy Savile's depravities, was a family man in his late 40s. As a 14-year old boy, he, his 13-year old brother (in the press later

---

[2168] James Hanning and Paul Cahalan, "Special Report: Police Revisit the Grim Mystery of Elm Guest House," *Independent*, December 16, 2012.

[2169] Keir Mudie, "VIP Paedophile Files: The Sick Web of High=Powered and well-Connected Child Abusers," *Mirror*, March 21, 2015.

identified as deceased Peter Hatton-Bornshin[2170]) were frequently trafficked from 8 miles away to the Elm Guest House within a year after their 1978 placement in Grafton Close Children's Care Home in Richmond.[2171] Told that they were in for "a treat," upon arrival at the Barnes guest home they were lured into drinking hard cider and competing in beer guzzling contests to first intoxicate and sedate the VIPs' targeted prey. Then they were ordered to dress into girls' fairy costumes for picture taking (no doubt for blackmail purposes) with disgusting older, well-dressed men with upper class accents, constantly pawing at them as paying house guest patrons, salivating as they verbally compared notes - "he's cute," and "oh isn't he nice."

The boys were then coerced into hideous hide and seek games before the perverted sickos moved in for the kill, committing the most vile acts sexually assaulting the youth. As he recounted his trauma years, he broke down in tears. Their father had died in an industrial accident and then their mother committed suicide, placing them in the UK Care System. The horror they experienced while trapped in UK's "Care System" as Grafton Close residents caused his brother ten years out of the system to commit suicide over his abusive, tormented past. The courageous surviving orphan concluded:

The people responsible have blood on their hands. I shouldn't think my brother is the only one to have taken his life because of this. I'm speaking out now because I want justice done for me and for my brother. What went on was absolutely disgusting. When we told the staff at the care home what was happening at Elm they used to say 'They are friends, they are good people.' No one was listening to us. It's taken 30 years for anyone to listen.[2172]

A month prior to this article, in January 2013, a police raid had taken place at the home of child campaigner-social worker Mary Moss who a quarter century earlier had befriended Carole Kasir, gaining access to many of Carole's Elm House documents. From their confiscated items the police discovered that South African pedophile Peter Glencross was instrumental in turning Elm Guest House from a gay guest house to a boy brothel in the late 1970s.[2173] Glencross operated out of Holland along with his boss, the Spartacus underground network founder - ex Catholic priest John Stamford, who had fled the UK to the Netherlands after a conviction for sending child pornographic material through the mail. Spartacus maintained a membership in Britain alone of 25,000 followers. From his office on the outskirts of Amsterdam, Stamford was the publisher of Spartacus International, a directory of worldwide resources marketed for adult

---

[2170] Richard Pendlebury and Stephen Wright, "Revealed: Face of Boy Abused in Elm House Scandal as Catholic priest and Head of Boys' Home are Arrested," *Daily Mail*, February 6, 2013.

[2171] Keir Mudie and Nick Dorman, "Elm Guest House Scandal: First Victim of Paedo Guest House Breaks his Silence," *Mirror*, February 2, 2013.

[2172] Keir Mudie and Nick Dorman, https://www.mirror.co.uk/news/uk-news/first-victim-of-elm-guest-house-1572073.

[2173] David Pallister and David Hencke, "Files Reveal who turned Elm Guest House into Paedo Brothel," *Exaro News*, February 2, 2013.

predators bent on abusing boys and Glencross was assigned the task of establishing boy brothels like Elm Guest House all around the world. In effect, it was a perfect, albeit most sinister, unholy union between the likes of the CIA-MI5/MI6-Mossad blackmailers and Spartacus "boy loving," sickos, among them sexually compromised and controlled VIP perverts from around the globe.[2174]

A Spartacus advertisement in the *Capital Gay* newspaper touting a 10% discount for Spartacus club members at the Elm Guest House is believed to be an encoded message informing homosexual pedophiles that children were readily available for sex.[2175] Just eight months after the June 19, 1982 law enforcement house raid at Elm, the *Sunday People* explicitly exposed Stamford's pedo-holiday tours, boasting where the best havens in the world for sex with boys younger than 12 could easily be arranged, mentioning Sri Lanka and the Philippines in particular as pedophile paradises.[2176] Of course the despicable sex tourism and sex slave trafficking industries promising illicit sex with children in Asia have spread like a cancer to the earth's four corners as a global blight. Currently sex trafficking falls just behind illegal arms on its way to overtaking drug sales as the largest, yet fastest growing, most profitable illegal trade on the planet.[2177]

Eventually in 1995 at only 56 years of age, John Stamford wound up dead in a Belgium prison from a heart attack, another apparent victim of the common fate befalling criminals who know too much just days ahead of standing trial for sexual abuse.[2178] Undoubtedly the criminal cabal knew Stamford's prosecution posed a serious liability to high-powered VIP pedophiles in Britain and Europe alike.

Up to 1983 the Kasirs entertained many British Establishment figures at their spacious Edwardian three-story guest home with regularly scheduled parties held day and night featuring trafficked in children predominantly from Grafton Close Home to satisfy the lustful, demented tastes of MPs, cabinet ministers, entertainers, judges, police commissioners, spy chiefs, high level civil servants, clergy, top businessmen, lawyers and doctors, no different from the elite pedophile rings that were simultaneously springing up in the US, Europe and Australia (through CIA and friends).

Though the Kasirs owned and operated the hotel-turned-boy brothel, from the get-go it was implicitly a joint British intelligence services' operation not unlike the Mossad sponsored Jeffrey

[2174] "Spartacus Boys and the CIA," *aangirfan.blogspot.com*, April 10, 2016.

[2175] Murun Buchstansangur, "The Spartacus Paedophile Network was Exposed by the Sunday People in February 1983," *spotlightonabuse.wordpress.com*, May 23, 2013.

[2176] Roger Insall, "Child Vice Holidays," *Sunday People/spotlightonabuse.wordpress.com*, February 6, 1983.

[2177] Ewelina U. Ochab, "The World's Fastest Growing Crime," *Forbes*, July 29, 2017.

[2178] David Hencke and David Pallister, "Elm Guest House Scandal: Coded Advert that gave Signal to Perverts," *Mirror*, February 2, 2013.

Epstein's web of Caribbean-Palm Beach-Manhattan child honey-traps, as the modern mechanism used to sexually blackmail targeted politicians, judges, royalty, entertainers, and high-end VIPs for obvious international cabal control purposes. By the late 1970s, underage children had already become the preferred honey trap commodity, holding more bang for the buck than old fashioned heterosexual adultery or even homosexuality in the shady world of sexual blackmail and global espionage.

Sexual blackmail threatening to expose the perversions of royalty and powerful members of the elite for money had been around for well over a century,[2179] but especially over this last half century, the elite bloodline puppet masters increasingly utilized blackmail to control leaders from around the world by deploying the global intelligence community led by the CIA as blackmailers as well as chief engineers and child pimping procurers. Hence, in Britain the dot connecting links of MI5/MI6 fingerprints are left at every single pedo-crime scene – from the Elm Guest House,[2180] Northern Ireland's Kincora Boys Home[2181] to the North Wales Bryn Estyn scandal.[2182] All are interconnected as irrefutable evidence confirming that care home children from Northern Ireland, Jersey in the Channel Islands and North Wales have been systematically trafficked into London to be victimized by VIPs at Elm Guest House as well as posh flats at Dolphin Square.[2183]

Jet setting British VIPs are also known to travel abroad to abuse children in Northern Ireland, Jersey Island, North Wales and European cities like Amsterdam within the larger international pedophilia network,[2184] that is whenever they're not being showered with perks and money bribes by Zionists sponsoring free trips to Israel.[2185] The mushrooming Israeli pedo-network will be covered in a later chapter. Additionally, evidence shows that MI5 has regularly brought in foreign diplomats and dignitaries from mainland Europe, America and elsewhere to both London's Elm Guest House and North Wales, videotaping their sexcapades as evidential leverage for blackmailing foreign dignitaries as well.[2186]

It's an ugly sick world at the top of the power pyramid that systemically misuses innocents in this most appalling, diabolical way as the common currency of elitist blackmail bait. Luciferians running this planet have gotten away with it for far too long and their age-old addictions to

---

[2179] "Royals Linked to Pedo Ring," *aangirfan.blogspot.com*, December 1, 2014.

[2180] Charles Frith, "MI5 and IRA VIP Paedo Abuse/Blackmail at Elm Guest House," *charlesfrith.blogspot.com*, October 19, 2013.

[2181] Ian Drury, "MI5 'Hid' Child Abuse at Boys' Home: Former Army Intelligence Officer Claims Security Chiefs Told him to 'Stop Digging' when he Reported possible Paedophile Ring," *Daily Mail*, April 7, 2015.

[2182] "North Wales Paedophile Ring, Top People, the Police and Security Services," *aangirgan.blogspot.com*, July 5, 2005.

[2183] "International Network – Whistleblower Kerr," *aangirfan.blogspot.com*, December 4, 2017.

[2184] Nico Hines, "How Thatcher's Government Covered-up a VIP Pedophile Ring," *The Daily Beast*, June 3, 2015.

[2185] Daniel Kraemer, "MPs Sign up for £2m of Free Overseas Trips," *BBC*, October 18, 2018.

[2186] "North Wales Paedophile Ring, Top People, the Police and Security Services."

both young flesh and blood literally feed their unquenchable thirst for absolute power and control. Soaring to unprecedented demonic heights today like never before, the pedophilia business is the devil's playground and must be eradicated if the human species is to survive, much less evolve and thrive.

Early in 1982 the Scotland Yard was tipped off by a boy asserting that he was sexually abused by none other than Thatcher cabinet secretary Leon Brittan. The victim was terrified of repercussions for revealing the abuse done to him and other children victimized on an ongoing, near daily basis at Elm Guest House at 27 Rocks Lane on the Barnes Common. Shortly after he spilled the beans on his VIP sexual predators, the youth disappeared altogether, never to be seen nor heard from again, one victim among many missing and murder cases. Good, honest rank and file cops wanted to bring justice for this vanished boy and his many child peer victims being gravely, savagely harmed for life. But once the initial investigation confirmed that household names belonging to such powerful men running the country were identified as the prime suspects, what may have begun as a local police probe was quickly taken over by the British security services and Metro's Special Branch as is always the standard custom in the United Kingdom.

To prove that it was British intelligence services that abruptly ended Metro's policing operation in order to eliminate incriminating evidence in the subsequent cover-up, just six days after MP Tom Watson's House of Commons speech in October 2012 linking a widespread VIP pedophile ring to Westminster and Downing Street, the *Daily Star* published a highly revealing article with the explosive headline "Tory Paedo Cover-up."[2187] A former Met detective who had worked on the original case in early 1982 disclosed to the *Daily Star* that he and his team of investigators were told they must immediately halt their police inquiry. The still angry, frustrated, honest copper explained:

It was a case of 'get rid of everything, never say a word to anyone.' It was made very clear to me that to continue asking questions would jeopardise my career.[2188]

The 1982 police investigation determined that the then current Home Office Secretary Leon Brittan was among the top VIPs abusing boys at Elm Guest House reportedly younger than ten.[2189] The police source said that MI5 had vetted Brittan prior to his becoming a Thatcher cabinet minister and that both security services and Thatcher were already well aware of his illicit sexual proclivities with underage boys, as has been proven repeatedly with her other

---

[2187] Jonathon Corke, Tony Bushby and Deborah Sherwood, "Tory Paedo Cover-up," *Daily Star*, October 28, 2012.
[2188] Jonathon Corke, Tony Bushby and Deborah Sherwood, https://www.dailystar.co.uk/news/latest-news/279380/TORY-PAEDO-COVER-UP.
[2189] Jeff Edwards, "Cover-up Bid in Vice Scandal," *News of the World/spotlightonabusee.wordpress.com*, August 8, 1982.

royally knighted, demented minister monsters like Peter Morrison and Peter Hayman among a startling number of purposely selected VIP creeps atop her government.[2190]

It's simply by sinister elitist design that so many of the most powerful political puppets are mentally ill perverts (recall from Chapter 1 that pedophilia is listed among psychiatric disorders) who get rewarded for indulging in their despicable psychopathology and systematically cherry picked to occupy the highest offices as easily controllable pawns doing the Zionist-Masonic-Illuminati bidding[2191] - making war on the planet permanent,[2192] enslaving the global population in insurmountable usury debt,[2193] now topping over $244 trillion where near half the world lives on $5.50 a day,[2194] while rapidly poisoning the earth[2195] to kill off at least 90% of the human species.[2196] The more suffering inflicted on humanity, the more these Luciferian beasts are rewarded with more power to harm, at least that's the way they think and by observation, it appears to be true.[2197]

Because Scotland Yard discovered VIP heavyweights were perpetrating pedophilia crimes at the Elm Guest House, on short order Special Branch was called in to shut the policing operation down. As the lead agency within British intelligence reportedly setting up nationwide sexual blackmail operations, MI5/MI6 worked with the likes of Sir Jimmy, Peter Righton and Colin Peters and even murdering thugs like Sidney Cooke and his clan to serve as both dutiful procurers and avid partakers of children primarily from UK care homes and rent boy runaways off the mean streets of London. As ravenous child sodomizers feeding and exploiting the same child pipeline network, more than solid evidence links Sir Jimmy Savile, Peter Righton, Sidney Cooke and Colin Peters supplying children to the likes of such VIP politicians as Sir Leon, Sir Cyril Smith and dozens of other sirs pathologically serving themselves in government.[2198]

Recall from an earlier Savile chapter how for years Elm Guest House proprietor Harry Kasir boasted Jimmy Savile among his best friends, allegedly taking tea with him countless

---

[2190] Jonathon Corke, Tony Bushby and Deborah Sherwood, https://www.dailystar.co.uk/news/latest-news/279380/TORY-PAEDO-COVER-UP.

[2191] "To Battle Against The Jesuits: The Banker's Illuminati was to Counter the Roman Catholic Christians!" *politicalvelcraft.org.*

[2192] Gunar Olsen, "Corporate Media Want nothing less than Permanent War," *truthdig.com*, February 1, 2019.

[2193] Paul Adams, "Usury: Weapon of Control and Enslavement – Part 1 of 2," *Activist Post*, November 4, 2013.

[2194] Michael Snyder, "Global Debt Tops 244 Trillion Dollars as 'nearly half the World Lives on less than $5.50 A day,'" *Zero Hedge*, January 18, 2019.

[2195] Makia Freeman, "Why are the Elite Poisoning the Planet?" *The Freedom Articles*, July 26, 2013.

[2196] Mike Adams, "Globalist Plan to Exterminate 90% of Mankind Begins now: 'Useless Eaters' must be Eliminated, say Globalists," *Natural News*, November 18, 2018.

[2197] "Masonic Initiation,"*freeworldfilmworks.com.*

[2198] Justin Penrose, "The Net Closes: Ex-Tory Chief Faces Child Sex Arrest over Claims Girl was Raped and Boys were Abused," *Mirror*, February 16, 2013.

occasions.[2199] MI5 had its web of go-to procurers and pimps that lined up VIPs at Elm and Dolphin Square with a steady diet of supplied victims. By the way, a Savile cohort and fellow derelict *BBC* DJ showing up on the Elm House guest list is none other than serial pedophile Chris Denning, still serving time after multiple child sex convictions.[2200] Unlike his *BBC* colleague Sir Savile, Denning was too low on the pecking order to avoid punishment.

From the last chapter we learned that Peter Righton was considered the foremost policy expert on the UK Care Home System and like Sir Jimmy, enjoyed unlimited access to exploit and abuse hundreds if not thousands of victims in children's homes and special schools throughout the nation and beyond. His 1992 slap-on-the-hand fine of £900 minus any jail time for possessing child pornography met with another "order from above" prematurely closing down his police investigation was no doubt due to Righton's international trafficking reach to such notorious pedo-havens as Malta and Holland as well as Denmark and Sweden that to this day still awaits full exposure.[2201] Among Righton's closest pedophile buddies sharing boy toys between them is convicted, currently imprisoned Charles Napier, whose half-brother is the longstanding Tory MP John Whittingdale.[2202] The MP brother's vociferous condemnation of Savile after exposure was hypocritically absent when it came to the outing of his own brother's crimes. Child protection officer Peter McKelvie's testimony and longtime quest to unveil Righton and Napier's powerful links to the UK pedo-establishment is the very reason why MP Tom Watson in October 2012 proclaimed in Parliament:

The evidence file used to convict Peter Righton, if it still exists, contains clear intelligence of a widespread paedophile ring. One of its members [PIE treasurer-Foreign Office teacher Charles Napier] *boasts of his links to a senior aide* [Foreign Office diplomat-PIE member Peter Hayman, convicted of child porn] *of a former prime minister* [Margaret Thatcher who blocked stripping Hayman of his knighthood[2203]], *who says he could smuggle indecent images of children from abroad* [Cairo, Egypt]. *The leads were not followed up, but if the files still exist, I want to ensure that the Metropolitan police secure the evidence, re-examine it and investigate clear intelligence suggesting a powerful paedophile network linked to Parliament and No 10.[2204]*

[2199] Fiona O'Clerigh and Mark Watts, "Met Detectives told of Jimmy Savile's Link to Elm Guest House," Exaro News, February 16, 2013.

[2200] "The Mary Moss Elm Guest House VIP Paedophile Party List," *cigpapers.blog*, April 29, 2013.

[2201] "Wanted Pedo – Peter Righton's Network," *cathyfox.wordpress.com*, April 2, 2018.

[2202] Paul Peachey, "Tory MP's Half-Brother Charles Napier Sentenced to 13 years over 'Prolific' Child Sex Abuse," *Independent*, December 23, 2014.

[2203] Chris Hastings, "Thatcher allowed Paedophile to keep Knighthood: Late former Prime Minister Blocked Plans to Strip Sir Peter Hayman of Honour," *Daily Mail*, May 16, 2015.

[2204] Lisa O' Carroll, "MP calls for Inquiry into possible Paedophile Ring Link to Parliament," *The Guardian*, October 24, 2012..

Napier knows a whole lot and not telling. We're still waiting for the full truth to come out, with no help from the long faltering Home Office fiasco – Theresa May's anything but Independent Inquiry.

As the tireless former child protection team manager who supplied key information resulting in Peter Righton's 1992 conviction as well as Tom Watson's 2012 Commons speech, Peter McKelvie has uncovered historical evidence of child sexual abuse committed by anywhere from 10 to 20 MPs and Lords still needing to be investigated in Operations Fernbridge and Midland focusing on VIP abuse at the Elm Guest House, Dolphin Square and other locations.[2205] Along with MP Watson, 138 other Parliament members were convinced that an independent inquiry into VIP government abuse investigating crimes over the last three or four decades is necessary due to the widespread cover-up by criminal obstructionists at both Westminster and 10 Downing Street. Of course that also means that an overwhelming majority of over 500 lords and MPs are not in favor of any inquiry into government child sexual abuse. I wonder why?

Initially in the early days of Fernbridge, yet more overt evidence of cover-up appeared. In 1982, the same year the Elm Guest House was raided, UK Customs Officer Maganlal Solanki employed at the Dover point of entry seized a package of child pornography consisting of three 8mm films, three video cassettes and an order form discovered in the possession of Russell Tricker.[2206] One of Tricker's videotapes included footage of Leon Brittan sexually abusing a young boy.[2207] That video was labeled "LB," matching the exact same initials as the only minister in the 1982 UK government.

But this is no first, recall that Sir Leon was captured on film before. From a March 2014 *Mirror* article:

They [Met Police] *are understood to have already spoken to the ex-minister about another video that places him at a sex party involving teenage boys three decades ago. Now they are expected to speak to the customs officer.[2208]*

After a two hour hold in 1982, Customs released Russell Tricker free to enter England minus his child porn videos that were then allegedly handed over to MI5. Placing child abuse videos into the hands of the security services agency chiefly responsible for both creating and protecting the British pedophilia blackmail network is just exactly what the MI5 boss Sir Leon would want.

[2205] Gordon Rayner and David Barrett, "'More than 10' Politicians on List Held by Police Investigating Westminster 'Paedophile Ring,'" *The Telegraph*, July 4, 2014.

[2206] Keir Mudie and Mark Conrad, "Ex-Tory Minister 'Pictured in Child Sex Abuse Video' Confiscated by Customs at Dover in 1982," *Mirror*, March 29, 2014.

[2207] Tim Tate, "The Politician, the Paedophiles, the Police & Press, *timtate.co.uk*, August 4, 2015.

[2208] Keir Mudie and Mark Conrad, https://www.mirror.co.uk/news/uk-news/ex-tory-minister-pictured-child-sex-3300248.

They don't call it security services for nothing. But the question becomes, whose security is served? Definitely not the abused children. Brittan's sick secret was safe with MI5, ensuring that such explosive evidence that could take down the entire Thatcher government would never see the light of day. It would later be learned that Russell Tricker was a PIE member whose job as a coach driver ferrying underage boys back and forth from Britain to Amsterdam[2209] also worked alongside the likes of MI5 agent-fellow PIE member and pedo-procurer John Rowe and Spartacus advertising agent Peter Glencross to convert Elm Guest House from a gay B&B to shielded VIP pedophile sex orgy haven. And just like his MI5 boss Leon Brittan, John Rowe was also a frequent visitor at the Elm House boy brothel.

Onetime English teacher Russell Tricker was among an army of English expatriated predators living in the Dutch capital, forced to leave UK after getting caught buggering, then opportunistically profiteering from child sex trafficking as well as making and distributing child pornography. Besides the tape with "LB's" initials on it, another confiscated video tagged "GB10," according to a child abuse victim, is nothing short of a sweet shop catalogue serving up fresh Great Britain boys for sex slave orders within the international pedophilia network typically featured through organizations like Spartacus Magazine. After several minutes of train footage, yet another video entitled "Amsterdam Tramway Museum" suddenly switches to showcasing European boys on fully displayed abuse for salivating perverts to order, a slight variation of the window prostitutes in the city's red light district, except they're legal and child abuse isn't. The Amsterdam Tramway Museum was simply Tricker's front company for his trafficking ring, no different from the CIA always creating fronts for its nefarious illegal undercover operations worldwide. Toff Travel and Toff Apartments were another angle of twisted Trickster's business web, masquerading behind his other child trafficking job as a coach driver ferrying young sex slaves across the channel.[2210]

Claiming he was merely an innocent courier having no idea of the contents inside his seized brown paper package in 1982, he was a free man. But as of 1992, the vile trickster's Tricker treats could trick no more, running into a temporary obstacle when convicted of child sex abuse back in Holland. But like the notorious Warwick Spinks (discussed in more depth later in this chapter), perhaps because Tricker was also an early player in the London-Amsterdam pedo-nexus, he only did 5 months of a two and a half year sentence while his abused victim soon wound up murdered.[2211] While the sicko criminals constantly go scot free, their victims commonly get re-victimized to death.

[2209] Nick Davies, "Paedophilia is easy 2: How a Paedophile Murder fell apart," *The Guardian*, November 27, 2000.
[2210] "Warwick Spinks & Co." *brynalynvictims.blogspot.com*, June 8, 2013.
[2211] Keir Mudie and Mark Conrad, https://www.mirror.co.uk/news/uk-news/ex-tory-minister-pictured-child-sex-3300248.

Customs Officer Maganlal Solanki had yet another, this time direct encounter with Leon Brittan himself at the Port of Dover also during the 1980s.[2212] Spotting Sir Leon's chauffeur driving suspiciously, the diligent customs agent pulled the vehicle over and subsequently discovered yet more child pornography films in the cabinet secretary's personal possession. Solanki confiscated them but just like Tricker except with even less waiting time, Sir Leon was allowed on his way. But Fernbridge detectives confirmed that they were in the process of being able to procure both Tricker's and Brittan's highly incriminating illegal videotapes. Apparently journalist-documentarian Tim Tate was able to learn from a Fernbridge insider that UK law enforcement held the videotape with conclusive evidence against Leon Brittan, yet purposely sat on it, keeping it from public exposure and the government's highest profile pedophile out of prison while still alive.

Also according to Tim Tate based on a recovered document from Richmond council archives, on the night of the Elm Guest House raid in June 1982, apparently the only young boy discovered inside the brothel was allegedly taken into police custody and interviewed that evening by a detective and a supposed social worker by the name of Andrew Neil Kier. But Kier was no typical Richmond social worker but the Officer-in-Charge (OiC) of Grafton Close Home, the victim supply source for Elm Guest House.[2213] With advance notice, of course no subsequent news accounts of the raid mention any boys from Grafton Close Children's Home ever being present at Elm Guest House on the night of June 19th, 1982. It would make no sense for standard protocol to be breached where a Richmond social worker fails to accompany the Special Branch raid on the Elm House unless the prearranged plan was to remove the only young child in the house - Harry and Carole Kasir's 10-year old son Eric from his home on 27 Rocks Lane and place him as the newest resident at Grafton Close Home that night.[2214] And so it's more than likely that Eric Kasir is yet another Elm Guest House abuse victim, and that VIP monsters like Leon Brittan sodomized him too.

Eric Kasir as the only young boy found inside Elm Guest House that night explains why Grafton Close Home's OiC Andrew Neil Kier was designated as the accompanying raid "social worker," since it had already been decided that Eric Kasir's new home would be Grafton Close Children's Home, ironically the very source of trafficked in victims abused by VIP guests at Elm. This premeditated arrangement also goes far in explaining why the Grafton Close fall guy arrested in the Elm Guest House scandal would eventually be Kier's deputy head John Stingemore rather than mystery man Kier himself who's rarely mentioned for his part in supplying sacrificial lambs

---

[2212] Tim Tate, http://timtate.co.uk/blog/the-politician-the-paedophiles-the-police-press/.

[2213] "Neil Kier Given Elm Guest House Raid Job," *Alternative News Network*, February 23, 2013.

[2214] "The Mary Moss Elm Guest House VIP Paedophile Party List," https://cigpapers.blog/2013/04/29/the-elm-guest-house-vip-paedophile-party-list/.

to the VIP child slaughterhouse.[2215] Also the single count charge directly involving Elm Guest House abuse that Stingemore was facing at his upcoming 2014 trial no doubt would've implicated his partner-in-crime Andrew Neil Kier. So conveniently for Kier, just before trial Stingemore was suddenly dead from an alleged heart attack. Andrew Neil Kier was off the hook, never in trouble with the law and never properly investigated by police because he was more than likely part of the MI5 blackmail operation. That same year 1982 Stingemore was reportedly hit with a sexual assault charge and terminated from Grafton Home but since the scandal was swiftly covered up, Stingemore was granted a 30-year reprieve to harm yet more boys it turns out in East Sussex. More on this later.

It wasn't until MP Watson's speech on the post-Savile 2012 House of Commons floor that eventually launched Fernbridge to eventually bring down the lowest hanging rotten fruit at Elm - John Stingemore. With Fernbridge and Midland in dire need of suspects after millions of tax paid pounds invested to uncover the Westminster scandal, similar to post-Savile Yewtree, in February 2013 Stingemore was thrown under bus as the pedo-cabal's sacrificial slime ball along with his unpriestly Catholic friend Tony McSweeney who'd also been shielded for decades. Meanwhile, back in 1983 Andrew Neil Kier was quietly permitted to move on after two years as Grafton Home OiC and throughout the decades has clearly been protected from accountability, reportedly considered a witness and never a suspect by Fernbridge investigators.

But a handwritten note from child campaigner Mary Moss based on conversations with Elm Guest House victims says different, exposing Andrew Neil Kier in all his perversions:

Systematically buggered by Kier and other older boys. Too frightened to complain. Introduced to H by Keir. He used to ring & tell them were (sic) to go to pick them up and take to mens homes[2216]

The three nameless MPs often referred to in the August 1982 press coverage of the Elm Guest House scandal as interrupted guests the night of the raid may well have included popular young Tory MP Jocelyn Cadbury elected to Parliament in a major upset in 1979.[2217] With his father linked to Knights of Malta, the 36-year old heir to the Cadbury Brothers chocolate empire was questioned by police over the Elm House affair.[2218] Having an older brother and sister already dying mysterious, tragic young deaths, barely a month after the Elm Guest House raid in an apparent suicide, on July 31, 1982 Jocelyn Cadbury allegedly shot himself with a shotgun blast

[2215] "The Child Abuse Network – Top Names – Part Two," *aangirfan.blogspot.com*, January 29, 2015.
[2216] "Neil Kier Given Elm Guest House Raid Job," https://alternativenewsnetwork.wordpress.com/2013/02/23/neil-kier-given-elm-guest-house-raid-job/
[2217] "Mysterious Cadbury Death," *aangirfan.blogspot.com*, December 5, 2015.
[2218] "Was Owner of Elm Guest House who kept List of Secret VIP Visitors Murdered? Newly Discovered Files…" *goodnessandharmony.wordpress.com*, November 11, 2017..

to the head at his parents' Birmingham estate.[2219] Yet no one has been able to figure out his motive when golden boy had so much going for himself and according to friends never appeared depressed or suicidal before snuffing himself. If it was related to the raid, it's not like a VIP at Elm Guest House had anything to worry about as all have been fiercely protected. And if murdered, why and by whom? At the time, MP Cadbury was also Parliamentary Private Secretary (PPS) to then Minister of State for Industry Norman Lamont, among the most powerful men in the British government.

A well-known journalist was told that a decade prior to his death, a young victim is alleged to have reported Cadbury to her doctor, calling him a "sadistic pedophile."[2220] Another reputable reporter claimed that Cadbury killed himself just two days after police had interviewed him about his involvement at the Elm Guest House. Might Cadbury have been among the three alleged MPs reportedly caught at the Elm Guest House the night of the raid, and if so, was Jocelyn the MP referred to when the only young child at the house "was rescued from horrific sexual assault" per a July 2014 *Telegraph* article?[2221]

Aside from disclosing to journalist Mike James in 1986 that future Labor Prime Minister Gordon Brown is a satanic pedophile (see last chapter), Lord Norman Lamont possesses his own share of shady elitist ties to organizations as a faithful Rothschild employ, leading member of the Cambridge mafia, the Privy Council, the powerful Pilgrims Society, head of Le Cercle and Savile friend appearing on Jim'll Fix It,[2222] in one way or another all linked to the unholy marriage between covert intelligence and high finance pillage and plunder, and its darker, hidden hand in illegal arms sales[2223] and the global pedophilia network.[2224] In the meantime, the man who thought the world of both his fallen PPC as well as Sir Leon, slammed Met Police for investigating historical child abuse.[2225] Wonder what deep dark secrets he has to hide making him so nervous and upset over historic child abuse investigations?

The currently retired police officer who originally interviewed the one boy found in Elm Guest House in the 1982 raid was tracked down by Fernbridge police in 2014. The former officer described the victim as the most sexualized child he had ever observed. In 2014 this abuse

[2219] "Heir to Candy bar Fortune Dies of Apparent Suicide," *UPI*, August 1, 1982.
[2220] "Was Owner of Elm Guest House who kept List of Secret VIP Visitors Murdered? Newly Discovered Files."
[2221] David Barrett, Tim Tate and Christopher Hope, "Westminster Paedophile Ring Allegations: Scotland Yard Detectives Trace 'Victim,'" *The Telegraph*, July 6, 2014.
[2222] Charles Savoie, "More Rothschild Linkage to the Pilgrims," *silvermarketnewsonline.com*, October 2018.
[2223] Joel van der Reijden, "The Pilgrims Society: A Study of the Anglo-American Establishment; Rockefeller, Mellon, Luce, Rothschild, Cecil, Windsor, the Federal Reserve, WWII, the CIA, and so much more," *isgp-studes.com*, July 17, 2008.
[2224] "Le Cercle: Clerical Fascism and the Pedophocracy Part III," *visupvew.blogspot.com*, April 30, 2016.
[2225] "Was Owner of Elm Guest House who kept List of Secret VIP Visitors Murdered? Newly Discovered Files."

survivor – now an entrepreneur in his early 40s residing in the United States – informed journalists from *The Telegraph* that he was sexually assaulted by at least one "senior MP."[2226]

This retired detective who interviewed the boy reported that the victim claimed he had been sodomized by at least nine men at Elm Guest House, but appeared surprised that the police were even involved since he'd apparently been repeatedly told that "Uncle Leon" "at the big house" (referring to Westminster/10 Downing Street) would take care of any problems that arose.[2227] This again sounds more like the words coming from a young boy who'd been living at 27 Rocks Lane, not a trafficked in child from Grafton Close. No doubt with customers like a naked Sir Leon photographed with naked boys, and tea buddies like Sir Jimmy, the Kasirs must have had a false sense of inflated security and impunity while also begrudgingly paying an extortion police fee for added protection.

Immediately the interviewing officer realized "Uncle Leon" was Thatcher Minister Leon Brittan. Fernbridge police were perplexed that the council document failed to either mention "Uncle Leon" or include the boy's signature. The retired officer explained that since the boy had been interviewed late at night, Andrew Neil Kier and the Special Branch officer agreed he could sign it in the morning after getting some sleep. But the next morning the child apparently "acted out" and allegedly refused to sign. This explanation may be a cop-out as the more likely reason the signature was never obtained may have more to do with the boy's last name.

When the interviewing officer from 1982 was then asked why the "Uncle Leon" reference was omitted from the original report, the former copper quickly grew agitated over the Official Secrecy Act leaving him vulnerable to prosecution, loss of pension and/or death. But with such crucial evidence left conspicuously hanging, Fernbridge sent a US Marshall previously on secondment to Metropolitan Police to interview the key witness in America. Though he initially did cooperate, by the time Scotland Yard was ready to dispatch detectives to speak more at length with him, he suddenly changed his mind.[2228] Eric initially stood by his original allegation that "Uncle Leon" Brittan, UK Home Secretary, sexually abused him. But someone or something got to Eric to make him suddenly change his mind, no doubt the extreme likelihood that the state murdered his own mother for talking too much. Also during Operation Fernbridge, police raided his father Harry Kasir's Richmond flat in January 2013, the same month they raided Mary Moss's domicile, in efforts to remove the last traces of VIP Elm House

---

[2226] David Barrett, Tim Tate and Christopher Hope, https://www.telegraph.co.uk/news/uknews/crime/10950138/Westminster-paedophile-ring-allegations-Scotland-Yard-detectives-trace-victim.html.

[2227] Tim Tate, http://timtate.co.uk/blog/the-politician-the-paedophiles-the-police-press/.

[2228] David Barrett, Tim Tate and Christopher Hope, https://www.telegraph.co.uk/news/uknews/crime/10950138/Westminster-paedophile-ring-allegations-Scotland-Yard-detectives-trace-victim.html.

evidence. After that, Harry Kasir reportedly planned to leave Britain to join his son in Connecticut.[2229]

Also understandable, Harry Kasir has chosen to deny that VIPs ever victimized kids (much less his own) at his Elm Guest House, insisting right to the bitter end that his three story eight room hotel only served gay consenting adults. Meanwhile, the key witness capable of blowing up the entire Elm Guest House cover-up, revealing the sordid filthy truth is the proprietors' long-lost son. But again, since the cabal murdered his mother, it's understandable he'd prefer leaving his abusive past behind him, rather than risk assassination even a generation later. Even without his explicit testimony, enough bits and pieces of truth have emerged to form a clear picture of what diabolical hell went down for kids trapped at 27 Rocks Lane between 1977 and 1983.

Eric Kasir's vacillation over telling what he knows segues into addressing the pertinent topic of victims changing their minds over time about talking to authorities of their past abuse. This has always been a major problem over the years as children far more than adults do not report their sex crimes, and only one in 10 adults report sexual assault. When the power differential between offender and victim is so extreme as in the Westminster scandal, especially when taking the dismal outcome into account of those who've tried to honestly report their abuse in the past, but are never listened to, or are punished, they rightly conclude that it's unsafe to bother to trying to speak up. When thousands of abuse victims throughout the decades whose firsthand allegations never resulted in any justice, only an enduring record of nonstop cover-up and subsequent retraumatized pain, it's rendered institutions of law enforcement and the judiciary unworthy of trust. The rigged system stacked so against child victims, keeps the powerful perpetrators in the drivers' seat banking on victims giving up. Until the system is radically changed and made safe for victims to speak up, where the result is that justice is served, nothing will change.

Unfortunately this is the all too common outcome when hundreds of thousands of victims' past abuse disclosures have fallen on deaf ears and been summarily rejected, smeared and dismissed with no action taken against the perpetrators, producing a deep distrust and doubt that testimony given years later would be any different, more credible or effective in facilitating their long-awaited justice. To have to relive past traumas in the face of providing yet more agonizing detailed evidence years later that's consistently failed to deliver a single conviction to any VIP pedophiles delivers the natural consequence of deterring already reluctant victims from ever coming forth again. To victims for all too obvious reason, UK law enforcement's disgustingly shameful track record covering-up pervasive elite sexual abuse justifiably relegates all legal authorities as thoroughly untrustworthy and criminally complicit. When the top-on-

---

[2229] David Hencke and Fiona O'Clerigh, "Elm Guest House: 'Boy Brothel Boss' Haroon Kasir to leave Britain for America," *Mirror*, February 16, 2013.

down system is historically so morally bankrupt, corrosively corrupt and grossly unjust, this is the resultant frustratingly painful pattern. Eventually victims give up trying to report abuse, especially when the one-sided power differential between perpetrator and victim has proven so unbreakably fixed and stacked against them.

Official channels like Theresa May's Inquiry or the Metro police are not purveyors of truth at all because as systemically deployed truth suppressors, their built-in purpose at all cost is simply to whitewash and maintain status quo of the tightly sealed cover-up. Otherwise, the plethora of collected photos and videos graphically proving Leon Brittan and other famous pedophiles would have been made public eons ago. By design, Metro's Fernbridge and Midland investigations hit a brick wall just as they were supposed to, complete with designated fraudsters to effectively smear all honest victims, not for lack of them offering real evidence to prosecute but simply because the system is so irreversibly rigged against truth and justice ever prevailing in a British court of law. Predictably by 2016 both VIP investigative operations were shut down in utter failure and waste, and still not a noteworthy creep or peep's been heard or brought to justice from either a courtroom or the IICSA currently on artificial life support a full half decade after its proposal.

The half dozen years that Britain's IICSA has dragged on, the national "independent" inquiry finally got around to examining the Elm Guest House scandal beginning late last 2018. The Home Office dictated format protecting status quo denial of any child sex abuse occurring at the Elm Guest House consisted of IICSA questions directed to Met Police Commander Neil Jerome, representing UK law enforcement's account of the Elm Guest House findings. Commander Jerome's sent back answers to said questions as official police response. Needless to say, the February 2019 IICSA report simply denied all allegations of abuse at Elm Guest House in yet another predictable whitewash of UK pedophilia history.[2230] The one exception is the 10-year old picked up the night of the house raid and placed into Grafton Close, the very group home supplying the victims. Jerome admitted the 10-year old boy's allegations were supported by medical forensics, though Jerome insisted the rest of all the abuse allegations were not confirmed by police, which is a total lie and a whitewash.

The British Establishment will never come clean, too many gatekeeping pedo-foxes ensure that the massive cover-up will continue on forevermore. The Scotland Yard, Crown Prosecution Service and the IICSA alike are all rabbit holed deep in complicit criminal cover-up and they should all be indicted for gross obstruction and perversion of justice.

That can only happen when courageous victims as seasoned survivors resolutely unite in solidarity (like the Shirley Oaks Survivors Association as the prototype model) to empower and

---

[2230] "D.7: Allegations Connected to Elm Guest House," *iicsa.org.uk*.

give voice to bravely speak out against their rapists, regardless of the unpunished criminals' power, status or position. But because as separate individuals the victim's voice has systematically been drowned out, negated and silenced by elites' consistent non-response, overuse of D-notices, libelous lawsuit threats, harassment and/or death, truth suppression is their reigning M.O. allowing aging perpetrators to successfully hide behind a colluded cover-up decade after decade after decade. An approaching critical mass soon to be reached among informed, educated and impassioned world citizens for justice, committed to supporting survivors' truth is the people's most powerful weapon of elite mass destruction. Clearly it's the elite that can't handle the truth, running like cockroaches for the nearest safe cover(up) of darkness. Like so called "Murun Buchstansangur's" valuable website,[2231] it's up to us to keep the "spotlight on abuse" using the light of truth as both our guide and weapon.

For one solid week in June 1984, two full years after the Elm Guest House raid, mainstream newspapers across Britain and even America ran story after story of rumors circulating about an unnamed Thatcher minister caught having sex with boys during the so called "Cabinet Secretary scandal."[2232] The press at the time reported that it could be the sex scandal of the century,[2233] and, had the UK elite not resorted to its blatant cover-up, it definitely would have. Margaret Thatcher's then Home Secretary Leon Brittan was again the thinly veiled VIP culprit, although with so many of her gay pedophile minister pals craving little boys, it could have just as easily been "eeny meeny miny mo." (See Chapter 22)

The London newspapers reported that the government countered the "assassination by gossip" and "trial by media rumors" by sternly vowing it would not be tolerated. The prime minister herself threatened any publication that named the rumored pedophile minister would immediately be slapped with a costly libel suit. By month's end, Iron Lady's aggressively viperous response effectively shut down all further coverage, just like two years earlier when after little more than a week of newspaper frenzy, breaking headlines about the most infamous of all VIP boy brothels - the Elm Guest House - was suddenly silenced for the next several decades, likely with more D-notices.

During that final week of June 1984, one publication - *Private Eye Magazine*, went so far as to identify Leon Brittan as the alleged child abuser but made sure to call the allegation a smear leaked by a disgruntled rogue element within MI5 in retaliation for the home secretary warning he'd impose a major MI5 shakeup for "mishandling" the April 1984 Libyan embassy attack when London constable Yvonne Fletcher was gunned down.[2234] Another lame explanation given for

---

[2231] Murun Buchstansangur, "Spotlight," *spotlightonabuse.wordpress.com*.
[2232] Murun Buchstansangur, "Leon Brittan and the 1984 'Cabinet Minister Scandal,'" *spotlightonabuse.wordpress.com*, April 19, 2014.
[2233] Mike Ambrose, "Whitehall Fears Sex Scandal," *Morning Starspotlightonabuse.wordprss.com*, June 23, 1984.
[2234] "Cabinet Minister Scandal," *Private Eye/spotlightonabuse.wordpress.com*, June 26, 1984.

MI5 "spooks and loonies" to make up such a "lie" about Britain's first Jewish home secretary is the Zionistas' old familiar standby – anti-Semitism. But forensic evidence soon emerged to indicate the 1984 embassy gunfire volley was a CIA led false flag in cahoots with MI5 to whip up Thatcher tag team support for Reagan/Bush's vilification of Libya's Muammar Gaddafi,[2235] the same criminal element echoed years later in 2011 with Hillary's hideous reaction upon learning that her assassination hit on Gaddafi was successful:

We came, we saw, he died, [hee, hee, hee].[2236]

The treasonous Bush-Clinton-Obama cabal still lives on in today's deep state havoc.

The now defunct *Private Eye* rag did have strong links to MI5.[2237] On top of a Jewish Home Secretary being the MI5 boss in 1984, by that time British security services were heavily controlled by Thatcher's security advisor - bloodline Jew Lord Victor Rothschild. In short, MI5 in 1984 was not anti-Jewish at all. At the height of the scandal, the *Private Eye* article went out of its way to emphasize that Brittan was innocently maligned, definitely not a pedophile but simply a target of a maliciously false, racist smear campaign, reportedly already confirmed by *News of the World*.

In a ploy to convince the head of the Press Association, Leon Brittan cunningly invited him into his office expressly to read the article as proof of the home secretary's "martyrdom."[2238] So the "MI5 leak" was strategically and timely inserted with the intent to take the heat off its "venerable" yet unfairly maligned leader Sir Leon. At that very same time with Brittan losing/destroying two incriminating dossiers as the deserving object of unshakeable multiple abuse allegations over the ensuing decades, regardless of how hard the police, the complicit media and the corrupt UK politics machine try to cover-up his pedo-crimes, far, far too much evidence has long implicated Sir Leon as a slithering prolific serial pedophile.

British security agencies had set up the Elm Guest House as a boy brothel with a sauna and both hidden and unhidden cameras (for child porn purposes) installed in every room (a la Jeffrey Epstein style) to serve as a sexual blackmail operation to control not only British VIPs but elites flown in from Europe as well. Recurring media coverage reported in 1982, in 1984, and again every year since 2012 (once deceased Savile was publicly outed) that a litany of police probes and whistleblowers have confirmed surveillance evidence exists of video footage and numerous photographs of Brittan in action along with pedo-porker pig Sir Cyril Smith, royal traitor Sir

---

[2235] "Yvonne Fletcher Murdered by Our Spooks," *aangirfan.com*, September 1, 2011.

[2236] Paul Craig Roberts, "Hillary's War Crime: The Murder of Muammar Gaddafi. 'We Came, we Saw, he Died,'" *Global Research*, October 21, 2016.

[2237] "Leon Brittan and Private Eye," *aangirfan.com*, November 1, 2014.

[2238] Guy Adams, "Are the Vile Paedophile Allegations against Leon Brittan a Sinister MI5 Smear Plot?" *Daily Mail*, October 31, 2014.

Anthony Blunt, our old friend Sir "Kitty" and a host of other decked out, totally compromised VIPs either entering, frolicking inside or departing Elm Guest House. As is often the case when it comes to the voracious appetites of dead sexual predators, Fernbridge detectives played it safe confirming Cyril Smith visited Elm Guest House.[2239] The fat man was reportedly even banned from Elm Guest House for a short spell after breaking a toilet seat and refusing to pay for it.[2240] On another visit he got stuck in the sauna and had to be hoisted out.[2241] Like Sir Leon, Sir Cyril was a guesthouse party regular.

Longtime social worker and child protection consultant Chris Fay testified that he had viewed compromising photographs of Brittan taken with young boys dating back to the early 1980s.[2242] Reportedly abusing boys as young as 8, 9 and 10, a nude Lord Brittan in one photo is allegedly wearing only a scanty French maid apron with a naked youth sitting on his lap.[2243] Recall another photo lost and found at a London train station a few years earlier depicting Sir Kitty dressed in women's underwear surrounded by underage boys that in a flash was scooped up immediately by dispatched thugs from Special Branch, Britain's longtime organized crime fixers. Reportedly that photo was used by Mossad to manipulate and control the aging superstar to pay homage to Zionist controlled Israel, which explains his frequent Tel Aviv trips.

But ultimately it was Iron Lady's Home Office minister as the Lithuanian Jewish central pedo-gatekeeper from 1982-85 whose job was in charge of both British intelligence as well as all police operations, ensuring every investigation into pedophilia was called off and every dossier given him was lost or destroyed. While still alive during the post-Savile Operation Fernbridge, only once in a long pedo-career was Sir Brittan ever even questioned by detectives under caution over his alleged rape committed years earlier on a teenage girl,[2244] yet even that critical piece of evidence was lost when someone accidentally-on-purpose "forgot" to push the record button.[2245] Right up to Leon Brittan's January 2015 death, Metro Police was purportedly still investigating fresh historic child abuse claims against him.[2246] But like all his fellow derelict VIP monsters before and after him – Sir Jimmy, Sir Cyril, Sir Ted, and subsequently Sir Greville to

[2239] "Sir Cyril Smith 'Visited Alleged Sex Abuse Guest House,'" *BBC*, September 13, 2013.
[2240] James Hanning and Paul Cahalan, "Cyril Smith named in Barnes Abuse Case," *Independent*, January 27, 2013.
[2241] Steven Swinford, "'Influential' Politician Visited Guest House at Centre of Child Sex Investigation," *The Telegraph*, April 18, 2014.
[2242] Levi Winchester, "Leon Brittan 'Attended Paedophile Parties in Notorious Brothel,'" *Express*, January 25, 2015.
[2243] "Nightmares at Elm Guest House," https://www.youtube.com/watch?v=ORU5x-ryedU; interview transcript, http://google-law.blogspot.com/2014/01/elm-guest-house-scandal-how-child-abuse_5191.html/
[2244] Jamie Merrill, "Leon Brittan Exclusive: Tory Peer Questioned by Police over Rape Allegation," *Independent*, July 6, 2014.
[2245] Martin Beckford, "Scotland Yard Failed to Record the only time it Quizzed Leon Brittan: Report Reveals String of Blunders by Met Police over Historic Sex Abuse Allegations," *Daily Mail*, February 7, 2016.
[2246] Mark Conrad, "Former Home Secretary was subject to Major Investigation by Police at time of his Death," *Exaro News*, January 24, 2015.

name a handful, unpunished, aging child rapists exit this planet without facing their victims who are consistently denied their day in court.

So let's do a quick recap of Lord Leon's known and confirmed sex crime history against underage children. Over the years he's undoubtedly had multiple accusers from the sex orgies at Elm Guest House and Dolphin Square alone, not to mention the one in South Yorkshire, he's been frequently naked while photographed with naked boys, he's played the child molesting villain abusing a boy in kiddie porn, was caught possessing child pornography videos by the same government agent who also separately observed Brittan on film abusing a child, was accused of date raping a teenage girl, was called in for police questioning but never recorded, was responsible for losing or destroying at least three different pedo-dossiers, and by as early as 1984, he was already being rumored and virtually outed as the most offending pedophile amongst Thatcher's platoon of pedophile ministers. Yet his widow was awarded a million tax-paid pounds worth of police apologies in undeserved compensation while all his countless victims received no justice at all but for nearly all, only a lifetime of pain and hardship. For sake of his victims, we need to finally uncover the full truth and nothing but the truth so help us God.

Another important survivor's story released through the *Sunday People* links two serial predators Peter Righton and Cyril Smith to sex orgies at both the Elm Guest House and Dolphin Square. While stuck in the UK Care System and groomed and abused by Righton and his VIP pedo-network from age 11 in 1977 until age 16, in April 2013, the man in his forties disclosed what he observed while on one of Righton's trips to a local London park.[2247] The boy witnessed Righton get out of the car and walk over to talk to a very obese man that the victim later identified on TV. While speaking to the famous MP, Righton would regularly look back over at the boy and Smith each time would nod and smile at him. As mentioned earlier, Peter Righton was one of Britain's major child procurers delivering boys in the UK Care System to VIP pedophile politicians and high level civil servants, corroborated by the abuse survivor recalling that networker Righton would often boast of his bigwig contacts so high up in government. In the informant's words:

People have talked about a paedophile ring working in the UK. This was not just a ring – it's more like the Olympic rings, interlocking on a large scale. It went everywhere. I believe it went to the heart of the Establishment. It needs to be investigated properly.[2248]

After sharing his story with the press, the man said he was planning to talk to detectives at Metro working Operations Fernbridge and Midland investigating child abuse committed by Westminster members. Unfortunately as in every other UK police operation, Fernbridge and

---

[2247] Keir Mudie, "New Victim Links Notorious Paedophile to VIP Child Abuse Network, *Mirror*, April 6, 2013.
[2248] Keir Mudie, https://www.mirror.co.uk/news/uk-news/new-victim-links-notorious-paedophile-1815932.

Midland also made sure to fail at arresting and charging any MPs, conveniently because of so much "lost and destroyed," "unsubstantiated" evidence.

A closer look at listed frequent Elm House guest Colin Peters is also very telling.[2249] Despite his and a buddy's arrest in their early 20s for committing child sexual abuse in Naples, Italy back in 1967, swiftly patched over by diplomatic immunity and their Foreign Office boss Robin Jasper,[2250] the British government saw fit to strangely seal the record of their Naples arrest at the National Archives for the next 87 years until 2056.[2251] In 2015 after the *Sunday Times* raised the question over why would two junior Foreign Office employees Colin Peters and colleague Alastair Laing's pedo-crimes be locked away for nearly a century, the Home Affairs ministers "agreed" to look into it.[2252] In view of the fact that Oxford educated barrister-career diplomat Peters was essentially set free to abuse boys again and again over the next couple decades, at both the Elm Guest House and then in 1989 caught running the largest known pedophile ring in British history,[2253] the question begs answering why 22 years earlier Peters' buggery crime in Italy would be so guardedly shielded from the public.

It's been speculated that Peters and Laing were procuring young Italian boys for such British cultural luminaries as WH Auden who for years rented a villa on Ischia in the Bay of Naples, regularly entertaining guests like Benjamin Britten[2254] and EM Forster[2255] as well as employing the services of underage local Neapolitan rent boys.[2256] The then UK Minister for the Arts, Baroness Jennie Lee, may have rushed to their aid to not only protect British Empire's most acclaimed national treasures of arts and letters but also the internationally expanding pedophilia network as well. The same year that adult homosexuality (21 and over) was no longer deemed a state crime in Britain, the government may well have been invested in protecting both its world famous gay pedophile icons living abroad as well as its Foreign Service pedo-pimps, unwilling to risk public disclosure until 2056. Again to the depraved establishment it's a no-brainer, protecting pedophile VIPs ranks a far higher priority than protecting a few street urchins from Italy or the UK.

[2249] "The Mary Moss Elm Guest House VIP Paedophile Party List," https://cigpapers.blog/2013/04/29/the-elm-guest-house-vip-paedophile-party-list/.
[2250] "Crown Office Appointments – Foreign Office," *The London Gazette*, May 24, 1966, p. 6128, Robin Jasper pdf.
[2251] "Arrest of Alastair Laing and Colin Peters, Members of HM Diplomatic Service, in Naples," *nationalarchives.gov.uk*.
[2252] Tom Harper, "Sex Abuse File Shut until 2056," *The Sunday Times*, March 29, 2015.
[2253] Mark Burdman, "Paedophiles Arrested in Britain: More Powerful than the Mafia," *EIR*, February 17, 1989.
[2254] Martin Kettle, "Why we must talk about Britten's Boys," *The Guardian*, November 21, 2012.
[2255] Brook Allen, "Reconsidering E.M. Forster," *Truthdig*, December 23, 2009.
[2256] Dame Alun Roberts, twitter.com, January 21, 2019.

Speaking of the arts and pedophiles, Colin Peter's fellow shielded partner-in-crime in Italy - Alastair Laing - went on to become art curator and author for the National Trust,[2257] as well as co-author of a book with the queen's art curator-Soviet spy traitor-fellow pedo Sir Anthony Blunt and Blunt protégé architectural historian Christopher Tadgell,[2258] who's married to prominent Somerset Tory MP Jacob Rees-Mogg's mother-in-law who's an ex-MP herself.[2259] Mogg's 2007 wedding guests included a couple known Elm guests as well. Lord Peter Brooke whose online essay on man-boy love is on full display[2260] as well as Peter and Virginia Bottomley. As Health Minister she played a key role in closing Righton's criminal investigation while all three Peters – Colin, Brooke and Bottomley made the infamous Elm House guest list... small world amongst the pedo-elite.[2261] Yet another Elm Guest visitor is deceased Tory MP Solicitor General of Scotland, mentioned in previous chapters as pedo-gatekeeper Esther Rantzen's adulterous lover boy Sir Nicholas Fairburn.[2262]

Another little dark chapter to add in the unending book of British pedophilia cover-ups on Health Minister Virginia Bottomley's watch (1992-95) involves a claim that the Hereford and Worcester head of social services for 20 years David Tombs went to senior civil servants in her health ministry while apparently she was busily closing down the police investigation on Peter Righton after his 1992 arrest. David Tombs, an office colleague of whistleblowing child protection manager Peter McKelvie, had access to the local police investigation on Righton and his VIP cronies in UK government and abroad, clearly indicating that a Westminster pedophile network was flourishing.[2263] With such a childcare expert and UK policy kingpin like Peter Righton under criminal investigation as a serial pedophile, on behalf of UK Health Minster Virginia Bottomley, UK Chief Inspector of Social Services Sir William Utting requested from David Tombs a report based on the Righton police probe findings with social services' recommendations on how to prevent future child abuse in the face of predators operating within the UK Care System.[2264] It was Peter McKelvie who wrote the report in 1993 alerting the Health Department of the alarming trend that pedophiles like Righton and Westminster VIPs pose to thousands of at-risk youth, having infiltrated all levels within the UK Care System. It included specific recommendations necessary to tackle the national pedophile ring engulfing

---

[2257] "Curator's Interview," *ezin.codart.nl*, spring 2013..

[2258] Anthony Blunt, Alastair Laing and Christopher Tadgell, *Baroque and Rococo Architecture and Decoration* (New York: Harper & Row), 1978.

[2259] Sebastian Shakespeare, "Jacob gets Hitched, old-Tory Style," *Daily Mail*, January 14, 2007.

[2260] Peter Brooke, "What is a 'Paedophile?'" *peterbrooke.org*.

[2261] "The Mary Moss Elm Guest House VIP Paedophile Party List," https://cigpapers.blog/2013/04/29/the-elm-guest-house-vip-paedophile-party-list/.

[2262] Greg Christison, "Esther's Horror at Fairbairn Child Sex Allegations," *Express*, July 21, 2014.

[2263] Keith Perry, "Warnings of Westminster Paedophile Network 'Ignored' because 'there were too many,'" *The Telegraph*, July 12, 2014.

[2264] Murun Buchstansangur, "The Peter Righton Case: Recommendations that were Ignored by Department of Health," *spotlightonabuse.wordpress.com*, November 30, 2013..

Britain, urging deployment of a joint police-social worker investigation team.[2265] Though the report was sent, Health Minister Bottomley completely ignored it, shutting down the ongoing Righton police investigation.

David Tombs as head of social services urgently also tried bringing the Westminster pedophilia network to the health department's attention as a major "national concern." During a July 2014 *BBC* Radio 4 program, David Tombs stated:

It was coming across to me at the time that there were names there that were linked into the establishment, if you like.[2266]

His dire warning of grave "national concern" to a senior health official drew the following reply, in David Tombs' words:

I was told that I was probably wasting my time, that there were — and the words used were along these lines — that there were 'too many of them over there.' Now, I was talking about paedophilia. I was in the Department of Health and the 'over there' to me indicated, although the words weren't used, within Parliament or within Government and Whitehall.[2267]

So on the one hand while the Health Minister's ignoring McKelvie's report and shutting down the police probe because it's implicating pedophiles atop the government, one of Baroness Bottomley's senior civil servants openly admits there's too many pedophiles in government to even bother trying to deal with them. Keep in mind this rampant pedo-epidemic and cover-up comes during the post-Thatcher years of the 1990s. Again, it's not about a particular era, leader or party because British culture-bred pedovore vultures running the United PEDO Kingdom have been doing it seamlessly and with full impunity for nearly a century.

Chapter 8 covered the satanic ritual abuse at daycare facilities throughout the 1980s from the controversial McMartin case in Southern California to military daycares at West Point and the Temple of Set's Lt. Col. Michael Aquino's Presidio scandal. Chapter 10 further exposed Col. Aquino as a master mind control, programming wizard and pedophile in the CIA-Tavistock-MK Ultra Monarch mind control programs exported worldwide. Evolving from the Babylonian-Cabbalistic-Egyptian rooted deities that are currently still practiced today in various forms as Satanism, the Illuminati Order, Freemasonry, Knights of Malta, Jesuits to Luciferianism, the

[2265] Peter McKelvie, "A Personal Viewpoint," *spotlightonabuse.wordpress.com*, 1993, https://spotlightonabuse.files.wordpress.com/2013/11/personalreport.jpg
[2266] Keith Perry, https://www.telegraph.co.uk/news/uknews/crime/10963499/Warnings-of-Westminster-paedophile-network-ignored-because-there-were-too-many.html.
[2267] Keith Perry, https://www.telegraph.co.uk/news/uknews/crime/10963499/Warnings-of-Westminster-paedophile-network-ignored-because-there-were-too-many.html.

ruling elite have for centuries engaged in occult rituals involving blood sacrifice and satanic ritual abuse (SRA) of children (also addressed in earlier chapters).

The inner club of powerful pedophiles and their enablers often are members of these malevolent secret societies. When in the 1980s satanic ritual abuse caught America's attention by storm, the CIA pedophile scientists swiftly dipped into their bag of tricks, pushing back with dubbing the sociological phenom gripping the nation as "satanic panic," followed by their next rabbit out of the hat called the False Memory Syndrome, "scientifically" backed up by the FM Foundation to plant the seed of doubt in every abuse victim's testimony, chalking it up to kids and misguided adults' overactive imaginations and paranoia, i.e., nothing to see here folks, no such thing as satanic ritual child sex abuse.

Just as the CIA labeled critical thinkers and doubters questioning the official government's false narrative behind the JFK assassination as "conspiracy theorists" as the forevermore M.O. calling card to instantly instill doubt and disbelief toward those intelligent enough to be skeptical of authoritarian lies. Embedded into the mass media propaganda machine, these CIA false labels are simply fabricated machinations strategically unleashed to shape, manipulate and control mass public opinion and perceptions of consensus reality within mainstream popular culture. In effect, the cunning elite are masters at turning the gullible masses into easily brainwashed, mind-controlled, misinformed, enslaved, non-thinking, robotic automatons addictively placated, mesmerized and distracted by addictive, button-pushing magic, while insidiously programmed to reject, scorn and ridicule those still capable of engaging in critical thinking, original, independent thought, or those who readily see through the government bullshit behind regularly staged false flags of state-sponsored terrorism at times killing its own citizens (3,000 on 9/11). This deceptive, sleight of hand defense mechanism utilizing cognitive dissonance to instantly on cue evoke a blindness through disbelief effectively burying and smothering the truth unfortunately has been extremely successful. So when child abuse victims' allegations are made, they're easily discarded or rarely taken seriously, especially when it's the famous perpetrators participating in satanic ritual abuse. Too unbelievable say the naysayers and deceivers as the Luciferian way to utilize propaganda as a WMD to systematically negate, obscure and silence the truth, discrediting and marginalizing those who seek it over elite's nonstop lies and calculated mass manipulation.

This temporary diversion can now come full circle, returning to the lovely Bottomleys. As a former psychiatric social worker turned Health Minister, after closing down the Righton police inquiry and suppressing evidence proving links to the Westminster VIP pedo-scandal, in 1994 Virginia implored British social workers and childcare workers "to take heed" of a report her health department financed, written by her friend and scholar Jean La Fontaine, claiming that there's no such thing as satanic ritual abuse.[2268] Upon the report's release, Bottomley arrogantly declared that the "myth of satanic abuse" has been thoroughly exposed.

While over the last 31 years the Baroness has been Governor of the Fabian founded London School of Economics where she earned her master's degree (recall also Margaret Oppenheimer's alma mater),[2269] for decades her pal Jean La Fontaine as LSE's anthropology emeritus professor has faithfully provided the "scientific" cover to subvert public exposure and awareness that organized ritual abuse is both real and far more prevalent than commonly known. Jean La Fontaine's latest application of her lifelong work helped a high court judge in 2015 declare the alleged satanic cult's reported ritual child sex abuse in the Hampstead scandal a complete hoax.[2270] This story and its cover-up will be fully dissected in Chapter 26.

The genius Stanley Kubrick wasn't murdered for nothing four days after his near final editing cut on "Eyes Wide Shut," boldly revealing the elite's inner secrets of perversion, occult ritual and death. With his next scheduled pet project purported to be an exposé on the rulers' obsessional agenda with pedophilia, the treacherous crime cabal had seen enough of Stanley Kubrick. The man knew too many secrets and had the audacity to want to share them with the world. He often would remind his wife:

Be suspicious of people who have, or crave, power. Never, ever go near power. Don't become friends with anyone who has real power. It's dangerous.[2271]

It's as if he knew his own tragic fate, an all too common outcome of those who "step out of line and the man come take you away" as Stephen Stills once wrote. Staged murder made to look like suicide or in Stanley's case a heart attack is untraceably common, and yet another running theme of this book befalling dozens who knew too much. Be it through academia, mass media or hired assassins, the elite's waging an all-out war on truth on countless fronts with a hi-tech arsenal of lethal weaponry we don't even know about.[2272]

The evildoers in control of this planet that regularly practice organized satanic ritual abuse and murder of children en masse of course would rather have us all believing it doesn't exist at all. Deferring to a post on the bold, feisty Chris Spivey website entitled "The Who's Who of Satanic Abuse," a list of alleged members belonging to or affiliated with a particular British satanic cult or coven that includes such luminaries as both the former health minister Virginia Bottomley and Professor La Fontaine in addition to Ted Heath, Dame Margaret Hodge, Lord Peter

---

[2268] Rose Waterhouse, "Satanic Abuse Dismissed as 'Myth' by Government Inquiry: Report Blames Evangelical Christians and 'Specialists' for the Scare which led to Investigations," *Independent*, June 3, 1994.
[2269] "Virginia Bottomley," *howlingpixel.com*.
[2270] Barbara Hewson, "The Hampstead Cult that wasn't: the Satanic Panic Revisited," *Spiked*, March 23, 2015.
[2271] Jon Ronson, "After Kubrick" *The Guardian*, August 18, 2010.
[2272] Christopher Spivey, "The Who's Who of Satanic Child Abuse," *chrisspivey.org*, January 30, 2014.

Mandelson and other likeminded ministers, lords and MPs.[2273] It appears to have been compiled during the years leading up to 2010 by an organization called the Ritual Abuse Information Network & Support (RAINS), an advocacy support group for ritual abuse victims, in this case a mind control SRA victim diagnosed with dissociative disorder named Helen G.

Since former Tory Prime Minster Ted Heath from 1970 to 1974 was mentioned in previous chapters and the paragraph above, this blackmail controlled Luciferian pedophile-murderer-traitor who sold Britain's national sovereignty to the international cabal behind the European Union was involved as noted earlier in PIE, Jersey Island pedophilia and murder with procurer Savile and abusing boys in Northern Ireland's Kincora scandal. But according to *The Sun*, the Wiltshire police probe apparently interviewed women claimants who as young girls maintain that Edward Heath sexually attacked children as a member of a satanic pedophile cult run by their own parents.[2274] They accused the cult of engaging in ritual child sacrifice in churches and woodlands in southern England as well as Africa, stabbing, maiming, torturing and slaughtering up to 16 children from babies to teenagers, then as cannibals resorting to blood drinking and consuming organs. This of course would support other allegations like the one mentioned above that Ted Heath was a satanic cult participant.

After a thorough albeit heavily challenged and controversial investigation named Operation Conifer begun in 2015, in February 2017 Wiltshire Chief Constable Mike Veale gave "120%" confidence behind the alleged 30 people who came forth with allegations of abuse against Heath being "genuine."[2275] Veale said their accounts are "strikingly similar" and "totally convincing," corroborating their veracity. At one point, Heath had no less than five police forces investigating him - the Met, Wiltshire, Hampshire, Kent and Jersey.[2276] But his political power ensured cover-up. Veale's inquiry included 42 allegations from seven alleged victims from 1956 to 1992 that police claim today would require questioning under caution.[2277] Turns out Heath's name was also on that dossier Barbara Castle gave to Don Hale in 1984 that Special Branch thugs swiftly scooped up. Of course David Icke outed him as a murdering pedophile-Satanist in his 1998 book *The Biggest Secret,* but too few were listening then a full seven years ahead of Heath's death in 2005.[2278] Jimmy Savile's nephew Guy Marsden has also gone public to report

[2273] Tom Burghardt, "'Non-Lethal' Weapons: Where Science and Technology Service Repression," *Global Research*, July 10, 2008.

[2274] Laura Burnip, "Heath Linked to a Murderous Paedophile Ring that Killed 16 Kids," *The Sun*, February 20, 2017.

[2275] Simon Walters, "Sir Edward Heath was a Paedophile, says Police Chief: Astonishing Claim is made that the former PM is Guilty of Vile Crimes 'Covered up by the Establishment,'" *Daily Mail*, February 18, 2017.

[2276] Simon Walters, https://www.dailymail.co.uk/news/article-4238188/Sir-Edward-Heath-paedophile-says-police-chief.html.

[2277] Nico Hines, "The Mysterious Case of the 'Pedophile' Prime Minister, Sir Edward Heath," *Daily Beast*, October 5, 2017.

[2278] David Icke, "Pedophile and Child Killing," *biblotecapleyades.net*, January 17, 2013.

that Edward Heath sexually abused Guy's 4-year old buddy at a swank London party in the 1970s.[2279]

Now for a last look at fellow Tory, thin-skinned hubby Sir Peter Bottomley. Thatcher's former transportation minister sure knows how to get around. In addition to Elm Guest House and Monday trips across the Channel, a most memorable trip to Brussels on May 29, 1985 placed Peter Bottomley at the Heysel Stadium disaster where 39 rowdy, hapless football fans were crushed and trampled to death.[2280] Two years later the queen honored knight happened to be at the Kings Cross underground station fire that killed 31 on the evening of November 18, 1987.[2281] Rent boys in an underground café at Kings Cross may have been targeted by what's now been concluded to be a very deadly arson fire.[2282] And just like clockwork, two years later again Sir Peter witnessed the Kegworth air disaster on January 8, 1989 when 44 passengers died. Unclear whether the lucky man was one of 79 passengers who survived or just happened to observe the tragedy while at the East Midlands Airport that day. Bottomley did not appear to be among the 300 guests attending the 30-year commemoration ceremony at Leicestershire in January 2019.[2283] Bottomley's first close encounter with death during his harrowing 80s decade of disasters came while representing the British Council of Churches attending the funeral of assassinated Archbishop Oscar Romero in El Salvador on March 30, 1980, when 14 mourners around him were mercilessly gunned down.[2284]

Imagine in less than one decade the odds of one man surviving four extremely deadly close calls and, at 74-years old today, still be alive to tell his grandkids, not to mention Sir Peter not slowing down as senior Conservative Member of Parliament for the last 44 years.[2285] But then it appears that all his traumas from the 1980s may have caught up to both him and his wife in the 1990s. Her bizarre, reactive, anti-children's crusade as health minister and his volatile, erratic, highly irrational, acting out misbehavior speak volumes. For instance, in a March 1993 article for the *Independent*, journalist Beatrix Campbell responds to the health minister's call to get tough on disciplining children under her brand of health care:

[2279] Russell Myers, "Jimmy Savile's nephew Claims Sir Edward Heath Abused his 14-year old Pal at London Party," *Mirror*, August 6, 2015.
[2280] "Heysel Disaster 1985," YouTube video, 5:50, posted on July 23, 2013.
[2281] Paul Harper, "When was the Kings Cross Fire in 1987, how many Victims were Involved in the Disaster and what's Changed at the Station?" *The Sun*, November 16, 2017.
[2282] Kings Cross Fire, Dolphin Square, Boy-Brothels, Suspicious Deaths, Murderous Arson and the VIP Child-Abuse Connection," *The Coleman Experience/holliegreigjustice.wordpress.com*, April 22, 2014..
[2283] Lara Keay, "'I still Shake when I fly': Survivor of Kegworth Air Disaster who 'didn't know whether he was alive or Dead' recalls moment 47 were Killed in British Midland Plane Crash on M1 30 years ago," *Daily Mail*, January 8, 2019.
[2284] "San Francisco Archbishop's Account of Oscar Romero's Funeral," *National Catholic Reporter*, March 24, 2015.
[2285] "Peter Bottomley: Biography," *fampeople.com*.

Mrs Bottomley's attitude is a symptom of the public's retreat from its awareness of children's pain. Her vaunted vocation as a social worker ended when the new age began. Her message, indeed Britain's message, is simple: when children don't oblige by being innocent victims, when they are demanding and difficult, when they are awkward accusers, and when they don't care whom they hurt, including themselves, then adults are absolved. No longer ashamed, we blame the victim.[2286]

While his wife Virginia was busy betraying at-risk kids in 1993, hubby Peter was doing his own anti-child thing too. In 1993 when a staff member working at Melanie Klein children's home in Greenwich was being investigated for his sexual debauchery abusing and contributing to the delinquency of underage girls, MP Bottomley rushed to the abuser's defense, barging in to interrupt a council disciplinary hearing with his unprovoked, off-the-wall tirade.[2287] An even more disgraceful meltdown on full public display was exhibited when the ranting madman tried in vain to halt Thames television from filming an investigation on the case. Not only did Sir Peter insist the program not move forward, but screamed in rage at the Thames board for allowing it. It was as if he was the sexual abuser being accused. What does that man have to hide if he never abused a child?

To put it mildly, neither Mr. nor Mrs. Bottomley were acting the least bit kid-friendly in 1993. As Beatrix Campbell alluded, the 1990s were even more unsafe for British children than the preceding decade when MP whistleblower Geoffrey Dickens first tried to alert the government about pedophilia amongst his peers. Was Sir Peter Bottomley unraveling because his name was being bandied about as an Elm Guest House regular, the notorious house of horror gnawing at the heart of the Westminster VIP scandal? Or perhaps it was those Monday Club cruises to Amsterdam and Brussels. Or maybe he was suffering from PTSD survivors' guilt. In any event, Bottomley was bottoming out, allowing all the rumors to rattle his cage to the extreme, only leaving observers with the impression that either the loose cannon was having a nervous breakdown or he was a man with much too much to hide for his own good. Eventually he threatened libelous action against any and all who dared make reference to his association with child sexual abuse.

Scalawag Magazine pointed out that he'd been groomed from a very early age for bigger and better things, yet the height of his political career prematurely eclipsed as mere Junior Minister for Northern Ireland, while his baroness wife's pinnacle reached the much higher perch as Health Minister.[2288] Perhaps his questionable past and psychological instability as the ticking

---

[2286] Beatrix Campbell, "When in Doubt, Blame the Children," *Independent/spotlightonabuse.wordpress.com*, March 24, 1993.

[2287] Simon Regan, "Shame and Scandal in the Family," *Scalawag/spotlightonabuse.wordpress.com*, 1993.

[2288] Simon Regan, https://spotlightonabuse.wordpress.com/2013/03/08/bottomley-bottoms-out-1993/

time bomb undermined and arrested his ambitious climb to the top. Or just one too many personal traumas from the 1980s.

In 1986 - two years into Virginia Bottomley's 21-year Parliamentary stretch, Dame Esther Rantzen began her *BBC* ChildLine operation reportedly filtering out calls from child victims of VIP sex abuse. It's rather telling that in a February 1989 *Daily Mirror* article covering the biggest pedophile ring bust in British history, that the final paragraph be devoted to soliciting Esther Rantzen's reaction. The ChildLine pedo-gatekeeper was promoting the idea that Britain urgently needed "a Ministry of Children" a full decade and a half before pedo-enabling Tony Blair made Esther's wish come true, selecting his former neighbor and Esther's Jewish "pedo-sister" Dame Oppenheimer the nation's first minister of children.[2289] It's as if the elite's diabolical plan had already been mapped out years in advance, which is exactly how the Luciferian planetary controllers operate.

Skip ahead just four years to 1993 and we have on full display the health minister in charge of the UK Care System and her longtime MP husband blatantly not operating in the best interest of children. If only Britain followed the immediate advice of gatekeeper Rantzen and had a caring, nurturing minister of children like Dame Oppenheimer Hodge whose maltreatment towards her own poor Islington kids at that time was finally being exposed in the press, how under Margaret's loving care, kids were being sexually mauled and attacked every single day on her watch. Margaret and Virginia's system of care was crawling with so many child sexual predators that their public records were clearly protecting. Leave it for another decade before the "compassionate" Prime Minister Tony Blair to finally implement Dame Esther's splendid idea to create the position especially for Dame Margaret to so fiercely protect rapists, I mean children. Again, regardless of decade, leader, party, male or female, those entrusted with the responsibility of taking care of children, by their own overt actions on public record took care of rapists first and children last.

By far the biggest theme of these books on modern pedophilia is that the same protected child sodomizing VIP criminals keep getting away with it their whole lives through, with few if ever caught and brought to justice. As a semi-notable on par with Peter Righton, it took Met's Operation Hedgerow (1987-89) to finally temporarily stop career Foreign Office diplomat-serial pedophile Colin Peters (with nearly two dozen others' arrests as well), resulting in their 1989 convictions and his eight year prison sentence.[2290] Police determined this enormous pedophile ring procured mostly local runaways off the English streets and public toilets as well as from one of his crime partner's cleaning business and youth football club. But despite the QC Foreign

---

[2289] Ted Oliver, "Mr Evil's Child Sex Gang are Locked up, *Daily Mirror/spotlightonabuse.wordpress.com*, February 4, 1989.
[2290] "Operation Hedgerow, Part 2," *scepticpeg.wordpress.com*, January 4, 2018..

Office barrister's London based sex ring having links to the much wider international pedophilia and child pornography network stretching to Italy (recall Naples 1967 sealed till 2056), Asia and the US, Operation Hedgerow was too underfunded and understaffed to follow up on its critical global leads.[2291] Reporting on the case in 2013, the *Independent* stated:

[Colin Peter's pedophile ring] *was used by highly placed civil servants and well-known public officials.[2292]*

A prominent MP and a member of high society were also implicated in the Hedgerow bust. But because trespassing on the cabal's worldwide pedo-operations was taboo even back in 1989, the two lead detectives' chain of command requests to expand the operation and establish a specialized international pedophilia unit were summarily rejected, especially once high society VIPs like a House of Lords peer and a West London vicar emerged as suspects. One of two lead detectives behind Operation Hedgerow, the retired Detective Chief Superintendent Roger Gaspar went on record in 2014:

I was warned off... 'Don't open the box, you will never get the lid back on.' I was warned not to open the box to find what else is going on because it would just carry on and on.[2293]

Hmm... kind of like the IICSA and UK's never-ending cover-up.

Despite making 23 arrests resulting in 14 convictions compiling evidence of abuse of at least 150 boys in the biggest pedophile police operation in UK history to-date, after two years Operation Hedgerow was shut down in 1989 with no further media coverage exposing this tip of the global pedo-iceberg. Again, another police probe got too close to pedophiles at the top of the predator food chain caught sprouting their international tentacles far and wide. And let's face it, Colin Peters along with the likes of Peter Righton and Jimmy Savile were among the elite's prime crime players busily working, in Jimmy's own words, "undercover" with MI5 and MI6, coordinating pedophile rings serving the British Establishment VIPs nationwide and far beyond, but most importantly, serving the control matrix through its globalized blackmail apparatus.

In its ever-expanding control over blackmail operations, even further back in the 1970s, MI5 made sure to infiltrate Britain's largest, most influential pedophile organization - the Paedophile Information Exchange (1974-1984).[2294] A longtime civil servant turned

---

[2291] Operation Hedgerow, Part 2," https://scepticpeg.wordpress.com/2018/01/04/operation-hedgerow-pt-2-dont-open-the-box-you-will-never-get-the-lid-back-on/.

[2292] Martin Hickman, "Police Failings put dozens of Children at Risk from Notorious Paedophile Gang," Independent, November 4, 2013.

[2293] James Fielding, "Exclusive: 'I was Warned off' says Detective involved in Historic Paedophile Probe," *Express*, December 21, 2014.

[2294] Tim Tate and Ted Jeory, https://www.express.co.uk/news/uk/485529/Special-Branch-funded-Paedophile-Information-Exchange-says-Home-Office-whistleblower.

whistleblower at the Home Affairs Office maintains that Metro's Special Branch funded PIE in the late 1970s and early 80s as a subversive means of implementing sexual blackmail control over PIE member politicians.[2295] Recall former MI6 deputy head Sir Peter Hayman was an active PIE member with a particular penchant for sexually fantasizing about torture and murder of children.[2296]

With Scotland Yard's Special Branch having infiltrated PIE, Met Police obtained possession of a PIE membership list in 1984.[2297] Additionally, the same week in 1983 that MP Geoffrey Dickens submitted a 40 page dossier on infiltrated pedophiles high up in government, the Scotland Yard also sent Home Office Secretary Sir Leon a PIE dossier outing 15 known pedophiles.[2298] The then pedo-enabling Director of Public Prosecutions Sir Thomas Hetherington also received a copy. Yet he too sat on it. But more on Sir Thomas the protector later. Of course pedophile Leon Brittan proceeded to do what he did best, lose and destroy all evidence, especially when it incriminated himself and/or his VIP pedo-pals. Unsurprisingly, Brittan also refused to take action to abolish the Paedophile Information Exchange that Dickens had railed against, passively allowing public exposure pressure to disband the group by 1984.[2299]

Geoffrey Dickens used Parliamentary privilege to name diplomat and MI6 deputy director Sir Peter Hayman as a pedophile due to a package found on a bus belonging to the pervert containing child pornography.[2300] Yet while lesser known P. I. E. members were prosecuted and jailed in 1978 on either the same or lesser charge of conspiring to corrupt public morals as a mere member, Hayman was protected and later knighted by the queen. In January 2015 a secret 37 page file was released by National Archives detailing Margaret Thatcher and her then Attorney General Michael Haver's preoccupation over concealing Sir Peter Hayman's sick habits from going public in anticipation of Dickens threat to expose him in Parliament.[2301]

For four years between 1981 and 1985 the courageous MP Geoffrey Dickens spoke continually of a Westminster-Downing Street pedophile ring linked to child pornography and organized

[2295] Tim Tate and Ted Jeory, "Exclusive: Secret service Infiltrated Paedophile Group to 'Blackmail Establishment,'" *Express*, June 29, 2014.

[2296] Tom McTague, "Top British Diplomat was Focus of Secret Government File sent to Margaret Thatcher about 'Unnatural' Sexual Behaviour," *Daily Mail*, January 30, 2015.

[2297] Tim Tate, "PIE and the Independent Child Abuse Inquiry," *timtate.co.uk*, February 3, 2017.

[2298] Stephen Swinford, "Leon Brittan was given Second Paedophile Dossier," *The Telegraph*, July 7, 2014.

[2299] Chris Greenwood, "Brittan Refused call to Ban Paedophile Support Group PIE: Tory said he wanted to see if existing Laws would be adequate to deal with the group," *Daily Mail*, June 4, 2015.

[2300] Peter Walker, "Secret 1981 File Naming Senior Diplomat as Paedophile is Released to Public," *The Guardian*, January 30, 2015, https://www.theguardian.com/politics/2015/jan/30/sir-peter-hayman-paedophile-file-national-archives-inquiry-child-abuse.

[2301] Peter Walker, https://www.theguardian.com/politics/2015/jan/30/sir-peter-hayman-paedophile-file-national-archives-inquiry-child-abuse.

crime, recognizing the evil and "vast sums" made abusing children on camera.[2302] Geoffrey spoke of "big, big names – people in positions of power, influence and responsibility" involved in child abuse. How correct he was.

For calling attention to such a disturbingly taboo topic, MP Dickens was a very brave and honorable man surrounded by pedophiles and wolves in his midst. On November 29, 1985 he spoke for the final time about the scourge engulfing all around him and his nation:

The noose around my neck grew tighter after I named a former high-flying British diplomat on the Floor of the House. Honourable Members will understand that where big money is involved and as important names came into my possession so the threats began. First, I received threatening telephone calls followed by two burglaries at my London home. Then, more seriously, my name appeared on a multi-killer's hit list.[2303]

Yet for the trouble of telling the ugly truth, Geoffrey Dickens paid a price. The vast majority of his peers scoffed and laughed at him... again, the usual treatment of a truth telling whistleblower bold enough to utter such shocking allegations. And in an evil system, the good guys always get punished with character or bodily assassination while the bad guys always remain protected and even rewarded. After his 1985 speech until his death at 64 in 1995, the 16-year MP never raised the topic of pedophilia again, perhaps because he feared assassination for him and his family. Dickens' widow also allegedly destroyed her husband's only dossier copy because she thought it was too "toxic," probably code word for lethal.[2304]

After Met Police submitted its PIE dossier to its Home Office boss Sir Leon and it too was lost or destroyed, it fails to absolve Britain's largest police force from its moral and legal duty and responsibility to make life safe from its long list of 300 known criminals.[2305] And a high number of PIE members from that 1984 list were serial sexual offenders who acted out their perverted desires for many more years. In fact, a slew from that list were later arrested, often times even decades later.[2306] But back in 1983 up to the time of their arrests, the Met Police Services (MPS) grossly failed to protect hundreds of child victims from self-confessed, known pedophiles, a most serious and grave dereliction of duty that an apology can never excuse.[2307] One member

---

[2302] "Tory MP Warned of Powerful Paedophile Ring 30 years ago," *Independent*, February 22, 2013.

[2303] "Tory MP Warned of Powerful Paedophile Ring 30 years ago," *Independent*, February 22, 2013.

[2304] Richard Pendlebury and Stephen Wright, "Leon Brittan's Faulty Memory and a Ticking Timebomb that could shake Westminster: Tory Peer faces Questions over 1980s Files Complied by MP Geoffrey Dickens on Westminster Paedophile Ring," *Daily Mail*, July 2, 2014.

[2305] James Hanning, Tim Tate and David Connett, "Paedophile Register of Controversial Group Ignored by Police," *Independent*, March 19, 2016.

[2306] Tim Tate, http://timtate.co.uk/category/blog/.

[2307] Matthew Weaver, "Met Police Apologises for Failing to Protect Children at Risk of Abuse," *The Guardian*, November 25, 2016.

was arrested 27 years later. Imagine how many young lives could have been saved from the lifetime damage and suffering caused by the reoffending crimes of 300 degenerates.

The most pressing question becomes why didn't Metro Police Services (MPS) do anything to stop known pedophiles from hurting children? The answer no doubt lies in the same reason the Met had virtually every investigation of a pedophile ring shut down prematurely from "orders from above." Clearly the MPS follow(ed) orders to let child abusers remain free to repeatedly harm children, especially if the perps happen to be MPs, lords and cabinet ministers. So the question becomes was there ever an explicit order, as in all the police probes stopped from "on high," not to investigate or surveil these identified men known to be on the prowl for their next child victim? And if so, who? Also from the notorious Elm Guest House list alone[2308] as well as media covered chief constables outed for their pedo-crimes,[2309] [2310] it's more than evident that police chiefs too often turn out to be pedophiles themselves (not to mention order-following enablers),[2311] and in the same way Sir Leon refused to out himself, senior pedo-police officers no doubt criminally resort to the same self-preservation tactics.

Investigative journalist Tim Tate in recent years has pressed the IICSA to thoroughly examine the Met's pervasive, systemic failure to protect children, in this case, passively sitting on a list of known PIE pedophiles.[2312] But despite the fourth presiding IICSA chair Alexis Jay's stated objective to probe PIE regarding its VIP connections, no official criticism or substantive uncovering of police failures have emerged from her "independent" inquiry during the past four years since it began. The latest foot in the mouth statement out of Jay's doublespeak dribble from a March 4, 2019 *Daily Mail* article:

The inquiry wishes to make clear that the fact certain individuals will be named during the public hearing does not mean that the allegations against them are true. This investigation is not examining the truth or otherwise of individual allegations. The inquiry is simply addressing issues of grave public concern.[2313]

Quite a radical departure from the tough talk from the Inquiry's official Twitter account back at its 2015 outset:

2308 Rickeo, "The Elm Guest House List," *freeandfearless.org.uk*, July 27, 2017.
2309 "Soham Force Police Chief Charged with Child Abuse," *Daily Mail*, November 14, 2005.
2310 Steven Morris, "Ex-Police Chief Gordon Anglesea Jailed for Child Sexual Abuse," *The Guardian*, November 24, 2016.
2311 "Chef Constable Accused in Child-Abuse Scandal. No Acton in 9 Months," *The Skwawkbox*, August 16, 2017.
2312 Tim Tate, http://timtate.co.uk/category/blog/.
2313 Fionn Hargreaves, "Former MI5 Spy Chief will be the first Spy Chief to give Evidence at Child Sex Abuse Inquiry over Links with a Tory MP," *Daily Mail*, March 4, 2019.

We'll conduct objective fact-finding inquiry into allegations of abuse by people of public prominence associated w. Westminster[2314]

The IICSA is an artificial prop set up by the pedo-elite to merely appease British citizens, offering the illusion the government is actually doing something about the epidemic, all for show without teeth or backbone to make a bit of difference. As Westminster, the Scotland Yard and the Home Office has mismanages this IICSA fiasco, none are willing or able to take a hard honest look at themselves and do the self-policing required to flush out the cold hard self-incriminating facts, much less out themselves for perverting and obstructing justice.[2315] Yet even the most casual observer can readily see that the emperor wearing no clothes has been committing criminal cover-up for decades. Like the zillion past inquiries before it, unwilling to examine the mountains of UK child abuse and more mountains of cover-up evidence, the IICSA has only proven itself to be yet one more enormous smokescreen for gross incompetence leading to more avoidance and more cover-up. Only the cabal pedophiles while harming another young child are loving it.

The IICSA as a poorly staged Home Office production of half-truths has chosen to focus almost exclusively on Church of England and Catholic Church horror, so far sidestepping the elephant in the room, the wider web of horror inflicted on children by a powerful network of so called famous government leaders, several of whom have been Home Office ministers. Though the cherry-picked victims providing abuse testimony at clerical run schools have a history of horrendous trauma that deserve a public forum as well, the bulk of the pedophilia at the heart of the British government's been forever covered up and so far conveniently glossed over by this sorry excuse of an inquiry.

Merely scratching the surface with Rochdale's Cambridge House hostel and Knowl View residential school abuse only touching on the relative safe zone of one obesely dead whale is hardly getting to the core truth. And then for the IICSA to pass off the blatant lie, concluding that no "deliberate cover-up" of Cyril Smith's over 40-year crime spree occurred is an insult to any human's intelligence with half a brain.[2316] The Inquiry panel also bogusly claims that police never quite possessed enough evidence to prosecute the queen's knight when everyone in his giant shadow knew full well he was a pedo-monster with incredible amounts of incriminating evidence over the years to secure a number of convictions.

Moreover, the timing of the stretched out Brexit saga designed to overshadow the feeble, never-ending now four-year run of the Independent Inquiry into Child Sexual Abuse are both

---

[2314] Inquiry CSA Twitter account, *twitter.com*, November 27, 2015.

[2315] Tim Tate, "Knaves or Fools? The Home Office and the IICSA," *timtate.co.uk*, October 18, 2016.

[2316] Kim Pilling, "Rochdale Abuse: Authorities showed 'total lack of Urgency' in Tackling Historic Sex Abuse of Boys," *Independent*, April 12, 2018.

scheduled to culminate at the same time in March 2019.[2317] These two co-timed events are no accident. With the March 29th official EU exit, Brexit's been set up to provide sleight of hand distraction drawing attention away from the inquiry's scheduled public hearings on the Westminster VIP cover-up.[2318] If it is anything like the Rochdale/Smith whitewash, this inquiry will go down as another duly noted government scam, a forgettable footnote in history books. Rather than expose the VIP child fuckers at the top of the predatory food chain, which would be the natural targeted objective of any actual independent inquiry, so far it's just been another sugarcoated version of nauseating cover-up. Meanwhile, a vast pedophilia network remains alive and well, feasting off the flesh and blood of child victims in today's booming global sex trafficking slave trade. Unless radical truth bombs begin surfacing in March, the IICSA will be regarded as the devil's charade. Hence, the Brexit debacle's been scheduled to take center stage.

As the "Jimmy Savile" of the British government, Liberal Democrat Cyril Smith and the infamous DJ's criminal lives ran an uncanny parallel course, intertwining constantly as close friends with the same addiction cut from the same predatory cloth active during the same five decades. Britain's two most prolific, high profile predators met each other at a medieval banquet in 1977 when Cyril sang and Savile invited the politician onto his Clunk Clink show.[2319] Together they shared the same sick sadistic passion for destroying upwards of thousands of young lives, getting away with their countless crimes linked to many of the same crime scenes - Elm Guest House, Northern Ireland's Kincora,[2320] the Moors outside Scarborough and Manchester.

Both were openly rumored to be serial pedophiles for many decades but never served one day in prison. Born less than two years apart (the younger Smith in 1928), their crime sprees spanned the same marathon stretch from the 1950s to their year apart deaths (Smith in 2010, Savile in 2011). And they were both knighted by the queen as major players in the same pedophilia network, fully shielded by the uppermost echelons of British Establishment power structure - the government, royalty, police, intelligence agencies and Crown Prosecution Service. And early on in their illustrious careers, both Savile and Smith gravitated to immersing themselves tirelessly into philanthropic youth charities as the convenient cover to seize unlimited opportunity to prey on a deep reservoir of defenseless kids in care.

As a Rochdale businessman, council member turned mayor in 1966, Cyril Smith helped establish Cambridge House hostel for troubled youth, Knowl View special school for the learning

---

[2317] Daniel Uria, "May Delays Vote on final Brexit deal due to Brussels Negotiations," *UPI*, February 24, 2019.
[2318] Owen Bowcott, "Child Abuse Inquiry to cover 'Concealment of Evidence against MPs,'" *The Guardian*, January 31, 2018.
[2319] Steve Robson, "Paedophile MP Cyril Smith 'Admitted Spanking Boys to Police in the 1960s' and was Friends with Jimmy Savile," *Daily Mail*, November 29, 2012.
[2320] "International Network – Whistleblower Kerr," *aangirfan.blogspot.com*, December 4, 2017.

disabled, the youth charity Rochdale Childer and, at one point, was governor of 29 local schools.[2321] Uncovered Knowl View documents indicate that up to a quarter of the children at the school may have suffered sexual and physical abuse by Cyril Smith and friends.[2322] The staff is accused of dereliction of duty in its failure to protect its vulnerable young students with learning disabilities.

Like Savile, Smith's orchestrated "altruistic arrangement" at multiple youth facilities gave him free day and night access with keys to buildings to waddle from classroom to classroom and children's center to children's center with no questions asked, typically playing the depraved role of either "medical examiner" or disciplinarian or both in his abuse ritual of young boys. He'd unlock the door to boys' bedrooms at Cambridge House and order youngsters to take their clothes off. His stated deceitful purpose:

I've been told you're ill and I've come to examine you.[2323]

Three to four times the size of his victims and overpowered by his authoritative, intimidating presence, one victim recollects:

I remember his eyes watching me like a beast sizing up its prey. In the folds of fat around his neck I could see rivulets of sweat. Shaking with fear, I did as I was told. He bent down and clasped me with huge hands like shovels. Suddenly he grasped my private parts and began to squeeze. I screamed. Violence flashed in his eyes. 'Now, now, lad. I'll have none of your petulance. This is for your own good. I'm checking to see if there's anything wrong with you,' he said, as he forced his way between my thighs again.[2324]

Thirteen survivors of Smith's abuse have come forward at Cambridge and Knowl View alone, indicating a likelihood of perhaps hundreds more during his near half century reign of terror, with his first confirmed incident dating back to 1961 grooming a Christmas carol choirboy. Eight brave boys from Cambridge House made abuse allegations against Cyril Smith as far back as the 1960s.[2325] Most of his victims were unaware of his political title, only that the "fat man" as they called him was "Mr. Rochdale," and everyone in town knew Cyril Smith to be an extremely

[2321] Simon Danczuk, "'I've come to Examine you': From Bogus Medical Examinations to Punishment Beatings, how Paedophile Cyril Smith used his Powerful Public Image to Abuse Boys, *Daily Mail*, April 11, 2014.

[2322] David Hencke, "Cyril Smith: New Evidence of Cover up of the Liberal Democrat's Leading Child Sex Abuser," *daviidhencke.com*, September 12, 2013, https://davidhencke.com/2013/09/12/cyril-smith-new-evidence-of-cover-up-of-the-liberal-democrats-leading-child-sex-abuser/.

[2323] Simon Danczuk, https://www.dailymail.co.uk/news/article-2602869/How-paedophile-Cyril-Smith-used-powerful-public-image-abuse-boys.html.

[2324] Simon Danczuk, https://www.dailymail.co.uk/news/article-2602869/How-paedophile-Cyril-Smith-used-powerful-public-image-abuse-boys.html.

[2325] Steve White, "He did Sexually Abuse Boys: Authorities Admit Cyril Smith was Paedophile," *Mirror*, November 27, 2011.

powerful local Godfather-like figure. The lifetime bachelor made his mother the "First Lady of Rochdale."

No matter if you're awakened in the middle of the night and forced downstairs to a room where the waiting fat man demanded a blow job, or if you had an allergy to eating meat and the big man brought a plate full of ham sandwiches and ordered you to eat, nothing else mattered.[2326] Smith stuffed the sandwich down his victim's throat and within seconds, when the young boy became sick, the sadistic, enraged punisher delivered a swift backhand paw swipe with such force that the boy's head hit the wall, causing a gash requiring stitches at the local emergency hospital room and knocking out his front teeth. But just like Sir Jimmy, victims were either disbelieved or deemed too powerless to go up against the most famous big man of Rochdale.

As Smith ascended to national prominence within the Liberal Party becoming an MP from 1972 to 1992, just as Sir Jimmy's crimes were hidden in plain sight, both utilized the mass media to cultivate their larger-than-life, iconic personas that helped conceal their diabolical natures and insatiable appetites for perversion and wickedness. While Savile's abuse was known to both police and *BBC*, Smith's too was well-known to police as well as Westminster. But with their link to the power establishment knowing the inside dirty lowdown on scores of other VIP pedophiles, their open secret was kept secure, tightly sealed in complicit cover-up, a lifetime guarantee until after their deaths.

However, just 7 years into his two decades in Parliament, in May 1979 a little local monthly paper called the *Rochdale Alternative Press* known as RAP ran the front-page headline "Strange Case of Smith the Man," graphically detailing the MP's systematic abuse of boys at Cambridge House.[2327] The astounding newspaper article printed in one of the two editors' cellars was the culmination of checking out barroom rumors firsthand with staff, former residents and nine victims (four with signed affidavits) along with local police accounts that confirmed the shocking reality of what was going on. The powerful Smith the Man threatened a libel suit that he never carried out for obvious reasons that the truth is not libelous. Though the story immediately created quite the local stir, with larger London newspapers descending on Rochdale and the RAP editors for interviews, like all similar complaints, evidence and persistent rumors over the years, other than one more *Private Eye* piece rehashing the RAP fact sheet, it too passed and Big Cyril of Rochdale prevailed, increasing his voting majority at his next election. Smith's working class, man-of-the-people charm as a regular on the TV talk show circuit and countless public appearances, along with help from fellow VIP peers, police, security services and the CPS, the fat man managed

---

[2326] Simon Danczuk, https://www.dailymail.co.uk/news/article-2602869/How-paedophile-Cyril-Smith-used-powerful-public-image-abuse-boys.html.
[2327] Andrew Malone, "Chilling Claims that Cyril Smith Child Abuse Scandal was Concealed to Avoid Crisis at Westminster," *Daly Mail*, November 23, 2012.

to thrive for the next three decades before succumbing to cancer in 2010. Upon both Smith and Savile's passing, the queen honored evil giants were revered as "national treasures," prior to the truth of their darker sides posthumously emerging in sensational shocking exposure.[2328]

At fat man's 80th birthday party, Liberal Democrat party leader Nick Clegg touted such praise as:

[Smith was] *a beacon for our party in the Seventies and Eighties.*

And upon fat man's death two years later, Clegg gushed:

He was a friend to everybody in Rochdale. Cyril Smith was a larger-than-life character and one of the most recognisable and likeable politicians of his day.[2329]

Clegg, I got news for you - your demagogue was not a friend to the hundreds of his victims in Rochdale or anywhere else.

MP Cyril Smith represents the embodiment of corrupt collusion and cover-up at the highest levels - the nefarious nexus between criminal politician and his protectors - the police, DPPs, intelligence services and fellow pedo club members. In both the Savile and Smith cases, decent rank and file cops were repeatedly thwarted trying to bring justice to victimized children, putting away the beast only to be reprimanded and ordered to stand down, muzzled and threatened with prosecution under the Official Secrets Act.[2330] Smith was in detectives' crosshairs for prosecution at least three times,[2331] while Savile was investigated in at least seven probes.[2332]

When police discovered indecent photos of children in Smith's car, suddenly a mysterious call from London arrived with instructions not to charge him.[2333] The serial molester was apprehended on numerous occasions at the St. James Park public toilets in London for gross indecency but orders from above were delivered like clockwork to always bail his lard ass out. In 1981 police set up surveillance of a flat in the Coronation Buildings in pedo-infested Lambeth, less than a mile from Parliament. Cyril Smith and a senior member of British

[2328] Simon Danczuk, "Knighted by Steel and Eulogised by Clegg: Cyril Smith and the Indelible Shame of the Liberal Party," *Daily Mail*, April 11, 2014.

[2329] "Former Liberal Democrat MP Cyril Smith Dies," *BBC*, September 3, 2010.

[2330] Nick Hopkins and Jake Morris, "Cyril Smith Child Abuse Inquiry 'Scrapped after his Arrest,'" *BBC*, March 17, 2015..

[2331] "Sir Cyril Smith 'Sexually Abused' Young Boys and Avoided Prosecution three times, Police say," *Huffington Post*, November 27, 2012.

[2332] Ryan Sabey and Amanda Ravell Walton, "Evil MP Cyril Smith and Jimmy Savile were Close Friends for Four Decades," *The Sun*, November 29, 2012.

[2333] Simon Danczuk, https://www.dailymail.co.uk/news/article-2602869/How-paedophile-Cyril-Smith-used-powerful-public-image-abuse-boys.html.

intelligence were caught on tape attending a sex orgy.[2334] Police picked him up and detained him a few hours before his release. The sergeant wanting to hold him was warned. After a police instructor leaked that there were 144 formal abuse complaints against Smith, she was abruptly silenced and reassigned. That's the screwed up system. Like the child victims, good cops wanting justice are always punished or threatened.

It's worth interjecting here that although Elm Guest House may be the most infamous of all locations where VIP child abusers gathered for orgies through several highly organized, convergent pedophile rings, it's definitely not the only place. Recall the plan to franchise the Elm brand to bring a boy brothel to every community. Though typically victims from Grafton Close Home and other children's residential facilities across Britain were sexually assaulted by staff and occasional outsiders in their own care homes, besides Elm Guest House, youth were frequently transported to other private homes as in Lambeth's Coronation Buildings or Dolphin Square flats or individual estates belonging to VIPs in the Greater London area and beyond. Plus it was also common for children from other areas in England, Wales and Northern Ireland to likewise travel to sex parties in any number of destinations around London and elsewhere. At times boys and girls from London were trafficked to other distant locales such as Northern Ireland, North Wales, and Jersey Island or abroad to Amsterdam and other cities. Elm House victims maintain they were brought to Amsterdam to be further abused there.[2335]

As alluded to earlier, Britain's pedophilia network was rapidly expanding throughout the 1980s both nationwide and internationally. Security services and a growing web of infiltrating homosexual pedophiles saturating social services, education and the burgeoning sex tourism trade, interfacing with likeminded senior civil servants, local and national politicians and top law enforcement personnel had built a vast pedophilia network that was both thriving and fairly well-insulated by the early 1980s. Hence, it's almost by fluke that tip of the iceberg scandals like Elm Guest House broke out at all as the ever-tightening grip of secrecy and deception grew during the unfolding national cover-up.

An MI5 memo surfaced at the October 2017 IICSA hearings showing that the Director of Public Prosecution (DPP), the queen knighted gatekeeper who decides what cases get prosecuted or not, Sir Thomas Hetherington in 1979 lied to the press insisting that no record of a police inquiry from 1970 existed exposing Cyril Smith as a child abuser.[2336] Though for decades MI5 was fully aware that Smith was repeatedly accused by countless victims, but as the "defender of the realm" (not to mention primary architect of UK's pedo-network), its primary responsibility was never to expose but only to protect pedophiles. Of course like any

---

[2334] "Cyril Smith, This is Your Life: A Timeline," *needleblog.wordpress.com*, January 7, 2015.

[2335] James Hanning and Paul Cahalan, "Abuse Victims were 'Trafficked Abroad,'" *Independent*, February 3, 2013..

[2336] Robert Mendick, "MI5 knew of Cover-up over Cyril Smith Child Abuse, Inquiry hears," *The Telegraph*, October 9, 2017.

intelligence agency, to this very day British security services have always attempted to fulfil their duty to ensure that pedophilia blackmail operations remain hidden, intact and covered up. And as another integral player in this evil scheme, so have all the DPPs throughout modern British history also protected the freedom and reputations of scores of child rapists from the VIP Establishment.

Hetherington was simply doing his expected job lying to the media in order to cover up VIP sex crimes, just as his DPP predecessor Sir Norman Skelhorn in 1970 chose to minimize and cover-up Smith's depravities, claiming not enough credible evidence to secure a conviction. This tactical decision came after eight young men independently corroborated each other's accounts, reporting that long before Smith was even an MP, he'd been sexually molesting boys at Cambridge House in the 1960s. But Skelhorn claimed the victims were not to be trusted.[2337] See how victims are routinely and historically treated, as if they're the criminals? From 1889 to this 1970 case right up to the present, child victims from the poor class are routinely double punished and invariably the criminal elite are shielded and allowed to escape justice to abuse again and again. Fact - the UK legal system has absolutely nothing to do with justice at all, delivering only injustice. In a letter to the Chief Constable, DPP Skelhorn in 1970 also lied:

[The claims] *were somewhat stale and without corroboration. Further, the characters of some of these young men would be likely to render their evidence suspect.*[2338]

Always it's the victims on trial, never the VIP perps.

During that same year in 1979 when pedo-protecting Hetherington lied to the press about a previous police inquiry into Smith abuse, at a Liberal Party election meeting held at a volunteer's flat in Manchester, Sir Cyril made his grand appearance. After his 29 stones broke a chair and then flustered, taking a seat next to a 14-year old boy, Smith's impulse control lapsed and he groped the lad's genitals who screamed so loudly in front of the shocked, silenced crowd, it instantly created a scandalous public scene.[2339] The couple at the flat hosting the event were appalled and bitterly complained to the party headquarters in London. The Liberal Party's official response was to offer them £200 in hush money to cover any "inconvenience" caused. As the party leader at the time, David Steel has claimed he never heard of this incident. But after reading the *Private Eye* article that same year in 1979 outing Smith, Steel maintains that he confronted Big Cyril and simply took his word at face value that he never abused children. Yet in 1988 Lord David Steel recommended the sexual predator for knighthood despite being told of

[2337] Martin Evans, "Sir Cyril Smith's Family 'Deeply Saddened' as Police Admit he Escaped Abuse Charges," *The Telegraph*, November 28, 2012.
[2338] Martin Evans, https://www.telegraph.co.uk/news/uknews/crime/9707609/Sir-Cyril-Smiths-family-deeply-saddened-as-police-admit-he-escaped-abuse-charges.html.
[2339] Simon Danczuk, "How Liberals offered Hush Money to Hide Cyril Smith's Abuse," *Daily Mail*, April 3, 2015.

Smith's numerous abuse allegations.[2340] Let's face it, if you're part of the pedophilia club, the system never fails to reward you with its royal blessings as virtually every suspected or known VIP pedophile is a royally honored knight.

In 1985 Director of Public Prosecutions Hetherington made a special trip over to the West End Central police station in person to demand that Metro's Operation Circus be shut down as police surveillance had captured in photos senior politicians, entertainers and a Scotland Yard commander abusing rent boys in Piccadilly Circus.[2341] In September 2015 it was discovered that this treasure trove of VIP evidence of child abuse documentation previously placed in a Special Branch registry and stored in police archives has suddenly gone missing. While the red docket files apparently disappeared from archives, the so called X4 files of unsubstantiated information on pedophiles believed to have been "a goldmine" were shredded. Dozens of police probe shutdowns and episodes of disappearing evidence are the cornerstone to cover-up.

Though apologists commonly claim if the same incriminating evidence was presented to CPS today against any VIP regardless of status, an arrest and prosecution would most certainly follow since there's been a major sea change in cultural perspective regarding institutionalized child abuse. Is that why still not one MP or minister has ever been charged and gone to prison? This is just more bullshit rhetoric used frequently as an excuse to explain away the massive unending cover-up still ongoing today.

Attorney Alan Collins, who represents abuse victims, states:

It would appear there's still sometimes this underlying attitude that when it comes to child abuse allegations that the children, the victims, are not necessarily believed.[2342]

Just like the Elm Guest House and Jimmy Savile scandals, on multiple occasions in 1970, 1979, and again in both 1998 and 1999, compelling evidence to prosecute Smith was criminally ignored, blocked and repeatedly covered up in conspiracy by police, MI5, DPPs and CPS in spite of the open secret swirling around this diabolical MP's entire political career.[2343]

Assigned Lancashire Special Branch officer Tony Robinson went public in 2012 reporting that he inadvertently stumbled upon a very thick dossier deliberately hidden away in a Special Branch safe in Lancashire during the 1970s containing a plethora of complaints compiled over the years

[2340] Sophie Jane Evans, "Lib Dem Leader put Paedophile MP Cyril Smith forward for Knighthood 'even after he was told of Abuse Allegations,'" *Daly Mail*, February 23, 2014.

[2341] "Historic VIP Child Sex Abuse Cop Files go Missing," *oye.news*, September 20, 2015..

[2342] Martin Evans, https://www.telegraph.co.uk/news/uknews/crime/9707609/Sir-Cyril-Smiths-family-deeply-saddened-as-police-admit-he-escaped-abuse-charges.html.

[2343] Martin Evans, https://www.telegraph.co.uk/news/uknews/crime/9707609/Sir-Cyril-Smiths-family-deeply-saddened-as-police-admit-he-escaped-abuse-charges.html.

by dozens of Smith victims.[2344] Robinson asserts that he then received a call from an MI5 officer requesting that the dossier be sent to London ASAP. Tony Robinson also said that the Director of Public Prosecutions had previously reviewed the file. Proof the dossier had already passed through the DPP's hands was self-evident:

Written across the top of it were the words: 'No further action, not in the public interest. DPP,' [adding]: *The police now say the file is lost. It seems like there was a complete cover up to me.*[2345]

Ya think? Another "missing dossier" to join the slew of destroyed evidence is but one more confirmation that MI5 and Special Branch's criminal responsibility and priority #1 is to seize and disappear all "loose ends" in "defense of the realm" in order to keep evidence of VIP pedophilia covered up at all cost.

Recall from the last chapter in the early to mid-1990s the heroic efforts of Dr. Liz Davies, calling urgent attention to the out of control pedophilia inside Margaret Hodge's dozen Islington care homes, ultimately hauling her painstakingly collected hardcore evidence into a Metro Police superintendent's office. He apologetically informed Liz that more powerful figures than him still control what gets exposed and what is systematically covered up and concealed, regretfully disclosing:

I won't be able to investigate here at Scotland Yard.[2346]

Clearly the supe was alluding to higher-ups in Special Branch, the security services, the British government and their puppet masters in control of the massive child abuse cover-up. Former Special Branch Lancashire Detective Tony Robinson said after he'd gone public in 2012 divulging the call he received years ago from MI5 in London ordering the immediate transfer of that hefty Smith dossier to MI5 headquarters, the now 85-year old in failing health said in 2014 that he received another call from an old boss warning him he'd be prosecuted for violating the Official Secrets Act if he talks to the press again.[2347] This is the cabal weapon ensuring the cover-up continues. That's why MP John Mann's sponsored 2015 bill calling for amnesty went down in defeat. Nothing has changes as virtually the entire British government is still guiltily in on the nonstop cover-up.

[2344] Steven Swinford, "Sir Cyril Smith Sex Abuse Dossier Seized by MI5," *The Telegraph*, November 14, 2012.
[2345] Steven Swinford, https://www.telegraph.co.uk/news/uknews/crime/9678697/Sir-Cyril-Smith-sex-abuse-dossier-seized-by-MI5.html.
[2346] Nico Hines, https://www.thedailybeast.com/how-thatchers-government-covered-up-a-vip-pedophile-ring?ref=scroll.
[2347] Don Hale, "Exclusive: MPs Face Sex Abuse Arrests!" *Daily Star*, November 30, 2014.

In each and every scandal from Jersey, Islington and Lambeth to Elm Guest House, Savile and Smith, in order to protect the security services' engineered pedophilia network and sexual blackmail operations, missing and destroyed files in every single case is the name of the game under the pretext of "national security" to keep the tightest lid on United Kingdom's longtime cover-up. Though the decision not to prosecute Smith is said to have come "from the top," spanning several prime ministers in office at the time,[2348] it bears in mind to recognize that "the top" is not the elite's selected puppet politicians "running" the country. Again, the most important decisions that make, break or save a particular government or entire British Establishment, virtually always originate with the bloodline puppet masters pulling the strings controlling the planet.

Another Lancashire Police officer doggedly in pursuit of Cyril Smith sex crimes also repeatedly ran into a brick wall. The now 86-year old 35-year police force veteran Jack Tasker was threatened by his higher-ups on a number of occasions.[2349] Facing loss of job, career and livelihood along with a two year prison sentence and exorbitant fines, in 1981 Tasker and his team of undercover detectives were abruptly forced to cease operations and turn in months and years of hard evidence on Smith. After painstakingly collecting a massive amount of surveillance building a strong criminal case against MP Cyril Smith and a number of his peers as well as a senior intelligence head and high ranking police commanders all caught on videotape and in pictures abusing trafficked boys from care homes at sex parties at Elm Guest House, Dolphin Square and other locations, it turned out all for naught as the cover-up of the century was already well underway.

Just prior to this monumental setback, the vice squad actually had arrested Smith and held him for several hours at the police station before his release. But that wasn't the first time Det. Tasker had the fat man in his grasp. Eight of Smith's victims as far back as 1969 had reported abuse to Tasker's investigative unit while Smith was still a Rochdale council member.[2350] Tasker questioned Smith, stating he had the stuttering, sweating pig near breaking point. But Tubby's mommy, soon-to-be "First Lady of Rochdale," just happened to be a cleaning woman at the police station who overheard the rumors and word quickly got back to her big momma's boy. The next thing Jack Tasker knew was:

[2348] Andrew Malone, https://www.dailymail.co.uk/news/article-2237627/Cyril-Smith-child-abuse-Chilling-claims-Smith-child-abuse-scandal-concealed-avoid-crisis-Westminster.html.

[2349] Don Hale, "Exclusive: Cyril Smith was Linked to Paedo Brothel Murder Probe says Ex-Cop," *Daily Star*, December 7, 2014.

[2350] Don Hale, https://www.dailystar.co.uk/news/latest-news/414072/Cyril-Smith-was-linked-to-paedo-brothel-murder-probe-says-ex-cop.

We were ordered to stop. We were visited by a superintendent and a chief superintendent. They were from the Lancashire Police HQ at Hutton.[2351]

Detective Jack explained his "superiors" forced him to unlock a drawer containing all the files on Smith.

They told me to take everything out that relates to this case and added 'We mean everything, every scrap of paper and every note you've ever made'. They said we would be back in uniform if anything went wrong.[2352]

Now all these years later, still fearing loss of pension and still facing threat of prosecution, the only way for former police officer octogenarians like Tasker and Robinson to freely report their earlier investigative findings from a half century ago is through either granting them amnesty or repealing the Official Secrets Act.

In 2015 anti-child abuse campaigner turned former Rochdale MP Simon Danczuk (he too has been neutralized as alluded to in a previous chapter) stated:

He [Smith] *was protected because he knew of other paedophiles in the networks in which he operated and had he been prosecuted, then I think those other people would have been named by Smith and that's why they ensured that he was never put before the courts.*[2353]

With his Smith investigation shut down again in 1981, former detective Jack Tasker maintains that Cyril Smith was yet another major supplier (just like his buddy Savile) to the VIP network.[2354] Moreover, Tasker asserts that a powerful spy web (MI5) obstructed all law enforcement efforts to arrest and convict the serial child predator, citing the same reason - fear that if the fat man was arrested, he wouldn't hesitate to bring down with him scores of fellow VIP sickos in politics, entertainment, the high courts, police and security services.[2355] Also similar to suspicions surrounding his satanic DJ pedo-pal Sir Jimmy, detective Tasker believes Smith could have been involved in murder at the Elm Guest House:

[2351] Don Hale, https://www.dailystar.co.uk/news/latest-news/414072/Cyril-Smith-was-linked-to-paedo-brothel-murder-probe-says-ex-cop.

[2352] Don Hale, https://www.dailystar.co.uk/news/latest-news/414072/Cyril-Smith-was-linked-to-paedo-brothel-murder-probe-says-ex-cop.

[2353] Nick Hopkins and Jake Morris, https://www.bbc.com/news/uk-31908431.

[2354] Don Hale, https://www.dailystar.co.uk/news/latest-news/414072/Cyril-Smith-was-linked-to-paedo-brothel-murder-probe-says-ex-cop.

[2355] Jaya Narain and Martin Robinson, "Cyril Smith was Spared Court because he would have Exposed other high-profile Child Abusers says former Police Detective," *Daily Mail*, March 16, 2015.

Smith's name even cropped up in talks with colleagues as a possible suspect for a murder at the Elm Guest House in London, where we knew Cyril was a regular visitor. I believe he was supplying kids for a lot of powerful people.[2356]

Just as Savile was entrusted by the pedo-saturated Thatcher government to keys to the pedo-kingdom's asylums, so was Smith. According to Jack Tasker:

Smith was a regular visitor to Buckley Hall Detention Centre, which was full of boys. He used to come and go as he pleased. People who worked there told me he had his own set of keys – not to the perimeter but to the interior. He used to come in, pick his keys up and wander around alone. He was allowed access to anywhere inside and could have anything he wanted.[2357]

So many striking parallels shared between this psychopathic Smith-Savile duo seem to run on infinitely – all by sinister design of course. Protected by MI5, both were dominantly aggressive, larger-than-life public figures creating a culture of sexual predation and exploitation around them that invited and enabled other pedophiles to operate safely within their social professional territory to get away with their flagrantly vile child sex crimes. Both were conduits for MI5 spreading the pedophilia network.

A Rochdale HIV prevention specialist reported to the council that men as far away as Sheffield would come to Rochdale's Knowl View just to prey on young boys with learning disabilities. Smith's unprecedented clout and influence in Rochdale sheltered other pervs with the same deviant habits from run-ins with the law.[2358] After all, they owned and relished touting their reputations as Godfathers. In effect, both Savile and Smith were co-opted as undercover pedo-operatives for UK security services to spread and expand the pedophilia network. And partially as a result, Rochdale became a pedo-haven for pedophile gangs flourishing in the city for decades (the out-of-control UK pedo-gangs to be covered exclusively in Chapter 27).

As untouchables, both Smith and Savile closely operated within UK's shared pedophile network together, playing "undercover" linkage roles throughout the care home and NHS system… another reason MI5 had both their backs and that each has been implicated in virtually every British scandal. Theresa May's Home Office controlled "dependent inquiry" lost whatever little credibility it had back in April 2018 when it concluded that no "deliberate cover-up" by Rochdale authorities was ever found and that police never quite had the goods on the beast.[2359] Two boldface lies.

[2356] Don Hale, https://www.dailystar.co.uk/news/latest-news/414072/Cyril-Smith-was-linked-to-paedo-brothel-murder-probe-says-ex-cop.

[2357] Don Hale, https://www.dailystar.co.uk/news/latest-news/414072/Cyril-Smith-was-linked-to-paedo-brothel-murder-probe-says-ex-cop.

[2358] Simon Danczuk, https://www.dailymail.co.uk/news/article-2602869/How-paedophile-Cyril-Smith-used-powerful-public-image-abuse-boys.html.

[2359] Cambridge House, Knowl View and Rochdale Investigation Report, *IICSA*, April 2018.

So let's do a quick recap on this over-bloated, dangerous asshole's history. For decades Smith had his way as the king of Rochdale abusers. He and a number of other VIP buddies like Sir Leon and Sir Jimmy reputedly raped boys procured by the murdering Sidney Cooke gang[2360] at the Elm Guest House among several other locations.[2361] Smith also hooked up with another notorious pedophile networker specializing in schools and care homes – Peter Righton.[2362] Like his fellow high level cohorts Righton and Savile, Smith also took full advantage of possessing keys to countless youth facilities as an MI5 protected serial offender.

Cyril's diddling days likely started in the late 1950s when lads were observed frequently entering his business from the rear and placed him under surveillance according to CID Mike Smith.[2363] At least three times Lancashire Police collected enough evidence to turn it over to CPS and put him away but, as always, Britain's CPS aka Chief Pedophile Savior insisted never enough evidence.[2364] Senior Liberals in his party knew he was a pedophile, yet said nothing.[2365] Up till two years before Cyril's parliamentary career began, longtime Liberal Party leader Sir Jeremy Thorpe was Smith's friend and ally as a fellow raving child rapist.[2366] Thorpe's successor David Steel also knew, yet it didn't stop him from promoting the child sodomizer for knighthood.[2367] And with MI5 vetting, queenie - the royal pedophile rewarder - also had to know. Pedophilia has rule over and controlled Britain for a very long time.

Now you can see why in May 2013 the Greater Manchester Police (GPS) suddenly decided to abort an ongoing inquiry into Sir Cyril, declining to even take up the National Society for the Prevention of Cruelty to Children's (NSPCC) offer to assist in a joint fact-finding investigation into the prolific abusing Liberal chief party whip.[2368] Though at the height of the Jimmy Savile revelations in late November 2012, GMP held a press conference announcing Smith was a prolific abuser who today would be prosecuted, requesting victims to contact police in Manchester's freshly opened police inquiry, seemingly all gung ho at the time to unravel the full

---

[2360] Justin Penrose, https://www.mirror.co.uk/news/uk-news/former-tory-faces-child-sex-1714162.

[2361] Stephen Wright and Richard Pendlebury, "Timebomb at Elm Guest House: Pop stars, a Bishop and a top Politician Appear on a List Seized by Police Investigating Child Abuse at the London Hotel in the 1980s," *Daily Mail*, February 1, 2013.

[2362] Keir Mudie, https://www.mirror.co.uk/news/uk-news/new-victim-links-notorious-paedophile-1815932.

[2363] "Cyril Smith, This is Your Life: A Timeline," https://theneedleblog.wordpress.com/2015/01/07/cyril-smith-this-is-your-life-a-timeline/comment-page-1/.

[2364] Vikram Dodd and Rajeev Syal, "Cyril Smith Abuse Claims: 'Decision not to Prosecute would not be made today,'" *The Guardian*, November 27, 2012.

[2365] Rajeev Syal, "Senior Liberals 'were aware of Cyril Smith Child Abuse Allegations,'" *The Guardian*, February 26, 2013.

[2366] Tony Rennell, "The Sickest Establishment Cover-up of all: How the Great and the Good let Jeremy Thorpe get away with Sex Abuse... and gave a Green Light to Monsters like Cyril Smith and Jimmy Savile," *Daily Mail*, July 29, 2016.

[2367] Sophie Jane Evans, https://www.dailymail.co.uk/news/article-2566158/Lord-David-Steel-paedophile-MP-Cyril-Smith-forward-knighthood-told-abuse-allegations.html.

[2368] Nick Fielding, "Police Abandon Probe into Cyril Smith's Sexual Abuse of Boys," *Exaro News*, May 13, 2013.

truth.[2369] Yet less than six months later, Manchester's enthusiasm to dig deeper was already spent or more like never genuine. With all that was publicly surfacing on Smith's crimes, the pedo-protecting GM Police were afraid what other bombshells might be unhinged. And unlike Yewtree, no sacrificial lambs of washed up celebs would be in the offing, only headliner MPs, lords and ministers at the heart of the pedophile saturated government would be exposed and the crime cabal simply could not permit that. So the GMP probe was suddenly a no-go, a most predictable outcome when it comes to UK police inspecting VIP pedo-scandals. If no stone was left unturned on all 29 stones of lard-ass Sir Cyril, the entire British pedophilic empire would have crumbled into ashes, VIP monsters would finally be rightfully rotting in their own prison cell hell on earth and the world would be a better, safer place for both children and adults alike.

Media efforts to explain this top criminal politician's longtime impunity typically also cite the politics of the day when a weak Conservative and then Labor Party strategically took turns courting Liberals to capture the coalition majority.[2370] But again, it goes far deeper than fickle party politics. Britain's encrusted pedophilia network consisting of establishment VIPs from every major party has always been immune from public exposure and accountability right from the start. There's nothing new here. The evil fucks that are the elite powerbrokers on this earth have operated above all human-made laws as unreachable, untouchable, godlike creatures ruling over this planet for millenniums. The truth is that basic and simple.

Look no further than how the elite has managed to do it, utilizing mass media to maintain global idolatry toward the British (actually German Nazi) royal family and its personal history steeped in pedophilia, Freemasonry and Nazi-fascism. Their dark depraved truth has been carefully concealed by the international crime cabal's media propaganda machine so that an adoring, misinformed public can continue fawning and marveling over their every move and latest baby bump tribalism. Quite a nice PR setup they got going to conceal their real history. As part of today's celebrity worshipping culture, it provides titillating Soap Opera Theater designed to entice a duped masses into remaining blind over the controllers' continual rape and pillage of both our babies and our earth. But more on the despicable royals' story awaits in Chapter 30.

Speaking of masonic royalty, it's worth mentioning that the queen's hubby Prince Philip, 66 years a card carrying Freemason,[2371] atop his expressed wish list is the demented desire to reincarnate as a killer virus to wipe out millions of people in the elite's overpopulation hoax.[2372]

[2369] Steve White, https://www.mirror.co.uk/news/uk-news/cyril-smith-was-paedophile-police-admit-1459987.

[2370] Andrew Malone, https://www.dailymail.co.uk/news/article-2237627/Cyril-Smith-child-abuse-Chilling-claims-Smith-child-abuse-scandal-concealed-avoid-crisis-Westminster.html.

[2371] "Prince Philip, Duke of Edinburgh, Reaches 60 years as a Member of the Craft," *Freemasonry Today*, September 5, 2013.

[2372] "Prince Philip, in his own Words: We need to 'Cull' the Surplus Population," *bibliotecapleyades.net*, August 25, 1997.

Looking into a crystal ball, the Duke of Edinburgh's favorite number must be 666. The queen's hubby and the queen's cousin Prince Edward, current Duke of Kent, recently the former grand master of all UK Freemasonry,[2373] personify the crown's rule over the highest degrees of the masonic brotherhood worldwide, synonymous with New World Order Luciferianism.[2374]

As such, the Freemasonry-Zionism nexus is heavily infiltrated and seamlessly embedded deep within the queen's Commonwealth, particularly its justice system, police and security services all covertly tied to both proliferation of pedophile rings and their scandalously sealed cover-up.[2375] At this point, we know all too well that the Luciferian matrix controllers have at their beck and call the global intelligence community as their private army of fanatical foot soldiers subversively, dutifully promoting worldwide pedophilia both covertly through child sex trafficking slavery and subliminally through mass media sleaze as mere lifestyle choice of the rich and famous in a "monkey see, monkey do" imprinting sequence.

Regarding the indelible MI5 presence on the London centerpiece scandal - the Elm Guest House, British intelligence services back in the late 1970s and early 1980s were reportedly hard at work partnering with the international Spartacus Club, catering to homosexual pedophiles on the prowl the world over, preying on boy victims within the larger global pedo-network.[2376] Information on boy brothels worldwide, published in the Spartacus International publication was allegedly supplied by various intelligence blackmail operators - chiefly the CIA.[2377]

One such promoter provides yet another key link between MI5 and the Elm Guest House boy brothel - John Rowe, the intelligence liaison who allegedly organized trips to Amsterdam for members of the ultra-right wing Conservative group known as the Monday Club, many of whom were reportedly also frequent Elm House guests.[2378] MI5 operative John Rowe was largely responsible for trafficking British care home kids and rent boys to the world's pedo-snuff center - the Netherlands.[2379] As an infiltrating MI5 PIE member as well, this high-flying pedophiling secret agent man suggested the use of Spartacus Magazine to advertise Elm Guest House. And when in London, Rowe's frequent houseguest from Amsterdam was none other than Spartacus commercial manager and pedo-party ringleader - South African Peter Glencross.[2380]

[2373] Ian Cobain, "Freemasonry Explained: A Guide to the Secretive Society," *The Guardian*, February 4, 2018.

[2374] Anthony Forwood, "Freemasons (Luciferians): They are Bound by Oaths to Protect each other — No Matter what," *humansarefree.com*, December 2016.

[2375] Tom Harper, "Revealed: How Gangs used the Freemasons to Corrupt Police," *Independent*, January 13, 2014.

[2376] "Spartacus Boys and the CIA," http://aanirfan.blogspot.com/2014/07/spartacus-boys-and-cia.html.

[2377] "The CIA Runs the Pedophile Rings," *aangirfan.blogspot.com*, November 17, 2014.

[2378] "'Child Sex' Used to Control the World," *aanirfan.blogspot.com*, July 1, 2014.

[2379] Nick Davies, "When Sex Abuse can lead to Murder," *The Guardian*, November 27, 2000.

[2380] "The Power of Paedophile connections in Europe and the United Kingdom," *google-law.blogspot.com*, July 9, 2013.

These guys' perverse world vision planned to incorporate, expand and franchise the Elm Guest boy brothel model not just nationwide but far beyond.[2381] Recall how Margaret Hodge and her pedovores infiltrating her and other boroughs and social services were proliferating into a far wider secret club network across the British Isles, a likely reason why Blair chose her as UK's first Children's Minister, to replicate her fine work in their old Islington stomping grounds throughout the world's pedo-epicenter Britain as the ruling elite's global beta test. These derelicts Rowe, Glencross, Stamford, Tricker among many others were the early "visionaries" laying the demonic groundwork for a pedophile ring coming soon to a neighborhood near you.

Along with pedo-pimp Terry Dwyer, John Rowe was instrumental in bringing the global pedophilia guide Peter Glencross and Carole Kasir together, resulting in Elm Guest House's shift away from serving the needs of just adult homosexuals to satiating the warped tastes of pedophile predators for its bread and butter with ample supply of gravy and a cherry on top.

It turns out that John Rowe has an older brother Michael Stuart **Ro**we whose gay partner **Ra**lph A. **W**illiams formed a company using parts of their names called RAWRO Investments Limited.[2382] As the Elm Guest House "money men," RAWRO is on record paying for the installation of the sauna room at the Elm Guest House, its "state of the art" bondage toys and sophisticated videotaping system (for its early 80s time) as well as advertisements in the local gay paper *Capital Gay*. Michael Stuart Rowe often styled himself a wannabe Captain Michael Stuart Rowe or Captain Paul Rinehart, utilizing many fake names because at the time Elm was busted, Michael was a 39-year old hustler out to make his fortune using the Elm Guest brand for marketing VIP pedo-parties sexually abusing trafficked in boys from local homes under Richmond council care.

After things went south at Elm, in later years Michael Stuart Rowe turned extremely litigious against business partners losing every lawsuit in the late 1980s and 90s, all ultimately thrown out of court. In one of his letters that found its way into court records, Michael Stuart Rowe claims at 8-years old he was sexually abused by his father and passed around papa's pedo-ring operating in the early 1950s, alluding to "scores to settle" by suing his father over his deceased mother's estate. Apparently his conscience can't be bothered to factor in all the suffering the many victims that his Elm House affiliation brought. Michael Stuart Rowe's name can be found online listed as both an officer for several now defunct corporations[2383] as well as litigant in lawsuits.[2384] Also Jonathon Patrick Rowe, alias John Rowe, born five years after Michael in 1948 and also listed as an officer in one of the same out-of-business companies that Michael ran, is ex-MI5 John Rowe currently comfortably retired in Australia. Both Rowe brothers appear to still

---

[2381] "Boylinks – USA, UK, Europe, the World," *aangirfan.blogspot.com*, July 11, 2013.
[2382] "The Elm Guest House Money Men," *7493021a.wordpress.com*, Jun 4, 2013.
[2383] "Michael Stuart Rowe," *companydirectorcheck.com*.
[2384] "Spook 666 – The Devil's Agent," *forum.davidicke.com*, October 5, 2013.

be alive today. But likely not so well in view of their Elm Guest House misadventures' still unpaid karmic debt, apparently granted yet another free pass by the now defunct Operation Fairbridge. In the same way it isn't in the crime cabal's best interest to open up the Cyril Smith Pandora's box, neither is it the Elm Guest House. IICSA won't touch it that's for certain.

In between pimping duties via his own rent boy agency called Lord Fox, John Rowe's friend Terry Dwyer (aka Terry Allen) allegedly carried on a homosexual affair for two years with notorious Conservative Party MP Harvey Proctor.[2385] But Dwyer proudly boasted that he also supplied his MP lover with up to six boys a week for his sensual pleasures.[2386] Lying to save his MP seat when more of his boy-toy victims kept emerging in the press, in 1987 the shamed Proctor came under increasing pressure to resign. A litany of S&M beating and spanking allegations from teenage and early 20s "schoolboys" eventually led to his downfall. Pretending to be their kinky headmaster, an overzealous Proctor would use a cane, slipper and his hand pummeling their bare ass bottoms for punishment, and then delight in taking snapshots of their welt-reddened asses for lusty nostalgic memory, which in court sealed his guilty verdict. Ultimately his multiple victims' confessions caught up to Harvey, convicting him of four counts of gross indecency.[2387] But with paying a modest fine of just £1,450,[2388] the disgraced ex-MP avoided jail time.[2389] So what else is new?

During the 1970s and 1980s when not immersed in scandal, Harvey Proctor was also a staunch member of the infamous Monday Club,[2390] the same clique alleged to take young boys on holiday excursions to Amsterdam, compliments of MI5 buddy John Rowe and others like Russell Ticker. Unsurprisingly, MP Proctor was also reportedly an Elm Guest House regular. Chris Fay, former campaigner for the National Association of Young People in Care (NAYPIC), based on conversations with Carole Kasir between 1988 to 1990, stated that he observed Harvey Proctor's name on her guest list.[2391] Though that original list may have disappeared as a result of several police raids intended to eliminate every trace of VIP Elm House abuse, an online handwritten version posted by Fay's colleague Mary Moss prior to her house raid fortunately remains.[2392]

[2385] Christian Gysin, Peter Kane, Anton Antononowicz and Georgina Walsh, "Seamy Secrets of the Lord Fox," *Sunday Mirror/spotlightonabuse.wordpress.com*, May 21, 1987.

[2386] Terry Lovell, "Spanking MP: The Shocking Truth," *The People/spotlightonabuse.wordpress.com*, September 28, 1986.

[2387] "Proctor's Mates have a Whip-Round," *The People/spotlightonabuse.wordpress.com*, July 12, 1987.

[2388] Ian McKerron and Kim Willsher, "Proctor Fined £1,450 in Spanking Scandal," *Daily Mail/spotlghtonabuse.wordpress.com*, May 21, 1987.

[2389] James Hanning, "Former Tory MP Harvey Proctor: I was about to Kill myself, but an Act of Kindness Saved my life," *Independent*, May 6, 2015.

[2390] James Hanning, https://www.independent.co.uk/news/people/former-tory-mp-harvey-proctor

[2391] Rajeev Syal, "Zac Goldsmith Urged to Withdraw Paedophile Ring Allegations," *The Guardian*, October 14, 2015.

[2392] Rickeo, https://www.freeandfearless.org.uk/elm-guest-house-list.

Additionally, similar to Proctor's fellow Tory MP Portillo (covered in last chapter), the scandal-prone former politician Harvey was also apparently on record as a frequent holiday guest in Morocco's North African neighbor Tunisia, arrested after a naked Arab boy was discovered hiding under his bed.[2393]

In 1988 fresh out of Parliament and knowing what he knew about the illicit sex lives of the Westminster rich and famous, Proctor convinced over a dozen of his political cronies to contribute sizeable investments in his brand new business enterprise, the colorful kinkster's newly opened fancy shirt shop at a couple of posh locations only to have them go belly up a dozen years later with several buddies "losing their shirts" up to £100,000.[2394] In the post-Savile Operations Midland and Fernbridge investigating Parliamentary pedophiles, more victims came forth to claim Proctor had abused them at sex parties in the 1980s. A source close to the 2014 police inquiry reported to the *Mirror* that:

Proctor's name has repeatedly been mentioned by at least two alleged victims. He is going to be of key interest.[2395]

In March 2015 Proctor's residence was raided and he was questioned under caution.[2396] But no doubt emboldened by Lord McAlpine and Cliff Richard's legal successes at overturning and suppressing past pedophilic associations and winning millions for their stress in a pedo-cabal pushback, in May 2018 as a distraught, self-confessed depressive, the 71-year old Proctor filed a libel lawsuit for £1 million against the Scotland Yard and his main accuser "Nick" who was conveniently outed by the establishment as an alleged fraud and is currently facing a criminal trial that in one fell swoop strangely wipes away all other countless victims' legit allegations over the years. Apparently their accusations don't mean jack shit against all VIP pedophiles, fully insulated and protected by the corrupt, rigged UK legal system that effectively guarantees the national cover-up policy continues infinitum.[2397]

Back in 1987 when MP Proctor was enflamed in scandal, his onetime lover-boy procurer Terry Dwyer also ran into his own legal difficulties as owner-operator of an illegal London gay club-massage parlor where both drugs and rent boy sex were served on a platter as the main attraction.[2398] But shortly after Dwyer's bust and conviction, appeal court judges in 1988 freed

[2393] Terry Lovell and Phil Hall, "Arrested," *The People/spotlightonabuse.wordpress.com*, March 15, 1987.

[2394] Padraic Flanagan, "Tories Lose their Shirts on Harvey," *Sunday Express/spotlightonabuse.wordpress.com*, July 30, 2000..

[2395] Murun Buchstansangur, "Harvey Proctor, Cottonrose Ltd., and the Conservative Party," *spotlightonabuse.wordpress.com*, October 16, 2014.

[2396] Mike Sullivan, "Cops Raid Home of Ex-MP Harvey Proctor," *The Sun*, March 5, 2015.

[2397] Martin Evans, "Former Tory MP Harvey Proctor Sues Accuser and Scotland Yard for £1m," *The Guardian*, May 4, 2018.

[2398] "Den of Sex Man is Jailed," *The Hull Daily Mail/theneedleblog.wordpress.com*, February 25, 1988.

him on the technicality that his first trial judge was alleged to allow inadmissible evidence, thus granting the pimping druggie-pedophile his freedom.[2399] You think Dwyer's deep anal connections to Parliament, MI5 and their massive global pedo-ring just may have something to do with his overly-lenient brush with the law?

As long as we're still on the topic of disgraced former MP Harvey Proctor, as a bona fide Monday Clubber, that ultra-Conservative group begun in 1961 as a Le Cercle offshoot that remained a loyal supporter of Apartheid South Africa and is still big on repatriating immigrants back to their ancestral homes,[2400] Proctor and another prominent MP and Monday Club member Sir Peter Bottomley landed on Elm House guest lists and as such, their indelible connection to the London-Amsterdam pedophile network lives on. Of course Harvey Proctor made claims he never even heard of the Elm Guest House[2401] and former Tory minister and longtime Worthing MP Sir Bottomley in recent years threatened to sue over his name associated with any pedophile ring.[2402] But like it or not, links between the nightmare on Elm and Monday Club's rent boy trips to the child porn capital across the Channel linger on... sorry Sir.

Though Derek Laud hasn't shown up on any Rocks Lane party guest list yet, this sometime Dolphin Square resident and longtime Tory Party fixture as fixer, advisor, lobbyist, Iron Lady speechwriter, friend of Lady Camilla Duchess of Cornwall, 2005 Big Brother contestant and sadistic pedophile-VIP child procuring monster[2403] has been named the first black member of the Monday Club[2404] as well as the first non-white Master of Foxhounds in New Forest, Dame Esther's pedo-hunting grounds... a regular modern Renaissance man with a pathologically dark pedo twist. Derek's name will resurface again as a headliner in Chapter 29, per a *Scallywag Magazine* article exposing the kiddie mover and shaker in the North Wales pedophilia scandal.[2405] As of late, Derek's been laying low in South Africa, distancing himself from the Monday Club, his Conservative Party and criminally shameful past that's yet to catch up to him.

A couple of other Monday Clubbers[2406] also on the nightmare at Elm's guest list include Peter Campbell and Richard Miles.[2407] Peter Campbell died in 2011 at age 78. The Reading University

---

[2399] Judith Halliday, "City Club Boss Wins his Liberty," *The Hull Daily Mail/theneedleblog.wordpress.com*, May 28, 1988.

[2400] "Meet the Conservative Monday Club – Racist Roots and Extremism," *True Publica*, November 22, 2017.

[2401] "The Mary Moss Elm Guest House VIP Paedophile Party List," https://cigpapers.blog/2013/04/29/the-elm-guest-house-vip-paedophile-party-list/.

[2402] Jason Groves, "I'll Sue if anyone Links me to Untrue Paedophile Claims, says Tory Grandee Sir Peter Bottomley," *Daily Mail*, July 7, 2014.

[2403] Christopher Spivey, "Derek! Who the F*** is Derek?" *chrisspivey.org*, January 19, 2013.

[2404] "Big Brother's Tory is 'Friend of Camilla,'" *Daily Mail*, June 3, 2005.

[2405] Angus James, "Lord McAlpine and the Paedophile Ring," *Scallywag Magazine*, 1994.

[2406] "Monday Club," *scepticpeg.wordpress.com*, February 21, 2016.

professor, author and founding chairman of the Conservative Group for Homosexual Equality (CGHE) was glowingly written up as some kind of pioneering gay rights hero in an obit-*Telegraph* fluff piece,[2408] conveniently overlooking his pedophilic tendencies and criminal misbehavior. Also unmentionable was the fact his personally edited CGHE newsletter "strongly recommended" visits to the infamous Barnes boy brothel.[2409] Also omitted were the child porn videos graphically depicting boys being raped and tortured made and distributed at the very same Elm Guest House he patronized. *Exaro News* obtained a copy of Campbell's newsletter with a handwritten note scrawled by pedo-Prof Peter asking:

I have now inserted the entry about the hotel but can't find the text about the Dutch venture – could you please let me have another copy?[2410]

"The Dutch venture" refers to the frequent Amsterdam trips child sex traffickers like MI5's John Rowe was coordinating for members of the Monday Club like Peter Campbell, Harvey Proctor and the rest of the gay preying, London to Amsterdam "boy-lovers."

In the June 1982 raid of the Elm Guest House, Carole Kasir had her and Harry's 10-year old son Eric and daughter by a previous marriage taken away and placed in Richmond social services care homes, not exactly the safest places for youth. Two years before she died in 1990, Carole's psychiatrist referred her to two child protection officers, NAYPIC's Mary Moss and Chris Fay, for assistance trying to advocate getting her son back, strategically withheld in the UK Care System as a control mechanism to keep Carole quiet for the last eight years. The elite was growing nervous over how far Carole might go to "spilling the beans." In meetings with Carole, she'd haul out a thick cardboard box filled with her personal papers, legal documents, letters, receipts, her diary, plus near two dozen known photographs and guest lists pertaining to her Elm House and its VIP clientele, calling it her "life insurance."

Though Carole stubbornly refused to hand over any of the material, posted internet copies of handwritten notes jotted down by Mary and Chris include a list of alleged guest house attendees compiled during a series of meetings over many months with Carole Kasir prior to her "accidental" death. Eventually gaining Carole's trust, Mary Moss was given copies of some highly revealing pertinent documents. Towards the end, Chris finally was able to convince Carole to at least share photocopies of her VIP party pics. All the while, Special Branch had

[2407] "The Mary Moss Elm Guest House VIP Paedophile Party List," https://cigpapers.blog/2013/04/29/the-elm-guest-house-vip-paedophile-party-list/.

[2408] "Professor Peter Campbell," *The Telegraph*, June 15, 2005.

[2409] Kier Mudie and David Hencke, "Paedo Brothel Advertised in Tory Leaflet: Party's Gay Link to Guest House," *Mirror*, January 26, 2013, https://www.mirror.co.uk/news/uk-news/paedo-brothel-elm-guest-house-1558001.

[2410] Kier Mudie and David Hencke, https://www.mirror.co.uk/news/uk-news/paedo-brothel-elm-guest-house-1558001.

Chris, Mary and Carole under very close surveillance. But the day Chris Fay arranged to pick up the photos, Carole Kasir was suddenly found dead.

Testifying at Carole Kasir's inquest, Chris Fay and Mary Moss, a private investigator and host of other witnesses including Carole's longtime doctor all emphasized blatant anomalies surrounding her death, questioning the cabal-puppet coroner Dr. John Burton's official narrative - death by suicide. No doubt based on the coroner's sterling performance at this sham of a death inquiry, Queen Elizabeth promoted him to coroner of the Queen's Household[2411] so that 7 years later the murdering royals had a "safe pair of hands" to make certain the Princess Diana-Dodi Al-Fayed assassination could be written off as pure accident. Similarly, Jill Dando's fiancé Dr. Farthing a few years after she was out of the way gets promoted to the queen's doctor. Once you prove yourself a trusted member of the cabal's "inner pedo-club," you're suddenly promoted to the royal household or bestowed knighthood... a constant pattern.

A number of witnesses insisted that Carole Kasir's two alleged suicide notes were fake, clearly not in her own handwriting. Only her drug dealing, addicted hustler boyfriend David Issett signed off on her note as authentic. But that's all that was needed for the state's official bogus conclusion - suicide by insulin overdose.

This convenient false verdict defies a number of flagrant inconsistencies. The only syringe mark on Kasir's entire body found on her ass cheek was determined to be three days old, defying all laws of science to stay alive and then fatally overdose three days later. It's the same impossible absurdity as a "suicide" with two bullet holes in the head. Also those who knew her best insist that Carole always injected herself in her arm, never her butt. Because the cabal's hired "faithful hand" was running into vehement opposition from the inquest peanut gallery, he adjourned the inquest for two weeks per Chris Fay allegedly pending the outcome of ordered lab tests.

But without mentioning lab results steady hands reconvened, barring all contentious witnesses, sneaking through his blatant order-following verdict. By the time the inquest conclusion was announced, the UK press had once again been muzzled with a D-notice silencing the truth that Carole was yet another assassination victim for simply knowing too much (like so many before and after her), deemed too risky a threat of bringing down the pedo-cabal.[2412] Only Canadian and Japanese news broadcasters approached Chris Fay for an alternative POV to counter the state's official cover-up lie.

[2411] "How much does he earn? No 21: Dr. John Burton, Coroner for West London," *Independent*, March 13, 1994.
[2412] "Nightmares at Elm Guest House," Chris Fay interviewed by Bill Maloney, posted October 14, 2013, 1:05:16.

Shortly before Fernbridge was closed, the Met police told MP Tom Watson that all the Kasir inquest papers had been destroyed.[2413] Yet a year after the Elm Guest House investigation ended, it was learned the police claim of destroyed inquest documents proved [once again] false. It seems lots of misinformation about Carole Kasir's been fed into the propaganda machine, like she was never born in Germany under the name Weichman as had always been reported, but born Carole Linda Jones in West Riding, Yorkshire, England.[2414] "Destroyed" documents found in November 2017 indicate her own GP doctor for 14 years concluded she did not commit suicide. Nor did the toxicology report even bother checking for contents in her stomach or any of the syringes or vials placed at the crime scene.

This newfound evidence uncovered over a year ago had campaigners and even MP Andrew Brigden demanding a new inquest.[2415] Despite it looking even more obvious that Kasir was murdered, these new revelations failed to either reopen Fernbridge or impact the ongoing "official" independent inquiry in any discernable way, reinforcing the common knowledge that both police and government investigations into themselves and their criminal role in cover-up has never been about pursuit of any real truth or justice. The IICSA won't even touch the Elm House scandal, nor Northern Ireland's Kincora, both for the all too obvious reason that the pedo-cabal would be exposed wide open and come tumbling down.

In view of this latest development, a source close to the original aborted police investigation of Elm Guest House back in the early 1980s had this to say:

I don't think there's any doubt this place [Elm Guest House] *is at the centre of things.*[2416]

Immediately following Carole's 1990 murder, over the next three months, Chris and Mary attempted to set the public record straight, feeling certain Kasir's untimely fate was the result of foul play. As such, they along with other witnesses and even Elm House abuse victims were threatened and intimidated by Special Branch officers applying undue pressure to keep their mouths shut or else.[2417] And based on Carole's fate, it was perfectly clear what the "or else" meant. Fay recalls the horrific stress that the government henchmen - thugs that they are - put him and others through, no different from how the Mafia and Kosher Nostra operate:

[2413] David Hencke, "Exclusive: How newly found "Destroyed" Papers Revive the Mystery of the Notorious Gay and Paedophile Elm Guest House," *davidhencke.com*, November 12, 2017.

[2414] David Hencke, https://davidhencke.com/2017/11/12/exclusive-how-newly-found-destroyed-papers-revive-the-mystery-of-the-notorious-gay-and-paedophile-elm-guest-house/.

[2415] Keir Mudie and David Hencke, "Was Owner of Paedophile Palace who kept Secret List of VIP Visitors Murdered?" *Mirror*, November 11, 2017.

[2416] Keir Mudie and David Hencke, https://www.mirror.co.uk/news/uk-news/secret-files-prove-carole-kasir-11506791.

[2417] James Fielding, "'Police Gunman told me to Ignore Paedophiles,' says ex-Child Protection Officer, *Express*, October 20, 2013.

At one point they had me up against a wall by my throat with a gun at my head telling me in no uncertain terms that I was to back away if I knew what was good for me. A colleague of mine [Mary] had the same treatment, as did a number of the volunteers. Victims who were actually abused at Elm House were also physically stopped from coming to speak to us at the NAYPIC office in North London. I witnessed Special Branch officers manhandling them and turning them away with a warning to keep their mouths shut. It was blatant, it was open, they were acting like gangsters. In the end we had to meet victims at a local community centre without the knowledge of the police to hear what they had to say. NAYPIC was given the identities of senior politicians who formed part of an alleged paedophile ring at the heart of government. I was told by the police implicitly, 'We do not want you to come to us with big names.'[2418]

As an exclamation point for dramatic effect, three bullet holes were shot through Chris's kitchen window.[2419] In all, Chris Fay stated that he worked with and knew as many as 11 Grafton Close victims of VIP abuse at the Elm Guest House. The Scotland Yard reported that a dozen underage boys were on file after the raid accusing VIPs at the Elm Guest House of criminal abuse.[2420] Chris Fay's account witnessing the ruthless cover-up firsthand appears authentic. One can easily see why the criminal elite felt compelled to attack Chris Fay's credibility by attaining a 2011 fraud conviction to smear his name and reputation.[2421] Fay also maintains that according to Carole Kasir, the Elm Guest House raid on June 19, 1982 was carried out by a unit of spooks attached to Special Branch called Special Patrol Group, not the regular Metro police that had the premises under surveillance for several months prior to the raid. Shortly before the goon squad's assault on Elm, the Met investigation was abruptly shut down. In Chris Fay's words:

The police say it was done by a local force, but I know it was done by Special Branch.[2422]

In a highly informative interview filmed in September 2013, Chris Fay offers his take on the Elm Guest House scandal-cover-up with tenacious anti-child abuse advocate, onetime child abuse victim and Pie and Mash filmmaker Bill Maloney.[2423] Chris maintains that Carole was given a one day advance notice of the planned raid by a Sinn Fein leader that went by the name of Gary

---

[2418] James Fielding, https://www.express.co.uk/news/uk/437954/Police-gunman-told-me-to-ignore-paedophiles-says-ex-child-protection-officer.

[2419] James Hanning and Paul Cahalan, "Elm Guest House Investigation: Former Senior Cabinet Minister Faces Rape Investigation," *Independent/cigpapers.blog*, July 21, 2013.

[2420] James Hanning and Paul Cahalan, https://www.independent.co.uk/news/uk/crime/special-report-police-revisit-the-grim-mystery-of-elm-guest-house.

[2421] Robert Mendick, "'VIP Child Abuse Ring' Accuser Served time in Prison for Fraud," *The Telegraph*, September 26, 2015.

[2422] Stephen Wright and Richard Pendlebury, https://www.dailymail.co.uk/news/article-2272253/Timebomb-Elm-Guest-House-Pop-stars-bishop-politician-appear-list-seized-police-investigating-child-abuse-London-hotel-1980s.html#axzz2Jjhe2wpl.

[2423] "Nightmares at Elm Guest House," https://www.youtube.com/watch?v=ORU5x-ryedU.

Walker, who even offered fake passports if the Kasirs needed to urgently leave the country. In an April 2014 article the *Daily Mail* also mentions "figures from the National Front and Sinn Fein" were patrons at the Elm Guest House.[2424] It's also been reported that Sinn Fein President and MP Gerry Adams whose father and younger brother Liam, Gerry's onetime Sinn Fein underling, were both confirmed pedophiles.[2425] If a Sinn Fein leader partied at Elm, it very likely was Liam, convicted years later of raping his own daughter from age 4 to 11. His deteriorating marriage, his final years abusing his young daughter and separation from his ex-wife all coincided with the years he probably ended up at the Elm Guest House operation. MI5 at both Kincora and Elm Guest House took full advantage using underage boys as honey trap blackmail currency to control IRA leaders.[2426] This fact will be confirmed in detail in Chapter 28 covering the Kincora scandal.

If it's true, that key figure(s) from the Irish Republican Army in 1982 at the bloody height of the Northern Ireland-UK conflict were involved in the same sex orgies abusing boys at parties right alongside UK's Home Office Minister Leon Brittan as part of an MI5 sexual blackmail operation in South West London, with 60 Special Branch officers invading the boy brothel under the Terror Act of 1976, it has to be a cover-up of the highest priority, a top secret humdinger, forever destined by the pedo-elite to remain permanently buried deep in illusory ashes of the dustbin graveyard of all cover-up graveyards. But the truth has a resilient way of resurrecting itself to bite the criminal deceivers and life destroyers right between their sinful loins, regardless of cabal efforts to squirm, dodge, suppress and escape both public exposure and its unpaid massive, soul-killing karmic debt.

In December 2013 a police insider working the case back in 1982 made this poignant observation:

The real unlawful activity was underage sex. The police should have been able to make the other charges stick, but the boys were only ever interviewed with a view to them being witnesses against Carole, not as kids who were abused themselves.[2427]

In other words, law enforcement never had any intention of going after the VIP pedophiles, only using the child victims as witnesses to hang a minimal "dirty house" conviction on Carole and Harry Kasir while grabbing her kids to keep the Kasirs from outing the diabolical operation that would've brought down the entire British Establishment.

[2424] Richard Pendlebury and Stephen Wright, "Was this Woman Murdered to Cover up Cyril Smith's Sex Ring? After a week of Devastating Revelations, this may be the most Devastating Question yet," Daily Mail, April 18, 2014.
[2425] "False Memory Syndrome," *Broadsheet*, October 31, 2014.
[2426] "Gerry Adams, IRA, MI6, Sex," *aangirfan.blogspot.com*, January 1, 2018.
[2427] James Hanning and Paul Cahalan, https://www.independent.co.uk/news/uk/crime/special-report-police-revisit-the-grim-mystery-of-elm-guest-house.

Interesting to note that the media never covered the raid until 50 days after the fact. But once the 50 days had passed since the Special Branch busted the Elm Guest House, from August 7-17, 1982 virtually every national newspaper in the UK covered the Elm House scandal daily. Yet after the 17th, with the exception of only the local gay pro-pedo paper the *Capital Gay* running a story on the Kasir trial outcome in 1983 and limited coverage of Carole Kasir's "accidental" 1990 death, no press dared touch the Elm Guest House for the next 30 years until autumn 2012. For years the nation's most disturbing, biggest sex scandal in British history, cutting straight into and through the heart of the government, has been effectively silenced by a massive media blackout in order to propagate the nation's biggest, unending, top-down cover-up of all time. The media's been complicit in this criminal operation as well.

Though the Elm House scandal from 1982 to 2012 was kept virtually secret from the public, in 2014 it was learned that in November 2002 Tony Blair's Home Secretary David Blunkett received a letter from a whistleblowing trade union official specifying that Elm House was used as a boy brothel by VIP politicians in the early 1980s.[2428] Of course in 2002 the Blair government was busy with its own pedophile scandals to cover-up - between Lords Janner, Boatteng and Mandelson. To Blunkett's credit, he did write back saying he was referring the matter to his own Home Office which three weeks later replied that it was turning the matter over to the Deputy Prime Minister John Prescott's office, which in turn urged the whistleblower to communicate his complaints to Richmond's Local Government Ombudsman, which in turn directed him to take the matter up with the police. And of course as always, the police did nothing.

So there you have it. See how impossible it is in the UK to get any real results reporting child abuse - past or present? As is typical of bureaucracy, child abuse and cover-ups, everyone gives you the runaround and in the end, no one takes responsibility and nothing ever gets done. What's more is that child abuse scandals and their political perps have always been open secrets. No doubt many of the 650 members of Parliament know exactly who the child sodomizers among them are, just like the US Congress. Remember the party whips' little black books? It's all used as a control mechanism. All of this only goes to show that most politicians just don't give a shit if poor kids in their own country (much less another) are being used and abused, tortured and killed. The facts speak for themselves.

To come full circle, the primary source of the Westminster VIP victims at the Elm Guest House came from Grafton Close Care Home that the Richmond authorities saw fit to close the same year the state decided to close out Carole Kasir's life. Both buildings at the center of this scandal - Grafton and Elm - were quickly converted to private flats as if - out of sight, out of

---

[2428] James Fielding, "Labour was told in 2002 about Child Sex Scandal," *Express*, November 23, 2014.

mind - the horror story from the early 1980s never really happened. If walls could talk, living in either home would be hard not to listen... as disturbing as the messages would be.

The *Daily Express* first broke the Elm Guest House story on August 7, 1982 with the headline "Security Alert over New Vice Scandal." The article references a police investigation uncovering the involvement of:

At least three MPs, a member of staff at Buckingham Palace, and leading lawyers, doctors and City businessmen have been questioned during inquiries.[2429]

The *Express* stated that undercover police had identified 30 prominent men caught up in illegal vice activities and that security services were concerned with:

Fears that some of the men involved might have been subjected to blackmail.[2430]

Bingo! That's the whole name of the game and reason why MI5 set up the Elm House operation to begin with. *Capital Gay* magazine ran an article stating that the Scotland Yard was vehemently, predictably disputing the security "fears," denying that VIPs were involved at all.[2431] While lawyers representing the Kasirs were threatening libel suits, Attorney General Sir Michael Havers receptively pledged that he would look into potential violations by the "sensational" press. Worried about lawsuits, all media coverage suddenly plunged to zero after the 17th of August. Obviously, the brothel owners, the police, security services and VIP pedophiles in government, churches, high courts and entertainment all collectively have a vested interest in covering up their criminality. From the very beginning decades ago to the present, nothing has changed.

The pedophilia establishment in Britain is the only candidate possessing both unlimited means and by far the most motivation for such an extensive, unprecedented cover-up. On the other hand, with all the flack and grief heaped upon the accusers, they have the least to show or gain from honestly and bravely coming forth to report their traumas to the authorities. Other than one victim-complainant secretly receiving an undisclosed compensation as an obvious hush money payoff from Richmond council, there's been no record of any other Elm Guest House abuse victim who has ever gained financially.[2432] So with the detective's proverbial "means and motive" test, the only clear winner in the Elm Guest House debacle are the VIP pigs who've

---

[2429] Don Coolican, "Security Alert over new vice Scandal," *Daly Express/spotlightonabuse.wordpress.com*, August 7, 1982.

[2430] Don Coolican, https://spotlightonabuse.files.wordpress.com/2013/02/dexp_1982_08_07_001security_1detail3.jpg.

[2431] "Attorney General to Probe London Brothel Reports," *Capital Gay/spotlightonabuswordpress.com*, August 1982.

[2432] David Hencke, "Did Richmond Council Pay 'Hush Money' to Cover up the Elm Guest House Child Abuse Scandal?" *davidhencke.com*, February 4, 2013.

gotten away with raping and sodomizing scores of innocent young boys. No one else has anything to gain from their respective involvement at Elm or Grafton, least of all those who maintain that abuse occurred.

The August 1982 media also reported that the police inquiry had begun three months earlier in May although based on firsthand neighborhood accounts, police surveillance began long before a month prior to the June raid. The last line in the *Express* alludes to all the evidence and statements being compiled would soon be sent to their go-to DPP cover-upper Sir Thomas Hetherington, who as alluded earlier was another queen knighted gatekeeper protecting the pedo-queendom from 1976 to 1987, systematically covering up evidence of abuse while refusing to prosecute notorious VIP child rapists like Cyril Smith, Jimmy Savile and Leon Brittan.

The breaking *Express* article also compared the Elm Guest House debauchery to the 1889 boy brothel scandal located at 19 Cleveland Street in West London, where homosexual princes, earls and dukes from the aristocratic class were busted paying for sex with teenage messenger boys from the Royal Post Office.[2433] But the criminals from the privileged class all escaped prosecution, never spending one day in jail while the sexually exploited underage rent boys were each given 4-9 months hard labor sentences.[2434] Even the journalist who uncovered the truth exposing the elite's guilty sodomizers was sued, convicted of libel and sentenced to a year of hard prison labor. Clearly the Cleveland scandal set the precedent for what was to come, establishing the British historic tradition of protecting criminal sickos from the royal family and elitist class at the expense of punishing their underage victims and truth tellers a full century in advance of the Elm House Westminster scandal. In traditional Britain, some things never change.

Time for another "lost" dossier tale. In 1984 the pedo-establishment encountered another incriminating file that fell into the lap of respected *Bury Messenger* newspaper editor Don Hale.[2435] As if being responsible for losing/destroying MP Geoffrey Dickens' as well as Scotland Yard's dossiers doesn't make Leon Brittan guilty enough of massive criminal cover-up, the pedophile Home Office Secretary successfully eliminated a third dossier containing compelling evidence that Labor peer and former cabinet secretary Barbara Castle handed over to Don Hale as well. When she brought Don the explosive documents, she explained that he was not her first choice as editor of the relatively small newspaper. But since it was her local paper and she trusted Don, in his recollected words:

[2433] Colin Simpson, Lewis Chester and David Leitch, *The Cleveland Street Affair* (London: Little, Brown) 1976, *bookfinder.com*.

[2434] "The Cleveland Street Scandal," *clevelandstreetscandal.com*.

[2435] Nico Hines, "How Thatcher's Government Covered up a VIP Pedophile Ring," *Daily Beast*, June 3, 2015.

She was saying, 'I've been everywhere else, I've been to the nationals, nobody would touch it with a barge pole, but what do you think?' As a journalist of course I was interested. Barbara never said he [Brittan] was a pedophile, she was just very, very hostile about him. 'He's the last person you want this to go to,' she said, which inferred that he was somehow involved.[2436]

In his 2015 *Daily Beast* interview, the longtime, highly respected editor unveiled his sad yet unsurprising story of how Special Branch detectives forcibly removed yet more incriminating files from Hale's office that again outed a number of VIP pedophiles operating at the heart of the British government. Don Hale had perused through the dossier just long enough to realize that Sir Leon was more than aware of the Westminster pedophile ring:

[Brittan] *was mentioned in everything you picked up, his fingerprints were over everything, he was the instigator.*[2437]

Don Hale's first angry visitor arrived the next morning, all 400+ pounds of the Parliament icon Cyril Smith barged into Hale's office less than 24 hours after Barbara Castle had dropped off her potentially damaging bombshell. News through the pedo-secret service grapevine travels faster than the speed of British history's fattest politician, but not by much. The editor described how Sir Cyril Smith charged at him screaming:

He was frothing at the mouth and really shouting and spitting in my face. He was straight at me like a raging lion; he was ready to knock me through the wall. He said to me quite clearly, 'I know who's given you this, it's Barbara Castle.' I wouldn't say who it was, but it was pretty obvious he knew. He's a hell of a sized guy, he's over six feet tall and he's huge; took up three seats. He's not a guy you could deal with easily, he was a horror.[2438]

Though Don Hale valiantly defied the big man's threats and demands, refusing to hand over the papers, the following morning three vehicles pulled up and a belligerent squad of 15 Special Branch officers burst into the newspaper offices with both a search warrant and D-notice. Two of them pushed Don up against the wall similar to Chris Fay's Special Branch episode in order to retrieve what Cyril couldn't the day before. The government thugs insisted that the files were stolen property belonging to Home Office and they promised to arrest Hale should he breathe a word. Again, in his own long-awaited words:

[2436] Nico Hines, https://www.thedailybeast.com/how-thatchers-government-covered-up-a-vip-pedophile-ring?source=DDMorning&via=newsletter.
[2437] Tomas Hirst, "Leon Brittan and the Westminster Child Abuse Scandal: 'His Fingerprints were over everything,'" *Business Insider*, March 6, 2015.
[2438] Nico Hines, https://www.thedailybeast.com/how-thatchers-government-covered-up-a-vip-pedophile-ring?source=DDMorning&via=newsletter.

These bully boys come storming in, they said, 'We're not here to negotiate. Hand them over or we'll arrest you now.' I couldn't argue, because as soon as you opened the files it had got 'Not to be removed', 'Confidential' and 'For your eyes only'—all these sort of things on them. I wouldn't have had a hope in hell legally. I would have ended up in prison and the story would have gone nowhere.[2439]

More than three decades later, after Metro Police Service found abuse survivors' allegations of systematic torture and sexual assault fully credible, Don Hale finally could lift the lid on what he was privy to, confirming not only that top level politicians, high ranking police officers, spies, judges, members of the royal palace household and entertainers were child raping criminals but that a major cover-up of the first order has remained tightly in place ever since.

Don Hale maintains that the 1984 dossier that Barbara Castle gave him was comprised of detailed Home Office files that definitively prove that Brittan as head of the internal pedo-investigation took what one might say an extremely active, self-serving role throughout the process, the exact opposite of his later initial denial and then vague, nondescript public accounting of any dossier placed in his possession:

He really had his finger on the pulse, he wanted to know everything about it; all the documents were cc'd back to Leon Brittan or it was an instruction directly from Leon Brittan.[2440]

Don Hale asserts that the dossier exposed 16 MPs from both the House of Commons and Lords and about 30 high ranking notables from the Church of England, private schools and major corporations as all being active PIE members.[2441] With the ridiculously strict UK libel laws, Hale knew he could not publicly out these pedophiles but planned to report that the Home Office was in the process of investigating these individuals which would have placed Brittan's office on notice that the public awaits his results.

MI5 and MI6 always relied on the Metro's now defunct Special Branch to carry out "undercover" dirty work in order to maintain their plausible deniability M.O. in keeping a safe public distance from revealing what really goes on at the seedy underbelly of power.[2442] The June 19, 1982 "police" raid on MI5's Elm Guest House blackmail operation was no different. A media blackout went into immediate effect at the time of the raid lasting nearly two months,

---

[2439] Nico Hines, https://www.thedailybeast.com/how-thatchers-government-covered-up-a-vip-pedophile-ring?source=DDMorning&via=newsletter.

[2440] Nico Hines, https://www.thedailybeast.com/how-thatchers-government-covered-up-a-vip-pedophile-ring?source=DDMorning&via=newsletter.

[2441] Nico Hines, https://www.thedailybeast.com/how-thatchers-government-covered-up-a-vip-pedophile-ring?source=DDMorning&via=newsletter.

[2442] David Rose, "Spies and their Lies," *New Statesman*, September 27, 2007.

undoubtedly so authorities could destroy as much confiscated evidence as possible, lining up all their ducks in a row for the media to downplay both Elm's importance and police findings.

Contrary to the major media coverage that began on August 7, 1982 and spanned the next 10 days, the purpose of the raid conveniently fell under "national security" auspices via the Prevention of Terrorism Act of 1976, having zero to do with it being a vice raid or rescuing child victims or prevention of further harm to children. As such, the raid was intentionally timed to net a minimal number of criminals as no boys from Grafton Close Home were even present in the house despite it being a Saturday night when normally the sex parties would be in full swing. The Special Patrol Group, the unit within Special Branch, carried out the raid that automatically carried a gag order prohibiting press coverage. Bottom line, the raid was never meant to protect children but simply to protect liability of VIP pedo-criminals from any and all accountability. Too many incriminating photos and video evidence were still at-large and in full damage control mode, the controllers desperately moved in to cap any further risk of leaked exposure to the public, confiscating on site lots of compromising photographs, guest lists, whips, chains, ropes and stockpiles of child pornographic material in obscene photos as well as videos.

When Elm Guest House was ransacked by the 60-men strong raiding party with flashing lights in the night, it created quite the public stir and spectacle for residents on and near the Barnes Common.[2443] Novelist Jilly Cooper who was a frequent dog walker on the Barnes Common described the night of the house raid in one of her books:

We then had lots more lurid details about vicars and MPs caught 'in flagrante,' running out of the brothel into the night in their underpants.[2444]

During its early 1980s heyday, neighbors of the Elm Guest House were painfully aware of the sex orgies and strange happenings associated with that notorious guest house. It was common knowledge Elm was a house of sodomizing ill repute. A teenage girl told her mother that while passing by the place one night, she observed through open curtained windows a bunch of naked men cavorting about inside.[2445] The neighborhood was also aware of the unmarked police van with the cameras carrying out surveillance. Another neighbor pointed out that the police presence was all too obvious:

[2443] Murun Buchstanslagur, "Keith Vaz and the Mystery of Barnes Common," *spotlightonabuse.wordpress.com*, February 15, 2015.

[2444] David Pallister, "Locals spoke of 'the Activities' at Guest House n Police Probe," *Exaro News*, December 15, 2015.

[2445] Stephen Wright, https://www.dailymail.co.uk/news/article-2272253/Timebomb-Elm-Guest-House-Pop-stars-bishop-politician-appear-list-seized-police-investigating-child-abuse-London-hotel-1980s.html#axzz2Jjhe2wpl.

They were there all the time. Police hiding behind the trees to look at the property was a running joke with the neighbours.[2446]

The Barnes brothel was drawing increasing unwanted attention leading to growing tensions within the community from worried neighbors who knew that children were being abused inside the three story dwelling at 27 Rocks Lane by the men in all the fancy cars constantly seen coming and going.[2447] As an open secret that young boys were routinely brought in to be sexually abused by older well-dressed men, numerous complaints were lodged with local representatives at Richmond council but seemingly to no avail. After many weeks of neither lifting a finger to stop the rampant pedophilia crimes nor respond to the community's mounting concerns, local authorities were coming under increasing pressure to intervene, ultimately forcing Special Branch's hand to execute its raid.

Bottom line, MI5's sleaze racket of sexual blackmail operations had become such a public nuisance in Barnes as potentially explosive liability risking VIP exposure, if it got out publicly, it would've undoubtedly brought down the Thatcher government. MI5 and Special Branch were frantically pressed into action. The Elm Guest House was raided with the intent of securing as much incriminating evidence as possible, tying up loose ends that otherwise threatened to destroy the British Establishment.

At the time future prominent Labor MP Keith Vaz happened to be the Richmond council solicitor running for Parliament in that same Richmond and Barnes district. Years later when asked on Twitter if he'd heard anything about the Elm Guest House affair, he succinctly answered "no." Yet just days after the infamous raid and over a month prior to the national publicity onslaught, Keith Vaz was quoted in the local *Richmond & Barnes Times* reacting to the community's growing fears for the safety of its women and children:

The police have to show a real presence on the common. It may be that they are opposed to vigilante groups but it is not unnatural for people who feared for their safety to protect themselves to do so. It is a terrible indictment on the authorities that people may have to do so.[2448]

Doesn't it seem a bit odd that the Richmond MP candidate would be so on top of the dangers and urgent need for greater police protection for his neighborhood constituents, to the extent that he was publicly promoting vigilantism, yet remains completely oblivious to the horrific

---

[2446] James Hanning and Paul Cahalan, https://www.independent.co.uk/news/uk/crime/special-report-police-revisit-the-grim-mystery-of-elm-guest-house.

[2447] David Hencke, David Pallister and Fiona O'Cleirigh, https://www.exaronews.com/police-twice-failed-to-probe-paedophile-ring-at-guest-house.

[2448] "Round the Clock Common Patrol," *Richmond & Barnes Times*, July 1982.

crimes being committed against children just days after the "big bust" that was the then talk of the town, not to mention the coming national media hype weeks later?

This is the same man who less than a decade later in 1991 publicly defended his mentor and longtime pedophile Lord Greville Janner, claiming on the Commons floor that Janner was "the victim of a cowardly and wicked attack" while near two dozen of his victims had provided sufficient evidence for Leicestershire police to prosecute,[2449] especially after Janner's feeble "no comment" response to police questioning.[2450] Clearly Vaz helped "convince" police and CPS to drop the case against his child abusing friend. And then in 2016, Vaz the hypocrite was caught red-handed embroiled in a rent boy sex scandal of his own,[2451] exposed for desperately trying to bribe his two rent boys on a promise he'd "fly them around the world."[2452] Hypocrisy is Keith Vaz's middle name. While ruling over committee legislation on Class A drugs and vice prostitution, from his near .5£m "sex shack" a mere half mile from his over 2£m family home, the married father of two was busily calling his rent boys to make sure their upcoming rendezvous included plenty of cocaine and poppers for his next adulterous, paid for sodomy services.[2453]

On top of that bombshell, according to a commenter on the *aangirfan* website, after Vaz was elected as Leicester East MP in 1987, hired movers transporting his personal belongings to London found under his mattress a copy of Spartacus Magazine, Iron Boy and other homosexual pedophile child pornography.[2454]

Meanwhile under a longstanding House of Commons ethical standards probe over his rent boy romp, Keith Vaz has used the exact same evasive and "cowardly" tactic as his pedophile mentor when Janner avoided prosecution for decades of serial child sex abuse claiming the last couple years of his life that he was too ill from dementia, all the while actively participating in the House of Lords right up to his decrepit end.[2455] And just like his derelict Jewish buddy from Leicester West, the longest running Asian MP from Leicester East has maintained he also is "too

[2449] Jay Rayner, "Keith Vaz helped Kill a 90s Probe into the Greville Janner Claims: Why is he Silent now?" *The Observer/The Guardian*, April 25, 2015.

[2450] Sean O'Neil, "Police Missed Chances to Question Janner," *The Times*, April 27, 2015.

[2451] Abe Hawken, "Keith Vaz Quits after being Caught up in Rent-Boy Scandal... but Suggests he was Drugged during the Encounter with Eastern European Prostitutes," *Daily Mail*, September 4, 2016.

[2452] Nick Dorman and Dan Warburton, "Keith Vaz Branded a 'Liar' by Male Escorts as they Reveal Shamed MP Offered to Fly them around the World," *Mirror*, September 10, 2016.

[2453] Nick Dorman, "Married MP Keith Vaz tells Prostitutes in his Flat: 'Bring Poppers... we need to get this Party started," *Mirror*, September 4, 2016.

[2454] "Mysterious Keith Vaz," *aangirfan.blogspot.com*, September 11, 2016.

[2455] Martin Robinson, "Why is Labour Peer Lord Janner not being Prosecuted because he has Dementia? At least 19 Defendants Suffering with the Disease have been Convicted for Sex Crimes... and ten were in the past year," *Daily Mail*, April 20, 2015.

ill" to answer for his ethical standards violations while photographed with big smiles regularly attending party functions around the globe.[2456]

As of February 2018 the corrupt politician nicknamed "Vaz-eline" may be facing yet a new police probe having to answer an Unexplained Wealth Order, amassing more than a £4m property empire that allegedly includes 8 homes in UK alone with more in India on a less than £75,000 annual MP salary.[2457]

While chairman of the powerful Home Affairs select committee for a decade and a half, his committee's website posted online the full names of four abuse victims testifying before the IICSA, breaking the law by grossly violating their confidentiality, resulting in their death threats from abusers.[2458] As the 15-year gatekeeping leader of the parliamentary committee that holds sway over police investigations into child sex abuse, this ultra-friendly pedo-protector no doubt has the dirty lowdown on the entire British VIP pedo-establishment. For that reason alone, his nonstop scandals never seem to stick to this Vaz-eline greased Teflon man. To this very day the disgraced pervert has managed to retain his permanent Leicester seat in Parliament, currently serving on the "Justice" Committee while living his life of luxury as an "untouchable."[2459] Sound eerily familiar to the Cyril Smith saga?

Recall how UK's pedophile Prime Minister Ted Heath's chief whip - Tim Fortescue - admitted in a 1995 interview that party leaders in the British government regularly bail out fellow MPs with pedophilia problems by using their cover-up protection as blackmail leverage to manipulate and control pedo-politicians to vote their way forevermore. Scum at the top of all major Western governments use their inside knowledge of their peers' pathological crimes as a form of insurance protection vis-a-vis former Congressman Anthony Weiner's laptop file he titled under his "life insurance."[2460] In other words, the child raping insiders are well aware of each other's deviant criminality and as long as their dirty secrets stay safe with them, all remain mutually protected in their own demonic VIP sicko club way.

In the case of MP Keith Vaz, if all his corrupt, perverse scandals ultimately result in his peers demanding his resignation, because his reign of power as longtime Home Affairs chairman afforded him full access gathering the dirt on virtually all the VIP establishment's illicit bad

---

[2456] Claire Duffin and Daniel Martin, "Labour Veteran Keith Vaz says he's too Ill to be Investigated over Party with Male Escorts...but is fit enough to Travel the World and Cut Ribbons," *Daly Mail*, February 9, 2018.
[2457] Tim Skulthorpe, "Labour Grandee Keith Vaz Faces new Probe into his Property 'Empire' after Tory MP writes to the Police," *Daily Mail*, February 18, 2018.
[2458] "British Sex Abuse Victims get Death Threats," *Press TV*, January 30, 2015.
[2459] Richard Wheeler, "MPs back Keith Vaz Appointment to Justice Select Committee," *Independent*, November 1, 2016.
[2460] Joachim Hagopian, "Breaking Sex Scandal from Weiner's Laptop may be the Smoking Gun that will bring down the Clintons for good," *sott.net*, November 4, 2016.

habits, parliamentary members with much to hide know that Vaz would not hesitate to throw them all under the bus exposing their illegal embarrassing secrets as well. So in effect, Keith Vaz is able to hold on to his permanent "safe" seat in Westminster because it would be suicidal for any of his fellow perverts to try and eject him… exactly the same identical dynamic that kept Sir Cyril Smith securely in power throughout his 82 years on earth.

In April 2014 more sleaze in UK's other major party was revealed when a high ranking Conservative source admitted that all the dirt on MPs (primarily pedophilia), meticulously recorded by party whips in their infamous "black books" up till 2010 were destroyed for fear that the public would find out how criminally sick their leaders are through Freedom of Information requests.[2461] So in this era of social media, to prevent leaks and bread crumb trails of incriminating evidence, in the current decade the sleaze is all handled strictly through verbal communication only.

In 2014 amidst the ongoing police investigations of Operations Fernbridge and Midland delving into the political elite's historic child abuse, fresh new revelations have erupted. Tory MP Mark Menzies was busted for rent boy sex with an underage Brazilian and David Cameron's government was under fire. Amongst MPs and lords, a rising wave of drunken sexual passes, sexual harassment and sexual assaults were being perpetrated against underage staffers, party aides and researchers. Plus sex orgies at tax paid expense uncovered at annual party conference hotels were the latest scandals rocking Westminster.[2462] One young victim disclosed how pathologically entitled those in power are:

A lot of MPs think they have almost got a right to try it on with junior staff, male or female. They are almost affronted if the staff don't go along with it.[2463]

All this filth in recent years only demonstrates that child abuse never ceased after the 1970s and 80s but only continues to this day among the degenerate VIPs atop the British government.

This diabolical political system doesn't just protect high level criminals from all accountability, it also rewards them. A classic illustration is Sir Peter Morrison, the Tory MP from Chester (1974-1992) and Thatcher's Parliamentary Private Secretary (PPC). The homosexual pedophile was repeatedly caught sexually abusing boys but merely cautioned with police warnings. Morrison was implicated in the North Wales scandal as well as at both Dolphin Square and Elm Guest House. Despite Thatcher's bodyguard Barry Strevens warning her Morrison and so many of her top lieutenants were pedophiles, in 1990 she made Sir Peter her campaign manager anyway.

[2461] Ben Glaze, "Tories 'Black Book of Sleaze' and how they Destroyed all Evidence of MPs' Wrongdoing," *Mirror*, April 13, 2014.

[2462] James Lyons, "David Cameron Prepares himself for Damaging Allegations of Tory Sexual Harassment and Sleaze," *Mirror*, April 11, 2014.

[2463] James Lyons, https://www.mirror.co.uk/news/uk-news/david-cameron-prepares-himself-damaging-3402667.

The serial child predator was protected right up to his 1995 fatal heart attack and then even further protected three years later when in 1998 his public toilet cottaging with young boys was covered up.[2464] That year an editor and a reporter from the *Mirror* were onto Morrison but tried in vain to acquire a copy of the child rapist's arrest record as law enforcement ensured it was blocked. It took until 2002, 7 years after his death, before Sir Peter was finally exposed publicly as yet another monster atop London's pedo-paradise government and not till 2012 as a North Wales pedo-ring abuser.[2465]

Where you have the queen, the prime minister and law enforcement actively going out of their way to both shield and reward deranged VIPs recklessly living out their sick perversions above the law till death do them part, you have Great Britain, the pedophilia epicenter of the world.

Former Thatcher health minister and pedo-gatekeeper MP Edwina Currie made a July 24, 1990 entry in her diary, yet waited 22 years later before making it public, saving her juicy tidbit quote below to boost her book sales:

Peter Morrison has become the PM's PPS. Now he's what they call 'a noted pederast',' with a liking for young boys; he admitted as much to Norman Tebbitt when he became deputy chairman of the party, but added, 'However, I'm very discreet' – and he must be![2466]

It takes one to know one. Jewish pedo-princess Edwina who carried on a four year adulterous affair with PM John Major in the 1990s not only signed off on handing the Broadmoor keys over to lunatic predator Savile to take over the asylum, but as of January 2014 Currie herself stands accused of child sexual abuse by then 45-year old Andrew Ash. Ferried down from his care home in Northern England to London's VIP sex parties, Andrew told the *Express* that a drunken female MP (later implicated to be Currie[2467]) was laughing while goaded by peers into sexually assaulting him when he was 13 at one of their many pedo-orgies.[2468] Currie's matter-of-fact admission that Morrison's habit of raping teenage boys was an open secret speaks volumes, but even more so does Andrew Ash's bombshell. In all likelihood, Sir Peter Morrison was made Thatcher's PPS **because** he was an easily controlled blackmail-able sexual deviant.[2469] Promoting and knighting an incompetent alcoholic frequently observed sleeping at his desk guarantees loyalty to both his party and his crime cabal for protecting his flagrant illicit activities. And with Ash's revelations, the same can be said for Madame Currie as well.

[2464] James Lyons, "Norman Tebbit admits he heard Rumours top Tory was Paedophile a decade before Truth Revealed," *Mirror*, July 8, 2014.

[2465] James Lyons, https://www.mirror.co.uk/news/uk-news/norman-tebbit-admits-heard-rumours-3826206.

[2466] James Lyons, https://www.mirror.co.uk/news/uk-news/norman-tebbit-admits-heard-rumours-3826206.

[2467] "Friends of Israel," *aangirfan.blogspot.com*, September 5, 2018.

[2468] James Fielding, "Female MP Abused Boy in Care," *Express*, January 12, 2014.

[2469] Murun Buchstansangur, "The Dirt Book: How Sexual Abuse of Children is used for Political Gain, *spotlghtonabuse.wordpress.com*, May 11, 2013.

Abuse survivor Andrew Ash also maintains he was trafficked to Amsterdam on a number of occasions where he claims the infamous murderous gang leader Sidney Cooke forced him to film another boy being raped by a pedophile.[2470] Like fellow child murderer-rapist-pimping procurer Warwick Spinks, Cooke is also believed to have made snuff films in Holland. Having lived through so much horrific trauma, Andrew grew increasingly frustrated after providing 70 hours divulging highly incriminating allegations to Metro's Paedophile Unit. Knowing that the police were in possession of a video with Andrew in the same frame as a senior male MP that abused him, yet never seeing any action taken by law enforcement to hold the VIP criminals accountable, the brave survivor decided to go public with his story in January 2014, stating:

All I want is justice and for the truth to come out because these people have been protected for far too long.[2471]

A high profile pedophile mentioned in the last chapter, the murderous snuff filmmaker-distributor Warwick Spinks has been allowed to escape justice too many times for him not to be considered also "protected" by the pedo-elite. After kidnapping a 14-year old boy in Sussex in the early 1990s, then drugging, abusing and pimping him in Amsterdam, he sold the victim to a Dutch brothel.[2472] Spinks was also secretly caught on tape peddling a video featuring a 10-year old boy who was tortured and killed on camera. Finally in 1995 the monster was tried, convicted and began a 7-year sentence that on appeal was reduced to five, and while released in 1997 on license after only two years, he fled right back to Europe to resume his lucrative sex slave trade operation. Spinks' criminal ties to Amsterdam and beyond involve not only the making of deadly pornographic films with underage boys but also child trafficking to Holland and numerous other cities in Germany, Poland and the Czech Republic.

Described as "one of Britain's most dangerous pedophiles" and called the "Pied Piper of Pedophiles," finally after 15 years as a fugitive in Europe, he was captured in Prague and extradited back to UK in November 2012. But incredibly, he was freed from prison again on a loophole after only four months. As of March 2013, Spinks was once again free to resume his predatory sick life back in Prague, thumbing his nose at a complicit, impotent British justice system. With his long gruesome criminal history committing the most egregious offenses imaginable, for him to have seemingly gotten away with it, it's all too obvious that this widely alleged sadistic rapist-killer has to be protected by the pedo-elite.

Warwick Spinks is the most infamous of hundreds of English child sodomizers on the run over the last several decades, escaping to pedo-friendly Holland with its laxly enforced child sex

---

[2470] James Fielding, https://www.express.co.uk/news/uk/453381/Female-MP-abused-boy-in-care.
[2471] James Fielding, https://www.express.co.uk/news/uk/453381/Female-MP-abused-boy-in-care.
[2472] Brian Flynn, "'Most Violent Paedo' Freed on Loophole… and back Ogling Teens," *The Sun*, August 3, 2013.

trafficking laws.[2473] Spinks and scores like him from Britain have been instrumental in Amsterdam's booming international pedo-sex tourism-child porn snuff film industry.[2474] With Dutch law enforcement claiming insufficient evidence to prosecute swarms of British pedo-expats like Spinks, and UK law enforcement maintaining both lack of resources to investigate and jurisdiction to intervene, the conveniently created safe haven city of Amsterdam not only attracts child traffickers, child rapists and child pornographers from all over the world, but also the VIP predator network from the UK, EU and Europe as a go-to safe zone stopover.[2475]

The Sun reported in December 2014 that while Spinks was supplying young boys to a Parliament member traveling to Amsterdam, the same MP became involved in the murder of a boy filmed in a snuff movie at the Blue Boy vice club.[2476] Less than a week after the article was published, Spinks actually registered a formal complaint against the *Sun* contending it violated four accuracy and ethics clauses but the Independent Press Standards Association ruled in favor of Rupert Murdoch's newspaper that no breaches occurred.[2477]

A source for the police investigating Spinks in the 1990s stated:

Officers were told Spinks knew the MP and arranged a tour to Amsterdam. While there he went to the Blue Boy bar, where Spinks was running a brothel. The MP was said to have been present when a boy died during an orgy which was being filmed.[2478]

This more than explains why Spinks has repeatedly been brazenly let off the hook, because like fellow murderer-trafficker Cooke, Spinks also provided rent boy services to Westminster VIP pervs, with at least one MP allegedly an accomplice in one of his snuff films.

Respected veteran journalist Nick Davies wrote an eye-opening exposé for *The Guardian* on this very topic of British pedophiles setting up shop in Holland:

After speaking to paedophiles and their victims and to police and social workers in Britain, Holland and Germany, we have uncovered the inner workings of an international paedophile ring. Its roots spring from Amsterdam, where, in the late 1980s, a group of exiled British paedophiles set up a colony. Taking advantage of Dutch tolerance towards sexual behaviour, they exploited the freedom of the gay community in the city as cover to enact their fantasies and to make money from them.[2479]

[2473] Janene Pieters, "Netherlands Criticized for Lenient Child Sex Trafficking Policy," *NL Times*, November 23, 2015.
[2474] "Revisited: UK-Amsterdam Paedophile Snuff Movie Connection," *21st Century Wire*, July 12, 2014.
[2475] "Warwick Spinks and Violent Sex Rings," *aangirfan.blogspot.com*, November 17, 2012.
[2476] Mike Sullivan and Tom Morgan, "MP 'was at Snuff Film Lad's Murder,'" *The Sun*, December 6, 2014.
[2477] "02292-14 Spinks v The Sun," *ipso.co.uk*, April 28, 2015.
[2478] Mike Sullivan and Tom Morgan, https://www.thesun.co.uk/archives/news/580588/mp-was-at-snuff-film-lads-murder/
[2479] Nick Davies, "When Sex Abuse can lead to Murder," *The Guardian*, November 26, 2000.

Since Davies described conditions up to when he wrote his article in 2000, the same year the Dutch brothel industry was made legal, the situation in Amsterdam apparently has only grown significantly worse. As of 2018 most legal prostitution zones in the Netherlands have been closed and over a third of all window brothels are reportedly out of business including Amsterdam's famous red light district. A proposed law if passed by the Dutch Senate would make it a crime to pay for sex with pimped, trafficked, or otherwise coerced prostitutes. Since 2000, rather than reduce human trafficking as expected, legalizing the sex trade has only opened up a floodgate in the illegal, unlicensed sex industry,[2480] especially pimping trafficked underage boys and girls, creating a vast black market for the London-Amsterdam pedo-connection, extending the global network in all four directions. As a result, an abolitionist movement toward the sex trade appears to currently be underway in the Netherlands.

For the longest time, no doubt because establishment sickos either participate and/or consume the horrendous torture-death scenes filmed on camera, the official word from UK law enforcement always denied that snuff films even existed, claiming police never encountered any in all of their so called investigations.[2481] Finally, British police could no longer pretend to be deaf and dumb in their denial. In May 2014 *Express* ran an article announcing that Lancashire police raided a house in February 2013, seizing "the world's first known 'snuff' child pornography video."[2482] The 22-year old low-life arrested on the scene received a mere 8-month prison sentence for possessing it along with a number of other deplorable child rape and torture videos confiscated. Upon arrest, beyond admitting he'd downloaded the film from a "file sharing program," he refused to disclose any further details. But obviously he is a bottom feeder in the much larger worldwide snuff film-child pornography network where billions of dollars are gained by the lowest of the lowest scum on earth. Police had acted on a tip from the Russian government as most of the other videos in the home featured even younger victimized Russian girls.

This particular snuff film depicted a blonde American girl likely around 14 who was savagely raped, strangled and then sexually victimized again, then ultimately rolled up tightly in a clear plastic sheet and dragged away by the murderer who appears to be her stepfather or father.[2483] All those viewing this highly disturbing 20-minute video footage concluded it is both authentic and the victim was actually filmed being killed. But here's the clunker. British police appallingly sat on this murder evidence for a full year prior to even contacting US law enforcement. In

---

[2480] Julie Bindel, "The Red Light District of Amsterdam could soon be a Distant Memory – here's why," *Independent*, February 13.

[2481] Tim Tate and Ted Jeory, "Police did nothing to track down Victim of Child Porn Snuff Film," *Express*, May 11, 2014.

[2482] Tim Tate and Ted Jeory, https://www.express.co.uk/news/uk/475207/Police-did-nothing-to-track-down-victim-of-child-porn-snuff-film.

[2483] Tim Tate and Ted Jeory, https://www.express.co.uk/news/uk/475207/Police-did-nothing-to-track-down-victim-of-child-porn-snuff-film.

other words, a whole year was allowed to elapse with zero effort made to track down either the identity of the murderer or the victim. As a solution to this problem, anti-child abuse campaigner MP Tom Watson called for an independent national child exploitation investigative agency that specializes in child pornography, similar to America's Operation Predator that's reportedly arrested 8,000 pedophiles since it was implemented in 2003.

From the Home Office which centrally controls all UK law enforcement operations, Britain has long been a pedophilia enabling haven. Award winning journalist Nick Davies has written a series of disturbingly incisive, detailed articles exposing child abuse in Britain and Europe. He wrote how UK police are allocated abundant funding and resources to combat drugs and property theft, yet law enforcement historically drags its feet investigating child sex abuse. In the macho ranks of police work, aggressively pursuing child rapists is insanely considered "soft women's work" in the policing business.[2484] After navigating past a plethora of systemic barriers yet credited with solving the 1994 London East End rape-murder case of 9-year old Daniel Handley, Detective Superintendent Ed Williams had this perplexing observation based on his firsthand experience:

Child protection is not macho. Those who are involved in it are looked at askance by Met police officers.[2485]

The Bristol police force for a time back in the late 1990s remained the lone exception. A young sergeant named Rob Jones and one hardworking Crown Prosecution barrister named Brendan Moorehouse together practically singlehandedly led a small dedicated team facing constant cutbacks and shutdown on a shoestring budget to proactively make a David vs. Goliath difference in shattering a persistent pedophile ring that had flourished in the area for 20 years, resulting in over a dozen convictions. It was this police crew that bridged awareness of the much wider pedophilia web stretching to Europe from Britain and the deadly pedo-trafficking ring and child porn industry booming in Amsterdam to London and beyond.[2486]

The monumental efforts of this barebones Bristol police pedophile unit and its local CPS one man operation became the nation's onetime model for putting child rapists behind bars with a near 100% conviction rate versus everywhere else in the country that's closer to zero, before it was ultimately shut down from lack of funding.[2487] A case in point for the near zero conviction rate as the UK norm, recall the conscientious efforts of Hereford and Worcester social services

---

[2484] Nick Davies, "Paedophilia is easy 1: How Police finally Caught up with a Network of Child Abusers," *The Guardian*, November 25, 2000.

[2485] Nick Davies, "Most Secret Crime: System Failure," *The Guardian*, June 5, 1998.

[2486] Nick Davies, "Paedophilia is easy 2: How a Paedophile Murder Inquiry Fell apart," *The Guardian*, November 27, 2000.

[2487] Nick Davies, https://www.nickdavies.net/2000/11/25/paedophilia-is-easy-how-police-finally-caught-up-with-a-network-of-child-abusers/.

director David Combs and his district's whistleblower Peter McKelvie whose evidence convinced MP Tom Watson's PM confrontation in 2012 on the House floor that launched Operations Fairbank, Fernbridge and Midland in search of VIP pedos (totaling one conviction), Hereford and Worcester's efforts to protect their children go over and above most all other social services in Britain.

Yet while both of those valiant child protectors were on duty in 1991 and 1992, a district outcome review revealed that out of a total of 148 abuse cases in Hereford and Worcester, 141 of the suspected child abusers were never charged.[2488] Out of the 7 derelicts charged, only one was convicted and imprisoned out of the total of 148 child abuse cases at less than 1% (a pathetic .0068% rate), and again that's one of the better social service departments in the entire nation. With the system set up to favor pedophiles while failing children, a disturbing trend has emerged. While an increasing number of abusers have been reported, the number being successfully prosecuted has significantly been reduced.[2489]

Yet when Bristol a few years later with its skeleton crew racked up a near 100% conviction rate, showing the rest of the country how to really protect children by proactively pursuing abusers by first tracking down victims, rather than embrace the model and expand it nationwide, the powers-that-shouldn't-be made certain its contract was not renewed. Recall that this same sad fate also shut down Operation Hedgerow in 1989 after it uncovered the largest pedophilia network in UK history while repeated requests to expand the operation were also rejected. See how the system operates? It goes out of its way every single time to protect the sickos at the expense of the innocents.

Rather than build off Bristol's unprecedented success, holding the mighty purse strings, the Home Office instead ensured its demise by never allocating a single pound worth of assistance since the crime of pedophilia conveniently doesn't qualify among its "best value performance indicators" of reported crimes.[2490] Each nation meticulously keeps records on stolen motor vehicles, all property damage and every conceivable reported crime, but when it comes to missing kids, police haven't a clue. And even when reported, it historically falls on deaf ears.

Nearly a quarter century ago based on a Home Office inquiry, it was learned that policing child abuse in the UK drastically needed "a radical improvement in the investigation and prosecution of offenders," requiring an urgent focus on proactively targeting child rapists, increasing both its responsiveness to victims as well as increase the miniscule minority of children willing to

---

[2488] Nick Davies, https://www.nickdavies.net/1998/06/05/system-failure/.

[2489] Nick Davies, https://www.nickdavies.net/1998/06/05/system-failure/.

[2490] Nick Davies, https://www.nickdavies.net/2000/11/25/paedophilia-is-easy-how-police-finally-caught-up-with-a-network-of-child-abusers/.

report sex offenses.[2491] 32 officers surveyed from ten Child Protection Units across the country unanimously delivered a blistering wake-up call that their units were sorely lacking resources, were undertrained, understaffed, unsupported and disrespected. Despite this scathing assessment way back in 1995, the Home Office has done very little to improve the lot of police officers shouldered with the responsibility of protecting kids, again no doubt by calculated design.

A November 2017 report found that despite being warned that Scotland Yard was placing children in increasing danger, the Constabulary Inspectorate determined that in 135 CSA cases examined, 93% of the Met's responses were deemed substandard.[2492] While more children in the UK Care System go missing, increasingly falling victim to pedophilic crime, severe police budget cuts and higher workload demand in the Child Protection Unit are only making matters more dire. Aside from weaker child protection and alarming rates of missing children, other areas of growing concern also include child sexual exploitation and detained children in police custody.

This comes after the 2016 report was so terrible that quarterly audit inspections were implemented on an emergency basis in order to every three months measure corrective progress and results. But the vast majority of recommendations had not even been initiated. Over 20 years after the stinging Home Office critique, the November 2016 report faulted the Met for still being stuck on its obsession to meet its target on car thefts and burglaries rather than make its priority stopping child rapists from abusing children.[2493] In short, the Home Office has only set the Met up for continued failure with £400m slashed from its budget and maintaining a longstanding policy of low priority investment in protecting children at-risk. In other words, this only confirms the realty that a political lack of will still exists in changing the UK system that's been long past broken for decades.

Despite the magnitude of this ever-glaring pedophilic epidemic, Home Office policy continues failing to fund police effort to fight against child abuse. And all those high priced, tax-paid, post-Savile police operations to investigate VIP pedophiles apparently were all for show, netting virtually zero results, providing the excuse to deny any more money spent on either historic much less current child abuse. Saving poor kids from viperous high level predators just isn't a priority in Britain, never has and never will... unless the people finally rise up in righteous anger and demand that something be done about it... like the International Tribunal for Natural Justice (ITNJ) and reconciliation commissions for starters.

[2491] Nick Davies, https://www.nickdavies.net/1998/06/05/system-failure/.

[2492] Vikram Dodd, "Met Police still Failing on Child Protection Policies, Report finds," *The Guardian*, November 23, 2017.

[2493] Henry Botkin, "'Serious errors' by Met Police put Children at Risk - Damning Report," *The Telegraph*, November 25, 2016.

With the system clearly built to shield child abusers from prosecution, especially powerful ones, it was only through the heroic local enterprise by a few remarkable individuals working together in Bristol that this onetime exception to the general rule ever broke out of the control box. The bureaucratic inertia of a rigid standard national policy of total non-interest and lack of commitment in eradicating child abuse, beginning with the gatekeeping Home Office ministers like Brittan or May extended to order-following, pedo-enabling police chiefs and DPPs, has allowed the vast pedophilia network throughout the UK, particularly serving the VIP establishment, to essentially thrive unimpeded for over a century now. The very few city police departments that include pedophile units are grossly understaffed and underfunded, and limited to focusing primarily on child pornography which in this internet age has also proliferated like wildfire.[2494] Sadly, disgracefully, Britain's political will to protect children is still absent. Instead to this very day, its priority remains diabolically protecting the pedophilia network over its own children's welfare and well-being.

Nick Davies offers two essential conditions that have always been nefariously met that permit VIP criminals to continue getting away with the wholesale rape and slaughter of the innocents:

Power is the fabric of a paedophile ring, essential first to subjugate the children, whose passivity is essential for the adults' indulgence; and second, where possible, to neutralise the authorities who might otherwise frustrate its activities.[2495]

Silencing the voice of children as victims and maintaining centralized control over shutting down police probes are the two primary M.O.s that the pedo-establishment utilizes to maintain its forever cover-up, along with the Official Secrecy Act.

When the frustrated admission that the UK child protection system is completely broken is unanimously shared by social workers, police and customs specialists alike, and echoed by senior government and top law enforcement officials responsible for overseeing this unconscionable mess, you know something at the core level is irreparably wrong and amiss. Two decades ago Nick Davies heard repeatedly from those working within this abomination of a failed system that:

They say that the power is with the paedophiles, then finally you begin to see the real horror, that we have put our trust in a child protection system that doesn't protect the children.[2496]

Nick spent years reporting from the trenches and has dozens of examples to prove the overwhelming truth that the British legal system chooses to protect child rapists and not

---

[2494] Nick Davies, https://www.nickdavies.net/1998/06/05/system-failure/.

[2495] Nick Davies, "Behind the Screen of Anonymity: Tales of Powerful Men Abusing Children," *The Guardian*, October 1, 1997.

[2496] Nick Davies, https://www.nickdavies.net/1998/06/05/system-failure/.

children. He cites a transport police officer opening a bus station locker and stumbling upon a suitcase full of photos depicting naked children in forced sexual poses.[2497] He handed the evidence over to police and social services only to have it collect dust for the next seven years before some detectives happening to investigate local care home abuse decided to match the photos with their findings that suddenly opened up numerous new leads. And that was a fluke as more often than not evidence is either lost, destroyed or sits around forever untouched.

Then there's the two far more egregious cases of two 2-year old girls oozing with pus from their vaginas diagnosed with gonorrhea at the same children's forensic center, but the monsters that did this to them both walked as the system could not hold them.[2498] The fact that child sex abuse is the most under-reported crime of all and the Home Office only acknowledges and finances policing for reported crimes directly results in virtually 100% of all child sex abusers in Britain getting away with the sickest of crimes.[2499] Factor in perps who run the nation and it's a done deal, VIPs routinely raping and ruining young lives with total impunity is simply a permanent job perk - none have ever been charged and throughout Britain's sorry-ass history none have ever gone to jail. Something's gone terribly wrong.

The abysmal conviction record of pedophiles is having a detrimental effect on social workers who are less responsive in meeting the needs of abuse victims such as delaying initial contact with the child's family or caregivers, providing timely medical examinations and interviewing the accused.[2500] In part this can be attributed to the extreme unlikelihood that any alleged perpetrator will ever be prosecuted, much less convicted. Also a skewed court emphasis on rigid adherence to making sure the child complainant's case complies with the Memorandum of Good Practice which was only meant to be a guide has judges throwing cases out right and left, denying justice and letting abusers off the hook on technicalities while in contrast the defendant's counsel is permitted to rake a child witness over the coals. A lack of sensitivity and understanding of the child's capacity and psychological development by attorneys and judges again heavily tilts the legal system to the suspect's advantage.

Yet another case in point among hundreds indicating the system favors child abusers over children. Prior to John Mann becoming a Labor MP for Bassetlaw and pointing out in 2015 Jeremy Corbyn's "missing" record protecting abused children (covered in the last chapter), Mann was a solicitor and member of the controversial Lambeth council. While investigating insurance fraud in Dolphin Square, he kept hearing about sex orgies involving children and

[2497] Nick Davies, https://www.nickdavies.net/1998/06/05/system-failure/.
[2498] Nick Davies, https://www.nickdavies.net/1998/06/05/system-failure/.
[2499] Nick Davies, https://www.nickdavies.net/1998/06/05/system-failure/.
[2500] Nick Davies, https://www.nickdavies.net/1998/06/05/system-failure/.

brought the disturbing matter to a couple Scotland Yard detectives back in 1988.[2501] Like all the rest of the police inquiries, three months later the detectives said the case was closed on orders from "those at the top." Meanwhile at the very same time, "those at the top" of UK's law enforcement were keen on shutting down Operation Hedgerow after it had inadvertently tapped into the international pedo-network despite its success as Britain's largest pedophilia bust in history. Note how every time the police encounter the larger child raping network, those in control will issue an immediate cease and desist order. Every single time this pattern's repeated.

In December 2014 MP Mann was back once again trying to defy this impenetrable blue-lined wall of protection and cover-up, this time handing over to Scotland Yard a list he reportedly compiled based on feedback from the public-at large identifying 22 MPs involved in what Mann believed was at least five major pedophile rings catering to the perverted compulsions of dozens of Westminster and Downing Street members.[2502] Of the near two dozen on the list, as of 2015 three were current members of the House of Commons and three were still active members in the House of Lords. The rest were either retired or dead, with 13 of them former ministers. For what it's worth, the list's political party breakdown is 14 Conservatives, 5 from Labor and 3 from other parties. Overoptimistic in late 2014 that arrests were pending, MP Mann asserted:

It would be inconceivable in some cases that they are not now interviewed by police about these allegations. Some of the evidence is incredibly strong.[2503]

But unfortunately the well-intentioned MP fighting an uphill battle was wrong. No Westminster arrests have been made during the half decade since police were allegedly re-investigating historic VIP child abuse. Though Met Police re-questioned Harvey Proctor (already convicted in 1987 of S&M but not CSA) and the late Leon Brittan (only once interviewed over the 1967 alleged rape of a teenage girl, sabotaging it by failing to record it), Scotland Yard still ended up forced to eat crow, apologizing to Brittan's widow, Proctor and the aging General Bramall, and coughing up a million pounds apiece for Bramall and Leon's widow. This humiliating 180 degree turnaround occurred not long after the *Mirror* in February 2013 claimed that Leon Brittan's arrest was eminent, that Met's Paedophile Unit Commander Peter Spindler had already met with his senior officers finalizing the former minister's pending arrest.[2504] But at the last minute

[2501] Rebecca Camber, "MP 'told Police about VIP Paedophile Ring's Parties 26 years ago': Labour's John Mann claims he handed Evidence of Abuse over to Scotland Yard but Investigation was Shelved," *Daily Mail*, November 16, 2014.
[2502] David Barrett, "Five Westminster Paedophile Rings Probed by Scotland Yard," *The Telegraph*, December 21, 2014.
[2503] David Barrett, https://www.telegraph.co.uk/news/uknews/crime/11306575/Five-Westminster-paedophile-rings-probed-by-Scotland-Yard.html.
[2504] Justin Penrose, https://www.mirror.co.uk/news/uk-news/former-tory-faces-child-sex-1714162.

shit always happens when the deck's pre-rigged. Once Brittan and Janner were spared the inconvenience of facing charges prior to keeling over, it's likely that the Met never bothered to even interview the other 20 MPs on Mann's pedo-list. And as of 2016, police operations into all historic VIP abuse have since been closed. And with Cliff's 2018 legal victory, the public will never know if famous people are ever questioned or arrested.

So where does all this leave us? Aging child rapists in high places still alive today whose names have been identified by accusers over the years will all safely go to their graves unpunished for ruining hundreds if not thousands of defenseless children's lives. Of course again this is simply the Luciferian way - do as much harm and damage to others on earth as you can and be guaranteed the reward of gaining more power to inflict even more suffering and pain on more victims, all the while assured of living out your days protected with immunity. That so far unbreakable travesty must soon be broken.

To ensure no public access to records of the June 1982 Elm Guest House raid ever becomes available through Freedom of Information requests, the Crown Prosecution Service (CPS) file holding all official actions and evidence legally taken after the raid were destroyed on April 11, 2007.[2505] No wonder no VIP pedophiles have ever been held accountable for their crimes, the British government has maintained a longstanding policy of simply destroying or "disappearing" any and all evidence and documents that are the least bit incriminating. In fact Crown Prosecution Service SOP mandates that all records be destroyed after only three years. The criterial exception by which files don't get destroyed after three years falls under "Long Term Interest." The Elm Guest House file remained open for just over a quarter century most likely due to the following stipulations - "security/terrorism, secret/top secret and famous, eminent or notorious people." Also noteworthy is the not surprising fact that Elm House records were destroyed just prior to Tony Blair leaving office, which per last chapter is characterized by so many D-notices, lost/destroyed criminal evidence and nonstop pedophilia cover-up.

After all, so much is at stake whenever senior members from the royal palaces, cabinet ministries, the Westminster government, and top brass from both police and national security services are all caught diddling kids in horrific rape and sodomy catering to the elite's most degenerate, sick pathologies utilized to guarantee Luciferian control over puppet leaders, world politics and indeed human history.

Hence, there's no way that the June 1982 raid at the Elm Guest House on Rocks Lane was a local vice squad operation but had to be a national security services recovery operation to confiscate and safeguard as much incriminating evidence as possible to protect VIP child sex

---

[2505] "CPS File on Elm Guest House Suspects was Destroyed in 2007," *spotlightonabuse.wordpress.com*, August 7, 2014.

offenders atop the British government. As long as their despicable habits are sealed off to escape public attention, the compromised, controlled and deranged puppets are kept in "power," remaining completely under continual diabolical control to submit to Lucifer's ungodly will.

Aside from the original 40-page Geoffrey Dickens dossier and Scotland Yard's two-year PIE probe dossier both handed over in November 1983 and then subsequently "lost," compliments of Home Office Minister Lord Brittan, eventually in 2014 the lost evidence morphed into an admitted 114 disappeared files pertaining to VIP politicians sexually abusing children.[2506] But then come to find out, by its own admission from 1979 to 1999, the UK government has systematically lost or destroyed a phenomenal, staggering total of 2,074 pedo-related files.[2507] This fact alone proves that Britain's central government is in the business of protecting its VIP pedophiles. Another incriminating numerical fact is that despite the police in 2015 releasing the official number of 261 so called VIP pedophile suspects found during its 30 post-Savile policing pedo-operations (135 in media entertainment, 76 politicians, 43 in music industry and 7 in sports),[2508] UK law enforcement has defiantly refused to both identify and follow up with the resulting status of these 261 VIP pedophile suspects.[2509] That too is nothing short of a blatant, in-our-face cover-up as well. By refusing to disclose, are we to believe nothing ever happened to these suspects?

When Mark Sedwill, the permanent secretary at the Home Office, confessed about the 114 missing files, self-righteous bluster was heard from home affairs select committee chair pedo Keith Vaz, urgently needing to get to the bottom of who the guilty culprit must be.[2510] And like always, that was the last we heard, no one has been named as the responsible party for losing 114 files, much less 2,074. But not surprisingly, the thousands of lost files never quite made it to mainstream news either. That's because it implicates the entire government in the cover-up. Yet no one in London has ever or will ever be charged with destruction of evidence, willful obstruction and perversion of justice, criminal corruption or cover-up, just as not one VIP pedophile has ever been brought to justice. Again, same old sad, pathetic story.

Various accounts covering the Elm Guest House raid characterize the policing operation as a page right out of an old keystone cop fiasco with undercover Special Branch officers just several

---

[2506] Patrick Sawer and Tim Ross, "Whitehall Child Sex Inquiry: The 114 Files 'Lost,'" *The Telegraph*, July 5, 2014.
[2507] "Appendix C: Table of Files Recorded on RMSys 1979 to 1999," gov.uk.
[2508] Loulla-Mae Eleftheriou-Smith, "VIP Child Sex Abuse Probe: Police Investigate more than 1,400 People including Politicians and Celebrities, *Independent*, May 20, 2015.
[2509] "'261 VIPs' Child Sex Abuse: Cover-up Equals Conspiracy to Pervert Course of Justice," *undercoverinfo.wordpress.com*, May 29, 2015.
[2510] Patrick Sawer and Tim Ross.

days earlier conspicuously infiltrating the guest house as fellow pedo-patrons.[2511] The lead officer reportedly feigned a fake arm sling injury with attached hidden microphone alleged to have accidentally gone off, signaling the greenlight for 60 officers strong to storm the house of ill repute apprehending the Kasirs, their 10-year old son, a 17-year old rent boy masseuse and nine pedo-clients caught on the premises, three of whom were reportedly MPs, and five of whom as later described in court were naked watching "a thoroughly obscene" child porn video.[2512] On top of that, as a giveaway that this tactical event was staged, Richmond social services that had been serving as the child pipeline facilitator for Elm Guest House were previously tipped off days in advance of the raid, explaining why no Grafton Close residents were present.[2513]

The only Grafton Close representative there that night was with the Special Branch raiding party – Andrew Neil Keir, the care home officer-in-charge who until that day by all reports had been a child victim procurer for Elm Guest House, and since he was in the direct employ of and in cahoots with Richmond social services director Louis Minster, himself a known guest house visitor, even the most casual observer would properly conclude that the raid was a staged event in a damage control recovery operation in order to obtain and destroy evidence that could potentially bring down the Thatcher government.

As a potent bargaining chip to keep the Kasirs in check from blowing the lid off MI5's covert blackmail operation, their son was taken into custody and placed at none other than the pedo-haven - the Grafton Close Children's Home.[2514] No Elm House arrests resulted in prosecution, other than the Kasirs after a number of charges were dropped leaving them to each pay a £1,000 fine for the ever-so-minor offense of running a disorderly house, their brief trial culminating with a suspended sentence in April 1983.

What does all this tell us? It was a high level top down cover-up to both shield the Thatcher government from ruin as well as salvage and maintain status quo on UK's pedophilia blackmail operations. With a constant cover-up ever since, the pedophilia at the top of the British Establishment has remained virtually unscathed and ongoing to this day, just operating slightly more discreetly under the radar. But all the constantly recurring holes and anomalies as each new scandal surfaces serve as proof that a massive cover-up is irrefutable regardless of the elite's nonstop feeble attempt to deceitfully suppress the truth.

[2511] Richard Pendlebury and Stephen Wright, https://www.dailymail.co.uk/news/article-2608177/Was-woman-murdered-cover-Cyril-Smiths-sex-ring.html.

[2512] Mark Conrad and David Pallister, "Revealed: Carole Kasir and her Squalid life at Elm Guest House, *Exaro News*, April 1, 2015.

[2513] Mark Conrad, "Richmond Council 'was Alerted to Allegations of Child Sex Abuse,'" *Exaro News*, February 23, 2013.

[2514] "The Child Abuse Network – Top Names – Part One," https://angirfana.blogspot.com/2015/04/the-child-abuse-network-top-names-part_5.html.

More evidence of a cover-up emerged when confidential police records from 1983 were leaked to the press in 2013 in the Savile aftermath.[2515] As a Grafton Close Children's Home resident, a victim at Elm Guest House reported VIP pedo-crimes to the Scotland Yard in 1983 a year after the authorities raided the brothel. But no doubt on orders from on high again the Metro Police Services (MPS) stood down and failed to further investigate the boy's claims of sex abuse, obviously already known by MPS, Special Branch and MI5. In April 2013 leaked files show how the police interviewed a second boy in 1983 who had corroborated the allegations made by the first victim. After all the potentially damaging VIP pedophilia evidence had been confiscated in the June 1982 raid, by 1983 with the cover-up in full swing, Metro was not about to rock the boat and begin protecting abused and still at-risk children, following strict orders from Special Branch and MI5 to no longer investigate the rampant abuse any further. The Met was fully responsible for dereliction of duty in failing to protect child victims as well as overt obstruction of justice in a willful conspiratorial cover-up of all available evidence led by Britain's pedo-elite.

So police consistently ignored 16 Grafton Close residents' accounts of abuse in 1982 after the Elm Guest House raid,[2516] and again a year later when two more boys came forth to report abuse in 1983. Yet Richmond-on-the-Thames council in charge of social services and its care homes as well as law enforcement both chose to ignore the boys' serious allegations. Disgracefully, as always this latest uncovered evidence of two more victims reporting in 1983 only confirms the already cold hard fact that priority has always been to protect powerful rapists over defenseless abused children. Muzzled by Special Branch and MI5, Met police kept quiet and took no further action, letting more innocent boys become VIP predator victims.

The second Grafton Close resident, now in his late 40s, explained:

I had known that the police had forgotten about this, and were always on the fringe of what was happening. At the time, I knew that there was something wrong. But as a child, I was not sure what.[2517]

In a 2014 effort to motivate retired police officers, social workers, witnesses and informants to contact investigators working on Operations Fernbridge and Midland delving into historic VIP abuse, author of the Cyril Smith exposé Rochdale MP Simon Danczuk and MP John Mann began calling for amnesty for former officers forced to sign gagging orders or fearing their pensions

[2515] David Hencke and Mark Conrad, "Richmond Files Reveal Failure to Pursue Claim of Child Sex Abuse," *Exaro News*, April 27, 2013.

[2516] David Pallister, "Revealed: Diaries and Receipts for Guest House in Police Probe," *Exaro News*, December 19, 2012.

[2517] David Hencke and Mark Conrad, https://www.exaronews.com/richmond-files-reveal-failure-to-pursue-claim-of-child-sex-abuse.

would be cut off.[2518] Anti-child abuse MP John Mann actually sponsored an amendment to the Official Secrets Act in February 2015 granting immunity to former police, civil servants and witnesses that would prohibit prosecution for providing evidence on historic child sexual abuse.[2519] But Tories and Social Democrats voted against it.

A month later shortly before becoming Prime Minister, Theresa May offered this rather feeble response:

If people are giving evidence of child abuse I would not expect them – I would hope them not to be prosecuted under the Official Secrets Act.[2520]

That hesitant and weak utterance was purposely designed to not convince anyone to come forth. The Mann amendment failed because the majority in the British government insist that no change in the Official Secret Acts law is necessary to protect whistleblowers from reporting what they know. But history has only shown that for many decades child sexual abuse whistleblowers have consistently been harassed, threatened, smeared and disbelieved. And the Official Secrets Act as existing law most certainly does have the teeth to throw truth tellers in jail just like the 1889 Cleveland scandal did.

A disappointed, exasperated John Mann told *BBC* Radio 4:

Police officer after police officer have told me that the Official Secrets Act and fear of breaching it are a bar to them.[2521]

This is just one typical example of the multiple barriers that purposely remain in place within Britain's legal system intended to effectively inhibit full disclosure of the damning truth that would deliver long overdue justice to the powerful child rapists still lurking inside and out of the government. It appears that MPs voted against the amendment to once again protect the child eating monsters among them. It strongly suggests that throughout all the British institutions of power, be it the Parliament, the prime minister's office, the high courts, CPS or top law enforcement, the system is irreparably rigged with pedophiles and pedophile protectors who may well comprise the majority in the halls of government.

[2518] David Barrett, Tim Tate and Christopher Hope, https://www.telegraph.co.uk/news/uknews/crime/10950138/Westminster-paedophile-ring-allegations-Scotland-Yard-detectives-trace-victim.html.
[2519] Patrick Wintour and Matthew Weaver, "No Change in Law Needed to Protect Child Abuse Whistleblowers, says Tory," *The Guardian*, March 17, 2015.
[2520] Jaya Narain and Martin Robinson, https://www.dailymail.co.uk/news/article-2997971/Cyril-Smith-held-paedophile-sex-party-police-told-cover-face-prosecution-Official-Secrets-Act.html.
[2521] Patrick Wintour and Matthew Weaver, https://www.theguardian.com/politics/2015/mar/17/police-told-drop-child-abuse-case-against-cyril-smith-whistleblower.

Though Parliament balked at amnesty, within a week after Danczuk raised the issue in 2014, it immediately prompted 40 informants to come forth with yet more allegations of VIP abuse.[2522] One was the retired detective that interviewed the 8-year old victim in 1982, recently stating that he was required to sign a gag order at the time prior to his investigation shutdown. But over three decades later his recollection of criminal events also remained consistent with the victim's recalled disclosure, only reinforcing the already voluminous body of cumulative cover-up evidence conveniently buried with the "out of sight, out of mind" 2015 closures of Operations Fernbridge and Midland.

Those two policing operations directed at the heart of the British government, by design have failed miserably to hold VIP pedophiles accountable. Not unlike Yewtree, either zero VIP offenders ended up prosecuted or a minor token player winds up convicted to appease the public. Long ago a likely majority of British citizens have realistically concluded that the most powerful politicians who are flaming child sodomizers are unreachable in a thoroughly rigged system designed to ensure that they remain free to live out their unimpeded lives above the law till death do them part. Operation Midland came up totally emptyhanded and Fernbridge sent one pervert priest to prison for a relative short stint of three years. That's it. Otherwise, all the VIPs have gotten away and continue getting away with their thousands and thousands of ungodly predatory crimes. All the so called inquiries numbering over 30 different policing operations into pedophilia in Britain have pathetically next to nothing to show for themselves, at grave cost to both the taxpaying public and its complete lack of faith in its irreversibly corrupt government.

In February 2013 while probing Elm Guest House child abuse as part of Fernbridge, the Scotland Yard finally arrested the former deputy head of Grafton Close Home - John Stingemore - for sexually abusing boys under his care years earlier.[2523] Along with his procuring boss Andrew Neil Keir who to this day remains a free man, it was Stingemore who was responsible for both trafficking his Grafton sex slaves eight miles away to the Elm Guest House as well as largely responsible for the suicide of one of his victims - 28-year old Peter Bornshin. Peter's abuse at 13 and 14 from frequent Elm House trips drove him at 28 to take his own life with a drug overdose.[2524] Meanwhile at 72, his pimping abuser Stingemore died just days ahead of his scheduled trial. Was the odd timing of Stingemore's death the result of knowing too much, posing a serious enough liability for guilty VIPs he once partied with?

[2522] David Barrett, Tim Tate and Christopher Hope, https://www.telegraph.co.uk/news/uknews/crime/10950138/Westminster-paedophile-ring-allegations-Scotland-Yard-detectives-trace-victim.html.

[2523] Stephen Wright and Richard Pendlebury, "Revealed: Face of Boy Abused in Elm House Scandal as Catholic Priest and Head of Boys' Home are Arrested," *Daily Mail*, February 6, 2013.

[2524] Tim Wood, "Priest Cleared of three more Counts, but Convicted of making three Indecent Images," Exaro News, February 27, 2015.

Or could it have also served as a direct warning to Stingemore's religious friend arrested on the same day in February 2013 who was due to also go on trial with him. Decades earlier, Stingemore provided easy child access for his pedo-priest buddy, Catholic vicar Tony McSweeney to sexually assault boys from Grafton Close. It was Father McSweeney as Grafton's part-time chaplain who played "good cop" to Stingemore's "bad cop."[2525] McSweeney was also a chaplain of the Norwich City football club and in 1990 officiated the wedding of world heavyweight champ Frank Bruno, the Freemason pictured shaking hands with the Yorkshire Ripper while their mutual satanic friend Sir Jimmy smugly looked on.[2526]

Though denying he ever committed sexual abuse, McSweeney did admit to making trips to Holland with Stingemore to purchase and distribute child pornography, the world's child snuff film capital.[2527] In 1998 the priest was even caught possessing child porn videos and indecent photos of children but of course the police and church just looked the other way and allowed him to move on to do more damage elsewhere.[2528] A couple of high profile British Catholic bishops quietly helped him transfer to East Anglia.[2529]

As the only formal police operation specifically designated to investigate VIP abuse at Elm Guest House, Fernbridge resulted in the conviction of zero VIPs, just one lowly, previously protected, pervert priest while dozens of infamously known monsters were explicitly captured on police surveillance, MI5 blackmail videos as well as Carole Kasir's photographs along with her guest sign-in list, diary entries and Mary and Chris' handwritten notes. Despite plenty of victims' firsthand accounts, including at least 18 Grafton Close boys identified as "recruited" Elm House victims,[2530] and so much other blatantly solid evidence still available, not one other arrest and conviction resulted outside this one fallen ex-priest that wasn't even directly connected to Elm House crimes. McSweeney is already a free man having served his 3-year sentence.[2531] All the rest of the guilty famous pedophiles remain free, unimpeded to strike again and again with total impunity to this very day. Once again the Elm Guest House story plays out the pathetically shameful running theme - at the world's pedophilia epicenter, some things never change.

[2525] Jenny Stanton, "Catholic Priest Accused of Abusing Boys 'was Caught with Child Porn and Sex Toys but was just Moved on by the Church and Escaped Police Charges," Daily Mail, February 18, 2015.
[2526] Ray Bullock, "The Devil in Control of Washington, Donald J. Drumpf, Roseanne Barr, Kathy Griffin and Joan Rivers," mindcontrolblackassassins.com, June 12, 2017.
[2527] Tim Wood, https://www.exaronews.com/tony-mcsweeney-found-guilty-of-abusing-boy-at-grafton-close.
[2528] Jenny Stanton, https://www.dailymail.co.uk/news/article-2959046/Catholic-priest-accused-abusing-boys-caught-child-porn-sex-toys-just-moved-church-escaped-police-charges.html.
[2529] Richard Pendlebury, "A Paedophile Priest, two Bishops and a Sickening Conspiracy of Silence: He married Frank Bruno and said Mass for Delia Smith. But behind the Glitz was one of the Catholic Church's Dirtiest Secrets," Daily Mail, March 4, 2015.
[2530] David Pallister, https://www.exaronews.com/revealed-diaries-and-receipts-for-guest-house-in-police-probe.
[2531] "Anthony McSweeney Case: Abuse Priest Failings Found," BBC, April 23, 2017.

By its own factual history, the only accurate conclusion to be drawn is that the United Kingdom lacks both the moral and political will and integrity to protect its "expendable" children trapped in its abominable [Don't] Care System. That said, the same can be said for North America, Australia, the rest of Europe and many other nations around the world as well. Where family court systems exploit and prey upon economically disadvantaged populations, creating a growing subclass of throwaway children [and adults if they live that long], provide the essential pipeline for the booming child sex trade resulting in history's fastest growing, most profitable illicit industry on earth, all because a relative handful of sub-humans atop this predatory food chain have been allowed to enjoy untouchable impunity for centuries. Recall from an earlier chapter that one very brave state Senator Nancy Schaefer from Georgia (along with her husband) paid the ultimate price in March 2010 for blowing the whistle on this tragic, disgraceful worldwide reality where a bounty's been placed on the head of each child sold from the child welfare system into the global pedophilia trafficking industry.[2532] Lethal consequences befalling those exposing this explosive alarming secret is intended to deter others from revealing the truth.

According to Operation Fernbridge, in addition to the 1982 Elm Guest House cover-up of ongoing VIP abuse, yet another unexplained failure to investigate the scandal occurred in 2003 when police were again informed that in the late 1970s and early 80s, children from the local Richmond care homes were brought in to "work" at the guest house operating as a child brothel for ministers and MPs.[2533] Terry Earland, director of Richmond children's services from 1981 to 2003, originally reported child abuse in 1982 to both the police and his colleagues on Richmond council.

Because the Special Branch raid accomplished its nefarious objective to secure and withhold all further evidence, upon approaching retirement two decades later, Terry Earland again met with police furnishing all he knew of the rampant abuse two decades earlier. Unhappy with law enforcement's blatant stonewalling in 2003 and 2004, Earland registered a formal grievance with the Independent Police Complaints Commission (IPCC) in 2004.[2534] Despite heaps of overwhelming evidence, IPCC also failed to respond for the all too obvious reason - orders from on high again. So with Fernbridge in 2013, it was role reversal time in Met's turn to investigate IPCC's part in the cover-up in 2004. Of course as always, nothing more on that probe was ever heard again.

[2532] Brian Shilhavy, "Senator Nancy Schaefer: Did her Fight against CPS Child Kidnapping Cause her Murder?" *Health Impact News/medicalkidnap.com*, April 27, 2015.
[2533] David Hencke, David Pallister and Fiona O'Cleirigh, "Police 'twice Failed to Probe Paedophile Riing at Guest House," *Exaro News*, December 14, 2012.
[2534] Mark Conrad, "Met Investigates Police Watchdog over Richmond 'Paedo Ring,'" *Exaro News*, April 22, 2013.

Recall from last chapter that in 2004 the Blair government was flagrantly engaging in its own batch of major pedophilia cover-ups, protecting his Home Office minister Paul Boateng in the Lambeth scandal and D-noticing Operation Ore to shield Lord Mandelson while facing intense growing pressure over his minister of children Oppenheimer-Hodge to resign for her appalling pedo-record that began the same year Elm Guest House was raided.

Terry Earland emphatically stated:

My modus operandi at that time [1982] *was always that if there was an allegation of abuse, it was referred to the* [Scotland Yard] *child-protection unit.*[2535]

Yet Terry's boss Louis Minster, head of Richmond's social services from 1975 to 1984, plus a conspicuous name on the infamous guest list, claimed in February 2013 that he never heard of any child abuse at either the Elm Guest House or Grafton Close Home:

There was never any... There were a couple of child abuse cases – violence in the families, and what have you. But the answer would be no. There were no inquiries at all.[2536]

The 81-year old Minster now living a comfy retired lifestyle on a hilltop residence in Malta, a notorious pedo-bastion dating back to the Peter Righton days whom he knew, prefaced his denial of knowing any abuse or raid or inquiry ever occurred on his watch by making sure to mention he currently suffers from memory problems, thus establishing "plausible deniability," adding:

I have never heard of them. I read it on Google the other evening.[2537]

Yet Terry Earland insists that he told Minster, the Richmond council and the Met police about the abuse. So one of them is clearly lying and my bet is on Minster as the boldface liar trying to cover his own guilty ass. It's on record that twice Minster pulled the file belonging to the second 14-year old boy that reported VIP abuse, a highly unusual fact in and of itself, particularly since the boy was no longer under the care of Richmond social services.[2538] When 2012 political journalist of the year David Hencke called Minster in Malta in 2013 to clear up this most glaring discrepancy, Minster feebly pretended he wasn't Minster.[2539]

[2535] Mark Conrad, https://www.exaronews.com/richmond-council-was-alerted-to-allegations-of-child-sex-abuse.
[2536] Mark Conrad and Alison Winward, "Richmond's Ex-Head of Social Services 'Unaware' of 'Paedo Ring,'" *Exaro News*, February 9, 2013.
[2537] Mark Conrad and Alison Winward, https://www.exaronews.com/richmonds-ex-head-of-social-services-unaware-of-paedo-ring.
[2538] David Hencke, "Elm Guest House Abuse Scandal: 'Paedo Police Ignored 16-year-old Victim,'" *Mirror*, April 27, 2013..
[2539] David Hencke, "The Mad World of Louis Minster- the Man who Denies he is there," *davidhencke.com*, May 2, 2013.

Despite his confessed memory impairment, by October the following year 2014, suddenly the 83-year old's recall was as lucid as ever, answering question after question posed by a local reporter from Malta, explaining that in 1982 Terry Earland did in fact brief him prior to that June house raid:

The police had asked to carry out inspections and interviews in the presence of a social worker and I had instructed Earland to take care of it since it was his responsibility.[2540]

Notice his euphemistic wording, calling a police raid an "inspection." And who from Richmond social services gets sent to accompany Special Branch on the guest house raid? Not a Richmond social worker per protocol but the Grafton Close Home Officer-in-Charge Andrew Neil Keir, who with deputy head pedo-John Stingemore were the very pimps trafficking their group home boys to the nightmare on Elm.[2541]

Minster claims he was never interviewed by police or ever under any investigation, and that:

Last March, I got a phone call from the Metropolitan Police who informed me that the Director of Public Prosecutions had decided not to use me as a witness.[2542]

Again, more euphemism as by all rights, Minster should have been a suspect a long time ago, not a witness. Seems the Richmond council and the Met would be equally motivated to sweep under the rug every last trace of the Elm Guest House scandal and their part in the cover-up since it's more than obvious both have much to criminally hide and avoid explaining.

The notorious list of Elm Guest House visitors posted on the internet by Mary Moss not only includes then Richmond social services director Louis Minster but also Richmond council's lauded education director as well. Apparently Richmond Director of Education and former Wandsworth Chief Constable Donald Naismith has never been taken to task to explain how his name as a longtime London borough educator (1974-1994) wound up as an Elm houseguest.[2543] A 1994 queen honored CBE recipient,[2544] to this day the retiree is also apparently enjoying his golden years as a renowned author and expert in UK education.[2545] When the borough's social services director and the education director are both pedophiles, they could easily arrange

[2540] Jurgen Balzan, "Expat Denies Involvement in Richmond Paedophile Ring Cover-up," *Malta Today*, October 28, 2014.
[2541] "Nightmares at Elm Guest House," https://www.youtube.com/watch?v=ORU5x-ryedU.
[2542] Jurgen Balzan, https://www.maltatoday.com.mt/news/world/45482/expat_denies_involvement_in_richmond_ paedophile_ring_coverup.
[2543] "The Child Abuse Network - Top Names - Part Two," *aangirfan.blogspot.com*, January 29, 2015.
[2544] "1994 Birthday Honours," *wikipedia.org*.
[2545] Jim Greenhalf, "Lessons under the Iron Lady," *Telegraph & Argus*, April 8, 2013.

through school record photos of all the Richmond boys in care homes be featured in the Spartacus catalogue so that VIPs had the pick of the litter at Elm Guest House.[2546]

Aside from incest, professions with daily access to children - teachers, coaches, Boy Scout leaders and social workers, childcare workers, babysitters - all too commonly turn out to be the child abusers. In addition to London borough social services and education directors, another Elm Guest House identified visitor is senor Westminster social worker Steve Everett. And yet another semi-notable from "the list" is George Tremlett, former Greater London Council leader, bookstore owner, journalist and David Bowie biographer (Bowie himself an accused pedophile[2547]).[2548]

Several more now deceased Westminster politicians wound up on the Elm Guest House list. Tory MP Charles Irving[2549] was yet another Monday Club member and advisor to Peter Campbell's CGHE, was knighted in 1990 and his prominent family owned a hotel chain.[2550] Another politician on "the list" is Labor MP Ron Brown who died in 2002.[2551]

Yet another fairly big name on that infamous Elm Guest House list is Labor MP Stuart Bell from Middlesbrough, elected in 1983 until he died in October 2012.[2552] In 1987 Stuart Bell played a reactionary, highly inflammatory role in the nation's largest single CSA case up to that time.[2553] In his home Cleveland County MP Bell libelously accused pediatricians and child abuse specialists of falsely making up allegations when they allegedly determined that 123 kids likely suffered sexual abuse. It also turns out that one of the abuse victims' father accused Bell but an alleged innocent man was tried and convicted for the crime despite the father's strong suspicion that the actual perpetrator was VIP Stuart Bell,[2554] whom the queen knighted in 2004.[2555]

[2546] "The Mary Moss Elm Guest House VIP Paedophile Party List," *cigpapers.blog*, April 29, 2013.

[2547] Caroline Howe, "David Bowie's Sex Addiction Drove him to Sleep with 13-year-old Groupies, Engage in Wild Orgies and declare he was Bi-Sexual with a 'Permanent Erection' - but he turned down an offer to 'F*** a warm Dead Body,'" *Daily Mail*, August 17, 2017.

[2548] "French Shocked about Geoffrey Dickens, the Elite Paedophiles and the Missing Dossier," *google-law.blogspot.com*, March 7, 2013.

[2549] Patrick Cosgrave, "Obituaries Sir Charles Irving," *Independent*, April 3, 1995.

[2550] Stephen Leece, "Filthy Britain Part 2: Rape, Lies and Videotape: The Elm Guest House Story," *Shout Out UK*, October 21, 2013.

[2551] Dominic Gover, "Who Were the Paedophiles at the Heart of the British Political Establishment?" *International Business Times*, July 10, 2014..

[2552] "The Power of Paedophile connections in Europe and the United Kingdom."

[2553] Tim Tate, "Cleveland: Unspeakable Truths," *spotlightonabuse.wordpress.com*, May 30, 2013.

[2554] "Boylinks – USA, UK, Europe, the World," https://aangirfan.blogspot.com/2013/07/boylinks-usa-uk-europe-world.html.

[2555] Julia Langdon, "Sir Stuart Bell Obituary," *The Guardian*, October 14, 2012.

No surprise that a number of police officers were among the list of Elm Guest House regulars as a manifestation of pedo-foxes guarding the Elm child victim henhouse.[2556] Among them Deputy Constable (DC) Chris Carter from Richmond Criminal Investigative Department (CID) and DC Ron Thornton also of Richmond CID, DC David Lines of Barnes CID, Police Constable (PC) Rodrick Smeaton, PC Alan Jones from Special Branch[2557] and two Women Police Constables - retired 30-year Metro Sergeant Sheila McInnes and WPC Elizabeth Meredith. Another guest list name belongs to then Met Police Constable and likely current 62-year old former Met Police Inspector, pro-EU supporter Chris Wicks, who surfaced in a *Mirror* article confronting philandering ex-Tory Foreign Minister-Brexiteer Boris Johnson in a restaurant in Greece over last New Year's holiday.[2558]

To further lend credence to allegations that a number of law enforcement pedophiles were regular Elm Guest House visitors, a child actor Dr. Who - Lee Towsey, the 16-year old masseuse employed for five months at the time of the June 1982 Special Branch raid, claims he had sex with three police officers at the brothel, likely with one or more of the above named guests. Speaking to *The Mail on Sunday* in April 2014 after reporting his experiences to Fernbridge detectives in 2012, Lee stated that Carole Kasir complained that she was forced to pay for "a police Christmas fund" as an extortion fee to Richmond police for "protection" during Elm's years of operation.[2559] Towsey also corroborated that Carole kept a list of high profile customers in a black book as her "insurance policy." Carole also mentioned the prominent cabinet minister as a regular house guest later determined to be Leon Brittan. It was Lee who informed MP Simon Danczuk upon release of his book on Cyril Smith that there were "much bigger fish" far "higher up the food chain" at Elm,[2560] referring to Sir Leon, though at sweet 16 Lee had a sexual encounter with "Big Cyril as well:

[2556] "The Mary Moss Elm Guest House VIP Paedophile Party List," https://cigpapers.blog/2013/04/29/the-elm-guest-house-vip-paedophile-party-list/.

[2557] "French Shocked about Geoffrey Dickens, the Elite Paedophiles and the Missing Dossier," http://google-law.blogspot.com/2013/03/french-shocked-about-geoffrey-dickens.html.

[2558] Ben Glaze and Andy Lines, "Boris Johnson and Girlfriend spent New Year in Greek Villa where he took his Family," *Mirror*, January 10, 2019.

[2559] Paul Cahalan and Ian Gallagher, "I had Underage Sex with Police Officers at Guest House used by 'VIP Paedophile Ring': Astonishing Allegations by Masseur who worked as a 16-year-old at Notorious Party Venue 'used by Politicians, Judges and Pop Stars,'" *Daily Mail*, April 10, 2014.

[2560] Steven Swinford, https://www.telegraph.co.uk/news/politics/liberaldemocrats/10775360/Influential-politician-visited-guest-house-at-centre-of-child-sex-investigation.html.

Carole told me not to let him in the sauna, as he had got stuck in there before and they had to take the door off to get him out. Smith wanted me to strip naked and massage him. I was also forced to watch as he masturbated.[2561]

The first time the underage masseuse had sex at the brothel with a policeman was in February 1982:

One came round in the first month. He was early 20s, good-looking, not the usual sort who went to the house.[2562]

The next occasion that Lee encountered the young police officer was when Elm was raided and the Kasirs and Lee were taken to the police station. Towsey also maintains that in April he had sex with another undercover officer that must have been from Special Branch as he was a member of the raiding party. But Lee said:

He came back about three weeks later and hired a room. He stayed two nights and on the second night his partner stayed too. I ended up having sex with them. Afterwards they asked how much and I told them that they were not clients and felt insulted they wanted to pay me.[2563]

At the time of the June raid, Lee was charged with assisting in the management of the brothel but was later dropped. That summer Towsey acquired another job working in the kitchen of a bingo hall where his father would pick him up after his shift. One day three policeman arrived at the usual time in place of his father. Lee said:

One of them was at the station following the raid. They told me they could pick me up at any time and told me keep my mouth shut. I never told anyone, not even my family.[2564]

Lee Towsey explained that despite a couple of calls from police since contacting him in 2012, he feels frustrated because no police action has been forthcoming after reporting his abuse as an underage victim at the hands of three lawbreaking pedophile cops, adding:

[2561] Paul Cahalan and Ian Gallagher, https://www.dailymail.co.uk/news/article-2608695/I-underage-sex-police-officers-guest-house-used-VIP-paedophile-ring-Astonishing-allegations-masseur-worked-16-year-old-notorious-party-venue-used-politicians-judges-pop-stars.html.
[2562] Paul Cahalan and Ian Gallagher, https://www.dailymail.co.uk/news/article-2608695/I-underage-sex-police-officers-guest-house-used-VIP-paedophile-ring-Astonishing-allegations-masseur-worked-16-year-old-notorious-party-venue-used-politicians-judges-pop-stars.html.
[2563] Paul Cahalan and Ian Gallagher, https://www.dailymail.co.uk/news/article-2608695/I-underage-sex-police-officers-guest-house-used-VIP-paedophile-ring-Astonishing-allegations-masseur-worked-16-year-old-notorious-party-venue-used-politicians-judges-pop-stars.html.
[2564] Paul Cahalan and Ian Gallagher, https://www.dailymail.co.uk/news/article-2608695/I-underage-sex-police-officers-guest-house-used-VIP-paedophile-ring-Astonishing-allegations-masseur-worked-16-year-old-notorious-party-venue-used-politicians-judges-pop-stars.html.

I am considering legal action against the Met. I shut the door on it once and I want to shut the door on it again and move on.[2565]

In 2013 Operation Fernbridge detectives were in search of the alleged two dozen aforementioned photos of this infamous motley crew of pervert guests reportedly photographed with their victims by the likely murdered brothel owner Carole Kasir. Of course if these photos have not already been destroyed, both security services and Met police have had in possession their own sets of elusive incriminating photos. As alluded to earlier, towards the end of her life, Carole Kasir befriended Mary Moss and was alleged to have given her copies of damaging VIP documents and photos. After three decades since the Elm House closure, the more recent 2013 Fernbrdge raid on Mary Moss' home was never intended to bring belated justice to the unpunished VIPs as no suspect has ever been arrested, much less convicted. But again it was another overt attempt to collect and remove perhaps the last vestige of smoking gun evidence to make certain VIP pedophiles stay out of both jail and the headlines.

In 2012 the police scoping exercise - Operation Fairbank - was conducted to determine if a further criminal investigation - Operation Fernbridge - would be warranted. It was. The Fernbridge objective ostensibly was to determine why prior police investigations were prematurely shut down in 1982 and never got off the ground in 2004,[2566] and the active role that Richmond council played in the abuse and cover-up.[2567] The Liberal Richmond council leader from November 1983 to 2001, the knighted Sir David Williams, said there's no evidence of child abuse that he's aware of.[2568] Yet Scotland Yard determined that the council paid out a rather hefty sum of hush money to an alleged Elm House child abuse victim. So Sir David wasn't being totally honest in his emphatic denial of abuse.

Lasting over two years in duration but closed by March 2015, unfortunately Operation Fernbridge amounted to no more than the same going-through-the motion posturing, under the false pretense of "leaving no stone unturned," as pedo-enabling PM David Cameron promised in order to placate a riled up public fresh off the Jimmy Saville revelations, demanding answers and justice that in Britain appear destined to never come to fruition.[2569] The most obvious reason for Scotland Yard's long history of aborted inquires and impotent inaction is

[2565] Paul Cahalan and Ian Gallagher, https://www.dailymail.co.uk/news/article-2608695/I-underage-sex-police-officers-guest-house-used-VIP-paedophile-ring-Astonishing-allegations-masseur-worked-16-year-old-notorious-party-venue-used-politicians-judges-pop-stars.html.
[2566] David Hencke, David Pallister and Fiona O'Cleirigh, https://www.exaronews.com/police-twice-failed-to-probe-paedophile-ring-at-guest-house.
[2567] David Pallister and David Hencke, "Police Investigate Richmond Council over VIP Paedophile Ring," *Exaro News*, January 26, 2013, https://www.exaronews.com/police-probes-richmond-council-over-vip-paedophile-ring.
[2568] David Hencke, https://davidhencke.com/2013/02/04/did-richmond-council-pay-hush-money-to-cover-up-the-elm-guest-house-child-abuse-scandal/.
[2569] Dawn Papple, "Prime Minister David Cameron 'no Stone left Unturned' in UK Child Sex Abuse Cover-up Investigation," *Inquisitr*, July 8. 2014.

because as mere lackeys on the pecking order totem pole, they simply follow their stand down orders from the Home Office or MI5. Like all previous cover-ups from the 1980s through the 2000s, all the post-Savile police probes exploring the Westminster-Downing Street connection have also proven to be more of the same unending cover-up.

It doesn't take millions of taxpayer pounds and years to figure out that powerful pedophiles will never voluntarily expose themselves. And as long as the highest ranking police, spies, judges and politicians are either pedophiles or pedophile enablers, the ending of the story will always stay the same. But all over the world the truth is finally breaking through their previously impenetrable walls and the guilty predators will soon be exposed and some will be held accountable before they too die off from old age.

Child victims through the ages have virtually always been ignored, disbelieved, or, if they present damaging enough evidence against VIP sickos, they become targeted for murder, character assassination, anything to eliminate them as threats to the status quo crime cabal. Child campaigner Chris Fay who gathered incriminating evidence against Leon Brittan from Carole Kasir prior to her sudden death was subsequently prosecuted and convicted for investment fraud in 2011, effectively neutralizing him thereafter as a fully credible witness to the public.[2570] Today's precarious situation where all the prior allegations once deemed "credible and true" from now alleged "fantasist" Nick (as if he is the only accuser in the world), claiming horrific torture and abuse at both Elm Guest House and Dolphin Square, witnessing three alleged child murders at the hands of VIPs, suddenly in 2016 were all declared false, automatically casting unfair doubt and dispersions on countless actual victims and their true claims.

In early 2018 the so called Nick, whose actual name Carl Beech was released by the judge[2571] after the 50-year old was initially arrested on charges of possessing and making indecent images of children.[2572] But currently Beech awaits his criminal trial scheduled for March 2019 on charges of perverting justice and fraud.[2573] See the pattern here? Ex-MP Danczuk was alleged to have sexted a 17-year old girl and raped his first wife while asleep, in effect ruining his parliamentary career as a child abuse advocate.[2574] Seems one by one the biggest threats to the status quo pedo-cover-up are all effectively neutralized one way or another. The more

---

[2570] Sam Tonkin, "Social Worker who Accused Leon Brittan and other VIPs as being Members of an Alleged Paedophile Ring was Convicted of Fraud in 2011," *Daily Mail*, September 27, 2015.

[2571] "Carl Beech, 50 Named as 'Westminster Paedophile Ring' Accuser," *Exaro News*, December 18, 2018.

[2572] Tom Wells, Chris Pollard and Alex West, "'Nick' Nicked Fantasist known only as 'Nick' who Sparked £3million VIP Paedo Probe held over Child Sex Offenses," *The Sun*, February 7, 2018.

[2573] Martin Evans, "VIP Paedophile Accuser 'Nick' to stand Trial Accused of Perverting the course of Justice and Fraud," *The Telegraph*, November 18, 2018.

[2574] Dan Bloom, "Shamed MP Simon Danczuk Denies Ex-Wife's Claims he is a 'Predator' who had Sex when she was Asleep," *Mirror*, January 4, 2016.

serious and damaging the accusations are to the pedo-elite, the more certain accusers' reputations will be attacked, smeared and destroyed.

With Operation Midland probing possible VIP murders, costing Briton taxpayers £3m and resulting in not even one single arrest, and Metro Police Services having to humiliatingly apologize to ex-MP pervert Proctor, General Bramall and Leon Brittan's widow, the latter two granted £100,000 each in compensation for the alleged false accusations against them, along with Sir Cliff Richard's July 2018 landmark court victory, the pedo-elite's pushback effectively seals the deal.[2575] No famous pedophile still alive in Britain will be brought to justice at the earth's pedophilia epicenter. The aforementioned VIPs' guilt or innocence notwithstanding, powerful child rapists' 2018 pushback have won and the current IICSA ensures that abysmal, shameful outcome.

The more the pedo-elite can waste taxpayer money on fruitless boondoggle witch hunts against so called innocent accused VIP victims, the less believable real victims of child abuse automatically become and the less public support for costly, failed police investigations into historic child sex abuse. The criminal elite's ultimate aim is to render the thousands of victims who've been abused by prominent pedophiles throughout the years null and void, where they're neither heard nor do they matter, as if their abuse never really happened at all. Of course that would be a grotesque travesty of justice and we cannot allow any legal system to reach such an abominable state of filth as in Britain. In effect, the cabal agenda is to censor, silence and deny the massive, glaring, overwhelming evidence that irrefutably speaks for itself, regardless of whatever gargantuan effort is made to cover it all up. Finally, if abuse victims figure that the corrupt UK justice system is so corrupt and so rigged against the truth ever winning or counting in a British court of law, no one will ever press charges, much less undergo the enduring stress and pressure of a long drawn out court process or even be sufficiently resolute to report crimes in the first place, reasonably concluding neither the legal system nor the police can ever be trusted.

Even an establishment bigwig, former 5-year Director of Public Prosecutions Keir Starmer has admitted:

Many, if not most, still do not have sufficient confidence in our criminal justice system to come forward in the first place and report what has happened to them... The prevalence figures for domestic violence and abuse set out in a report by the Early Intervention Foundation last week remind us that this is far from a historical matter. For many victims the adversarial journey through our courtrooms is such an ordeal that most vow never to repeat it. The way some

---

[2575] Scott D'Arcy, Met 'to pay Lord Bramall and Lady Brittan £100,000 after Raiding Homes in Doomed Child Abuse Investigation,'" *Independent*, September 2, 2017.

victims and witnesses in the sex-grooming trials were treated makes very uncomfortable reading for any politician, lawyer or judge... Even when a case is sensitively handled, the adversarial system does not always serve victims well.[2576]

... Or at all. One victim echoing the DPP's statement above who was abused by high powered pedophile criminals from age 9 to 16 had this to say:

The authority is not what stops people from speaking out, it's the fear that is instilled by these people. It appears the cover-ups did happen and it makes survivors very wary because you don't know who you can have confidence in to report.[2577]

There's good reason why the criminal justice system is not called the victims' justice system, because when the rich and powerful are the criminals, always they're protected and always the victims re-victimized. With all the power and resources in their favor, the VIP pedophile strategy is counting on the above scenario to only continue on indefinitely since it's worked so well for them for so long. The entire court system needs a complete drastic overhaul if anything's to ever change. Again, Keir Starmer has called for "a radical shift in attitude and approach" in the existing criminal justice system, advocating a specific and enforceable new victims' law, concluding:

We could start by retiring the description 'criminal justice system' and conceive instead of a criminal justice service fit for victims.[2578]

But as gatekeepers too many pedophiles have long infiltrated Britain's rotten-to-the-core legal system, ensuring that the outcome stays fixed and controlled so that VIP child rapists always remain free while too many abuse victims, suffering immeasurably, tragically die too young. For this sad, pathetic realty to ever change, we citizens of the world must unify as one formidable force for good to make it happen.

In the meantime, survivor groups like the Shirley Oaks Survivors Association (SOSA) stand out as a model of the way to go to mobilize power and support for vindicated recognition and at least recover long overdue financial compensation. It's still not satisfactory justice until the criminals are fairly punished in a court of law but better than no justice at all. Abuse survivor organizations can also be instrumental in assisting police to gather evidence for prosecution as SOSA helped put a pedophile priest behind bars as noted in the last chapter.

[2576] Owen Bowcott, "Former Director of Public Prosecutions calls for Victims' Law," *The Guardian*, February 3, 2014.

[2577] Nico Hines, https://www.thedailybeast.com/how-thatchers-government-covered-up-a-vip-pedophile-ring?ref=scroll.

[2578] Owen Bowcott, https://www.theguardian.com/law/2014/feb/03/former-director-public-prosecutions-victims-law-keir-starmer.

As yet another example of the pedo-foxes guarding the henhouse, in this case UK's justice system, let's examine one high court judge who in 2013 was appointed as the queen's personal legal advisor.[2579] A few months after his royal upgrade, Appeal Court Judge Adrian Fulford was having to answer charges that in 1979 he was founder of the campaign group called Conspiracy Against Public Morals that openly supported and defended the rights of pedophiles. He attended strategy meetings with PIE chairman Tom O' Carroll, later found guilty of possessing child pornography, and organized protests outside the courtrooms where PIE leaders were on trial for conspiracy to corrupt public morals. A pamphlet from the organization that Fulford founded claimed that if children were allowed to have sex with adults, it would free them from the oppression of the state and their parents.

The barrister's activism motivated him to make a speech at a 1980 PIE rally defending pedophile rights, acknowledged in PIE's newsletter Magpie thanking him by name for delivering the best speech of the day. While a volunteer at the same infamous civil rights group - NCCL (currently known as Liberty) - that embraced PIE as an affiliate partner that also came back to bite Labor leaders Patricia Hewitt, Harriet Harman and Jack Dromey in the ass in March 2014, also stung Lord Judge Fulford. Despite clear evidence he was actively supporting pedophiles having sex with kids, when confronted over his past reprehensible behavior, the razor sharp legal mind of Queen's Counsel suddenly went dull and limp, claiming he had no recollection of the pro-pedophile organization he founded nor any of his actions defending their "rights" that despite his denial remain a matter of clear public record. In his own deceitful words:

I have no memory of having been involved with its foundation or the detail of the work of this campaign.[2580]

Rather than be honest and cop to it, he went on a self-righteous rant about how he would never be in favor of anyone or any group that sexually abuses children and insists he has never advocated lowering the age of sexual consent from 16. Regardless of his lame excuses and double talk scrambling to do damage control, the facts plainly speak for themselves.

That said, when a Supreme Court judge was assigned to investigate the nitty gritty of his PIE-friendly past, Fulford was exonerated and cleared of any misconduct... pretty predictable in the nation that consistently protects child rapists.[2581] This pathetic episode is just one more piece of factual evidence blatantly showing how judicial members of an enabling royal elite are entrenched in positions of gatekeeping power to ensure that the pedophilia epidemic stays

---

[2579] Martin Beckford, "High Court Judge and the Child Sex Ring: Adviser to Queen was Founder of Paedophile Support Group to Keep Offenders out of Jail," *Daily Mail*, March 8, 2014.
[2580] Martin Beckford, https://www.dailymail.co.uk/news/article-2576451/High-court-judge-child-sex-ring-Adviser-Queen-founder-paedophile-support-group-offenders-jail.html.
[2581] "Lord Justice Fulford Cleared: Top judge with links to Paedophile Group Cleared of Allegations of Misconduct," *Daly Mail*, July 5, 2014.

shielded as much as sinisterly possible from public exposure, thereby guaranteeing that the diabolical cover-up continues on indefinitely.

For the umpteenth time, shortly after Labor MP Tom Watson's confrontational outburst on the House of Commons floor directed at the flustered Prime Minister David Cameron in October 2012, reminding the world once again of the unfinished business of reckoning with the still covered-up Westminster pedophilia scandal, in January 2013 the Metro Police was once again compelled to relook into historic child sexual abuse under Operation Fairbank turned Fernbridge in what the *Daily Mail* was calling perhaps "the biggest Establishment cover-up" ever.[2582] Then two years later in March 2015, the *Independent* Police Complaints Commission (IPCC), the same outfit that refused to investigate Elm Guest House in 2004, jumped on the insincere, "give-victims-a-voice" bandwagon to announce:

[It] *is to investigate 14 referrals detailing allegations of corruption in the Metropolitan Police Service in relation to child sex offences dating from the 1970's to the 2000's.*[2583]

These allegations involve the numerous aborted police investigations into pedophilia from orders on high, the withholding of evidence against VIPs, a conspiracy within the Met to protect high ranking politicians and sexual abuse committed by senior police personnel. But just when VIP probes were fizzling out with Fernbridge and Midland closed, this IPCC investigation begun in March 2015 also appears to have run its dead-end course as well. So much for investigations into the Westminster cover-up.

Three months after the IPCC announced its 2015 investigation into the widespread Westminster cover-up, MP John Mann warned:

Without a question there is cover-up at the highest level.[2584]

Mann insisted that the British Establishment is still blocking revelations about "systemic" child abuse going public. He believes "hundreds of thousands of people" are "just starting to come forward" with allegations - and they are just "the tip of the iceberg."[2585] In the near four years since John's statements, it seems the Establishment may be winning this war to suppress the truth as investigation after investigation has failed to bring even one VIP to justice and with no

---

[2582] Stephen Wright and Richard Pendlebury, "A Timebomb at Elm Guest House: Pop Stars, a Bishop and a Top Politician appear on a List Seized by Police Investigating Child Abuse at the London Hotel in the 1980s," *Daily Mail*, February 2, 2013.

[2583] Mark Conrad, "Scotland Yard's 'Charge Sheet' for Cover-up on 'VIP Paedophiles,'" *Exaro News*, March 21, 2015..

[2584] Ben Glaze, "Child Sex Abuse is still being Covered up at 'the highest level' Warns Campaigning MP," *Mirror*, June 23, 2015.

[2585] Ben Glaze, https://www.mirror.co.uk/news/uk-news/child-sex-abuse-still-being-5934709.

police inquiry left now to probe historic child abuse, it doesn't look good for the home team still fighting for the truth to come out.

Under the false cover of Fernbridge pledging to finally conduct a real investigation into VIP child abuse, on an early morning in January 2013, the Establishment launched a decisive assault in its continued cover-up when police raided the central London residence of child protection social worker Mary Moss, searching to eliminate the last incriminating evidence known to be still at large. Along with other important documents entrusted her by Carole Kasir before her death, the alleged Elm Guest House list was recovered. Fortunately for us Mary had smartly beat the boys in blue to the punch, uploading the list of boy brothel patrons online before they stole (and no doubt destroyed) more key documents from her home. To this day copies of Mary and Chris's handwritten notes listing the brothel's VIP guests can still be found online,[2586] and infamous child rapists from the Establishment were outed anyway, a rare win for the truth and the public's right to know.

But first the caveat... though child abuse at Elm Guest House is clearly irrefutable, alleged visitors who often signed in at the boy brothel under fake names are included on Mary Moss's online list as the result of handwritten notes written by Mary and her fellow colleague Chris Fay. Also posted online are some of Mary's additional notes from hours of meeting at length with Carole Kasir. However, the accuracy of her online documents cannot be verified as gospel truth since they're based on hearsay information supplied by Mary via Carole Kasir, whose word cannot always be relied upon.

With this qualifier in mind, the following paragraphs cover the alleged VIP sex orgy guests and other notables listed as visitors. Three are so called pop stars. "Kitty" aka superstar Sir Cliff Richard apparently joined by another aging early 1960s heartthrob-turned-actor Jess Conrad as well as a third singer named Ron Wells aka Gladys. Other listings include a bishop that may well be Prince Charles' Anglican Church pal former Bishop Peter Ball linked to pedophilia crimes in East Sussex, home of former Grafton Close Home's deputy head John Stingemore as a transporter of boys to the Elm Guest House.[2587] Among senior MPs aside from Sir Cyril Smith are Monday Club members mentioned earlier, Harvey Proctor and still active MP Sir Peter Bottomley. An official from the royal household is also listed (actually both the queen's lead bodyguard Michael Trestrail as well as Buckingham Palace senior aide Richard Langley have been implicated),[2588] also a senior MI5 officer (the usual suspect - MI5 royal traitor Anthony Blunt who signed in as Anthony Goldstein and also linked to Kincora scandal as well), an MI6

[2586] "The Mary Moss Elm Guest House VIP Paedophile Party List," https://cigpapers.blog/2013/04/29/the-elm-guest-house-vip-paedophile-party-list/.

[2587] "Bishop Ball, Savile, Elm Guest House, Sevenoaks, MI5..." *aangirfan.blogspot.com*, April 1, 2014.

[2588] "Buckingham Palace at the Centre of a Vast Paedophile Network," *robinwestenra.blogspot.com,* December 4, 2019.

officer (likely Peter Hayman as former MI6 deputy director), and a prominent business mogul (possibly related to Guy Blackburn-Hamilton, alleged son of Westland Helicopters chairman).[2589]

Another name worth noting is Barry Haddon, an alleged child pornographer that Mary Moss' notes claim he supplied child porn to Proctor, was a fellow child procurer and close associate of Terry Dwyer who also knew John Rowe and Peter Glencross.[2590] Both Dwyer and Haddon were also boy toy suppliers and apparently protected by higher-ups on the food chain. Haddon's black book "diary" contains a number of senior police officers such as Detective Chief Inspector Chris Sage and a Brent police surgeon named Dr. David Foster.[2591]

A cartoonish underworld figure named Patrick Puddles is also listed as an alleged frequent Elm guest with a particular taste for posing for photo sessions with young boys in the sauna room.[2592] David Issett, the cabal stooge claiming to be Carole's boyfriend who signed off on her two "suicided" notes, insisted his former boss "Patsy" would never be caught up in pedophilia.[2593] An ironic twist coming from an alleged pedophile himself. According to local papers, Issett was linked to a child pornography ring involving Grafton Close Home victims and convicted pedophile-pornographer David Hamilton-Grant, extradited from Cyprus, Turkey.[2594] Now deceased, Patsy Puddles was a police protected local businessman, property owner[2595] and major child porn distributor with a distribution circuit from London to Amsterdam, Rotterdam, Germany and Cyprus.[2596]

Notice the Elm Guest House attracted those who abuse exploitable naked children not only for sex with high rollers willing to pay top dollar to rape and torture, but also a converging parasitic swarm commercially exploiting boys for indecent photos and videos for sordid profit. The Nightmare at Elm House was a den of iniquity in the worst possible way and don't think for a minute Mr. and Mrs. Kasir didn't know it,[2597] leaving their own young son to be allegedly victimized.

Finally, among the motley Elm guest crew arrived the post-WWII British Nazi leader Colin Jordan of the National Socialist Movement financed by his heiress wife Dior, not the National

---

[2589] "Elm Guest House: Mary Moss Leaked Documents," scrbd.com.

[2590] "Harvey Proctor and Cliff Richard Child Sex Abuse Raids: The 'Evidence' that Links them," undercoverinfo.wordpress.com, March 8, 2015.

[2591] "Elm Guest House: Mary Moss Leaked Documents," https://www.scribd.com/doc/253517687/ELM-GUEST-HOUSE-Mary-Moss-Leaked-Documents-authenticity-unverified.

[2592] "The Pedophile Elite London had Branches in the Netherlands," no2abuse.com, March 5, 2013.

[2593] Richard Pendlebury and Stephen Wright, https://www.dailymail.co.uk/news/article-2608177/Was-woman-murdered-cover-Cyril-Smiths-sex-ring.html.

[2594] "Elm Guest House: Carole Kasir Inquest - 1990," slepticpeg.wordpress.com, October 18, 2017.

[2595] "Is Britain Safe; Boy Brothel Cover-up," aangirfan.blogspot.com, April 19, 2014..

[2596] "Elm Guest House; David Hamilton-Grant; Denham Gilbart-Smith," aangirfan.blogspot.com, February 13, 2013.

[2597] "Nightmares at Elm Guest House," https://www.youtube.com/watch?v=ORU5x-ryedU.

Front as reported on the Moss list,[2598] and a Sinn Fein leader who signed in with the alias Gary Walker.[2599] Just as Northern Ireland's Kincora scandal shows British intelligence working covert sexual blackmail with both sides in the Irish-UK conflict, with pedophile leaders from both sides raping boys side by side at London's Elm Guest House, it likewise demonstrates the larger sobering reality that all so called political conflicts and wars in this world are artificially manufactured, planned creations, executed by the same pedophilic elite that virtually owns and controls the entire planet. With centralized control their juggernaut, the ruling elite is presently engaged in a genocidal war against humanity, leading to the endgame scenario of fascist totalitarian tyranny that enslaves the surviving, heavily depopulated, powerless servant class. This is what humans who value freedom, currently targeted in the cabal's crosshairs, are facing in this 11th hour. Out of this Elm Guest House saga emerges many cautionary lessons.

Over the years countless allegations have also persisted of pervasive child sexual abuse at orgies held inside many of the 1250 private luxury flats within the enormous Dolphin Square complex in Pimlico, less than a mile from the Parliamentary buildings where as many as 100 MPs have made their home.[2600] The 1930s dungeon-like chambers are steeped in dark mystery and scandal. Famous old generals and admirals, spies, politicians, writers and royalty frequently make Dolphin Square their home.[2601] M5 and MI6 chiefs have targeted the largest residential block in all of Europe as one humongous sexual blackmail honey trap. After a number of victims and witnesses have come forth since 2012 to report that they were trafficked to flats at Dolphin Square and abused and tortured by MPs and other VIPs, including children allegedly murdered, drawing no response from Metro Police, the Independent Police Complaints Commission in 2015 specified that Dolphin Square would be one of the prime allegations to investigate the Met Police for apparently covering up widespread abuse.[2602]

Recall that boys and girls from care homes throughout the British Isles were trafficked to Dolphin Square parties. Outspoken survivor Richard Kerr from Northern Ireland's Kincora Boys' Home has asserted that he was sexually assaulted by VIPs at both Elm Guest House and Dolphin Square.[2603] Boys from North Wales Bryn Estyn Home were trafficked to Dolphin sex orgies.[2604]

[2598] Dominic Gover, "Westminster Paedophile Scandal: Current MPs named 'again and again' in Calls to Sex Abuse Helpline," *International Business Times*, July 8, 2014.

[2599] Stephen Wright and Richard Pendlebury, https://www.dailymail.co.uk/news/article-2272253/Timebomb-Elm-Guest-House-Pop-stars-bishop-politician-appear-list-seized-police-investigating-child-abuse-London-hotel-1980s.html.

[2600] Patrick Strudwick, "Child Abuse Survivor calls for Inquiry into Police Handling of his Dolphin Square Allegations," *Buzzfeed*, May 7, 2016.

[2601] Henry Porter and Anabel Davidson, "Another Dark Chapter for London's most Scandalous Address," *Vanity Fair*, December 22, 2014, https://www.vanityfair.com/style/scandal/2014/12/scandal-dolphin-square-london.

[2602] "Dolphin Square Named in List of Allegations Probed by IPCC," *ITV News*, March 16, 2015.

[2603] "Kincora Child Sex Abuse Victim Richard Kerr: I was Molested by Powerful People at Dolphin Square and Elm Guest House in London," *Belfast Telegraph*, April 7, 2015.

And of course, it goes without saying, if you happen to be a resident trapped in a London borough care home such as Richmond's Grafton Close or in Islington or Lambeth, from the 1970s through the 1990s and likely beyond, you were likely sexually assaulted in Dolphin Square.[2605]

Scalawag had this to say about Derek Laud, the Tory go-to advisor-fixer-pimp in the 1980s and 1990s:

Derek Laud ran a Pimlico PR agency called Ludgate Communications... in cahoots with [scandal ridden ex-MP] *Ian Greer Associates. Ludgate Communications was at the very hub of our investigation into allegations... At his Pimlico flat, and selected addresses in Dolphin Square nearby, Laud threw parties.*[2606]

Laud's Ludgate pedo-party planner reportedly supplied care home boys from every which direction, funneled straight into his perverted friends' grasps. Boys from North Wales were taken to Laud's fellow lobbyist buddy Ian Greer's Dolphin Square flat to be abused by Tory MPs.[2607] It was in Ian Greer's office that former child actor-anti-child abuse activist Ben Fellows was allegedly molested by soon-to-be Home Office Minister Kenneth Clarke while a camera on a nearby table reportedly captured it concealed from a bag.[2608] Ben also alleges that he too was sexually abused at Dolphin Square parties.

The dual purpose of inviting selected politicians and VIPs to parties is not only to provide the sick sadistic lustful pleasure for powerful, despicable, likeminded criminals but more importantly to gain blackmail control over mostly key Conservative Members of Parliament. Former MI5 operative David Shayler has said that MI5 has fitted many of the Dolphin residences with one way mirrors and hidden cameras for the usual purpose of sexual blackmail.[2609] Since security services headquarters are in close proximity, and a heavy influx of a spy presence at the Pimlico complex on the Thames has been well documented historically,[2610] just like Elm Guest House, Dolphin Square pedophilia is also a sexual blackmail operation.

[2604] James Gillespie and Josh Boswell, "Care Home Paedophile 'Supplied Boys for Whitehall Parties," *The Times*, November 30, 2014.

[2605] "Friends of Israel," *aangrfan.blogspot.com*, September 5, 2018.

[2606] "Child Rapes at Flats Linked to MI5 – Dolphin Square in Pimlico," *aangirfan.blogspot.com*, July 13, 2014.

[2607] "Child Rapes at Flats Linked to MI5 – Dolphin Square in Pimlico," https://aanirfan.blogspot.com/2014/07/child-rapes-at-flats-linked-to-mi5.html.

[2608] "Child Rapes at Flats Linked to MI5 – Dolphin Square in Pimlico," https://aanirfan.blogspot.com/2014/07/child-rapes-at-flats-linked-to-mi5.html.

[2609] Christopher Spivey, "Harvey Proctor and the Dolphin Square Apartment Complex," *chrisspivey.org*, December 17, 2018..

[2610] "Wimpole Muse, Chapter 2 – Dolphin Square" *wimpolemuse.blogspot.com*, September 21, 2016..

A deeper look at how Shirley Porter, Jewish heiress daughter of Sir John Cohen, founder of Tesco supermarket chain, ran her Tory controlled Westminster council as a Kosher Nostra, illustrates the unholy marriage between London's dirty trick politics and Dolphin Square's flourishing cottage industry led by predatory pedophiles like Laud and Greer, supplying fresh young boy meat to dozens of degenerate Westminster VIPs. The queen honored Dame Shirley and her Tory council henchmen's gentrified gerrymandering to push the homeless, unemployed and otherwise poor "riff raff" Labor Party voters out of Westminster to dominate a gay-Tory-pedo playground monopolizing control over both the Westminster borough and its Dolphin Square Tory pedophile ring.[2611] In the late 1980s the district auditor busted her and her cronies' illicit operation, rigging votes in the "homes for votes" corruption scandal, and charged her £42m for bilking council funds, of which only £7000 was recovered, seized from her belongings left behind in London.[2612] Though disgraced publicly back in Britain, as a dual Israeli first citizen, it didn't stop her from living the life of luxury in Israel with hubby Sir Leslie Porter, the Tel Aviv University Chancellor. In 2002 she shamelessly declared herself worth only £300,000, about one-thousandth her actual estimated worth, hidden in offshore accounts in Guernsey, British Virgin Islands and Swiss banks. Shirley surely made out like a bandit as the convicted fraudster eventually settled in 2004 with a £12m payment out of the total £42m she stole from Westminster council funds.[2613]

Originally an Oxford educated Jewish Laborite, Dr. Julian Lewis switched gears to cut his Tory teeth as deputy head researcher at his Conservative Party's Central Office in Smith Square from early to mid-1990s before becoming the Zionist Tory MP for New Forest East in 1997, Esther R's old stomping [alleged child burial] grounds.[2614] As of 2015 the current chair of the powerful Defense select Committee, steeped in high finance and covert arms sales, MP Lewis has reportedly frequented Dolphin Square flats linked to pedo-sex parties.[2615] According to abuse victims who were former residents of North Wales care homes, in addition to being victimized in North Wales (covered in Chapter 26), they also claim they were trafficked to sex parties at Dolphin Square as well as Hampshire County just west of London as part of a national pedo-ring tied to prominent Tories. A *Scalawag Magazine* article reporting the young men's tragic fate contends:

There have been many allegations that Hampshire County Council, through the influence of Derek Laud and his friend Julian Lewis, is a central player in a national paedophile ring supplying

---

[2611] "Friends of Israel," https://aanirfan.blogspot.com/search?q=shirley+porter.

[2612] Andy McSmith and Justin Huggler, "Sleaze Scandal Strips Dame Shirley Porter of her Title," *Independent*, July 6, 2003.

[2613] Matt Weaver, "Dame Shirley Pays out £12m in Housing Scandal, *The Guardian*, July 5, 2004.

[2614] "Rita Ora and the VIP Child-Abuse Connection," *thecolemanexperience.wordpress.com/holliegregjustice.wordpress.com*, February 2, 2016.

[2615] "Letter to the Noor Inayat Khan Memorial Trust," *scribd.com*, February 9, 2016.

young boys from care systems to VIPs... The alleged victims of VIP abuse who died in the fire in Palmeira Avenue Hove (Brighton) in 1991 had also linked Laud, Lewis, and Greer, to the circumstances of the abuse they said they had suffered in care.[2616]

Other known Tory MPs with more than a passing connection with Laud, Greer and Dolphin Square orgies are Sir Edward Leigh,[2617] Sir Peter Lilley,[2618] Sir Michael Portillo,[2619] Michael Brown,[2620] David Nicholson[2621] and Robert Banks.[2622] Because *Scalawag* magazine was exposing Tory pedophiles, it was Julian Lewis who finagled a court order on a bogus claim the magazine was delinquent in its lease payments, changing *Scalawag*'s office locks overnight and seizing the magazine's assets.[2623] The alleged pedophile's dirty tricks campaign against his nemesis continued when he managed to covertly entrap *Scalawag* editor Simon Regan on tape vowing to reduce Lewis' New Forest votes in his 1997 MP election bid.[2624] A four day trial ruled in Lewis' favor with a judgment against Regan breaching an obscure electoral law.

And so the pedo-Establishment neutralized another anti-child abuse threat, ensuring that *Scalawag* went out of business. Regan soon died after a brief illness in 2000 following his co-editor brother's freak fatal car accident in Cyprus in 1996. Gloating over his coup d'état, when a *Scalawag* article accurately incriminated the subsequently convicted pedophile police superintendent Gordon Anglesea who died in prison, Julian Lewis rushed to his aid supplying him with *Scalawag* distributors and printers as ammo for him also to sue the muckrakers as well... birds of a feather.[2625]

Numerous firsthand accounts of abuse have been reported to the police, with understandably only a few willing to forego their right to confidentiality to talk to the press. One such compelling disclosure came from a middle aged man named Michael, interviewed by an ITV news reporter.[2626] Michael verbalized how on Friday afternoons as special outings considered "a treat," he and other residents from his care home were transported in a van south to London for the weekend to attend VIP sex parties. Friday night it might be at a flat in Dolphin Square

---

[2616] "Nick versus Lord Bramall," *aangirfan.blogspot.com*, January 1, 2019.

[2617] "Letter to the Catholic Union," *scrbd.com*, February 10, 2016.

[2618] "Letter to Herts Aid," *scribd.com*, February 3, 2016.

[2619] "BBC Broadcaster Michael Portillo; Alleged Child Sexual Abuse," *scribd.com*, January 27, 2016.

[2620] "Conservative Sex," *aangirfan.blogspot.com*, October 10, 2015.

[2621] "David Nicholson MP," *scribd.com*..

[2622] "Julian Lewis, Harvey Proctor, Keith Vaz, Edward Leigh...," *aangirfan.blogspot.com*, June 19, 2015.

[2623] "Child Rapes at Flats Linked to MI5 – Dolphin Square in Pimlico," https://aanirfan.blogspot.com/2014/07/child-rapes-at-flats-linked-to-mi5.html

[2624] Ian McQuaid, "England's Dreaming #14: Scalawag – UK's Great, Forgotten Satirical Rag," *theransomnote.com*.

[2625] David Hooper, "Libelled Politicians," *julianlewis.net*, extract from *Reputations under Fire: Winners and Losers in the Libel Business* (London: Little, Brown and Company), 2000, p.369-71.

[2626] "Dolphin Square Child Abuse: 'Michael' Abuse Victim Speaks," YouTube video, 14:35, *butlincat.com*, November 9, 2012.

and the next night a mansion in a ritzy borough estate in London or another flat at "the Dolphin." During the day on Saturday the boys would attend sightseeing tours but at plush parties late into the evening, they would be plied with plenty of alcohol and drugs while selected by well-dressed pedophiles for various degrading forms of sex abuse.

For one summer in the early 1980s while in his early teens nearly every weekend he would actually look forward to his getaways to London town as an adventure and reprieve from his dull weekday routine at his group home, accepting the sexual abuse as a mere tolerated price to pay for temporary admission into this unknown and exciting world of the high life, a momentary fleeting escape from his poor working class roots to a brief glimpse encounter observing how the wealthy and powerful live and party. Michael's stoic, almost matter-of-fact, yet casually open attitude toward accepting sexual abuse as an unpleasant price to pay appears perhaps his defensive coping mechanism while presenting himself before the rolling news camera. Or perhaps years of therapy afforded him the opportunity to emotionally distance himself from his past schoolboy trauma when speaking about it years later.

The IPCC police commission's decision in 2015 to probe further into the cover-up of abuse at Dolphin Square stemmed from how the Met Police has refused to properly investigate the reported rapes of multiple victims resulting from consistent stand down orders from above. One abuse survivor whose actual name is David, currently in his early fifties, came from a loving family that moved to the iconic countryside of Lincolnshire when he was just turning 15. His friendly neighbor Gordon Dawson was among the respected town leaders, a local ombudsman, active in the Anglican Church diocese, quickly becoming friends with David's parents.[2627] Gordon taught David how to hunt and shoot rabbits. Little did the naïve boy or his unsuspecting parents know he was being classically groomed by a serial child sexual predator.

Like so many victimized boys at 15, David reacted to the sexual abuse by withdrawing socially into a private, confused world of shame and dread. As a desperate attempt to get away, ultimately David told his parents how much he hated school and wished to return to his old one two hours away in Cambridgeshire. But then the family friend Dawson offered to pick him up on Fridays. Next came an invitation to London for the weekend and a night at the theater. Because his parents completely trusted this seemingly warm, generous man taking a "mentor's" interest in their shy youngest of three sons, David felt trapped and frozen in fear to tell anyone.

So like fellow abuse survivor Michael, it was off to spending numerous weekends in the bustling capital London, staying at London's Dolphin Square in 1982. The wealthy landowner from

---

[2627] Patrick Strudwick, "This is what happens when you Report Historical Sexual Abuse to the Police," *Buzzfeed*, May 7, 2016.

Lincolnshire trafficked David at least 10 times into the big city to his Dolphin Square luxury flat where David claims he was carnally assaulted repeatedly by Dawson and other men. David explained that they would regularly attend dinners at London restaurants where they'd meet up with Dawson's friends, reportedly MPs, senior military officers, prominent businessmen, and members of the Church of England's General Synod. Sometimes other young boys were present at the restaurant as well.[2628] After dining, they would reconvene at one of the Dolphin Square flats for after dinner drinks to gorge on their boy toy dessert.

As the church's governing body, the general synod periodically meets several times a year in Westminster. As of March 2018, the IICSA heard public testimony and complaints from witnesses and victims like David amongst a total of 3,300 child sex abuse allegations committed by Queen Elizabeth's Church of England.[2629] Between all her sex offending knights and perverted clergy, CSA is simply their Luciferian way of life.

Even prior to David reporting his abuse to Lincolnshire Police, in December 2006 an officer gave the child rapist a heads up call that he would be arrested after receiving allegations from Dawson's other sexually abused victims.[2630] What's worse is when David did report Dawson's crimes to police just two months later in February 2007, that same police officer again leaked to Dawson that he'd be rearrested, unbelievably adding that David was his latest accuser.[2631] This grossly unethical if not illegal deference shown Dawson gave him ample opportunity to destroy incriminating evidence and clearly endangered David's life with potential violent retribution. Standard police protocol would confiscate an arrestee's gun collection as precaution against either suicide or homicide. Within 90 minutes of that February phone call, Dawson allegedly shot himself in the head, preventing any real justice for David. Though the police quickly wrote it off as suicide, later falsely proclaiming it to the press, in fact the coroner recorded Dawson's death as an open verdict.[2632] With the local perpetrator deceased and out of the way, Lincolnshire Police instantly washed its hands of the case, refusing to investigate any further. Moreover, the criminal leads David reported of sexual abusers at Dolphin Square were completely omitted from the Lincolnshire Police records. Even the IPCC in 2007 refused to touch the case, no doubt due to implicating Dolphin Square VIPs. It turns out that Gordon Dawson had a long record for abusing boys as young as five dating back to 1964 right up to at

---

[2628] Patrick Strudwick, https://www.buzzfeed.com/patrickstrudwick/this-is-what-happens-when-you-report-historical-sexual-abuse?utm_term=.pjGRmvWez#.rrLVeQ4wr.

[2629] "Queen-led Church of England Faces 3,300 Sexual Abuse Allegations," *Press TV*, February 11, 2018.

[2630] Patrick Strudwick, https://www.buzzfeed.com/patrickstrudwick/child-abuse-survivor-calls-for-inquiry-into-police-handling.

[2631] Patrick Strudwick, https://www.buzzfeed.com/patrickstrudwick/this-is-what-happens-when-you-report-historical-sexual-abuse?utm_term=.pjGRmvWez#.rrLVeQ4wr.

[2632] Patrick Strudwick, "Police Commissioner says 'Lessons must be learnt' from Historical Sex Abuse Exposé," *Buzzfeed*, May 26, 2016.

least 1986… another despicable example of a protected VIP allowed to harm children for decades because of his influence and power, locally as well as in London.[2633]

After Scotland Yard's Operation Fairbank had publicly appealed for victims to come forth with evidence as part of its overarching inquiry into historic Westminster abuse, in 2015 David decided to once again report Dawson and his VIP friends' sexual crimes to police a second time, providing two days' worth of allegations backed up by documents supporting his Dolphin Square abuse claims along with his prior complaint to police 8 years earlier.[2634] It was then that David found out that two of Dawson's friends and co-owners of the Pimlico flat were never even interviewed by police. But David was reassured by the Met detectives interviewing him that his case had just cause to be reopened. Yet several days later, Met police notified David that Dolphin Square was suddenly off limits, specifying that:

There is nothing further for us to investigate here. The information that we discussed doesn't fall within the remit of [Operation] Fairbank or the Metropolitan Police.[2635]

Trying to get answers finally drew an email response from Detective Sergeant James Townly explaining:

It is not feasible for the police to investigate every potential or convicted paedophile for links to others. In an ideal world we would very much like to identify all offenders and identify their links to other paedophiles and networks [but] sadly that does not happen.[2636]

A final email from Townly specified that because David could not supply names of VIPs at the restaurants or the Dolphin Square flats, "this is not sufficient for a crime report." Despite knowing the names of Dawson's two partners sharing the same Dolphin flat, because they were not known to Met Police, they wanted no part. Again bottom line, neither Fairbank nor Midland really wanted any part in uncovering and bringing to justice any of the powerful VIP criminals that abused David or any other child. This dereliction of duty perverting the course of justice was completely unacceptable, prompting David to go public. Clearly the circled wagons had once again closed in rapid order to shield off any further exposure of VIP pedo-crimes committed at Dolphin Square… i.e., the same old, same old.

[2633] Patrick Strudwick, https://www.buzzfeed.com/patrickstrudwick/this-is-what-happens-when-you-report-historical-sexual-abuse?utm_term=.pjGRmvWez#.rrLVeQ4wr.

[2634] Patrick Strudwick, https://www.buzzfeed.com/patrickstrudwick/child-abuse-survivor-calls-for-inquiry-into-police-handling.

[2635] Patrick Strudwick, https://www.buzzfeed.com/patrickstrudwick/this-is-what-happens-when-you-report-historical-sexual-abuse?utm_term=.pjGRmvWez#.rrLVeQ4wr.

[2636] Patrick Strudwick, https://www.buzzfeed.com/patrickstrudwick/this-is-what-happens-when-you-report-historical-sexual-abuse?utm_term=.pjGRmvWez#.rrLVeQ4wr.

Keith Best, chief executive of the victims' group called Survivors UK, said that Lincolnshire made "grave errors" only to be compounded by Met's flagrant obstruction of justice to cover up, adding:

The current unsatisfactory situation not only leaves considerable suspicion but also a massive discouragement to others to come forward in similar cases.[2637]

With added pressure from the negative press, compliments of *Buzzfeed* that took up David's righteous cause, once the survivor filed his formal complaint with IPCC, it may have ultimately swayed the police watchdog to look into Met's "alleged" cover-up, i.e., its outright refusal to even touch Dolphin Square debauchery.

In May 2016 a new Lincolnshire police commissioner tried putting his best spin forward:

A number of lessons were learned in relation to best practice and fed back to the Public Protection Unit[2638] [i.e., don't tell the arrestee he's going to be arrested beforehand, don't tell him who his latest accuser(s) are and confiscate all his guns prior to arrest, all SOP police practice everywhere except when VIPs are the criminals].

The Lincolnshire police superintendent issued a belated apology to David with the usual rhetoric that if the same investigation occurred today, it would have been handled differently... famous last words oftentimes heard before. Yet regardless of today or yesterday, the outcome always remains the same – no justice for VIP perps at the expense of no justice for victims. Apologies and rhetoric don't mean shit – today's system still fully protects sodomizers and inflicts double the pain and trauma on child victims.

As a postscript in the final days of 2016, a full decade after the first botched investigation-cover-up was willfully, prematurely closed, Lincolnshire Police finally conceded that it would reopen David's case against Dawson.[2639] Of course small consolation, it changes nothing and likely was only done to appease the persistent bad publicity coming from *Buzzfeed*, providing a temporary reprieve from David's lifelong troubles. And the IPCC promise in 2015 to thoroughly re-investigate the Met's mishandling and cover-up at Dolphin Square? Whatever happened with that? Another "out of sight, out of mind" gloss over conveniently forgotten four years later. Child fuckers inside their palaces are toasting "long live the royal Commonwealth's cover-up of the centuries."

[2637] Patrick Strudwick, https://www.buzzfeed.com/patrickstrudwick/child-abuse-survivor-calls-for-inquiry-into-police-handling.
[2638] Patrick Strudwick, "Historical Child Sex Abuse Case Reopened after Buzzfeed News Investigation," *Buzzfeed*, December 31, 2016.
[2639] Patrick Strudwick, https://www.buzzfeed.com/patrickstrudwick/police-reopen-child-sexual-abuse-case-following-buzzfeed-new.

In 1985 the Met Police responded to an emergency call claiming that a boy of about 11 years of age appeared to be taken against his will into one of the Dolphin Square flats by adult men.[2640] Upon arrival at the riverside complex, police discovered in the living room of one of the first floor units a makeshift film studio with expensive camera and lighting equipment still on. The occupants apparently were in a mad rush to escape filming their last scene. But there was no further criminal evidence at that time to go on - until a few months later. A child pornographic video was seized in a police raid in Soho's West End depicting two well-dressed men filmed from the neck down sexually abusing a boy about 11 from the same recognized Pimlico apartment.[2641] During the 15-minute footage, the two abusers disrobed revealing their middle aged paunches with one showing a scar below his navel.

Thirty years later detectives working Operation Midland hoped to take advantage of forensic advances that might provide additional clues to aid in identifying the boy who'd now be in his 40s as well as his abusers. Reports of children murdered at Dolphin Square sex orgies under Operation Midland motivated law enforcement's renewed interest in the Westminster-Dolphin Square pedo-scandal, particularly because of the all too obvious history of Establishment cover-up. But it too apparently went nowhere just like Midland with no leads or subsequent arrests. And just like the VIP child rapists at Elm Guest House, the Dolphin Square pedophiles also got away with their sick depravities.

With all the post-Savile outrage and the ensuing public pressure to investigate and prosecute VIP child abusers, it didn't take long for the pedo-Establishment to predictably begin its pushback campaign. Teamed with the government-owned *BBC*, and the Lord McAlpine retraction, by 2015 British media claims of a "witch hunt" were well underway. In October that year a *Daily Mail* headline read "I'm the latest victim of sex abuse witch-hunt, says ex-MP: VIP police quiz former backbencher" with the first sentence out the starting gate:

A former MP became the latest victim of Labour's child sex abuse 'witch-hunt' yesterday.[2642]

The elite's old familiar "divide and conquer" tactic pitting Labor versus Tory Party politics is the first giveaway to the elite's media manipulation. Reality check #1 – just as the planetary controllers control both parties in UK and US, in fact all major political parties virtually everywhere especially in the Western world are saturated with compromised, controlled and well-protected pedophiles. The second is the pejorative term "witch hunt" used to describe in order to nullify the thousands of actual child abuse victims' claims that are true.

[2640] James Fielding, "Boy's Rape Filmed in Dolphin Square," Express, August 23, 2015.

[2641] James Fielding, https://www.express.co.uk/news/uk/600117/Boy-rape-filmed-notorious-Dolphin-Square.

[2642] Darnel Martin, Andy Dolan and Emily Kent Smith, "I'm the latest Victim of Sex Abuse Witch-Hunt, says ex-MP: VIP Police Quiz former Backbencher," *Daily Mail*, October 12, 2015.

The oft quoted alleged fake victim-fantasist "Nick" whose reportedly fraudulent allegations, once believed by Met Police as highly "credible" and "true," singlehandedly spawned the £3m Operation Midland boondoggle netting zero arrests is about to go on trial in March 2019 for perverting the course of justice and fraud. Immediately the Establishment seizes the opportunity to promote the false notion of an overzealous "witch hunt" that encourages fantasists like Nick and Darren to jump on the CSA bandwagon for press attention or money at the expense of poor old war heroes like General Lord Bramall or the *Daily Mail's* "ex-MP" like poor old, long suffering Harvey Proctor, or the martyred Sir Lord Leon trashed after his passing when no longer able to properly defend himself against this vengeful, wicked and groundless scheme to demonize these "innocent" VIPs being unfairly vilified, crucified and skewered by an out-of-control public lynch mob mentality. This is elitist propaganda caught turning the pendulum table with VIP rapists once again granted "get out of jail cards" while it's back to the abuse victims who end up on trial as fantasist, untrustworthy criminals.[2643]

As mentioned earlier, this is just more of the same old "satanic panic as mere myth," and the "false memory syndrome" designed to negate actual child abuse memories and experiences.[2644] The rulers employ the CIA to conjure up these clever little catchy, play-on-word fabrications as their weapons to suppress the truth. Hence, aluminum tin foiled, hat wearing "conspiracy theorists" are constantly promoting "false flag" accusations, making up outrageous, "not-to-be-believed" lies against our much maligned, upstanding leaders and governments. Bush's post 9/11 speech illustrates the point: "Let us never tolerate outrageous conspiracy theories."[2645]

Throw in poor little Kitty and his Elm Guest House super injunctions,[2646] his 2018 court victory over the police and *BBC* and his £5m payout (see Chapter 5) barring the free press and people's right to know when famous suspects are arrested, and you have the ruling elite's highly effective pushback agenda aiding and abetting the pedo-cabal's continual rape of our innocents to guarantee permanent impunity for all VIP rapists. The elite's rigged legal system and multibillion dollar propaganda blitz ensure that the truth stays hidden so that powerful child rapists can safely go to their graves unburdened by consequences.[2647] As a countermeasure to cut through their 24/7 bullshit lies, the purpose of this A-Z fully documented sourcebook exposé on modern pedophilia is to shine the spotlight on all the pedo-cockroaches so they can no longer pull the wool over our eyes and, under the false cover of their artificially created

---

[2643] "'Witch Hunt' – The Abusers 'get out of Jail Free' Card," *oye.news*, October 13, 2015.
[2644] Catherine Bennett, "After the Lessons of the 1990s Satanic Abuse Panic, why was 'Nick' believed?" *The Guardian*, February 10, 2018.
[2645] "Bush Addresses the UN – tells the World no 911 Discussions," YouTube video, 0:15, posted June 4, 2006.
[2646] Janet Street-Porter, "People like Cliff Richard Deserve Anonymity if they haven't been Charged with a Crime – but MPs under Investigation for Misconduct certainly do not," Independent, July 20, 2018.
[2647] "Historic Child Abuse Victims become the Guilty as the Establishment Turn the Tables," *oye.news*, October 5, 2015.

Luciferian darkness, roam freely to continue at will destroying thousands upon thousands of young people's lives the world over. The truth is finally out there and there's no place left to hide for these sick fucks.

With so called fantasists like Nick and Darren notwithstanding, plenty of legitimate abuse victims like the aforementioned David have come forth to share their harrowing abuse experiences at Dolphin Square. But with zero convictions resulting from the now closed Operations Midland and Fernbridge (save one minor ex-priest) and the IPCC and IISCA fizzling down and out into oblivion, despite all of these high profile productions ostensibly designed to investigate Westminster VIP abuse, it's as if the hundreds of victims reporting horrific abuse at Elm and Dolphin sex orgies through the years never happened at all when overwhelming evidence confirms that in fact it did. That shows you how hard working overtime the pedo-cabal's been to magically make the Westminster scandal go away once and for all. But the genie of lies and deception cannot be put back in the bottle because too much truth is already out there.

Yet another survivor of sex crimes at the Dolphin Square complex also named David went public with his story in May 2015. During his three month stay in London in 1975, a 20-year old David reports that he was coerced and threatened to attend sex parties at various locations including "the Dolphin" where he was forced to perform paid for sex acts with prominent MPs, senior military officers, judges and businessmen.[2648] He claims that little boys as young as 8 were being savagely abused. To help get him through the traumatic events, he immersed himself in alcohol and drugs. One of the sex parties had the pedophiles celebrating Margaret Thatcher's promotion to becoming Tory Party leader in February 1975 in anticipation of her reign as the prime minister pedo-queen throughout the 1980s. The 60 year old abuse survivor in 2015 reported his sexual assaults to the press, disclosing that he observed Peter Hayman at parties abusing young boys as well as Peter Righton. David recalled how at a soiree in Notting Hill, he witnessed two brothers, one 8 and the other 10, drugged and forced to sexually assault each other for the sick viewing pleasure of drunken and vile dirty old men. When he attempted to intervene, he maintains that he was beaten unconscious. David also said he was coerced into performing a sex act on two politicians. In his words:

[2648] Amanda Williams, "I was Sexually Abused at Paedophile Parties: Victim of 1970s tells of being Forced to Perform Sex Acts as Senior Tories Celebrated Thatcher Victory," *Daily Mail*, May 5, 2015.

I was totally humiliated. And from then it started. I was drawn into this web where I was taken to these parties, I would be meeting individuals for sex. Just totally trapped. Then began my descent into drinking, taking drugs. It was just a nightmare.[2649]

Another link to Dolphin Square pedophiles is Roddam Twiss, disgraced son of Frank Twiss, the famed Admiral of the British Fleet and the queen's envoy in the House of Lords' Black Rod.[2650] As a 27-year old teacher in 1967, Roddam Twiss was convicted of stripping, beating and sexually assaulting five boys as young as 11 and sentenced to three years. This perv has pretty much been into S&M on the rent boy scene ever since. As of 2004 he's also a convicted fraudster of a conman, stealing £1.2million of his investors' money and doing more time for that lowlife caper.[2651] His past associates include Lennie Smith who Twiss at one time rented to. Smith is a member of the infamous Sidney Cooke gang, convicted of rape, torture and murder of many boys, including Jason Swift.[2652] In 2018 MP Andrew Brigden called for Roddam to be summoned to the IICSA for his role as a rent boy procurer for Westminster pedophiles.[2653]

Two detectives investigating Cyril Smith years ago observed the MP taking an underage boy to Roddam's flat. When they approached their superiors for the go-ahead to surveil Twiss, they were called off since the Twiss senior was then the queen's envoy in the House of Lords. For a hardcore pedophile like Twiss who's been a frequent Dolphin Square visitor for many decades, to call it the "den of iniquity," you know disgustingly sick shit is the Square's main faire. Twiss would regularly visit his close friend millionaire playboy Mervyn Greenway who lived there. Twiss has said, "Mervyn knew everyone in high places," and of course that's most helpful to a pimping procurer for VIPs at the Dolphin among a number of other safe pedo-havens around town.[2654]

Despite the so called fantasists, former Scotland Yard detectives that investigated child abuse allegations at Elm House and Dolphin Square knew Westminster VIPs were vultures hurting children with impunity:

[2649] Amanda Williams, https://www.dailymail.co.uk/news/article-3068950/I-abused-Establishment-paedophile-parties-Victim-1970s-Dolphin-Square-ring-tells-forced-perform-sex-acts-senior-Tories-celebrated-Thatcher-victory.html.

[2650] Glen Owen and Paul Cahalan, "Summon the Son of ex-Black Rod to Child Sex Abuse Probe, MP Demands after Mail on Sunday Revealed his Links to VIPs and Rent Boys, *Daily Mail*, May 19, 2018.

[2651] Patrick Sawer, "Â£1.2m Fraud of Black Rod's Son," *Evening Standard*, July 29, 2004.

[2652] "Twiss, Dolphin Square, Jason Swift, the Navy," *aangirfan.blogspot.com*, May 14, 2018.

[2653] Glen Owen and Paul Cahalan, https://www.dailymail.co.uk/news/article-5749103/Summon-son-ex-Black-Rod-child-sex-abuse-probe-MP-demands.html.

[2654] "Twiss, Dolphin Square, Jason Swift, the Navy, http://aanirfan.blogspot.com/2018/05/twiss-dolphin-square-jason-swift-navy.html.

There was a significant paedophile group in Parliament who were untouchable to the police.[2655]

I would add they still are. But the truth is making them increasingly nervous. Even a pedo-cabal insider let the truth slip out. A candid elitist in a rare moment dared to admit the truth in July 2014 when former Thatcher minister Lord Norman Tebbit confessed that "there may well have been" a political cover-up of pedophilia in the 1980s, and as the leader of the Tory Party whose job was to cover it all up, he should know.[2656] When so many stay silent or continue lying through their false teeth, it's refreshing to know that at least one Establishment figure mustered the guts to at least momentarily cop to what's most undeniable.

In the same 2014 *BBC* article, of all people, Dame Margaret Oppenheimer-Hodge is quoted saying there's been "a veil of secrecy over the establishment" for far too long... talk about the pot calling the kettle black! This too is an old elitist tactic, using the propaganda machine to put out a morsel of truth intended to de-vilify and distance proven past criminality. As Minister of Children, Hodge allegedly pressed PM Blair to issue a D-notice suppressing the Nene report in 2004 that also determined a high profile pedophile ring was rampantly abusing boys in 16 London care homes.[2657] Any new finding that was confirming what she'd begun in Islington and Lambeth in the 80s and early 90s had spread to more London boroughs by 2004 while Britain's Minister of Children, no questions asked had to be covered-up.

If child sexual abuse is so tightly concealed in a massive UK cover-up, then torture and murder are too. Sometimes all three heinous crimes are committed by VIP untouchables. Among the running main themes of this book is what happens to those individuals who know too much for the deadly system to tolerate. That's when strange, mysterious, unexplained deaths are most apt to occur, like improbable suicides with two bullet holes through the head or sudden disappearances or untraceable heart attacks or lethal accidents, OD injections and other untimely fates that so often coincide with upcoming court appearances.

Another abrupt ending of a life is the suspicious death of 65-year old Sir John Stradling Thomas, Tory MP of Monmouth from 1970 to his March 1991 death. The MP was found dead in his Dolphin Square flat, reportedly just hours prior to speaking about deadly child abuse and its cover-up involving Westminster peers and prominent senior officials in NHS and UK Care System.[2658] In 1990 and 1991 Sir John embarked on a series of correspondences with former Health Minister Tony Newton, Attorney General Patrick Mayhew and Home Secretary Earl

[2655] Fiona Keating, "MPs in Westminster Paedophile Ring Were 'Untouchables' Claims Former Special Branch Officer," *IB Times*, November 23, 2014.

[2656] "Child Abuse 'may well have been' Covered up – Norman Tebbit," *BBC*, July 6, 2014.

[2657] "Sex in Schools," *aangirfan.blogspot.com*, February 3, 2015.

[2658] Sally Baker, "Criminals are getting away with it," *drsallybaker.com*, May 22, 2018.

Ferrers, apparently making unwanted waves inquiring into dozens of covered up deaths of children in Suffolk care, many disabled.[2659]

Sir John may have stumbled upon and opened a Pandora's Box that quickly closed in on him at his Dolphin Square flat on March 29, 1991... that Pandora's Box being lethal Tavistock methods using guinea pig drug experimentation on disabled children at an NHS contracted facility in Suffolk County called Beeches, among a large number of other children's facilities throughout Britain.[2660] Both Islington and Hackney sent children with cerebral palsy to Beeches where 43 children mysteriously died between 1954 and 1972.[2661] Only two of the 43 children had inquests. Evidence shows major cover-up collusion between a host of authorities in Suffolk alone, including the County Council, County National Health Service, Suffolk Police and Police Crime Commissioner... not to mention Suffolk's long related history of child sexual abuse.[2662] MP Thomas may well have been digging his own grave at the infamously shady Dolphin Square complex, digging and probing into dirty business considered off limits to MPs with a conscience. Plus one would think the sudden death of a knighted, upstanding MP for 21 years would draw more press. There's absolutely nothing on his cause of death. Predictably, Operation Midland that rightfully should have taken up this entire matter never did. And with a rabbit hole running this deep, nor will the IICSA whitewash.

A year after MP Thomas's death, in 1992 when the well-connected, overly protected child procurer Peter Righton was busted for possessing and distributing child pornography, Lord Henniker opened up his Suffolk estate Thornham Magna as the founding PIE member's next residence for several years.[2663] Recall that Margaret Hodge as Islington council leader was sending vulnerable at-risk children from her pedo-infested care homes to Thornham Magna under the Islington-Suffolk Project, using the estate as an educational and recreational center. With the likes of Righton, his convicted pedo-lover Alston and their convicted pedo-friend Napier all granted free access to the boy toy sweet shop, it's highly suspected that more children were sexually assaulted there. At all cost UK upholds its longstanding pattern protecting VIP pedophiles while child advocates trying to safeguard targeted kids from harm or uncover past child abuse and murder are targeted themselves for abuse and murder. Lucifer has always had a home in Freemason country.

Another Tory MP who died a suspicious death also found lifeless in his Dolphin Square flat was MP Iain Mills (covered in Chapter 21). Though a supposed teetotaler and never seen publicly

[2659] Richard Card, "Suffolk County Council - Social Services Directors," *whatdotheyknow.com*, September 18, 2017.
[2660] "Aston Hall, Kendall House, Mind Controlled Kids, Gravesend," *aangirfan.blogspot.com*, April 15, 2017.
[2661] Richard Card, "Islington Council Raise Inquiry into 43 Child Care Deaths at one Care Home," *change.org*.
[2662] Elite Sex; Suffolk – Updated," *aangirfan.blogspot.com*, May 22, 2015.
[2663] Stewart Payne and Eileen Fairweather, "Country House Hideaway of Disgraced Care Chief," *Evening Standard/spotlightonabuse.wordpress.com*, May 6, 1993.

consuming alcoholic beverages, MP Mills was discovered two days after his January 1997 demise with empty gin bottles around him and a high content of alcohol allegedly in his bloodstream that old "faithful hands," cabal coroner Dr. Paul Knapman automatically ruled alcohol poisoning.[2664] Iain Mills had been a close friend and ally of MP Geoffrey Dickens who died little more than a year earlier, and speculation that Mills also was growing increasingly intolerant and disgusted by the rampant Dolphin Square sex orgies at the expense of abused trafficked children may have led to his premature departure at only 57. And speaking of another Chapter 21 strange and suspicious death at the Dolphin pedo-haven, 64-year old Judge Rodney McKinnon allegedly fell to his death and Knapman insisted it was suicide despite the strong objection from Rodney's brother who was also a judge.

Though so called Nick's three witnessed murders of abused child victims at Dolphin Square are now allegedly untrue, plenty of murdered boys associated with the Elm Guest House and Dolphin Square scandals remain fact. Two of the highest profile, still unsolved disappearance-murder cases are 15-year old Martin Allen in 1979 followed less than two years later by 8-year old Vishal Mehrotra in 1981.

Kevin Allen was just 18 months older than his brother Martin. As teenage sons of head chauffeur of the Australian high commissioner, the Allen family lived in the caretaker's 5-bedroom cottage located just behind the commissioner's residence at Stoke Lodge on the famous Kensington street Hyde Park Gate where the DeBeers jewelry family were neighbors and Winston Churchill lived and died.[2665] At the underground basement of the Canberra House down the street from the Australian Embassy, for pocket change Kevin and Martin would regularly wash the commissioner's custom car fleet.

But then on Guy Fawkes Night, November 5th, 1979, Martin was last seen at the Kings Cross tube station heading home after visiting his oldest brother. A witness reported to the press at the time that he identified Martin being held by a six foot blonde man by the scruff of the neck on the subway train.[2666] Moreover, coverage of the Elm Guest House raid in August 1982 stated that the investigation into the two missing boys in 1979 and 1981 was reopened and widened to link them with the dirty business a short distance away at the Elm Guest House among other houses of ill repute around London. But then the outcome of this "widening" investigation was never again reported because, like all the rest of the VIP police inquiries into pedophilia, it was ordered shut down not only to conceal child sex abuse but very likely murder as well.

[2664] "Who are the Queen's Lord Lieutenants?" *whale.to*.

[2665] Jaquelin Magnay, "A Missing Boy and the Australian High Commission in London," *The Australian/spotlightonabuse.wordpress.com*, January 31, 2015.

[2666] Murun Buchstansangur, "Was the Scotland Yard Investigation into Missing Boys Closed down?" *spotlightonabuse.wordpress.com*, February 9, 2013.

In recent years it has come to light that whenever the father's crew of five chauffeurs were already booked, a temporary chauffeur rental service on the other side of the Thames would be hired for fill-in drivers, one of whom was pedophile-serial murderer Sidney Cooke.[2667] Known to procure and traffic children to VIP bigwig parties at nearby Elm Guest House, the Dolphin Square complex and other select locations around London including even Amsterdam, the Cooke gang "Dirty Dozen" regularly grabbed boys from off the street as well as care homes to deliver abuse victims to sex orgies.

When a 17-year old Kevin Allen was asked by the lead detective what he believed happened to his younger brother, Kevin said he thought that Martin had been abducted by a higher or elite person. According to Kevin, the investigator pointed his finger at Kevin, threatening:

You shouldn't be saying things like that, you could get hurt.[2668]

From an incisive January 2015 article in *The Australian*, drawing links to the VIP pedophile ring:

For more than 30 years, the activities of this incredibly well-connected pedophile network was apparently protected from scrutiny through the issuing of government D-notices, which prevent media publication of anything deemed to affect national security. It is believed this stymied police investigations. Hundreds of files relating to the disclosures and evidence about the VIP pedophile ring have since gone missing. Kevin says the files relating to Martin's disappearance have been destroyed twice.[2669]

The article goes on to reference the abruptly disbanded 1986 police probe into the VIP pedo-ring just one day before the scheduled arrest of Leon Brittan, Cyril Smith and 14 other high profile figures photographed attending an orgy in North London, victimizing boys picked up at Kings Cross.[2670] It's more than plausible that Martin Allen was also picked up at Kings Cross, kidnapped, dropped off and sexually abused by VIPs, only to be disposed of by the likes of the Sidney Cooke gang, ultimately covered up by police at the behest of the criminal Establishment.

On the celebrated day when Prince Charles married Lady Diana on July 29, 1981, an 8-year old boy named Vishal Mehrotra suddenly vanished after watching the wedding precession with his

---

[2667] Jaquelin Magnay, https://spotlightonabuse.wordpress.com/2015/02/01/a-missing-boy-and-the-australian-high-commission-in-london-31-01-15/.

[2668] Jaquelin Magnay, https://spotlightonabuse.wordpress.com/2015/02/01/a-missing-boy-and-the-australian-high-commission-in-london-31-01-15/.

[2669] Jaquelin Magnay, https://spotlightonabuse.wordpress.com/2015/02/01/a-missing-boy-and-the-australian-high-commission-in-london-31-01-15/.

[2670] Jaquelin Magnay, https://spotlightonabuse.wordpress.com/2015/02/01/a-missing-boy-and-the-australian-high-commission-in-london-31-01-15/.

family.[2671] While his family went shopping afterwards, used to walking to and from school every day on his own, the boy headed the short distance home alone, apparently reaching within 300 yards of his Putney residence before disappearing. Vishal was last seen less than a mile from Elm Guest House. Though several witnesses claimed they'd seen men with a young Asian boy, the leads grew cold. Then a few months later in February 1982 in a wooded area in West Sussex, a skull and rib cage were found and identified as Vishal's remains. Months later the father, a Wimbledon court magistrate, recorded a 15-minute phone conversation from a man believed to be in his 20s who shared that he believed that Vishal was apprehended by those associated with the Elm Guest House VIP pedophile ring. But when the father brought the new piece of evidence to the police, he soon was disappointed:

... Instead of investigating it, they just pooh-poohed it and I never heard anything about the tape again. The whole thing went cold. At that time I trusted the police. But when nothing happened, I became confused and concerned. Now it is clear to me that there has been a huge cover up. There is no doubt in my mind.[2672]

Despite insisting that 20,000 people were interviewed by police, as soon as Scotland Yard learned that judges and politicians were implicated, the interest in finding Vishal Mehrotra's killers apparently went no further. Again the now 92-year old Sidney Cooke, currently serving two life sentences linked to nine murdered boys, was named at least eight times in a heavily censored police report on the missing 8-year old boy's murder.[2673] Cooke had worked at fairgrounds and records show that at the time of Vishal's abduction, two fairs were in the area. Released through a 2015 Freedom of Information request, large blocks of the police report were redacted, obviously because the Scotland Yard has much to hide in its cover-up protection of child raping VIPs. An informant in the review made the statement that "Cooke and his associates" claimed at least 12 victims, including an "Asian boy."

Police kept secret from Vishal's family that four or five suspects were questioned and released, and the senior officer admitted that suspects' alibis were not carefully checked.[2674] The shoddy murder investigation also failed to follow up a shoe found in the bog next to Vishal's remains nor two people observed throwing a sack over the fence where the bones were found. In short, the police purposely sabotaged solving the case in order to shield the Westminster pedo-ring.

[2671] Bill Gardner, "Father Claims Scotland Yard Covered up Son's Murder by Westminster Paedophiles," *The Telegraph,* November 18, 2014.

[2672] Bill Gardner, https://www.telegraph.co.uk/news/uknews/crime/11239535/Father-claims-Scotland-Yard-covered-up-sons-murder-by-Westminster-paedophiles.html.

[2673] Jonathan Corke, "Paedophile Sidney Cooke's Potential Links to Murder of Boy, 8, Ignored by Police, *Mirror,* May 30, 2015.

[2674] Nicola Fifield and Jonathan Corke, "VIP Paedophile Murders: Police didn't tell Family about Quizzing Suspects in Killing of Boy aged eight," *Mirror,* April 4, 2015.

And despite the IPCC watchdog in 2015 including Scotland Yard ignoring the Elm Guest House tipoff as one of 14 allegations it would pursue, again nothing ever came out of that either.

Sidney Cooke and his "Dirty Dozen" gang ultimately were convicted of torturing and murdering three boys – 7-year old Mark Tildesley lured from a fairground Cooke was working in 1984, a year later 14-year old Jason Swift from a Margaret Hodge Islington care home in 1985 and abducted 6-year old Barry Lewis in 1991. But the lead detective Roger Stoodley who provided evidence to secure the three convictions by 1992 under Operation Orchid feels near certain that 17 more abduction-murders were committed by this same evil gang throughout the 1980s into the early 90s.[2675] Cooke and his gang supplied boys grabbed off the street, recruited rent boys from the public toilets and trafficked care home boys to VIP orgies at both Elm Guest House and Dolphin Square as well as Kensington, North London and other locations. Besides being a fairground worker, Cooke also worked as a chauffeur and has been linked to both the Martin Allen and Vishal Mehrotra abduction-murders that fit his gang's M.O. profile. But because police inspections at Elm Guest House, Dolphin Square, Lambeth and North London, Manchester were all consistently closed as soon as Westminster MPs, Downing Street ministers, high court judges, senior police commanders and security services were implicated as suspects, all policing actions in Britain have been immediately suspended and records destroyed. The cover-up must go on.

With Operations Fairbank, Fairbridge and Midland opened during the post-Savile revelations, it was hoped by all VIP victims and both the Allen and Mehrotra families that justice can finally be done but because the pedophile Establishment is still in control protecting all prominent pedophiles still alive in its inner elite club, no VIPs have been arrested much less convicted. Then in 2015 when the IPCC was launched to investigate Scotland Yard's blatant cover-ups at both Dolphin Square and the Vishal Mehrotra murder, hopes again were raised but it too was for mere public appeasement just like the IICSA. As said before, the British government, including law enforcement and its judicial system, are all saturated with slithering low life criminal scum and they will never be willing to reveal the full truth and take responsibility for their heinous crimes against children. And the same can be said for their just as guilty counterparts in North America, Europe, Australia and likely most of the rest of the world as it's a global scourge we are facing now. Worldwide truth and reconciliation commissions are necessary.

One of the Scotland Yard detective sergeants working on the original 1981 Mehrotra murder case, Jackie Malton, whose career inspired the Helen Mirren ITV series "Prime Suspect," as

---

[2675] Steph Cockroft, "Notorious Paedophile Gang 'could have Covered up 17 Child Murders and be Linked to VIP Guest House,'" *Daily Mail*, November 20, .

much as admitted a police cover-up took place.[2676] Just days earlier in November 2014, Vishal's father had revealed that the police had refused to investigate the taped phone conversation of a young male prostitute stating his son was very likely taken in by a Westminster pedophile ring operating out of the Elm Guest House, leaving the father to conclude the tape was refused because it implicated "judges and politicians," forcing the police to engage in a huge cover-up. After retiring from the Met in 1997 as detective chief inspector, Jackie has now gone on record stating that the investigation she worked on for four months in 1981, attempting in vain to solve Vishal's abduction and murder case, may have been compromised by the "power of politicians," adding:

During my time in the police there was a feeling of misuse of power. There were a lot of powerful people saying, 'Don't you know who I am?' There was also a strong sense of the power of Parliament and of politicians. It was very much a case of 'Do as you are told.'"[2677]

After four months on the case, Jackie was reassigned elsewhere. Weeks later Vishal's father submitted the taped conversation. She now concedes that the recording may have been ignored and the murder covered up because of powerful senior Westminster politicians. She went on to surmise:

There is clear evidence that something was happening at that [Elm] guesthouse. If nothing has been done about it in retrospect, then Mr Mehrotra is right. Either the police disbelieved it, or they covered it up one way or another... Some inquiries would come to an end when someone senior said, 'That's enough.' I remember a case where there was an MP accused of cottaging and it all kind of disappeared... Politicians were very much in power, and the police officers' voices could often not be heard [just like the voiceless child victims].[2678]

Many players both big and small have been part of Britain's mammoth pedophilia network and its equally mammoth cover-up. A few rotten ones on the bottom go to jail, the rest live above the law.

On July 8, 2014 Dr. Jon Bird from the National Association for People Abused in Childhood (NAPAC) spoke to the press about his observations based on the high volume of alleged victims calling in to report historic child sex abuse crimes committed by powerful VIPs, independently reporting virtually the same 10 high profile abusers:

[2676] Bill Gardner, "Metropolitan Police Detective's Fears of Westminster Paedophile 'Cover-up,'" *The Telegraph*, November 19, 2014, https://www.telegraph.co.uk/news/uknews/crime/11242273/Metropolitan-Police-detectives-fears-of-Westminster-paedophile-cover-up.html.

[2677] Bill Gardner, https://www.telegraph.co.uk/news/uknews/crime/11242273/Metropolitan-Police-detectives-fears-of-Westminster-paedophile-cover-up.html.

[2678] Bill Gardner, https://www.telegraph.co.uk/news/uknews/crime/11242273/Metropolitan-Police-detectives-fears-of-Westminster-paedophile-cover-up.html.

The names of people in very high places – politicians, senior police officers and even some judges – have been going around as abusers for a very long time. Since the Jimmy Savile revelations, there's been a sea change in the way police and the CPS respond to these sort of complaints and now, at last, it looks like these people are going to be investigated.[2679]

Investigated? Don't get your hopes up Dr. Jon. For all the countless official probes, reviews and reports, again none of the major perps in government have ever been arrested, prosecuted, convicted or imprisoned for raping a child – NONE! What may have been your sincere optimism welcoming the long-awaited "sea change" a half decade ago now appears to be a mere transitory case of false hope. Sea change or no sea change, not one VIP pedophile has ever spent a full day in jail for his sordid crimes, despite Theresa May's sham of a long, drawn out, sputtering "independent inquiry" into government abuse. She, it and Brexit are but one big cruel joke unleashed on the good people of Britain who've once again been had and hoodwinked.

Though Dr. Bird specifies that the same 10 pedophile names that keep coming up include "senior police officers and even some judges," a current consensus of most identified VIP pedos, aside from Prince Charles' childhood mentor and uncle Lord Mountbatten and his favorite trio Sir Jimmy Savile, Sir Anthony Blunt and Bishop Peter Ball, the following politicians might make the Top 10 List of pervert politicians: Sir Cyril Smith, Sir Leon Brittan, Sir Greville Janner, Sir Peter Hayman, Sir Peter Morrison, Sir Ted Heath, Sir Nicholas Fairburn, Sir Peter Mandelson, Sir Paul Boatteng and ex-MP Harvey Proctor. Dishonorable mentions could easily go to Lord Boothby and MP Tom Driberg from the 1950s and 60s but it's unlikely that enough child victims would still be alive to name them in 2014 as their abusers. Spared is Sir Peter Bottomley – he may just blow a gasket. Notice of the Top 10 every single one of these alleged high-profile child abusers but one have been granted knighthood by the queen, with the vast majority already escaped to their rotting graves unpunished.

Shifting from perpetrator to victim, the extensive pedophilia network that runs both inside and outside of Great Britain from local to national to international is both widespread and sadly heavily-travelled by trafficked care home children that the system makes a national policy of betraying instead of protecting for well over a century now. Between civil servants in social services, NHS, education, UK security services to politicians in local and national government, care home kids were and still are a cheap commodity systemically shuffled from one geographical location to the next to be abused again and again and again. It too became UK national policy. The ratlines most often converge on London as Britain's pedo-wheel hub but they branch out in every direction to Jersey Island, Amsterdam, Brussels, Portugal, Wales,

---

[2679] Dominic Gover, https://www.ibtimes.co.uk/westminister-paedophile-scandal-current-mps-named-again-again-calls-sex-abuse-helpline-1455805.

508

Northern Ireland, Scotland and well beyond. Children within national care systems are even exchanged as well. Recall from Chapter 4 Righton's trade with Malta. Or from last chapter victims from Islington routinely sent for abuse in Jersey and vice versa. A massive criminal network of moving child victims back and forth for VIP abuse to virtually everywhere in the world captures just a glimpse into the world's largest illegal operation that's reached an unprecedented, industrial, pandemic scale today, in case you're a member of the shrinking minority still believing the MSM fake news of denial.

Just over a decade ago it was discovered that in addition to Islington's policy of swapping children with Jersey Island, social services from the city of Birmingham were also busted, illegally dropping off kids in the pedophilia haven of Jersey and then losing track of them.[2680] This only came to light during the police investigation into Jersey's deathtrap care home Haut de la Garenne after 100 bone fragments and 65 teeth of dead children were unearthed. Liberal Democrat MP from Birmingham John Hemming said:

The Government has refused to order councils to check properly because it does not want to open a can of worms, on the links between abusers in England and Jersey… The system nationally is not properly accountable. Children are taken into care never to be seen again… They are stalling because they are embarrassed by the size of the problem, and because it involves English authorities, too.[2681]

In other words, social services all around Britain will not be checking into their records any time soon, nor will police, NHS or Home Office require it because it would only prove that it's simply been UK's longtime national policy to misuse its children from its underclass as scorned, disposable objects to be tortured and destroyed by its deranged elite for a very long time. This page as yet another dark chapter was only uncovered after MP Henning requested his district's social services check account records that showed Birmingham had made payments to Jersey from 1960 to 1990. Remember, the UK maintained a long history of banishing over 150,000 of its children to other Commonwealth countries (which Jersey is part of) for further abuse as a national policy. So this problem at the world's pedo-epicenter is systemic.

The fact remains that a quarter century after veteran journalist-Channel 4 presenter Jon Snow's scathing critique in a 1996 *Guardian* article of "the UK Care System" has only gone from bad to worse in the level of abuse heaped on the disposable British youth population.[2682] Snow's 1996 appraisal was painfully accurate describing how children too early in their young lives fall victim

---

[2680] Eileen Fairweather, "Birmingham Council Ilegally Sent Children into Care in Jersey, MP Report Reveals," *Daily Mail*, August 4, 2008.

[2681] Eileen Fairweather, https://www.mailonsunday.co.uk/news/article-1041035/Birmingham-council-illegally-sent-children-care-Jersey-MP-report-reveals.html.

[2682] Jon Snow, "True Scandal of the Child Abusers," *The Guardian/spotlightonabuse.wordpress.com*, June 6, 1996.

into a spiraling cycle of systemic failure, delivering human suffering at the most unsettling, most profound levels. Beginning with the dire family conditions of austerity and impoverishment that typically give way to the overreaching authoritarian UK family court system, secretly exploiting families and forcing hapless British kids into residential placement or foster care often far from home in a national care system that delivers the farthest thing from genuine care.

Through no fault of their own, children have virtually forever been helplessly trapped in a multi-tiered system set up to fail and harm them at every turn, starting with rampant sexual abuse at their care homes only to be farmed out and trafficked by organized pedophile rings, too often ending up raped and sodomized by their nation's most powerful beasts atop the predatory food chain entrusted to deliver the very "care" system that is systematically failing and destroying them, and has been operating this way for well over a half century. Moreover, as a national policy to ship unwanted British children off to Australia, New Zealand, Canada, South Africa, and what's now Zimbabwe for further abuse is unconscionable, yet leave it to the world's pedo-epicenter to perpetrate this despicable crime against 150,000 youth for centuries up to 1974.[2683] The UK Care System is arguably the most egregious, most heinous institutionalized mind fuck ever put on innocent kids imaginable.

With the average "shelf life" of trafficked child sex slaves only two years, this lethal cycle of abuse invariably involves drug addiction, plied throughout by pimping perpetrators at every level for obvious control purposes. At any point along this death trap road, young people attempting to escape the system go missing, and the growing number exceeding 10,000 each year alone in Britain only find themselves preyed upon as runaway rent boys and girls aging out of the system at 18 if they even live that long.[2684] With Jon Snow citing 23 years ago that 75% of kids leaving the system have no educational qualifications, it's far worse now with dropout rates rising all the time.[2685] Both minors and young adults without formal education or legitimate means of self-support, prostitution becomes an all too common fate for survival, followed by early death by murder, disease or suicide, whichever comes first. And with estimates of 11 million sexually abused British citizens out of a total population of near 67 million, one in four women and one in six men in the UK are the walking wounded.[2686]

With human slavery and pedophilia reaching an unprecedented, off the chart scale across this pandemic globe, unless we citizens of the world do something now to change this ungodly bottom line reality, the child raping Luciferians in control may destroy us all. Robotics,

---

[2683] Tom Symonds, "The Child Abuse Scandal of the British Children sent abroad," *BBC*, February 26, 2017.
[2684] Tim Stickings, "More than 10,000 Children in Care went Missing last year amid Fears of Exploitation by Child Grooming Gangs," *Daily Mail*, April 21, 2018.
[2685] Kate Loveys, "Britain's Neets Shame: New Study Reveals UK has one of Worst Dropout Rates in Developing World," *Daily Mail*, September 14, 2011.
[2686] "Child Sex Abuse a National Health Epidemic, Government Adviser Warns," *The Guardian*, December 8, 2014.

automation, transhumanism and artificial intelligence are making over 90% of us "useless eating" humans obsolete, so just as the queen's husband's wet dream is to kill us off as a contagious virus, the rest of his planetary controlling ilk want nearly all of us dead. As repeatedly mentioned, their genocidal war against humanity being fought right now is down to either us or them. Marked in the murdering criminals' crosshairs, we the peace-loving citizens of the world have the right to defend ourselves and our children by holding them accountable for all their countless atrocities and crimes against humanity.

Over recent years and decades, the tragically common fate of sexually abused children has befallen millions worldwide and with the sex slave industry currently at an all-time shameful high in recorded history, it's high time we stewards of the earth finally begin protecting our most precious resources, starting with our children from the monsters who for millenniums have ruled over and are fast destroying our only living habitat. Since today we know more about the pedophilia scourge than at any previous time in human history, the profiteers behind the child sex slave trade are the very same planetary controlling profiteers behind our fiat, debt-based economic slavery system, our perpetual state of war and our world's sixth mass life extinction, the first one whose known cause is the deranged subhuman species in control. Before the real Homo sapiens perish at the hands of these bloodthirsty cannibals, it's urgent we take decisive action to employ organizations like the International Tribunal for Natural Justice (ITNJ) to learn more from the victim-survivors and ascertain the extent of global child abuse,[2687] leading to truth and reconciliation commissions to hold those most guilty criminals at the very top fully accountable. The bottom line - at this ever-late hour, again it's literally down to either us or them. For our own self-preservation as a human species, we must fight our identifiable enemy now! Tomorrow may be too late.

[2687] "International Tribunal for Natural Justice," https://www.itnj.org/.

Index

C

516

527

529